T0321702

Intelligent Multidimensional Data Clustering and Analysis

Siddhartha Bhattacharyya
RCC Institute of Information Technology, India

Sourav De
Cooch Behar Government Engineering College, India

Indrajit Pan
RCC Institute of Information Technology, India

Paramartha Dutta
Visva–Bharati University, India

A volume in the Advances in Data Mining and
Database Management (ADMDM) Book Series

www.igi-global.com

Published in the United States of America by
IGI Global
Information Science Reference (an imprint of IGI Global)
701 E. Chocolate Avenue
Hershey PA, USA 17033
Tel: 717-533-8845
Fax: 717-533-8661
E-mail: cust@igi-global.com
Web site: http://www.igi-global.com

Library of Congress Cataloging-in-Publication Data

Library of Congress Cataloging-in-Publication Data

Names: Bhattacharyya, Siddhartha, 1975- editor. | De, Sourav, 1979- editor. |
    Pan, Indrajit, 1983- editor. | Dutta, Paramartha, editor.
Title: Intelligent multidimensional data clustering and analysis / Siddhartha
    Bhattacharyya, Sourav De, Indrajit Pan, and Paramartha Dutta, editors.
Description: Hershey, PA : Information Science Reference, [2017] | Includes
    bibliographical references and index.
Identifiers: LCCN 2016043162| ISBN 9781522517764 (hardcover) | ISBN
    9781522517771 (ebook)
Subjects: LCSH: Cluster analysis. | Image processing--Mathematics. |
    Biomedical engineering--Mathematics.
Classification: LCC QA278.55 .I57 2017 | DDC 519.5/3--dc23 LC record available at https://lccn.loc.gov/2016043162

This book is published in the IGI Global book series Advances in Data Mining and Database Management (ADMDM)
(ISSN: 2327-1981; eISSN: 2327-199X)

Advances in Data Mining and Database Management (ADMDM) Book Series

David Taniar
Monash University, Australia

ISSN:2327-1981
EISSN:2327-199X

Mission

With the large amounts of information available to organizations in today's digital world, there is a need for continual research surrounding emerging methods and tools for collecting, analyzing, and storing data.

The **Advances in Data Mining & Database Management (ADMDM)** series aims to bring together research in information retrieval, data analysis, data warehousing, and related areas in order to become an ideal resource for those working and studying in these fields. IT professionals, software engineers, academicians and upper-level students will find titles within the ADMDM book series particularly useful for staying up-to-date on emerging research, theories, and applications in the fields of data mining and database management.

Coverage

- Profiling Practices
- Association Rule Learning
- Quantitative Structure–Activity Relationship
- Decision Support Systems
- Information Extraction
- Data Mining
- Cluster Analysis
- Factor Analysis
- Text Mining
- Database Testing

IGI Global is currently accepting manuscripts for publication within this series. To submit a proposal for a volume in this series, please contact our Acquisition Editors at Acquisitions@igi-global.com or visit: http://www.igi-global.com/publish/.

Titles in this Series

For a list of additional titles in this series, please visit: www.igi-global.com

Emerging Trends in the Development and Application of Composite Indicators
Veljko Jeremic (University of Belgrade, Serbia) Zoran Radojicic (University of Belgrade, Serbia) and Marina Dobrota (University of Belgrade, Serbia)
Information Science Reference • copyright 2017 • 402pp • H/C (ISBN: 9781522507147) • US $205.00 (our price)

Web Usage Mining Techniques and Applications Across Industries
A.V. Senthil Kumar (Hindusthan College of Arts and Science, India)
Information Science Reference • copyright 2017 • 424pp • H/C (ISBN: 9781522506133) • US $200.00 (our price)

Social Media Data Extraction and Content Analysis
Shalin Hai-Jew (Kansas State University, USA)
Information Science Reference • copyright 2017 • 493pp • H/C (ISBN: 9781522506485) • US $225.00 (our price)

Collaborative Filtering Using Data Mining and Analysis
Vishal Bhatnagar (Ambedkar Institute of Advanced Communication Technologies and Research, India)
Information Science Reference • copyright 2017 • 309pp • H/C (ISBN: 9781522504894) • US $195.00 (our price)

Effective Big Data Management and Opportunities for Implementation
Manoj Kumar Singh (Adama Science and Technology University, Ethiopia) and Dileep Kumar G. (Adama Science and Technology University, Ethiopia)
Information Science Reference • copyright 2016 • 324pp • H/C (ISBN: 9781522501824) • US $195.00 (our price)

Data Mining Trends and Applications in Criminal Science and Investigations
Omowunmi E. Isafiade (University of Cape Town, South Africa) and Antoine B. Bagula (University of the Western Cape, South Africa)
Information Science Reference • copyright 2016 • 386pp • H/C (ISBN: 9781522504634) • US $210.00 (our price)

Intelligent Techniques for Data Analysis in Diverse Settings
Numan Celebi (Sakarya University, Turkey)
Information Science Reference • copyright 2016 • 353pp • H/C (ISBN: 9781522500759) • US $195.00 (our price)

Managing and Processing Big Data in Cloud Computing
Rajkumar Kannan (King Faisal University, Saudi Arabia) Raihan Ur Rasool (King Faisal University, Saudi Arabia) Hai Jin (Huazhong University of Science and Technology, China) and S.R. Balasundaram (National Institute of Technology, Tiruchirappalli, India)
Information Science Reference • copyright 2016 • 307pp • H/C (ISBN: 9781466697676) • US $200.00 (our price)

www.igi-global.com

701 E. Chocolate Ave., Hershey, PA 17033
Order online at www.igi-global.com or call 717-533-8845 x100
To place a standing order for titles released in this series, contact: cust@igi-global.com
Mon-Fri 8:00 am - 5:00 pm (est) or fax 24 hours a day 717-533-8661

Prof. (Dr.) Siddhartha Bhattacharyya would like to dedicate this book to his father Late Ajit Kumar Bhattacharyya, mother Late Hashi Bhattacharyya, beloved wife Rashni and his maternal uncles Late Ratan Mukherjee, Late Bimal Bhattacharya, Mr. Adinath Chatterjee and Late Anup Mukherjee

Dr. Sourav De would like to dedicate this book to his son Mr. Aishik De, wife Mrs. Debolina Ghosh, father Mr. Satya Narayan De, mother Mrs. Tapasi De and sister Mrs. Soumi De

Dr. Indrajit Pan would like to dedicate this book to his father Mr. Sitansu Kumar Pan, mother Mrs. Ratna Pan and wife Subhamita

Prof. (Dr.) Paramartha Dutta would like to dedicate this book to his father Late Arun Kanti Dutta and mother Mrs. Bandana Dutta

Editorial Advisory Board

Table of Contents

Detailed Table of Contents

Chapter 1
Marlene Goncalves, Universidad Simón Bolívar, Venezuela
José N. Mendoza, Universidad Simón Bolívar, Venezuela

Since the huge volume of data that is generated today, businesses need to have tools to efficiently manage such data. MonetDB is a column-oriented database management system which has shown to have better query processing time with respect to row-oriented systems. The main objective of this chapter is to propose a physical design strategy that improves query execution times in MonetDB. The proposed physical design strategy was empirically studied for 18 TPC-H queries. The experiments were conducted on the basis of cold cache. Each of the queries were executed first using the proposed physical design strategy in this work and then without any physical design. The reported results show that the runtimes using physical design strategy are better for all queries with a minimum percentage improvement of 29%. Also, they showed that the improvement was statistically significant by means of statistical tests.

Chapter 2
Bülent Başaran, Bilecik Şeyh Edebali University, Turkey
Fatih Güneş, Bilecik Şeyh Edebali University, Turkey

Data clustering can be associated with and used in many research methodologies and application areas. In this chapter, the basics of data clustering and some kind of its applications are given with examples and a real data set. The examples show data types and help to explain basic clustering algorithms. The real data help to classify countries in terms of their computer and internet proficiency levels. After examining the resulting clusters obtained from four different basic methods according to eight computer and internet proficiencies, it is found that the regional closeness of countries and being outside of a union are the major drivers of those clusters' formation. This application gives some possible future research area extensions to researchers about clustering the same or other countries by different proficiencies and unions.

Chapter 3

Neelu Khare, VIT University, India
Dharmendra S. Rajput, VIT University, India
Preethi D, VIT University, India

Many approaches for identifying potentially interesting items exploiting commonly used techniques of multidimensional data analysis. There is a great need for designing association-rule mining algorithms that will be scalable not only with the number of records (number of rows) in a cluster but also among domain's size (number of dimensions) in a cluster to focus on the domains. Where the items belong to domain is correlated with each other in a way that the domain is clustered into classes with a maximum intra-class similarity and a minimum inter-class similarity. This property can help to significantly used to prune the search space to perform efficient association-rule mining. For finding the hidden correlation in the obtained clusters effectively without losing the important relationship in the large database clustering techniques can be followed by association rule mining to provide better evaluated clusters.

Chapter 4

Shashi Mehrotra, Birla Institute of Technology, India
Shruti Kohli, Birla Institute of Technology, India

It is needed to organize the data in different groups for various purposes, where clustering is useful. The chapter covers Data Clustering in the detail, which includes; introduction to data clustering with figures, data clustering process, basic classification of clustering and applications of clustering, describing hard partition clustering and fuzzy clustering. Some most commonly used clustering method are explained in the chapter with their features, advantages, and disadvantages. A various variant of K-Means and extension method of hierarchical clustering method, density-based clustering method and grid-based clustering method are covered.

Chapter 5

Seikh Mazharul Islam, RCC Institute of Information Technology, India
Minakshi Banerjee, RCC Institute of Information Technology, India
Siddhartha Bhattacharyya, RCC Institute of Information Technology, India

This chapter proposes a content based image retrieval method dealing with higher dimensional feature of images. The kernel principal component analysis (KPCA) is done on MPEG-7 Color Structure Descriptor (CSD) (64-bins) to compute low-dimensional nonlinear-subspace. Also the Partitioning Around Medoids (PAM) algorithm is used to squeeze search space again where the number of clusters are counted by optimum average silhouette width. To refine these clusters further, the outliers from query image's belonging cluster are excluded by Support Vector Clus-tering (SVC). Then One-Class Support Vector Machine (OCSVM) is used for the prediction of relevant images from query image's belonging cluster and the initial retrieval results based on the similarity measurement is feed to OCSVM for training. Images are ranked from the positively labeled images. This method gives more than 95% precision before recall reaches at 0.5 for conceptually meaningful query categories. Also comparative results are obtained from: 1) MPEG-7 CSD features directly and 2) other dimensionality reduction techniques.

Data mining has great contributions to the healthcare such as support for effective treatment, healthcare management, customer relation management, fraud and abuse detection and decision making. The common data mining methods used in healthcare are Artificial Neural Network, Decision trees, Genetic Algorithms, Nearest neighbor method, Logistic regression, Fuzzy logic, Fuzzy based Neural Networks, Bayesian Networks and Support Vector Machines. The most used task is classification. Because of the complexity and toughness of medical domain, data mining is not an easy task to accomplish. In addition, privacy and security of patient data is a big issue to deal with because of the sensitivity of healthcare data. There exist additional serious challenges. This chapter is a descriptive study aimed to provide an acquaintance to data mining and its usage and applications in healthcare domain. The use of Data mining in healthcare informatics and challenges will be examined.

Chapter 7

The CAD is a relatively young interdisciplinary technology, has had a tremendous impact on medical diagnosis specifically cancer detection. The accuracy of CAD to detect abnormalities on medical image analysis requires a robust segmentation algorithm. To achieve accurate segmentation, an efficient edge-detection algorithm is essential. Medical images like USG, X-Ray, CT and MRI exhibit diverse image characteristics but are essentially collection of intensity variations from which specific abnormalities are needed to be isolated. In this chapter a robust medical image enhancement and edge detection algorithm is proposed, using tree-based adaptive thresholding technique. It has been compared with different classical edge-detection techniques using one sample two tail t-test to exam whether the null hypothesis can be supported. The proposed edge-detection algorithm showing 0.07 p-values and 2.411 t-stat where $\alpha = 0.025$. Moreover the proposed edge is single pixeled and connected which is very significant for medical edge detection.

Different graph theoretic approaches are prevalent in the field of image analysis. Graphs provide a natural representation of image pixels exploring their pairwise interactions among themselves. Graph theoretic approaches have been used for problem like image segmentation, object representation, matching for different kinds of data. In this chapter, we mainly aim at highlighting the applicability of graph clustering techniques for the purpose of image segmentation. We describe different spectral clustering techniques, minimum spanning tree based data clustering, Markov Random Field (MRF) model for image segmentation in this respect.

Chantana Chantrapornchai, Kasetsart University, Thailand
Aree Kaegjing, Silpakorn University, Thailand
Sathaporn Srakaew, Silpakorn University, Thailand
Warot Piyanuntcharatsr, Silpakorn University, Thailand
Songchok Krakhaeng, Silpakorn University, Thailand

Data mining has been a popular technique. It has been for many applications in many areas nowadays. In this chapter, we are interested in utilizing architecture features and apply data mining techniques for a computer design. Since data mining requires lot of collected data for building models, the relevant data needs to be properly generated. We demonstrate the applications and their methodology starting from data set generation, feature extraction, modeling and evaluations. Important characteristics of the architecture are considered for data set generation and feature extractions: particularly, the instruction set, and memory access pattern features. The chapter utilizes these features given with observations for building the models for cache prediction, branch prediction, and malware detection.

Abhishek Basu, RCC Institute of Information Technology, India
Susmita Talukdar, Infosys Ltd., India

In this paper, a saliency and phase congruency based digital image watermarking scheme has been projected. The planned technique implants data at least significant bits (LSBs) by means of adaptive replacement. Here more information is embedded into less perceptive areas within the original image determined by a combination of spectral residual saliency map and phase congruency map. The position of pixels with less perceptibility denotes the most unimportant region for data hiding from the point of visibility within an image. Therefore any modification within these regions will be less perceptible to one observer. The model gives a concept of the areas which has excellent data hiding capacity within an image. Superiority of the algorithm is tested through imperceptibility, robustness, along with data hiding capacity.

Swati Aggarwal, NSIT, India
Venu Azad, Government Girls PG College, India

In the medical field diagnosis of a disease at an early stage is very important. Nowadays soft computing techniques such as fuzzy logic, artificial neural network and Neuro- fuzzy networks are widely used for the diagnosis of various diseases at different levels. In this chapter, a hybrid neural network is designed to classify the heart disease data set the hybrid neural network consist of two types of neural network multilayer perceptron (MLP) and fuzzy min max (FMM) neural network arranged in a hierarchical manner. The hybrid system is designed for the dataset which contain the combination of continuous and non continuous attribute values. In the system the attributes with continuous values are classified using the FMM neural networks and attributes with non-continuous value are classified by using the MLP neural network and to synthesize the result the output of both the network is fed into the second MLP neural network to generate the final result.

Due to microarray experiment imperfection, spots with various artifacts are often found in microarray image. A more rigorous spot recognition approach in ensuring successful image analysis is crucial. In this paper, a novel hybrid algorithm was proposed. A wavelet approach was applied, along with an intensity-based shape detection simultaneously to locate the contour of the microarray spots. The proposed algorithm segmented all the imperfect spots accurately. Performance assessment with the classical methods, i.e., the fixed circle, adaptive circle, adaptive shape and histogram segmentation showed that the proposed hybrid approach outperformed these methods.

Enhancing the energy efficiency and maximizing the networking lifetime are the major challenges in Wireless Sensor Networks (WSN).Swarm Intelligence based algorithms are very efficient in solving nonlinear design problems with real-world applications.In this paper a Swarm based Fruit Fly Optimization Algorithm (FFOA) with the concept of K-Medoid clustering and swapping is implemented to increase the energy efficiency and lifetime of WSN. A comparative analysis is performed in terms of cluster compactness,cluster error and convergence. MATLAB Simulation results show that K-Medoid Swapping and Bunching Fruit Fly optimization (KMSB-FFOA) outperforms FFOA and K-Medoid Fruit Fly Optimization Algorithm (KM-FFOA).

Chapter 14

This chapter aims to study the use of Hybridization of intelligent techniques in the areas of bioinformatics and computational molecular biology. These areas have risen from the needs of biologists to utilize and help interpret the vast amounts of data that are constantly being gathered in genomic research. Also describes the kind of methods which were developed by the research community in order to search, classify and mine different available biological databases and simulate biological experiments. This chapter also presents the hybridization of intelligent systems involving neural networks, fuzzy systems, neuro-fuzzy system, rough set theory, swam intelligence and genetic algorithm. The key idea was to demonstrate the evolution of intelligence in bioinformatics. The developed hybridization of intelligent techniques was applied to the real world applications. The hybridization of intelligent systems performs better than the individual approaches. Hence these approaches might be extremely useful for hardware implementations.

Chapter 15

Deepthi P. Hudedagaddi, VIT University, India

B. K. Tripathy, VIT University, India

With the increasing volume of data, developing techniques to handle it has become the need of the hour. One such efficient technique is clustering. Data clustering is under vigorous development. The goal of clustering is to determine the intrinsic grouping in a set of unlabeled data. Several data clustering algorithms have been developed in this regard. Data is uncertain and vague. Hence uncertain and hybrid based clustering algorithms like fuzzy c means, intuitionistic fuzzy c means, rough c means, rough intuitionistic fuzzy c means are being used. However, with the application and nature of data, clustering algorithms which adapt to the need are being used. These are nothing but the variations in existing techniques to match a particular scenario. The area of adaptive clustering algorithms is unexplored to a very large extent and hence has a large scope of research. Adaptive clustering algorithms are useful in areas where the situations keep on changing. Some of the adaptive fuzzy c means clustering algorithms are detailed in this chapter.

Preface

Commonly used as a preliminary data mining practice, data preprocessing transforms the data into a format that will be more easily and effectively processed for the purpose of the users. There are a number of data preprocessing techniques: data cleaning, data integration, data transformation and data reduction. The need to cluster large quantities of multi-dimensional data is widely recognized. Cluster analysis is used to identify homogeneous and well-separated groups of objects in databases. It plays an important role in many fields of business and science. Existing clustering algorithms can be broadly classified into four types: partitioning, hierarchical, grid-based, and density-based algorithms. Partitioning algorithms start with an initial partition and then use an iterative control strategy to optimize the quality of the clustering results by moving objects from one group to another. Hierarchical algorithms create a hierarchical decomposition of the given data set of data objects. Grid-based algorithms quantize the space into a finite number of grids and perform all operations on this quantized space. Density-based approaches are designed to discover clusters of arbitrary shapes. These approaches hold that, for each point within a cluster, the neighborhood of a given radius must exceed a defined threshold. Each of the existing clustering algorithms has both advantages and disadvantages. The most common problem is rapid degeneration of performance with increasing dimensions, particularly with approaches originally designed for low-dimensional data. To solve the high-dimensional clustering problem, dimension reduction methods have been proposed which assume that clusters are located in a low-dimensional subspace. However, this assumption does not hold for many real-world data sets. The difficulty of high-dimensional clustering is primarily due to the following characteristics of high-dimensional data:

- High-dimensional data often contain a large amount of noise (outliers). The existence of noise results in clusters which are not well-separated and degrades the effectiveness of the clustering algorithms.
- Clusters in high-dimensional spaces are commonly of various densities. Grid-based or density-based algorithms therefore have difficulty choosing a proper cell size or neighborhood radius which can find all clusters.
- Clusters in high-dimensional spaces rarely have well-defined shapes, and some algorithms assume clusters of certain shapes.
- The effectiveness of grid-based approaches suffers when data points are clustered around a vertex of the grid and are separated in different cells.

To sum up, the classical techniques lack in one way or other as regards to faithful analysis and clustering of multidimensional data owing to inherent uncertainties in assumptions and heuristic choices. It is in this scenario that the soft computing paradigm can be effectively used to arrive at effective and productive throughputs.

The book would surely come to the benefits of several categories of students and researchers. At the students' level, this book can serve as a treatise/reference book for the special papers at the masters level aimed at inspiring possibly future researchers. Newly inducted PhD aspirants would also find the contents of this book useful as far as their compulsory courseworks are concerned. At the researchers' level, those interested in interdisciplinary research would also be benefited from the book. After all, the enriched interdisciplinary contents of the book would always be a subject of interest to the faculties, existing research communities and new research aspirants from diverse disciplines of the concerned departments of premier institutes across the globe. This is expected to bring different research backgrounds (due to its cross platform characteristics) close to one another to form effective research groups all over the world.

The present edited volume comprises 15 well-versed chapters spanning across varied domains of multidimensional data clustering and analysis.

Since the huge volume of data that is generated today, businesses need to have tools to efficiently manage such data. MonetDB is a column-oriented database management system which has shown to have better query processing time with respect to row-oriented systems. Chapter 1 proposes a physical design strategy that improves query execution times in MonetDB. The proposed physical design strategy was empirically studied for 18 TPC-H queries. The experiments were conducted on the basis of cold cache. Each of the queries were executed first using the proposed physical design strategy in this work and then without any physical design. The reported results show that the runtimes using physical design strategy are better for all queries with a minimum percentage improvement of 29%. Also, they showed that the improvement was statistically significant by means of statistical tests.

In Chapter 2, the basics of data clustering and some kind of its applications are given with examples and a real data set. The examples show data types and help to explain basic clustering algorithms. The real data help to classify countries in terms of their computer and internet proficiency levels. After examining the resulting clusters obtained from four different basic methods according to eight computer and internet proficiencies, it is found that the regional closeness of countries and being outside of a union are the major drivers of those clusters' formation. This application gives some possible future research area extensions to researchers about clustering the same or other countries by different proficiencies and unions.

Clustering creates meaningful and useful clusters to analyze and describe the real world for discovering interesting patterns in areas such as, information retrieval, pattern recognition in biological sequence data, etc. Existing clustering approaches suffer from rapid degeneration of performance with increase in dimensions; particularly those are designed for low-dimensional data and due to ineffective cluster evaluation and analysis of multidimensional data owing to inherent uncertainties. ARM is a useful technique that can be used to extract association rules or sets of frequent patterns. These AR leads to potential knowledge to detect the regularities and path in large databases for designing scalable association-rule mining algorithms that will find the number of records in a cluster but also the number of dimensions in a cluster to focus on the domains. Chapter 3 illustrates the fidelity and properties of the ARM technique with recourse to its applications in detail.

Chapter 4 covers data clustering in detail, which includes; introduction to data clustering with figures, data clustering process, basic classification of clustering and applications of clustering, describing hard partition clustering and fuzzy clustering. Some most commonly used clustering methods are also explained in the chapter with their features, advantages, and disadvantages. A variant of K-Means and extension method of hierarchical clustering method, density-based clustering method and grid-based clustering method are also covered.

Chapter 5 proposes a content based image retrieval method dealing with higher dimensional feature of images. The kernel principal component analysis (KPCA) is done on MPEG-7 Color Structure Descriptor (CSD) (64-bins) to compute low-dimensional nonlinear-subspace. Also the Partitioning Around Medoids (PAM) algorithm is used to squeeze search space again where the number of clusters are counted by optimum average silhouette width. To refine these clusters further, the outliers from query image's belonging cluster are excluded by Support Vector Clustering (SVC). Then One-Class Support Vector Machine (OCSVM) is used for the prediction of relevant images from query image's belonging cluster and the initial retrieval results based on the similarity measurement is feed to OCSVM for training. Images are ranked from the positively labeled images. This method gives more than 95% precision before recall reaches at 0.5 for conceptually meaningful query categories. Also comparative results are obtained from (1) MPEG-7 CSD features directly and (2) other dimensionality reduction techniques.

Data mining has great contributions to the healthcare such as support for effective treatment, healthcare management, customer relation management, fraud and abuse detection and decision making. The common data mining methods used in healthcare are Artificial Neural Network, Decision trees, Genetic Algorithms, Nearest neighbor method, Logistic regression, Fuzzy logic, Fuzzy based Neural Networks, Bayesian Networks and Support Vector Machines. The most used task is classification. Because of the complexity and toughness of medical domain, data mining is not an easy task to accomplish. In addition, privacy and security of patient data is a big issue to deal with because of the sensitivity of healthcare data. There exist additional serious challenges. The objective of Chapter 6 is to provide a descriptive study aimed to provide an acquaintance to data mining and its usage and applications in healthcare domain. The use of data mining in healthcare informatics and challenges is also examined.

CAD is a relatively young interdisciplinary technology, which has a tremendous impact on medical diagnosis, specifically cancer detection. The accuracy of CAD to detect abnormalities on medical image analysis requires a robust segmentation algorithm. To achieve accurate segmentation, an efficient edge-detection algorithm is essential. Medical images like USG, X-Ray, CT and MRI exhibit diverse image characteristics but are essentially collection of intensity variations from which specific abnormalities are needed to be isolated. In Chapter 7, a robust medical image enhancement and edge detection algorithm is proposed, using tree-based adaptive thresholding technique. It has been compared with different classical edge-detection techniques using one sample two tail t-test to examine whether the null hypothesis can be supported. The proposed edge-detection algorithm shows 0.07 p-values and 2.411 t-stat where a = 0.025. Moreover, the proposed edge is single pixeled and connected which is very significant for medical edge detection.

Different graph theoretic approaches are prevalent in the field of image analysis. Graphs provide a natural representation of image pixels exploring their pairwise interactions among themselves. Graph theoretic approaches have been used for problem like image segmentation, object representation, matching for different kinds of data. Chapter 8 mainly aims at highlighting the applicability of graph clustering techniques for the purpose of image segmentation. Different spectral clustering techniques like minimum spanning tree based data clustering, Markov Random Field (MRF) model for image segmentation are discussed in this respect.

Data mining has been a popular technique in many applications. In Chapter 9, the authors focus on utilizing architecture features and apply data mining techniques for computer design. Since data mining requires lot of collected data for building models, the relevant data needs to be properly generated. The authors demonstrate the applications and their methodology starting from data set generation, feature extraction, modeling and evaluations. Important characteristics of the architecture are considered for data set generation and feature extractions: particularly, the instruction set, and memory access pattern features. The chapter utilizes these features given with observations for building the models for cache prediction, branch prediction, and malware detection.

In Chapter 10, a saliency and phase congruency based digital image watermarking scheme has been projected. The planned technique implants data at least significant bits (LSBs) by means of adaptive replacement. Here more information is embedded into less perceptive areas within the original image determined by a combination of spectral residual saliency map and phase congruency map. The position of pixels with less perceptibility denotes the most unimportant region for data hiding from the point of visibility within an image. Therefore, any modification within these regions will be less perceptible to one observer. The model gives a concept of the areas which has excellent data hiding capacity within an image. Superiority of the algorithm is tested through imperceptibility, robustness, along with data hiding capacity.

In the medical field diagnosis of a disease at an early stage is very important. Nowadays soft computing techniques such as fuzzy logic, artificial neural network and Neuro- fuzzy networks are widely used for the diagnosis of various diseases at different levels. In Chapter 11, a hybrid neural network is designed to classify the heart disease data set the hybrid neural network consist of two types of neural network multilayer perceptron (MLP) and fuzzy min max (FMM) neural network arranged in a hierarchical manner. The hybrid system is designed for the dataset which contain the combination of continuous and non-continuous attribute values. In the system the attributes with continuous values are classified using the FMM neural networks and attributes with non-continuous value are classified by using the MLP neural network and to synthesize the result the output of both the network is fed into the second MLP neural network to generate the final result.

Due to microarray experiment imperfection, spots with various artifacts are often found in microarray image. A more rigorous spot recognition approach in ensuring successful image analysis is crucial. Chapter 12 proposes a novel hybrid algorithm for this purpose. A wavelet approach is applied, along with an intensity-based shape detection simultaneously to locate the contour of the microarray spots. The proposed algorithm is able to segment all the imperfect spots accurately. Performance assessment with the classical methods, i.e., the fixed circle, adaptive circle, adaptive shape and histogram segmentation shows that the proposed hybrid approach outperforms these methods.

Enhancing the energy efficiency and maximizing the networking lifetime are the major challenges in Wireless Sensor Networks (WSN). Swarm Intelligence based algorithms are very efficient in solving nonlinear design problems with real-world applications. In Chapter 13, a Swarm based Fruit Fly Optimization Algorithm (FFOA) with the concept of K-Medoid clustering and swapping is implemented to increase the energy efficiency and lifetime of WSN. A comparative analysis is performed in terms of cluster compactness, cluster error and convergence. MATLAB Simulation results show that K-Medoid Swapping and Bunching Fruit Fly optimization (KMSB-FFOA) outperforms FFOA and K-Medoid Fruit Fly Optimization Algorithm (KM-FFOA).

Chapter 14 aims to study the use of Hybridization of intelligent techniques in the areas of bioinformatics and computational molecular biology. These areas have risen from the needs of biologists to utilize and help interpret the vast amounts of data that are constantly being gathered in genomic research. It also describes the kind of methods which were developed by the research community in order to search, classify and mine different available biological databases and simulate biological experiments. This chapter also presents the hybridization of intelligent systems involving neural networks, fuzzy systems, neuro-fuzzy system, rough set theory, swam intelligence and genetic algorithm. The key idea was to demonstrate the evolution of intelligence in bioinformatics. The developed hybridization of intelligent techniques was applied to the real world applications. The hybridization of intelligent systems performs better than the individual approaches. Hence these approaches might be extremely useful for hardware implementations.

With the increasing volume of data, developing techniques to handle it has become the need of the hour. One such efficient technique is clustering. Data clustering is under vigorous development. The goal of clustering is to determine the intrinsic grouping in a set of unlabeled data. Several data clustering algorithms have been developed in this regard. Data is uncertain and vague. Hence uncertain and hybrid based clustering algorithms like fuzzy c means, intuitionistic fuzzy c means, rough c means, rough intuitionistic fuzzy c means are being used. However, with the application and nature of data, clustering algorithms which adapt to the need are being used. These are nothing but the variations in existing techniques to match a particular scenario. The area of adaptive clustering algorithms is unexplored to a very large extent and hence has a large scope of research. Adaptive clustering algorithms are useful in areas where the situations keep on changing. Chapter 15 details some of the adaptive fuzzy c means clustering algorithms which are widely used in a variety of applications especially image processing.

The primary objective of the present endeavor is to bring a broad spectrum of multidimensional data clustering and data analysis applications under the purview of hybrid intelligence so that it is able to trigger further inspiration among various research communities to contribute in their respective fields of applications thereby orienting these application fields towards intelligence. Once the purpose, as stated above, is achieved a larger number of research communities may be brought under one umbrella to ventilate their ideas in a more structured manner. In that case, the present endeavor may be seen as the beginning of such an effort in bringing various research applications close to one another. By academically coming closer to one another, research communities working in diversified application areas involving multidimensional data viz. true color images, videos, big data, would be more encouraged to form groups among themselves paving way for interdisciplinary research. Speaking from the scholastic view, this is a formidable achievement in which the present endeavor may be thought of as the maiden facilitator. It may however be noted that there are good amounts of contributions of the application of hybrid soft computing in various fields. However, any such previous effort has remained application specific, that is, aimed at identifying a specific application domain where the ingredients of hybrid soft computing have been applied quite effectively. But, to the best of our knowledge, efforts to bring in multiple domains of multidimensional data within one framework are not very frequent. In that sense, this appears to be the first such effort to accommodate cross platform applications of hybrid soft computing. Moreover, efforts of hybridization are very meager in the literature. Once successful, this will become an encouragement towards further research of interdisciplinary nature by providing scope to various research communities to come together through such an effort.

Siddhartha Bhattacharyya
RCC Institute of Information Technology, India

Sourav De
Cooch Behar Government Engineering College, India

Indrajit Pan
RCC Institute of Information Technology, India

Paramartha Dutta
Visva-Bharati University, India

Chapter 1
A Physical Design Strategy for Datasets with Multiple Dimensions

Marlene Goncalves
Universidad Simón Bolívar, Venezuela

José N. Mendoza
Universidad Simón Bolívar, Venezuela

ABSTRACT

Since the huge volume of data that is generated today, businesses need to have tools to efficiently manage such data. MonetDB is a column-oriented database management system which has shown to have better query processing time with respect to row-oriented systems. The main objective of this chapter is to propose a physical design strategy that improves query execution times in MonetDB. The proposed physical design strategy was empirically studied for 18 TPC-H queries. The experiments were conducted on the basis of cold cache. Each of the queries were executed first using the proposed physical design strategy in this work and then without any physical design. The reported results show that the runtimes using physical design strategy are better for all queries with a minimum percentage improvement of 29%. Also, they showed that the improvement was statistically significant by means of statistical tests.

INTRODUCTION

Relational databases have been essential for applications in the last decades. Likewise, there is the promise of giving to organizations, Data Base Management Systems (DBMS) that covers all application needs, e.g., systems for handling data related to sales, orders, human resources and analysis for decision-making.

With respect to the promise to cover all the needs of applications, it has not been fulfilled at all, since it has given greater prominence to transaction processing in order to support core applications of the companies. These applications are known as Online Transactional Processing (OLTP) and its main feature is the need to constantly perform read and write operations on the data. Therefore, DBMS as PostgreSQL, Oracle and MySQL are suitable for online transactions because they are optimized for the

DOI: 10.4018/978-1-5225-1776-4.ch001

insertion, modification and deletion of data stored in databases. On the other hand, applications that support the data analysis have been developed separately and not necessarily with relational DBMS, but with other tools that require a better performance when the user works with them. This application type is known as Online Analytical Processing (OLAP) and its operations are primarily read.

In this sense, there are two possibilities to cover the need of DBMS for OLAP applications. The first possibility is to utilize DBMS that are regularly used in OLTP applications. This first option may be a mistake because the way in which data is physically stored into databases for the support of OLTP and OLAP applications are totally different. Firstly, in OLTP databases, the tuples are arranged in rows and are stored in disk blocks. Moreover, OLAP databases are based on star schemes and compression of attributes by columns using dictionaries.

On the other hand, traditional DBMS that normally work with OLTP applications have seen the need to reinvent themselves to be able to deal with OLAP applications. For example, CitusDB is a PostgreSQL extension for working with a storage model by columns.

The second possibility is to look for other DBMS that are suited to the type of work in OLAP applications. In this context, it has lately increased interest in column oriented DBMS or Column-Stores because they have better performance on data managed by OLAP systems w.r.t. row oriented DBMS or Row-Stores. In fact, several works reveal that the performance of Column-Stores is better compared to Row-Stores. Particularly, if MonetDB is compared against CitusDB, the improvement is not significant and MonetDB continues having best runtimes in most of the queries.

Since the second option is the best, in this chapter, we study the physical design of MonetDB. MonetDB was selected because it is a DBMS open and pioneered in the use of columns as physical structure for storing data. In addition, MonetDB is not obsolete, far from it, has a very active community and participate in major projects, especially in Europe (MonetDB, 2015).

Finally, experimental studies have been conducted on MonetDB using cold cache without any physical design. Thus, in this chapter we propose a physical design strategy in order to improve the performance on cold cache taking into account the specific characteristics of MonetDB.

This chapter is comprised of six sections in addition to Section 1 that introduces the problem. Section 2 describes column-oriented database management systems, execution plans, the physical design, and the MonetDB execution model. Section 3 introduces the strategy for physical design in MonetDB. In Section 4, the performance of the proposed strategy will be empirically evaluated. Finally, the future research directions and conclusion of this chapter will be pointed out in the Sections 5 and 6, respectively.

BACKGROUND

This section describes column-oriented database management systems, execution plans, the physical design, and the MonetDB execution model.

Column Stores

Column-oriented database management systems, also known as column stores, are an alternative to row-oriented database management systems (row stores) and have gained importance in recent years by the rise in analytical applications where queries are based on processing large amounts of data and calculating aggregate functions such as averages, sums and maxima.

There are two main differences between column stores and row stores. First, database inside column stores are partitioned vertically in columns, that is, each column of a table is stored separately from other columns (Abadi, 2008). In addition, the data processing when executing a query is different from the traditional processing because the column-stores process an entire column at a time while the row-stores process one tuple at a time traversing the execution tree generated by the database management system from the leaves to reach the root.

The main advantage of column-oriented database management systems is that they allow direct access to the necessary columns in order to answer analytical queries. For example, let ra, rb and rc be the columns of a table R to be accessed in a query. Column-oriented database management systems retrieve only the columns ra, rb and rc from disk to main memory and evaluate aggregate functions necessary to process them. In consequence, there is a better use of the main memory. On the contrary, row-stores access the whole table and process tuple to tuple in order to project the necessary columns (ra, rb and rc) and return the result.

Execution Plan

An execution plan is a set of operations to be executed in a certain order to answer a query. Some relational algebra operators to be evaluated in an execution plan are the following:

- **Projection (π):** This operator retrieves a subset of columns from a table (relation). It is mainly used as one of the last operators during the query execution because it allows only to return the columns that the user want as a result.
- **Selection (σ):** This operator filters the tuples of a relation that meet the specified predicate. For example, if R is a relation with an integer attribute ra, then the selection $\sigma_{ra=10}\left(R\right)$ returns all tuples of R whose ra value is equal to 10.
- **Join ($\bowtie$):** It is an operator that is based on combining two different relations by a common attribute. In the most general form, a join between two relations can be defined as a Cartesian product preceded by a selection with the condition that the common attributes are equal. For example, if R and S are relations with a common attribute att, the join is $R \bowtie_{R.att=S.att} S = \sigma_{R.att=S.att}(R \times S)$.

It is noteworthy that the join is the most expensive operator of the Relational Algebra; therefore, its evaluation has a great impact on the query performance. The main evaluation algorithms or physical operators used to evaluate the join operator are nested-loop join, block-nested loop join, sort-merge join and hash join (Ramakrishnan & Gehrke, 2003).

- **Group By:** The idea of this operator is to divide the relationship in non-overlapping groups of tuples. Each of these groups consists of tuples having the same value for one or several attributes, known as grouping attributes (Elmasri & Navathe, 2015).

In general, all execution plans are represented by a binary tree (Ramakrishnan & Gehrke, 2003). Each leaf of the tree is a relationship and each internal node corresponds to an operator. When executing a query, the tree is traversed from the leaves to the root. Each operator (node) requires the result from its children and each intermediate result will serve as input to the immediate parent node.

Figure 1. A left-linear tree

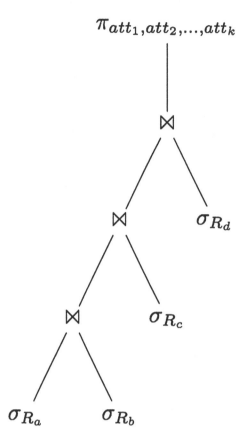

The tree shape can be different according to the database database system. The tree examples in this chapter are left-linear trees. The main feature of left-linear trees is that each operator has a table as its right child and each left child is a subtree. For example, in Figure 1. A left-linear tree1 is a left linear tree. It can be noted that each right node represents a specific relationship: R_b, R_c and R_d.

Physical Design

The physical design aims to achieve a good performance when working with data stored in relational databases. Thus, the physical design is an activity that includes not only create a configuration on a database, but also all actions that can ensure a good performance (Elmasri & Navathe, 2015).

On the other hand, decisions for the physical design of a database include indexing and Denormalization. The indices are data structures that enable fast access to data. It is characterized by establishing an order among the data that is on disk, that is, data are sorted from the index point of view.

When the indices have several fields, it is important to choose the order among the attributes to create the index. Generally, heuristics to establish order among the attributes of the index is the selectivity of the predicates of the indexed attributes. The selectivity of a predicate is the ratio of tuples in a relation that meets the predicate (Lynch, 1988). Empirically, the selectivity of a predicate p is calculated using the Equation 1.

$$S = \frac{Tuples_p(R)}{Cardinality(R)} \tag{1}$$

where $Tuples_p(R)$ is the number of tuples in the relation R that meet the predicate p and $Cardinality\big(R\big)$ is the number of rows contained in the relation R. For example, consider a relation R and a predicate $att_1 = k$. The selectivity of this predicate is the ratio of tuples that result after applying this predicate to the relation R.

Moreover, it is desirable to have a normalized database in order to reduce redundancy and avoid problems that may require more processing time to maintain the consistency of the database (Elmasri & Navathe, 2015).

Sometimes, the database may be denormalized in order to have better performance in the execution of queries. When a query is executed in a normalized database, it is necessary to execute the joins between tables because many of the attributes are separated into separate tables. Since the join operation is expensive, the join materialization may be a solution. The join materialization consists of pre-computing the join and storing its result. The join materialization is a process known as denormalization and its disadvantage is the redundancy which must be controlled due to the database consistency. A denormalized database is a problem when working with OLTP applications because it is needed controls to maintain consistency for each change that occurs in the database. However, this chapter focuses on physical design strategies for OLAP databases where reads and updates do not predominate. In consequence, denormalization can be a viable option as physical design proposal.

MonetDB

MonetDB is an open source relational database management system and has been developed by the CWI Database Architecture group since 1993 (Abadi, Boncz, Harizopoulos, Idreos, & Madden, 2013). It is a column-store focused on analytical applications; processing of analytical applications is based on queries and large amounts of data are updated from time to time. Additionally, it provides an engine with data structures and algorithms for efficient execution on columns in memory.

The data are physically organized according to the vertical fragmentation, i.e., each of the columns of a table is stored in a binary structure known as BAT (Binary Association Table). Each BAT is composed of object identifiers (OID) and the corresponding values. A BAT takes the form of two arrays in memory; one array is for identifiers and the other one is for the particular value. OIDs are sorted sequences of numbers generated by the system to identify each tuple (Abadi et al., 2013).

Each table is internally represented by a collection of BATs. For example, there are n BATs to represent a table R with m columns in MonetDB and a tuple t of the table R has the same OID in the associated BATs. In consequence, it is said that the identifiers are shared (they are the same) for all BATs associated with the columns of the table R and the OID order allows efficient reconstructions between BATs when it is needed. Indeed, a sequence sorted by the OIDs allows implicit identifiers. Therefore, finding a specific identifier i is to identify the position i at the array of individual values. Also, searching a particular value given a position is constant ($O(1)$).

Furthermore, the MonetDB algebra is based on the BAT algebra which is a low level algebra optimized to work with BATs and scalar values as entries. Intermediate results are always stored as intermediate BATs. MonetDB uses late materialization which allows to work with BATs throughout the query execution and it constructs and materializes the rows just before sending the final result. Also, each BAT algebra operator has a corresponding MAL (MonetDB Assemblee Language) instruction which is implemented as a simple operation on arrays; MAL is an assembly language (Idreos, Groffen, Nes, Manegold, Mullender, & Kersten, 2012).

To illustrate the MonetDB execution model, consider Figure 2. Data organization in relational databases and MonetDB2 which shows how two tables are represented in relational databases and in MonetDB. In traditional databases, data are organized by rows while MonetDB stores data in vertically partitioned tables. For example, the Orders table is decomposed in multiple tables by MonetDB; one table for each attribute. Each vertically partitioned table is composed of the object identifiers (OID) and the attribute values.

Moreover, Figure 3 shows a query on the tables Orders and Customer in order to retrieve dates and shipping priorities for customer´s orders between March 15, 1992 and March 15, 1995 that are in the building market segment and whose status is 'F'.

Figure 2. Data organization in relational databases and MonetDB

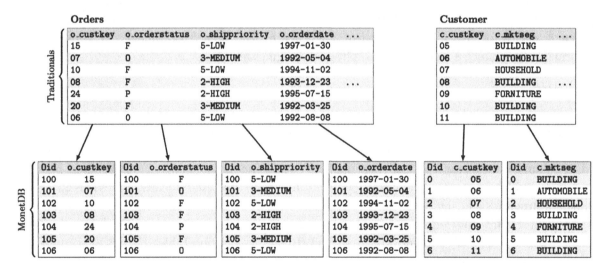

Figure 3. Sample query on orders and customer

```
1   SELECT O.ORDERDATE,  O_SHIPPRIORITY

2   FROM CUSTOMER,  ORDERS

3   WHERE C_MKTSEG          = 'BUILDING'

4       AND C_CUSTKEY       = O.CUSTKEY

5       AND O.ORDERDATE     > DATE '1992-03-15'

6       AND O.ORDERDATE     < DATE '1995-03-15'

7       AND O.ORDERSTATUS = 'F'
```

Figure 4. Approximate plan generated by MonetDB for the query on orders and customer

```
1   tmp1            = select(o_orderdate,1992-03-15, 1995-03-15)
2   tmp2            = reconstruc(o_orderstatus, tmp1)
3   tmp3            = select(tmp2, 'F')
4   input_orders    = reconstruc(o_custkey, tmp3)
5   tmp4            = select(c_mktseg, 'BUILDING')
6   input_customer  = reconstruc(c_custkey, tmp4)
7   join_result     = join(input_orders, input_customer)
8   tmp5            = voidHead(join_result)
9   tmp6            = reconstruc(o_orderdate, tmp5)
10  tmp7            = reconstruc(o_shippriority, tmp5)
11  result          = (inter6, inter7)
```

In summary, the SQL compiler of MonetDB translates from SQL to MAL in order to generate an execution plan. When MonetDB receives the query from Figure 3, creates an execution plan; an approximate plan is expressed at high level in Figure 4.

With respect to the plan in Figure 4, the database management system may decide to evaluate the selection operators in order to reduce the number of rows to be processed by the joins. Subsequently, it may execute the joins and other operators needed to answer the query.

Particularly, for the query on orders and customer presented in Figure 3, each step of the execution plan in Figure 4 is as follows:

1. In Step 1, the database management system evaluates the selection whose order date is between "03/15/1992" to "03/15/1995" and returns a set of OIDs, this is, $tmp1 = \{101, 102, 103, 105, 106\}$.

The variable $tmp1$ corresponds to the rows whose values met the selection condition and it is shown in Figure 5(a).

2. In Step 2, the coincidences between the $tmp1$ values and the identifiers of the o_orderstatus column are sought. Thus, a result table $tmp2 = \{(101, O), (102, F), (103, F), (105, F), (106, O)\}$ is built in Figure 5(b); $tmp2$ can be seen as a subset of the o_orderstatus column which has less data to be processed in the next selection.

3. The Step 3 in Figure 4 proceeds with the last selection for the orders table. Thus, $tmp3 = \{102, 103, 105\}$ is a set ordered of identifiers on $tmp2$. The variable $tmp3$ contains those identifiers that met the condition that the status of orders is "F" and it is shown in Figure 5(c).

4. The Step 4 in Figure 4 receives those data that meet all the selection conditions on the orders table and proceeds to find the coincidences between $tmp3$ and the identifiers of o_custkey. As result, Figure 5(d) shows $input\_orders = \{(102, 10), (103, 8), (105, 20)\}$ which will be input for the join operator.

Figure 5. Steps of execution plan on the orders table

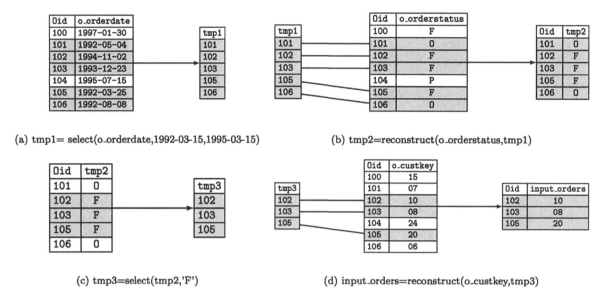

(a) tmp1= select(o_orderdate,1992-03-15,1995-03-15)

(b) tmp2=reconstruct(o_orderstatus,tmp1)

(c) tmp3=select(tmp2,'F')

(d) input_orders=reconstruct(o_custkey,tmp3)

Similarly, the Step 5 in Figure 4 filters the c_mktseg column whose value is "BUILDING" and produces the set of identifiers $tmp4 = \{0,3,5,6\}$.

The Step 6 in Figure 4 obtains the coincidences between the identifiers of the c_custkey column and $tmp4$. This intermediate column is named $input\_customer = \{(0,05),(3,08),(5.10),(6,11)\}$ and will be the input to the join operator in Step 7. These steps are represented in Figure 6.

Subsequently, the Step 7 in Figure 4 executes the join operator between input_orders and input_customer, and is represented in Figure 7(a). The table $join\_result = \{(102,5),(103,3)\}$ contains the identifiers corresponding to the column values that met the join condition, i.e., the first column of join_result corresponds to the identifiers of the orders table and the second column includes the identifiers of the customer table. Finally, Steps 8-11 project the expected answer from the join result. The query results are displayed in Figure 7(b).

Figure 6. Steps of execution plan on the customer table

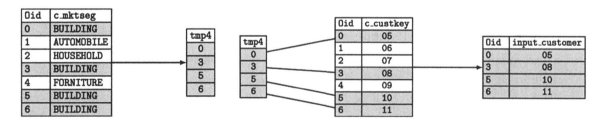

(a) tmp4= select(c_mktseg,'BUILDING')

(b) input_customer=reconstruct(c_custkey,tmp4)

Figure 7. Final steps of the execution plan

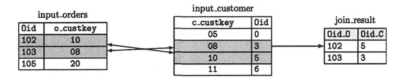

(a) join_result= join(input_orders, input_customer)

result

o_orderdate	o_shippriority
1994-11-02	5-LOW
1993-12-23	2-HIGH

(b) Final result

Related Work

Recent research on analytical processing has attracted much interest in the database community. Particularly, denormalization is a method that can improve query performance because eliminates the need for a join. In some works, the authors discussed how to incorporate denormalization into a database design methodology (Sanders & Shin, 2001; Shin & Sanders, 2006) and the authors concluded that the denormalization may improve query performance when there is a clear understanding of application requirements. In (Shin & Sanders, 2006), the denormalization is examined under several scenarios showing its effect on the query performance. (Costa, Cecilio, Martins, & Furtado, 2011) proposed an alternative storage in order to store the denormalized star schema model eliminating cost for processing joins. Additionally, column-oriented databases have been studied due to the interest of the research community and the industry. The column-oriented database management systems (columns stores) have proven to be faster in terms of time than traditional row-oriented systems. (Idreos et al., 2012) described the last two decades of the Monetdb technology and its future evolution. (Kemper & Neumann, 2011) introduced a hybrid system that can handle both OLTP and OLAP. (Xin, Rosen, Zaharia, Franklin, Shenker, & Stoica, 2013) presented a data warehouse system on large clusters. (Färber, May, Lehner, Große, Müller, Rauhe, & Dees, 2012) described the integration of transactional and analytical workload at the same time within a database management system. (Raman, Lohman, Malkemus, Mueller, Pandis, Schiefer, Attaluri, Barber, Chainani, Kalmuk, KulandaiSamy, Leenstra, Lightstone, Sharpe, Sidle, Storm, Zhang, & Liu, 2013) integrated techniques for processing column-organized tables that enhance Business Intelligence queries. Lastly, the activity whose purpose is to improve the query performance over a database management system is known as the physical design. In this sense, this chapter proposes a strategy based on denormalization and sorting for the database physical design using the column-oriented database management system, MonetDB.

PHYSICAL DESIGN ON THE TPC-H BENCHMARK USIGN MONETDB

Although MonetDB has properties that allow to have good runtimes for most queries based on OLAP schemes, it is still possible to improve its performance by applying physical design techniques.

The aim of this section is to describe the strategy that has led to the proposed physical design in this chapter. The proposed strategy will be described incrementally in base of how MonetDB executes queries without any physical design. Subsequently, the use of indexes is incorporated into the proposed strategy. Then, the denormalization is included in the proposed strategy and finally, the proposed strategy is introduced basing on denormalization and data sorting.

The strategy outlined in this chapter is directly dependent on the query characteristics. For example, the number of tables, operators involved and if there are nested queries.

To illustrate the proposed strategy, consider the query 3 of the TPC-H benchmark which is shown in Figure 8. The query 3 retrieves the shipping priority and potential revenue of the orders having the largest revenue among those that had not been shipped as of a given date in a specific market segment (TPC, 2013). The query 3 is characterized by a join between customer, order and lineitem, a selection condition on a column of customer, a selection condition on a column of orders, and a selection condition on a column of lineitem.

In addition, Figure 9 shows the logic plan used by the optimizer and the intermediate code generated by the SQL MAL compiler. The logical plan on the left image of Figure 9 is represented by a left-linear tree. The intermediate code on the right image of Figure 9 is expressed at high level and hides details of the MAL language in order to facilitate its explanation.

Figure 8. Shipping priority query
TPC, 2013.

```
 1  select
 2          l_orderkey,
 3          sum(l_extendedprice * (1 - l_discount)) as revenue,
 4          o_orderdate,
 5          o_shippriority
 6  from
 7          customer,
 8          orders,
 9          lineitem
10  where
11          c_mktsegment = 'BUILDING'
12          and c_custkey = o_custkey
13          and l_orderkey = o_orderkey
14          and o_orderdate < date '1995-03-15'
15          and l_shipdate > date '1995-03-15'
16  group by
17          l_orderkey,
18          o_orderdate,
19          o_shippriority
20  order by
21          revenue desc,
22          o_orderdate;
```

Figure 9. A logic plan and explain in MAL algebra

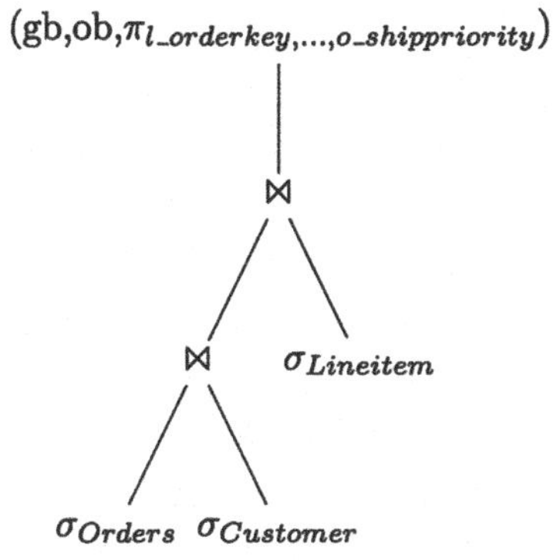

(a) An execution tree

```
tmp1 = select(o_orderdate,1995-03-15, '<')
tmp2 = reconstruc(o_custkey, tmp1)
tmp3 = reconstruc(o_orderkey, tmp1)
tmp4 = select(c_mktsegment, 'BUILDING')
tmp5 = reconstruc(c_custkey, tmp4)
tmp6 = join(tmp2, tmp5)
tmp7 = select(l_shipdate,1995-03-15, '>')
tmp8 = reconstruc(l_orderkey, tmp7)
tmp9 = join(tmp3, tmp8)
sql.exportResult("l_orderkey",...)
```

(b) An execution plan in MAL

Furthermore, the arrangement of the relationships customer, lineitem and orders within MonetDB is displayed in Figure 10 which shows that each relationship has a set of columns for each attribute relevant to the query. Also, each attribute has one column associated with an object identifier (OID). It can be noted that identifiers are the same for each column of the same relationship; however this is not the case with respect to the columns associated with a different relationship. Indeed, the identifiers corresponding to the attributes of LineItem are different from those corresponding to the attributes of customer and orders.

Query Evaluation by MonetDB

The first strategy corresponds to the step by step execution of the intermediate code in Figure 9(b), i.e., is the traditional behavior of MonetDB when executing the query in Figure 8.

Figure 10. Arrangement of relevant attributes for the query 3 within MonetDB

lineitem

Oid	l_orderkey	Oid	l_extendedprice	Oid	l_discount	Oid	l_shipdate
10	205	10	27819.65	10	0.10	10	1996-03-13
11	206	11	42918.12	11	0.02	11	1996-04-12
12	207	12	16039.20	12	0.05	12	1997-01-28
13	208	13	32096.32	13	0.09	13	1993-12-14
14	209	14	2740.68	14	0.15	14	1994-01-16
15	210	15	87205.50	15	0.05	15	1994-02-02
16	211	16	47362.12	16	0.10	16	1994-10-16

customer

Oid	c_custkey	Oid	c_mktseg
0	05	0	BUILDING
1	06	1	AUTOMOBILE
2	07	2	HOUSEHOLD
3	08	3	BUILDING
4	09	4	FORNITURE
5	10	5	BUILDING
6	11	6	BUILDING

orders

Oid	o_orderkey	Oid	o_custkey	Oid	o_shippriority	Oid	o_orderdate
210	209	210	3281	210	5-LOW	210	1996-01-02
211	210	211	2120	211	3-MEDIUM	211	1996-12-01
212	211	212	1200	212	5-LOW	212	1998-07-21
213	212	213	4212	213	5-LOW	213	1995-11-03
214	213	214	3145	214	3-MEDIUM	214	1992-06-03
215	214	215	2002	215	2-HIGH	215	1996-09-20
216	215	216	4192	216	2-HIGH	216	1992-02-21

In Step 1 of Figure 9, a selection on the o_orderdate column is performed and those tuples whose dates are less than '3/15/1995' are retrieved. In Steps 2 and 3 of Figure 9, the columns o_orderkey and o_custkey belonging to the orders table are prepared from the result of Step 1. These columns are the input to the join operator between orders-customer and orders-lineitem, respectively. In Step 4 of Figure 9, those tuples whose value of c_mktsegment is equal to "BUILDING" are filtered. Similar to the Steps 2 and 3, the Step 5 in Figure 9 searches for matches between identifiers obtained as a result of step 4 and identifiers from the c_custkey column of the customer table. The Step 5 produces the input for the join operator which it is executed between the tables orders and customer in Step 6. The Step 7 in Figure 9 identifies a subset of identifiers corresponding to tuples whose l_shipdate values are greater than "15/03/1995". In Step 8 of Figure 9, an input for the join operator between the tables orders and lineitem is built. This is achieved from the column l_orderkey looking for coincidences between its identifiers and the identifiers resulting from Step 7. The Step 9 in Figure 9 performs the last join between the tables orders and lineitem for the query 3 of Figure 8. Finally, all internal MAL operations for projection and the clauses order by and group by are executed in Step 10 of Figure 9.

Briefly, this strategy has some limitations. First, it can be expensive to perform selections in the language MAL depending of conditions on the selected column, that is, if the column values are sorted or not. For example, the database management system must execute a full scan on the column when making a selection on an unsorted column. Second, the joins are still executing in the same manner as a traditional relational database management system, that is, if the join inputs correspond to primary and foreign keys, then the database management system can run a known algorithm such as a join index. Thus, executing a join in a database management system is quadratic complexity. However, the query evaluation by MonetDB can be improved when considering a major feature of vertically partitioned tables in MonetDB. The cost of performing intersections between columns of a same table is low because it shares their identifiers (OIDs). However, in this particular case, identifiers for the three tables involved in the query of Figure 8 are not shared (are different). In consequence, the database management system can not exploit the use of intersections between identifiers when performing the joins and its choice is to run the join operator traditionally.

Indexes

Since a scan is executed by MonetDB each time a selection on any column is performed, the index creation on the selected columns can be a technique of physical design to be applied. In this case, indexes on the columns o_orderdate, c_mktsegment and l_shipdate can be built in order to speed up searches on the columns whose values meet the conditions for selection operators.

Indexes can improve performance of selection operators because it is not necessary to scan all the values in one column. For example, if a B-tree is used then the cost is the tree height plus the cost of scanning the leaves that contain selected data.

On the other hand, an index by each column of the join operator can improve the query performance. However, MonetDB does not guarantee the index use during a query execution although allows its creation. Therefore, MonetDB decides when to access an index and there is no way to indicate the use of a particular index.

Join Materialization

The denormalization can be used as a technique of physical design because there is no control on the use of indexes by MonetDB. The denormalization avoids the cost of join evaluation during the query execution because the join is precalculated. Nevertheless, the denormalization generates an additional cost because the join is materialized in an intermediate table. Note that this cost is paid each time the data is updated but data changes are performed from time to time; data are not highly changeable. In addition, OLAP queries can be executed many times. Thus, the join materialization will reduce the processing time by each query execution. Moreover, the materialized join allows to share the same identifiers (OIDs) between vertically partitioned tables corresponding to the intermediate table. Thus, the identifiers are shared (equal) for all columns involved in the query. Figure 11 illustrates the vertically partitioned tables corresponding to the join materialization between customer-orders and orders-lineitem.

Despite the fact that denormalization avoids the cost of the join during query execution, the scan to be performed when a selection is run still has a complexity $O(n)$ because the columns do not have any predetermined order. Although the denormalization improves query execution avoiding the join evaluations, it can take advantage of the data sorting to further improve the query performance.

Denormalization and Sorting

In addition to pre-calculate the joins, data from the intermediate table can be sorted according to the selectivities of predicates in order to avoid scanning all data when the selections are evaluated. To illustrate this strategy, consider the selectivities in Table 1. Table 1 shows the selectivities for the columns

Figure 11. Join Materialization in an intermediate table for the query 3

intermediate

Oid	l_orderkey	Oid	l_extendedprice	Oid	l_discount	Oid	l_shipdate	Oid	c_custkey	Oid	c_mktseg
10	205	10	27819.65	10	0.10	10	1996-03-13	10	05	10	BUILDING
11	206	11	42918.12	11	0.02	11	1996-04-12	11	06	11	AUTOMOBILE
12	207	12	16039.20	12	0.05	12	1997-01-28	12	07	12	HOUSEHOLD
13	208	13	32096.32	13	0.09	13	1993-12-14	13	08	13	BUILDING
14	209	14	2740.68	14	0.15	14	1994-01-16	14	09	14	FORNITURE
15	210	15	87205.50	15	0.05	15	1994-02-02	15	10	15	BUILDING
16	211	16	47362.12	16	0.10	16	1994-10-16	16	11	16	BUILDING

intermediate

Oid	o_orderkey	Oid	o_custkey	Oid	o_shippriority	Oid	o_orderdate
10	209	10	3281	10	5-LOW	10	1996-01-02
11	210	11	2120	11	3-MEDIUM	11	1996-12-01
12	211	12	1200	12	5-LOW	12	1998-07-21
13	212	13	4212	13	5-LOW	13	1995-11-03
14	213	14	3145	14	3-MEDIUM	14	1992-06-03
15	214	15	2002	15	2-HIGH	15	1996-09-20
16	215	16	4192	16	2-HIGH	16	1992-02-21

Table 1. Selectivities for the columns involved in the query 3

c_mktsegment	o_orderdate	l_shipdate
0.20	0.49	0.54

c_mktsegment, o_orderdate and l_shipdate because they allow to filter data in the query 3. The amount of data to be filtered is estimated by the selectivity. In particular, the condition on c_mktsegment is the less selective. Its selectivity is 0.20. This value indicates that the estimated result is 20% of the data once the selection is evaluated.

Also, suppose the intermediate table in Figure 12 where data are sorted by the selectivity of the columns in Table 1.

1. First, the intermediate table is sorted by the less selective attribute, c_mktsegment.
2. Second, those tuples with the same value of c_mktsegment are ordered by the second less selective attribute, o_orderdate.
3. Third, those tuples with the same value in c_mktsegment and o_orderdate are sorted by the third less selective attribute, l_shipdate.

Thus, the table is sorted in the same way as when specifying the clause ORDER BY c_mktsegment, o_orderdate, l_shipdate. It can be noted that Figure 12 shows an intermediate table for a row oriented database management system when MonetDB actually stores the data in vertically partitioned tables.

Moreover, the importance of sorting by selectivity has to do with the amount of data to be processed in the evaluation of each selection operator. For example, consider 100 million tuples, data independence and the data sorting by c_mktsegment, o_orderdate and l_shipdate. The first selection on c_mktsegment returns an estimated 20% (20 million tuples) of the initial data. Once the data are filtered based on the first selection, the second selection on o_orderdate returns an estimated 9.8 million of tuples $\left(100 * 0.2 * 0.49\right)$. Similarly, once the data are filtered based on the two first selections, the third selection on l_shipdate returns an estimated 5.2 million of tuples $\left(100 * 0.2 * 0.49 * 0.54\right)$.

Figure 12. Table sorted by selectivity

Intermediate

c_mktsegment	o_orderdate	l_shipdate	l_orderkey	
AUTOMOBILE	1992-05-04	1992-06-14	312	
AUTOMOBILE	1992-05-04	1992-06-14	101	
AUTOMOBILE	1992-05-04	1992-06-25	198	
...	...	...	...	...
AUTOMOBILE	1994-11-02	1994-11-30	204	
AUTOMOBILE	1994-11-02	1994-12-02	199	
AUTOMOBILE	1995-07-15	1995-08-12	254	
AUTOMOBILE	1995-07-15	1995-08-15	320	
BUILDING	1993-12-23	1994-01-10	908	
BUILDING	1993-12-23	1994-01-17	751	
BUILDING	1993-12-23	1994-02-21	114	
...	...	...	...	...
BUILDING	1997-01-30	1997-02-03	745	
BUILDING	1997-01-30	1997-02-13	622	
BUILDING	1997-01-30	1997-03-24	103	
BUILDING	1997-01-30	1997-03-30	809	
...	...	...	...	...

However, the amount of data to be processed for each selection can be larger and the query performance can be lower if another data sorting is performed. Suppose a second case where data are sorted by l_shipdate, o_orderdate and c_mktsegment. The first selection on l_shipdate returns an estimated 54% of the initial data, i.e., 54 million tuples. Note that in this case the estimated number of tuples exceeds 20 million when data were sorted first by c_mktsegment. For the second selection on o_orderdate, the estimated result is 26.4 million tuples $\left(100 * 0.54 * 0.49\right)$. Once more, in this case, the estimated number of tuples exceeds 9.8 million when data were sorted first by c_mktsegment and o_orderdate. Finally, the third selection on c_mktsegment retrieves an estimated 5.2 million $\left(100 * 0.54 * 0.49 * 0.2\right)$.

The following running illustrates how MonetDB executes the query under this strategy. First, MonetDB selects data based on the c_mktsegment column, returning a set of identifiers for rows whose values are 'BUILDING'. Then, from the o_orderdate column and the set of identifiers resulting from the first step, MonetDB builds an intermediate subset ($inter0$) from the o_orderdate column. This subset is sorted and is equal to

$$\left[\begin{matrix} \left(id_1, 1993-12-23\right), ..., \left(id_j, 1997-01-30\right), \\ \left(id_{j+1}, 1997-01-30\right), \left(id_{j+2}, 1997-01-30\right), ... \end{matrix}\right].$$

Similarly, after performing the selection on $inter0$, a subset sorted by o_orderdate and l_shipdate is produced when l_shipdate is regarded. Consequently, MonetDB is accessing smaller subsets of data according to the order established by the selectivities (from less selective to more selective), which is similar to using composite indexes by traditional database management systems.

Therefore, our strategy is proposed as a technique that takes advantage of the sorting and the join materialization. This strategy may improve performance of selections because data are ascendingly sorted by selectivity. Also, join materialization allows to share the same identifiers between vertically partitioned tables, and in consequence, subsequent reconstructions of selections can be faster. However, there are two particular cases. The first case is when the query has grouping without selection, i.e., the query has a group by clause without a where clause. The second case is when the from clause contains one table and a where clause. In the first case, the strategy of denormalization and sorting varies since the order of the intermediate table is based on columns of the GROUP BY clause. For the second case, the strategy assumes an order of the intermediate table according to the selectivities without join materialization. In this case, the intermediate table does not contain the join pre-calculation because the query has only one table.

To illustrate the first case, consider the query 18 of the TPC-H benchmark which is shown in Figure 13. The query 18 retrieves the 100 customers who have an order quantity above a certain level (TPC, 2013). The query 18 is characterized by a join between customer, order and lineitem, a nested query and a group by clause. The query 18 groups columns of the customer and order tables, and includes columns in the join condition (c_custkey and o_orderkey).

One of the physical operators for the grouping (the group by clause) is based on sorting. This type of operator sorts the data by the columns that are in the group by clause and then scans the sorted data in order to discard duplicate values or calculate the aggregate function that may be in the select clause. Because the query 18 has no selection condition and the join is evaluated before a grouping (the group by clause), the proposed strategy consists of materializing the join with the data sorted by the columns

Figure 13. Large volume customer query
Source: TPC, 2013.

```
1  select
2      c_name ,
3      c_custkey ,
4      o_orderkey ,
5      o_orderdate ,
6      o_totalprice ,
7      sum( l_quantity )
8  from
9      customer ,
10     orders ,
11     lineitem
12 where
13     o_orderkey in (
14         select
15             l_orderkey
16         from
17             lineitem
18         group by
19             l_orderkey having
20                 sum( l_quantity ) > 300
21     )
22     and c_custkey = o_custkey
23     and o_orderkey = l_orderkey
24 group by
25     c_name ,
26     c_custkey ,
27     o_orderkey ,
28     o_orderdate ,
29     o_totalprice
30 order by
31     o_totalprice desc ,
32     o_orderdate ;
```

in the group by clause. Thus, the evaluation of join and grouping may be advantaged because data is being sorted by the columns of the grouping which contain columns considered in the join.

In addition to pre-calculate the joins, data from the intermediate table can be sorted according to the columns of the group by clause. The intermediate table is sorted by c_name, c_custkey, o_orderkey, o_orderdate and o_totalprice. Thus, the table is sorted in the same way as when specifying the group by clause. With our strategy, Monetdb only scan data and for the groups with the same values in c_name, c_custkey, o_orderkey, o_orderdate and o_totalprice, Monetdb calculates the aggregate function (sum). The sorting for evaluating the group by clause is not required.

To illustrate the second case, consider the query 6 of the TPC-H benchmark which is shown in Figure 14. The query 6 retrieves the amount of revenue increase after eliminating certain company-wide discounts in a given year in a given percentage range (TPC, 2013). The query 6 is characterized by one table in the from clause, and four selection conditions on the attributes of lineitem.

Three indices may be defined on the columns l_shipdate, l_discount and l_quantity. These indices may improve the query performance because of data order. Nevertheless, MonetDB does not guarantee the index use during a query execution although allows its creation. Therefore, this strategy may not be used because there is no way to indicate the use of a particular index in Monetdb. Also, the join materialization strategy can not be utilized since there is no join in the query 6.

However, data may be sorted according to the selectivities of predicates in order to avoid scanning all data when the selections are evaluated. To exemplify this strategy, consider the selectivities in Table 2. Table 2 shows the selectivities for the columns l_discount, l_shipdate and l_quantity because they allow to filter data in the query 6. In particular, the condition on l_discount is the less selective. Its selectivity is 0.08. This value indicates that the estimated result is 8% of the data once the selection is evaluated.

Thus, the data is sorted by the most selective attribute, l_discount. Those tuples with the same value of l_discount may be ordered by the second less selective attribute, l_shipdate. Those tuples with the same value in l_discount and l_shipdate are sorted by the third less selective attribute, l_quantity. This is, the table is sorted in the same way as when specifying the clause ORDER BY l_discount, l_shipdate, l_quantity.

Moreover, sorting by selectivity may filter a high volume of data. For example, consider 100 million tuples, data independence and the data sorting by l_discount, l_shipdate, l_quantity. The first selection on l_discount returns an estimated 8% (8 million tuples) of the initial data. Once the data are filtered based on the first selection, the second selection on l_shipdate returns an estimated 1.2 million of tuples

Figure 14. Forecasting revenue change query
Source: TPC, 2013.

```
1 select
2     sum(l_extendedprice * l_discount) as revenue
3 from
4     lineitem
5 where
6     l_shipdate >= date '1994-01-01'
7     and l_shipdate < date '1995-01-01'
8     and l_discount = 0.06
9     and l_quantity < 24;
```

Table 2. Selectivities for the columns involved in the query 6

l_discount	l_shipdate	l_quantity
0.08	0.15	0.46

$(100 * 0.08 * 0.15)$. Similarly, once the data are filtered based on the two first selections, the third selection on l_quantity returns an estimated 552 thousand tuples $(100 * 0.08 * 0.15 * 0.46)$.

However, the amount of data to be processed for each selection can be larger and the query performance can be lower if another data sorting is performed. Suppose a second case where data are sorted by l_quantity, l_shipdate, l_discount. The first selection on l_quantity returns an estimated 46% of the initial data, i.e., 46 million tuples. Note that in this case the estimated number of tuples exceeds 8 million when data were sorted first by l_discount. For the second selection on l_shipdate, the estimated result is 6.9 million tuples $(100 * 0.46 * 0.15)$. Once more, in this case, the estimated number of tuples exceeds 1.2 million when data were sorted first by l_discount and l_shipdate. Finally, the third selection on l_discount retrieves an estimated 552 thousand tuples $(100 * 0.46 * 0.15 * 0.08)$.

The following running illustrates how MonetDB executes the query under this strategy. First, MonetDB selects data based on the l_discount column, returning a set of identifiers for rows whose values are 0.06. Then, from the l_shipdate column and the set of identifiers resulting from the first step, MonetDB builds an intermediate subset ($inter0$) from the l_shipdate column. This subset is sorted. Similarly, after performing the selection on $inter0$, a subset sorted by l_discount and l_shipdate is produced when l_shipdate is regarded. Consequently, MonetDB is accessing smaller subsets of data according to the order established by the selectivities (from less selective to more selective), which is similar to using composite indexes by traditional database management systems.

Strategy According to The Type of Queries

In summary, the strategy characteristics used in accordance with the characteristics of queries are shown in Table 3. Note that the denormalization and sorting by selectivity is represented in the second row of Table 3. The strategy characteristics of the first and third rows are variants of the strategy characteristics of the second row.

Those queries with characteristics presented in the fourth row of Table 3, the proposed strategy does not work because they have nestings, ourterjoin and the predicates exist and in. As future work, we plan to define a new strategy since the evaluation of such queries is highly expensive. It can be noted that typical optimizers do a poor job in presence of nested queries and they may identify better execution plans with equivalent queries without nesting. Sometimes, a nested query may be rewritten as an equivalent query without nesting.

Table 3. Strategy summary

Query Characteristics	Strategy Characteristics
One table and selection conditions	Sorting by selectivity
Two or more table, joins and selection conditions	Denormalization and sorting by selectivity
Two or more table, joins and grouping	Denormalization and sorting by columns in the group by clause
Nested queries (with the predicates exist and in) and outerjoin	No strategy

EXPERIMENTAL STUDY

In this section, the experimental study is reported. First, it begins by describing the metrics and the configuration that were considered in this experimental study. Second, it continues by comparing the physical design strategy proposed against the MonetDB evaluation.

Experimental Design

Datasets and Queries

This study was conducted on synthetic datasets. Synthetic datasets consist of data generated by DBGEN (TPC, 2013). The TPC-H benchmark offers a random data generator known as DBGEN. A benchmark is a way to measure performance on a system and this term is also used as a tool that provides a set of elements to measure the performance of an object (Gray, 1992).

TPC-H is a benchmark for decision support which has a set of queries and business-related data (TPC, 2013). Conceptually, the test database of this benchmark does not represent any particular business and its purpose includes a number of points for any interested organization. The scheme of this test database covers business relations which exist between customers and suppliers in countries from various regions. These relations involve orders, items and parts, and include attributes such as pricing and promotions, inventory, costs and profits, supply management and market analysis. Additionally, this benchmark has 21 queries and one view. All the queries require input parameters for their execution. The benchmark documentation suggests using a random generator of parameters. However, the TPC-H documentation contains randomly generated parameters for all queries in order to check the correctness on the results obtained by executing each of the queries (TPC, 2013). Thus, these parameters were used in the experimental study this chapter to study the query performance.

The use of this benchmark brings two main benefits:

1. Exploring large amounts of data. In fact, the benchmark provides flexibility to scale the database that is used to perform the experiments by a factor ranging from 1 to 100,000. Thus, a test database can have an approximate size from 1 GB to 100,000 GB. Particularly, the experimental study of this chapter has been performed in a 30 scale, i.e., 30 GB of data for the test database. The database size generated by DBGEN is defined by an attribute called SF. By default, the database size is 1 GB of data (SF = 1). DBGEN generates eight load ASCII files corresponding to tables from the TPC-H scheme (TPC, 2013).
2. Complex queries execution. It uses several operators available in database management systems in order to analyze their performance. Moreover, the complexity and the large number of data available within the database offer the possibility to generate an intensive work by the database server enabling better study their behavior under stress. Finally, the queries are suitable for online analytical processing which is ideal to analyze the performance of the database management system MonetDB (MonetDB, 2015).

In this experimental study, we ran our strategy on 18 TPC-H queries because characteristics of the queries 4, 13, 20 and 22 make the proposed strategy does not work. Thus, we plan to study the characteristics of these queries as a future work in order to modify this strategy or propose a new strategy able to improve the performance of this query type.

Metrics

To study the query performance, the number of reading and writing blocks and the total execution time were reported. On one hand, the number of reading and writing blocks corresponds to the number of blocks that the database server read or wrote from disc while executing a query. To obtain the number of blocks, the TRACE command was used for each query. The TRACE command allows to create a log called tracelog where information about query performance can be found. In particular, the tracelog includes reads and writes performed. Since the information is broken down by each MAL statement executed by the database server, the number of reading and writing blocks was summed to calculate the total number of reading and writing blocks. On the other hand, the total execution time represents the time in milliseconds elapsed from when the SQL query is sent to when the first set of responses is received. The total execution time usage was measured by means of the option --interactive of mclient; mclient is the MonetDB command-line tool.

Experimental Environment

The experimental study was conducted on a computer INTEL®CoreTMi7-3770 3.40GHz with 8GB of memory and 500GB of hard disk. MonetDB v11.17.21 "Jan2014-SP3" (64-bit, 64-bit oids) was installed with all utilities on Debian 3.2.60 with AMD architecture 64. Before running a query, we cleaned the cache and used this computer in exclusive mode to avoid keeping data in main memory that could benefit any of the strategies.

Impact of the Proposed Physical Design on the Query Performance

This experiment was performed in order to experimentally determine that the runtime and the number of reading and writing blocks when processing TPC-H queries with physical design strategy proposed in this chapter are better with respect to traditional query evaluation by MonetDB.

Figure 15 contains a bar chart that graphically shows the execution times of 18 TPC-H queries. The X axis has the Qi queries where i represents the query number and the Y axis corresponds to time units of milliseconds.

Figure 15 shows that runtimes are better when using the proposed physical design strategy. Since the characteristics of the proposed strategy, query execution times are lower with respect to traditional MonetDB evaluation. Firstly, the join execution is avoided because the join is precalculated into an intermediate table. Secondly, the full scan may be avoided because the intermediate table is sorted by selectivity of columns involved in the selection predicates. Thus, smaller datasets are retrieved as the selection predicates are evaluated. Thirdly, data from the intermediate table share the same object identifiers, that is, the set of identifier values are equal for each column. Therefore, reconstructions between columns are extremely fast since they are processed as arrays in memory.

To validate the results, have been performed statistical tests to determine which of the two possibilities described in the experiments is better, that is, if the execution times obtained by applying the proposed physical design for the 18 TPC-H queries represent a significant improvement over the times of MonetDB. These times are shown in Table 4.

Figure 15. Execution times in MonetDB with and without physical design

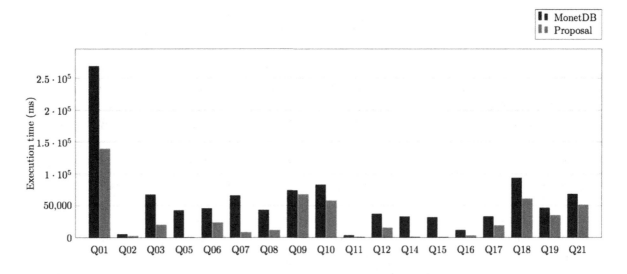

Table 4. Execution times for 18 TPC-H queries with or without physical design

Query	MonetDB	Strategy
Q01	269230.827	139170.925
Q02	5258.143	2422.05
Q03	67660.636	19819.35
Q05	42581.971	299.664
Q06	45834.826	23311.352
Q07	66042.868	8086.016
Q08	42903.105	11269.341
Q09	74014.565	67805.423
Q10	82703.775	57834.156
Q11	3392.667	812.351
Q12	36665.607	15012.516
Q14	32630.302	961.735
Q15	31617.7	432.048
Q16	11599.048	3132.215
Q17	32764.731	18718.081
Q18	93414.148	60902.177
Q19	46551.41	34784.777
Q21	68366.192	51187.795

A Shapiro-Wilk test was performed for each sample in order to determine if the data corresponding to the resulting times for both possibilities follow a normal distribution (ETH, 2015). A $p - value < 0.0001$ has resulted for the sample related to MonetDB execution times, and a $p - value = 0.0006$ has been obtained for the sample corresponding to the proposed physical design strategy. Both $p - values$ indicate that there is statistically significant evidence that the samples do not follow a normal distribution.

Since the statistical evidence shows that the data does not follow a normal distribution, it is appropriate to apply a statistical test that does not require such a condition. The statistical test that adapts to this situation is the nonparametric (Moore & McCabe, 2009), known as the Wilcoxon signed-rank with dependent samples (Berenson & Levine, 2012), because the samples are related by the query number. When this test is applied, a $p - value < 0.0001$ is obtained. This result evidences that there is a statistically significant difference between the times obtained by executing queries using the physical design strategy ($Mdn = 16870$) and MonetDB ($Mdn = 44370$).

Moreover, Figure 16 graphically reports the number of blocks read by MonetDB without physical design and when the proposed physical design strategy is applied. The X axis contains the query identifiers and the Y axis corresponds to the number of reading blocks.

Fewer blocks may be read because no join is executed; an intermediate table is built with the attributes necessary to execute the query. In the case of the query 21, the number of reading blocks is not reduced because it has a set of nested queries that run on the table with the largest number of tuples (lineitem).

Thus, statistical tests were applied to analyze whether the results obtained in terms of readings by MonetDB using the proposed strategy are statistically significant on the execution of 18 TPC-H queries without any physical design. The amounts of reading blocks are shown in Table 5.

Initially, a Shapiro-Wilk test (ETH, 2015) was conducted to determine if the sample data in Table 5 follow a normal distribution. In this sense, a sample was taken for MonetDB execution and the proposed physical design. Subsequently, the following results were obtained: a $p - value = 0.007$ for the first sample and a $p - value = 0.0006$ for the second sample. Both $p - values$ are such that there is statistically significant evidence that the samples in Table 5 do not follow a normal distribution.

Figure 16. Number of data blocks read by MonetDB with and without physical design

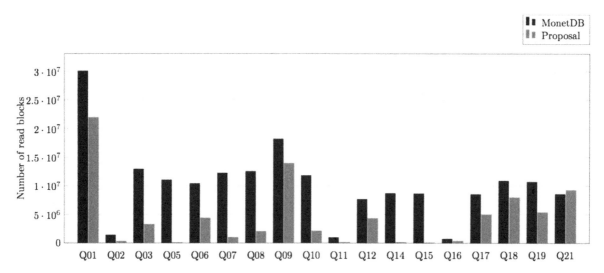

Table 5. Blocks read when executing 18 TPC-H queries with and without physical design

Query	MonetDB	Strategy
Q01	30071272	21944728
Q02	1392592	314992
Q03	12929096	3273008
Q05	11008112	68368
Q06	10392448	4385536
Q07	12232976	992760
Q08	12517488	2015840
Q09	18180408	13916360
Q10	11797296	2094144
Q11	963160	140576
Q12	7668088	4346984
Q14	8703624	110176
Q15	8644712	51016
Q16	727440	357160
Q17	8552864	5003376
Q18	10879968	7975008
Q19	10714688	5398392
Q21	8579272	9266376

Afterward, the Wilcoxon signed-rank test (Berenson & Levine, 2012) was applied with samples dependent on the query number because it does not require that samples follow a normal distribution. This nonparametric test produced a $p - value < 0.0001$ and therefore, there is a statistically significant difference between the readings obtained when running queries with the proposed strategy ($Mdn = 2.684$ million) and MonetDB ($Mdn = 10.55$ million).

Additionally, Figure 17 shows the number of blocks written by MonetDB when executing 18 TPC-H queries. The graphical representation used is a bar chart for two possibilities: i) blocks written by MonetDB without any associated physical design; ii) blocks written by MonetDB when the proposed physical design strategy is considered. On the X axis are the identifiers of the Qi queries and the Y axis has the number of writing blocks.

Finally, statistical tests were used to determine whether the results obtained in terms of the number of blocks written are statistically significant, i.e., tests for data samples represented in Table 6. The first column of Table 6 is the number of blocks written by MonetDB when executing queries without any physical design, and the second column contains the number of blocks written by MonetDB when running queries using the proposed physical design.

Firstly, a Shapiro-Wilk test was performed in order to determine if the sample data in Table 6 follow a normal distribution (ETH, 2015). The test returned a $p - value < 0.0001$ for the samples corresponding to the number of blocks written by MonetDB without physical design and with the proposed strategy. In both cases, $p - values$ are such that there is statistically significant evidence that the samples in Table 6 do not follow a normal distribution.

Figure 17. Number of data blocks written by MonetDB with and without physical design

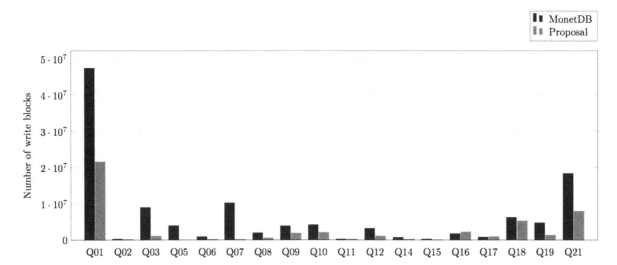

Table 6. Blocks written to run 18 TPC-H queries with and without physical design

Query	MonetDB	Strategy
Q01	47335104	21509104
Q02	270256	160472
Q03	8967360	1095696
Q05	3943128	23136
Q06	893704	171256
Q07	10236080	113704
Q08	1962576	578592
Q09	3857784	1864856
Q10	4163640	2081096
Q11	261512	246256
Q12	3178072	1112968
Q14	719952	193536
Q15	264696	64376
Q16	1754928	2222512
Q17	818120	922328
Q18	6175200	5275280
Q19	4752920	1344608
Q21	18326120	7961680

Secondly, the nonparametric statistical test known as Wilcoxon signed-rank (Moore & McCabe, 2009) was used with samples dependent on the query number (Berenson & Levine, 2012). This test was selected because it does not require that samples follow a normal distribution. This test returned a $p - value = 0.0001$ and therefore, there is a statistically significant difference between the writings obtained when executing queries with the proposed strategy ($Mdn = 1.009$ million) and with MonetDB ($Mdn = 3.518$ million).

FUTURE RESEARCH DIRECTIONS

The proposed physical design strategy is based on denormalization and sorting. This strategy improved those queries characterized by joins, selections and groupings. However, although we do not report processing times in this chapter, the proposed strategy equaled or worsened processing times when it was applied to outer joins or nested queries with the predicate "exists" and the operator "in". This type of query has a high computational cost because the database management system must compare all rows against all rows. Therefore, the strategy of how MonetDB evaluates such queries must be analyzed in depth in order to propose a physical design strategy that achieves a better performance. In this sense, to continue the study of the four TPC-H queries for which the proposed strategy was not designed, we plan to study the operation of the operators that prevented the improvement, for example, the predicate "exists" and the operator "in" which are generally presented with nested queries.

Moreover, it can materialize joins considering several queries. In this work, the joins were materialized by each query. Nevertheless, several queries may contain joins between the same tables. In this way, we can also propose a strategy that efficiently materializes joins given a set of queries.

Lastly, the experimental study was performed on a centralized database but MonetDB offers 5 optimizers which consist of a sequence MAL functions that will be executed to transform the execution plan generated at first for a query (MonetDB, 2015). Each optimizer has its benefits and was developed for certain situations. The minimal pipe is the default optimizer and is the minimum necessary to run the server. The default pipe can improve the performance when working with large tables. It distributes the work parallelly. The no mitosis pipe is identical to default but without horizontal fragmentation. It is used when there are problems with the fragmentation. The sequential pipe can improve performance when working with large tables, but it does not distribute the work in parallel. The recycler pipe try to reuse the intermediate BATs generated during the execution. As future work, we plan to extend the experimental study to analyze the behavior of the optimizers when working on several stations in parallel.

CONCLUSION

This chapter has unveiled a physical design proposal for database of the TPC-H benchmark and has also presented results indicating that there is a substantial improvement in the query performance in MonetDB when the physical design strategy proposed in this work is used. Performance is measured in terms of execution times and the number of reading and writing blocks.

The proposed physical design reported in this work is based on the denormalization and ordering of attributes that are part of operators capable of filtering or helping in some way to accelerate the query execution. There is a cost associated with the creation of an intermediate table (denormalization) because the join is precomputed and this step takes considerable time. However, the TPC-H queries are based on OLAP and are frequently executed, and therefore, paying this price seems worthwhile.

To support the results obtained, an experimental study has been conducted. In this study, 18 from the 21 TPC-H queries were considered using cold cache. In the experimental study, execution times and reads and writes were reported when executing queries making use of the proposed physical design and without physical design.

According to the reported results, query performance is better when the proposed physical design was used. In addition, statistical tests were done to validate the results. Non-parametric tests were chosen because they statistically demonstrated that sampled data were not normally distributed. Based on statistical tests, it was proved that the resulting runtimes for 18 queries using the proposed physical design were better with a statistically significant difference. Something similar happened for reads and writes. Statistical tests also showed that readings and writings performed by using the proposed strategy were lower with a statistically significant difference with respect to execute the 18 TPC-H queries without any physical design.

REFERENCES

Abadi, D., Boncz, P., Harizopoulos, S., Idreos, S., & Madden, S. (2013). The design and implementation of modern column-oriented database systems. *Foundations and Trends in Databases*, 5(3), 197–280. doi:10.1561/1900000024

Abadi, D. J. (2008). *Query execution in column-oriented database systems* (PhD Thesis). Massachusetts Institute of Technology. Retrieved from http://cs-www.cs.yale.edu/homes/dna/papers/abadiphd.pdf

Berenson, M. L., & Levine, D. M. (2012). *Basic business statistics: Concepts and Applications* (12th ed.). Boston, MA: Prentice Hall.

Costa, J. P., Cecílio, J., Martins, P., & Furtado, P. (2011). ONE: A Predictable and Scalable DW Model. Data Warehousing and Knowledge Discovery Lecture Notes in Computer Science.

Elmasri, R., & Navathe, S. B. (2015). *Fundamentals of Database Systems* (7th ed.). Boston, MA: Pearson.

ETH. (2015). *Seminar for Statistics. Shapiro-wilk normality test*. Retrieved May 15, 2015, from http://stat.ethz.ch/R-manual/R-devel/library/stats/html/shapiro.test.html

Färber, F., May, N., Lehner, W., Große, P., Müller, I., Rauhe, H., & Dees, J. (2012). The SAP HANA Database -- An Architecture Overview. *A Quarterly Bulletin of the Computer Society of the IEEE Technical Committee on Data Engineering*, 35(1),28–33.

Gray, J. (1992). *The Benchmark Handbook: For Database and Transaction Processing Systems*. San Francisco, CA: Morgan Kaufmann Publishers.

Idreos, S., Groffen, F., Nes, N., Manegold, S., Mullender, K. S., & Kersten, M. L. (2012). Monetdb: Two decades of research in column-oriented database architectures. *A Quarterly Bulletin of the Computer Society of the IEEE Technical Committee on Data Engineering*, 35(1), 40–45.

Kemper, A., & Neumann, T. (2011). HyPer: A hybrid OLTP&OLAP main memory database system based on virtual memory snapshots. In *Proceeding of the 27th International Conference on Data Engineering*, (pp, 195-206). Hannover, Germany: IEEE. doi:10.1109/ICDE.2011.5767867

Lynch, C. A. (1988). Selectivity estimation and query optimization in large databases with highly skewed distribution of column values. In *Proceedings of the 14th International Conference on Very Large Data Bases (VLDB)*, (pp. 240-251). San Francisco, CA: Morgan Kaufmann Publishers Inc.

Monet D. B. B. V. (2015). *The column-store pioneer*. Retrieved May 15, 2015, from http://www.monetdb.org/Home

Moore, D. S., & McCabe, G. P. (2009). *Introduction to the Practice of Statistics* (6th ed.). New York, NY: W. H. Freeman and Company.

Ramakrishnan, R., & Gehrke, J. (2003). *Database Management Systems* (3rd ed.). New York, NY: McGraw-Hill.

Raman, V., Lohman, G. M., Malkemus, T., Mueller, R., Pandis, I., Schiefer, B.,... Liu, S. (2013). DB2 with BLU acceleration: so much more than just a column store. *Proceedings of the VLDB Endowment*, *6*(11), 1080-1091. doi:10.14778/2536222.2536233

Sanders, G., & Shin, S. (2001). Denormalization effects on performance of RDBMS. In *Proceedings of the 34th Annual Hawaii International Conference on System Sciences*. Maui, HI: IEEE Computer Society.

Shin, S. K., & Sanders, G. L. (2006). Denormalization strategies for data retrieval from data warehouses. *Decision Support Systems*, *42*(1), 267–282. doi:10.1016/j.dss.2004.12.004

Transaction Processing Performance Council (TPC). (2013). *TPC Benchmark H Standard Specification Revision 2.17.0, 2014*. Retrieved May 15, 2015, from http://www.tpc.org/tpc_documents_current_versions/pdf/tpc-h_v2.17.1.pdf

Xin, R. S., Rosen, J., Zaharia, M., Franklin, M. J., Shenker, S., & Stoica, I. (2013). Shark; k: SQL and Rich Analytics at Scale. In *Proceedings of the 2013 International Conference on Management of Data (SIGMOD)*, (pp. 13-24). New York, NY: ACM. doi:10.1145/2463676.2465288

KEY TERMS AND DEFINITIONS

Column-Store: A database management system that vertically partitions and stores the tables by set of columns.

Denormalization: The process of storing the calculation of a join. In this process the changes made during normalization are reversed because of performance reasons.

Execution Plan: Set of operators to be executed in a certain order to answer the query.

Index: A data structure used to access data quickly.

Join: Operator used to combine information from two or more tables.

Physical Design: An activity that involves determining storage structures and access structures for ensuring good performance of the queries.

Row-Store: A database management system that stores table data as rows.

Vertically Partitioned Table: A Vertically Partitioned Table is a table whose data are stored as key-value.

Chapter 2
Data Clustering

Bülent Başaran
Bilecik Şeyh Edebali University, Turkey

Fatih Güneş
Bilecik Şeyh Edebali University, Turkey

ABSTRACT

Data clustering can be associated with and used in many research methodologies and application areas. In this chapter, the basics of data clustering and some kind of its applications are given with examples and a real data set. The examples show data types and help to explain basic clustering algorithms. The real data help to classify countries in terms of their computer and internet proficiency levels. After examining the resulting clusters obtained from four different basic methods according to eight computer and internet proficiencies, it is found that the regional closeness of countries and being outside of a union are the major drivers of those clusters' formation. This application gives some possible future research area extensions to researchers about clustering the same or other countries by different proficiencies and unions.

INTRODUCTION

Increasing diversity of customer expectations becomes one of the major concerns for all kinds of companies and institutions when they try to promote and maintain their businesses in today's competitive markets. This consumption based diversity increases the kinds of components, parts, equipment, products, data and knowledge in all fields. It is not possible to deal with that much diversity without any standardization for companies in order to survive for a long time because desirably driven needs are too many to offer. Standardization necessitates classification to make categories that each one of them contains a certain number of similar members. These groups are homogenous in certain levels and they are called clusters.

Without any clustering, parts production and data processing are very difficult and time consuming. For example, if a part family or cluster is structured with similar parts, the production processes of them are also similar. Therefore, it is possible to assign a certain number of machines to produce them specifically and there is no confusion at all. In a call center with an answering machine for example, certain numbers are dedicated for certain operations and any client must dial just the exact number that

DOI: 10.4018/978-1-5225-1776-4.ch002

is needed for the operation. Without clustering data, any server has to deal with all kinds of attributes of the data under process. This situation makes the server a bottleneck server and the time spending on each datum is increased. Data clustering facilitates handling and processing the data and makes possible to assign right server to them.

There are a certain number of data clustering methods to use. Each one of them has its own characteristics and can be used to a specific kind of data structures. The results of these methods on the same data can be different. When the same data set is identified with different measurement units, the results of these different units will also be different even if the same clustering method is used on them. It is advisable to use different clustering methods on a given data set to compare resulting patterns in order to find a suitable one for the researcher's purpose (Martinez & Martinez, 2005; Nisbet et al., 2009). The purpose of this chapter is to describe these methods with remarkable examples. This chapter also makes possible to find out advantages and disadvantages of them. The reader will be able to learn how to classify the data, how the methods differ from each other, and which one is the most applicable for his/her data structure.

APPLICATION AREAS OF DATA CLUSTERING

Because it is the most widely used technique for grouping data, and separation of the data into groups according to some attributes is necessary in many processes, procedures, disciplines, and strategic issues, data clustering has many application areas spread all over the life. Those areas include pattern recognition, data analysis, image processing, outlier detection, market segmentation, facilities layout, natural sciences etc. Aggarwal and Reddy (2014) approach those issues from the application domains in which the clustering problem arising point of view. They listed the problem areas as intermediate step for other fundamental data mining problems, collaborative filtering, customer segmentation, data summarization, dynamic trend detection, multimedia data analysis, biological data analysis, and social network analysis. DeSarbo and Mahajan (1984) approach them from external and/or internal information (reasons) on the objects to be classified. External reasons do not depend on the physical resemblances of the objects whereas internal reasons depend on those physical resemblances of the objects. Punj and Stewart (1983) present marketing research application areas. Those areas are market segmentation, identifying homogeneous groups of buyers, development of potential new product opportunities, test market selection, and general data reduction. Gong and Richman (1995) give the application areas of atmospheric science research. Wilk and Pelka (2013) give numerical data application areas such as classification of people, plants, animals and chemical elements, and symbolic data application areas such as data mining, artificial intelligence, machine learning research, cognitive psychology research and conceptual clustering.

After examining and deepening insights into those literature approaches, the application areas of data clustering are decided to be classified into following three points of views and recent studies related to them are given:

Item Based Clustering

- **Object Clustering:** The goal of object clustering methods is to partition an attribute of objects into subgroups such that those in each particular group attribute of objects are similar to each other than to those of other groups. According to the types of objects that can be assessed in two different forms;

- **Real Objects:** Clustering of real objects means exploring and manipulating of the items in their environment and comparing new objects to familiar ones. Objects will be compared or clustered with describing measurable attributes of objects (e.g., short, long, heavy, similarity, dissimilarity)
- **Virtual Objects:** "Virtual object" is defined as an object that does not exist in the real world. In evaluating of virtual items, objects are characterized by their position in the Euclidean space and naturally, dissimilarity between two objects is defined by their Euclidean distance (Yiu & Mamoulis, 2004). In this type of objects, data can be composed of a number of records stored in a database or figures in computer games

Subject Clustering

- **Behavioral (Psychological):** Cluster analysis of psychological distress and illnesses is often used in medical researches. A study made in this area shows us that health-related behaviors are clustered in adolescents (Busch et al., 2013).
- **Contextual:** Contextual clustering (or text clustering) is the application of cluster analysis to textual documents. It has applications in document organization, indexing, topic extraction, customer segmentation and fast information getting or filtering (Aggarwal & Zhai, 2012).
- **Time Based Clustering:** Data are called in cluster analysis static if all their attribute values do not change with time, or change negligibly. Clustering of time-dependent data, separated into three groups depending on their history such as historical, current and futuristic. Historical data remains the best way to forecast the future. For example creating a new financial model requires some assumptions about the underlying assets and the most used way here needs to be used historical data or personal experience or instinct.

Actual data represents the current state such as instant traffic flows in cities or arrival/departure rate of *an* airport.

To predict the future outcomes such as weather forecast, world population or financial crisis have been major subjects of scientists, and data mining has become one of the most referenced techniques in this area.

- **Action Based Clustering:** Data also can be categorized into 2 groups based on their stability and moving (Mobile). Data clustering in a network of mobile smart phones or prediction of mobile user routes from cellular data can be given as an example for moving data. Stable data can be defined as data unchangeable as depending on location.

DISTANCE MEASURES AND DATA EXAMPLES

Distances, in other words dissimilarities, or similarities between data items need to be calculated beforehand in order to apply most of data clustering methods. There are two commonly used data types in data clustering: interval and binary. There are many similarity and dissimilarity coefficients or distance measures (more than 20) in literature that can be used for binary data (Yin & Yasuda, 2005; Yin & Yasuda, 2006). There are a certain number of distance measures that can be used for interval data also.

An example is given in Table 1 for interval data and another similar example is given in Table 3 for binary data in order to explain how the methods work. Let us assume that there are 12 parts needed to be clustered in a production facility. Each part has four attributes to separate from the others. Part numbers and their attributes are given in Table 1 as interval data.

The most widely used distance measures for interval data are 'Euclidean' (Equation 1), 'Squared Euclidean' (Equation 2), 'City-block (Manhattan)' (Equation 3) and 'Mahalanobis' (Equation 4) expressed in equations below.

$$d_{ij} = \left\{ \sum_{i=1}^{k} \left(X_{ik} - X_{jk} \right)^2 \right\}^{1/2} \text{ Euclidean} \tag{1}$$

where,

dij is distance (dissimilarity) between objects i and j,

k is number of attributes,

Xik is the value of attribute k of object i,

Xjk is the value of attribute k of object j.

$$d_{ij} = \sum_{i=1}^{k} \left(X_{ik} - X_{jk} \right)^2 \text{ Squared Euclidean} \tag{2}$$

Table 1. Example of interval data sets

Parts	Length (cm)	Diameter (cm)	Number of Holes	Production Time (Minute)
P1	50	3	4	20
P2	20	6	8	16
P3	36	10	3	14
P4	42	14	9	14
P5	18	4	2	8
P6	26	6	2	22
P7	2	12	5	10
P8	30	11	4	16
P9	4	5	2	6
P10	50	8	6	15
P11	24	3	3	17
P12	16	10	3	9

Table 3. Example of binary data sets

Parts	Thread Cutting	Paint Work	Furnace Heating	Aluminum Alloy
P1	1	0	1	1
P2	1	1	0	1
P3	0	0	1	0
P4	1	0	0	1
P5	0	1	1	0
P6	0	1	0	1
P7	1	1	1	1
P8	1	0	1	0
P9	1	1	0	0
P10	0	1	0	1
P11	1	0	1	0
P12	0	0	1	1

$$d_{ij} = \sum_{i=1}^{k} \left| X_{ik} - X_{jk} \right| \text{City-block (Manhattan)} \tag{3}$$

$$d_{ij} = \left[\left(X_{ik} - X_{jk} \right) C^{-1} \left(X_{ik} - X_{jk} \right)' \right]^{1/2} \text{Mahalanobis} \tag{4}$$

where C is the covariance matrix of all data.

The distance between P1 and P2 in Table 1 is calculated by Euclidean distance as follows.

$$d_{12} = \sqrt{(50-20)^2 + (3-6)^2 + (4-8)^2 + (20-16)^2} = 30.676$$

The squared Euclidean distance is 941. The City-block (Manhattan) distance is calculated as follows.

$$d_{12} = \left| 50-20 \right| + \left| 3-6 \right| + \left| 4-8 \right| + \left| 20-16 \right| = 41$$

For Mahalanobis distance, inverse of the covariance matrix of all data is needed. This matrix is given directly here because its calculation is quite long.

$$C^{-1} = \begin{bmatrix} 0.0072 & -0.0005 & -0.0117 & -0.0138 \\ -0.0005 & 0.1053 & -0.0869 & 0.023 \\ -0.0117 & -0.0869 & 0.2797 & -0.0106 \\ -0.0138 & 0.023 & -0.0106 & 0.0747 \end{bmatrix}$$

Therefore, the Mahalanobis distance between P1 and P2 is as follows:

$$d_{12} = \sqrt{\begin{bmatrix} (50-20) + (3-6) \\ +(4-8) + (20-16) \end{bmatrix} C^{-1} \begin{bmatrix} (50-20) + (3-6) \\ +(4-8) + (20-16) \end{bmatrix}'} = 3.223$$

Table 2 gives only the distances between P1 and the other parts in terms of above mentioned distance measures. This table shows how big these measures differ from each other.

Table 2. Dissimilarities (distances) between P1 and the other parts

	P2	P3	P4	P5	P6	P7	P8	P9	P10	P11	P12
Euclidean	30.676	16.793	15.684	34.249	24.352	49.860	21.909	48.166	7.349	26.192	36.428
Sqr. Euclid.	941	282	246	1173	593	2486	480	2320	54	686	1327
City-block	41	28	30	47	31	68	32	64	12	30	53
Mahalanobis	3.223	2.480	3.259	2.564	2.862	3.960	2.701	3.224	1.715	1.730	3.060

The similar example for parts in Table 1 can be given in binary format also. Let us assume that we have 12 parts to be clustered again and their 4 needed processes will help us to cluster them. The first three processes of the parts are whether or not they need thread cutting, paint work, and furnace heating. The last process or attribute is whether or not they contain aluminum alloy. Table 3 shows the binary data of this example. If any part needs any of these processes, there is 1 input value at the cross section of that part and the process. If the part does not need this process, the input value is 0 for that corresponding process.

Some of the similarity coefficients that can be used for binary data are Simple matching, Hammann, Jaccard, Ochiai, Rogers and Tanimoto, and Russel and Rao. They are given in Table 4 and the notes of Table 4 explain their notations (Yin & Yasuda, 2005).

For the binary example given in Table 3, simple matching, Hammann, and Jaccard coefficients between P1 and P5 are calculated as follows.

The binary data of them are these:

P1: 1, 0, 1, 1
P5: 0, 1, 1, 0

For this data $a = 1$, b = 2, c = 1, d = 0.

Simple matching:

$$s_{15} = \frac{1+0}{1+2+1+0} = 0.25$$

Hammann:

$$s_{15} = \frac{(1+0)-(2+1)}{(1+0)+(2+1)} = -0.5$$

Table 4. Similarity coefficients for binary data

Coefficients	Similarity Expression (*Sij* =)	Range
1. Simple matching	$(a+d)/(a+b+c+d)$	0 – 1
2. Hammann	$[(a+d)-(b+c)]/[(a+d)+(b+c)]$	−1 – 1
3. Jaccard	$a/(a+b+c)$	0 – 1
4. Ochiai (Cosine)	$a/[(a+b)(a+c)]^{1/2}$	0 – 1
5. Rogers and Tanimoto	$(a+d)/[a+2(b+c)+d]$	0 – 1
6. Rusell and Rao	$a/(a+b+c+d)$	0 – 1

Notes: a: the attribute exists in both items; b: the attribute exists in item i but does not exist in item j; c: the attribute exists in item j but does not exist in item i; d: the attribute does not exist in both items.

Jaccard:

$$s_{15} = \frac{1}{1+2+1} = 0.25$$

Table 5 gives only the similarities between P1 and the other parts in terms of above mentioned similarity coefficients for binary data in Table 3. Table 5 shows how big these measures differ from each other.

As can be seen in Table 2 and 5, significant numerical differences can occur between different methods and coefficients. Therefore, the final solution of any coefficient or method can be different. The size and members of the clusters can change accordingly. This is not the only problem that the analysts can experience. If the measurement scales of attributes (variables) are different, resulting distance measures or similarity coefficients may be ambiguous. In the parts data in Table 1 for example, the measure of first two attributes are centimeters, the third one is amount, and the fourth one is minute. There are big differences between the ranges of these attribute series. On the other hand, if the production time unit is chosen as seconds instead of minutes, there will be big differences in results also (Churchill, 1995).

Because of those reasons, standardizing the data before clustering is important for most of the times. Converting each variable (attribute) to standard Z scores is the most widely used form of standardization. A variable's Z scores are calculated by subtracting each number in the series from the mean and dividing by the standard deviation. Comparisons between variables are much easier and if the scale of the variable is changed (e.g. meter-centimeter, second-minute), no differences occur on the final clustering results when the data are standardized (Hair et al., 2010). Conversely, standardization may remove some natural relationship reflected in the scaling of the variable. If the data are measured roughly of the same magnitude for each variable, it is better not to standardize them (Churchill, 1995). In addition to this, standardization may not give any significant changes on the results for some data. Because of these reasons and in order to give comparable solutions to researchers, interval data example in Table 1 are calculated without standardization when the clustering methods are explained, and then the clustering results are given for both unstandardized and standardized data in the following sections.

CLUSTERING METHODS

Before describing the methods, there is one important thing to realize that clustering and classification are different in nature. In generally speaking, clustering methods are unsupervised learning methods because they do not require training data (Nisbet et al., 2009). Conversely, classification techniques

Table 5. Similarity coefficients between P1 and the other parts

	P2	P3	P4	P5	P6	P7	P8	P9	P10	P11	P12
1. Simple matching	0.500	0.500	0.750	0.250	0.250	0.750	0.750	0.250	0.250	0.750	0.750
2. Hammann	0.000	0.000	0.500	-0.500	-0.500	0.500	0.500	-0.500	-0.500	0.500	0.500
3. Jaccard	0.500	0.333	0.667	0.250	0.250	0.750	0.667	0.250	0.250	0.667	0.667
4. Ochiai (Cosine)	0.667	0.577	0.816	0.408	0.408	0.866	0.816	0.408	0.408	0.816	0.816
5. Rogers and Tanimoto	0.333	0.333	0.600	0.143	0.143	0.600	0.600	0.143	0.143	0.600	0.600
6. Russel and Rao	0.500	0.250	0.500	0.250	0.250	0.750	0.500	0.250	0.250	0.500	0.500

necessitate training data. Although classification techniques seem to be different from clustering, they can be used for clustering purposes also

Clustering is a predictive model that you get a prediction class of model such as estimating temperature of the next day or identify factory department of any new product in production line in plants. Gleen and Cooper (1987) divided clustering methods into four categories: hierarchical, partitioning, overlapping, and ordination. Because overlapping, such as graph theoretic approach, and ordination, such as factor analysis and multidimensional scaling, are mainly used for different applications other than clustering and they are somewhat different from this chapter's coverage, they are not explained here. Hierarchical methods are divided into two categories: agglomerative and divisive (Gleen & Cooper, 1987; Hair et al., 2010; Martinez & Martinez, 2005). Agglomerative hierarchical methods begin with each case (object) as a separate cluster and at every steps in the clustering procedure, two of the clusters are merged. It continues until a single cluster, which contains all cases, stands alone. Divisive methods are the reverse of agglomerative methods. They begin with a single cluster containing all cases and divide the cases into two or more clusters until all of the cases form their own one-member clusters. Agglomerative methods are more popular because divisive methods face problems of computational complexity. Partitioning methods are known as nonhierarchical methods and included in k-means clustering.

Clustering can be shown mathematically as follows:

Let $T = \{\}$ be a database and each represents a data items

Let $C = \{\}$ be a set of m clusters

each should be included in a class

Each is separate class and each class includes its own records

There are various types of clustering algorithms for predicting continuous variables or categorical variables from a set of continuous predictors or categorical factors. In the scope of data mining algorithms has developed many techniques for clustering processes, including "Bayesian algorithm", "based on the decision tree algorithms", "k-means", "neural networks" and "K-nearest neighbor algorithm" (Silahtaroglu, 2008).

Among below-explained methods, k-means, fuzzy c-means and hierarchical clustering are unsupervised, and k-nearest neighbor, and support vector machines, decision trees including ID3, C4.5, SLIQ and SPRINT algorithms are supervised.

K-Means Clustering

K-means method was first developed by MacQueen (1967). This method can be applied by using one of the two procedures. The steps of the first procedure are as follows:

1. Specifying the initial number of clusters.
2. Dispersing each data item to these clusters randomly or by using a method.
3. Calculating the distances of each item to each cluster centroids (mean coordinate). Squared Euclidean distance is widely used for this purpose. Each item is included to the nearest cluster. All cluster centroids are calculated again.

4.   Repeating the third step until there is no item to be assigned.

Only the step two is different for the second procedure. In second procedure, initial seed points are formed. It is not necessary to include all data items to these seed points at the beginning.

According to first procedure in k-means clustering, we need to separate all objects (cases, parts) into clusters. Let us assume that we need only two clusters and the parts between P1 and P6 belong to one and between P7 and P12 belong to the other cluster. These procedures can be applied for both interval and binary data without any difference. All calculations and steps are the same. Let us explain this procedure for interval data in Table 1. Centroid coordinates are calculated in Table 6.

Squared Euclidean distances of P1 to Cluster 1 is $(50 - 32)^2 + (3 - 7.167)^2 + (4 - 4.667)^2 + (20 - 15.667)^2 = 360.583$ and to Cluster 2 is $(50 - 21)^2 + (3 - 8.167)^2 + (4 - 3.833)^2 + (20 - 12.167)^2 = 929.083$. The Squared Euclidean distances of all parts to clusters are shown in Table 7. The last column of Table 7 shows whether the part goes to the other cluster or stays in the cluster that is currently belongs to. The minimum distance between the part and the clusters is chosen and the part moves accordingly.

In terms of the new structures of clusters, the centroid coordinates are calculated again. These steps are repeated until there is no possible revision that is until every part stays in its own cluster. After the second iteration of the algorithm as shown in Table 7, the resulting clusters are as follows.

C1 = {P1, P3, P4, P6, P8, P10}

C2 = {P2, P5, P7, P9, P11, P12}

The standardized version of resulting clusters will be as follows:

C1 = {P5, P6, P7, P9, P11, P12}

C2 = {P1, P2, P3, P4, P8, P10}

The second procedure in k-means clustering is formation of clusters based on initial seed points. This is the only difference from the steps of first procedure. In the parts example of interval data given in Table 1 again, let us assume that two initial seed points are specified as P11 and P12. The coordinates of P11 are 24, 3, 3, 17, and the coordinates of P12 are 16, 10, 3, and 9.

Table 6. Initial centroid coordinates

	$\bar{X}_1$	$\bar{X}_2$	$\bar{X}_3$	$\bar{X}_4$
{P1, P2, P3, P4, P5, P6}	$\dfrac{\sum_{i=1}^{6} X_i}{6} = 32$	$\dfrac{\sum_{i=1}^{6} X_i}{6} = 7.167$	$\dfrac{\sum_{i=1}^{6} X_i}{6} = 4.667$	$\dfrac{\sum_{i=1}^{6} X_i}{6} = 15.667$
{P7, P8, P9, P10, P11, P12}	$\dfrac{\sum_{i=7}^{12} X_i}{6} = 21$	$\dfrac{\sum_{i=7}^{12} X_i}{6} = 8.167$	$\dfrac{\sum_{i=7}^{12} X_i}{6} = 3.833$	$\dfrac{\sum_{i=7}^{12} X_i}{6} = 12.167$

Table 7. Distances of all parts to clusters

	Iteration 1				Iteration 2		
	Distance to Cluster 1	Distance to Cluster 2	Based on Minimum Distance		Distance to Cluster 1	Distance to Cluster 2	Based on Minimum Distance
Cluster 1							
P1	360.58	929.08	Stays in Cluster 1	P1	163.58	1390.47	Stays in Cluster 1
P2	156.58	37.75	Goes to Cluster 2	P3	21.583	504.81	Stays in Cluster 1
P3	29.58	232.42	Stays in Cluster 1	P4	64.25	873.47	Stays in Cluster 1
P4	168.25	505.08	Stays in Cluster 1	P6	209.92	268.81	Stays in Cluster 1
P5	271.92	47.08	Goes to Cluster 2	P8	87.58	299.81	Stays in Cluster 1
P6	84.58	129.75	Stays in Cluster 1	P10	126.58	1318.47	Stays in Cluster 1
Cluster 2							
P7	955.58	381.75	Stays in Cluster 2	P2	379.92	78.81	Stays in Cluster 2
P8	19.25	103.75	Goes to Cluster 1	P5	547.92	35.47	Stays in Cluster 2
P9	889.25	340.42	Stays in Cluster 2	P7	1426.92	174.81	Stays in Cluster 2
P10	326.92	853.75	Goes to Cluster 1	P9	1362.92	131.14	Stays in Cluster 2
P11	85.92	59.75	Stays in Cluster 2	P11	259.92	150.14	Stays in Cluster 2
P12	311.25	39.08	Stays in Cluster 2	P12	594.92	19.81	Stays in Cluster 2

Squared Euclidean distances of P1 to seed point P11 is $(50 - 24)^2 + (3 - 3)^2 + (4 - 3)^2 + (20 - 17)^2 = 686$ and to seed point P12 is $(50 - 16)^2 + (3 - 10)^2 + (4 - 3)^2 + (20 - 9)^2 = 1327$. Because the minimum is the distance of P11 (686), P1 is joined to P11. The new centroid coordinates of {P1, P11} are calculated as follows:

$$\overline{X}_1 = \frac{50 + 24}{2} = 37$$

$$\overline{X}_2 = \frac{3 + 3}{2} = 3$$

$$\overline{X}_3 = \frac{4 + 3}{2} = 3.5$$

$$\overline{X}_4 = \frac{20 + 17}{2} = 18.5$$

The coordinates of P12 are the same. New distances to seed points are calculated again. P2 is the next part to calculate its distances. Squared Euclidean distances of P2 to seed point {P11, P1} is $(20 - 37)^2 + (6 - 3)^2 + (8 - 3.5)^2 + (16 - 18.5)^2 = 324.5$ and to seed point {P12} is $(20 - 16)^2 + (6 - 10)^2 + (8 - 3)^2 + (16 - 9)^2 = 106$. Because the minimum is the distance to the seed point {P12} (106), P2 is joined to {P12}. The new centroid coordinates of {P12, P2} are calculated. This procedure is repeated for all remaining parts. Table 8 shows all of the distances from seed points to all parts. The last column of Table 8 shows which seed point that the part belongs to in terms of the minimum distance. This situation forms the clusters also.

In terms of the second procedure, the resulting clusters are as follows:

C1 = {P11, P1, P3, P4, P6, P8, P10}

C2 = {P12, P2, P5, P7, P9}

The standardized version of resulting clusters will be as follows:

C1 = {P11, P1, P2, P5, P6, P9}

C2 = {P12, P3, P4, P7, P8, P10}

If the initial seed points were P1 and P2, the resulting clusters would be as follows:

C1= {P1, P3, P4, P8, P10}

C2= {P2, P5, P6, P7, P9, P11, P12}

The standardized version of resulting clusters will be as follows:

C1 = {P1, P3, P5, P6, P9, P11, P12}

C2 = {P2, P4, P7, P8, P10}

As can be seen the new cluster formation of the seed points P1 and P2, remarkable differences occurred from cluster formation of the seed points P11 and P12. Therefore, the resulting clusters highly depend on the initial seed points in the second procedure of k-means clustering. K-means clustering is computationally faster and produces tighter clusters than hierarchical clustering (Sharma et al., 2012, Singhal et al., 2013, Fahad, et al. 2014).

Table 8. Distances of all parts to seed points P11 and P12

	Seed Point 1	**Seed Point 2**	**Joining**	**Cluster Members**
P1	686	1327	S1	{P11, P1}
P2	324.5	106	S2	{P12, P2}
P3	70.5	336.5	S1	{P11, P1, P3}
P4	238.5	626.5	S1	{P11, P1, P3, P4}
P5	424.625	48.5	S2	{P12, P2, P5}
P6	186.625	205.125	S1	{P11, P1, P3, P4, P6}
P7	927.156	293.625	S2	{P12, P2, P5, P7}
P8	14.9063	438.6563	S1	{P11, P1, P3, P4, P6, P8}
P9	852.227	74.65625	S2	{P12, P2, P5, P7, P9}
P10	391.477	1906.039	S1	{P11, P1, P3, P4, P6, P8, P10}

For the binary data in Table 3, k-means clustering procedures can be applied without any changes or similarity coefficient calculations. Because of this reason, without any explanation of the procedures again, Table 9 and 10 show the binary data example results of both procedures in k-means clustering. As described earlier for the interval data example, initial clusters of the first procedure are also the same for the binary data example. Initial seed points of the second procedure are also the same of P11, P12 and P1, P2 as explained above.

Table 9. Distances of all parts to clusters

	Iteration 1				Iteration 2		
	Distance to Cluster 1	**Distance to Cluster 2**	**Based on Minimum Distance**		**Distance to Cluster 1**	**Distance to Cluster 2**	**Based on Minimum Distance**
Cluster 1							
P1	0.861	0.722	Goes to Cluster 2	P2	0.560	1.653	Stays in Cluster 1
P2	0.861	1.056	Stays in Cluster 1	P4	0.760	1.510	Stays in Cluster 1
P3	1.194	1.056	Goes to Cluster 2	P6	0.360	2.082	Stays in Cluster 1
P4	0.861	1.056	Stays in Cluster 1	P10	0.360	2.082	Stays in Cluster 1
P5	1.194	1.056	Goes to Cluster 2	P12	1.160	1.224	Stays in Cluster 1
P6	0.861	1.389	Stays in Cluster 1				
Cluster 2							
P7	0.861	0.722	Stays in Cluster 2	P1	1.360	0.796	Stays in Cluster 2
P8	1.194	0.722	Stays in Cluster 1	P3	2.160	0.796	Stays in Cluster 2
P9	1.194	1.056	Stays in Cluster 2	P5	1.960	0.939	Stays in Cluster 2
P10	0.861	1.389	Goes to Cluster 1	P7	1.160	0.939	Stays in Cluster 2
P11	1.194	0.722	Stays in Cluster 2	P8	2.360	0.367	Stays in Cluster 2
P12	0.861	1.056	Goes to Cluster 1	P9	1.560	1.224	Stays in Cluster 2
				P11	2.360	0.367	Stays in Cluster 2

Table 10. Distances of all parts to seed points P11 and P12

	Seed Point 1	**Seed Point 2**	**Joining**	**Cluster Members**
P1	1.0000	1.0000	S1	{P11, P1}
P2	2.2500	3.0000	S1	{P11, P1, P2}
P3	2.0625	1.0000	S2	{P12, P3}
P4	0.5625	2.2500	S1	{P11, P1, P2, P4}
P5	2.8906	1.2500	S2	{P12, P3, P5}
P6	1.6406	1.8125	S1	{P11, P1, P2, P4, P6}
P7	1.1602	1.8125	S1	{P11, P1, P2, P4, P6, P7}
P8	1.8525	1.3125	S2	{P12, P3, P5, P8}
P9	1.3525	1.8281	S1	{P11, P1, P2, P4, P6, P7, P9}
P10	1.1194	2.5781	S1	{P11, P1, P2, P4, P6, P7, P9, P10}

In terms of the second procedure, the resulting clusters are as follows:

C1 = {P11, P1, P2, P4, P6, P7, P9, P10}

C2 = {P12, P3, P5, P8}

If the initial seed points were P1 and P2, the resulting clusters would be as follows:

C1= {P1, P3, P5, P8, P11, P12}

C2= {P2, P4, P6, P7, P9, P10}

K-Nearest Neighbor Clustering

K-nearest neighbor (KNN) clustering is based on Cover and Hart's (1967) nearest neighbor pattern classification study. In this clustering method, there are initially specified classes and a certain number of sample data points that belong to these classes. The classes of these sample data points are specified initially. Which classes are these sample data points belonged to are definitely specified beforehand. Those data are called labeled data. If data items do not belong to any class at the beginning, they are called unlabeled data. A vector of a number of attributes represents each data point. Any sample *x* input vector is assigned to a class in which its nearest neighbor is located. The steps of *K*-nearest neighbor algorithm are as follows (Keller et al., 1985):

1. Let $W = \{x_1, x_2, ..., x_n\}$ be a set of *n* labeled samples (training set).
2. Input a sample vector *y*, of unknown classification.
3. Specify *K* nearest neighbor, $1 \leq K \leq n$
4. Compute distance from *y* to *xi*.
5. If $i \leq K$, include *xi* in the set of *K*-nearest neighbors.
6. If *xi* is closer to *y* than any previous nearest neighbor, delete farthest in the set of *K*-nearest neighbors and include *xi* in the set of *K*-nearest neighbors.
7. Determine the majority class represented in the set of *K*-nearest neighbors.
8. If a tie exists, compute sum of distances of neighbors in each class that tied. If no tie occurs, the first choice is to classify *y* in the class of minimum sum, the second choice is to classify *y* in the class of last minimum found, and the third choice is to classify *y* in the majority class.

For the parts example of interval data in Table 1, a training set must be specified first in order to apply KNN classification algorithm. Let us specify P1, P2, P3 and P4 as the training set. In this training set, let us specify P1 and P2 as the members of first class and P3 and P4 as the members of second class. In order to be a member of one of these two classes for any part in the data other than in the training set, *K*-nearest neighbors of that part in the training set is calculated. *K* cannot exceed the number of elements in the training set so that the maximum value of *K* is 4 here. Let *K* is equal to 3 and find out the first-three-nearest neighbors of P5 using Euclidean distance.

- Euclidean distance of P1-P5 is 34.25 and rank order of it is 4.
- Euclidean distance of P2-P5 is 10.39 and rank order of it is 1.
- Euclidean distance of P3-P5 is 19.92 and rank order of it is 2.
- Euclidean distance of P4-P5 is 27.59 and rank order of it is 3.

The first-three-nearest neighbors are taken into account according to rank orders. Only one of them is in the first class. On the other hand, two of them are in the second class. This means that P5 is closer to the second class and it belongs to that one. For each remaining part, K-nearest neighbors are calculated and the parts are assigned to classes. The training set does not change throughout the algorithm. Table 11 shows the rank orders of each parts. For example, P9 belongs to second class when K is 3. It belongs to first class when K is 2 because the nearest one is taken although one of them is in Class 1 and the other one is in Class 2. For example, P10 belongs to Class1, Class1, Class 2, and Class 1 when K is 1, 2, 3, and 4 respectively. Table 12 shows the rank orders of each parts in terms of the standardized data.

KNN depends on the researcher's subjective judgement when choosing the training data set, the classes, and how many nearest neighbors in it (Miner et al., 2012). If irrelevant variables are included the algorithm, the classification accuracy decreases (Nisbet et al. 2009). Some advantageous aspects of the KNN method, on the other hand, are easy implementation, and relatively simple and fast calculation (Singhal et al., 2013).

Fuzzy C-Means Clustering

In order to apply fuzzy c-means (FCM) method in data clustering, a $\mu k(xjk)$ matrix must be prepared. An element in this matrix shows that the membership of item j to the cluster which is structured by attribute k. For example, a linear membership function (5) can be used for this purpose.

Table 11. Nearest distance rank orders of interval data of parts example

		P5	P6	P7	P8	P9	P10	P11	P12
Class 1	P1	4	4	4	4	4	1	4	4
	P2	1	1	1	2	1	4	1	1
Class 2	P3	2	2	2	1	2	3	2	2
	P4	3	3	3	3	3	2	3	3

Table 12. The standardized version of Table 11

		P5	P6	P7	P8	P9	P10	P11	P12
Class 1	P1	3	1	4	4	3	2	1	4
	P2	2	3	2	2	2	4	3	2
Class 2	P3	1	2	1	1	1	1	2	1
	P4	4	4	3	3	4	3	4	3

$$\mu(x) = \begin{cases} 1, & b < x \\ \dfrac{(x-a)}{(b-a)}, & a < x \le b \\ 0, & x \le a \end{cases} \tag{5}$$

In this linear membership function, b is upper and a is lower limit for this attribute. If any element has this attribute as much as bigger than upper limit, this element will be a full (1) member of this cluster. If the element has this attribute smaller than the lower limit, it is not at all (0) a member of this cluster.

The next thing to do is to prepare a U starting classification matrix (6) which is consists of X elements, c piece of clusters and subject to (7), (8) and (9) constrains.

$$U = \begin{matrix} & \begin{matrix} X_1 & X_2 & X_3 & \cdots & X_n \end{matrix} \\ \begin{matrix} 1 \\ 2 \\ 3 \\ \vdots \\ c \end{matrix} & \begin{bmatrix} u_{11} & u_{12} & u_{13} & \cdots & u_{1n} \\ u_{21} & u_{22} & u_{23} & \cdots & u_{2n} \\ u_{31} & u_{32} & u_{33} & \cdots & u_{3n} \\ \vdots & \vdots & \vdots & \ddots & \vdots \\ u_{c1} & u_{c2} & u_{c3} & \cdots & u_{cn} \end{bmatrix} \end{matrix} \tag{6}$$

$$0 \le u_{ij} \le 1 \,, i = 1, 2, \ldots, c; j = 1, 2, \ldots, n \tag{7}$$

$$\sum_{i=1}^{c} u_{ij} = 1 \,, j = 1, 2, \ldots, n \tag{8}$$

$$\sum_{j=1}^{n} u_{ij} > 0 \,, i = 1, 2, \ldots, c \tag{9}$$

Constraint 7 ensures that all elements in the matrix are fuzzy numbers between 0 and 1. Constraint 8 ensures that any classified X element can be a member of any clusters with different membership degrees. Here, 1 defines full membership and 0 defines full non-membership. The sum of memberships of any element cannot exceed 1. If the sum of memberships of any element is equal to 1, this means that the element is completely represented by existing clusters in hand. Constraint 9 ensures that any cluster must have at least an element with a membership degree greater than 0. That is, it is unnecessary to present an empty cluster. For the sum of any row in the matrix, there is no other constraint except being greater than 0.

Although FCM method was first developed by Bezdek (1981), it is based on an objective function and a "Pickard loop" algorithm taken from Ruspini's (1970) study. The last structure of the algorithm developed by Bezdek is as follows:

Step 1: Specify and determine below components.
1.   A fuzzy clusters matrix showing data attributes and consisting of $\mu k(xjk)$ elements.

2. The number of clusters denoted by c. $(2 \leq c \leq n)$
3. A degree of fuzziness denoted by m. $(1 \leq m \leq \infty)$
4. A stopping criterion denoted by ε. $(\varepsilon > 0)$
5. A 'U^0' fuzzy classification matrix that shows initial membership degrees and provides the conditions of constraints 7-9 (The superscript of U is not the zero exponent of U. It shows that 'U^0' is a beginning matrix. This matrix is randomly specified in general).

Step 2: Form a 'V' cluster centers matrix by using Equation 10.

$$v_{ik} = \frac{\sum_{j=1}^{n} (u_{ij})^m \mu_k(x_{jk})}{\sum_{j=1}^{n} (u_{ij}^m)} \tag{10}$$

Step 3: Form a new 'U^1' fuzzy classification matrix by using Equation 11 (The superscript of U is not an exponential calculation. It shows the iteration number.).

$$u_{ij} = \frac{1}{\sum_{l=1}^{c} \left(\frac{\sum_{k=1}^{p} (\mu_k(x_{jk}) - v_{ik})^2}{\sum_{k=1}^{p} (\mu_k(x_{jk}) - v_{lk})^2} \right)^{1/(m-1)}} \tag{11}$$

Step 4: Calculate '$Jm(U,V)$' by using Equation 12 which shows that the sum of total weighted squared distances of the elements from the centers of clusters.

$$J_m(U,V) = \sum_{j=1}^{n} \sum_{i=1}^{c} u_{ij}^m \sum_{k=1}^{p} (\mu_k(x_{jk}) - v_{ik})^2 \tag{12}$$

Step 5: If this iteration's '$Jm(U,V)$' value minus the value of previous one is equal or smaller than ε stopping criterion, stop the algorithm. If not, go to Step 2.

If value of m in Step 1 is chosen closer to infinity, the fuzziness degree of the final solution will be very high. This fuzziness degree shows how clusters are overlapped each other. If $m = 1$, a crisp partitioning occurs. This means that any data point is just belong to only one cluster when the algorithm finished. Usually, m is chosen between 1 and 2 in literature. If a big value is chosen, the membership degrees become to equal for all clusters so that no cluster can be distinctly identified from the other clusters.

For the interval data of parts example in Table 1, let $x1$, $x2$, ..., $x12$ are the columns of initial U^0 matrix and $c = 2$ (two clusters) as given below. The cluster memberships in this matrix are randomly specified. For the rows of $[\mu k(xjk)]$ matrix, let $x1$, $x2$, ..., $x12$ are the parts and for the columns of the matrix, let $k1$, $k2$, $k3$, and $k4$, are the length, diameter, number of holes, and production time attributes respectively. Let $m = 2$ and $\varepsilon = 0.0001$, fuzziness degree and stopping criterion respectively.

$$U^0 = \begin{array}{c|cccccccccccc} & x_1 & x_2 & x_3 & x_4 & x_5 & x_6 & x_7 & x_8 & x_9 & x_{10} & x_{11} & x_{12} \\ \hline c_1 & 0.4 & 0.6 & 0.9 & 0.1 & 0.6 & 0.3 & 0.2 & 0.8 & 0.4 & 0.9 & 0.7 & 0.2 \\ c_2 & 0.6 & 0.4 & 0.1 & 0.9 & 0.4 & 0.7 & 0.8 & 0.2 & 0.6 & 0.1 & 0.3 & 0.8 \end{array}$$

$$[\mu_k(x_{jk})] = \begin{array}{cccc} k_1 & k_2 & k_3 & k_4 \\ \begin{bmatrix} 50 & 3 & 4 & 20 \\ 20 & 6 & 8 & 16 \\ 36 & 10 & 3 & 14 \\ 42 & 14 & 9 & 14 \\ 18 & 4 & 2 & 8 \\ 26 & 6 & 2 & 22 \\ 2 & 12 & 5 & 10 \\ 30 & 11 & 4 & 16 \\ 4 & 5 & 2 & 6 \\ 50 & 8 & 6 & 15 \\ 24 & 3 & 3 & 17 \\ 16 & 10 & 3 & 9 \end{bmatrix} \end{array}$$

In terms of this given values, because $c = 2$, there will be two cluster centers. Because the number of attributes is four, the dimensions of cluster centers matrix V will be 2×4. The $v11$ element of this matrix is calculated as follows:

$$v_{11} = \frac{\begin{array}{l}(0,4^2 \times 50) + (0,6^2 \times 20) + (0,9^2 \times 36) + (0,1^2 \times 42) + (0,6^2 \times 18) + (0,3^2 \times 26) + \\ (0,2^2 \times 2) + (0,8^2 \times 30) + (0,4^2 \times 4) + (0,9^2 \times 50) + (0,7^2 \times 24) + (0,2^2 \times 16)\end{array}}{0,4^2 + 0,6^2 + 0,9^2 + 0,1^2 + 0,6^2 + 0,3^2 + 0,2^2 + 0,8^2 + 0,4^2 + 0,9^2 + 0,7^2 + 0,2^2}$$
$$= 31,8438$$

Therefore, cluster centers matrix V is;

$$V = \begin{bmatrix} 31.84383 & 7.438287 & 4.148615 & 14.54408 \\ 23.34748 & 8.94695 & 4.687003 & 13.24668 \end{bmatrix}$$

The distance of part j to cluster center i is calculated by Equation 13.

$$\sqrt{\sum_{k=1}^{p}\left(\mu_k(x_{jk}) - v_{ik}\right)^2} \tag{13}$$

For example, the Euclidean distance of P1 to the first cluster center is denoted by $d11$.

$$d_{11} = \sqrt{(50-31.84383)^2 + (3-7.438287)^2 + (4-4.148615)^2 + (20-14.54408)^2} = 19.47137 \, .$$

The square root operation in $d11$ is not necessary for the operations in Equation 11. Therefore, without square root operation, it is equal to 379.1341. The squared Euclidean distances matrix D is;

$$D = \begin{vmatrix} 19.47 & 12.62 & 5.05 & 13.04 & 15.84 & 9.82 & 30.54 & 4.27 & 29.31 & 18.27 & 9.41 & 17.02 \\ 28.14 & 6.20 & 12.83 & 19.82 & 9.37 & 9.98 & 21.81 & 7.52 & 21.21 & 26.76 & 7.26 & 8.72 \end{vmatrix}$$

New element $u11$ in the new formed U^1 fuzzy classification matrix by using Equation 11 is;

$$u_{11} = \cfrac{1}{\left(\cfrac{19.47}{19.47}\right)^1 + \left(\cfrac{19.47}{28.14}\right)^1} = 0,5910$$

New fuzzy classification matrix U^1 is;

$U^1 =$

	x_1	x_2	x_3	x_4	x_5	x_6	x_7	x_8	x_9	x_{10}	x_{11}	x_{12}
c_1	0.591	0.329	0.718	0.603	0.372	0.504	0.417	0.638	0.420	0.594	0.436	0.339
c_2	0.409	0.671	0.282	0.397	0.628	0.496	0.583	0.362	0.580	0.406	0.564	0.661

The first iteration result of Equation 12 is;

$(0.4^2 \times 19.47) + (0.6^2 \times 28.14) + (0.6^2 \times 12.62) + (0.4^2 \times 6.20)$
$+(0.9^2 \times 5.05) + (0.1^2 \times 12.83) + (0.1^2 \times 13.04) + (0.9^2 \times 19.82) + (0.6^2 \times 15.84) + (0.4^2 \times 9.37)$
$+(0.3^2 \times 9.82) + (0.7^2 \times 9.98) + (0.2^2 \times 30.54) + (0.8^2 \times 21.81) + (0.8^2 \times 4.27) + (0.2^2 \times 7.52)$
$+(0.4^2 \times 29.31) + (0.6^2 \times 21.21) + (0.9^2 \times 18.27) + (0.1^2 \times 26.76) + (0.7^2 \times 9.41) + (0.3^2 \times 7.26)$
$+(0.2^2 \times 17.02) + (0.8^2 \times 8.72) = 109.2731$

Table 13 shows the results of Equation 12 for 20 iterations of the algorithm.
Because $\varepsilon = 0.0001$ (stopping criterion) and the difference of $Jm(U,V)$ values between iteration 19 and 20 is less than 0.0001, the algorithm stops. Cluster membership results of 20th iteration are shown below.

$U^{20} =$

	x_1	x_2	x_3	x_4	x_5	x_6	x_7	x_8	x_9	x_{10}	x_{11}	x_{12}
c_1	0.678	0.277	0.877	0.735	0.206	0.514	0.327	0.677	0.312	0.696	0.401	0.181
c_2	0.322	0.723	0.123	0.265	0.794	0.486	0.673	0.323	0.688	0.304	0.599	0.819

Table 13. Iteration results of Equation 12

Iteration No.	$Jm(U,V)$	Iteration No.	$Jm(U,V)$	Iteration No.	$Jm(U,V)$	Iteration No.	$Jm(U,V)$	Iteration No.	$Jm(U,V)$
1	109.2731468	5	80.86810981	9	80.19748818	13	80.15224939	17	80.14800739
2	83.74320786	6	80.51307089	10	80.17464027	14	80.15019675	18	80.14779487
3	82.42814701	7	80.33137991	11	80.16251419	15	80.14903784	19	80.14767382
4	81.48998722	8	80.24197315	12	80.15591032	16	80.14838081	20	80.14760483

Maximum cluster memberships are the criteria when deciding which parts belong to which clusters. The clusters are shown below:

C1 = {P1, P3, P4, P6, P8, P10}

C2 = {P2, P5, P7, P9, P11, P12}

As can be seen in the U^{20} matrix, for example P3 ($x3$) strongly belongs to cluster 1 (0.877) but it also belongs to cluster 2 at 0.123 membership level. Therefore, FCM method gives flexibility to formation of clusters. Conversely, it requires long computational time and it is sensitive to the initial guess and noise (Singhal et al., 2013, Fahad et al., 2014). Besides giving flexibility to cluster formation, for example Ghosh and Dubey (2013) found K-means algorithm consumes less elapsed time than FCM algorithm and FCM produces close results to K-means clustering.

Table 14 gives the iteration results of $Jm(U,V)$ values in terms of the standardized data.

Cluster membership results of 8th iteration for standardized data version are shown below.

$U^8 =$

	x_1	x_2	x_3	x_4	x_5	x_6	x_7	x_8	x_9	x_{10}	x_{11}	x_{12}
c_1	0.508	0.503	0.503	0.502	0.493	0.505	0.493	0.505	0.493	0.509	0.504	0.487
c_2	0.492	0.497	0.497	0.498	0.507	0.495	0.507	0.495	0.507	0.491	0.496	0.513

The standardized version of resulting clusters will be as follows:

C1 = {P1, P2, P3, P4, P6, P8, P10, P11}

C2 = {P5, P7, P9, P12}

Table 14. The standardized data version of Table 11

Iteration No.	$Jm(U,V)$	Iteration No.	$Jm(U,V)$	Iteration No.	$Jm(U,V)$	Iteration No.	$Jm(U,V)$
1	13.61325317	3	11.04934932	5	11.0479301	7	11.04792495
2	11.05526258	4	11.04818819	6	11.04789867	8	11.04796021

Hierarchical Clustering

Hierarchical clustering is one of the useful techniques in data clustering although it is more sensitive for noisy data (Verma et al., 2012). Distances, in other words dissimilarities, between objects (cases) need to be calculated beforehand in order to apply this method. For the parts example of interval data in Table 1, the Euclidean distances are given in Table 15.

There are several linkage methods in hierarchical clustering: single linkage, complete linkage, average linkage, Ward's method, centroid clustering, and median clustering. Single, complete and average linkage methods are explained here. Table 16 shows the single linkage method applied on the parts data in terms of Euclidean distance measures given in Table 15. Single, complete and average linkage methods begin with rank ordering distance measures from smallest to biggest. The third column of Table 16 gives this Euclidean distance rank orders. In order to explain single linkage method, giving all distances is not necessary because the algorithm stops at Step 17. The last column of the Table 16 gives what happens in corresponding steps. There must be at least one same part between pairs in order to merge or cluster them together. This rule is applied for complete and average linkage also. Until Step 3, there are no same parts between pairs (or clusters) and therefore no reason to merge them. Because of this reason, pairs form their own clusters in Steps 1, 2, and 3. In Step 4, P2 goes to cluster 1 and merges with that cluster according to single linkage method because its partner P11 is already in cluster 1. This rule is enough to merge any part or cluster to another cluster for single linkage method. In other words, the shortest distance is enough for a part or a cluster to become a member of another cluster. The only rule must be satisfied is the existence of a same part in both clusters. Therefore, cluster 1 enlarges as {P6, P11, P2} in Step 4. The other steps are developed using the same procedure in Table 16.

On the other hand, according to complete and average linkage methods merging procedure is not that much simple. According to complete and average linkage methods at step 4 in Table 16, all distances between P2 are checked first. The distance between P2 and P6 is 10.39, and between P2 and P11 is 7.14. In complete linkage method, P2 cannot be a member of cluster 1 until the level of linkage dis-

Table 15. Euclidean distances of interval data parts example

	P1	P2	P3	P4	P5	P6	P7	P8	P9	P10	P11	P12
P1												
P2	30.68											
P3	16.79	17.35										
P4	15.68	23.52	9.38									
P5	34.25	10.39	19.92	27.59								
P6	24.35	10.39	13.45	20.81	16.25							
P7	49.86	20.12	34.35	40.45	18.25	27.66						
P8	21.91	11.87	6.48	13.49	16.16	9.00	28.67					
P9	48.17	19.82	33.38	40.47	14.18	27.22	8.83	28.57				
P10	7.35	30.15	14.49	10.49	33.24	25.40	48.44	20.35	47.14			
P11	26.19	7.14	14.21	22.14	10.91	6.24	24.86	10.10	22.93	26.72		
P12	36.43	10.30	20.62	27.44	6.48	16.91	14.32	15.72	13.38	34.71	13.30	

Table 16. Single linkage method

Steps	Pairs	Linkage Distances	Cluster Formation
1	P6-P11	6.24	Begins to form Cluster 1: {P6, P11}
2	P3-P8	6.48	Begins to form Cluster 2: {P3, P8}
3	P5-P12	6.48	Begins to form Cluster 3: {P5, P12}
4	P2-P11	7.14	P2 goes to Cluster 1: {P6, P11, P2}
5	P1-P10	7.35	Begins to form Cluster 4: {P1, P10}
6	P7-P9	8.83	Begins to form Cluster 5: {P7, P9}
7	P6-P8	9.00	Cluster 1 and 2 merge, called Cluster 12: {P6, P11, P2, P3, P8}
8	P3-P4	9.38	P4 goes to Cluster 12: {P6, P11, P2, P3, P8, P4}
9	P8-P11	10.10	
10	P2-P12	10.30	Cluster 12 and 3 merge, called Cluster 123: {P6, P11, P2, P3, P8, P4, P5, P12}
11	P2-P5	10.39	
12	P2-P6	10.39	
13	P4-P10	10.49	Cluster 123 and 4 merge, called Cluster 1234: {P6, P11, P2, P3, P8, P4, P5, P12, P1, P10}
14	P5-P11	10.91	
15	P2-P8	11.87	
16	P11-P12	13.30	
17	P9-P12	13.38	Cluster 1234 and 5 merge, called Cluster 12345: {P6, P11, P2, P3, P8, P4, P5, P12, P1, P10, P7, P9}

tances reaches the biggest distance that is 10.39. In average linkage method, P2 cannot be a member of cluster 1 until the level of linkage distances reaches the average distance 8.765 that is (10.39 +7.14)/2. The average linkage method tries to mediate between single and complete linkage methods but needs extra calculations in each step. Table 17 shows the linkage distances when the clusters are formed and enlarged for three explained methods. The standardized data version of Table 17 is given in Table 18.

Single linkage algorithm is the most versatile among other linkage methods. It is very sensitive if an error in the data exists no matter how small it is (Milligan & Cooper, 1987). Single linkage can form long chains with dissimilar items at opposite ends within the same cluster. This is called chaining problem. Complete linkage eliminates the chaining problem. Average linkage method tends to generate clusters with small within-cluster variation (Hair et al., 2010). Single, complete, and average linkage methods do not take the cluster structure into account (Martinez & Martinez, 2005).

Another useful illustration of showing cluster formation is a graphical presentation called dendrogram. A dendrogram is a tree diagram that one of its axes presents objects to be clustered and the other one presents linkage distances which portrays the steps in the hierarchical procedure (Hair et al., 2010). It shows the nested structure of the partitions (Martinez & Martinez, 2005). The graph connects the lines of the objects in each linkage distance. It is possible to see all clusters in all linkage levels on a dendrogram. When choosing a linkage distance level, drawing a parallel line to the objects (cases) axis from that distance depicts how many clusters are formed in that level and what are the members of these clusters. Figure 1 shows three dendograms produced for three explained linkage methods. Figure 2 is the standardized data form of Figure 1. As in the parts example for interval data, the objects to be clustered are parts here.

Table 17. Linkage distances and cluster formations of methods

Steps	Single		Complete		Average	
	Linkage Distances	Cluster Formation	Linkage Distances	Cluster Formation	Linkage Distances	Cluster Formation
1	6.245	{P6, P11}	6.245	{P6, P11}	6.245	{P6, P11}
2	6.481	{P3, P8}	6.481	{P3, P8}	6.481	{P3, P8}
3	6.481	{P5, P12}	6.481	{P5, P12}	6.481	{P5, P12}
4	7.141	{P6, P11, P2}	7.348	{P1, P10}	7.348	{P1, P10}
5	7.348	{P1, P10}	8.832	{P7, P9}	8.767	{P2, P6, P11}
6	8.832	{P7, P9}	10.392	{P2, P5, P12}	8.832	{P7, P9}
7	9.000	{P6, P11, P2, P3, P8}	13.491	{P3, P8, P4}	11.436	{P3, P8, P4}
8	9.381	{P6, P11, P2, P3, P8, P4}	16.912	{P2, P5, P12, P6, P11}	13.010	{P2, P6, P11, P5, P12}
9	10.296	{P6, P11, P2, P3, P8, P4, P5, P12}	21.909	{P1, P10, P3, P8, P4}	16.619	{P1, P10, P3, P8, P4}
10	10.488	{P6, P11, P2, P3, P8, P4, P5, P12, P1, P10}	27.659	{P2, P5, P12, P6, P11, P7, P9}	20.275	{P2, P6, P11, P5, P12, P7, P9}
11	13.379	{P6, P11, P2, P3, P8, P4, P5, P12, P1, P10, P7, P9}	49.860	{P1, P10, P3, P8, P4, P2, P5, P12, P6, P11, P7, P9}	27.757	{P1, P10, P3, P8, P4, P2, P6, P11, P5, P12, P7, P9}

Table 18. The standardized version of linkage distance and cluster formations

Steps	Single		Complete		Average	
	Linkage Distances	Cluster Formation	Linkage Distances	Cluster Formation	Linkage Distances	Cluster Formation
1	0.753	{P3, P8}	0.753	{P3, P8}	0.753	{P3, P8}
2	1.009	{P5, P9}	1.009	{P5, P9}	1.009	{P5, P9}
3	1.356	{P7, P12}	1.356	{P7, P12}	1.356	{P7, P12}
4	1.385	{P6, P11}	1.385	{P6, P11}	1.385	{P6, P11}
5	1.625	{P3, P8, P7, P12}	1.735	{P3, P8, P10,}	1.697	{P3, P8, P10}
6	1.659	{P3, P8, P7, P12, P10}	1.958	{P6, P11, P1}	1.878	{P6, P11, P1}
7	1.694	{P3, P8, P7, P12, P10, P5, P9}	2.629	{P3, P8, P10, P2}	2.146	{P5, P9, P7, P12}
8	1.799	{P6, P11, P1}	2.738	{P5, P9, P7, P12}	2.309	{P3, P8, P10, P6, P11, P1}
9	1.902	{P3, P8, P7, P12, P10, P5, P9, P6, P11, P1}	2.808	{P3, P8, P10, P2, P4}	2.503	{P3, P8, P10, P6, P11, P1, P2}
10	2.137	{P3, P8, P7, P12, P10, P5, P9, P6, P11, P1, P4}	4.165	{P3, P8, P10, P2, P4, P6, P11, P1}	2.997	{P3, P8, P10, P6, P11, P1, P2, P5, P9, P7, P12}
11	2.149	{P3, P8, P7, P12, P10, P5, P9, P6, P11, P1, P4, P2}	4.825	{P3, P8, P10, P2, P4, P6, P11, P1, P5, P9, P7, P12}	3.464	{P3, P8, P10, P6, P11, P1, P2, P5, P9, P7, P12, P4}

Figure 1. Dendrograms of parts data according to Euclidean distances

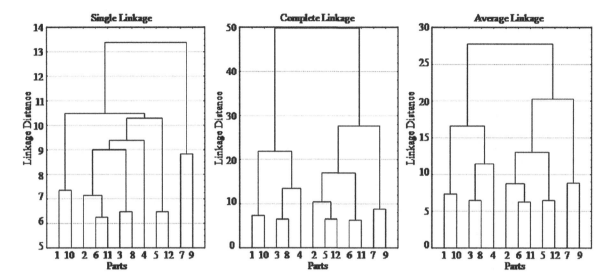

Figure 2. The standardized data form of Figure 1

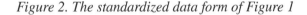

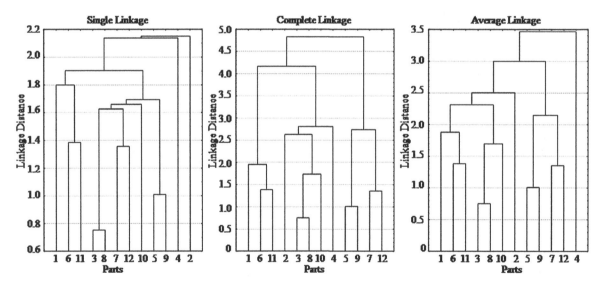

One of the important things that effects seriously the final results of hierarchical clustering is the kind of distance measure. Euclidean distance is used to make clusters so far. Under the different distance measures however, hierarchical clustering results may show a big difference. For example, Table 19 shows the Mahalanobis distances of parts data. One of the most important aspects of Mahalanobis distance is the inclusion of covariance matrix of all data in calculation. When calculating the distances between two parts the only concern is not the attributes of these two parts but the covariance matrix of all data. This distance measure normalizes by standard deviations and also compensates for the intercorrelations of the variables (Morrison, 1967). Because of this reason, data standardization is not needed when Mahalanobis distance is used. Therefore, the distances in Table 19 are the Mahalanobis distances

Table 19. Mahalanobis distances of interval data parts example

	P1	P2	P3	P4	P5	P6	P7	P8	P9	P10	P11	P12
P1												
P2	3.22											
P3	2.48	4.05										
P4	3.26	3.04	2.64									
P5	2.56	3.49	2.46	3.55								
P6	2.86	3.69	2.72	4.05	3.70							
P7	3.96	2.88	2.84	2.83	3.16	3.07						
P8	2.70	3.49	1.14	2.41	2.93	2.04	2.11					
P9	3.22	3.31	2.81	3.69	0.98	3.70	2.58	2.99				
P10	1.72	3.29	1.99	1.97	2.41	3.69	3.54	2.43	3.04			
P11	1.73	2.42	2.61	3.46	2.15	2.05	2.84	2.36	2.29	2.62		
P12	3.06	3.56	1.41	2.69	1.87	3.03	1.86	1.55	1.74	2.47	2.47	

of standardized data at the same time. Figure 3 shows the dendrogram of Mahalanobis distances of three linkage methods explained above.

For the binary data example in Table 2, a similarity coefficient must be chosen and calculated for each part pairs. Because the similarities between parts are taken into account this time, the algorithm starts with the biggest similarity, goes through the shortest, and linkages occur accordingly. However, if the researcher wants to use a software package on clustering and the package works with dissimilarities (distances) only, the conversion is possible. In order to convert similarity coefficients ranging 0-1 in Table 4, the coefficient needs to be subtracted from 1 and then it can be used as a dissimilarity.

Figure 3. Dendrograms of Parts Data according to Mahalanobis distances

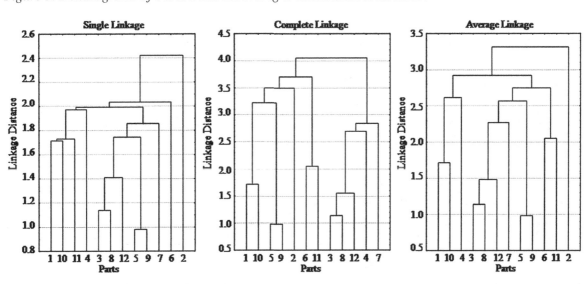

Decision Trees

As a person it is difficult to decide what to do on the weekend. There are several things to do on the weekend that you actually enjoy doing such as going to a party, spend your time with friends or going to cinema. The choice is sometimes made for you, if you are feeling sick or lazy, then you need to rest at home, if there is a new film at cinema you can go to the cinema. You are looking for a nice algorithm that will you decide what to do each weekend without thinking about it every weekend. Decision Trees is a graphical representation format of the event that resulting from the first stage to reach the final result.

Decision trees are one of the most widely used algorithms for classification problems and one of the predictive modelling approaches used in statistics, data mining and machine learning. Compared to other methods is easier to configuration and understand. The idea of a decision tree is that we break classification down into a set of choices about each feature in turn, starting at the root (base) of the tree and progressing down to leaves, where we receive the classification decision. The trees are very easy to understand, and can even be turned into a set of if-then rules, suitable for use in a rule induction system.

However, decision trees are beneficial for focusing discussion when a group must have a decision. Decision Trees is used often in data mining problems to simplify complex challenges and evaluate the cost-effectiveness of research and business decisions. For example, in Table 20 has classified any product according to its attributes such as length, diameter and number of holes. So can be decide on based these results class of any product that comes new in the process line in the fabric plant.

Below have been studied algorithms ID3, C4.5, SLIQ and SPRINT which produce reasonable decision trees.

ID3

ID3 algorithm uses entropy to find distinctive feature of variables for clustering which describes the amount of impurity in a set of features. The entropy of a dataset S is minimal when all included items are members of the same class. Since the goal of decision tree mining is to split the input data by class membership, the problem can be reduced to a minimization of the overall partition entropy (Dunham, 2003). Value of entropy will reach its maximum value when all probabilities are equal.

Table 20. Attributes of any product that comes new in the process line in the fabric plant

Parts	Length (cm)	Diameter (cm)	Number of Holes	Production Time (Minute)
P1	>40	<=5	3<...<=6	>=20
P2	<=20	5<...<=11	>6	10<...<20
P3	20<...<=40	5<...<=11	<=3	10<...<20
P4	>40	>11	>6	10<...<20
P5	<=20	<=5	<=3	<=10
P6	20<...<=40	5<...<=11	<=3	>=20
P7	<=20	>11	3<...<=6	<=10
P8	20<...<=40	5<...<=11	3<...<=6	10<...<20
P9	<=20	<=5	<=3	<=10
P10	>40	5<...<=11	3<...<=6	10<...<20

Figure 4. A simple decision tree to determine production time of items

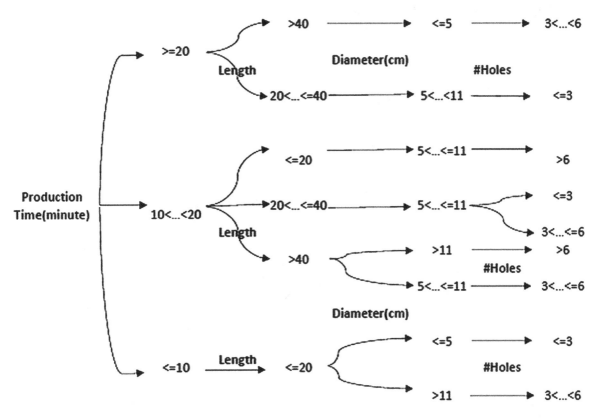

Entropy can be described mathematically as follows:

Given the probabilities $\langle p_1, p_2, ..., p_n \rangle$ and the sum of the probabilities should be 1.

$$\sum_{i=1}^{n} p_i = 1,$$

entropy is defined as

$$H(s) = H\left(p_1, p_2, ..., p_n\right) = \sum \left(p_i \log\left(\frac{1}{p_i}\right)\right)$$

Entropy is used to determine the which feature to choose next and that gives us the node of the tree to help classify the data. We just have to work out how to apply it.

Information gain will be calculated as follows:

- The ID3 algorithm computes this information gain for each feature and chooses the entropy which produces the highest value.
- It continuous until end of the tree by choosing the feature with the highest information gain at each stage.

Figure 5. A Graph of entropy, detailing how much information is available from finding out another piece of information given what you already know

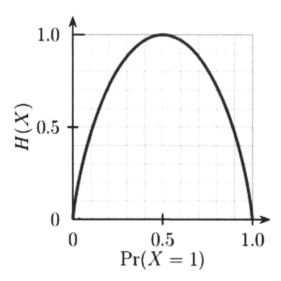

$$Gain(D : S) = H(D) - \sum_{i=1}^{n} P(D_i)H(D_i)$$

When desired to construct a decision tree according to Table 2, root node will be calculated as shown in Table 22.

First will be calculated current entropy.

According to the frequency table; with

$$H(p_1, p_2, p_{3,}, ..., p_n) = \sum p_i \log(\frac{1}{p_i}))$$

$$= \frac{4}{20} \times \log 5 + \frac{10}{20} \log 2 + \frac{6}{20} \log \frac{20}{6} = 0,4470$$

Entropy is calculated for variable length, Entropi for >40:

$$= \frac{2}{5} \times \log \frac{5}{2} + \frac{2}{5} \times \log \frac{5}{2} + \frac{1}{5} \log 5 = 0.4579$$

for $20 < ... \leq 40$

$$= \frac{1}{4} \log 4 + \frac{3}{4} \log \frac{4}{3} = 0.2442$$

Table 21. Table of length, diameter, #holes, production time of items

Parts	Length (cm)	Diameter (cm)	Number of Holes	Production Time (Minute)
P1	>40	<=5	3<...<=6	>=20
P2	<=20	5<...<=11	>6	10<...<20
P3	20<...<=40	5<...<=11	<=3	10<...<20
P4	>40	>11	>6	10<...<20
P5	<=20	<=5	<=3	<=10
P6	20<...<=40	5<...<=11	<=3	>=20
P7	<=20	>11	3<...<=6	<=10
P8	20<...<=40	5<...<=11	3<...<=6	10<...<20
P9	<=20	<=5	<=3	<=10
P10	>40	5<...<=11	3<...<=6	10<...<20
P11	20<...<=40	<=5	<=3	10<...<20
P12	<=20	5<...<=11	<=3	<=10
P13	<=20	<=5	3<...<=6	10<...<20
P14	>40	>11	<=3	>=20
P15	<=20	5<...<=11	>6	10<...<20
P16	<=20	<=5	3<...<=6	<=10
P17	<=20	>11	3<...<=6	10<...<20
P18	<=20	>11	3<...<=6	10<...<20
P19	<=20	5<...<=11	3<...<=6	>=20
P20	>40	5<...<=11	<=3	<=10

Table 22. Frequency distribution of the three types of production time

	Frequency
>=20	4
10<...<20	10
<=10	6

for ≤ 20

$$= \frac{1}{11} \log 11 + \frac{5}{11} \log \frac{11}{5} + \frac{5}{11} \log \frac{11}{5} = 0.4058$$

Total weight:

$$= \frac{0.4579}{4} + \frac{0.2442}{5} + \frac{11}{20} \times 0.4058 = 0.3856$$

Calculated information gain for length:

$$= 0.4470 - 0.3856 = 0.0614$$

Entropy is calculated for variable Diameter, for ≤ 5

$$= \frac{\log 6}{6} + \frac{\log 3}{3} + \frac{\log 2}{2} = 0.4391$$

for $5 < \ldots \leq 11$

$$= \frac{2}{9}\log\frac{9}{2} + \frac{5}{9}\log\frac{9}{5} + \frac{2}{9}\log\frac{9}{2} = 0.4321$$

for > 11

$$= \frac{1}{5}\log\frac{5}{2} + \frac{3}{5}\log\frac{5}{3} + \frac{1}{5}\log 5 = 0.3524$$

Total weight:

$$= \frac{6}{20} \times 0.4391 + \frac{9}{20} \times 0.4321 + \frac{5}{20} \times 0,3524 = 0.4142$$

Calculated information gain for Diameter:

$$= 0.4470 - 0.4142 = 0.032$$

Entropy is calculated for variable #Holes:

for ≤ 3

$$= \frac{2}{8}\log 4 + \frac{2}{8}\log 4 + \frac{4}{8}\log 2 = 0.4515$$

for

$3 < \ldots \leq 6$

$$= \frac{2}{9}\log\frac{9}{2} + \frac{5}{9}\log\frac{9}{5} + \frac{2}{9}\log\frac{9}{2} = 0.4321$$

for > 6

$$= \frac{3}{3}\log 1 = 0$$

Total weight:

$$= \frac{8}{20} \times 0.4515 + \frac{9}{20} \times 0.4321 + \frac{3}{20} \times 0 = 0.3750$$

Calculated information gain for #Holes:

$$= 0.4470 - 0.3750 = 0.072$$

Now we have gains for variables as follows:

gain(length) = 0.0614

gain(diameter) = 0.032

gain(#holes) = 0.072

value, #Holes, will be selected as the root node of the biggest variables;

After this step will be calculated the gains for length and diameter based on values of #Holes and herein node will be identified. Then will be established the tree by applying respectively the same procedure for other branches. As it can be seen, the method is recursive algorithm.

C 4.5

'C4.5' algorithm is a natural extension of the ID3 algorithm and it has some advantages according to ID3. In 'C4.5' algorithm the missing values are not considered on data set. So in calculating gain ratio only non-missing records are used and C4.5 estimates missing values from data that are present. However, this algorithm also takes into accounts qualitative variables. Thus can be created more sensitive and meaningful trees. In ID3 algorithm the variables are divided into several sub-sections, and this separation can cause excessive learning. To avoid this Quinlan used following gain ratio instead of information gain (Quinlan, 1987).

Figure 6. Calculated root node #Holes

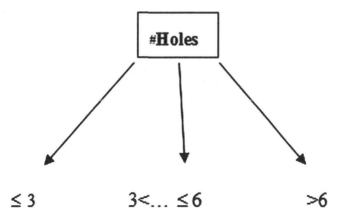

With pseudocode decision tree algorithm can be expressed as follows:

- Control of best situation
- Find the normalized information gain ratio from splitting on *a*
- Let *a* be the feature with the highest information gain
- Create a decision node that separates on *a_best*
- Iterate on the sublists supplied by separating on *a_best*, add these nodes as children of *node* (Kotsiantis, 2007)

The GainRatio measure is defined in terms of the earlier Gain measure, as well as this Split Information, as follows:

$$GainRatio(S, A) = \frac{Gain(S, A)}{SplitInformation(S, A)}$$

Continue with results in ID3.
Information (S,A) for length:

$$= \frac{5}{20} \log \frac{20}{5} + \frac{4}{20} \log 5 + \frac{11}{20} \log \frac{20}{11} = 0.4331$$

Gain Ratio:

$$= 0.4470 / 0.4331 = 1.03$$

Information (S,A) for diameter:

$$= \frac{6}{20} \log \frac{20}{6} + \frac{9}{20} \log \frac{20}{9} + \frac{5}{20} \log 4 = 0.4634$$

Gain Ratio:

$$= 0.4470 / 0.4634 = 0.9646$$

Information (S,A) for #Holes:

$$= \frac{8}{20} \log \frac{20}{8} + \frac{9}{20} \log \frac{20}{9} + \frac{3}{20} \log \frac{20}{3} = 0.4388$$

Gain Ratio:

$$= 0.4470 / 0.4388 = 1.0187$$

58

The attribute with the smallest gain ratio will be appointed as root or next node.

SLIQ (Supervised Learning in Quest)

SLIQ is a decision tree based algorithm that can be used for the classification of both quantitative and categorical data. And pre-sorting technique is used during the creation of the tree to reduce the cost of the evaluation of numerical data. It is important to sort the data when dealing with numerical data to find the optimal separating of branches. In relation to other data mining algorithms SLIQ executes faster and results in compact trees.

While ID3 and C4.5 algorithms are working according to the principle depth-first, SLIQ algorithm creates at the same time a lot of leaves by acting with the idea breadth-first. SLIQ uses Gini-Index in separation process to branches and uses a fast algorithm by creating subsets of the categorical data. SLIQ also uses a new tree-pruning algorithm that is low-cost, and results in compact and closed trees.

Furthermore, in process of pruning of the tree used principle of MDL (Minimum Description Length). "*Minimum description length* (MDL) uses an information theoretic measure (Rissanen, 1978). Moreover, this model can be applied to big data, which can be stored only in hard disks and difficult to keep in memory.

SLIQ algorithm is fast as well as creates decision trees which produces good results. With all of these techniques enables SLIQ to scale for large data sets and classify data sets irrespective of the number of classes, attributes, and examples (records), thus making it an attractive tool for data mining (Mehta et al., 1996).

SPRINT (Supervised Learning in Quest)

In this section we also study SPRINT, which is the initial version of the SLIQ. SPRINT removes all of the storage constraints and is fast and scalable. As mentioned earlier, ID3, C4.5 and also CART work according to the principle depth-first and to reach best allocation criteria of branches data will be sorted on each node. However, SLIQ uses separate list for each variable and do sorting process only once. In this aspect SPRINT and SLIQ have similarity with each other. However, SPRINT differs from the algorithm using different data structures (Shafer et al., 1996).

SPRINT firstly prepare a separate list of attributes for each attribute. So will be occur tables in database as the number of variables (Table 23, examp of lists). While the tables will be sorted according to the continuous attribute which contain continuous variables, other table will be sorted according to the order number. The first lists obtained from the training set are associated with the root of the classification tree. As the tree is grown and nodes are split to create new children, the attribute lists belonging to each node are partitioned and associated with the children. When a list is partitioned, the order of the records in the list is preserved; thus, partitioned lists never require resorting (Shafer et al., 1996).

Histograms, denoted as C_{above} and C_{below}, are used to determine class distribution of the attributes at a given node, which are under consideration for splitting. Gini-Index is used for criteria for splitting to the sub-branches of the nodes as in the same SLIQ algorithm. Gini index for any data set K will be calculated as follows:

$$gini(K) = 1 - \sum p_i^2$$

Table 23. Example of attribute lists

Age	Class	Rid	Car Type	Class	Rid
17	Large	1	Crossover	Large	0
20	Compact	5	Sports	Compact	1
21	Compact	0	Sports	Compact	2
66	Large	4	Crossover	Large	3
36	Mid-Size	2	Hatchback	Mid-Size	4
43	Large	3	Crossover	Large	5

where p_i is the relative frequency of class i in K. If set of K divided into subsets as K_1 ve K_2, value of $gini_{split}(K)$ of the divided sets is calculated as follows;

$$gini_{split}(K) = \frac{n_1}{n_2} gini(K_1) + \frac{n_2}{n_2} gini(K_2)$$

SPRINT algorithm is applied as follows according to data of Table 2. First splitting criteria is calculated for the length attribute;

$$gini(for > 40) = 1 - \left(\left(\frac{2}{5}\right)^2 + \left(\frac{2}{5}\right)^2 + \left(\frac{1}{5}\right)^2 \right) = 0.64$$

$$gini(20 < ... \leq 40) = 1 - \left(\left(\frac{1}{4}\right)^2 + \left(\frac{3}{4}\right)^2 \right) = 0.37$$

$$gini(\leq 20) = 1 - \left(\left(\frac{1}{11}\right)^2 + \left(\frac{5}{11}\right)^2 + \left(\frac{5}{11}\right)^2 \right) = 0.58$$

$$gini_{split}(length) = \left(\frac{5}{20}\right) \times 0.64 + \left(\frac{4}{20}\right) \times 0.37 + \left(\frac{11}{20}\right) \times 0.58 = 0.553$$

The same procedure will be applied for other attributes, diameter and #holes, and root node will be selected which has the smallest value of $gini_{split}$.

Support Vector Machines (SVM)

Support vector machines are supervised learning models with associated machine learning algorithms, which have been developed as the other methods to solve clustering problems. SVM's are one of the very simple and effective method in this field. As examples of application areas of SVM can be given handwriting recognition, face recognition, 3-D object recognition, voice recognition, speaker recognition and text classification. It is possible to separate the 2 groups with drawing a borderline between them in a plane. Consider the example in Figure 7, there are many classifier lines that can split the data, but here is the goal to find optimal function, that maximizes the distance between margin and nearest data of each groups.

To perform this operation, need to be draw 2 border line which are parallel and near to each other, and with approximation of these borderline to each other will be generated new common boundary line. Consider the 2 group in Figure 8.

In this way the two groups are shown on a two dimensional plane. This plane and dimensions can be thought of as a feature. For each input in the system is made feature extraction and obtained different points which are show each input on the 2 dimensional plane. Classification of the points mean that the classification of the feature extraction of the entries. The consisted range between 2 groups above can be defined as tolerance(offset). The definition of each point in the plane can be described with the following notations:

$$D = \left\{ (x_i, c_i) \mid x_i \in R^p, c_i \in \{-1, 1\} \right\}_{i=1}^n$$

The above notation can be read as follows; Both of x and c are point in the vector space and c is the point of indicating that the value -1 or +1. The set of points go from i=1 to n. So this notation refers to the point that in the Figure 8. Considering that this show on the hyperplane. Each point on this notation can be defined by the following equation.

$$wx - b = 0$$

Figure 7. Optimal separating hyperplane

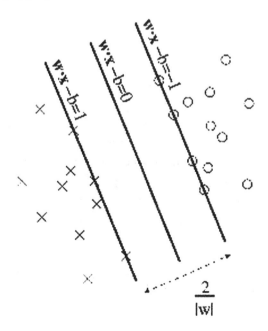

Figure 8. 2 groups with borderline

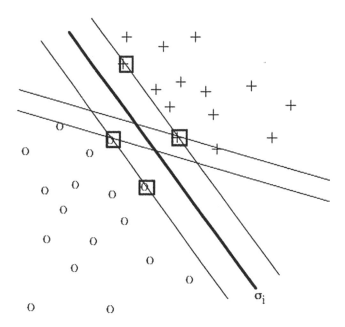

Here, w (is known as the weight vector) is the perpendicular normal vector to the hyperplane and x is the changing parameter of the point and b is bias. According to the above equation b/||w|| value gives us the difference in distance between the two groups. Above we named this difference tolerance(offset). To maximize the distance between groups, shown above in the Figure 8, is used 2/||w|| formula in the equation. So the distance between lines is determined as 2 units.

So the following equations are obtained according to the above:

$$wx + b = -1$$

$$wx + b = 1$$

In fact, this equation is a consequence of the presence of the highest value obtained by removing the right. And also problem with these equations is accepted as linearly separable. Hyperplane is not able to have one-way between the two groups. An example of this is shown in Figure 9.

Separation way of the data sets with SVM can be linear separable or non-separable. Being able to divided as linear case, the data may be separated directly by a hyperplane. As mentioned above, the set of vectors is said to be optimally separated by the hyperplane if it is separated without error and the distance between the closest vector to the hyperplane is maximal (Steve,1998). There may be many linear plane that separates data sets belonging to different classes but purpose of the SVM to find hyperplane that maximizes the distance between data sets of different groups.

In case of linear separable, data can be divided into 2 classes by linear plane. But in practice, this situation may not always be available. So data cannot be separated from each other by a linear plane. Figure 10 shows us 2 cases of SVM:

Figure 9. Hyperplane between groups

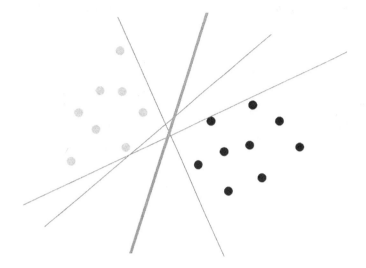

Figure 10. Representation of the SVM with linear or non-linearly separable case

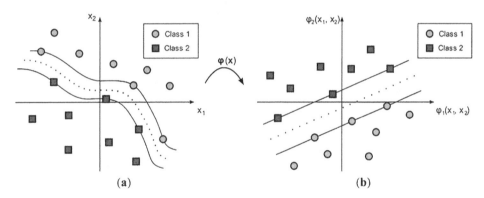

1. A linearly separable case, where the hyperplane splits green circles from red squares; and
2. A non-linearly separable case, where no hyperplane splits all of the green circles from the red squares (Gonzales et al., 2014).

In cases, where data cannot be linear separated, non-linear classifiers can be used instead of a linear classifier. For linear inseparable cases, data in low dimension space are mapped into a high dimension space using a kernel function, so as to transform a low-dimensional inseparable problem into high-dimensional linear separable problem (Chen, 2013). Such conditions require a more complex and detailed decision boundary. SVM increases the dimensionality of the input space m_0 to feature space of dimension m_f by applying nonlinear transformation, denoted by φ(·). Thus this transformation, φ(·), provides to reduce the misclassification probability in the transformed feature space (Gonzales et al., 2014).

The transformation shown in Figure 11 can be described mathematically as follows:

$$w^T \phi(x) + b = 0\,;\ x \in R^{m_0} \text{ and } \phi(x) \in R^{m_f}$$

Figure 11. Support Vector Machine classifier with a nonlinear kernel; function $\varphi(\cdot)$ is the nonlinear transformation mapping vectors from (a) the input space to (b) the feature space.

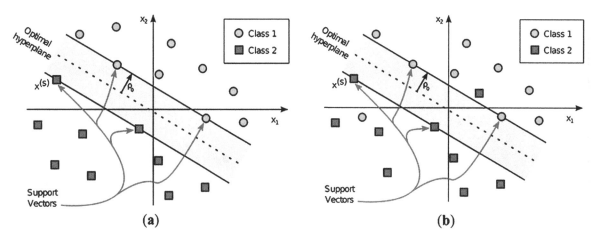

Optimal weight vector can be expressed using Lagrange multipliers method as follows:

$$w = \sum_{i=1}^{N} a_i d_i \phi(x_i) \; ; \; a_i : \text{Lagrange multiplier coefficients}$$

Decision boundary can be written as:

$$\sum_{i=1}^{N} a_i d_i \phi(x_i)^T \phi(x) + b = 0$$

After renaming $t_i = a_i d_i$ and $K(x_i, x) = \phi(x_i)^T \phi(x)$, decision function can be denoted as follows:

$$y = \sum_{i=1}^{N} t_i K(x_i, x) + b$$

Thus the classification is done by determining the sign of the output value, decision function y. If sign(y) = +1, then this input is identified as class +1 and if otherwise as class −1. The most well-known and commonly used nonlinear kernel functions are sigmoids, radial basis functions (RBF) and polynomials.

- Radial basis function can be described as

$$K(x,y) = \exp(-\gamma \left\| x - y \right\|^2) \, ,$$

γ is a user-defined parameter

- Sigmoid kernel function can be described as

$$K(x,y) = \tanh(\gamma(x^T y))$$

- Polynomial kernel function can be described as

$$K(x,y) = \tanh(\gamma(x^T y) + c_0)^d,$$

d is the polynomial degree.

The most important advantage of the SVM is to solve the problems by converting to the quadratic optimization problem. Thus, the number of transactions in the learning phase of the solution to the problem are decreasing and solution can be reached faster than other algorithms (Osowski et al., 2004). Therefore, it is possible to classify the large amount of data in an easy way. In addition, the performance of the classification due to the optimization-based, is more successful than other techniques in terms of computational complexity and usability (Nitze et al., 2012).

AN APPLICATION ON EUROPEAN COUNTRIES

The level of computer and internet usage differ from country to country. The computer and internet abilities of people and how computers and internet involve throughout the commerce, enterprises, and institutions determine any nations' professional usage level of these kind of technology. Countries can be classified by the similarities in the proficiency levels of computer and internet usage. Some countries are closed to each other whereas some others are far away according to this proficiency.

This application is based on the second-hand data taken from Eurostat which is the official statistics institution of European Union (EU). The European Economic Community (EEC) was constructed in 1958 and had six members: Belgium, Germany, France, Netherlands, Luxembourg, and Italy. Denmark, Ireland, and United Kingdom in 1973; Greece in 1981; Portugal and Spain in 1986 joined to EEC. The name of EEC has changed to European Union (EU) in 1993. Austria, Finland, and Sweden in 1995; Cyprus, Czech Republic, Estonia, Hungary, Latvia, Lithuania, Malta, Poland, Slovakia, and Slovenia in 2004; Bulgaria and Romania in 2007; Croatia in 2013 joined to the EU. Today, the EU has 28 member countries and Albania, Montenegro, Serbia, the former Yugoslav Republic of Macedonia, and Turkey are the candidate countries of the EU membership (European Union, accessed: June 12, 2016).

When classifying the European countries in terms of computer and internet proficiencies, it is possible to observe whether or not the EU entry years and membership status of those countries are also similar to the resulting cluster structures. If it is similar, it may be possible to say that early memberships to EU increases the computer and internet proficiency levels of the countries. Additionally, it may also be possible to say that being still outside of the EU decreases this proficiency levels of the countries. With these possibilities in mind, the explanations in Table 24 and the data in Table 25 have been taken from the web site of the official statistics institution of EU (Eurostat, accessed: June 3, 2016).

Several data clustering methods are used on the data in Table 25 and the results are shown in Table 26. In order to easy interpretations, the number of clusters are specified as 3 for each method except

Table 24. Descriptions of the data in Table 25 (Eurostat)

Column in Table 25	Description
A	Individuals who have carried out 5 or 6 of the computer related activities. % of individuals aged 16 to 74. Computer skills are measured using a self-assessment approach, depending on how many computer-related tasks have been carried out, without these skills being assessed, tested or actually observed. 5 or 6 of the following activities have been done: copied/ moved a file/folder, copy/cut/paste to move information on the screen, used basic arithmetic formulae, compressed/zipped a file, connecting and installing new devices or written a computer program.
B	Persons employed using computers connected to the internet. Persons employed using computers with access to World Wide Web. Percentage of total employment. All enterprises, without financial sector (10 persons employed or more).
C	Share of persons who cannot afford a computer. Household type variable (HHTYP): Total. Income situation in relation to the risk of poverty threshold (INCGRP): Total.
D	Enterprises - computers: devices and communication systems. Enterprises having a web site or homepage. Percentage of enterprises. All enterprises, without financial sector (10 persons employed or more).
E	E-commerce, customer relation management (CRM) and secure transactions. All enterprises, without financial sector (10 persons employed or more). Percentage of enterprises. Enterprises having received orders via computer mediated networks.
F	Individuals using the internet to buy or order online content. % of individuals aged 16 to 74. Online content: films, music, electronic books, magazines, newspapers, e-learning material, computer software (incl. Computer and video games and software upgrades). Within the last 12 months before the survey for private use.
G	Employees - devices to access the internet. Persons employed using computers with access to World Wide Web. Percentage of total employment. All enterprises, without financial sector (10 persons employed or more).
H	Enterprises purchasing via internet and/or networks other than internet. Enterprises having purchased via computer mediated networks. Percentage of enterprises. All enterprises, without financial sector (10 persons employed or more).

hierarchical clustering because of the distinct separation for Iceland. However, the results of hierarchical clustering can be interpreted as three clusters because Iceland forms a cluster with single membership.

As can be seen from Table 26, different clustering methods give different results even if the data are the same. The structure of the clusters depends on the number of clusters, the specification of parameters inside the method, the kind of distance measure, and data standardization.

The results in Table 26 show that Turkey, FYRM, and Romania tend to be in the same cluster for each method. The same tendency is also true for Denmark, Finland, Sweden, and Norway. It is interesting to see that geographical closeness supports these tendencies. However, for the other countries it is not possible to say the same thing. In addition to this, with several exceptions, it is hard to say that the EU membership years determine the level of computer and internet proficiency because very different membership years exist in the same clusters. According to membership status, the only support is given by Turkey and FYRM. Both of these countries are not the EU members yet and they are in the same clusters for each method. The similar interpretation can be given for Bulgaria and Romania too. Both of these countries enter the EU lastly in the same year and they are also in the same clusters for each method. Therefore, it may possible to say that according to membership status to EU, the proficiency levels of computer and internet usage of the countries can be similar.

Table 25. Percentages of computer and Internet proficiencies of European countries (Eurostat)

Country	A	B	C	D	E	F	G	H
	2014	2015	2014	2015	2015	2014	2015	2015
Belgium	24	50c	2.3	81	26	15	50c	43
Bulgaria	15	25	17.4	48	9	1	25	13
Czech Republic	27	37	3.5	83	25	2	37	56
Denmark	39	71	0.9	92	27	23	71	72e
Germany	30	52	3.0	87	27	26	52	54
Estonia	37	42	3.6	80	15	11	42	23
Ireland	26	46	5.3	75	32	18	46	47
Greece	30	38	10.8	61	7	2	38	11
Spain	33	49	7.2	75	18	9	49	26
France	33	53	2.3	67	21	17	53	43
Croatia	22	45	5.3	71	20	5	45	22
Italy	26	41	2.0	71	10	5	41	38
Cyprus	23	39	3.2	72	11	3	39	22
Latvia	30	49	10.3	59	10	4	49	35
Lithuania	34	39	6.8	77	19	5	39	27
Luxembourg	42	44	1.1	79	10	36	44	32
Hungary	24	35	11.1	64	14	4	35	31
Malta	26	46	2.9	83	19	14	46	26
Netherlands	27	61	1.2	90	25	20	61	47
Austria	34	52	1.8	87	18	20	52	68
Poland	21	38	5.0	65	12	5	38	21
Portugal	34	36	7.3	61	20	10	36	23
Romania	7	30	19.8	45	8	3	30	14
Slovenia	31	48	3.7	83	22	6	48	28
Slovakia	25	39	6.5	79	15	13	39	22
Finland	46	70	1.7	95	19	24	70	51
Sweden	38	72	0.7	90	28	34d	72	44
United Kingdom	33	56	5.0	81	23	39	56	51
Iceland	38	100e	0.6	85e	34e	37	100e	72e
Norway	42	67	0.3	80	29	45	67	56
FYRM	20	28	13.6	52	4	1	28	6
Serbia	9a	39e	16.6	74e	22e	0a	39e	40e
Turkey	15	26	39a	65	12	2	26	15b

Notes: FYRM: Former Yugoslav Republic of Macedonia. a As of 2009; b As of 2010; c As of 2012; d As of 2013; e As of 2014.

Table 26. Results of the analysis

Clustering Method	Resulting Clusters (C)
K-means (based on the first procedure)	C1: Denmark, Finland, Sweden, Iceland, Norway C2: Bulgaria, Greece, Croatia, Cyprus, Hungary, Poland, Portugal, Romania, FYRM, Serbia, Turkey C3: Belgium, Czech Republic, Germany, Estonia, Ireland, Spain, France, Italy, Latvia, Lithuania, Luxembourg, Malta, Netherlands, Austria, Slovenia, Slovakia, United Kingdom
KNN ($K = 3$, Euclidean distance) The training sets: C1: Denmark, Norway C2: Serbia, Turkey C3: Belgium, Slovakia	C1: Denmark, Norway, Germany, Netherlands, Austria, Finland, Sweden, United Kingdom, Iceland C2: Serbia, Turkey, Bulgaria, Greece, Romania, FYRM C3: Belgium, Slovakia, Czech Republic, Estonia, Ireland, Spain, France, Croatia, Italy, Cyprus, Latvia, Lithuania, Luxembourg, Hungary, Malta, Poland, Portugal, Slovenia
FCM	C1: Denmark, Germany, Netherlands, Austria, Finland, Sweden, United Kingdom, Iceland, Norway C2: Belgium, Czech Republic, Estonia, Ireland, Spain, France, Croatia, Italy, Cyprus, Latvia, Lithuania, Luxembourg, Malta, Portugal, Slovenia, Slovakia, Serbia C3: Bulgaria, Greece, Hungary, Poland, Romania, FYRM, Turkey
Hierarchical Clustering (average linkage, Euclidean distance, unstandardized)	C1: Iceland C2: Latvia, Italy, Portugal, Hungary, Poland, Cyprus, Croatia, Greece, Slovenia, Malta, Spain, Slovakia, Lithuania, Estonia, Serbia, Czech Republic C3: Turkey, FYRM, Romania, Bulgaria C4: Norway, Sweden, Finland, Denmark, Luxembourg, Austria, United Kingdom, Netherlands, Germany, France, Ireland, Belgium

CONCLUSION

Data clustering is necessary for both practitioners and researchers in order to easy understanding about the nature of the problems to be solved and the decisions to be decided. It plays an important role to facilitate data processing and gives initial perspectives for further analysis and applications also. Many methods have been developed and many application areas can be found for data clustering. Among the application areas, the clusters of countries, which is one of the focal points of this chapter, can be included. It is possible to find out more than one method applicable for the same data set. Therefore, the important thing here is to decide which method is the best for the available data structure. Conversely and unfortunately, there is no certain procedure for this decision process. On the other hand, it is possible to use several methods on the same data set and look at each results in order to find out the best formation of clusters.

In this chapter, after a brief explanation of application areas, the most popular data clustering methods are explained and illustrated with examples. A real data application on the computer and internet proficiencies of European countries is also included. The first contribution of this chapter to the literature is to provide a comprehensive illustrations of the methods for the readers with comparative explanations. The second contribution of it is to present a new approach to division of application areas of clustering for researchers. This approach not only can give some extensions on the domain topic to researchers but also can be a starting point for texts regarding data clustering. How data clustering can be used to find out the proficiency levels on any topic of a certain number of countries is the third contribution of this chapter. The European countries are analyzed in terms of the proficiency levels on computer and internet usage. Entrance years to the EU and membership status of the countries are taken as independent variables to search some supports for that reasoning. Therefore, it is possible to figure out this and different topics on the EU and other unions by clustering countries around the world in future researches.

REFERENCES

Aggarwal, C., & ChengXiang, Z. (Eds.). (2012). Comprehensive survey driven book on text mining with chapters contributed by prominent researchers in the field. In Mining Text Data. Springer.

Aggarwal, C. C., & Reddy, C. K. (2014). Data Clustering Algorithms and Applications. CRC Press.

Bezdek, J. C. (1981). *Pattern Recognition with Fuzzy Objective Function Algorithms*. Plenum Press.

Busch, V., & Van Stel, H. F. (2013). *Clustering of health-related behaviors, health outcomes and demographics in Dutch adolescents: A cross-sectional study*. BMC Public Health. doi:10.1186/1471-2458-13-1118

Chen, H., & Hu, J. (2013). *Proceedings of The Eighth International Conference on Bio-Inspired Computing: Theories and applications*. Springer.

Churchill, G. A. Jr. (1995). *Marketing Research Methodological Foundations*. The Dryden Press.

Cover, T. M., & Hart, P. E. (1967). Nearest neighbor pattern classification. *IEEE Transactions on Information Theory, IT-13*(1), 21–27. doi:10.1109/TIT.1967.1053964

DeSarbo, W. S., & Mahajan, V. (1984). Constrained classification: The use of a priori information in cluster analysis. *Psychometrika, 49*(2), 187–215. doi:10.1007/BF02294172

Dunham Margaret, H. (2003). *Data Mining Introductory and Advanced Topics*. Prentice Hall, Pearson Education Inc.

European Union. (n.d.). *EU Member Countries*. Retrieved from http://europa.eu/about-eu/countries/index_en.htm

Eurostat. (n.d.). *The Statistical Office of the European Union*. Retrieved June 3, 2016, from http://ec.europa.eu/eurostat/search?p_auth=TbvilBdy&p_p_id=estatsearchportlet_WAR_estatsearchportlet&p_p_lifecycle=1&p_p_state=maximized&p_p_mode=view&_estatsearchportlet_WAR_estatsearchportlet_action=search&text=computer

Fahad, A., Alshatri, N., Tari, Z., Alamri, A., Khalil, I., Zomaya, A. Y., & Bouras, A. et al. (2014). A survey of clustering algorithms for big data: Taxonomy and empirical analysis. *IEEE Transactions on Emerging Topics in Computing, 2*(3), 267–279. doi:10.1109/TETC.2014.2330519

Ghosh, S., & Dubey, S. K. (2013). Comparative Analysis of K-Means and fuzzy C-Means Algorithms. *International Journal of Advanced Computer Science and Applications, 4*(4), 35–39. doi:10.14569/IJACSA.2013.040406

Gong, X., & Richman, M. B. (1995). On the application of cluster analysis to growing season precipitation data in North America east of the Rockies. *Journal of Climate, 8*(4), 897–931. doi:10.1175/1520-0442(1995)008<0897:OTAOCA>2.0.CO;2

Gonzalez, R. R., Gomez-Gil, J., Gomez-Gil, F. J., & Martínez-Martínez, V. (2014). *An SVM-Based Classifier for Estimating the State of Various Rotating Components in Agro-Industrial Machinery with a Vibration Signal Acquired from a Single Point on the Machine Chassis*. Academic Press.

Gun, S. R. (1998). SVM for classification and regression. University of Southampton.

Hair, J. F., Black, W. C., Babin, B. J., & Anderson, R. E. (2010). *Multivariate Data Analysis, A Global Perspective*. Upper Saddle River, NJ: Pearson Prentice Hall.

John, S. (1996). SPRINT: A scalable Parallel Classifier for Data Mining. *22th International Conference on very large databases*.

Keller, J. M., Gray, M. R., & Givens, J. A. Jr. (1985). A fuzzy K-nearest neighbor algorithm. *IEEE Transactions on Systems, Man, and Cybernetics, SMC-15*(4), 580–585. doi:10.1109/TSMC.1985.6313426

Kotsiantis, S. B. (2007). Supervised Machine Learning: A Review of Classification Techniques. *Informatica, 31*, 249–268.

MacQueen, J. B. (1967). Some methods for classification and analysis of multivariate observations. In *Proceedings of the Fifth Symposium on Mathematical Statistics and Probability*. University of California.

Martinez, W. L., & Martinez, A. R. (2005). *Exploratory Data Analysis with MATLAB*. Boca Raton, FL: Chapman & Hall/CRC Press.

Mehta, M., Agrawal, R., & Rissanen, J. (1996). A fast scalable classifier for data mining. In *proceedings of 5th International Conference on Extending Database Technology: Advances in Database Technology*. Springer Verlag. doi:10.1007/BFb0014141

Milligan, G. W., & Cooper, M. C. (1987). Methodology review: Clustering methods. *Applied Psychological Measurement, 11*(4), 329–354. doi:10.1177/014662168701100401

Miner, G., Delen, D., Elder, J., Fast, A., Hill, T., & Nisbet, R. A. (2012). *Practical Text Mining and Statistical Analysis for Non-structured Text Data Applications*. Waltham, MA: Elsevier Inc.

Morrison, D. G. (1967). Measurement problems in cluster analysis. *Management Science, 13*(12), B-775–B-780. doi:10.1287/mnsc.13.12.B775

Nisbet, R., Elder, J., & Miner, G. (2009). *Handbook of Statistical Analysis and Data Mining Applications*. Burlington, MA: Elsevier Inc.

Nitze, I., Schulthess, U., & Asche, H. (2012). Comparison of machine learning algorithms random forest, artficial neural network and support vector machine to maximum likelihood for supervised crop type classification.*Proceedings of the 4th GEOBIA*.

Osowski, S., Siwekand, K., & Markiewicz, T. (2004). MLP and SVM Networks – a Comparative Study. *Proceedings of the 6th Nordic Signal Processing Symposium*.

Punj, G., & Stewart, D. W. (1983). Cluster analysis in marketing research: Review and suggestions for application. *JMR, Journal of Marketing Research, 20*(2), 134–148. doi:10.2307/3151680

Quinlan, J. R. (1987). Simplifying Decision Trees. *International Journal of Man-Machine Studies, 27*(3), 221–234. doi:10.1016/S0020-7373(87)80053-6

Rissanen, J. (1978, September). Modeling by shortest data description. *Automatica, 14*(5), 465–471. doi:10.1016/0005-1098(78)90005-5

Ruspini, E. (1970). Numerical methods for fuzzy clustering. *Information Sciences*, 2(1), 319–350. doi:10.1016/S0020-0255(70)80056-1

Sharma, N., Bajpai, A., & Litoria, R. (2012). Comparison the various clustering algorithms of weka tools. *International Journal of Emerging Technology and Advanced Engineering*, 2(5), 73–80.

Silahtaroglu, G. (2008). *Kavram ve Algoritmalarıyla Temel Veri Madenciliği*. Istanbul: Papatya Yayıncılık. (in Turkish)

Singhal, G., Panwar, S., Jain, K., & Banga, D. (2013). A comparative study of data clustering algorithms. *International Journal of Computers and Applications*, 83(15), 41–46. doi:10.5120/14528-2927

Verma, M., Srivastava, M., Chack, N., Diswar, A. K., & Gupta, N. (2012). A comparative study of various clustering algorithms in data mining. *International Journal of Engineering Research and Applications*, 2(3), 1379–1384.

Wilk, J., & Pelka, M. (2013). "Cluster analysis-symbolic vs. classical data", Acta Universitatis Lodziensis. *Folia Oeconomica*, 286, 205–213.

Yin, Y., & Yasuda, K. (2005). Similarity coefficient methods applied to the cell formation problem: A comparative investigation. *Computers & Industrial Engineering*, 48(3), 471–489. doi:10.1016/j.cie.2003.01.001

Yin, Y., & Yasuda, K. (2006). Similarity coefficient methods applied to the cell formation problem: A taxonomy and review. *International Journal of Production Economics*, 101(2), 329–352. doi:10.1016/j.ijpe.2005.01.014

Yiu, M. L., & Mamoulis, N. (2004). Clustering Objects on a Spatial Network. *Proceedings of the ACM Conference on Management of Data (SIGMOD)*.

KEY TERMS AND DEFINITIONS

Binary Data: A type of data that is represented with binary numerical system 0s and 1s, which are used from computers to store data.

Cluster: An ordered list of objects, which have similar characteristics.

Dendrogram: Dendrogram is a graphical presentation of the clusters to show its formation. It is treelike diagram and represents the distance or dissimilarity of the clusters. Axess of the dendrogram presents objects to be clustered and the other one presents linkage distances which portrays the steps in the hierarchical procedure.

Entropy: Statistical entropy is a probabilistic measure of uncertainty or ignorance. The entropy of a dataset S is minimal when all included items are members of the same class. Value of entropy will reach its maximum value when all probabilities are equal.

Gini Index: Gini coefficient is a measure of inequality of the distribution and value of this measure is between 0 and 1. Gini index is described as a percentage and is equal to the gini coefficient multiplied by 100.

Hyperplane: Hyperplane is n-1 dimensional subspace of a vector space that divides the space into two disconnected parts.

Interval Data: Interval scales are numeric scales which are ordered and represent also the exact differences between data.

Supervised Learning: Supervised Learning is a machine learning method which extrapolate function from training data that consist of a set of training examples.

Chapter 3
Association Rules– Based Analysis in Multidimensional Clusters

Neelu Khare
VIT University, India

Dharmendra S. Rajput
VIT University, India

Preethi D
VIT University, India

ABSTRACT

Many approaches for identifying potentially interesting items exploiting commonly used techniques of multidimensional data analysis. There is a great need for designing association-rule mining algorithms that will be scalable not only with the number of records (number of rows) in a cluster but also among domain's size (number of dimensions) in a cluster to focus on the domains. Where the items belong to domain is correlated with each other in a way that the domain is clustered into classes with a maximum intra-class similarity and a minimum inter-class similarity. This property can help to significantly used to prune the search space to perform efficient association-rule mining. For finding the hidden correlation in the obtained clusters effectively without losing the important relationship in the large database clustering techniques can be followed by association rule mining to provide better evaluated clusters.

INTRODUCTION

Clustering partitions data into Clusters that are meaningful and useful to analyze and describe the real world. It is known as a process of grouping physical or abstract objects into conceptually meaningful classes of similar objects. If meaningful cluster is the objective, then the cluster should extract the natural structure of the data. In many cases, cluster analysis only a useful starting point for other purposes, such as data summarization.

DOI: 10.4018/978-1-5225-1776-4.ch003

Clustering played an important role in discovering interesting data distributions and patterns for understanding, in areas such as, information retrieval, pattern recognition in biological or other sequence data, climate, psychology and medicine, business, machine learning, data mining or as pre processing step of data mining, etc. In context of utility, clustering is a technique to find out the most appropriate cluster prototype, these prototypes can serve as the base of various data analysis or data processing techniques such as, summarization, Compression and to efficiently finding nearest neighbour. Existing clustering approaches are divided into four categories:

- Partitioning,
- Hierarchical,
- Grid-Based, and
- Density-Based.

All these approaches are suffering from rapid degeneration of performance with increase in dimensions; particularly those are designed for low-dimensional data and due to ineffective cluster evaluation and analysis of multidimensional data owing to inherent uncertainties.

Association rule mining is a useful technique for discovering interesting relationships hidden in large data sets. Such hidden relationships can be extracted in the form of association rules or sets of frequent patterns. These association rules (AR) leads to potential knowledge to detect the presence of regularities and path in large databases. Rules represent the relations (in terms of co-occurrence) between pairs of items or among the items from different dimensions of large databases. Strength of rules are measured by: *support* and *confidence*, the rules which satisfy the minimum support and minimum confidence criteria, should be fixed in order to remove both that only trivial rules are retained and also that interesting rules are focused.

MULTIDIMENSIONAL DATA MODEL

The Multidimensional data model consists of three types; they are:

- Logical Multidimensional Data Model,
- Relational Multidimensional Data Model,
- Analytic Workspace Implementation Multidimensional Data Model.

LOGICAL MULTIDIMENSIONAL DATA MODEL

The Multidimensional data model is an integral part of On-Line Analytical Processing, or OLAP. Because OLAP is on-line, it must provide answers quickly; analysts pose iterative queries during interactive sessions, not in batch jobs that run overnight. And because OLAP is also analytic, the queries are complex. The multidimensional data model is designed to solve complex queries in real time.

The Multidimensional data model is composed of logical cubes, measures, dimensions, hierarchies, levels, and attributes. The simplicity of the model is inherent because it defines objects that represent real-world business entities. Analysts know which business measures they are interested in examining, which dimensions and attributes make the data meaningful, and how the dimensions of their business are organized into levels and hierarchies.

RELATIONAL MULTIDIMENSIONAL DATA MODEL

The Relational implementation of the multidimensional data model is typically a star schema or a snowflake schema. A star schema is a convention for organizing the data into dimension tables, fact tables, and materialized views. Ultimately, all of the data is stored in columns, and metadata is required to identify the columns that function as multidimensional objects.

In Oracle Database, you can define a logical multidimensional model for relational tables using the OLAP Catalog or AWXM. The metadata distinguishes level columns from attribute columns in the dimension tables and specifies the hierarchical relationships among the levels. It identifies the various measures that are stored in columns of the fact tables and aggregation methods for the measures. And it provides display names for all of these logical objects.

ANALYTIC WORKSPACE IMPLEMENTATION MULTIDIMENSIONAL DATA MODEL

Analytic workspaces have several different types of data containers, such as dimensions, variables, and relations. Each type of container can be used in a variety of ways to store different types of information. For example, a dimension can define an edge of a measure, or store the names of all the languages supported by the analytic workspace, or all of the acceptable values of a relation. Dimension objects are themselves one dimensional list of values, while variables and relations are designed specifically to support the efficient storage, retrieval, and manipulation of multidimensional data.

MULTIDIMENSIONAL DATA CLUSTERING

Clustering of multidimensional data is an important topic in pattern analysis and recognition, with very useful applications in many areas of research. Ismail and Kamel (1989) had showed that there are several techniques to cluster multidimensional data exist, which utilize different criteria and different methodologies. These techniques can be classified generally into three main categories:

1. Heuristic methods;
2. Graph theoretic methods, which include hierarchical clustering and the use of a minimum spanning tree; and
3. Methods based on the minimization of a specified objective function, which are sometimes called partitioning algorithms.

The proposed algorithm for clustering of multidimensional data in (Wan, et al., 1988) is summarized below:

1. Choose the hyper box with the largest weighted variance for further partition.
2. Project all data points in the hyper box onto each of the m coordinate axes. For each of the m projected distributions, calculate the optimal cut-point and the reduction of expected variance.

3. Partition this hyper box by the hyper plane perpendicular to the axis along which the reduction of expected variance is the largest. This hyper plane intersects this axis at the optimal cut-point.
4. Compute the weighted variance for each of the two smaller hyper boxes.
5. Repeat Steps 1 to 4 until the number of the hyper boxes reaches the required number of clusters.
6. Calculate the centroids of the resulting hyper boxes, which form the desired cluster centers.
7. Map each data point to its closest cluster center.

ASSOCIATION RULE MINING

Association rule mining can be defined formally as follows: $I = \{i_1, i_2, \dots, i_m\}$ is a set of literals, or items. For example, goods such as milk, sugar and bread for purchase in a store as items; and $A_i = v$ is an item, where v is a domain value of the attribute A_i, in a relation $R(A_1, A_2, \dots, A_n)$. Let X be an item set if it is a subset of I. For example, a set of items for purchase from a store is an item set; and a set of $A_i = v$ is an item set for the relation $R(PID, A_1, A_2, \dots, A_n)$, where PID is a key. Let $D = \{t_i, t_{i+1}, \dots, t_n\}$ is a set of transactions, called a transaction database, where each transaction t has t_{id} and $t - itemset$ such that, $t = (t_{id}, t - itemset)$. For example, a customer's shopping trolley going through a checkout is a transaction; and a tuple $(v_1, \dots, v_n)$ of the relation $R(A_1, A_2, \dots, A_n)$ is a transaction.

A transaction t contains an item set X iff, for all items, where $i \in X$, I is a $t - itemset$. For example, a shopping trolley contains all items in X when going through the checkout; and for each $A_i = v_i$ in X, v_i occurs at position i in the tuple $(v_1, \dots, v_n)$. There is a natural lattice structure on the item sets $2I$, namely the subset/superset structure. Certain nodes in this lattice are natural grouping categories of interest. For example, items from a particular department such as clothing, hardware, furniture, etc; and, from within say clothing, children's, women's and men's clothing, toddler's clothing, etc.

An item set X in a transaction database D has a support, denoted as $supp(X)$. (For descriptive convenience in this book, we sometimes use $p(X)$ to stand for $supp(X)$. This is the ratio of transactions in D containing X. Or

$supp(X) = |X(t)| / |D|$ where $X(t) = \{t \text{ in } D | t \text{ contains } X\}$.

An item set X in a transaction database D is called as a large, or frequent item set if its support is equal to, or greater than, the threshold minimal support $(minsupp)$ given by users or experts. The negation of an item set X is $\neg X$. The support of $\neg X$ is $supp(\neg X) = 1 - supp(X)$. An association rule is the implication $X \rightarrow Y$, where item sets X and Y do not intersect. Each association rule has two quality measurements, support and confidence, defined as the support of a rule $X \rightarrow Y$ is the support of $X \bigcup Y$; and the confidence of a rule $X \rightarrow Y$ is $conf(X \rightarrow Y)$ as the ratio

$|(X \bigcup Y)(t)| / X(t)$,

or

$supp(X \bigcup Y) / supp(X)$.

That is, support = frequencies of occurring patterns; confidence = strength of implication. In Support confidence framework, let I be a set of items in a database D, X, $Y \subseteq I$ be item sets, $X \cap Y = \varnothing$, $p(X) = 0$ and $p(Y) = 0$. Minimal support $(minsupp)$ and minimal confidence $(\min conf)$ are given by users or experts. Then $X \rightarrow Y$ is a valid rule if

1. $supp(X \cup Y) \geq minsupp$,
2. $conf(X \rightarrow Y) = supp(X \cup Y) / supp(X) \geq \min conf$,

where, $conf(X \rightarrow Y)$ stands for the confidence of the rule $X \rightarrow Y$

Mining association rules can be broken down into the following two sub problems:

1. Generating all itemsets that have support greater than, or equal to, user specified minimum support. That is, generating all frequent itemsets.

   Generating all rules that have minimum confidence in the following simple way: For every frequent itemset X, and any $B \subset X$, let $A = X - B$. If the confidence of a rule $A \rightarrow B$ is greater than, or equal to, the minimum confidence (or)

$supp(X) / supp(A) \geq \min conf$,

then it can be extracted as a valid rule.

The support-confidence framework is generally used as a framework for capturing a certain type of dependence among items represented in a database. This model measures the uncertainty of an association rule with two factors: support and confidence. However, the measure is not adequate for modelling all uncertainties of association rules. For instance, the measurement does not provide a test for capturing the correlation of two itemsets. Also, the support is limited in informative feedback because it represents the number of transactions containing an itemset but not the number of items.

In order to improve this framework, some measurements on the support and confidence of association rules, such as the chi-squared test model and collective strength based measure, have been recently proposed. These different measurements on support and confidence lead to different models for mining association rules. Hence, the measuring of uncertainty of association rules has recently become one of the crucial problems when mining association rules. In fact, the measurement of the uncertainty of an event has been a popular topic for research over the years. Mathematical probability theory and statistics offer many well-developed techniques for measuring uncertainty. Thus, there are many measuring models that can be applied for the estimation of the uncertain factors (supp and conf) of an association rule.

The issue of mining association rules was first addressed in 1993.They pointed out that there are some hidden relationships among the purchased items in transactional databases. For example, there are associations or relationships between items such as bread and milk, which are often purchased together in a single basket transaction. The mining results can help understand the customer's purchase behaviour, which might not have been previously perceived. An association rule is of the form $X \rightarrow Y$, where X and Y are both frequent item sets in the given database and the intersection of X and Y is an empty set, i.e., $X \setminus Y = B$. The support of the rule $X \setminus Y$ is the percentage of transactions in the given database that contain both X and Y, i.e., $P(X \setminus Y)$

The confidence of the rule $X \setminus Y$ is the percentage of transactions in the given database containing X that also contains Y, i.e., $P(Y \setminus X)$. Therefore, association rule mining is used to find all the association rules among item sets in a given database, where the support and confidence of these association rules must satisfy the user-specified minimum support and minimum confidence. The problem of association rule mining can be divided into two sub problems:

1. Finding frequent item sets with their supports above the minimum support threshold.
2. Using frequent item sets found in the Step 1 to generate association rules that have a confidence level above the minimum confidence threshold.

Therefore, many studies of association rule mining concentrate on developing efficient algorithms for frequent item set discovery. The following subsections summarize some of the most popular algorithms for frequent item set mining.

APRIORI-LIKE ALGORITHM

The first step of association rules mining is finding frequent item sets in databases. The complexity of an association rules mining system is heavily dependent upon the complexity of the corresponding algorithm for identifying frequent item sets. The following algorithm Frequent Itemsets is used to generate all frequent item sets in a given database D. This is the Apriori algorithm. The parameter db size is the total number of tuples in the database.

ALGORITHM FOR GENERATING FREQUENT ITEMSETS

Input: D = data set; minsupp = minimum support;
Output: L = frequent itemsets;
 Begin
Let frequent item set $L \leftarrow \{\}$;
Let frontier set $F \leftarrow \{\{\}\}$;
 while $F \leftarrow \{\}$ *do begin*
Association Rule–make a pass over the database D
Let candidate set $C \leftarrow \{\}$;
 $\forall$ Database tuples t, *do*
 $\forall$ Itemsets f in F, *do*
 if t Contains f Then *begin*
Let $C_f \leftarrow$ candidate item sets that are extensions of f and contained in t;
 $\forall$ Itemsets c_f in C_f do
 if $c_f \in C$ Then
$c_f.count \leftarrow c_f.count + 1$;
 else
$c_f.count \leftarrow 0$; $C \leftarrow C \cup \{c_f\}$;
 end
–consolidate

Let $F \leftarrow \{\}$;
$\forall$ Itemsets c in C *do begin*
if c.count / *dbsize* > *minsupp* Then
$L \leftarrow L \cup c$;
if c should be used as a frontier in the next pass then
$F \leftarrow F \cup c$;
end
end
end

The Apriori algorithm makes multiple passes over a given database. The frontier set for a pass consists of those item sets that are extended during the pass. In each pass, the support for certain item sets is measured. These item sets, referred to candidate item set, are derived from the tuples in the database and the item sets contained in the frontier set. Associated with each item set is a counter that stores the number of transactions in which the corresponding item set has appeared. This counter is initialized to zero when an item set is created. Initially, the frontier set consists of only one element, which is an empty set. At the end of a pass, the support for a candidate item set is compared to minsupp to determine whether it is a frequent item set. At the same time, it is determined whether this item set should be added to the frontier set for the next pass. The algorithm terminates when the frontier set becomes empty. The support count for the item set is preserved when an item set is added to the frequent/frontier set.

FP-GROWTH ALGORITHM

A frequent pattern tree (FP-tree) structure, which contains all the compact information for mining frequent item sets, and then proposed the FP-growth algorithm, which adopts a pattern segment growth approach to prevent generating a large number of candidate item sets. Their mining method only scans the whole database twice and does not need to generate candidate item sets, and so it is very efficient.

PARTITIONED CLUSTERING WITH ASSOCIATION RULES

Four partition based clustering algorithms are considered. K-Means algorithm, Medoids Partitioning around Medoids(PAM), CLARANS (Clustering Large Applications based on RANdomized Search).

K-MEANS ALGORITHM

The K-Means algorithm is a well known technique for performing clustering on objects in R_n . Each cluster is centred about a point called the centroid, where the centroids coordinates are the mean of the coordinates of the objects in the cluster. The algorithm can be summarized as follows:

1. Select k points to be the initial candidates for the cluster centroids. These points need not correspond to any of the objects.
2. Assign each object to the cluster associated with the closest centroid.

3. Recalculate the positions of the k centroids.
4. Repeat Steps 2 and 3 until the centroids become fixed.

K – MEDOIDS ALGORITHM

The K-Medoids algorithm, as used to produce the results of this paper, is an adaptation of the k-means algorithm. Rather than calculate the mean of the items in each cluster, a representative item, or Medoids, is chosen for each cluster at each iteration.

There are two advantages to using existing rules as the centres of the clusters. Firstly, a Medoid rule serves to usefully describe the cluster. Secondly, there is no need for repeated calculation of distances at each iteration, since the K- Medoids algorithm can simply look up distances from a distance matrix.

The K-Medoids algorithm can be summarized as follows:

1. Choose k objects at random to be the initial cluster Medoids.
2. Assign each object to the cluster associated with the closest Medoid.
3. Recalculate the positions of the K- Medoids.
4. Repeat Steps 2 and 3 until the Medoids become fixed.

PARTITIONING AROUND MEDOIDS (PAM)

Partitioning Around Medoids (PAM) also clusters objects about k Medoids, where k is specified in advance. However, the algorithm takes the form of a steepest ascent hill climber, using a simple swap neighbourhood operation. In each iteration Medoid object i and non-Medoid object j are selected that produce the best clustering when their roles are switched. The objective function used is the sum of the distances from each object to the closest Medoid.

CLARANS

CLARANS is a variant of PAM that uses the same neighbourhood operation but takes the form of a stochastic first-Bound hill climber. In each iteration, a Medoid object i, and non-Medoid object, j, are selected at random until the clustering produced when their roles are switched is better than the current clustering. No build phase is required; the algorithm starts with a randomly selected set of K-Medoids.

QUANTITATIVE ASSOCIATION RULE MINING METHOD WITH CLUSTERING (QARC_APRIORI)

An efficient algorithm named QARC_Apriori is proposed by Dong and Pi (2014). Firstly, to reduce the redundant attributes and lower the problem complexity, grey relational analysis method is applied. Secondly, each filtered attribute is partitioned into several subintervals, combining with K-Means clustering algorithm. During clustering, the outliers are removed to improve the accuracy of clustering results. Due to the different distributions and the scopes of attributes, the clustering centers are automatically adjusted. Moreover, the statistical information of each attribute is used to avoid repeatedly scanning the database.

Finally, all the quantitative association rules are mined by an improved Apriori algorithm. QARC_Apriori has Input such as raw satellite telemetry data; the parameters: *w1* (initial clustering threshold), *w2* (outliers threshold), *minsup* (minimum support threshold), *minconf* (minimum confidence threshold) and the resultant Output is the quantitative association rules. The experiments are conducted with the power supply data of a China's satellite from 2011.6.1 to 2011.9.1. The experimental data for quantitative association rules mining contains 1575196 records. It took four hours and three minutes to generate 930 frequent item sets and 517 quantitative association rules. It indicates that the proposed algorithm is suitable for generating quantitative association rules and it plays an important role for satellite on-orbit performance analysis.

QARC_Apriori algorithm is constituted with main three steps. The first step is to reduce the redundant attributes of the original data. All attributes with smaller correlation value are chosen. The second step is to discrete for each filtered attributes. Firstly, the values of each attribute are clustered by the statistics information based on K-means algorithm, after all outliers are detected and removed. Then the attribute domain is divided into disjoint intervals and each interval corresponds to a discrete value, according to the clustering results. The last step is to mine all quantitative association rules, which contains two phases: frequent item sets mining and association rules generation. The QARC_Apriori algorithm is described as follows.

ALGORITHM OF QARC_APRIORI

Input: Raw satellite telemetry data.
Parameters: w_1 (initial clustering threshold), w_2 (outliers threshold), minsup (minimum support threshold), minconf (minimum confidence threshold).
Output: Quantitative association rules.

A clustering scheme based on multiple dimensions for mining a complete set of inter-transaction association rules. This scheme has two phases:

1.   Generation of descriptions of clusters based on multi-dimensional semantic grouping; and
2.   Exploring associations between cluster descriptions/abstractions. The proposed scheme is used to successfully mine meaningful association rules from simulated data by (Ananthanarayana, et al., 2001).

Clustering classification multi-level association rule mining is proposed. This method combines the concept of hierarchical concept; the data of the generalization set processing, and uses SOFM neural network generalization into the database after the transaction. By introducing an internal threshold, there is no need to set the minimum support threshold, to generate the local frequent item sets as global candidate item sets in order to generate global frequent item set, enhancing the efficiency of multilevel association rules and accuracy.

Based on the theoretical research of the multi-level association rules mining, Top-K frequent pattern mining, SOFM clustering and classification methods, according to the problem in the traditional multi-level association rules mining based on the Apriori algorithm which is not adaptable to a large database by QingLan and DuanLongZhen (2013).A hybrid approach which finds the frequent XML documents by association rule mining and then clusters the XML documents by using classical k-means algorithm. The XML documents are used for finding the properties in web mining. Association rule based mining finds the temporal associations among XML documents. But this kind of data mining is not sufficient to retrieve the properties of every XML document.

Finding the properties for set of similar documents is better idea rather than to find the property of a single document. Hence, the key contribution of the work is to find the meaningful clustered based associations by association rule based clustering. The proposed approach was tested with real data of Wikipedia. When the dataset size is huge big data, both memory use and computational cost can still be very expensive as discussed by Muralidhar and Pattabiraman (2015). This study aims to propose a novel framework which clusters the data first and then followed by association rules mining. The first stage employs the ant system-based clustering algorithm (ASCA) and ant K-means (AK) to cluster the database, while the ant colony system-based association rules mining algorithm is applied to discover the useful rules for each group. The medical database provided by the National Health Insurance Bureau of Taiwan Government is used to verify the proposed method. The evaluation results showed that the proposed method not only is able to extract the rules much faster, but also can discover more important rules. The total searching time in all the clusters was 3.282 s, and it spent 3.875 s in mining the complete data. From mentioned above, this method mines association rule from different clusters and it takes 15.31% time in mining complete data. But it spends more than 1 h, which is hugely long time, in clustering analysis as shown by (Kuo, et al., 2007).

HIERARCHICAL CLUSTERING WITH ASSOCIATION RULES

(Tang, et al., 2009), a data mining system to discover the habitat area and migration route efficiently. A new hierarchical clustering algorithm is developed in the system to find sub-areas with a dense location points relative to the entire area. Then the Minimum Convex Polygon Home Range of bird species is calculated. Then, association analysis is used to discover the site connectedness and migration route between the discovered habitats.

Component flow the system in Figure 1, consists of four phases: pre-processing, clustering, home range calculation and sequence mining. The raw data of the habitat areas and the migration routes can be determined by high-tech GPS satellite telemetry that are usually large scale with high complexity. In this paper, the authors convert these biological problems into computational studies, and introduce efficient algorithms for the data analysis.

The key idea is the concept of hierarchical clustering for migration habitat localization and the notion of association rules for the discovery of migration routes. The idea of combining DBSCAN with a hierarchical clustering approach is to find the habitats with different levels of densities. The studies are conducted at the Qinghai Lake National Nature Reserve, Qinghai province, China. The data sets are received from Western Ecological Research Center which consists of 66796 and 22951 location data records for the 2007 survey and 2008 survey, respectively.

Clustering and association rule mining do provide an effective assistance for biologists to discover new habitats and migration routes of Wild bird species. A new hierarchical clustering algorithm is developed in the system to find sub-areas with a dense location points relative to the entire area. Then the

Figure 1. Component flow
Source: Tang, et al., 2009.

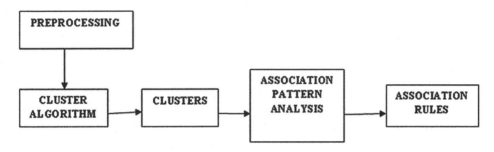

Minimum Convex Polygon Home Range of bird species is calculated. Then, association analysis is used to discover the site connectedness and migration route between the discovered habitats. Figure 2 shows a diagram and component flow of our system, which consists of four phases:

- Pre-processing,
- Clustering,
- Home range calculation, and
- Sequence mining.

A fast data association technique based on clustering and multidimensional assignment algorithms for multisensory – multi target tracking. Assignment-based methods have been shown to be very effective for data association. Multidimensional assignment for data association is an NP-hard problem and various near-optimal modifications with (pseudo-)polynomial complexity have been proposed. In multidimensional assignment, candidate assignment tree building consumes about 95% of the time. The fast data association algorithm partitions the problem into smaller sub-problem.

Figure 2.

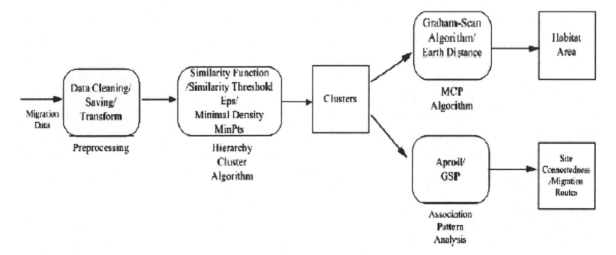

The clustering technique used to prune the number of candidate associations is a hierarchical algorithm which groups the measurements according to two parameters:

- A distance metric, and
- The sensor-origin of the measurement.

A clustering approach, which attempts to group measurements before forming the candidate tree, is developed for various target-sensor configurations. The effectiveness of the clustering algorithm combined with the multidimensional assignment problem is demonstrated on a number of scenarios with different target-sensor configurations. In all cases, there is a significant improvement in CPU time.

Simulation result shows a significant computational savings over the standard multidimensional assignment approach without clustering (Chummun, et al., 2001). An approach using a pattern-based clustering approach to group customer transactions. The new approach is based on segmenting the customer transactions: one that is based on the idea that there are natural behavioural patterns in different groups of transactions. An objective function is used in order to achieve a good clustering of customer transactions and presents an algorithm, GHIC which group customer transactions such that item sets generated from each cluster, while similar to each other, are different from ones generated from others.

The experimental result shows that GHIC generates a highly effective clustering of customer transactions. In order to compare the performance of GHIC, the following three methods were implemented:

1. Hierarchical k-means on data represented in items (the "K-Means- items" approach),
2. Hierarchical k-means on data represented in item sets (the "k-means-item sets" approach), and
3. GHIC on data represented in item sets.

The comparison between k-means-items and k-means-item sets evaluates whether the item sets representation is good since the two approaches share the same clustering algorithm but are applied on what is essentially different data formats. The comparison between k-means-item sets and GHIC evaluates the specific heuristic used in GHIC since the two use the same data format but different algorithms (Yang, et al., 2005). The notion of "closed interesting" item sets (i.e. closed item sets with high interestingness). This provides heuristics such as "super item" to efficiently mine these item sets and show that they provide significant dimensionality reduction over closed frequent item sets.

These item sets retain the "closeness" property of closed frequent item sets, but replace the minimum support requirement with achieving minimum threshold of a symmetric, statistically inspired objective interestingness measure. Using "closed interesting" item sets, this paper proposes a new, sub-linearly scalable, hierarchical document clustering method that outperforms state of the art agglomerative, partitioning and frequent-item sets based methods both in terms of clustering quality and runtime performance, without requiring the dataset specific parameter tuning. This method is evaluated with twenty interestingness measures and shows that when used to generate "closed interesting" item sets, and to select parent nodes, Mutual Information, Added Value, Yule's Q and Chi-Square offers the best clustering performance.

The proposed a new hierarchical document clustering approach, outperforms state of the art approaches on a large number of standard datasets, both in terms of accuracy and run-time performance. Using global cross-validation, a small number of interestingness measures generalize well to a large number of datasets, without requiring parameter tuning (Malik, et al., 2006). A new normalized distance metric to group association rules. Based on these distances, an agglomerative clustering algorithm is used to cluster the rules. Also the rules are embedded in a vector space by multi-dimensional scaling and clustered using a self organizing feature map.

A new distance metric between two association rules in this approach and propose a new grouping methodology using multi-dimensional scaling (MDS) and self organizing maps (SOMs). The results are combined for visualization. The proposed method is compared with various distance measures and illustrates subjective and objective cluster purity on results obtained from real data-sets. The data is represented at multiple levels of product hierarchy:

- Before extracting clustering, and
- Merging of association rules.

This may provide more abstract descriptions of the data's association rules that better captures the customer buying behaviour. By keeping track of the customer behaviour, a home-improvement store, for example, could make inferences on what project a specific customer is working on and provide exactly the right service to satisfy that customer's needs (Strehl, et al., 1999). The hierarchical clustering ensemble algorithm based on association rules (HCEAR) is proposed in this paper.

HCEAR makes use of the distribution of clustering memberships, combines m subset of Descartes with support degree of the association rules, and then achieves the partition by variation of hierarchical clustering. The optimal number of clusters is determined by the average degree of clustering using distribution of all clustering memberships and support degree of association rules. Then the variation of the hierarchical clustering algorithm was adopted for best partition. The algorithm implements clustering ensemble under full unsupervised condition. The algorithm adopts hierarchical clustering to partition points by making use of the distribution of results of all clustering memberships and the support degree of association rules.

Finally, the algorithm was applied in practice data and results show that the HCEAR is superior to anyone of the clustering memberships by Li and Chen (2009). The hierarchical clustering ensemble algorithm based on association rules (HCEAR) is proposed in this paper. HCEAR makes use of the distribution of clustering memberships, combines m subset of Descartes with support degree of the association rules, and then achieves the partition by variation of hierarchical clustering. The optimal number of clusters is determined by the average degree of clustering using distribution of all clustering memberships and support degree of association rules. Then the variation of the hierarchical clustering algorithm was adopted for best partition. The algorithm implements clustering ensemble under full unsupervised condition. The algorithm adopts hierarchical clustering to partition points by making use of the distribution of results of all clustering memberships and the support degree of association rules. Finally, the algorithm was applied in practice data and results show that the HCEAR is superior to anyone of the clustering memberships.

DENSITY BASED CLUSTERING WITH ASSOCIATION RULES

Many algorithms have been proposed for mining Boolean association rules, but they cannot deal with quantitative and categorical data directly. Although we can transform quantitative attributes into intervals and apply Boolean algorithms to the intervals. But this approach is not effective and is difficult to scale up for high-dimensional cases. An efficient algorithm, DBSMiner (Density Based Sub-space Miner), is proposed by using the notion of "density- connected" to cluster the high density sub-space of quantitative attributes and the gravitation between Grid /cluster to deal with the low density cells which may be missed by the previous algorithms. DBSMiner not only can solve the problems of previous approaches, but also can scale up well for high-dimensional cases.

Evaluations on DBSMiner have been performed using the car and the shuttle databases maintained at the UCI Machine Learning Repository. DBSMiner has several unique features. It is able to:

1. Dealing with the high dimension dataset and can deal with low density sub-space which may be missed by previous algorithms and
2. Only need to check the neighbour cell, needn't scan the whole space.

Experiments showed that DBSMiner is able to discover meaningful and interesting quantitative association rules while many existing data mining algorithms may miss in their mining process. The results indicate that DBSMiner is effective and can scale up to quite linearly with an increasing number of attributes (Yunkai, et al., 2008).

A density-based quantitative attribute partition algorithm for industrial database is proposed. The algorithm uses an improved density-based clustering algorithm to detect the clusters. The clusters are agglomerated to form the new clusters according to the proximity between clusters and the new clusters are projected into the domains of the quantitative attributes. So the fuzzy sets and the membership functions used for partition are determined.

The proposed algorithm is divided into several phases, where phase I is a clustering process of the improved density-based clustering algorithm, phase II is the agglomeration of the clusters, detected in phase I, to form the new clusters and calculating the centroid of the new clusters, and phase III is the establishment of the membership functions based on the projections of the new clusters and identifying the membership values of each quantitative attribute of the objects. The experiments were performed on a test database and a real industrial database and the results shows that the algorithm not only can partition the quantitative attributes of industrial database successfully but also with the higher partition effectiveness (Cao, et al., 2008).

CBSD (CLUSTERING BASED ON SORTED DENSE UNIT)

$INPUT(MinDen, f)$

1. Using a grid structure to quantize the object space into a finite number of cells, in this section, assume the number as k
2. Delete all the blank cells and such cell which has low density and has no high- density neighbour nearby. If a cell has low density but the attraction force between its high-density neighbours is greater than the minimum force f, then label it as cluster–able.
3. $cluster\_no = 0$; // no is the cluster number
4. $CS = \varnothing$; // CS are the cluster sets
5. Divide each attribute into t equal parts, initialize S;
6. Scan the database DB, for each transaction

7. $if(transeS_i)S_i.density + +$;
8. $\forall \ S_i$
9. $\{if(S_i.density \geq MinDen)$
10. $S = S * S_i\}$
11. $Sort(S)$; //sort in the descending order
12. Insert S into a list L;
13. $while(L \neq \varnothing)$
14. $\{cluster\_no + +$;
15. $c\_no = \varnothing$;
16. Get the first node P in L and set $P.cluster\_no = no$; add P into c_no;
17. $repeat = true$;
18. $while(repeat \ \& \ \& L \neq \varnothing)$
19. $\{repeat = false$;
20. Search all the node N in L which it can directly density-reachable from P or it is $N's$ density
21. if(in 20 found a node that can add to C no)
22. $repeat = true;\}$
23. $CS = CS * c\_no$; //add C no into the cluster sets;
24. $\} \ // \ end \ while(L \neq \varnothing)$
25. End

Algorithms for mining Boolean association rules have been well studied and documented, but they cannot deal with quantitative data directly. In this paper, a novel algorithm MQAR (Mining Quantitative Association Rules based on dense grid) which uses tree structure DGFP-tree to cluster dense subspaces is proposed, which transforms mining quantitative association rules into finding dense regions.

In this paper, a novel algorithm MQAR is proposed, which is easy to get rid of the noise and redundant rules by transforming the problem into finding regions with enough density and then map these dense regions to quantitative association rules. Also, MQAR proposed a new density and grid-based cluster algorithm which clusters database by finding dense subspaces in DGFP-tree and it can deal with higher dimensional database with scalable performance. MQAR not only can solve the conflict between minimum support problem and minimum confidence problem, but also can find the interesting quantitative association rules which may be missed by previous algorithms. To evaluate the effectiveness of MQAR, it is applied to the Stat log (Shuttle) data set maintained at the UCI Machine Learning Repository. The shuttle dataset has 43,500 transactions and contains 9 attributes all of which are numerical. From the results, it can be concluded that the execution times change in linear with the size of database.

Experimental results show that MQAR can efficiently find quantitative association rules. The advantages of MQAR are shown as follows:

1.   DGFP-tree compress the database effectively and no need to scan database many times;
2.   H' saves the support information of each grid units and save the time of calculating the support information of each grid;
3.   No need to generate lots of candidate units
4.   The new form is used to identify grid units which makes the finding of neighbour units effective (Junrui, et al., 2010).

A novel approach to subspace clustering is proposed to exhaustively and efficiently mine quantitative frequent item sets (QFIs) from massive transaction data for quantitative association rule mining. The numeric part of a QFI is an axis-parallel and hyper-rectangular cluster of transactions in an attribute subspace formed by numeric items. For the computational tractability, our approach introduces the adaptive density-based and Apriori-like subspace clustering. The QFI mining is used as the basis to mine QARs, and proposed a novel approach called *"QFIMiner"* having the following features:

1. The approach exhaustively mines all dense clusters supported by more than
2. Min_sup transactions in all subspaces formed by both numeric and categorical attributes of a given transaction data.
3. The clusters to be mined have axis-parallel and hyper rectangular shapes in the numeric attribute subspaces.
4. Interval values of numeric items are allowed in the transactions for mining.
5. The approach is virtually $O(N \log N)$ and tractable.
6. Its outstanding performance is demonstrated through the comparison with the past subspace clustering approaches and the application to practical and massive data (Washio, et al., 2005).

CONCLUSION

This chapter discusses various different types of clustering algorithms applied in association rules based analysis in multidimensional clusters. It also provides various algorithms proposed so far and can be extended to different applications.

REFERENCES

Ananthanarayana, V. S., Narasimha Murthy, M., & Subramanian, D. K. (2001). Multi-dimensional semantic Clustering of large databases for Association rule mining. Pattern Recognition, 939-941

Cao, H., Si, G., Zhang, Y., & Jia, L. (2008). A Density-based Quantitative Attribute Partition Algorithm for Association Rule Mining on Industrial Database.*American Control Conference Westin Seattle Hotel.*

Ceglar, A., & Roddick, J. F. (2006). Association mining. *ACM Computing Surveys, 38*(2), 1–42. doi:10.1145/1132956.1132958

Chummun, M. R., Kirubarajan, T., Pattipati, K. R., & Bar-Shalom, Y. (2001). Fast data association Using Multidimensional Assignment with Clustering. *IEEE Transactions on Aerospace and Electronic Systems, 37*(3), 898–913. doi:10.1109/7.953245

Dong, X., & Pi, D. (2014). An Effective Method for Mining Quantitative Association Rules with Clustering Partition in Satellite Telemetry Data.*Second International Conference on Advanced Cloud and Big Data.* doi:10.1109/CBD.2014.12

Ismail, M. A., & Kamel, M. S. (1989). Multidimensional data clustering utilizing hybrid search strategies. *Pattern Recognition, 22*(1), 75–89. doi:10.1016/0031-3203(89)90040-X

Junrui, Y., & Feng, Z. (2010). An Effective Algorithm for Mining Quantitative Associations Based on Subspace Clustering.*International Conference on Networking and Digital Society.*

Kuo, R. J., Lin, S. Y., & Shih, C. W. (2007). Mining association rules through integration of clustering analysis and ant colony system for health insurance database in Taiwan. Expert Systems with Applications, 794–808.

Li, T., & Chen, Y. (2009). Hierarchical Clustering Ensemble Algorithm based Association Rules.*5th International Conference on Wireless Communications, Networking and Mobile Computing.* doi:10.1109/WICOM.2009.5305676

Malik, H., & Kender, J. R. (2006). High quality, efficient hierarchical document clustering using closed interesting item sets.*Proceedings of the Sixth International Conference on Data Mining (ICDM'06).* IEEE. doi:10.1109/ICDM.2006.81

Muralidhar, A., & Pattabiraman, V. (2015). An Efficient Association Rule Based Clustering of XML Documents. *2nd International Symposium on Big Data and Cloud Computing (ISBCC'15), Procedia Computer Science.* doi:10.1016/j.procs.2015.04.024

QingLan, H., & Zhen. (2013). Multi-level Association rule mining based on clustering partition. *Third International Conference on Intelligent System Design and Engineering Applications.* IEEE.

Strehl, A., Gupta, G. K., & Ghosh, J. (1999). Distance Based Clustering of Association Rules.*Proceedings ANNIE Intelligent Engineering Systems through Artificial Neural Networks.*

Tan, P. N., Steinbach, M., & Kumar, V. (2007). *Introduction to Data Mining.* Pearson Education.

Tang, M., Zhou, Y., Cui, P., Wang, W., Li, J., Zhang, H.,... Yan, B. (2009). Discovery of Migration habitats and routes of Wild Bird Species by Clustering and Association analysis. Springer.

The multidimensional data model. (n.d.). Retrieved August 5, 2016, from https://web.stanford.edu/dept/itss/docs/oracle/10g/olap.101/b10333/multimodel.htm

Wan, S. J., Wong, S. K. M., & Prusinkiewicz, P. (1988). An Algorithm for Multidimensional data clustering. *ACM Transactions on Mathematical Software, 14*(2), 153–162. doi:10.1145/45054.45056

Washio, T., Mitsunaga, Y., & Motoda, H. (2005). Mining Quantitative Frequent Item sets Using Adaptive Density-based Subspace Clustering.*Fifth IEEE International Conference on Data Mining (ICDM'05).* doi:10.1109/ICDM.2005.100

Yang, Y., & Padmanabhan, B. (2005). Ghic: A Hierarchical Pattern-Based Clustering Algorithm for Grouping Web Transactions.*IEEE Transactions on Knowledge and Data Engineering, 17*(9), 1300–1304. doi:10.1109/TKDE.2005.145

Yunkai, G., Junrui, Y., & Yulei, H. (2008). An Effective Algorithm for Mining Quantitative Association Rules Based on High Dimension Cluster.*4th International Conference on Wireless Communications, Networking and Mobile Computing.* IEEE.

Zhang, C., & Zhang, S. (n.d.). *Association rule mining: models and algorithms.* Springer.

Chapter 4
Data Clustering and Various Clustering Approaches

Shashi Mehrotra
Birla Institute of Technology, India

Shruti Kohli
Birla Institute of Technology, India

ABSTRACT

It is needed to organize the data in different groups for various purposes, where clustering is useful. The chapter covers Data Clustering in the detail, which includes; introduction to data clustering with figures, data clustering process, basic classification of clustering and applications of clustering, describing hard partition clustering and fuzzy clustering. Some most commonly used clustering method are explained in the chapter with their features, advantages, and disadvantages. A various variant of K-Means and extension method of hierarchical clustering method, density-based clustering method and grid-based clustering method are covered.

INTRODUCTION

What Is Clustering?

Clustering is a method of grouping the objects based on their characteristics. The objects which are having similar characteristics are assigned the same group called cluster while the objects having different characteristics are assigned different cluster (Das, Abraham, & Konar, 2008). A cluster contains a collection of object, which is similar in nature, while different from the objects in another cluster. Thus, clustering means the grouping of the objects based on some similarity among objects. Objects belonging to a cluster are more similar to each other compared to the objects belonging to another cluster (Jain, Murty, & Flynn, 1999). Cluster analysis is an unsupervised learning i.e., no predefined class. A typical way to use cluster analysis is to get insight into data distribution or as a preprocessing step for other algorithms. The following figure is an example for clusters of various shapes.

Figure 1 shows cluster of three different shapes. One cluster has star objects, the other cluster has circle objects, and the third cluster has triangles. Each cluster has objects that are similar in shape while they are different from another cluster.

DOI: 10.4018/978-1-5225-1776-4.ch004

Figure 1. Three clusters

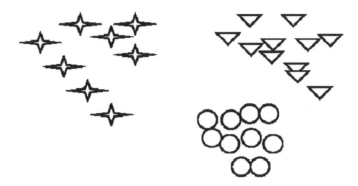

Applications of Clustering

Cluster analysis has a lot of applications, and being used in various fields such as used for artificial intelligence, spatial data analysis, image segmentation, document collection, multimedia data analysis or social media analysis, generating a concept summary of the data, pattern analysis, outlier detection, fraud detection, recommendation system, business, marketing, customer segmentation, and for preprocessing as an intermediate step (Das, Abraham, & Konar, 2008).

A lot of research has been conducted and is going on in the above-mentioned area. Still, a lot of scope is there for research in clustering, it can be effectively used to get insight from the data. Clustering analysis research is being widely going on.

Clustering is being used very often for the medical purpose. Medical sciences use clustering to identifying lump etc., using image segmentation. Clustering is being used in various ways for web applications. The web is being used as the largest repository. Search results contains title and snippets. Results clustered in a meaning full folder will facilitate user to search relevant result in quick manner (Kohli & Mehrotra, 2016).

Search engines cluster search results for a large number of web pages to represent them in more organized way. The Clusty is the most common example, which uses clustering for search result organization.

Clustering analysis is widely used to get insight from the data and used it for policy making and decision making in many business organizations. Clustering may be helpful in target marketing, document retrieval, grouping people in social network in our day to day life (Mehrotra & Kohli, 2016, March).

For the efficient marketing, customers are grouped into different types for targeting the prospective user segment (Jain, 2010). Users are segmented according to their income group, their life style, their interest, their past purchasing behavior, their age group etc.

For example, various income group can be presented in different clusters as given below:

Figure 2 shows three clusters of the different salary group people. One cluster is for the high-income group, and two others are for medium income group and low-income group.

Example 1

A retailer wants to know people to whom they can sell which car. For this purpose, they can create different groups of people based on their income. Customer data can be grouped into a low-income group,

Figure 2. Clusters of a different income group

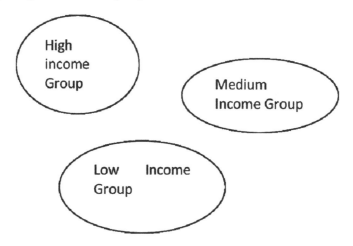

medium-income group, and high- income group, and to market for the car retailer will target the specific customer segment accordingly.

Example 2

A housing company can target specified income group for the specific housing scheme, such as they will target higher income group for HIG houses or for penthouses while lower income group are to be targeted for LIG houses.

TYPE OF ATTRIBUTE

The attributes can be of the following type:

1. **Quantitative Attributes:** Deals with the things which can be measured precisely, such as height, width, length etc. It can present some value, which may be of the following type:
   a. Discrete values is a count of some item or person, for example, a number of children or adults in the family. It can't be in fractions such as kids or adult family member can't be 2.5.
   b. Continuous values can be more precise, for example, the height of a person can be 5.6. Thus height is a continuous value.
   c. Interval variables are a numeric value and exact difference between the values. For example, annual income that is measured in dollars, $10,000, $15,000 and $20,000. Another example is temperature (degrees Fahrenheit).
2. **Qualitative Attributes:** Deals with characteristics of something which cannot be measured in numbers such as smell, color. It may be subdivided into following types:
   a. Nominal variables are used for labeling variables, for example, gender 1) Male 2) Female, another example is hair color 1) Brown 2) Black 3) Gray.
   b. Ordinal data deals with items which can be assigned to categories and that do have order, such as "Small", "Medium", "Large". Another example is ranking or quality evaluation of some item on a 1 to 10 scale. It shows 10 is the best and better than 9, which is better than 8 and so on.

SIMILARITY MEASURE

Grouping of data is performed on the basis of some similarity among the objects. The similarity among the objects is measured through some proximity measure. For measuring the similarity between objects, some proximity measure is used based on the type of attributes. To measure continuous attributes distance functions are used, while to measure the qualitative attributes, similarity measures are used. Some of the objects, which does not contain a particular type of variable, rather they contain mixed variables. These variables can be mapped into the interval (0,1) and then measures like Euclidean distance can be used, or they can be transformed into binary variables, and then binary similarity function can be used. The main disadvantages of using these methods are the information loss. The Euclidean distance measure is the most common distance measure used for measuring the closeness among the continuous attributes.

Following are some of the distance measures which are used to measure closeness among the objects.

Euclidean Distance

Euclidean distance measures the distance between the object, and Euclidean distance is defined as given below:

$$p=[p_1, p_2, \ldots \ldots p_n]$$

$$q=[q_1, q_2, \ldots \ldots q_n]$$

$$D(p,q) = \left(\sum_{t=1}^{n} |p_t - q_t|^2 \right)^{1/2} \tag{1}$$

where, two n dimensional data object are: $(p_1, p_2, \ldots, p_n)$ and $(q_1, q_2, \ldots, q_n)$.

The K-Means algorithm is the most popular clustering algorithm that uses Euclidean distance. It tends to generate hyper spherical cluster (Xu & Wunsch, 2005).

Mahalanobis Distance

Mahalanobis distance is the distance measure which gives the distance between the objects. Mahalanobis distance is defined as given below:

$$D(p,q) = \left| \left(p_1 - q_1 \right) \right| + \left| \left(p_2 - q_2 \right) \right| + \ldots + \left| \left(p_n - q_n \right) \right| \tag{2}$$

where, two data object are: $(p_1, p_2, \ldots, p_n)$ and $(q_1, q_2, \ldots, q_n)$. It tends to generate hyper ellipsoidal clusters (Xu & Wunsch, 2005).

Minkowski Distance

Minkowski distance measure can be considered as a generalization of the Euclidean distance and Mahalanobis distance. Minkowski distance is defined as given below:

$$D(p,q) = \left(\left| \left(p_1 - q_1 \right)^k \right| + \left| \left(p_2 - q_2 \right)^k \right| + \ldots + \left| \left(p_n - q_n \right)^k \right| \right)^{1/k}$$

(3)

where, two n dimensional data object are:

$(p_1, p_2, \ldots, p_n)$ and $(q_1, q_2, \ldots, q_n)$.

where k is a positive integer (Jensi & Jiji, 2014).

Cosine Similarity

The Cosine similarity is most commonly used document clustering. The Cosine similarity is defined as given below:

$$s(x,y) = \cos \alpha = \frac{x^t . y}{\left\| x \right\| \left\| y \right\|}$$

(4)

where x^t is a transposition of the vector x, ‖x‖ is the Euclidean norm of the vector x, ‖y‖ is the Euclidean norm of the vector y (Jensi & Jiji, 2014).

Jaccard Coefficient

Jaccard coefficient is defined as:

$$J(A,B) = \left(A \cap B \right) \big/ \left(A \cup B \right)$$

(5)

where A and B documents.

Clustering is applied in two modes which are as given below:

- **Crisp Clustering:** Data may belong to only one cluster in case of crisp clustering. Each object is allocated to a single cluster.
- **Fuzzy Cluster:** Data may belong to more than one cluster with a degree of membership. A fuzzy clustering method assigns a degree of membership to the each object in various clusters (Jensi & Jiji, 2014).

CLUSTERING PROCEDURE

Clustering process consists of following steps:

1. **Attribute Selection:** This step selects relevant attributes to be included for clustering, as all the attributes are not relevant for analysis. Properly selected attributes can significantly ease the workload.
2. **Design or Selection of Clustering Algorithm:** This step selects the proper proximity measure as various measures exist, and that directly affects the resulting cluster. The designing of the new clustering algorithm or choosing the existing clustering algorithm is also part of this step. A lot of clustering algorithms exist to solve various problems in specific fields, and many new algorithms coming up. No single clustering algorithm can be used to solve all the problems.
3. **Cluster Validation:** This step is performed for the evaluation of the output of a clustering algorithm. Different algorithm leads to different output; therefore evaluation of the derived clusters, based on some criteria is needed. Even the same algorithm with different parameters or even different input order may generate different output. Validity assessments are performed to access whether the generated output is meaningful. There are some test criteria that is to be performed to justify why one is choosing an algorithm rather than another algorithm. There are three types of validation studies which are used, as given below:
   a. **External Indices:** This test uses some pre-specified structure, which is used as a standard for the validation of the clustering solutions. The recovered structure is compared with the pre specified structure.
   b. **Internal Indices:** This test does not depend on the prior knowledge. It tests the clustering structure from the actual data and tries to determine whether the structure is appropriate for the data.
   c. **Relative Criteria:** This test focus on comparing the clustering structures for deciding the best reveal the characteristics of the objects. Two structures are compared to measure their relative merits.
4. **Results Interpretation:** The result should be easily and clearly interpretable so that the end user gets meaningful insight from the data, which will be effectively helpful in decision making (Xu & Wunsch, 2005).

REQUIREMENTS AND CHALLENGES

For the cluster analysis, there are many quality requirements and challenges, which are as given below:

1. **Ability to Deal with Different Types of Attributes:** There are many algorithms that work for numerical data, but does not work for text, multimedia, and mixture of different type data.
2. **Ability to Detect Clusters with Arbitrary Shapes:** There are some algorithms which generate spherical clusters only. Some algorithms are needed which can detect clusters of arbitrary shape.
3. **Ability to Handle with Noisy Data:** Most of the real world dataset contains noises, which affect the cluster quality, as most of the algorithms are sensitive to the noise.
4. **Ability to Deal with High Dimension Data:** Some clustering algorithms are not good at cluster high dimension data.
5. **Easy Interpretable:** Clustering result required to be interpretable (Han, Kamber & Pei, 2011).

CLUSTERING TECHNIQUES

Clustering algorithms are categorized as given below:

1. Hierarchical Clustering

Hierarchical clustering algorithm presents the data in the form of tree or dendrogram, and it recursively derived nested clusters. The cluster either starts from a single object in each cluster and, at the end, includes the entire object in one cluster or vice versa.

The root node of the tree represents the whole data set, and the leaf node represents the data object. The hierarchical clustering is helpful if the data contains some hierarchical relation, for example, species of organisms (Xu& Wunsch, 2005).

Hierarchical Agglomerative and Divisive Clustering

Hierarchical Agglomerative clustering starts with each object in a separate cluster. In this way, n clusters are formed, and after that clusters containing similar objects are merged. The merge operation continues until a single cluster is formed containing all the objects.

Hierarchical Agglomerative Clustering Algorithm (Jain, A. K., Murty, M. N., & Flynn, P. J. (1999))

1. Calculate the proximity matrix that contains the distance of each pair of objects. Each object is treated as a cluster.
2. Select the most similar pair of clusters according to the proximity matrix, and merge them into one cluster. This merges operation now to be reflected in proximity matrix by updating it.
3. Go to step 2, until all the objects are not assigned to one cluster.

Agglomerative clustering varies on various link, single-link and complete-link are the most common example of hierarchical clustering algorithms which are as given below (Jain, 2010).

Single Link Method

The Single-link method determines the distance between two clusters by the closest two objects in the different clusters. AGNES (Agglomerative NESting) is an example of single-linkage approach.

Figure 3 points the two closest objects of two clusters.

Advantages of Single Link method is that it can cluster non elliptical shapes objects.

The disadvantage of Single Link method is that it is sensitive to noise.

Complete Link Method

The complete linkage method uses the farthest distance of a pair of objects for the inter- cluster distance. DIANA is an example of complete link method, which considers the maximum distance between the closest neighboring objects.

Figure 3. Example of single link cluster

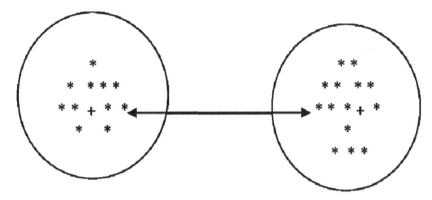

Figure 4. Example of complete link cluster

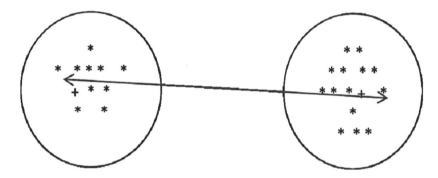

Figure 4 points two farthest objects of two clusters. Complete link method usually generates more compact clusters.

Disadvantage of the complete link method is, this method is sensitive to outliers.

Hierarchical Divisive Clustering

In the case of the hierarchical divisive algorithm, it starts with only one cluster containing all the objects and keeps on splitting based on some criterion until each cluster contain only one object (Jain, Murty, & Flynn, 1999). The computation cost of divisive clustering is very high. Two clustering algorithms named MONA and DIANA are the examples of the divisive clustering algorithm.

Drawbacks of Hierarchical Clustering

1. Hierarchical clustering is sensitive to noise and outliers.
2. Hierarchical clustering cannot correct misclassification i.e., once an object is assigned incorrectly, it can't be corrected again.
3. Hierarchical clustering has high computational cost, for most of the hierarchical clustering algorithm time complexity is $O(N^2)$, where N is the number of total objects. Thus, it is not suitable for the large data sets.

Many improved hierarchical clustering algorithms came up considering the need of large-scale data sets. Some of the examples are BIRCH, CURE, ROCK, and Chameleon.

BIRCH (Balanced Iterative Reducing and Clustering using Hierarchies)

BIRCH is an integration of agglomerative clustering with another clustering method. It is a multiphase clustering algorithm, and inclemently construct a hierarchical data structure, CF(Cluster Feature) tree. It is suitable for numerical data of large size.

BIRCH uses the clustering feature and clustering feature tree(CF tree).

CF = <N, LS, SS>

where

N: number of data points.

LS: Linear sum of N points: $\sum_{i=1}^{n} x_i$

SS: Square sum of N points: $\sum_{i=1}^{n} x_i^2$

For example, 3 points are given in a cluster, (3,4), (2,6), and (4,3).

$$CF = \left\langle 3, \left(3+2+4, 4+6+3\right), \left(3^2+2^2+4^2, 4^2+6^2+3^2\right) \right\rangle$$
$$= \left\langle 3, \left(9,13\right), \left(29,61\right) \right\rangle$$

A CF tree stores the clustering features for a hierarchical clustering, and it is a height balanced tree. The CF tree needs two parameters as given below:

- **Branching Factor:** Denotes the maximum number of children per nonleaf node.
- **The Threshold:** Denotes the maximum diameter of sub-clusters that can be stored at the leaf nodes.

Advantages of BIRCH

BIRCH overcomes the drawbacks of Agglomerative clustering methods. It has following advantages:

1. Scalability.
2. BIRCH is robust to outliers.
3. The problem of the undoing of the misclassification did in earlier the step.
4. The computational complexity of BIRCH is O(n), where n is the number of objects.

Disadvantages of BIRCH

1. Sensitive to insertion order of data point.
2. Clusters shape may not be very natural due to the size of the leaf nodes.
3. Clusters tend to be spherical.

CURE (Clustering Using Representatives)

CURE is an extension of hierarchical clustering, and it represents a cluster using a well-scattered representation points. Minimum distances between the representative's points are chosen. To represent representative points, there may have some points those will be closer to the center of the data point that may be considered as representative points. Choosing scattered points help CURE to capture clusters of arbitrary shapes. It incorporates the features of both single link and average link.

ROCK (A Hierarchical Clustering Algorithm for Categorical Attributes)

ROCK is a hierarchical clustering with link i.e., the number of common neighbors between the two objects. Rock works efficiently for categorical data. The ROCK considers the neighbors of a pair of points, and if these two point's neighbors are same, in that case, these two points may be merged into the same cluster. The neighbors of points are represented by links.

The sparse graph is constructed from a given data similarity matrix, and a threshold and the concept of shared neighbors is used. Then agglomerative hierarchical clustering is performed on the sparse graph.

CHAMELEON (A Hierarchical Clustering Algorithm Using Dynamic Modeling)

Chameleon measures the similarity based on dynamic modeling. Chameleon was developed to overcome the weakness of the algorithms: ROCK and CURE. As Chameleon considers similarity by accessing how objects are interconnected within a cluster, and the proximity of the cluster. Two clusters are merged only if the interconnectivity and closeness between two clusters are high (Anastasiu, Gao, & Buttler, 2011).

Chameleon work in two phases:

1. It clusters the objects relatively into small sub-clusters by using k-nearest-neighbor graph approach.
2. In the second phase, it uses an agglomerative hierarchical algorithm to merge the clusters.

The best feature of Chameleon is that it is able to generate clusters of complex objects efficiently.

2. Partitioning Algorithms

In the partitioning clustering, a number of partitions are created and assigns a set of objects into the partition with no hierarchical structure. A number of partitions are predefined, and groups the data by optimizing a specific objective function. Partitioning method is suitable for applications involving large data sets.

Following are the most common partitioning clustering algorithms (Cobos,Mendoza, & Leon, 2011):

- K-Means,
- K-medoids,
- Expectation Maximization.

K-Means Clustering Algorithm (Jain, Murty, & Flynn, 1999).

The K-Means algorithm starts with random initial partitions, and based on some similarity between the object and the center of the cluster, keep assigning the objects until there is no change. The main clustering objective of K-Means algorithm is the minimization of the dissimilarity among the objects and centroid of the corresponding cluster (Yang, Sun, & Zhang, 2009).

1. Select k cluster centers.
2. Assign each object to the cluster, which center is closest to the object.
3. Recalculate the cluster center with new cluster members.
4. Go to Step 2 till there is no change in the clusters.

There are three parameters, that K-Means requires are; k is the number of clusters, cluster initialization, and the distance metric. Initialization affects the k-mean output. Various initializations may generate different output (Jain, 2010).

Advantages of the K-Means Clustering Algorithm

K-Means clustering algorithm has following advantages (Das, Abraham, & Konar, 2008):

1. It is easy to implement.
The time complexity of the K-Means is O(tkn), where, n is the number of objects, k represents the number of clusters, and t represents the number of iterations.

k, t << n;

therefore it is suitable for large data sets.

Disadvantages of the K-Means Clustering Algorithm

However it has some drawbacks which are as given below (Das, Abraham, & Konar, 2008):

1. It requires a number of clusters to be defined in the starting itself.
2. K-Means is highly dependent on initialization conditions.
3. It can result to the local minima.
4. K-Means can be applied only on numerical data.
5. K-Means can detect cluster that is linearly separable.

Variant of the K-Means

Many variants of K-Means clustering algorithm has been developed considering various aspects of K-Means. Some variant tried to improve splitting and merging the clusters derived. Most common example using this technique is the ISODATA. Some other variant used other criterion function rather than centroid. Some of the most common variants are as follows:

- K-Medoids
- K-Median
- K-Modes

K-Medoids Clustering Method

K-Medoids instead of taking the mean value of the objects in a cluster uses medoid, which is the most centrally located object in a cluster. The K-medoids algorithm is similar to K-Means algorithm, except that considering the mean of the cluster, it focuses on centrally located object.

PAM (Partitioning Around Medoids) is the most common example of K-Medoids clustering method, and this was the first developed K-Medoids algorithm.

K-Median Clustering Method

The K-Median clustering method is more suitable where there are variation in the data. The K-Median uses following criterion function:

$$s = \sum_{j=1}^{k} \sum_{x \in c_j} \left| p - o_j \right|, \tag{6}$$

where s is absolute error o_j is the object of cluster c_j, and is representative of the cluster c_j, and p is the point in cluster c_j.

The representative object is the most centrally positioned object in the cluster. The K-median is less sensitive to outlier compared to the K-Means. K-Median uses

K-Mode Clustering Method

K-Mode is an extension of K-Means by replacing means of clusters with modes. K-Mode clustering method is suitable for categorical data and overcomes the issue with K-means, which cannot handle non-numeric data.

3. Fuzzy Clustering Method

In the case of fuzzy clustering, objects may belong to all the clusters, and the entire object will have a degree of membership. Fuzzy clustering is useful in the case where the boundary among the clusters is not clearly separated.

Example:

There are two crisp sets A and B as given below:

A={1,2,3,4,5}

B={6,7,8,9,10}

Clusters generated by a fuzzy clustering algorithm might generate two fuzzy clusters as given below:

Fa={(1,0.9), (2,0.7), (3, 0.7), (4,0.8), (5, 0.8), (6,0.3), (7,0.3), (8,0.0), (9,0.0), (10,0.0)}

Fb={(1,0.0), (2,0.0), (3,0.0), (4,0.0), (5,0.1), (6,0.7), (7,0.7), (8,1.0), (9,1.0), (10, 1.0)}

The above set represents the object and its membership value. Each object has a membership value in between [0,1].

FCM is the most popular fuzzy clustering algorithm. The fuzzy set concept can also be used for the hierarchical clustering. A hierarchical fuzzy clustering, named HUFC is proposed by Geva, that cluster the objects in the hierarchy, and objects are given a degree of membership. Fuzzy clustering approach overcomes one of the drawbacks of the hierarchical cluster, that once an object is assigned to a cluster incorrectly, it cannot be reassigned.

4. Graph Theoretic Clustering

The graph theoretic clustering approach is based on first generating the Minimal spanning tree(MST). Once a tree is created, largest length edges are deleted, which results in clusters. Single-link clusters are the result of the sub graphs of the minimum spanning tree. Complete-link clusters are the result of maximal complete sub graphs.

5. Density Based Clustering Method

Density-based clustering method based on density and a cluster is a maximal set of connected dense units in a subspace. Following are some of the most common example of density- based clustering method:

- DBSCAN,
- OPTICS,
- DENCLUE,
- CLIQUE.

Major features of the density based clustering approach are as given below:

- Discover clusters of arbitrary shape.
- Capable of handling noise.

The most common example of density based clustering; DBSCAN (Density based spatial clustering of applications with noise) is explained below:

DBSCAN (Density-Based Spatial Clustering of Applications with Noise)

DBSCAN clustering algorithm, developed by Ester in 1996, which searches for the dense regions. Data with a high-density area is treated as a cluster and the data with a low-density area is treated as noise. DBSCAN generates a new cluster from the if the neighborhood meets the user-specified density threshold.

Advantages of DBSCAN

1. It can filter noise.
2. It does not require a number of clusters to be defined.
3. Any shape clusters are formed based on density-reach ability mechanism (Yang & Ng, 2009).

Disadvantages of DBSCAN

1. It is not suitable for high dimensional data.
2. DBSCAN is sensitive to parameter setting (Jain, 2010).

6. Grid Based Approach

In the grid based approach individual regions on the data space are formed into a grid-like structure, and the grid specifies characteristics of data. It finds clusters i.e., a dense region of the cells in the grid structure. STING, CLIQUE, Wave Cluster and factual clustering (FC) are the example of grid-based clustering algorithms.

7. Evolutionary Clustering Method

Evolutionary algorithms are inspired by natural evolution process, using the evolutionary operators; selection, recombination, and mutation. The selection operator selects the individuals for the next generation. The recombination and mutation operators are used for the assortment of the population. An objective function, known as fitness function is used for evaluating the optimizing degree of the individuals, where each individual has it fitness value. Evolutionary approaches are parallel in nature.

Evolutionary clustering algorithms consist of genetic algorithm (GAs), evolutionary programming (EP), evolution strategies (ESs). Out of these, Genetic algorithms are the most popular approached used for cluster analysis.

Genetic Algorithms

Jhon Holland invented Genetic algorithms in the 1960s, and along with his students, it was developed during 1960s and 1070s at the University of Michigan (Fogel, 1997).

GAs inspired by biological evolution and based on Darwin theory survival of fittest. A population of solutions is used, and fitness of each individual is calculated using some objective function. Selection of individuals are performed based on the fitness of individual, and according to the fitness, individuals will be passed to next generation. As the generation's passes, the members of the population should get fitter and fitter, i.e. closer and closer to the solution.

Following are the components of the Genetic algorithm:

Individuals or chromosomes may be the feasible solutions in an optimization problem and usually encoded as a bit of string, and the population is the set of individuals.

Genetic Operators

Genetic algorithms involve three types of operators as given below (Goldberg, 2006):

- **Selection:** This operator selects the individuals for reproduction of offspring. There are various selection method which can be used for choosing the individual for the next generation.
- **Crossover:** This operator is used for exchange features of two individuals to produce two off springs. Crossovers may be, two parent crossover, three parent crossover, single-point crossover, two-point crossover, uniform crossover. Table 1 shows the example of two parent single-point and two-point crossover.
- **Mutation:** Randomly select the element and change it. For example, 0 is changed to 1or 1 may be changed to 0.
- **Fitness Function:** Fitness function takes a single chromosome as an input and returns a measure of the fitness value, i.e., the goodness of the solution.

Advantages of the Genetic Algorithm

Genetic algorithms overcome some of the drawbacks of the traditional clustering algorithm, such as genetic algorithms are able to cope with local optima, as they recombine and compare various candidate solutions simultaneously. Best solutions dominate and the bad solutions are eliminated due to mutation and selection (Das, Abraham, & Konar, 2008).

Table 1.

Single-Point Crossover																			
Parents										Offspring									
1	0	0	0	1	1	1	1	0	1	1	0	0	0	1	0	1	0	0	1
0	0	1	1	0	0	1	0	0	1	0	0	1	1	0	1	1	1	0	1
Two-Point Crossover																			
Parents										Offspring									
1	0	0	0	1	1	1	1	0	1	1	0	**1**	1	0	0	1	1	**0**	1
0	0	1	1	0	0	1	0	0	1	0	0	**0**	0	1	1	1	0	**0**	1

Disadvantages of Genetic Algorithm

Genetic algorithms (GAs) are sensitive to the selection parameters, such as the size of population, crossover and mutation probabilities.

CLUSTERING LARGE DATA SETS

With the rapid increase in the size of the database and use of the internet, clustering algorithms have to face many challenges. A lot of research work have been done and still going on. Following are some algorithms which are suitable for the large data sets.

1. **K-Means Clustering Algorithm:** The K-means algorithm is the most popular and simple to use (Cobos, Mendoza, & Leon, 2011, June). It is quite suitable for the large data sets, as its time complexity is O(nkt) and the space complexity is O(n + k), where n is the number of objects, k is the number of clusters, and t is.number of iterations. Thus, the complexity of K-Means algorithm comes to linear. Experimental result in (Mehrotra & Kohli, 2016) shows the K-means performs best among EM and Canopy clustering algorithm the K-Means algorithm takes less execution time (Mehrotra & Kohli, 2015, October). Many researchers have worked to overcome the drawbacks of K-Means algorithm and still the work is going on.

2. **CLARANS (Clustering Large Applications Based On Random Search):** It starts with a node as a current node, and checks out its neighbor for a better solution. The neighbor becomes the current node which has a lower cost. The current node becomes the winner node when the user specified maximum number neighbor is attained. This will continue until the termination condition is meet or user specified iteration are complete. The time complexity of the CLARANS is O(n), where n is the number of objects.

3. **The BIRCH (Balanced Iterative Reducing and Clustering) Algorithm:** The BIRCH algorithm stores the summary information about the candidate clusters in the CF tree data structure and the leaf node represents the clustering.

Every clustering algorithm has its own features such as K-Means uses Euclidean distance, and therefore, it tends to generate hyperspherical clusters. Thus, K-Means may not be effective, in the case where other geometric shape clusters are required.

CONCLUSION

Clustering is organizing the objects into meaningful groups, called a cluster. A cluster contains objects, which are similar in nature, while different from the objects in other clusters.

The similarity between objects is measured using some proximity measure. Some of the examples such as Euclidian distance, Manhattan Distance, Minkowski Distance, Mahalanobis Distance, Jaccard distance, Cosine similarity measure.

Cluster analysis has a lot of applications, such as it is being used for artificial intelligence, spatial data analysis, image segmentation, document collection, medical sciences, biology, and business decision making, marketing, and customer segmentation etc. Cluster analysis has also been used for preprocessing as an intermediate step.

Clustering techniques can be categorized as hierarchical clustering method, partition clustering method, density-based methods, grid-based methods, and evolutionary methods. Some variants of K-Means and hierarchical algorithms are developed.

A hierarchical method generates a tree structure, which includes two types methods:

1. Agglomerative clustering method,
2. Divisive clustering method.

A partitioning method generates k partitions called cluster, and each object is assigned to the partition, whose mean is closest to the object. The parameter k represents a number of clusters, and it is an iterative process. Some variants of K-Means are as given below:

*   K-Medoids,
*   K-Median,
*   K-Modes.

Fuzzy clustering method may assign objects to all the clusters, and the entire object will have a degree of membership. FCM is the most popular fuzzy clustering algorithm.

Evolutionary algorithms are inspired by natural evolution process, using the evolutionary operators; selection, recombination, and mutation. Evolutionary clustering algorithms consist of genetic algorithm (GAs), evolutionary programming (EP), evolution strategies (ESs).

Density-based clustering method based on density and a cluster is a maximal set of connected dense units in a subspace. Following are some of the most common example of density-based clustering method:

*   DBSCAN,
*   OPTICS,
*   DENCLUE,
*   CLIQUE.

Grid-based approach from the data space into a grid-like structure and the grid specifies characteristics of data. It finds clusters i.e., a dense region of the cells in the grid structure. Some of the examples of grid structure are as follows:

*   STING,
*   CLIQUE,
*   Wave Cluster,
*   Factual clustering (FC).

Exercise

1. What is clustering? Explain with example.
2. Describe the proximity measures with the formulas to measure closeness for different types data.

3. List the types of attributes.
4. Briefly, explain following clustering methods:
    a. Density based method
    b. Grid-based method
    c. Model-based method
5. Describe the application of clustering, and how it can be used in the various field.
6. The tuples mentioned represent objects: (44, 6, 46, 22), (40, 2, 36, 20). Perform following computation between the above mentioned two objects.
    a. Euclidean distance,
    b. Manhattan distance,
    c. Minkowski distance.
7. Describe the following clustering methods with their advantages and disadvantages.
    a. Hierarchical,
    b. Agglomerative,
    c. K-Means,
    d. K-median,
    e. BIRCH.
8. Map the following statement to the hierarchical clustering algorithm to which it pertains:

Objects are first partitioned using a tree structure, which is then clustered using other clustering algorithms.

*   BIRCH,
*   CHAMELEON,
*   CURE.

REFRENCES

Anastasiu, D. C., Gao, B. J., & Buttler, D. (2011, October). A framework for personalized and collaborative clustering of search results. In *Proceedings of the 20th ACM international conference on Information and knowledge management* (pp. 573-582). ACM. doi:10.1145/2063576.2063662

Cobos, C., Mendoza, M., & Leon, E. (2011, June). A hyper-heuristic approach to design and tuning heuristic methods for web document clustering. In Evolutionary Computation (CEC), 2011 IEEE Congress on (pp. 1350-1358). IEEE. doi:10.1109/CEC.2011.5949773

Das, S., Abraham, A., & Konar, A. (2008). Automatic clustering using an improved differential evolution algorithm. *Systems, Man and Cybernetics, Part A: Systems and Humans. IEEE Transactions on*, *38*(1), 218–237.

Fogel, D. B. (1997). An introduction to genetic algorithms: Melanie Mitchell. MIT Press.

Goldberg, D. E. (2006). *Genetic algorithms*. Pearson Education India.

Han, J., Kamber, M., & Pei, J. (2011). *Data mining: Concepts and techniques*. Elsevier.

Jain, A. K. (2010). Data clustering: 50 years beyond K-means. *Pattern Recognition Letters*, *31*(8), 651–666. doi:10.1016/j.patrec.2009.09.011

Jain, A. K., Murty, M. N., & Flynn, P. J. (1999). Data clustering: A review. *ACM Computing Surveys*, *31*(3), 264–323. doi:10.1145/331499.331504

Jensi, R., & Jiji, D. G. W. (2014). *A survey on optimization approaches to text document clustering.* arXiv preprint arXiv:1401.2229

Kohli, S., & Mehrotra, S. (2016), A clustering approach for optimization of search result. Journal of Images and Graphics, 4(1), 63-66.

Mehrotra, S., & Kohli, S. (2015, October). Comparative analysis of K-Means with other clustering algorithms to improve search result. In *Green Computing and Internet of Things (ICGCIoT), 2015 International Conference on* (pp. 309-313). IEEE. doi:10.1109/ICGCIoT.2015.7380479

Mehrotra, S., & Kohli, S. (2016). Application of clustering for improving search result of a website. In *Information Systems Design and Intelligent Applications* (pp. 349–356). Springer India. doi:10.1007/978-81-322-2752-6_34

Mehrotra, S., & Kohli, S. (2016, March). The Study of the Usage of Data Analytic and Clustering Techniques for Web Elements. In *Proceedings of the ACM Symposium on Women in Research 2016* (pp. 118-120). ACM. doi:10.1145/2909067.2909089

Xu, R., & Wunsch, D. (2005). Survey of clustering algorithms. *Neural Networks. IEEE Transactions on*, *16*(3), 645–678.

Yang, C. C., & Ng, T. D. (2009, June). Web opinions analysis with scalable distance-based clustering. In *Intelligence and Security Informatics, 2009. ISI'09. IEEE International Conference on* (pp. 65-70). IEEE.

Yang, F., Sun, T., & Zhang, C. (2009). An efficient hybrid data clustering method based on K-harmonic means and Particle Swarm Optimization. *Expert Systems with Applications*, *36*(6), 9847–9852. doi:10.1016/j.eswa.2009.02.003

Chapter 5
Dealing with Higher Dimensionality and Outliers in Content–Based Image Retrieval

Seikh Mazharul Islam
RCC Institute of Information Technology, India

Minakshi Banerjee
RCC Institute of Information Technology, India

Siddhartha Bhattacharyya
RCC Institute of Information Technology, India

ABSTRACT

This chapter proposes a content based image retrieval method dealing with higher dimensional feature of images. The kernel principal component analysis (KPCA) is done on MPEG-7 Color Structure Descriptor (CSD) (64-bins) to compute low-dimensional nonlinear-subspace. Also the Partitioning Around Medoids (PAM) algorithm is used to squeeze search space again where the number of clusters are counted by optimum average silhouette width. To refine these clusters further, the outliers from query image's belonging cluster are excluded by Support Vector Clus-tering (SVC). Then One-Class Support Vector Machine (OCSVM) is used for the prediction of relevant images from query image's belonging cluster and the initial retrieval results based on the similarity measurement is feed to OCSVM for training. Images are ranked from the positively labeled images. This method gives more than 95% precision before recall reaches at 0.5 for conceptually meaningful query categories. Also comparative results are obtained from: 1) MPEG-7 CSD features directly and 2) other dimensionality reduction techniques.

INTRODUCTION

High dimensional multiple array data and exponential information growth nowadays are being widely observed in the areas of multimedia retrieval, modern computer vision research (Ju, Sun, Gao, Hu, & Yin, 2015), social networking, text processing, gene expression dataset analysis etc., with respect to

DOI: 10.4018/978-1-5225-1776-4.ch005

both dimensionality and sample size. The dimensionality is being increased double in every 20 month or so (Jensen & Shen, 2008). This high-dimensionality not only increases computational overhead and memory requirements in algorithms, but also adversely affects their performance in real applications. These high-dimensional data however, are not often distributed uniformly in their ambient space; instead they lie in or close to a low-dimensional space or manifold (Torki, Elgammal, & Lee, 2010), (Zhang, Huang, & Wang, 2010). Obtaining the low dimensional features set from high-dimensional data has been a challenging problem in machine learning research. Knowledge acquisition, refining is only valuable when it can be used efficiently and effectively. The accumulated data may contain the noise because of the technological imperfection while capturing these data and the source of the data may produce noisy data. In medical domain any kind of the inadequacy in the imaging device may produce noisy medical images and may be the reason of wrong diagnosis. In social media data is unstructured in nature. The excellent formal or informal contents, spam, grammatical mistakes in those contents, wrong spelling and punctuation marks all these issues are prevalent in social media. The useful knowledge extraction from the data as mentioned is very difficult. The dimensionality reduction in this context is very effective to get rid of the noisy and redundant features. It refers both the feature extractions and feature selections. In feature extraction the original features space is translated into new feature space with smaller dimension and the semantic meaning is lost. In feature selection, a subset of the original features set is extracted by eliminating features with little or no predictive information by minimizing redundancy and maximizing relevance to the target such as the class labels in classification.

Theoretically, the problem of higher dimensional data can be given using a K-Nearest Neighbors (KNN) classifier (Hastie, Tibshirani, & Friedman, 2008). Suppose the inputs are uniformly distributed in the unit hypercube $[0, 1]^p$ and task is to make a decision for a test point **x's** belonging class by "growing" a hypercube around **x** until it contains a desired fraction **r** of the training data points. The expected edge length of this cube is given by $e_p(r) = r^{1/p}$ as $e(r)^d = r$. The p = 10 gives $e_{10}(0.01) = 0.01^{1/10} \approx 0.63$ and $e_{10}(0.1) = 0.1^{1/10} \approx 0.80$ indicate that to consider 1% or 10% of the data to form a local average, it requires to cover 63% or 80% of the range along each dimension around **x**. In this context the neighborhoods are no longer "local" in spite of the name "nearest neighbor". Reducing r will not help because then only fewer observations will be taken for average which results in higher variance. The following Figure 1 is illustrating this curse of dimensionality.

However, in the last couple of decades, a lot of progress has been observed in developing tools or formulating algorithms for dimensionality reduction and features selection (Celik, Logsdon, & Aase, 2014), (Jenatton, Obozinski, & Bach, 2010), (Kong, Wang, Teoh, Wang, & Venkateswarlu, 2005), (Lu, Plataniotis, & Venetsanopoulos, 2008).

In this chapter a content based image retrieval system will be discussed which can handle the issue of dimensionality and outliers. Searching for similar images corresponding to a query using text has commenced since 1970s. The "Content based image retrieval" was first addressed by Toshikazu Kato in 1992 on his research article "Database architecture for content-based image retrieval". He used color and shape like feature for image retrieval from a large database. This content based retrieval method is better than text based method since text based IR needs manual keywords annotation requires enormous human intervention. Moreover, tagging images by metadata cannot capture the diversity and ambiguity present in image. On other hand, the content based image retrieval (CBIR) system represents images by features vectors which are obtained from the color, shape, texture properties of images and retrieve similar images by computing the similarity score. The following Figure 2 gives a block diagram for content based image retrieval system.

Figure 1. The illustration of curse of dimensionality. The right figure shows that, for any dimensions p, the side-length of the sub-cube required to consider a fraction r of the volume of the data. For p=10, to capture 10% of the data it requires to capture 80% of the range of each dimension.

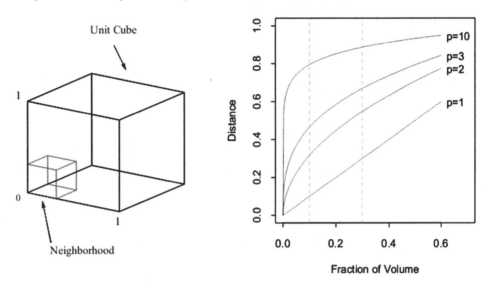

Figure 2. The block diagram of CBIR system

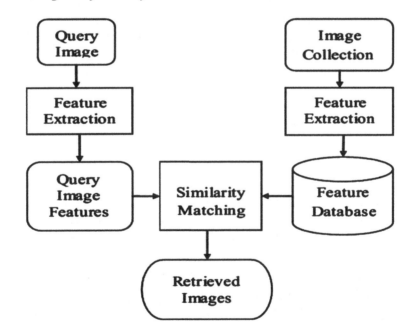

Motivation behind the Dimensionality Reduction

In the context of CBIR the large number of features may better represent the discriminative properties of visual contents of database images. But this fact also leads to dimensionality curse issue (Banerjee & Islam, 2015), (Lu, He, & Zeng, 2005). So, as a preprocessing step, feature selection or reduction is helpful for reducing dimensionality, removing irrelevant data, improving learning accuracy, and enhancing output comprehensibility. There are two basic kinds of feature selection algorithms, viz. filter and wrapper models (Jensen & Shen, 2008). The filter model chooses feature subsets independently of any learning algorithm and relies on various measures of the general characteristics of the training data. The wrapper model uses the predictive accuracy of a predetermined learning algorithm to determine the goodness of the selected subsets and is computationally expensive.

In the literature the dimensionality reduction techniques called Principal Component Analysis (PCA), Linear discriminant analysis (LDA) (Ju, Sun, Gao, Hu, & Yin, 2015), (Banerjee & Islam, 2015), (Lu, He, & Zeng, 2005), (Deng, Xiaofei, & Jiawei, 2007), (Dube, El-Saden, Cloughesy, & Sinha, 2006) have been used extensively in CBIR. The PCA projects the feature vectors into a lower dimensional subspace, in which the variance is maximized. It approximates the original data by a linear combination of the leading eigenvectors and it is unsupervised. The supervised dimensionality reduction method LDA encodes discriminatory information by finding directions that maximize the ratio of between-class scatter to within-class scatter. Image retrieval using PCA is based on the global statistics of features. Image Retrieval using Laplacian eigenmap has been proposed in (Lu, He, & Zeng, 2005), which produces efficient results by preserving local neighborhood information of data points but suffers from the problem of new data point, that is if image is absent in database.

The kernel PCA (Scholkopf, Smola, & Muller, 1998) is a nonlinear form of PCA, can efficiently compute principal components in high dimensional feature spaces. It gathers more information than PCA as it is related to the input space by some nonlinear mapping. Although efficient feature reduction is an important criteria as a remedy to curse of dimensionality for a particular query in CBIR, to speed up the retrieval process data clustering becomes more effective in contrast to sequential data search as the database size increases enormously; this is the other aspect of handling the curse of dimensionality. Still, selection of appropriate number of clusters for an unknown database is an important issue (Banerjee & Islam, 2015).

Motivation of Outlier Detection

It is also important to find out unusual, unrepresentative or outliers observations from the datasets because these abnormal, dissimilar and irregular patterns, as per the statistical point of view, deviate from normal generating mechanism of data objects in an input dataset in which majority data objects follow a common normal generating mechanism, may bias the estimates and produce misleading results (Aggarwal & Yu, 2001). The definition of Hawkins for outliers is that an outlier is an observation which deviates so much from the other observations as to arouse suspicions that it was generated by a different mechanism (Hawkins, 1980), (Williams, Baxter, He, Hawkins, & Gu, 2002). The accurate definition of an outlier relies upon hidden assumptions about the data structure and the used detection method. The difficulty of detection increases with the number of outliers and the dimension of the data because the outliers can be extreme in any growing number of directions.

Many motivating examples are in the literature for detecting outliers. For example (Barnett & Lewis, 1994), in 1949 in England, Mrs. Hadlum had given birth to a child which was happened 349 after Mr. Hadlum left for military service. Since the average gestation period for a human female is 280 days then the 349 days, statistically, is an outlier because 349 days are considered as a large observation or does that child belong to another female who conceived much later than Mrs. Hadlum. Outlier detection methods have been employed in several applications, such as identifying suspicious fraudulent transaction for credit card companies, identifying abnormal brain signals that may indicate the early development of brain cancers, detecting mislabeled data in a training data set, detecting an anomalous object in an image such as a land mine, voting irregularity analysis, data cleansing, network intrusion, severe weather prediction, geographic information systems, athlete performance analysis etc.

The most commonly used methods for outlier detection follows statistical approaches (Barnett & Lewis, 1994), (Hodge & Austin, 2004). The statistical properties of the data are used to decide whether a data points comes from the same distribution or not. So estimating underlying distribution of the data is important in this approach. There are two way to compute these distribution: parametric and non-parametric approaches (Barnett & Lewis, 1994; Hodge & Austin, 2004). In parametric approach a family of known distributions, for example, normal distribution, provide the data and the certain parameters are calculated to fit this distribution. However, it is not easy always to know the underlying distribution of the data in real world hence have little practical importance. On other hand the nonparametric methods estimate the density function from the data as well as the parameters of the model and hence give more flexibility. The problem in these approaches is that it requires large number of samples and is only preferable when large scale set is available. Moreover the estimation of the complete density of the data points rather than estimating the boundary around a data points may require too much data and can produce bad descriptions. In this case, to extract the boundaries of a data points the neural network (Hawkins, He, Williams, & Baxter, 2002) can be utilized. But choice of the size of the network, weight initialization and the stopping criterion, etc. for neural network training to extract boundaries of a data points create some difficulties. And also during the training of neural network it cannot deal with the local optimal solution.

Contribution of the Proposed Method

In this chapter a novel outlier detection method is presented based on support vector clustering (SVC) which is unsupervised and non-parametric approach (Yang, Estivill-Castro, & Chalup, 2002). In SVC the data sets are transformed by means of a Gaussian kernel into a high dimensional feature space in order to find the minimal enclosing sphere. Then this sphere transformed back to data space, where a set of contours each of which enclose the data points denotes a separate cluster of points. Actually a convex quadratic program problem is required to obtain the SVC model. These contours can be considered as cluster boundaries. If the width parameter, say q, of the Gaussian kernel is increased, the data space will incorporate more number of disconnected contours and hence produce more number of clusters. Moreover these contours can be considered as one describing valleys in probability distribution. As compared with neural network, the unwanted local minima in the training processes of SVC model can be avoided. The soft margin constant (say C) in SVC handles outliers by letting the sphere in feature space not to include all points.

Precisely, the proposed retrieval method in this chapter uses kernel principal component analysis for dimensionality reduction and then employs Partitioning Around Medoids (PAM) (Kaufman & Rousseeuw, 2008) algorithm for clustering considering the optimum number of clusters. The clusters are further processed using Support Vector Clustering (SVC) to remove possible outliers from the cluster containing the query. One-class support vector machine (Chen, Zhou, & Huang, 2001) is also used for classification as this classifier is biased to the learned concept of a particular category. Training samples are generated from displayed results obtained using KPCA-reduced CSD feature and L1 similarity distance. The proposed method (Banerjee & Islam, 2015) is compared with others dimensionality reduction techniques, namely, Principal Component Analysis (PCA), Factor analysis (FA), and Laplacian eigenmaps (LEM). The remaining sections are organized as follows: Section 2 describes the related work and section 3 gives mathematical background of Kernel PCA, Partitioning Around Medoids (PAM) and one-class SVM. Proposed method is discussed in section 4. Experiment and results are analyzed in the section 5. Section 6 concludes.

RELATED WORKS

Several Content Based Image Retrieval Systems have been developed in recent years for both the commercial and research purposes. The underlying design principles of these systems have a closer link with the proposed method in this book chapter. In this section few such CBIR systems, namely, QBIC (Marques & Borko, 2002), (Flickner, Sawhney, Niblack, Ashley, Huang, Dom, Gorkani, Hafner, Lee, Petkovic, Steele, & Yanker, 1995), Photobook (Pentland, Picard, Sclaroff, 1996), Netra, MARS, PicTo-Seek, VisualSEEk, PicHunter, SIMPLIcity (Wang, Li, & Wiederhold, 2001) will be mentioned.

QBIC

This is a first commercial Content Based Visual Information Retrieval system which was developed at IBM Almaden Research Center and pioneered many later developments. It can retrieve images corresponding to an example images, user-constructed sketches, and selected colors and texture patterns. As a color feature it uses the average (R,G,B), (Y,I,Q), (L,a,b), and MTM (Mathematical Transform to Munsell) coordinates and a k-bin (64 or 256) color histogram. As a texture representation of an image it uses the method proposed by Tamura et al. to compute coarseness, contrast, and directionality texture features. To compute shape descriptors it considers shape area, circularity, eccentricity, major axis orientation, and a set of algebraic moment invariants. An efficient indexing structure is created by Karhunen-Loeve Transform (KLT) for dimension reduction and R∗-tree. The current version of it also supports text-based keyword search which is coupled with content-based similarity search. It does not use relevance feedback methods.

Photobook

This is a set of tools and useful for browsing and searching images inte-ractively developed at MIT Media Lab. It allows user to select one or multiple images from the list and display a sorted list of images by measuring similarity score between selected image/images and the remaining images in the database. A new improved version of it is FourEyes which incorporates the relevance feedback mechanism for better performance.

Netra

This system was developed in UCSB Alexandria Digital Library (ADL) project which supports the objects or regions based image search. Prior to adding images in the database, images are segmented into homogeneous regions using robust segmentation algorithm and each of the regions is considered for feature (color, texture, shape, and location) extraction. It employs a compact color feature representation for segmented regions, compute texture feature based on Gabor wavelet decom-position, and shape representation using Fourier descriptors. It does not use relevance feedback.

MARS (Multimedia Analysis and Retrieval System)

It was originally developed at University of Illinois at Urbana-Champaign. It combines multiple visual features for suitable retrieval architecture instead of representing image by a single feature representation which helps in dynamically adaptation of different applications and different users. It exclusively uses relevance feedback mechanism which is coupled with query vector refinement, automatic matching tool selection, and automatic feature adaptation.

PicToSeek

It was developed at University of Amsterdam for web-based image search. Using the web crawlers this engine initially accumulates images from the web. Then those collected images are catalogued and classified into predefined categories and hence relevant features are computed. The users have the options for searching using image features, an ex-ample image, or simply browsing the pre-computed im-age catalog. The color and shape invariant features have been combined efficiently and relevance feedback mechanism also has been adopted in it.

SIMPLIcity

It uses robust image segmentation method to roughly classify images into indoor-outdoor, textured-non-textured, city-landscape, with-without people, and graph-photograph images manually. Then, a feature extraction method is selected as per the class label of the image. A new similarity measure is given to compute the distance between two images which are considered as a set constituting features vectors for each individual region.

VisualSEEk

It was developed at Columbia University. It allows queries using both the visual features and their spatial relationships. The user can draw regions and then positions them on a query grid, and assigns them properties of color, size, and absolute location. The combined regions location and its corresponding properties are used to be compared against all the images in the collection and the best candidates are retrieved. It does not use relevance feedback.

PicHunter

It was developed at NEC Research Institute, New Jersey. It employs relevance feedback mechanism and Bayes's rule to predict the target image given the users' actions.

Besides all the above mentioned retrieval systems many retrieval models have been proposed in the literature in order to tackle ever existing semantic gap problem between low-level features and the high-level concepts. This semantic gap problem has been tackle to some extents using relevance feedback mechanism. Recently, apart from using global feature, bag-of-visual-words model which can represent images at object level and build a visual dictionary by the clustering of local features of images can substantially reduce the semantic gap problem between low level features and high-levels semantics proposed in (Philbin, Chum, Isard, Sivic, & Zisserman, 2007).

Conventional CBIR approaches have used few fixed rigid similarity/distance function (such as euclidean distance or cosine similarity) which may not facilitate well in complex visual image retrieval tasks. That is why, in recent years, a surge of active research efforts have been observed to develop multiple distance/similarity measures on some low-level features using the machine learning techniques (Wang, Cai, Zhang, Pan, Weifeng, & Han, 2014). Learning to hashing or compact codes from high-dimensional image data which try to preserve semantic similarity is mentioned in the literature (Wang, Cai, Zhang, Pan, Weifeng, & Han, 2014). Another way to improve the feature representation is distance metric learning (DML) is also reported in the literature of CBIR which minimizes the distance between similar images and simultaneously maximizes the distance between dissimilar images (Wang, Cai, Zhang, Pan, Weifeng, & Han, 2014).

The well-know semantic gap issue of CBIR is being tackled by the deep learning framework by applying a state-of-the-art deep learning method, called, convolution neural networks (CNNs) for learning feature representations from image data, is reported in (Krizhevsky, Sutskever, & Hinton, 2012).

THEORETICAL BACKGROUND

Kernel Principal Component Analysis for Dimensionality Reduction

Kernel principal component analysis (KPCA) (Scholkopf, Smola, & Muller, 1998; Quan, 2012) follows the same concept of principal component analysis (PCA) for dimensionality reduction to increase the usefulness of PCA. The popular PCA can deal with the datasets which are linearly separable. In the real world the data points in the datasets may not be linearly separable. To reduce the dimensionality of these non-linearly separable datasets kernel tricks can be combined with PCA. The VC (Vapnik-Chervonenkis) theory says that mapping the dataset by a kernel into a higher dimensional space than the dimension of the input space provide us with greater classification power.

Suppose $\varnothing$ is a non-linear function which transforms the data points from the original D-dimensional feature space into an M-dimensional feature space F where $M \gg D$. This can be written by the following Equation:

$$\varnothing : R^D \to F, x_i \to \varnothing\left(x_i\right), \left(i = 1, ..., N\right) \tag{1}$$

Then the data points in the new feature space can be projected by the standard PCA to a low-dimensional subspace corresponding to the eigenvectors that capture most of the variance. Since the original feature space is augmented into an M-dimensional feature space F then applying standard PCA in this new feature space is very costly and inefficient. The kernel tricks fortunately are used to simplify the computation (Scholkopf, Smola, & Muller, 1998; Quan, 2012).

Firstly it is assumed that the projected new features have zero mean:

$$\frac{1}{N}\sum_{i=1}^{N}\varnothing(x_i) = 0 \tag{2}$$

Then the covariance matrix of the projected features is of size M×M is obtained by the Equation 3 is given below.

$$C = \frac{1}{N}\sum_{i=1}^{N}\varnothing(x_i)\varnothing(x_i)^T \tag{3}$$

Now the eigenvalues and eigenvectors of the covariance matrix are given by

$$Cv_k = \lambda_k v_k \tag{4}$$

where $k=1,2,\ldots,M$. From Equation 3 and Equation 4, we have

$$\frac{1}{N}\sum_{i=1}^{N}\varnothing(x_i)\left\{\varnothing(x_i)^T v_k\right\} = \lambda_k v_k \tag{5}$$

or

$$v_k = \frac{1}{\lambda_k N}\sum_{i=1}^{N}\{\varnothing(x_i)v_k\}\varnothing(x_i)^T \tag{6}$$

Now this $\{\varnothing(x_i)v_k\}$ produces a scalar quantity and hence the eigenvectors v_k can be expressed as linear combination of features by:

$$v_k = \sum_{i=1}^{N}a_{ki}\varnothing\left(x_i\right) \tag{7}$$

Now by substituting v_k in Equation 5 with Equation 7, we have

$$\frac{1}{N}\sum_{i=1}^{N}\varnothing(x_i)\varnothing(x_i)^T\sum_{j=1}^{N}a_{kj}\varnothing\left(x_j\right) = \lambda_k\sum_{i=1}^{N}a_{ki}\varnothing\left(x_i\right). \tag{8}$$

If we define the kernel function

$$K\left(x_i, x_j\right) = \varnothing(x_i)^T\varnothing\left(x_j\right) \tag{9}$$

and multiply both sides of Equation 8 by $\varnothing(x_l)^T$, we have

$$\frac{1}{N}\sum_{i=1}^{N}k\left(x_l,x_i\right)\sum_{j=1}^{N}a_{kj}k\left(x_i,x_j\right) = \lambda_k\sum_{i=1}^{N}a_{ki}k\left(x_l,x_i\right) \tag{10}$$

We can use the matrix notation

$$K^2a_k = \lambda_k NKa_k \text{ where } K_{i,j} = K\left(x_i,x_j\right) \tag{11}$$

and a_k is the N-dimensional column vector of a_{ki}:

$$a_k = [a_{k1},a_{k2},\ldots,a_{kN}]^T, \tag{12}$$

a_k can be solved by

$$Ka_k = \lambda_k Na_k \tag{13}$$

$$y_k\left(x\right) = \varnothing(x)^T v_k = \sum_{i=1}^{N}a_{ki}k\left(x,x_i\right) \tag{14}$$

If the projected datasets $\left\{\varnothing\left(x_i\right)\right\}$ does not have zero mean, we can use Gram matrix $\tilde{K}$ to substitute the kernel matrix K. The Gram matrix is given by

$$\tilde{K} = K - 1_N K - K1_N + 1_N K1_N \tag{15}$$

where 1_N is the *N×N* matrix with all elements equal to 1/*N*.

The power of kernel methods is that we do not have to compute $\varnothing\left(x_i\right)$ explicitly. We can directly construct the kernel matrix from the training data set $\{x_i\}$. Two commonly used kernels are the polynomial kernel

$$K\left(x,y\right) = (x^T y)^d \text{ or } K\left(x,y\right) = (x^T y + c)^d$$

where *c<0* is a constant, and the Gaussian kernel

$$K\left(x,y\right) = \exp\left(-\left\|x - y\right\|^2 / 2\sigma^2\right)$$

with parameter σ.

The steps of kernel PCA for dimensionality reduction can be summarized as:

1. Construct the kernel matrix K from the training data set $\{x_i\}$ using Equation 11.
2. Calculate the Gram matrix $\{X_i\}$ using Equation 15.
3. Use Equation 13 to solve for the vectors a_i (substitute K with $\tilde{K}$).
4. Finally, compute the kernel principal components $y_k(x)$ using the Equation 14.

Suppose we have equal number of 3-dimensional data points which are distributed on two concentric sphere surfaces is shown in Figure 3. Although the class labels are given in the data points but we are not using it. The standard PCA and KPCA are used to reduce this dataset into a 2-dimensional dataset. The standard PCA result is shown in Figure 4 does not bring out any structural information of the original data. In Figure 5 the result of polynomial kernel PCA is still not linearly separable. In Figure 6, the two classes are completely linearly separable by using the Gaussian kernel PCA.

Figure 3. 3D plot of the two-concentric-spheres synthetic data

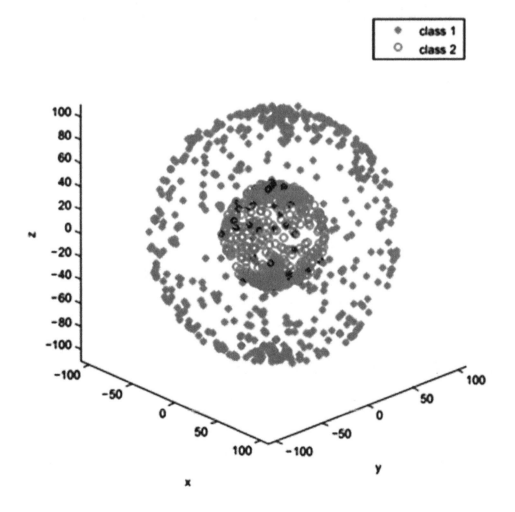

Figure 4. Standard PCA results for the two-concentric-spheres synthetic data

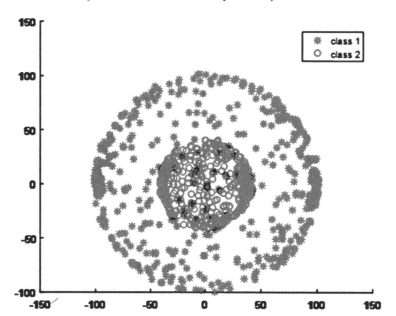

Figure 5. Polynomial kernel PCA results for the two-concentric-spheres synthetic data with d = 5

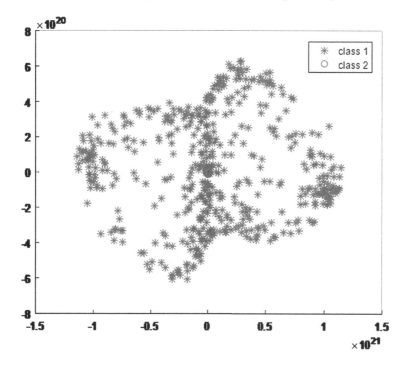

Figure 6. Gaussian kernel PCA results for the two-concentric-spheres synthetic data with $\sigma = 27.8$

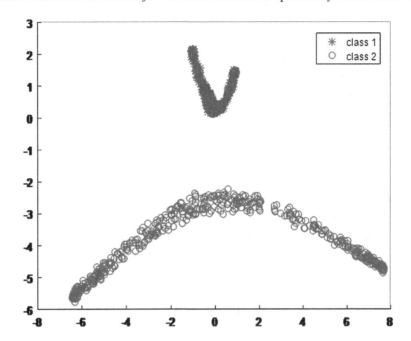

Clustering Algorithm: K-Medoids

K-Medoids (PAM) algorithm determines k partitions for n objects. Initially, it randomly selects the k representative objects as medoids, then updates these medoids by taking a non-medoid object for a cluster in order to find a medoid which minimizes the sum of squared distances of all the objects of the cluster to the cluster medoid. The time complexity of each iteration is $O(k(n-k)^2)$ that is costly for large value of n (number of data points) and k (number of clusters). The K-Medoids algorithm is below (Kaufman & Rousseeuw, 2008).

Algorithm 1. The Partitioning Around Medoids (PAM) Algorithm

Input: k number of clusters, a data set D containing n objects.
Output: k number of clusters.
Step 1: Choose randomly k data points from the whole dataset as the initial representative objects or seeds or medoids;
Step 2: Assign each of the remaining data points to its nearest representative object;
Step 3: Randomly select a non-representative object, d_{rand};
Step 4: Compute the total cost, **C**, of swapping representative object, d_j, with d_{rand};
Step 5: If **C** < 0 then swap d_j with d_{rand} to form the new set of k; representative objects;
Step 6: Repeat Step 2 and Step 5 until no change;
Step 7: Stop the process.

One Class Support Vector Machine

The OCSVM (Banerjee & Islam, 2015), (Chen, Zhou, & Huang, 2001) transforms input data into a high dimensional feature space using a kernel function and iteratively determines the maximal margin hyperplane which best separates the training data from the origin. The OCSVM may be viewed as a regular two-class SVM where all the training data lies in the first class, and origin is taken as only member of the second class. Thus, the hyperplane (or linear decision boundary) corresponds to the classification rule is:

$$f\left(x\right) = w, x + b \tag{16}$$

where w is the normal vector and b is a bias term. The OCSVM solves an optimization problem to find the rule with maximal geometric margin. To assign a label to a test sample x, if the condition $f(x)<0$ is true then the sample is non-relevant otherwise relevant.

Kernels

The optimization problem of OCSVM is obtained by solving the dual quadratic programming problem, is given by:

$$\min_{\alpha} \frac{1}{2} \sum_{ij} \alpha_i \alpha_j K\left(x_i, x_j\right), \text{ s.t. } 0 \le \alpha_i \le \frac{1}{vl} \text{ and } \sum_i \alpha_i = 1. \tag{17}$$

where α_i is a lagrange multiplier (or "weight" on example i such that vectors associated with non-zero weights are called "support vectors" and solely determine the optimal hyperplane), v is a parameter that controls the trade-off between maximizing the distance of the hyperplane from the origin and the number of data points contained by the hyper-plane, l is the number of points in the training dataset, and $K(x_i, x_j)$ is the kernel function. By using the kernel function to project input vectors into a feature space the nonlinear decision boundaries are incorporated. Given a feature map:

$$\varnothing : X \to R^N \tag{18}$$

where $\varnothing$ maps training vectors from input space X to a high-dimensional feature space and the kernel function can be defined as:

$$K\left(x, y\right) = \left\langle \varnothing\left(x\right), \varnothing\left(y\right)\right\rangle \tag{19}$$

The commonly used kernels are 'linear', 'radial basis function', and 'sigmoid'.

PROPOSED METHODOLOGY

In Figure 7 we have explained proposed methodology and the algorithmic steps are also given below.

Algorithm 2. Steps in the proposed methodology

Input: A query Image.

Output: Similar Images.

Step 1: Compute MPEG-7 CSD (64-bins) features of all the images in database.

Step 2: Employ KPCA to map feature vectors in lower-dimensional space.

Step 3: Now apply PAM algorithm to cluster the reduced dataset which is obtained in Step 2. Select the cluster containing the query by feature matching.

Step 4: Training Samples Collection - Display 36 nearest images with respect to query image using L_1 norm in KPCA - reduced space and mark relevant images to get training set.

Step 5: Test Samples Collection - Apply SVC to the cluster containing the query obtained in Step 3 to remove possible outliers.

Step 6: Train OCSVM using samples obtained in Step 4.

Step 7: Input test samples obtained in Step 5 in OCSVM for prediction (prediction label 1 is for positive sample and 0 for negative sample).

Step 8: Consider all positive samples obtained in Step 7 automatically using the labels of prediction.

Figure 7. Proposed method

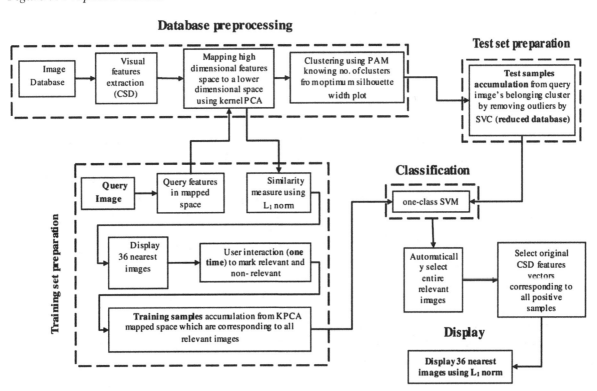

Step 9: Select original CSD (64-bins) feature vectors corresponding to all positive samples and calculate the similarity value by L_1 norm. Sort these similarity values in ascending order.

Step 10: Display the ranked images obtained in Step 9.

Feature Extraction

The Color Structure descriptor (CSD) (64-bins) as a visual features is extracted from each image employing an 8×8 -structuring element. Number of times a particular color is contained within the structuring element is counted using

$$c_0, c_1, c_2, \ldots, c_{M-1}$$

quantized colors. A color structure histogram can then be denoted by

$$h(m), \ m = 0, 1, 2, \ldots, M-1$$

where the value in each bin represents the number of structuring elements in the image containing one or more pixels with color c_m. The hue-min-max-difference (HMMD) color space is used in this descriptor (Salembier & Sikora, 2002).

Implication of Dimensionality with Similarity Function and Clustering

The L_1 or L_2-norm has been used as a similarity function as it popular in Minkowski space which is defined by:

$$L_k(x, y) = \sum_{i=1}^{d} \left(\left\| x^i - y^i \right\|^k \right)^{1/k},$$

where d is the dimensionality. The values of the parameter k other than 1 or 2 are not suitable for high-dimensional data (Williams, Baxter, He, Hawkins, & Gu, 2002), (Yang, Estivill-Castro, & Chalup, 2002) which can be inferred from the fact that for a certain data distribution, the relative difference of the distances of the closest and farthest data points of an independently selected point goes to 0 as the dimensionality increases, i.e.,

$$\lim_{d \to \infty} \frac{dist_{max} - dist_{min}}{dist_{min}} \tag{20}$$

From the above equation it is clear that the goodness of the grouping using PAM algorithm after the KPCA based reduction are obtained better and the numbers of clusters are reduced having more data points in the belonging cluster, in reduced search space.

Optimum Number of Clusters Counting Using Partitioning Around Medoids

Retrieving similar images from few nearest clusters are more effective than sequential search in large database. The PAM (Banerjee & Islam, 2015; Kaufman & Rousseeuw, 2008) is robust to outliers as it does not use optimization to solve the vector placement problem, instead uses actual data points to represent cluster centres. It is less susceptible to local minima than standard k-means during training where k-means often converges to poor quality clusters. It groups similar objects by minimizing sum of the dissimilarities of all the objects to their nearest medoids. The aim is to find the clusters C_1, C_2, ..., C_k that minimize following target function:

$$\sum_{i=1}^{k}\sum_{r \in C_i} d(r,m)$$

where for each i the medoid m_i minimizes

$$\sum_{r \in C_i} d(r,m)$$

where $d(r, m_i)$ indicates dissimilarity between r and m_i. The numbers of clusters are determined from optimum average silhouette width plot. For every point i, the silhouette width $silw(i)$ is calculated as follows: Let $p(i)$ be the average dissimilarity between i and other all points of the partition to which i lies. If i is only object in its belonging partition then $silw(i) = 0$ barring further computation.

For all remaining partitions C we get $d(i,C)$ = average dissimilarity of i to all objects of C. The smallest of these $d(i,C)$ is

$$q(i) \;=\; min \forall C \left(d\left(i, \; C \; \right) \right)$$

indicates the dissimilarity between i and its nearest partition obtained from minimum leads to Equation 21 and

$$max(avg(silw(C)), \forall C)$$

determines the number of clusters. For example, if number of clusters is k (where k = 2, 3, 4,..., 25) then silhouette width for every point is computed and average is found. Finally, the cluster number which gives the maximum average silhouette width plot is selected. In Figure 8 it is obvious that the number of clusters is 3 by taking up to 25 clusters.

$$silw(i) = (q(i) - p(i)) / max(p(i), q(i)) \tag{21}$$

Figure 8. Computation of number of clusters from optimum average silhouette width

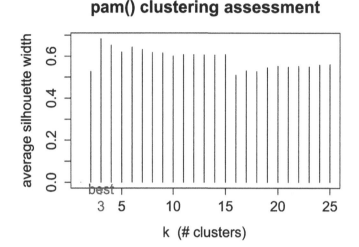

Outliers Detection Criteria by Support Vector Clustering

Suppose $\{X_i\}$ be a dataset with dimensionality d. The SVC computes a sphere of radius R and center a containing all these data. The outliers in the training set are decided by the distance from X_i to the center a should not be strictly smaller than R^2 (Banerjee & Islam, 2015), (Yang, Estivill-Castro, & Chalup, 2002). The computation of such smallest sphere under the auspices of solving minimization problem considering lagrangian formulation leads to the following expression to test an object x.

$$\left\| x - a \right\|^2 = \left(x \cdot x \right) - 2\sum_{i=1}^{N} \propto_i \left(x \cdot x_i \right) + \sum_{i}^{N}\sum_{j}^{N} \propto_i\propto_j \left(x_i \cdot x_j \right) \le R^2,$$

where $\propto_i$ is the lagrangian multipliers. Outliers are the data points that are located in boundary regions. If a test data x lies outside the cluster boundary then it is considered as a outlier and the necessary condition is $\propto_i \ge 0$. The Figure 9 illustrates this.

Computational Issues

In the proposed method the kernel principal component analysis (KPCA) is performed only once to reduce original data set in $O(n^3)$ times, where n is the number of data points. Next, the reduced dataset is clustered by PAM at least in quadratic times only once. The complexity associated with SVC is $O(n^2d)$ if the number of support vectors is $O(1)$ (where d is the number of dimensions of a data point). One Class SVM algorithm utilize sequential minimal optimization to solve the quadratic programming problem, and it takes time $O(dL^3)$, where L is the number of objects in the training dataset. The total complexity is involved mainly in SVC and OCSVM which are applied on reduced features and search space.

Figure 9. Illustration of outliers. The bounded support vectors, BVS, which are outside of each contour are treated as outliers

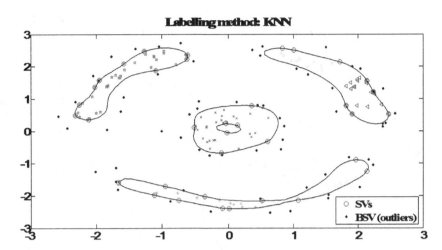

EXPERIMENT AND ANALYSIS

The results have been shown in Figure 10 to Figure 17 using SIMPLIcity (Banerjee & Islam, 2015; Wang, Li, & Wiederhold, 2001) database which includes 10 Semantic groups of African People and villages, Buses, Dinosaurs, Elephants etc. in diverse background. Each group consists of 100 images. Experiments are conducted extensively on each group. The performances evaluation is denoted by Recall rate and Precision rate. Let $N1$ be the number of images retrieved in top N positions that are close to a query image. Let $N2$ be the number of images in the database similar to the query. Evaluation standards, Recall rate *(R)* is given by $N1/N2 \times 100\%$ and Precision rate *(P)* are given by $N1/N \times 100\%$ (Banerjee & Islam, 2015).

The dimensionality of MPEG-7 CSD dataset has been reduced by the KPCA taking Gaussian function with *sigma=0.2* as a kernel function using "kernlab" R language Package. The OCSVM is employing radial basis function as a kernel using LIBSVM package with *c=0.01, gama= 0.00001*. Finally the predicted relevant images of OCSVM have been re-ranked using L_1-norm considering original CSD features of predicted set (Banerjee & Islam, 2015). The result of Figure 10 and Figure 11 indicate a query from the

Figure 10 and Figure 12 represent MPEG-7 CSD(64-bins) with L_1 norm, relevant/scope ratios 16/36 and 20/36 respectively, Figure 11 and Figure 13 represent proposed method, relevant/scope ratios 35/36 and 35/36 respectively, with KPCA projected dimension=1, OCSVM based prediction on query image's belonging filtered cluster chosen optimally using PAM. Here top-left most image is the query.

category of *elephant* bearing quite rich semantic information. Figure 10 conveys result with MPEG-7 CSD (64-bins) features using L_1-norm as a similarity measure. Figure 11 represents proposed method with KPCA projected dimension equals to one. The query image is the top left image. The comparative results show that the obtained precision in case of Figure 10 within the scope of 36 images is 44.44% and proposed method in Figure 11 gives 97.22% where semantically similar images have attained higher rank than Figure 10 in a reduced search space. The effectiveness of the proposed method is also observed in Figure 12 for the category "Bus". Here color structure descriptors have proven to be good features for retrieving buses not only for similar shapes but also for similar colors. Improvement of the results

Figure 10.

Figure 11.

Figure 12.

Figure 13.

both in term of precision and ranking are observed in Figure 13 compared to Figure 12. Institutively nonlinear KPCA based features mapping entails discriminating information of the CSD (64-bins) into a lower dimensional subspace. The performance is also improved as the original search space is reduced horizontally.

Figure 14 , Figure 15, and Figure 16 represent Average Precision vs. Number of Retrieved Images for categories African People and villages, Mountains and glaciers and Dinosaurs and Figure 17 represents Average Precision vs. Recall on overall database.

The results are compared with other unsupervised dimensionality reduction methods namely PCA with L_1-norm, laplacian eigenmaps with L_1-norm, factor analysis with L_1-normas well as L_2 and L_1 – norm on MPEG-7 CSD (64-bins) dataset. Average precision is chosen as a comparative measure because the precision gives a good measure within the displayed scope and it is not always possible to know the number of relevant image in advance for a particular query in an unknown database. The proposed method gives average precision 97% within the scope of 20 images for the category of African people is shown in Figure 14 and performs far well than the other techniques. In case of the category of mountain in Figure 15 the proposed method gives average precision 98% within the scope of 30 images and is far beyond far beyond other methods as shown in Figure 15. For the category of *dinosaur* in Figure 16 Factor analysis gives somewhat better result. Majority of the images are covered by the white background and lacking prominent color structure properties. Intuitively FA performs well because it is computed in terms of maximum likelihood estimate of the majority color information. Considering images from all categories the average precision vs. recall graph on the overall database is plotted in the Figure 17 is giving more than 95% precision before recall reaches at 0.5.

Figure 14.

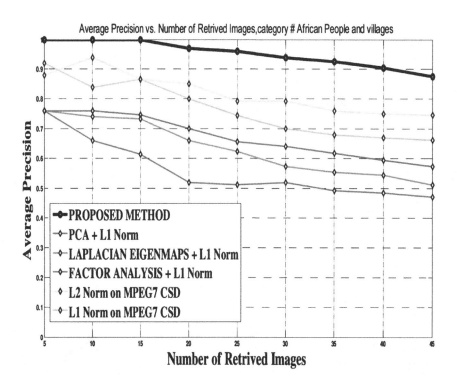

Figure 15.

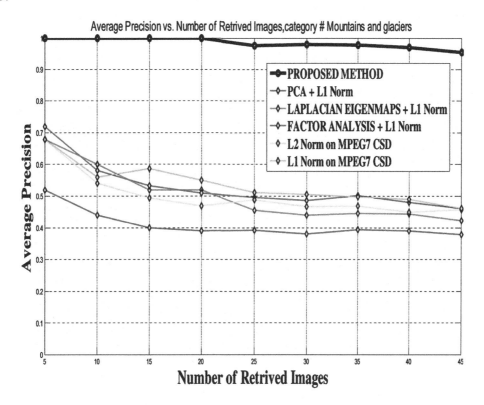

Figure 16.

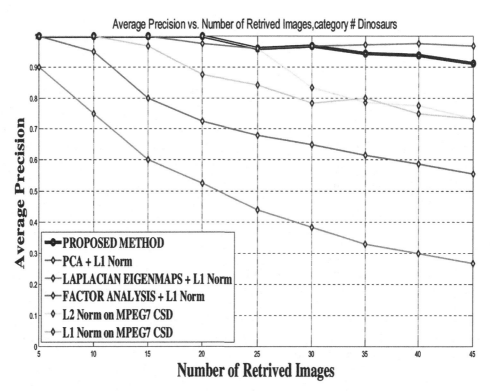

Figure 17.

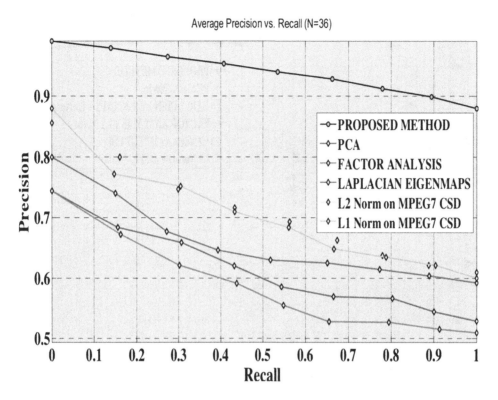

CONCLUSION

In this chapter a content based image retrieval method has been discussed for dealing with the issues of feature and search space reduction through KPCA and clustering techniques and outliers detection while trying to keep the semantic meaning intact. The MPEG-7 Color Structure Descriptor (CSD) (64-bin) alone performs satisfactorily for many categories and showing the potential to outperform many existing retrieval systems that apply several other MPEG-7 descriptors together for those categories. As a further scope of research we want to consider several newer datasets for different retrieval applications. We would also like to aggregate others MPEG7 features like edge histogram descriptors (EHD), homogeneous texture descriptors (HTD) and dominant color descriptors (DCD) etc. and extend the proposed method for object retrieval by unifying textual cues.

REFERENCES

Aggarwal, C., & Yu, P. (2001). Outlier Detection for High Dimensional Data. In *Proceedings of the ACM SIGMOD International Conference on Management of Data*. doi:10.1145/376284.375668

Banerjee, M., & Islam, S. M. (2015). Tackling Curse of Dimensionality for Efficient Content Based Image Retrieval, In *Pattern Recognition and Machine Intelligence: 6th International Conference, PReMI 2015*. Springer. doi:10.1007/978-3-319-19941-2_15

Barnett, V., & Lewis, T. (1994). *Outliers in Statistical Data*. Chichester, UK: John Wiley and Sons; doi:10.1016/0169-2070(95)00625-7

Celik, S., Logsdon, B., & Aase, S. I. (2014). Efficient dimensionality reduction for high-dimensional network estimation. In *Proc. 31st Int. Conf. Mach. Learn.*, (pp. 1953–1961).

Chechik, G., Sharma, V., Shalit, U., & Bengio, S. (2010). Large scale online learning of image similarity through ranking. *Journal of Machine Learning Research*, *11*, 1109–1135.

Chen, Y., Zhou, X. S., & Huang, T. (2001). One-class svm for learning in image retrieval. In *International Conference on Image Processing* (pp. 34-37).

Deng, C., Xiaofei, H., & Jiawei, H. (2007). Spectral regression: a unified subspace learning framework for content-based image retrieval. *Proceedings of the 15th international conference on Multimedia*.

Dube, S., El-Saden, S., Cloughesy, T. F., & Sinha, U. (2006). Content based image retrieval for MR image studies of brain tumors. *IEEE International conference on Engineering in Medicine and Biology*, (pp. 3337–3340).

Flickner, M., Sawhney, H., Niblack, W., Ashley, J., Huang, Q., Dom, B., & Yanker, P. et al. (1995). Query by image and video content: The QBIC system. *Computer*, *28*(9), 23–32. doi:10.1109/2.410146

Hastie, T., Tibshirani, R., & Friedman, J. (2008). The Elements of Statistical Learning: Data Mining, Inference, and Prediction (2nd ed.). Retrieved from https://web.stanford.edu/~hastie/local.ftp/Springer/OLD/ESLII_print4.pdf

Hawkins, D. (1980). *Identification of Outliers*. Chapman and Hall. doi:10.1007/978-94-015-3994-4

Hawkins, S., He, H. X., Williams, G. J., & Baxter, R. A. (2002). Outlier detection using replicator neural networks. In *Proceedings of the Fifth International Conference and Data Warehousing and Knowledge Discovery (DaWaK02)*.

Hodge, V. J., & Austin, J. (2004). A survey of outlier detection methodologies. *Artificial Intelligence Review*, *22*(2), 85–126. doi:10.1023/B:AIRE.0000045502.10941.a9

Jenatton, R., Obozinski, G., & Bach, F. (2010). Structured sparse principal component analysis. In *Proc. Int. Conf.Artif. Intell. Statist.*, (pp. 366–373).

Jensen, R., & Shen, Q. (2008). *Computational Intelligence and Feature Selection: Rough and Fuzzy Approaches*. Wiley-IEEE Press. doi:10.1002/9780470377888

Ju, F., Sun, S., Gao, J., Hu, Y., & Yin, B. (2015). Image outlier detection and feature extraction via L1-normbased 2Dprobabilistic PCA. *IEEE Transactions on Image Processing*, *24*(12), 4834–4846. doi:10.1109/TIP.2015.2469136 PMID:26292341

Kaufman, L., & Rousseeuw, P. J. (2008). *Partitioning Around Medoids (Program PAM)*. John Wiley & Sons, Inc.

Kong, W. L., Teoh, E. K., Wang, J.-G., & Venkateswarlu, R. (2005). A framework of 2D Fisher discriminant analysis: Application to face recognition with small number of training samples. In *Proc. IEEE Int. Conf. Comput. Vis. Pattern Recognit.*, (pp. 1083–1088).

Krizhevsky, A., Sutskever, I., & Hinton, G. E. (2012). Imagenet classification with deep convolutional neural networks. *Advances in Neural Information Processing Systems.*

Lu, H., Plataniotis, K. N., & Venetsanopoulos, A. N. (2008). MPCA: Multilinear principal component analysis of tensor objects. *IEEE Transactions on Neural Networks, 19*(1), 18–39. doi:10.1109/TNN.2007.901277 PMID:18269936

Lu, K., He, X., & Zeng, J. (2005). Image retrieval using dimensionality reduction. In J. Zhang, J. H. He, & Y. Fu (Eds.), Computational and Information Science (LNCS), (vol. 3314, pp. 775–781). doi:10.1007/978-3-540-30497-5_120

Marques, O., & Borko, F. (2002). MUSE: A content-based image search and retrieval system using relevance feedback. *Multimedia Tools and Applications, 17*(1), 21–50. doi:10.1023/A:1014679605305

Pentland, A., Picard, R. W., & Sclaroff, S. (1996). Photobook: Content-based manipulation of image databases. *International Journal of Computer Vision, 18*(3), 233–254. doi:10.1007/BF00123143

Philbin, J., Chum, O., Isard, M., Sivic, J., & Zisserman, A. (2007). Object retrieval with large vocabularies and fast spatial matching. *Computer Vision and Pattern Recognition, CVPR'07, IEEE Conference.*

Quan, W. (2012). *Kernel principal component analysis and its applications in face recognition and active shape models.* arXiv preprint arXiv:1207.3538

Salembier, P., & Sikora, T. (2002). *Introduction to MPEG-7: Multimedia Content Description Interface.* New York, NY: John Wiley & Sons, Inc.

Scholkopf, B., Smola, A., & Muller, K. R. (1998). Nonlinear component analysis as a kernel eigenvalue problem. *Neural Computation, 10*(5), 1299–1319. doi:10.1162/089976698300017467

Torki, M., Elgammal, A., & Lee, C. S. (2010). Learning a joint manifold representation from multiple data sets. In *Proc. IEEE 20th Int.Conf. Pattern Recognit.,* (pp. 1068–1071). doi:10.1109/ICPR.2010.267

Wang, H., Cai, Y., Zhang, Y., Pan, H., Weifeng, L. v., & Han, H. (2014). Deep learning for content-based image retrieval: A comprehensive study. *Proceedings of the ACM International Conference on Multimedia.* ACM.

Wang, J., Li, J., & Wiederhold, G. (2001). Simplicity: Semantics-sensitive integrated matching for picture libraries. *IEEE Transactions on Pattern Analysis and Machine Intelligence, 23*(9), 947–963. doi:10.1109/34.955109

Williams, G., Baxter, R., He, H., Hawkins, S., & Gu, L. (2002). A Comparative Study for RNN for Outlier Detection in Data Mining. In *Proceedings of the 2nd IEEE International Conference on Data Mining.* doi:10.1109/ICDM.2002.1184035

Yang, J., Estivill-Castro, V., & Chalup, S. (2002). Support vector clustering through proximity graph modeling. In *Proceedings of the 9th International Conference on Neural Information Processing, ICONIP '02* (pp. 898-903). doi:10.1109/ICONIP.2002.1198191

Zhang, J., Huang, H., & Wang, J. (2010). Manifold learning for visualizing and analyzing high-dimensional data. *IEEE Intelligent Systems, 25*(4), 54–61.

Chapter 6
For Better Healthcare Mining Health Data

Güney Gürsel
Command post of Gendarme Logistics, School ol of Technical and Auxiliary Forces, Turkey

ABSTRACT

Data mining has great contributions to the healthcare such as support for effective treatment, healthcare management, customer relation management, fraud and abuse detection and decision making. The common data mining methods used in healthcare are Artificial Neural Network, Decision trees, Genetic Algorithms, Nearest neighbor method, Logistic regression, Fuzzy logic, Fuzzy based Neural Networks, Bayesian Networks and Support Vector Machines. The most used task is classification. Because of the complexity and toughness of medical domain, data mining is not an easy task to accomplish. In addition, privacy and security of patient data is a big issue to deal with because of the sensitivity of healthcare data. There exist additional serious challenges. This chapter is a descriptive study aimed to provide an acquaintance to data mining and its usage and applications in healthcare domain. The use of Data mining in healthcare informatics and challenges will be examined.

INTRODUCTION

From primary care institutions to big healthcare centers, every healthcare organization uses an information system. These healthcare information systems (HCIS) store, process and retrieve healthcare data. Healthcare data is very valuable in today's world. By the help of rapidly developing healthcare informatics, there are efforts to use the valuable data stored electronically in HCIS databases to improve healthcare. Healthcare staff expects more than e-recording the data from HCISs. Besides using healthcare data for care giving, healthcare centers and academic centers use these data for education and research. Research in medical area is not limited to healthcare development such as developing new healing techniques and drugs. There are healthcare informatics fields such as structured data entry, constructing longitudinal patient data, image processing, etc. Any research area dealing with huge and valuable data such as medical domain requires creative techniques supported with computers and computer systems to utilize it. Data mining techniques are good examples for these required creative techniques.

DOI: 10.4018/978-1-5225-1776-4.ch006

Life expectancy has risen. We live longer when we compared to past. This improvement is tremendous for human being. But it has a cost. We spend more to healthcare when compared to past. The healthcare expenses are becoming unmanageable. Payers put pressure on healthcare organizations to decrease the cost. Then is it possible to decrease the cost while increasing the quality of healthcare? The answer is "it depends". It depends on the extent that we utilize the data and information we have.

It is stated that every healthcare institution uses an information system. During the daily healthcare service, every piece of patient data is recorded by means of HCISs. In short, we have huge amounts of patient data and it is growing every day. These huge amounts of data are called as "Big Data". These "Big Data" should be used to get information and knowledge. The most fundamental challenge about Big Data is to explore the large volumes of data and extract useful information or knowledge for future use (Wu, Zhu, Wu, & Ding, 2014).

Data mining is one of the techniques to utilize this valuable healthcare data. There are many different definitions available in the literature. Drawing from the literature, we can define data mining as the process of analyzing data and discovering knowledge, patterns, associations, rules, anomalies, sequences that are non-trivial, implicit, previously unknown and potentially useful from databases.

Healthcare institutions are geographically distributed to ease healthcare access. Data about a patient can be scattered into many HCIS databases. There should be a technique to handle these scattered data to analyze and mine. Distributed data mining deals with this scattered data problem and will be covered through the chapter.

Patient health data is very sensitive. Researches about patient health data should comply with some ethical and legal issues to protect patient privacy as well as data mining studies. Privacy is term used for notion of the confidentiality and access restrictions of patients' protected health information (PHI) which contains sensitive and personal information (Sun, Zhu, Zhang, & Fang, 2012). Patient privacy refers to any medical data (medical condition, test result, payment information, etc.) in any form (paper, electronic, etc.) that belongs to a patient, the meaning is about what is protected and who will be permitted to use this information (Upstate Medical University, 2011). Protecting patient privacy in data mining will be a part and it is examined in the chapter.

The complexity and toughness of the medical environment is common information in the literature. The complexity and toughness of the medical domain is a challenge to every technology and application as well as data mining. In this chapter, the challenges specific to data mining will also be examined.

This chapter is a descriptive study that examines the concepts, issues related and techniques used in data mining in healthcare big data. The purpose of the study is to give an idea about the data mining tasks and techniques used in healthcare.

The chapter is organized as follows: In the background section, the universal basics, not related to healthcare only, of data mining will be covered. The main part is in the heading of "MEDICAL DATA MINING" comprising the contribution of the data mining to the healthcare, data mining techniques used in healthcare, temporal data mining in healthcare, distributed data mining in healthcare, challenges, privacy and security issues, data mining for healthcare management. In the end, are the future research directions and conclusion parts interpreting the chapter.

BACKGROUND

Data Mining Basics

In this section, the universal basics, not related to healthcare only, of data mining will be examined. There will be a brief summary of data mining to give idea and get acquaintance. Not to digress from the main subject, details are left to reader; the references in the "Additional Reading" could help.

Data mining is the miracle of technology era. In the electronically stored big data, no matter what area is, companies are in a race to get useful knowledge to gain advantage in the ruthless competition of our age. To give an idea about what can data mining extract from the big data, we can give some examples as (Bramer, 2013):

- Analyzing satellite imagery,
- Analysis of organic compounds,
- Fraud detection,
- Electric load prediction,
- Financial forecasting,
- Medical diagnosis,
- Real estate valuation,
- Targeted marketing,
- Toxic hazard analysis,
- Weather forecasting.

In data mining, the critical part is the quality of data. Before data mining, we have to be sure that data has below features (Kantardzic, 2011):

- **Accuracy:** The data to be mined should be consistent, complete and true.
- **Having Right Data Type:** We have to ensure that the data is stored in the correct form. Numerical value should not be available in character form or vice versa.
- **Integrity:** There shouldn't be any conflicts in the data.
- **Consistency:** The form and the content should not change after integration of large data sets.
- **Being Not Redundant:** Redundancy is an issue that should be avoided or kept to minimum not only in data mining but also in database design. It is the replication of the same data in different tables of database. Redundant data may lead to problems in storing, accessing and analyzing the data.
- **Timeliness:** The time component of the data should be well organized and bias related to data time should be avoided.
- **Being Understandable:** The data should not have misleading form. The user and analyzer should clearly understand what the data stand for.
- **Complete:** Missing values are serious problems for data mining. It should also be kept to minimum.

The features given above are very critical. In real world, the data in the databases are so messy to deal with which is called as "dirty". They are mostly incomplete, erroneous (noisy) and inconsistent. In order to make the data have desired features given above, data preprocessing is done for data mining. Major tasks in data preprocessing can be listed as (Jiawei & Kamber, 2001):

- **Data Cleaning:** Filling missing values, smoothing noisy data, identifying or removing outliers and resolving inconsistencies.
- **Data Integration:** Integration of multiple databases, data cubes or files.
- **Data Transformation:** Normalization and aggregation.
- **Data Reduction:** Obtains reduced representation in volume but produces the same or similar analytical results.
- **Data Discretization:** Part of data reduction but with particular importance especially for numerical data.

Data mining tasks and techniques are confused and can be misused interchangeably. To eliminate the confusion, it is better to mention about what are data mining tasks and what data mining techniques are.

Data mining tasks are divided into two categories: Descriptive tasks and Predictive tasks. Some sources in literature name these categories as Supervised and Unsupervised. Descriptive tasks present the main characteristics of the data set, a summary of the data points making it possible to study important aspects (Jain & Srivastava, 2013). Descriptive tasks are undirected, find patterns in the data set and leave the interpretation of the patterns to the researcher in which the data speaks for itself (Jain & Srivastava, 2013).

Predictive tasks provide the researcher with the facility to predict an unknown (often future) value of a specific variable (Jain & Srivastava, 2013).

Namely, data mining tasks are:

- Classification,
- Clustering,
- Rule association,
- Description,
- Visualization,
- Outlier detection,
- Time series analysis.

In Classification, we try to find group memberships for the known and predefined labels (classes). Classification is a predictive data mining task.

In Clustering, there is no predefined and known class. Clustering tasks group the data into clusters according to their similarities.

Rule association is another predictive task that is used for searching relationships within data. Antecedent and consequent relationships, meaning which occurs before and after, which situations co-exist, etc. are the possible search criteria.

Description tasks are descriptive and they help us characterize the data. By the help of description tasks, data can be generalized, summarized and characterizations are determined.

Visualization tasks help us understand the results of data mining. Because some data mining techniques are hard to understand for the target managers, by means of visualization, result of data mining becomes accessible and comparable.

Outlier detection is easy to understand from its name. These tasks help us detect the data that are significantly different, we call them as outlier. Especially for fraud and abuse detection, outlier detection tasks are used.

Time series analysis tries to find patterns and rules depending on time.

As to data mining techniques, we can define them as the methods used to perform data mining tasks given above. The common techniques for data mining can be listed as:

- Artificial Neural Network (ANN),
- Decision Tree (DT),
- Genetic Algorithms (GAs),
- Regression and Correlation methods (such as Logistic Regression),
- Bayesian Networks,
- Support Vector Machines (SVMs),
- Similarity Measures (such as Nearest Neighbor Method),
- Fuzzy Logic,
- Hybrid techniques (such as Neuro-Fuzzy).

Artificial Neural Network (ANN) is the model that tries to emulate human nerve system into computer applications. ANN is an adaptive system that changes its parameters during the training phase, like human nerve system, model learns from the training set. In Figure 1, an ANN design example is given. Number of hidden layers depends on the case and the problem.

Decision Tree (DT) is a structure where each node denotes a test on an attribute value, each branch represents an outcome of the test and tree leaves represent classes or class distribution, it is a predictive model used for classification commonly (Jain & Srivastava, 2013). In Figure 2 an example of DT is given.

Genetic Algorithms approach is the effort to emulate natural evaluation into computer applications. The idea behind GAs is building a better solution by combining the good parts of other solutions just like nature does by combining the DNA of living beings (Jain & Srivastava, 2013).

Regression and Correlation methods (such as Logistic Regression) evaluates the strength of a relationship where regression is a predictive method of future values by fitting the current available values into a curve, and correlation is a descriptive method used to examine the degree of similarity (Jiawei & Kamber, 2001).

Figure 1. ANN example

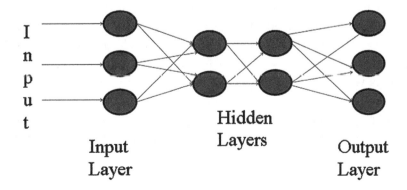

Figure 2. DT example

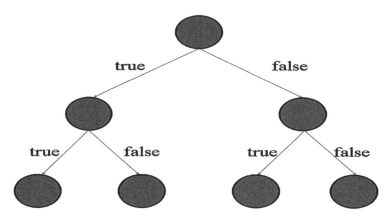

Bayesian Network is a statistical multivariate model for a set of variables which is defined in terms of two components, a qualitative component, a directed acyclic graph (DAG), and a quantitative component, a conditional distribution of each variable in the graph(Jensen & Nielsen, 2007).

Support Vector Machines are manly used for classification. It is a type of supervised machine learning method. The method is presented with a set of labeled data instances and the SVM training algorithm aims to find a hyper plane separating the given dataset into a discrete predefined number of classes consistent with the training set (Mountrakis, Im, & Ogole, 2011).

Similarity Measures are used for measuring the similarities in big data. Nearest Neighbor Method, Manhattan distance, and Euclidean distance are the most known forms of similarity measures.

Fuzzy logic is the multivalued logic attempting to emulate human reasoning in the computer applications. In fuzzy logic, instead of using hard borders such as 0-1, white-black, soft computing techniques are employed.

Hybrid techniques combine fuzzy logic methods with other methodologies such as neural network, genetic algorithms, Bayesian reasoning, machine learning, etc.

MEDICAL DATA MINING

Contribution of the Data Mining to the Healthcare

Healthcare service can have huge costs. Food consumed, bed occupied and related services for lodging, surgery preparation laboratory tests, radiology tests, surgery, post-surgery care and post-surgery control laboratory tests... expenditures for the inpatients increase the healthcare cost in a considerable manner. Payers of the healthcare put strong pressure on the healthcare institutions to decrease the costs. By the way, the toughest thing is the quality of the service must increase in spite of the decreased cost not to decrease the attractiveness of the healthcare institution.

USA spent 2 trillion dollars in 2008 for healthcare (which stands for 16.2% of gross domestic product) (AMA, 2010). Table 1 gives the top-ranked countries in healthcare expenditure (Speights, 2013).

Table 1. Countries with the highest healthcare expenditure in OECD

Rank	Country	Percentage in Gross National Product (%)	$ per Person Spent	Life Expectancy (Years)
1	USA	17.9	8,680	78.7
2	Netherlands	12	5,056	80.8
3	Germany	11.6	4,338	80,5
4	France	11.6	3,974	81,3
5	Switzerland	11.4	5,270	82.6
6	Canada	11.4	4,445	80.8
7	Denmark	11.1	4,464	79.3

Source: Speights, 2013.

As seen in Table 1, the expenditures are huge. These expenditures are not compatible with the life expectancy, USA is the first to spend but near last to have life expectancy whereas Switzerland is almost last to spend but first to have life expectancy.

American Medical Association's (AMA, 2010) proposal to reduce costs can be summarized as follows:

- Reduce the burden of preventable disease.
  - Reduction of the risk factors for disease;
  - Prevention of the onset of chronic illness;
  - Improvement of patient compliance with medications.
- Reduce nonclinical health system costs that do not contribute to patient care
- Make health care delivery more efficient.
  - Reduction of unnecessary use of services;
  - Increase in use of services with positive return on investment;
  - Increase in availability of information on the effectiveness of different treatments;
  - Improvement in management of chronic illness;
  - Reduction of medical errors.
- Promote value-based decision-making at all levels.

Achievement of all proposed solutions of AMA is directly dependent on the use of information and conversion of the information to knowledge.

Above, we mention that there is a pressure to decrease the costs, but at the same time the healthcare institutions have to increase the quality. Is this possible? The answer is "it depends". It depends on the extent that the managements of the healthcare institutions utilize the big data they have. There are some utilization techniques; one of them is data mining.

Although the discussion about what is data, what is information and what is knowledge took place long ago and these terms are clear in today's world, it will be useful to mention briefly in this chapter to avoid confusion. Data is the raw form and it has no meaning by itself. Wikipedia (2015) explains the relation between these three concepts in simple and understandable way. Difference between these three terms lies in the level of abstraction. Data is the first level, the raw and meaningless form. With interpreting, the data becomes information. Utilization of information brings the knowledge.

Returning back to our subject, it is said that almost all healthcare institutions use an information system. These systems collect and generate data. These data are not only about patient but also about medical devices, medical resources, their operating times, in short, every item related to healthcare. The healthcare data at hand are growing bigger and bigger as the time passes. The anonymous saying (it is everywhere but no sign about who is the owner) "Drowning in data, starving for information/knowledge" summarizes the situation. We need data mining to extract information and knowledge from these big data in healthcare, use this information and knowledge for decreasing the costs and increasing the quality.

Data mining help healthcare get (Hays, 2012):

- Question based answers,
- Anomaly based discovery,
- New Knowledge discovery,
- Informed decisions,
- Probability measures,
- Predictive modeling,
- Decision support,
- Improved health,
- Personalized medicine.

In the above items, it is clear that the profits of medical data mining are compatible with the proposed solutions of AMA given before. They are very tough to accomplish. All needs long time effort, discrete planning and powerful techniques.

In addition to Hay's list, Canlas (2009) added Evidence based medicine, Reduction of medical errors, Policy making in public health, Early diagnosis, Preventive medicine, Non-invasive diagnosis, Detection of adverse drug events (Canlas, 2009).

Other additional items to this list made by Desikan, Hsu, and Srivastava (2011) are:

- Fraud and abuse detection,
- Customer relationship management decisions of Healthcare organizations,
- Identification of effective treatments and best practices by physicians,
- More affordable healthcare services received by patients.

Association rules are the important aid of the data mining to the healthcare. It gives characteristics of certain information as a consequence or as an antecedent (Milovic & Milovic, 2012). This is very helpful for health professionals who are searching for the relations between diseases and lifestyles or demographics or between survival rates and treatment (Milovic & Milovic, 2012). The associations are used to help strengthen the claims regarding whether to engage or eliminate the rules in the knowledge model (Milovic & Milovic, 2012).

One of the most value adding contributions of data mining to the healthcare is in reimbursement field. Medicare, the national social insurance program administered by US government, declared that it wouldn't reimburse the healthcare organization for medical errors in 2009. This would lead serious cuts in the healthcare organizations. Reduction of medical errors, by means of data mining, not only gives way to more qualified service, but also helps elimination of the deserved fund cuts.

In addition to elimination of fund cuts, data mining also enables organizations to have accurate claims to the reimbursement companies. By the use of the information and knowledge discovered, underestimation or over billing risks will definitely be lower.

Data Mining Techniques Used in Healthcare Informatics

The data mining techniques/methods and data mining tasks may be a point of confusion in the literature as it is mentioned before. To avoid misunderstanding, before starting the section, it is better to clarify that in this chapter, classification, clustering, rule association, description and visualization are called as data mining tasks. The techniques/methods used accomplishing these tasks such as Artificial Neural Networks, Decision Tree, Logistic Regression etc. will be called as data mining techniques/methods.

In healthcare, HCISs record huge amount of data every day. But quality of the data decreases because of the complex nature of healthcare. It is previously mentioned that data should be clean to apply successful data mining applications. There are rigorous data mining tools to handle noisy data. But anyway the healthcare institutions should take measures to capture and store complete, consistent and accurate data for better data mining results.

Healthcare is an endless area for the data mining. So it is hard to tell any technique, not used in it. In this section of the chapter, the most common techniques will be examined and explained briefly.

The most common task used in medical data mining is the classification (Chen, Fuller, Friedman, & Hersh, 2005).

One of the application areas is the detection of tumors in radiology. Radiologists have difficulties in detection of tumors. The neural networks with back-propagation and association rule mining is commonly used for tumor classification in mammograms (Mishra, Padhy, & Panigrahi, 2013). The data mining is effectively used in the diagnosis of lung abnormality that may be cancerous or benign (Mishra, Padhy, & Panigrahi, 2013).

For the detection of high risk breast cancer groups, it is proved possible to find statistically significant associations with breast cancer by deriving a decision tree and selecting the best leaf (Sundar, Latha, & Chandra, 2012).

Statistical neural networks are effectively used for breast cancer diagnosis by applying several neural network structures (Sarvestani, Safavi, Parandeh, & Salehi, 2010).

In the Sundar, Latha, and Chandra's study (2012), results showed that SVM has better results for diabetes and heart disease whereas decision tree is better technique for liver disorders and breast cancer.

In the literature review of Kolçe and Frasheri (2012) for the data mining techniques used in the diagnosis and prognosis of diseases, DTs, ANNs and Bayesian algorithms appeared to be the most well-performing algorithms for diagnosis. For prognosis ANNs, Bayesian algorithms, DTs and Fuzzy algorithms came out to be the most well-performing algorithms respectively. In the same study, literature showed that, in diagnosis of cancer diseases ANNs, in heart diseases Bayesian algorithms and in other diseases DTs, in prognosis of cancer diseases again ANNs, in heart diseases ANNs and Bayesian algorithms are the most well performing techniques.

Temporal Data Mining in Healthcare Informatics

Time is a critical dimension in healthcare knowledge extraction because hidden patterns do not exist throughout the whole time period of healthcare monitorization but only in some time intervals with recurrent and periodic nature (Henriques, Pina, & Antunes, 2013).

Temporal data mining (TDM) can be defined as the attempt to search for interesting correlations and patterns in temporal databases (Bruno & Garza, 2012). TDM tries to discover qualitative and quantitative patterns in temporal databases or in datasets of discrete-valued time series (Lin, Orgun, & Williams, 2002). It has two popular threads (Lin, Orgun, & Williams, 2002):

- In the purpose of finding fully or partially similar patterns in temporal databases(similarity)
- In the purpose of finding fully or partially periodic patterns in temporal databases(periodicity)

Temporal Abstraction is the approach of dealing with time-related data in medical research in which methods give the opportunity to make abstract definition of temporal data by extracting the relevant features (Takabayashi, Ho, Yokoi, Nguyen, Kawasaki, Le, Suziki, & Yokosuka, 2007). It is the transformation of time-stamped data into interval based representation. Temporal Abstraction has two phases:

1. First one is extracting time-stamped data,
2. Second is extracting temporal specific relationships between these extracted data (Takabayashi, Ho, Yokoi, Nguyen, Kawasaki, Le, Suziki, & Yokosuka, 2007).

Batal, Valizadegan, Cooper & Hauskrecht (2012), has divided the clinical variable as medical variables (that uses the abstraction as **on** medication and **of** medication) and lab variables having two types of abstractions, trend abstraction (decreasing, steady, increasing) and value abstraction (e.g. very low, low, high, etc.).

To describe the relations between pairs of state intervals, Allen's temporal logic (1984) is used in TDM not in medicine but in general. Table 2 shows Allen's 7 relations between the time intervals A and B.

Table 2. Allen's temporal logic

Relation	Notation	Pattern	Name	Inverse Name
Before	A<B	| A | | B |	A before B	B after A
Meets	A m B	| A | | B |	A meets B	B is met by A
Overlaps	A o B	| A | | B |	A overlaps B	B is overlapped by A
Finishes	A f B	| A | | B |	A finishes B	B is finished by A
During	A d B	| A | | B |	A is during B	B contains A
Starts	A s B	| A | | B |	A starts B	B is started by A
Equals	A = B	| A | | B |	A equals B	B equals A

One of the most attractive applications of TDM is the extraction of temporal rules from data (Laboratory for Biomedical Informatics, 2015). In temporal rules, the consequent is related to the antecedent of the rule with a kind of temporal relationship, unlike association rules; in addition, a temporal rule suggests a cause-effect association between the antecedent and the consequent of the rule (Laboratory for Biomedical Informatics, 2015).

For example, by the help of TDM, a temporal rule extracted may be, "in many diabetic patients, the presence of hyperglycemia overlaps with the absence of glycosuria" (Patel, Hsu, & Lee, 2008). Another example can be "Low systolic blood pressure AND Low diastolic blood pressure frequently occur before high heart rate frequency" (Concaro, Sacchi,Cerra, Fratino, & Bellazzi, 2011).

Distributed Data Mining in Healthcare Informatics

Healthcare organizations are (and should be) distributed to facilitate easy access of public. In most countries, there is a chain of healthcare that is; the patient visits the primary care health institutions first, if it can't solve the problem, then secondary and third step health institutions are visited respectively. This type of healthcare organization brings some problems for healthcare informatics such as standardization of healthcare data, healthcare language problem (called as medical coding systems), electronic communication of the healthcare institutions, collection of patient data scattered to different healthcare institutions, etc. This issue is a challenge to healthcare data mining and will be mentioned in the following sections. There should be a distributed possibility to enable mining scattered healthcare databases and scattered health data of the same patient.

In Figure 3, we see an example of central data mining. All the data in the distributed HCIS databases are transferred to the center data warehouse first, and then they are processed.

In Figure 4, we see an example of distributed data mining. In this scenario, all the data are processed in the HCIS database cite locally, and the processed results are transferred to the center.

Figure 3. Central data mining

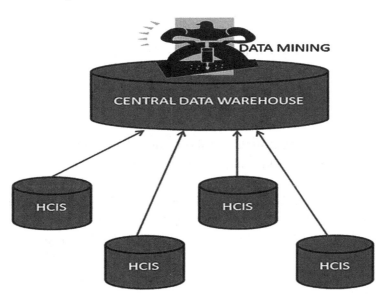

Figure 4. Distributed data mining

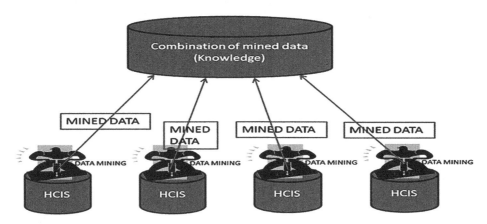

DDM has two possibilities: To process and analyze the data in the distributed centers separately or transfer all data to a center and analyze all centrally. The latter option somehow requires huge resources for the healthcare. There are efforts to have a central database for the patient data but all these efforts have the architecture to have summary data in the center and link them to the original source to avoid the requirement of huge resources and budget. Mining in this central architecture will be nonsense. Then the first option seems more suitable for healthcare

There are efforts to solve DDM in healthcare using agents. The terms agent-based DDM, DDM using intelligent mobile agents, etc. are available in the literature. In such approaches, the idea is deploying a data mining agent to the site and getting analysis from the agent to the center. There is no standard way to accomplish such approaches and it is not easy to perform. There are some studies in the literature having the same idea but proposing different designs.

Challenges for the Use of Data Mining in Healthcare Informatics

In every Introduction to Medical Informatics lecture, the complexity and toughness of the medical environment is emphasized. This "complexity and toughness" is a challenge to every information technology tool and application as well as data mining. In this section of the chapter, the challenges specific to healthcare data mining will be examined.

Heterogeneous Sources and Forms of the Data

In the previous section, scattered nature of the healthcare institutions is mentioned. This scattered structure is a challenge to the healthcare data mining applications and distributed applications are needed to handle this challenge.

The wide range of medical domain also fuels the heterogeneity. There are many different departments of medical domain such as clinics, laboratories, radiology, nuclear medicine, etc. All these departments may have different databases or have a common database if they are the part of the same institution. In either way, they have different type and format of data to mine. For example radiology data have images;

laboratory data have number type results whereas clinical data have texts. This "form heterogeneity" is also another challenge for healthcare data mining.

Data Heterogeneity may cause sampling, selection and spectrum bias (Kwiatkowska, Atkins, Ayas, & Ryan, 2007).

Disharmony between Medical and Computer Communities

This challenge is related to the "complexity and toughness" of the medical domain. It is not a specific healthcare data mining challenge but a challenge for all information technology applications. Medical users have tight schedule in dealing with care giving and are not volunteer to use any information technology that costs them additional time. Computer staff urges medical users to enter structured data to have them in computer processable form while medical users want to write down their needs as notes in papers because of the time consumed by dealing with computers.

In addition to this disharmony, the problems of accessibility in hospital exist such as: placing any hardware to sterile areas, entrance of technical staff to these areas for maintenance and fixing can be given as an example.

Legal and Ethical Issues

Privacy and security issues, their protection with the law are another item of challenge that healthcare data mining has to deal with. These issues will be examined in the next section thoroughly. Cios & Moore (2002) describe these challenges as follows:

- **Data Ownership:** Ownership of patient data is not clear. Whether the patients, the physicians, the healthcare institution or the insurance companies own the data collected from patients. The main regulation about the ownership of the data is the Health Insurance Accountability and Portability Act (HIPAA) Privacy Rule.
- **Fear of Lawsuits:** In medical communities, particularly in the Unites States, malpractice and other costly lawsuits is a matter of fear that constitutes a challenge to the application of healthcare data mining.
- **Privacy Issues:** Protecting patient privacy and doctor-patient confidentially constitutes another set of challenges to healthcare data mining. Administrators and researchers should pay utmost attention to privacy and security issues.

Non-Standard Data

This subject deserves being mentioned separately because of its being big challenge for healthcare data mining although it is mentioned in the heterogeneity of data part.

Physician's interpretations in clinical data are written in unstructured form which makes data mining difficult to perform (Milovic & Milovic, 2012). Even the high experienced specialists of the same area cannot agree on common terms that indicate the status of the patient. Different names are used to describe the same disease, different grammatical structures are used to explain the relations between medical entities (Milovic & Milovic, 2012). Although there are considerable efforts to constitute nomenclatures and classifications for structured medical data entry such as International Classification of

Diseases (ICD), Systematized Nomenclature of Medicine (SNOMED), International Classification of Nursing Practices (ICNP), still there is enormous size of non-standard data in medical domain. For this reason, data mining researchers have to spend great efforts for text mining applications in healthcare.

Noisy Data

In the previous parts, the tight schedule of healthcare staff is mentioned. This tightness brings many handicaps. Missing, corrupted, inconsistent data are some outcomes. In the time of care giving, the user does not think or care about the usefulness of the data he is entering and he miswrites (if it is obligatory field) or leave it blank. This missing, corrupted, inconsistent data is called as "noisy" in short. Noisy data is a big challenge for data mining. Surely there are data cleaning techniques in data mining to handle noisy data but it causes a bias anyway no matter how well it is handled.

Low Quality of Healthcare Data

In the past, HCISs are used to be designed for financial/billing purposes. This leads to low quality of patient data. Additionally, users' unwillingness to use HCIS contributes to low quality patient data. Unavailability of mobile HCIS usage is another source of low quality data. Especially bed site visits for inpatients, surgery side entries and emergency service operations need mobile data entry to HCIS. If there is no such opportunity, offline entry after a time period elapsed can cause incomplete, inconsistent or missing data in short noisy data.

Domain Participation

Healthcare data mining has different perspectives when compared to data mining in other fields. In the previous section "complexity and toughness" of the medical field is emphasized. This "complexity and toughness" needs domain expertise to perform successful data mining applications. To have both medical and data mining expertise is almost impossible so cooperation and team work is needed for healthcare data mining. This can be possible by either having a domain expert in the research team or convincing medical staff for cooperation.

Complexity of Data Mining Methods

Because each data mining algorithm has its own theoretical design, they require user parameters and end users usually do not have sufficient information about the parameters and their selection (Yoo, Alafaireet, Marinov, Pena-Hernandez, Gopidi, Chang, & Hua, 2012). When it is taken into consideration that data mining results are very sensitive to the parameter, it is a big problem for the success of the data mining task.

Dynamism of the Medical Domain

With the help of the technology, online scientific databases and increasing research funds, medicine is developing rapidly. New devices capturing and storing new forms of healthcare data are invented every day or the current devices are improving by additional facilities. New healthcare diagnosis and prognosis techniques are coming out. In this situation, healthcare data mining becomes a shooter to hit a moving target (Anne, 2011).

Privacy and Security of Patients in Healthcare Data Mining

Privacy and security of patient data became critical with the rapid development of electronic storage of data and HCISs. With the help of electronic facilities, the users get the possibility of accessing and storing vast amounts of data which they never had the ability when they were in paper form. As the data electronically stored in HCIS databases and the size increases, it whets many organizations' appetite. They want to mine and use them for different purposes, legal or illegal. To avoid misusage and confusion, it will be better for readers to give brief descriptions about what is intended with patient privacy and security.

Patient privacy refers to any medical data (medical condition, test result, payment information, etc.) in any form (paper, electronic, etc.) that belongs to a patient. The meaning is about what is protected and who will be permitted to use this information (Upstate Medical University, 2011). The Office for Civil Rights, a department of the United States Department of Health and Human Services, created the Health Insurance Portability and Accountability Act (HIPAA) in 1996 and it is updated regularly. HIPAA has privacy rule for patient privacy. This rule creates a national standard for US to protect medical records of patients. HIPAA privacy rule applies to all forms of patients' protected health information (PHI), whether electronic, written or oral (Center of Medicare & Medicaid Services, 2007).

Data miners should be well aware of what is patient privacy and show utmost effort to comply with the regulations arranging the issue. Otherwise they can harm patients. Data miners can also be subjected to penalties of violating patient privacy.

Security risks are available for all information systems and databases, medical research can add additional risks (Berman, 2002). To provide patient privacy, a privacy review board or institution review board is required to supervise every data mining project in the healthcare institutions (Cooper & Collman, 2005). In the universities, there exists an ethical review board to oversight the ethical issues of any candidate research project. Such a board should be constituted for privacy oversight of the researches related to the patient data.

To provide privacy, three approaches appeared to be common for using personal data in research and secondary analysis of organizations (Lowrance, 2002):

- Use of personal data only with the owner's consent,
- Use of personal data without explicit consent of the owner only in a public interest,
- Making the data anonymous before using.

In many countries, there are laws and regulations against the violation of privacy that apply serious sanctions up to loss of license. Bergman (2002) states that, "Researchers have no automatic right to review patient data. Besides developing strategies for minimizing patient risk, as described herein, investigators should take simple steps to characterize their compliance with human subject's requirements".

Security refers to safeguarding the patient privacy. The meaning is how the information will be protected (Upstate Medical University, 2011). Again HIPAA has a rule for security of the patient data which is called as HIPAA Security Rule.

Healthcare data miners should employ several important security practices such as (Cooper & Collman, 2005):

- An inclusion of a description of steps to minimize patient risks in the methods sections of research proposals and publication submissions
- For each session and query, good access control and authorization should be used.
- The removal of common identifiers (such as names, addresses) of the data subjects if possible.
- Institution of robust audit practices.
- Training for all principle investigators to reinforce their responsibilities.
- Applications of sanctions for violations of policy and/or procedures.
- Tracking the breaches and sanctions trends over time and usage of these trends in the process of security awareness and training.

Healthcare Informatics Fields of Data Mining

Medical domain is so huge and complex so application of fields of data mining is not an easy task to list. To give an idea about the contribution of data mining to the healthcare, the fundamental fields of data mining applications will be examined in this section.

Hospital Infection Control

Literature says nosocomial infections effect two millions of patients in the USA in each year in 2001 (Gaynes, Richards, Edwards, Emori, Horan, Alonso-Echanove, Fridkin, Peavy, & Tolson, 2001). Association rules can be drawn from culture and patient data obtained from the laboratory database and infection committee can review these rules periodically (Obenshain, 2004).

Standardized Reporting

Hospitals report many incidents and epidemic diseases to the government. Cluster and association analyses can show how risk factors are reported with the use of International Classification of Diseases and by reconstructing patient profiles (Obenshain, 2004).

Identifying High Risk Patients

Data mining applications can report patients that have high risks. This can aid caregivers to take some precautions and save lives (Obenshain, 2004).

Outlier Detection

Outlier Detection, can be also named as Anomaly detection, provides opportunity for identifying rare events in large datasets (Jacob & Ramani, 2012). Detection of extreme observations may prevent incorrect data and human error while at the same time presence of Outliers could lead to novel insights in clinical knowledge discovery (Jacob & Ramani, 2012).

Fraud and Abuse Detection

Healthcare is prone to fraud and abuse because of the huge amount of money it creates. Both healthcare providers and clients can commit fraud. In healthcare, the most common forms of provider fraud include (Patel, Hsu, & Lee, 2008):

- Billing for services not furnished,
- Misrepresenting the diagnosis to justify payment,
- Soliciting, offering or receiving a kickback,
- Unbundling or "exploding" charges,
- Falsifying certificates of medical necessity, plans of treatment and medical records to justify payment,
- Billing for a service not furnished as billed.

Client abuses can be card-sharing, acting in collusion with a provider for kickbacks, etc. (Patel, Hsu, & Lee, 2008).

Especially medical insurance companies employ data mining applications to detect whether healthcare claims are potentially fraudulent or erroneous, to reduce their losses related to fraud and abuse.

Treatment Effectiveness

Data mining can help about which courses of action prove effective by comparing and contrasting causes, symptoms and courses of treatments (Koh & Tan, 2011). Data mining also helps evolve standardized treatments for specific diseases (Koh & Tan, 2011). Also applications to facilitate early diagnosis, non-invasive diagnosis, determination of adverse drug effects can be made.

Healthcare Management

This section is examined thoroughly in upcoming sections.

Customer Relationship Management (CRM)

In the previous parts it is mentioned that healthcare institutions have to increase the quality. This increase comprises increasing the customer satisfaction as well as the services given. The customers could be patients, pharmacists, physicians or clinics. Detection of usage and purchase patterns and the eventual satisfaction they result in can be used to improve overall customer satisfaction, in many cases, purchasing and usage behavior prediction aid in designing proactive initiatives to reduce the costs and increase the customer satisfaction (Desikan, Hsu, & Srivastava, 2011).

Data mining applications can help healthcare to determine the preferences, usage patterns, current and future needs of individuals, whether a patient is likely to comply with prescribed treatment or whether preventive care is likely to produce a significant reduction in future utilization (Koh & Tan, 2011).

Reduction of Medical Errors

Medical errors are an important issue in healthcare. According to the report of Institute of Medicine (IOM) at least 44,000, may be as many as 98,000 patents die in the hospitals each year because of medical errors (Duan, Street, & Xu, 2011). Another study states that 195,000 people in the U.S. died due to potentially preventable, in-hospital medical errors out of 37 million patient records (Amin, Agarwal, & Beg, 2013). In addition to the loss of human lives, medical errors have a huge cost of both compensation and loss of reputation. It is seen that medical errors are harmful and costly. This is a giant problem to tackle with. One of the most important application fields of data mining is medical errors. By means of decision support facility, it can help reduce medical errors.

Data Mining for Healthcare Management

Healthcare management is a separate area of science in itself because of its importance and complexity. There are departments in universities about this issue, Master of Science and Ph.D. programs are available on this topic. Naturally there are job positions in the healthcare institutions as "Healthcare Manager". All the educations, researches, positions in healthcare management have one big goal: Managing the healthcare efficiently. Tasks of the healthcare managers can be described as optimization of clinical processes in medical and administrative quality terms as well as the cost/benefit relation (Milovic & Milovic, 2012).

Healthcare managers make very critical decisions about amount of supplies, number of employees, drug needs, hardware and software management, vacant beds required, maintenance needs,etc. These decisions must be on time, true and well supported. To do this, like all management branches, healthcare management needs the effective use of informatics maybe more than any other management field. They need approximate and healthy predictions.

Data mining applications are useful for better identification of and tracking chronic disease states and high-risk patients, for designing appropriate interventions and reducing the number of hospital admissions; claims would help healthcare management (Koh & Tan, 2011). By means of data mining, comparisons across healthcare groups of things such as practice patterns, resource utilization, length of stay, and costs of different hospitals be possible (Johnson, 2001), which are valuable information for the healthcare management.

Data mining can help healthcare managers to (Milovic & Milovic, 2012):

- Discover new hypothesis for indexes of quality for data, standards, plans and treatments;
- Check if the given quality for data, standards, plans and treatments indexes are still valid;
- Improve, strengthen and adjust the quality indexes for data, standards, plans and treatments;

Resource allocation is another field that data mining can help healthcare management. By detecting high risk areas, it should also predict the requirement and usage of various resources accordingly (Sharma & Speights, 2014).

One of the major problems in healthcare is stated as measuring the flow of patients through hospitals along with other healthcare facilities that are being used (Sharma & Mansotra, 2014). If healthcare managers can predict the length of stay of inpatients correctly, planning and management of hospital resources can be easier (Sharma & Mansotra, 2014).

Healthcare management is not limited to the management of a healthcare institution. It also encompass the public health services given, directed, supervised by governmental organizations. They need multiple sourced data mining applications to manage the public health. In this point, DDM applications are needed for this kind of healthcare management. These applications help managers manage some critical risks such as disease outbreak, epidemic diseases, some trends such as cost of healthcare, mortality rates, birth rates, appearance frequencies of the diseases, their sub information about the cities, ages, etc.

These examples about how data mining may help healthcare management can easily be augmented. The ability of data mining to associate rules and uncover hidden relations provides invaluable support to healthcare management both in organization level and governmental level. Key questions of the process of healthcare quality management are quality of data, standards, plans and treatments all of which can be acquired by the utilization of available data at hand.

FUTURE RESEARCH DIRECTIONS

Healthcare domain is dynamic and we named this issue as a challenge to the data mining. It is also a forcing motivation to the data mining applications in healthcare. This dynamism gives way to new horizons and more data mining applications will be employed to discover new patterns and associations.

In the view of the subjects examined in this chapter, future data mining studies seem to take place, not limited to but in considerable weight, in distributed data mining applications. Nowadays, hospital chains are emerging. All over a country or city, there exist a number of hospitals belonging to an organization. They have distributed solutions as well as central ones. Governmental prediction and management issues are another source of need for DDM applications. In short, needs for DDM applications are growing which is making the DDM a future progress area candidate.

Text mining algorithms are another candidate area of progress. Although the idea of HCIS force users to structured data entry, healthcare is not ready for a fully structured data entry and there are doubts if it can be provided fully. Radiology reports, surgery reports, Nuclear Medicine reports, anamnesis forms and more examples about healthcare are in fully text data form. For mining these data, text mining methodologies will get great efforts most probably.

The low quality of the medical data is mentioned throughout the chapter. In academic literature, these kinds of data are called as dirty and noisy. Although there are rigorous data mining algorithms available that deal with these problems, and there is a preprocessing phase of data mining, healthcare data deserves more research and development in this issue because of its bad reputation and nature.

While developing and improving data mining, patient privacy and security should be the first priority of concern. Health data is the most private data of a person. There may be so sensitive information that can make a person ashamed and upset. There may be some details even the person himself wants to forget. Because of the sensitivity of the data, there should be considerable future work for protecting the security and privacy of EPHI both by private sector and governmental bodies.

CONCLUSION

In the era of information and technology, data is too valuable. Every possibility that lit a light about what future can look like is very welcomed by the organizations. When it comes to healthcare, this importance increases exponentially, because human life is the main subject of the sector. By the help of the improvements in science, the deadly diseases are so trivial now that we do not fear anymore.

Data and its processing is a catalyzer to the improvement in all areas of science. In this era, information and knowledge is the power. Data is all over, the magic is to convert it to information and knowledge, to get the power.

Complexity and toughness of the medical domain makes use of information technologies mandatory. Its scattered nature, text loaded data forms, having the subject of human life and the pressure to decrease costs push healthcare managers to use data effectively and convert it to the information and knowledge. Accomplishment of these tasks is possible with the effective use of data mining.

ACKNOWLEDGMENT

Part of this study was presented at the 2nd International Conference on e-Health and Telemedicine ICEHTM 2014, on 22-24 May 2014, Istanbul/Turkey.

REFERENCES

Allen, J. F. (1984). Towards a general theory of action and time. *Artificial Intelligence*, *23*(2), 123–154. doi:10.1016/0004-3702(84)90008-0

American Medical Association. (2010). *Getting the most for our health care dollars: Medical liability reform.* Chicago, IL: American Medical Association. Retrieved on 30 December 2015 from http://www.allhealth.org/briefingmaterials/AMASharedDecisionMaking-1936.pdf

Amin, S. U., Agarwal, K., & Beg, R. (2013). Data mining in clinical decision support systems for diagnosis, prediction and treatment of heart disease. *International Journal of Advanced Research in Computer Engineering & Technology*, *2*(1), 218–223.

Anne. (2011). *Challenges for process mining in medicine.* Retrieved on 30 August 2013 from http://www.techcrunch.com

Batal, I., Valizadegan, H., Cooper, G. F., & Hauskrecht, M. (2012). A Temporal pattern mining approach for classifying electronic health record data. *ACM Transactions on Intelligent Systems and Technology*, *4*(4), 63. PMID:25309815

Berman, J. J. (2002). Confidentiality issues for medical data miners. *Artificial Intelligence in Medicine*, *26*(1-2), 25–36. doi:10.1016/S0933-3657(02)00050-7 PMID:12234715

Bramer, M. (2013). *Principles of data mining.* London: Springer-Verlag. doi:10.1007/978-1-4471-4884-5

Bruno, G., & Garza, P. (2012). Temporal pattern mining for medical applications. In *Data Mining: Foundations and Intelligent Paradigms* (pp. 9–18). Berlin: Springer. doi:10.1007/978-3-642-23151-3_2

Canlas, R. D., Jr. (2009). *Data Mining in Healthcare: Current Applications and Issues* (Unpublished master dissertation). Carnegie Mellon University, Australia.

Center of Medicare & Medicaid Services. (2007). *Security 101 for covered entities*. Retrieved on June 10, 2015 from: http://www.hhs.gov/ocr/privacy/hipaa/administrative/securityrule/security101.pdf

Chen, H., Fuller, S. S., Friedman, C., & Hersh, W. (2005). Knowledge management, data mining, and text mining in medical informatics. In Medical Informatics (pp. 3-33). Springer US. doi:10.1007/0-387-25739-X_1

Cios, K. J., & Moore, G. W. (2002). Uniqueness of medical data mining. *Artificial Intelligence in Medicine, 26*(1), 1–24. doi:10.1016/S0933-3657(02)00049-0 PMID:12234714

Concaro, S., Sacchi, L., Cerra, C., Fratino, P., & Bellazzi, R. (2011). Mining health care administrative data with temporal association rules on hybrid events. *Methods of Information in Medicine, 50*(2), 166–179. doi:10.3414/ME10-01-0036 PMID:21170468

Cooper, T., & Collman, J. (2005). Managing information security and privacy in healthcare data mining. In Medical Informatics (pp. 95-137). Springer US. doi:10.1007/0-387-25739-X_4

Desikan, P., Hsu, S., & Srivastava, J. (2011, April). *Data mining for health care management*. Paper presented at 2011 SIAM International Conference on Data mining, Mesa, AZ.

Duan, L., Street, W. N., & Xu, E. (2011). Healthcare information systems: Data mining methods in the creation of a clinical recommender system. *Enterprise Information Systems, 5*(2), 169–181. doi:10.1080/17517575.2010.541287

Gaynes, R., Richards, C., Edwards, J., Emori, T. G., Horan, T., Alonso-Echanove, J., & Tolson, J. et al. (2001). Feeding back surveillance data to prevent hospital-acquired infections. *Emerging Infectious Diseases, 7*(2), 295–298. doi:10.3201/eid0702.010230 PMID:11294727

Hays, T. (2012, December). *Medical data mining*. Speech made at The National Institute of Standards and Technology (NIST) Symposium. Retrieved on 30 December 2015 from http://www.nist.gov/healthcare/upload/Hays-Medical-Data-Mining-slides-for-web.pdf

Henriques, R., Pina, S., & Antunes, C. (2013). Temporal mining of integrated healthcare data: Methods, revealings and implications. *SDM IW on Data Mining for Medicine and Healthcare*, 52-60.

Jacob, S. G., & Ramani, R. G. (2012). Data mining in clinical data sets: A review. *International Journal of Applied Information Systems, 4*(6), 15–26. doi:10.5120/ijais12-450774

Jain, N., & Srivastava, V. (2013). Data mining techniques: A survey paper. IJRET. *International Journal of Research in Engineering and Technology, 2*(11), 1163–2319.

Jensen, F. V., & Nielsen, T. D. (2007). *Bayesian networks and decision graphs*. London: Springer. doi:10.1007/978-0-387-68282-2

Jiawei, H., & Kamber, M. (2001). Data mining: Concepts and techniques. San Francisco, CA: Morgan Kaufmann.

Johnson, D. E. (2001). Web-based data analysis tools help providers, MCOs contain costs. *Health Care Strategic Management, 19*(4), 16. PMID:11329971

Kantardzic, M. (2011). *Data mining: concepts, models, methods, and algorithms*. John Wiley & Sons. doi:10.1002/9781118029145

Koh, H. C., & Tan, G. (2011). Data mining applications in healthcare. *Journal of Healthcare Information Management*, *19*(2), 65. PMID:15869215

Kolçe, E., & Frasheri, N. (2012, September). *A literature review of data mining techniques used in healthcare databases*. Paper presented at the ICT innovations 2012, Ohrid, Macadonia.

Kwiatkowska, M., Atkins, M. S., Ayas, N. T., & Ryan, C. F. (2007). Knowledge-based data analysis: First step toward the creation of clinical prediction rules using a new typicality measure. Information Technology in Biomedicine. *IEEE Transactions on, 11*(6), 651–660.

Laboratory for Biomedical Informatics. (2015). Retrieved on September 11, 2015, from http://www.labmedinfo.org/translational/temporal

Lin, W., Orgun, M. A., & Williams, G. J. (2002). Mining temporal patterns from health care data. In *Data Warehousing and Knowledge Discovery* (pp. 222–231). Springer Berlin Heidelberg. doi:10.1007/3-540-46145-0_22

Lowrance, W. W. (2002). Learning from experience: Privacy and the secondary use of data in health research. *The Journal of Biolaw & Business, 6*(4), 30–60. PMID:15072055

Milovic, B., & Milovic, M. (2012). Prediction and decision making in Health Care using Data Mining. *International Journal of Public Health Science, 1*(2), 69–78.

Mishra, P., Padhy, N., & Panigrahi, R. (2013). The survey of data mining applications and feature scope. *Asian Journal of Computer Science & Information Technology, 2*(4), 43–58.

Mountrakis, G., Im, J., & Ogole, C. (2011). Support vector machines in remote sensing: A review. *ISPRS Journal of Photogrammetry and Remote Sensing, 66*(3), 247–259. doi:10.1016/j.isprsjprs.2010.11.001

Obenshain, M. K. (2004). Application of data mining techniques to healthcare data. *Infection Control and Hospital Epidemiology, 25*(8), 690–695. doi:10.1086/502460 PMID:15357163

Patel, D., Hsu, W., & Lee, M. L. (2008, June). Mining relationships among interval-based events for classification. In *Proceedings of the 2008 ACM SIGMOD international conference on Management of data* (pp. 393-404). ACM. doi:10.1145/1376616.1376658

Sarvestani, A. S., Safavi, A. A., Parandeh, N. M., & Salehi, M. (2010, October). Predicting breast cancer survivability using data mining techniques. In *Software Technology and Engineering (ICSTE), 2010 2nd International Conference on* (Vol. 2, pp. V2-227). IEEE. doi:10.1109/ICSTE.2010.5608818

Sharma, A., & Mansotra, V. (2014, March). Emerging applications of data mining for healthcare management-A critical review. In *Computing for Sustainable Global Development (INDIACom), 2014 International Conference on* (pp. 377-382). IEEE. doi:10.1109/IndiaCom.2014.6828163

Speights, K. (2013). 7 Countries with the highest health care costs. *Daily Finance*. Retrieved on September 14 2015 from http://www.dailyfinance.com/2013/06/15/7-countries-with-the-highest-health-care-costs/

Sun, J., Zhu, X., Zhang, C., & Fang, Y. (2012). Security and privacy for mobile health-care (m-Health) systems. In S. K. Das, K. Kant, & N. Zhang (Eds.), *Handbook on Securing Cyber-Physical Critical Infrastructure* (pp. 677–704). Elsevier. doi:10.1016/B978-0-12-415815-3.00027-3

Sundar, N. A., Latha, P. P., & Chandra, M. R. (2012). Performance analysis of classification data mining techniques over heart disease database. *International Journal of Engineering Science & Advanced Technology*.

Takabayashi, K., Ho, T. B., Yokoi, H., Nguyen, T. D., Kawasaki, S., Le, S. Q., & Yokosuka, O. et al. (2007). Temporal abstraction and data mining with visualization of laboratory data. *Studies in Health Technology and Informatics*, *129*(2), 1304. PMID:17911925

Upstate Medical University. (2011). *Protecting patient confidentiality and security*. Retrieved on September 1 2015, from www.upstate.edu/forms/documents/F84037.pdf

Wu, X., Zhu, X., Wu, G. Q., & Ding, W. (2014). Data mining with big data. *Knowledge and Data Engineering. IEEE Transactions on*, *26*(1), 97–107.

Yoo, I., Alafaireet, P., Marinov, M., Pena-Hernandez, K., Gopidi, R., Chang, J. F., & Hua, L. (2012). Data mining in healthcare and biomedicine: A survey of the literature. *Journal of Medical Systems*, *36*(4), 2431–2448. doi:10.1007/s10916-011-9710-5 PMID:21537851

ADDITIONAL READING

Brameier, M., & Banzhaf, W. (2001). A comparison of linear genetic programming and neural networks in medical data mining. Evolutionary Computation. *IEEE Transactions on*, *5*(1), 17–26.

Chen, J. Y., & Lonardi, S. (Eds.). (2009). *Biological data mining*. London: CRC Press.

Cios, K. J., & Kacprzyk, J. (2001). *Medical data mining and knowledge discovery*. New York, NY: Physica-Verlag.

Dua, S., & Acharya, U. R. (2011). *Data mining in biomedical imaging, signaling, and systems*. London: Auerbach Publications.

Epstein, I., & Blumenfield, S. (2001). *Clinical data-mining in practice-based research: Social work in hospital settings*. New York: Routledge.

Evfimievski, A., & Grandison, T. (2009). Privacy-preserving data mining. Handbook of Research on Innovations in Database Technologies and Applications: Current and Future Trends, 527-536. doi:10.4018/978-1-60566-242-8.ch056

Fu, T. C. (2011). A review on time series data mining. *Engineering Applications of Artificial Intelligence*, *24*(1), 164–181. doi:10.1016/j.engappai.2010.09.007

Gada, F. V., Yadav, K. R., & Shah, R. D. (2013). Data Mining in Medical Application for better Detection of Disease. *IJCER*, *2*(2), 173–176.

Giles, R., Epstein, I., & Vertigan, A. (Eds.). (2011). *Clinical data mining in an allied health organisation: A real world experience*. Sydney: Sydney University Press.

Iakovidis, D., & Smailis, C. (2012). A semantic model for multimodal data mining in healthcare information systems. *Studies in Health Technology and Informatics*, *180*, 574–578. PMID:22874256

Jensen, P. B., Jensen, L. J., & Brunak, S. (2012). Mining electronic health records: Towards better research applications and clinical care. *Nature Reviews. Genetics*, *13*(6), 395–405. doi:10.1038/nrg3208 PMID:22549152

Khan, A., Doucette, J., Jin, C., Fu, L., & Cohen, R. (2011, January). An ontological approach to data mining for emergency medicine. In 2011 Northeast Decision Sciences Institute Conference Proceedings 40th Annual Meeting. Montreal, Quebec, Canada (pp. 578-594).

Lavrač, N., & Zupan, B. (2010). Data mining in medicine. In Data Mining and Knowledge Discovery Handbook (pp. 1111-1136). Springer US.

Maulik, U., Bandyopadhyay, S., & Mukhopadhyay, A. (2011). Multiobjective genetic algorithms for clustering: Applications in data mining and bioinformatics. Springer USA.

Prather, J. C., Lobach, D. F., Goodwin, L. K., Hales, J. W., Hage, M. L., & Hammond, W. E. (1997). Medical data mining: Knowledge discovery in a clinical data warehouse. In *Proceedings of the AMIA Annual Fall Symposium* (p. 101). American Medical Informatics Association.

Raipure, G. S., & Gupta, S. R. (2013). Decision support system in medical science using OLAP & data mining. *International Journal Of Computer Science And Applications*, *6*(2), 248–254.

Ramakrishnan, N., Hanauer, D., & Keller, B. (2010). Mining electronic health records. *Computer*, *43*(10), 77–81. doi:10.1109/MC.2010.292

Rao, R. B., Sandilya, S., Scherpbier, H. J., & Warrick, T. R. (2012). U.S. Patent No. 8,214,224. Washington, DC: U.S. Patent and Trademark Office. Retrieved on Jan 01, 2016 from https://www.google.com/patents/US8214224

Smith, M. R., Wang, X., & Rangayyan, R. M. (2009). Evaluation of the sensitivity of a medical data-mining application to the number of elements in small databases. *Biomedical Signal Processing and Control*, *4*(3), 262–268. doi:10.1016/j.bspc.2009.04.001

Soni, J., Ansari, U., Sharma, D., & Soni, S. (2011). Predictive data mining for medical diagnosis: An overview of heart disease prediction. *International Journal of Computers and Applications*, *17*(8), 43–48. doi:10.5120/2237-2860

Tuffery, S. (2011). *Data mining and statistics for decision making*. John Wiley & Sons. doi:10.1002/9780470979174

Chapter 7
Adaptive Edge Detection Method towards Features Extraction from Diverse Medical Imaging Technologies

Indra Kanta Maitra
B. P. Poddar Institute of Management Technology, India

Samir Kumar Bandhyopadhyaay
University of Calcutta, India

ABSTRACT

The CAD is a relatively young interdisciplinary technology, has had a tremendous impact on medical diagnosis specifically cancer detection. The accuracy of CAD to detect abnormalities on medical image analysis requires a robust segmentation algorithm. To achieve accurate segmentation, an efficient edge-detection algorithm is essential. Medical images like USG, X-Ray, CT and MRI exhibit diverse image characteristics but are essentially collection of intensity variations from which specific abnormalities are needed to be isolated. In this chapter a robust medical image enhancement and edge detection algorithm is proposed, using tree-based adaptive thresholding technique. It has been compared with different classical edge-detection techniques using one sample two tail t-test to exam whether the null hypothesis can be supported. The proposed edge-detection algorithm showing 0.07 p-values and 2.411 t-stat where α = 0.025. Moreover the proposed edge is single pixeled and connected which is very significant for medical edge detection.

INTRODUCTION

Medical diagnosis process is dealt with patient's signs and symptoms of potential health problems to determine the disease accurately whereas clinical investigation procedure is a major backbone of accurate diagnosis apart from physical examination and past records. In statistical point of view, clinical investigation procedure is a classification test to confirm the diagnosis and to determine the follow up

DOI: 10.4018/978-1-5225-1776-4.ch007

actions. Typically the clinical investigation process is of two folds namely, invasive and non-invasive tests. Invasive tests mostly depend on open surgery, fine needle aspiration cytology (FNAC) etc. which involve puncturing of skin or incision. These processes are expensive, time consuming and pain staking. Non-invasive medical investigation techniques, on the other side, do not involve incision into the body or the removal of tissues. Medical imaging is one of the most important non-invasive investigation processes to aid the accurate diagnosis.

Medical Imaging

Medical imaging has been undergoing a revolution in the past decade with the advent of faster and more accurate devices. Medical image are images of the human body or parts of the body intended for clinical purposes of revealing or diagnosis of disease in medical science. Digital Radiography, Mammogram, Ultrasound (USG), Computed Tomography (CT), Magnetic Resonance Imaging (MRI) are some well accepted imaging techniques used for clinical diagnosis. The quality and characteristics of images obtained depend on the different sensors, parameters set by the operators and individual characteristics of the patients. Medical image analysis is critical in numerous biomedical applications such as detection of abnormalities, tissue measurement, surgical planning and simulation, and many more. Medical imaging is used to determine the relative change in size, shape and the spatial relationships between anatomical structures. The radiologists are particularly interested to observe the size, shape and texture of the organs and/or parts of organ for recognition, levelling and quantitive measurement of the specific objects and structures which are involved in the analysis of medical images.

Radiography is one of the most commonly used and oldest form of medical imaging. The ionizing radiation produce by X-ray technology determine the internal structure of a person depending on the density of body parts. Whereas mammography, interventional radiology, computed radiography, digital radiography and computed tomography (CT) are the different variant of conventional radiography. Radiographic image technology are typically used to evaluate broken bones, cavities, swallowed objects lungs, liver, pancreas, blood vessels, breast (mammography), etc. Diagnostic ultrasound in this field of medical imaging technology, also known as medical ultrasonography, uses high frequency sound waves to create images of the interior parts of the body. Ultrasound is often used to evaluate pregnancy, abnormalities in the heart and blood vessels, organs in the pelvis and abdomen symptoms of pain, swelling and infection. The most modern and effective medical imaging technology is Magnetic Resonance Imaging (MRI) which uses radio waves and a magnetic field to create detailed images of organs and tissues. MRI is often used to evaluate the blood vessels, abnormal tissue, breasts bones and joints organs in the pelvis, chest and abdomen.

Image Processing and CAD

Varieties of these machines and techniques can create picture of the structures and activities inside human body and the type of imaging used depends on the symptoms and the part of the body being examined. Generalized feature extractions from such images are difficult as they involve diverse technologies. The only commonality among all imaging technologies is the intensity features exhibited by them. DICOM (Digital Imaging and Communication in Medicine) image format is universally well accepted among all the above. In general, the grayscale image pixel is represented by 8 bits in DICOM format having 256 (2^8) grayscale colour intensities.

The above mentioned grey scale image information can be further enhanced by using image processing algorithms. Image processing is a procedure of converting an image into digital form and carrying out some operation on it, to extract further information from it and acquire an improved image. Mathematically image processing is defined as the processing of a two dimensional picture by computer algorithms. Necessity of digital image processing is due to two principal reasons the first being the improvement of pictorial information for human interpretation and the second being the processing of a scene data for an autonomous machine perception. It is the most sought after technique for identifying, isolating and extracting information from an image. The traditional image processing can be applied in the field of medical imaging and the different important feature information can be extracted. The extracted information need to be interpreted automatically to reduce the burden on the radiologist and deliver accurate decision making. Computer Aided Detection/Diagnosis (CAD) is the solution for the same.

Now a day's computer is a tool used in every discipline of study to solve critical problems. Different inter-disciplinary subject are evolving which is dealing with super specialised area of knowledge. Computer technology has had a tremendous impact on medical imaging. Radiology is using computer in the field of image interpretation process which introduces new flexibility into the system. This inter-disciplinary field is known as medical image processing and computer aided diagnosis (CAD) is the outcome of the same. By definition a CAD is a set of automatic or semiautomatic tools developed to assist radiologists in the detection and / or evaluation of medical images. Digital mammography accompanied with CAD can reduce huge work load on radiologists. CAD systems are not intended to replace radiologist but rather to assist them during image evaluation by prompting suspicious regions of breast.

The analysis of radiographic images using computer assistance is not new idea (Bick & Doi, 2000). In 1964, to determine the cardio-thoracic ratio on chest radiographs Meyers (Meyers, Nice, Becker, Nettleton, Sweeney, & Meckstroth, 1964) proposed an autonomous system. In 1967, a system for automated analysis of mammograms based on bilateral comparison was developed (Winsberg, Elkin, Macy Jr, Bordaz, & Weymouth, 1967); it was useful in screening normal examinations of mammography with routine viewing. An algorithm for detection of micro-calcifications on mammograms was developed (Tasto, 1975) in 1975, which were based on grey scale identification in a mammogram. These are some early evidence of CAD in radiology. Later with revolutionary development of digitisation techniques, improvement in the field of digital image processing algorithms and sufficient speed of computational power started to make practically feasible CAD applications.

A large number of research organisation and commercial establishments around the world are actively participating in research on CAD. Among several research initiatives, reviews are focusing on few of them which are really worthy (Doi, MacMahon, Katsuragawa, Nishikawa, & Jiang, 1999; Giger, Huo, Kupinski, & Vyborny, 2000; Karssemeijer, & Hendriks, 1997; Vyborny, & Giger, 1994; Cascio et al., 2006; Bellotti, Carlo, Tangora, & Nunzio, 2006; Masala, Tangaro, Quarta, 2006; Cerello et al., 2005; Bottigli, et al., 2006; Lauria, et al., 2006). The first CAD device to receive U.S. Food and Drug Administration (FDA) approval, the ImageCheckerM1000® by R2 Technology, Inc. (Los Altos, CA), was approved by premarket application (PMA) approval (P970058) on June 26, 1998. The initial product labelling was for use on routine screening mammograms, but on May 29, 2001, approval was granted for the expansion of the "Indications for Use" to cover diagnostic as well as screening mammograms (Technology Evaluation Center, 2002).

Image Segmentation

In CAD, image segmentation is an essential step, which partitions the medical image into different non-overlapping regions such that each region is nearly homogeneous and ideally corresponds to some anatomical structure or region of interest (ROI). The accuracy of CAD to detect abnormalities on medical image analysis requires a robust segmentation algorithm. This is considered as one of the first step in image analysis. The segmentation process refers to the decomposition of a screen into its constituent parts, such that each level of subdivision depends on the problem to be solved. Segmentation is discontinued once the Region of interest (ROI) in a specific application has been isolated and edge points of an image are obtained. The segmentation technique can be broadly classified into five main classes threshold based, edge based, region based, clustered based and water shaded based.

A grey level image consists of two main features, namely edge and region. The radiological images, specifically DICOM image are typically grey scale image. Segmentation algorithms for grey images are generally based on two basic properties of image intensity values; discontinuity and similarity. In the first category, the approach is to partition an image based on abrupt changes in intensity, which is the basic feature of image edge detection. Process of identification of sharp discontinuities within an image is called edges i.e. edges are significant local changes of intensity so, the discontinuities mean abrupt change of pixel intensity of image. Thus intensity causes basically geometric events and non-geometric events; geometric events basically discontinuity in entropy and/or colour depth and texture i.e. object boundary and discontinuity in surface and/or colour and non-geometric events basically direct reflection of light called specularity and inner reflection or shadow from other objects or same objects. In high level image vision, edge detection is used in interpretation of 3-D objects from 2-D images obtained from an image occulation in radiological imaging. The goal of edge detection is to produce a continuous line drawing from a screen from an image of that screen. Important features can be extracted from an image and these features can be used by high level computer vision algorithms for image analysis. Edge detection techniques provide an efficient means of non-invasive mapping/segmentation of the anatomy of an organ for further analysis like abnormalities. It can also be efficiently used to determine size, shape and spatial relationships between anatomical structures from the intensity distributions provided by radiological images.

Medical image are images of human body or parts of human body intended for clinical purposes for revealing abnormalities. Radiography, mammography, ultrasound, computed tomography and magnetic resonance imaging are some of the well accepted imaging techniques which are already discussed earlier. Among these heterogeneous technologies, generalized commonality is all these techniques uses intensity to represent the outcome. DICOM image format is universally well accepted for all the above imaging technologies. In this research a generalized edge detection technique for grey scale medical images has been proposed. Instead of using filter based edge detection technique a threshold based edge detection is used for its simplicity and dependency on intensity. The nature of thresholding used in the proposed method is adaptive. Thresholding is one of the generally used method for image segmentation. It is used to segregate the discontinuity by using an adequate threshold value. To accommodate the divergent imaging technology, proposed method uses adaptive threshold instead of global threshold to make it dynamic and image specific.

PREVIOUS WORKS

In image analysis, edge detection has a fundamental importance. The edge of a typical image characterise object boundaries and are therefore useful for segmentation, registration and identification of objects in a scene. Edge detection is one of the most commonly used operations in image analysis. An edge is defined by a discontinuity in colour values. In other words, an edge is the boundary between an object and the background.

The shape of edges in images depends on many parameters: the geometrical and optical properties of the object, the illumination conditions and the noise level in the images (Chidiac & Ziou, 1999). The importance of the classification is that it simplifies several problems in Artificial Vision and Image Processing, by associating specific processing rules to each type of edges (Ji & Haralick, 1999).

In practice, sampling and other image acquisition imperfections yield edges that are blurred, with the degree of blurring being determined by the factors such as quality of the image acquisition system, the sampling rate and illumination conditions under which the image is acquired. As a result, edges are more closely modelled as having a "ramp like" profile. The slope of the ramp is inversely proportional to the degree of blurring in the edge. The blurred edges tend to be thick and sharp edges tend to be thin (Gonzalez & Woods, 2007).

All edge detection algorithms are not involved with intensity change. Effects such as refraction or poor focus can result in objects with boundaries defined by a gradual and continuous change in intensity. Choosing a specific operator is dependent on responsiveness to such gradual change in intensity. Contemporary wavelet-based techniques describe the nature of the transition for each edge in order to distinguish edges. There are many edge detection methods which are based on the gradients in the image. The methods return non-zero values in the uneven regions that typically occur on the boundary between two diverse regions in an image. There are large numbers of edge detection algorithms available, each designed to be responsive to certain particular types of edges. The majority of different methods may be grouped into three broad ways:

1. The maximum and minimum values derived from the first derivative is useful to obtain the edges by the gradient method,
2. The second order derivative has helped to find the zero crossings and detect the edges in an image by the Laplacian method and
3. Other recent methods of medical edge detection used divergent techniques to derive the edge map. The first two categories may be treated as classical approaches whereas last one may be termed as medical image edge detection techniques.

Classical Approaches

An image gradient is a directional change in the intensity or colour in an image. Image gradients may be used to extract information from images. The gradient of a two-variable function image intensity function is at each image point a 2-D vector with the components given by the derivatives in the horizontal and vertical directions. At each image point, the gradient vector points in the direction of largest possible intensity increase, and the length of the gradient vector corresponds to the rate of change in that direction.

Roberts' Cross

Roberts Cross operator is one of the first edge detectors and was initially proposed by Lawrence Roberts in 1963 (Roberts, 1965). It is a differential operator. The idea is to approximate the gradient of an image through discrete differentiation which is achieved by computing the sum of the squares of the differences between diagonally adjacent pixels. According to Roberts, an edge detector should have the following properties, the produced edges should be well-defined, the background should contribute as little noise as possible, and the intensity of edges should correspond as close as possible to what a human would perceive. With these criteria in mind and based on then prevailing psychophysical theory Roberts proposed the following equations:

$$y_{i,j} = \sqrt{x_{i,j}} \text{ and } z_{i,j} = \sqrt{\left(y_{i,j} - y_{i+1,j+1}\right)^2 + \left(y_{i+1,j} - y_{i,j+1}\right)^2}$$

where x is the initial intensity value in the image, z is the computed derivative and i,j represent the location in the image. The results of this operation will highlight changes in intensity in a diagonal direction. One of the most appealing aspects of this operation is its simplicity; the kernel is small and contains only integers. However with the speed of computers today this advantage is negligible and the Roberts cross suffers greatly from sensitivity to noise (Davis, 1975). To perform edge detection with the Roberts operator, first convolve the original image, with the following two kernels:

$$\begin{bmatrix} +1 & 0 \\ 0 & -1 \end{bmatrix} \text{ and } \begin{bmatrix} 0 & +1 \\ -1 & 0 \end{bmatrix}$$

Let I(x,y) be a point in the original image and G_x(x,y) be a point in an image formed by convolving with the first kernel and G_y(x,y) be a point in an image formed by convolving with the second kernel. The gradient can then be defined as:

$$\nabla I_{(x,y)} = G_{(x,y)} = \sqrt{G_x^2 + G_y^2}$$

The direction of the gradient can also be defined as follows:

$$\theta_{(x,y)} = \arctan\left(Gy_{(x,y)} / Gx_{(x,y)}\right)$$

Sobel Filter

It is a discrete differentiation operator, computing an approximation of the gradient of the image intensity function. At each point in the image, the result of the Sobel operator is either the corresponding gradient vector or the norm of this vector. The Sobel operator is based on convolving the image with a small, separable, and integer valued filter in horizontal and vertical direction and is therefore relatively inexpensive in terms of computations. Mathematically, the operator uses two 3×3 kernels which are convolved with the original image to calculate approximations of the derivatives - one for horizontal changes, and one for vertical (Rosin & Ioannidis, 2003). If A is defined as the source image, and G_x and G_y are two images which at each point contain the horizontal and vertical derivative approximations, the computations are as follows:

$$G_y = \begin{bmatrix} -1 & -2 & -1 \\ 0 & 0 & 0 \\ +1 & +2 & +1 \end{bmatrix} * A \text{ and } G_x = \begin{bmatrix} -1 & 0 & +1 \\ -2 & 0 & +2 \\ -1 & 0 & +1 \end{bmatrix} * A$$

where * here denotes the 2-D convolution operation. The X-coordinate is here defined as increasing in the "right"-direction, and the Y-coordinate is defined as increasing in the "down"-direction. At each point in the image, the resulting gradient approximations can be combined to give the gradient magnitude, using:

$$G = \sqrt{G_x^2 + G_y^2}$$

Using this information, the gradient's direction can also be calculated:

$$\theta = \arctan\left(G_y / G_x\right)$$

where, for example, Θ is 0 for a vertical edge which is darker on the left side (Gonzalez & Woods, 2007).

Prewitt Filter

It is a discrete differentiation operator, computing an approximation of the gradient of the image intensity function. At each point in the image, the result of the Prewitt operator is either the corresponding gradient vector or the norm of this vector. The Prewitt operator is based on convolving the image with a small, separable, and integer valued filter in horizontal and vertical direction and is therefore relatively inexpensive in terms of computations. Mathematically, the operator uses two 3×3 kernels which are convolved with the original image to calculate approximations of the derivatives - one for horizontal changes, and one for vertical (Prewitt, 1970). If it is defined A as the source image, G_x and G_y are two images which at each point contain the horizontal and vertical derivative approximations, the latter are computed as:

$$G_x = \begin{bmatrix} -1 & 0 & +1 \\ -1 & 0 & +1 \\ -1 & 0 & +1 \end{bmatrix} * A \text{ and } G_y = \begin{bmatrix} -1 & -1 & -1 \\ 0 & 0 & 0 \\ +1 & +1 & +1 \end{bmatrix} * A$$

Compass Operator-Kirsch Operator

The kirsch edge detector detects edges using eight filters that are applied to the image. The eight filters are a rotation of a basic compass convolution filter. For comparison with Sobel and Prewitt operator here only two directions i.e. horizontal and vertical convolution kernels (3x3) are considered. The operator is calculated as follows for directions with 45° difference:

$$h_{n,m} = \max_{z=1,...,8} \sum_{i=-1}^{1}\sum_{j=-1}^{1} g_{i,j}^{(z)} \cdot f_{n+i,m+j}$$

where the direction kernels are:

$$g^{(1)} = \begin{bmatrix} +5 & +5 & +5 \\ -3 & 0 & -3 \\ -3 & -3 & -3 \end{bmatrix}, g^{(2)} = \begin{bmatrix} +5 & +5 & -3 \\ +5 & 0 & -3 \\ -3 & -3 & -3 \end{bmatrix}, g^{(3)} = \begin{bmatrix} +5 & -3 & -3 \\ +5 & 0 & -3 \\ +5 & -3 & -3 \end{bmatrix}, g^{(4)} = \begin{bmatrix} -3 & -3 & -3 \\ +5 & 0 & -3 \\ +5 & +5 & -3 \end{bmatrix}.$$

Second-Order Derivative Method

Some edge-detection operators are instead based upon second-order derivatives of the intensity. They essentially capture the rate of change in the intensity gradient. Thus, in the ideal continuous case, detection of zero-crossings in the second derivative captures local maxima in the gradient. In order to effectively detect intensity changes (edges), the operator needs to have two characteristics.

1. First, it must be a differential operator, taking either a first or second spatial derivative of the image.
2. Second, it should be capable of being tuned to act at any desired scale so that large filters can be used to detect blurry shadow edges, and small ones can be used to detect sharply focused fine detail in the image. This led to the so-called Laplacian-of-Gaussian edge operator.

Laplacian of Gaussian (LoG)

This is a compound operator that combines a smoothing operation, using a Gaussian-shaped, linear-phase FIR filter, with a differentiation operation, using a discrete Laplacian (Huertas & Medioni, 1986; Marr & Hildreth, 1980). The edges are identified by the location of zero crossings (recall that the second derivative changes sign in the vicinity of maxima of the first derivative). As Laplace operator may detect edges as well as noise (isolated, out-of-range), it may be desirable to smooth the image first by convolution with a Gaussian kernel of width

$$G_{\sigma}(x,y) = \left(1/\sqrt{2\pi\sigma^2}\right)\exp\left(-\left(x^2+y^2\right)/2\sigma^2\right)$$

to suppress the noise before using Laplace for edge detection:

$$\Delta\Big(G_\sigma\big(x,y\big)*f\big(x,y\big)\Big)=\Big(\Delta G_\sigma(x,y)\Big)*f\big(x,y\big)=LoG*f\big(x,y\big)$$

The first equal sign is due to the fact that

$$\frac{d}{dt}\Big(h\big(t\big)*f(t)\Big)=\frac{d}{dt}\int f\big(\tau\big)h\big(t-\tau\big)d\tau=\int f\big(\tau\big)\frac{d}{dx}h\big(t-\tau\big)dr=f\big(t\big)*\frac{d}{dt}h(t)$$

So it can obtain the Laplacian of Gaussian $\Delta G_\sigma\big(x,y\big)$ first and then convolve it with the input image. To do so, first consider

$$\frac{\partial}{\partial x}G_\sigma\big(x,y\big)=\frac{\partial}{\partial x}e^{-\left(x^2+y^2\right)/2\sigma^2}=\frac{x}{\sigma^2}e^{-\left(x^2+y^2\right)/2\sigma^2}$$

and

$$\frac{\partial^2}{\partial^2 x}G_\sigma\big(x,y\big)=\frac{x^2}{\sigma^4}e^{-\left(x^2+y^2\right)/2\sigma^2}-\frac{1}{\sigma^2}e^{-\left(x^2+y^2\right)/2\sigma^2}=\frac{x^2-\sigma^2}{\sigma^4}e^{-\left(x^2+y^2\right)/2\sigma^2}$$

Note that for simplicity the normalising coefficient $1/\sqrt{2\pi\sigma^2}$ is omitted. Similarly it can be acquired

$$\frac{\partial^2}{\partial^2 y}G_\sigma\big(x,y\big)=\frac{y^2-\sigma^2}{\sigma^4}e^{-\left(x^2+y^2\right)/2\sigma^2}$$

Now, have LoG as an operator or convolution kernel defined as

$$LoG\triangleq\Delta G_\sigma\big(x,y\big)=\frac{\partial^2}{\partial x^2}G_\sigma\big(x,y\big)+\frac{\partial^2}{\partial y^2}G_\sigma\big(x,y\big)=\frac{x^2+y^2-2\sigma^2}{\sigma^4}e^{-\left(x^2+y^2\right)/2\sigma^2}$$

2-D LoG can be approximated by a 5 by 5 convolution kernel such as

$$\begin{bmatrix} 0 & 0 & 1 & 0 & 0 \\ 0 & 1 & 2 & 1 & 0 \\ 1 & 2 & -16 & 2 & 1 \\ 0 & 1 & 2 & 1 & 0 \\ 0 & 0 & 1 & 0 & 0 \end{bmatrix}$$

The kernel of any other sizes can be obtained by approximating the continuous expression of LoG given above. However, this must make sure that the sum (or average) of all elements of the kernel has to be zero (similar to the Laplace kernel) so that the convolution result of a homogeneous regions is always zero.

The edges in the image can be obtained by these steps:

- Applying LoG to the image,
- Detection of zero-crossings in the image,
- Threshold the zero-crossings to keep only those strong ones (large difference between the positive maximum and the negative minimum). This last step is needed to suppress the weak zero-crossings most likely caused by noise.

Canny Edge Detection

The Canny edge detection algorithm (Canny, 1986) is known to many as the optimal edge detector and has shown that the first derivative of the Gaussian closely approximates the operator that optimizes the product of signal-to-noise ratio and localization. The algorithm then tracks along these regions and suppresses any pixel that is not at the maximum. The steps for canny edge detection is follows, Compute f_x and f_y

$$f_x = \frac{\partial}{\partial x}\left(f * G\right) = f * \frac{\partial}{\partial x}G = f * G_x$$

$$f_y = \frac{\partial}{\partial y}\left(f * G\right) = f * \frac{\partial}{\partial y}G = f * G_y$$

G(x, y) is the Gaussian function.
Gx (x, y) is the derivate of G(x, y) with respect to x:

$$G_x\left(x, y\right) = \frac{-x}{\sigma^2}G(x, y)$$

Gy(x, y) is the derivate of G(x, y) with respect to y:

$$G_y\left(x, y\right) = \frac{-y}{\sigma^2}G(x, y)$$

The performance of the canny algorithm (Canny, 1986; Pellegrino, Vanzella, & Torre, 2004) depends heavily on the adjustable parameters, σ, which is the standard deviation for the Gaussian filter and the threshold values. The σ also controls the size of the Gaussian filter. The greater the value for σ, the larger the size of the Gaussian filter. This indicates more blurring which is necessary for noisy images and also can detect larger edges. Gradient-based algorithms such as the Prewitt filter have a major drawback of being very sensitive to noise. The size of the kernel filter and coefficients are fixed and cannot be adapted to a given image. An adaptive edge-detection algorithm is necessary to provide a robust solution that is adaptable to the varying noise levels. The complexity of Canny edge detection algorithm is high compared to Sobel, Prewitt and Robert's operator but the algorithm performs better than all these operators under almost all scenarios.

Contemporary Methods

Apart from the above mentioned classical edge detection techniques there are several other contemporary methods which are not directly associated with convolution filter. Out of many, few are described here.

The Frei-Chen edge detection method (Frei & Chen, 1977) determines edge points on the size of the angle between the sub-image b and its projection on the edge sub-space. The Frei-Chen edge detector actually uses a combination of 4 pairs of wavelets. Two pairs are the first degree partial derivatives of the Gaussian smoothing function, which are sensitive to step edges and the other two pairs are second and fourth mixed partial derivatives of the Gaussian smoothing function, which are sensitive to Dirac edges. The citation by Zhang (Zhang, Ouyang, & Cham, 2009), the Viterbi algorithm has shown the hidden state to map the estimation and evaluate the result of the edge detection algorithm based on the coefficient obtained at each step. Whereas F. Jassim (Jassim, 2013) in his citation step by step edge detection on grey scale image preceded by denoising to smoothen the image pixel is followed. In this citation, the upper left pixel in the 2x2 window represents an edge and the differences observed visibly between the edges proposed and the standard edge detectors is shown. Instead of detectors for filtering purpose N.C Woods (Woods, Longe, & Roberts, 2012) used spammers to filter out the edges with the help of Optical Character Recognition. The global magnitudes of edges in an image are obtained from filtering the low level features which classified the image into spams. These algorithms are using diverge technologies like wavelet, thresholding etc. and the obtain results are significantly acceptable.

In the ideal case, the result of applying an edge detector to an image may lead to a set of connected curves that indicate the boundaries of objects. Thus, applying an edge detection algorithm to an image may significantly reduce the amount of data to be processed and may therefore filter out information that may be regarded as less relevant, while preserving the important structural properties of an image. Edges extracted from an image is often hampered by fragmentation, meaning that the edge curves are not connected, missing edge segments as well as false edges, thus complicating the subsequent task of interpreting the image data (Lindeberg, 1998). Edge detection is one of the fundamental steps in image processing, image analysis, image pattern recognition, and computer vision techniques (Zhai, Dong, & Ma, 2008).

Medical Image Edge Detection Techniques

In spite of the mathematical sophistication of these filter based techniques; the problem of finding true edges that correspond to physical boundaries of an object in an image is still a very difficult one. Thus several medical edge detection techniques are developed with new ideas. The recent developed algorithms in the field of medical edge detection are active contour or snake model, texture discrimination based, multi-scale based, contextual based Hopfield Neural Network, generic Algorithm, Bayesian edge detection, Fuzzy set based and linking to boundaries of low contrast Lesions.

Active Contour or Snake Model

Active contour or Snakes is defined as a framework in computer vision and it is popularly known method to delineate an object outline from a 2-D image. A snake (Kass, Witkin, & Terzopoulos, 1988) is an energy minimizing spline guided by external constraint forces and influenced by image forces that pull it towards features such as lines and edges. Snakes are active contour models: they lock into nearby edges, localizing them accurately. Scale-space continuation can be used to enlarge the captured region surrounding the feature. This methodology is based upon the utilization of deformable contours which conform to various object shapes and motions. Snakes can be used for edge and curve detection in medical imaging, segmentation, shape modelling and visual tracking (Yezzi, Kichenassamy, Kumar, Olver, & Tannenbaum, 1997). They proposed a novel geometric active contour model for segmentation and edge detection of MRI, CT and USG images. It is based on defining feature based matrices on a given image.

Texture Discrimination

One of the possible directions for the analysis of grey-level texture is the thresholding of the image followed by the analysis of the obtained binary texture. As medical images are fuzzy, edge detection based on texture characteristics is more effective than intensity based techniques. A generic methodology (Thangam, SaiDeepak, Rai, & Mirajkar, 2009) has been described for texture edge detection using multi-resolution and multi-scale filters on some modalities of medical images for discriminating, segmenting different texture regions and capturing texture edge information. First texture edge information is defined and an experimental work bench is presented for finding efficient range of values for Gabor function parameters to capture it. The true pixel count for a given location (x,y) in the image is given by:

$$T_{PC}\left(x,y\right) = \sum P_{ON}\left(x_i, y_i\right)$$

Then step by step approach is delineated to achieve the texture edge map. This method needs to be employed to minimize the ringing effect produced by this texture based filter method.

Multi-Scale Edge Detection

This method of edge detection and segmentation enhances the quality on natural images that can be improved significantly. It eliminates the need for explicit scale selection and edge tracking that exist at a wide range of scales and localizes these edges at finer scales. This method is based on multi-scale analysis (Hajj, Nguyen, & Chin, 1996) using filter banks and is adaptive to a large number of features. Initially, an optimal one-scale filter is designed for the required detection and then it is further extended to a set of multi-scale filters, which in turn are used in designing the filter bank that would provide the desired multi-scale responses. Subsequently, the scale space information is optimally combined in a maximum-a-posteriori (MAP) classifier, whose design depends on the desired feature and the resulting filter bank.

Contextual Based Hopfield Neural Network (CHNN)

A Hopfield network is a form of recurrent artificial neural network which was made popular by John Hopfield in 1982. It is guaranteed to converge to a local minimum, but convergence to a false pattern (wrong local minimum) rather than the stored pattern (expected local minimum) can occur. Chang (Chang, 2004) proposed a special design Hopfield neural network called Contextual Hopfield Neural Network (CHNN) for finding the edges of CT and MRl images. Different from the conventional 2-D Hopfield neural networks, the CHNN maps the two-dimensional Hopfield network at the original image plane. With the direct mapping, the network is capable of incorporating pixels' contextual information into a pixels' labelling procedure. As a result, the effect of tiny details or noises will be effectively removed by the CHNN and the drawback of disconnected fractions can be overcome.

Generic Algorithm

In the field of artificial intelligence, a genetic algorithm is a heuristic search that mimics the process of natural selection and it is routinely used to generate useful solutions to optimization and search problems. An algorithm is proposed by Gudmundsson (Gudmundsson, El-Kwae, & Kabuka, 1998) that detects well-localized, un-fragmented, thin edges in medical images based on optimization of edge configurations using a genetic algorithm (GA). Several enhancements were added to improve the performance of the algorithm over a traditional GA. The edge map is split into connected sub regions to reduce the solution space and simplify the problem. The edge-map is then optimized in parallel using incorporated genetic operators that perform transforms on edge structures. Adaptation is used to control operator probabilities based on their participation.

Morphological Filters

It is a tool for extracting components that are useful in the representation and description of the region shape such as boundaries for pre-processing or post-processing technique. Some relevant techniques for feature extraction have been discussed by several scholars. Morphological operations can be used for edge detection, segmentation and image enhancement. The basic set operations are dilation, erosion, opening, and closing. Morphological opening and closing operations perform similar nonlinear noise removal with litter or no loss of edge feature. The edge structure can be estimated by subtracting the morphological erosion. The morphological edge detector proposed by Peng (Peng & Rusch, 1991), obey threshold-linear superposition which means a complex grey-scale edge detector that is formulated by implementing simple binary edge detector subsections and summing their opted binary edges.

Bayesian Edge Detection

A Bayesian network is a probabilistic directed acyclic graphical model that represents a set of random variables and their dependencies based on some conditions. The probabilistic relationship can also be applied to derive edges. The method proposed by Kao (Kao, Pan, Hiller, & Chen, 1998), a discrete linear imaging model appropriate for clinical ultrasound B-scans is derived. Based on this model, a Bayesian restoration approach is developed that is currently designed for the generation of correct edges of medical ultrasound images. In this method, a priori information is incorporated in part by the use of line sites, which have numerical values between 0 and 1, as a way of evaluating the probability of the presence of edges between two neighbouring pixels. This auxiliary information is utilized to avoid smoothing across true edges and thus perform speckle reduction, edge detection, and region segmentation at the same time.

Fuzzy Set Based

Fuzzy logic is a form of many-valued logic in which the truth values of variables i.e. fuzzy values helps in the segmentation process of medical images. Zhang (Zeng, Tu, & Zhang, 2008) proposed a fast edge detection method basing on the combination of fuzzy subsets which involves partitioning the image into two portions: the edge portion and the non-edge portion. The latter one, as the main constituent of an image, consists of the object and its background. Removing the non-edge portion from an image, the remainder is nothing but the edge of this image. In this technique, the grey level histogram is partitioned into several sub-regions. Some operations are performed with the associated fuzzy subsets corresponding to those sub-edges in the sub-regions on the grey-level-square-difference histogram. Thus, the edge of this image is finally obtained.

Sequential Edge Detection and Linking to Boundaries of Low Contrast Lesions

This technique describes an algorithm (Liu, Bland, Williams, Schunck, & Meyer, 1989) for the optimal edge contour estimation in medical images without a priori shape models. An optimal and robust contour estimator is derived by minimization of a risk function, which measures the error from both inappropriate choice of edge contour and the noise model in the image. The result includes Huber's function. If a parametric statistical noise model and the Neyman-Pemon criterion are used, the result is an extension of maximum likelihood function. A recursive formula can be implemented by assuming independent random field and a Markov path model. The assumption of independent statistics can be satisfied by use of an autoregressive moving-average (ARMA) pre-processor. The problem of varying edge strength is lessened using an adaptive trimmed mean. The robust algorithm is implemented using a priority-tree (stack) structure.

Owing to the better performance of the medical edge detection, several alternatives methods are described above. Geometric active contour models are formulated for edge detection and segmentation of magnetic resonance imaging (MRI), computed tomography (CT), and ultrasound medical imagery whereas multi-scale edge detection is based on multi-scale analysis tested on echocardiographic images and can be applied to images suffering from severe noise degradation. Contextual based Hopfield Neural Network (CHNN) is proved to design more appropriate, more continued edge points than Laplacian-based, Canny's, and wavelet based methods. At the same time the Genetic algorithm (GA) can be applied on MRI, CT and USG to get the basic edge features and the detected edge is thin, continuous and well localized. Morphological operators are useful for medical images in comparison to linear edge detection since local variation of such are relatively small. The Bayesian restoration approach can be applied for USG images with reduced speckles and achieve edge detection and region segmentation. The Fuzzy-set Based approach is quite simple and effective to achieve the edge picture towards accurate determination of the sizes of atria cordis, mitral valve and ventricles of heart, etc. so as to judge the status of his/her heart and the degree of disease. Like Genetic algorithm, the Sequential Edge Detection and Linking to Boundaries of Low Contrast Lesions algorithm is effective for MRI and CT images.

The special characteristic features for medical edge detection like thin edge, continuity and relevant edge lines preservation can be achieved by the above mentioned algorithms. But these algorithms are not equipped for all types of medical imaging technologies and at the same time complexity of some of these algorithms are high and algorithms are complicated in nature. The generalised solution can only be achieved to develop an algorithm which is adaptive in nature. The proposed method of adaptive thresholding towards edge detection is developed, that aims to achieve a generalized solution for the same.

PROPOSED METHOD

Any grayscale image is represented as a two-dimensional array of pixel intensities. A grayscale image can be expressed as a combination of k intensity values with a certain frequency f(k) where k = 0 to n. In this research article a new structure is proposed to represent images using a modified full and complete binary tree that will accommodate both the intensity and frequency measures. The objective in constructing such a tree is to obtain an image with reduced number of colour, yet maintaining the full colour palette; thus achieving colour quantization at every tree level.

A binary tree can be defined as full binary tree if the entire node contains exactly two child nodes or it is leaf node and all leaf nodes must contains in the same level. Similarly a binary tree T with n levels is complete if all levels except possibly the last are completely full, and the last level has at least all its nodes to the left side. But in case of full and complete tree it must satisfy both the conditions laid down by their definitions. Hence it is possible to obtain a tree that is complete at all levels having all nodes and all child nodes; at the last level have only external nodes i.e. leaf node.

Here some of the basic functions are defined which are used in later algorithms:

```
Parent (i)
        Return
Left (i)
        Return 2i
Right (i)
        Return 2i+1
// Total number of nodes in a full and complete Binary Tree tNode (h)
        Return 2^(h+1) - 1
//The number of internal nodes (non-leaf nodes) in a full and complete Binary
Tree iNode (h)
        Return 2^h-1
//The number of external nodes (leaf nodes) in a full and complete Binary Tree
eNode (h)
        Return tNode (h) - iNode (h)
```

The proposed data structure, all the possible colour of an image can be represented by the leaf nodes of the said data structure i.e. if the image contains 2^n number of distinct colours then the tree will have 2^n leafs at level n. To represent a 256 grayscale DICOM image, it is required to construct a full and complete binary tree with leaf nodes at level 8 (as $2^8 = 256$). The node structure of the said binary tree

Figure 1. Full and complete binary tree

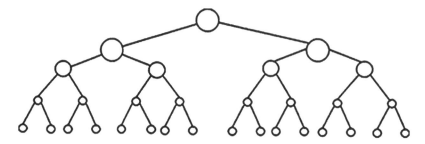

will contain pointers for left and right child along with image data. The data will have two components i.e. colour intensity and its frequency present in the image.

$$Node = \Big\{Node * Left, Node * Right, Int\ Intensity, Int\ Frequency\Big\}$$

The frequency of intensity of left child node f(L) and right child node f(R), whichever is greater, will be the intensity of the parent node. The frequency for the node will be the summation of f(L) and f(R).

$$Node.Intensity = \begin{cases} f\big(R\big) \cdot Intensity & if\ f\big(L\big) \cdot Frequency < f\big(R\big) \cdot Frequency \\ f\big(L\big) \cdot Intensity & if\ f\big(L\big) \cdot Frequency > f\big(R\big) \cdot Frequency \end{cases}$$

Initially, a tree is created having level n where 2^n = total number colour present in the image. The image bitmap is read in row major order. Each image pixel's intensity will be compared with the external nodes i.e. leaf nodes from left to right. If the intensity value matches frequency will be incremented by one otherwise consider the next node. At the end of the reading process, the tree contains frequency information of image data set at the external nodes in the tree.

The entire tree is constructed but only the leaf has image data. In the next phase, the intensity value of image data for all the intermediate nodes including the root node are required to be calculated. As per the proposed algorithm the parent node will hold the intensity value of the child node that has a greater frequency among the two child nodes. To achieve the same the tree has to be traversed in post-order method. According to the post-order traversal of tree the left child node and the right child node is traversed before the parent node, making it possible to compare the intensity frequencies of the child nodes. The intensity value of the parent node is updated based on the comparison results of the child nodes. This process is continued till the intensity value of the image data for root node is achieved.

The tree structure that is obtained by the above procedure contains the histogram of the original image with C grey shades at level n where C = 2^n and in every subsequent upper level contains n/2 number of grey shades. The intensity values of intermediate nodes can contain any grey shade value, thus preserving the original colour palette and performing uniform colour quantization at every level.

The manifestation of same density in different medical imaging technologies, are divergent. Even similar type of medical image may show different intensity characteristics, for example, MRI of brain and knee will exhibit significant intensity differences. Appropriate level of the aforesaid data structure can be utilized to accommodate different cases depending on the intensity characteristics to obtain optimal result. Moreover, to highlight or segment out a portion of any image intensity, different parts of multiple levels can be utilized. Say for example, to isolate a tumour that exhibit higher intensities than the rest of the image, it is possible to take a lower level for those high intensity parts, thus taking greater number of colour shades. For the rest of the image intensities a higher level is used with reduced number of colour shades.

Generation of Image Histogram

Image histogram is a graphical representation of the intensity distribution in a digital image. It exhibits the number of pixels for each intensity value. In mathematical term, a histogram is a function that counts the number of observations that fall into each of the disjoint categories. Let n be the total number of observations and k be the total number of disjoint categories, the histogram H_i meets the following.

$$n = \sum_{i=1}^{k} H_i$$

In this proposed method, colour intensities and their frequencies are extracted from the original image colour space to generate histogram. The extracted data are stored in the leaf nodes of proposed tree i.e. each leaf node representing individual disjoint intensity sequentially.

Generation of Level Histogram

LEVEL-HISTOGRAM is an important process to generate colour quantised histograms for each subsequent level of tree with reduces number of colour i.e. half number of colours upto the root in bottom-up mode. The way LEVEL-HISTOGRAM works:

- It will work for all leaf nodes i.e. iNode (h) + 1 to tNode (h).

Figure 2. (a) Original MRI image and (b) it's histogram of Level 0

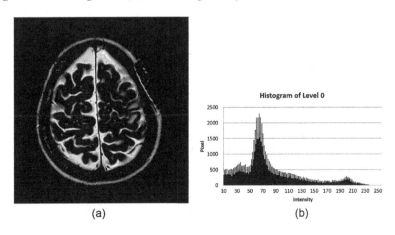

(a) (b)

Algorithm 1. Storing original colour space at leaf nodes of tree

```
ORGIGINAL-HISTOGRAM (Image, height, width)
Loop x← 1 to height
    Do Loop y← 1 to width
            Do      Intensity ← Image [x, y]
                    Tree [(iNode (h) + 1) + Intensity].count ← Tree [(iNode (h)
+ 1) + Intensity].count + 1
                    x←x +1
        y←y +1
Return Tree
```

- Compare frequency count of Tree[i] with child nodes i.e. Tree[Left(i)] and Tree[Right(i)], intensity of the larger will be propagated to parent intensity and sum of frequency count of children will be the frequency count of parent.
- The iteration will be terminated when the parent node is the root of tree.

Figure 3. (a) Histogram of Level 1, (b) histogram of Level 2 and (c) histogram of Level 3 of original MRI image of Figure 2

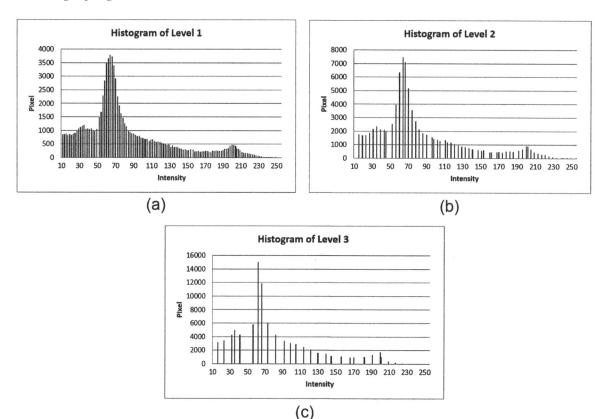

Algorithm 2. Generate quantize colour spaces in different level of tree

```
LEVEL-HISTOGRAM (Tree)
Loop x ← iNode (h) + 1 to tNode (h)
    Do Lcount ← Tree (x).count
        Loop y ← Parent (x) downto 0
            Do If x mod 2 ≠ 0
                        Then  Tree [y].intensity ← Tree [x].intensity
                                Tree [y].count ← Tree [y].count + Lcount
                ElseIf Tree [y].count < Tree [x].count
                                Then  Tree [y].intensity ← Tree
[x].intensity
                                        Tree [y].count ← Tree
[y].count + Lcount
                    x ← y
                    y ← Parent (x)
        x ← x + 1
Return Tree
```

Average Bin Distance (ABD) Calculation

In each level, half of intermediate colours bin are truncated depending on the condition stated above. This intermediate truncation will generate different bin distance in the histogram of particular level of the Tree. The process BIN-DISTANCE will calculate the average bin distance of that histogram. The Average Bin Distance (ABD) is the mean of different bin distance in the histogram. The way BIN-DISTANCE has been calculated.

- It will work for a particular height (h_i) of the Tree.
- The iteration will start from first node i.e. iNode (h_i) upto the last node i.e. tNode (h_i) of particular height of the Tree.
- Summing the intensity distance between all adjacent nodes sequentially and calculate average bin distance (ABD) dividing by the number of bins.

Calculation Maximum Difference Threshold (MDT)

In previous process, ABD of histogram of particular level of the Tree has been derived. CALCULATE-MDT process first segregates the bins into two categories namely, Prominent Bins and Truncated Bins. Prominent Bins are the points of histogram from where sharp change intensity values are recorded. Whereas, Truncated Bins has an insignificance difference of intensity with its adjacent bins. Prominent bins have a significant role to determine edges of an image. Using the prominent bins, CALCULATE-MDT process generates the Maximum Difference Threshold (MDT). The outline of CALCULATE-MDT:

- It will work for a particular height (h_i) of the Tree.

Algorithm 3. Calculate the average bin distance

```
BIN-DISTANCE (Tree, h)
TotBin ← 0
TotBinDist ← 0
Loop x ← iNode (h) + 2 to tNode (h)
    Do TotBin ← TotBin + 1
        TotBinDist ←TotBinDist + (Tree [x].intensity - Tree[x - 1].intensity)
        x ← x + 1
AvgBinDist ← TotBinDist / TotBin
Return AvgBinDist
Calculation Maximum Difference Threshold (MDT)
```

- The iteration will start from first node i.e. iNode (h_i) upto the last node i.e. tNode (h_i) of particular height of the Tree.
- It will compare the intensity difference of a node with its previous node with ABD. If intensity difference is greater than the ABD, it will be marked as prominent node else it will be marked as truncated.

Generation of Enhanced Image

In this process, the enhanced image will be generated from the original medical image. The New Intensity of a particular pixel has been calculated using the truncated histogram from the tree of a particular level. Initially mapping between original histogram at level (h-1) and the desired level histogram at level h1 has been done. From mapping process a particular intensity has been selected from the level histogram and checking has been performed whether the obtained intensity is prominent or not. If the obtained intensity is prominent one then it will be propagated to the image pixel, else the next higher prominent intensity will be selected from the level histogram to propagate.

Figure 4. Level 2 Histogram showing prominent bins along with other bins

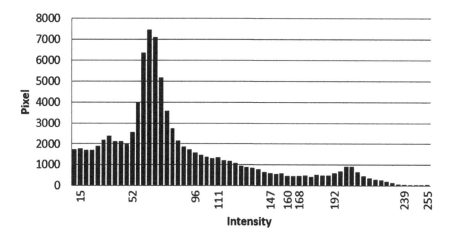

Algorithm 4. Calculation of MDT by identifying the prominent bins and truncate the non-prominent bins

```
CALCULATE-MDT (Tree, h₁)
Tree [iNode (h₁) + 1].prominent ←1
TotPrmBin ← 0
TotPrmBinDist ← 0
Loop x ← iNode (h₁) + 2 to tNode (h₁)
    Do If Tree [x].intensity - Tree [x - 1].intensity ≥ AvgBinDist
            Then   Tree[x].prominent ← 1
                        TotPrmBin ← TotPrmBin + 1
                        TotPrmBinDist ← TotPrmBinDist + (Tree [x].intensity
- Tree [x - 1].intensity)
            Else         Tree[x].prominent ← 0
        x ← x + 1
MDT ← TotPrmBinDist / TotPrmBin
Return MDT
```

Figure 5. (a) Enhanced MRI image and (b) graph showing prominent intensity distances in Level 2 of enhanced MRI image

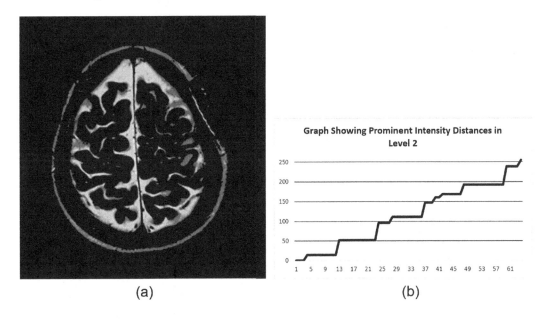

(a)   (b)

Generation of Horizontal and Vertical Edge Map

In the previous process, the enhanced image has been generated by using the level histogram of a desired level. In this part of the algorithms the horizontal edge map i.e. HozEdgeMapImage will be obtained using the aforesaid enhanced image. The process will scan the enhanced image in row major order. It will be started from the left most pixel from first row and terminated at the right most pixel of the last row. Here two consecutive pixels i.e. NewIntensity and NxtNewIntensity respectively are compared. If

Algorithm 5. Redraw the image using truncated histogram

```
REDRAW - IMAGE (Image, height, width, Tree, h₁, h)
Loop x ← 1 to height
   Do Loop y ← 1 to width
           Do    NewIntensity ← (Image [x, y] / (tNode (h) / tNode (h₁))) +
1
               If    Tree[iNode (h₁) + NewIntensity + 1].prominent ≠1
                     Then While Tree [iNode (h1) + NewIntensity + 1].prom-
inent ≠1
                                     Do    NewIntensity ← NewIntensity
- 1
               NewImage [x, y] ← NewIntensity
               y ← y + 1
       x ← x + 1
Return NewImage
```

the absolute value of the difference is greater than the MDT then the corresponding pixel position of the HozEdgeMapImage image will be set to 0 i.e. black else N i.e. white.

$$f\left(h\right) = \sum_{i=0}^{r}\sum_{j=0}^{c}P_{i,j} = \begin{cases} 0, & \left|P_{i,j} - P_{i+k,j}\right| > MDT \\ N, & \left|P_{i,j} - P_{i+k,j}\right| < MDT \end{cases}$$

Algorithm 6. Derive the horizontal edge of the image

```
HozEdgeMap (NewImage, height, width, MDT)
Loop x ← 1 to height
   Do flag← 1
       Loop y ← 1 to width
           Do If Flag = 1
                   Then   NewIntensity ←NewImage [x, y]
                 NxtNewIntensity ←NewImage [x, y]
               If    |NewIntensity − NxtNewIntensity |≥ MDT
               Then   Flag ← 1
                           HozEdgeMapImage [x, y] ← BLACK
               Else
                           Flag ← 0
                           HozEdgeMapImage [x, y] ← WHITE
                 y ←y + 1
       x←x + 1
Return HozEdgeMapImage
```

Figure 6. (a) Horizontal edge map and (b) vertical edge map in Level 2

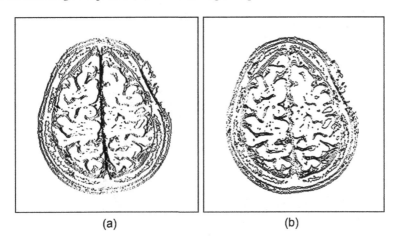

(a)   (b)

For vertical edge detection, algorithms is similar to the above horizontal edge detection algorithm except it sets pixels vertically i.e. in column major order rather than horizontally.

Generation of Final Edge Map

In previous two methods horizontal edge map and vertical edge map images has been obtained. In this process the horizontal and vertical edge map are superimposed in each other using logical OR operation.

$$EdgeMap = f\left(h\right) \vee f\left(v\right)$$

The superimposed output image will be the obtained edge of the medical image i.e. EdgeMapImage. It is the final outcome of the research paper which can be applicable to any medical image.

Algorithmic Complexity

The proposed Adaptive Edge Detection method is consist of seven discrete, sequential and mandatory algorithms. All the proposed algorithms are short, simple and dependent on the output of previous one.

Algorithm 7. Derive the edge of the image

```
EDGEMAP (HozEdgeMapImage, VerEdgeMapImage, height, width)
Loop x ← 1 to height
    Do Loop y ← 1 to width
            Do     EdgeMapImage [x, y] ←HozEdgeMapImage [x, y] OR VerEdge-
MapImage [x, y]
                    y ← y + 1
        x ← x + 1
Return EdgeMapImage
```

Figure 7. (a) Edge detection steps 1: The 6X6 pixel 2-D array of original image, (b) Edge detection steps 2: The 6X6 pixel 2-D array of image after performing the horizontal edge map image, (c) Edge detection steps 3: The 6X6 pixel 2-D array of image after performing the vertical edge map image and (d) Edge detection steps 4: The 6X6 pixel 2-D array of image after performing the Union showing complete edge map image

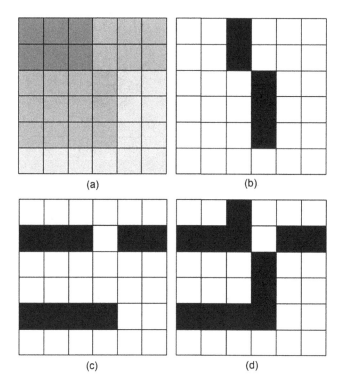

Figure 8. Derived edge of the MRI image in Level 2

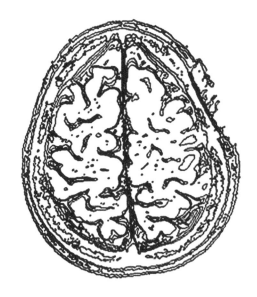

The method starts with the algorithm called ORGIGINAL-HISTOGRAM which captures the original medical image intensity information. The information are stored in leaf nodes. Here, the leaf node is starting from iNode (h) +1 to tNode (h) where h is the height of the tree. Assuming the image height = width = n then the running time of the algorithm is $\Theta(n^2)$ for all cases.

Now, the next algorithm i.e. LEVEL-HISTOGRAM is to propagate leaf node information to predecessor nodes i.e. internal nodes of the tree depending on the condition as stated. If it is assumed that the Tree with height h, the number of leaves is eNode (h) = 2^{h-1}, so, the outer loop will execute 2^{h-1} number of times. To traverse from a leaf to root, h-1 number of iteration is required. The inner loop will be executed (h – 1) times for each leaf node. So, the running time of the algorithm is exactly $\Theta(2^{h-1}.(h-1))$ for all cases i.e. Constant. The Average Bin Distance (ABD) is calculated by the algorithm entitled as BIN-DISTANCE. Here, if the Tree is height h, the loop will execute 2^{h-1} number of times at leaf node level whereas for intermediate level of Tree, loop will be executed in lesser number of times. Therefore, the upper bound of the running time will be $O(2^{h-1})$. The CALCULATE-MDT algorithm is to determine MDT by Identifying the Prominent Bins of specific level of the tree. The running time of the said algorithm is same as previous one i.e. $O(2^{h-1})$.

The next step of the method is to generate enhanced image from original medical image using RE-DRAW – IMAGE algorithm. If the height of the image h and width of the image w, then maximum number of iteration of loop is h * w. Thus, if h = w = n then the complexity of the above algorithm is $O(n^2)$. Algorithms to derive the Horizontal and Vertical Edge Map of the image, the running time will be always $O(n^2)$. Finally the Edge Map of the of the image is generated by EDGEMAP algorithm using horizontal and vertical edge maps and the algorithmic running time is also exactly $O(n^2)$. So, over all running time of the adoptive edge detection algorithm is $O(n^2)$.

EXPERIMENTAL RESULTS

Different medical images like digital radiograph, mammogram, MRI, computed tomography (CT scan) are used to obtain the results of the proposed algorithms. Here the proposed method is implemented on 247 number of digital radiograph images of chest lung nodules and non-nodules of the Japanese Society of Radiological Technology (JSRT) in cooperation with the Japanese Radiological Society (JRS), 322 number of mammogram images of the MIAS database, 485 number of mammogram images DEMS database, over 500 number of MRI and CT images of DICOM sample image sets provided by OsiriX and other medical images available in public domain. Apart from aforesaid medical dataset, the proposed algorithm is tested with some real life data given by some medical institutes but to maintain the medical ethics and anonymity of the patients those results are not considered for publication. For the experiment purpose different body parts are considered like breast, brain, chest, knee, abdomen, spine etc. to establish the robustness of the method. Some of the outputs of different types of medical images are cited in Figure 9 to Figure 12. After consulting with experts and by observation, it has been recognised in general that second level decomposition is most acceptable level for further investigation. In this level most of important edges are preserved leaving behind the redundant edges. Further decomposition may lead to loss of significant information related to edge. But at the same time different types of medical images like CT, MRI, Mammogram, Radiograph etc. exhibit best results in different levels depending on the body parts and the technical parameters like adaptive threshold etc.

Figure 9. Lung radiograph: (a) original image, (b) edge map with level 1 decomposition, (c) edge map with level 2 decomposition and (d) edge map with level 3 decomposition

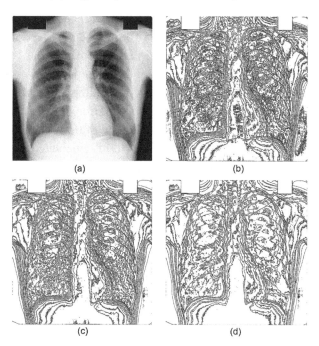

Figure 10. Breast mammogram: (a) original image, (b) edge map with level 1 decomposition, (c) edge map with level 2 decomposition and (d) edge map with level 3 decomposition

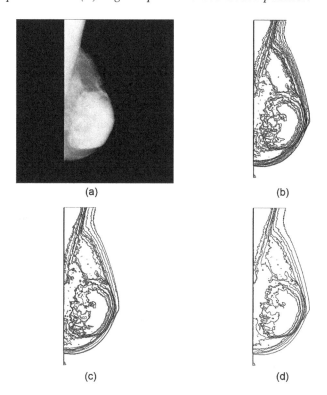

Figure 11. Knee MRI: (a) original image, (b) edge map with level 1 decomposition, (c) edge map with level 2 decomposition and (d) edge map with level 3 decomposition

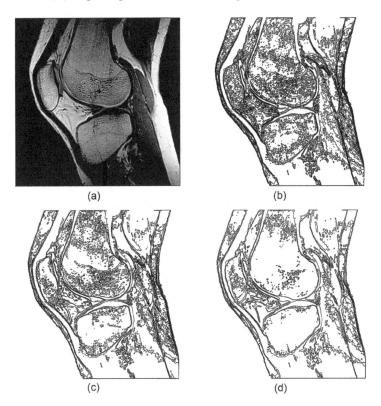

(a)   (b)

(c)   (d)

Figure 12. CT of abdomen with contrast: (a) original image, (b) edge map with level 1 decomposition, (c) edge map with level 2 decomposition and (d) edge map with level 3 decomposition

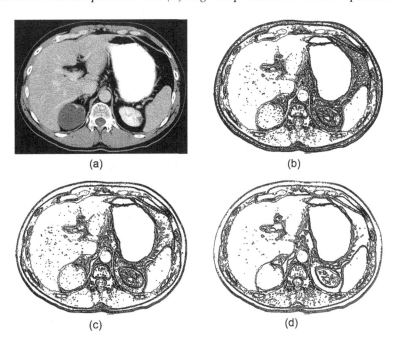

(a)   (b)

(c)   (d)

RESULTS EVALUATION

Performance evaluation in algorithm design is an important step that is commonly neglected. What constitutes an "acceptable" result differs significantly, and is often based on visual subjective opinion with very little quantitative endorsement (Maitra, Bhattacharjee, Bhattacharyya, Kim, & Bandyopadhyay, 2016). The accuracy is measured for the proposed algorithms using quantitative measures by comparing the obtained results representing an abnormality, as a "mask" with its equivalent "gold standard". The "gold standard" is obtained by manually drawing the region representing an abnormality within medical images. The boundary of the regions corresponding to the abnormality is manually traced by our medical expert to extract the region and generate a "ground truth (GT) image".

It is needed to derive a quantitative measure to get the accuracy of the proposed segmentation method. The "masks" derived is compared with the GT to obtain the measures of "True Positive (TP)","False Negative (FN)" and "False Positive (FP)"."True Positive" is denotes the intersection of obtained mask and GT indicating the actual match between the two. "False Negative" is the under-segmented region that is absent in "mask" whereas in "False Positive" it is the over segmented region that is absent in GT. By using these parameters on the output of all the images having abnormalities, the following results are obtained on different quality measures. As the GTs are obtained manually, there are some chances of human error. In view of that a standard estimated error rate may be $\pm 0.05\%$ in the following results.

COMPARATIVE ANALYSIS

The results obtained by the application of the proposed algorithm are compared with the results obtained from the six well-known classical methods namely, Roberts, Sobel, Prewitt, Kirsch, LoG and Canny. These six algorithms are considered as benchmark to standardise the proposed algorithm. The quality of the edge depends on probability of false edges, probability of missing edges, error in estimation of the edge angle, mean square distance of the edge estimate from the true edge, tolerance to distorted edges and other features such as corners and junctions. Considering the above facts, a relative comparison is done with proposed algorithm along-with benchmark algorithms. Initially, the mean value of the edge map pixel is obtained for all the algorithms by considering only the edge pixels that are present within

Table 1. Common measures used in the evaluation of the proposed method

Common Measures	Computation	Radiograph	Mammogram	MRI	CT
Accuracy (Percentage agreement)	ITNI+ITPI/ITNI+ITPI+IFPI+IFNI	0.9990	0.9992	0.9991	0.9995
Dice similarity coefficient (DSC)	2×ITPI/2×ITPI+IFPI+IFNI	0.9164	0.9446	0.9314	0.9668
Error rate	IFPI+IFNI/IFPI+IFNI+ITPI+ITNI	0.0009	0.0007	0.0008	0.0004
Sensitivity (Percentage of Correct Estimation)	ITPI/ITPI+IFNI	0.9606	0.9743	0.9680	0.9848
Specificity (True Negative Fraction/Rate)	ITNI/ITNI+IFPI	0.9521	0.9687	0.9609	0.9814
False Positive Fraction/Rate	1 – Specificity	0.0478	0.0312	0.0390	0.0185
Under estimation fraction (UEF)	IFNI/ITNI+IFNI	0.0004	0.0003	0.0003	0.0002
Over estimation fraction (OEF)	IFPI/ITNI+IFNI	0.0005	0.0004	0.0004	0.0002

the ROI of medical images. Table 2 shows the average relative frequencies of the detected edge pixels using the edge detection algorithms for the dataset. The ratio of edge pixels with respect to each other provides a definitive comparative statistics for the occurrence of edges.

These derived values are analysed using one sample two tail T-Test where Alpha is 0.025. A t-test is used in statistical hypothesis testing for checking whether the null hypothesis can be supported. It is used to determine, if two sets of data are significantly different from each other. The ratio of edge map pixels between each other as shown in the Table 3 is used to perform the one sample two tail t-test to show their relative acceptance.

Table 3 summarizes the t-test performed on the relative frequency for every method with other methods described. The result obtained show that there is no significant difference among Sobel, LoG, Canny and the proposed algorithm. The p-value of proposed algorithm shows a higher value in comparison with others. The t-statistics value of the proposed algorithm is very close to Sobel, LoG and Canny methods. It may be inferred that the edge map obtained from newly proposed method is acceptable.

The edge map obtained by the proposed algorithm is though similar to Sobel, LoG and Canny statistically but significantly better than them, as it forms a single pixel connected edge map rather than discrete edge pixels. This is extremely important for the image segmentation in medical image analysis. So, the occurrence of edge pixels that are connected with least sensitivity to noise is a remarkable achievement for the algorithm proposed in this research. The generalised comparative analysis of all the methods described including the proposed method is summarized in Table 4.

Table 2. Average of Relative Frequency (RF) of detected edge pixels

	Roberts	Sobel	Prewitt	Kirsch	LoG	Canny	Proposed Algorithm
Roberts	1	3.3216	7.2299	4.9079	3.9192	2.9313	2.6839
Sobel	0.3010	1	2.1766	1.4775	1.1799	0.8824	0.8080
Prewitt	0.1383	0.4594	1	0.6788	0.5420	0.4054	0.3712
Kirsch	0.2037	0.6767	1.4731	1	0.7985	0.5972	0.5468
LoG	0.2551	0.8475	1.8447	1.2522	1	0.7479	0.6848
Canny	0.3411	1.1331	2.4664	1.6743	1.3370	1	0.9156
Proposed Algorithm	0.3725	1.2376	2.6938	1.8286	1.4602	1.0921	1

Table 3. One sample two tail t-test result where α is 0.025

	Roberts	Sobel	Prewitt	Kirsch	LoG	Canny	Proposed Algorithm
Mean (μ)	0.2686	1.2793	2.9807	1.9699	1.5395	1.1094	1.0017
SD (s)	0.0877	1.0407	2.1266	1.4942	1.2152	0.9230	0.8461
Std Err	0.0358	0.4248	0.8681	0.6100	0.4961	0.3768	0.3454
t-Stat	7.5006	3.0110	3.4333	3.2292	3.1032	2.9442	2.8999
p-Value	0.0006	0.0297	0.0185	0.0232	0.0267	0.0320	0.0337
Significant Difference	Yes	No	Yes	Yes	No	No	No

Table 4. Comparison of the classical methods with the proposed method based on important parameters

Edge Operators	Convolution	Sensitivity to Noise	Single Pixel edge	Edge Continuity	Algorithm	Computational Time
Sobel	Yes	Yes	No	No	Simple	Slow
Roberts	Yes	Yes	No	No	Simple	Slow
Kirsch	Yes	Yes	No	No	Simple	Slow
Prewitt	Yes	Yes	No	No	Simple	Slow
LoG	Yes	No	No	No	Complex	Slow
Canny	No	No	No	No	Multi-Stage	Fast
Proposed Algorithm	No	No	Yes	Yes	Simple	Fast

CONCLUSION

Edge detection is very significant step in any image segmentation and analysis algorithm. Proper classification of regions based on local intensity characteristics leads to prominent edges that isolate different anatomical regions as separate objects. So, edge detection algorithm can be considered as pre-processing step towards feature extraction and abnormality detection. The proposed edge detection algorithm is capable to accommodate all types of medical images irrespective of make, brand and version. Due to its adaptive nature it is independent of common image properties like contrast, brightness etc. and produce same quality edge. Like all well accepted classical methods, the proposed algorithm is satisfying the conditions of edge quality discussed earlier. Moreover, the proposed algorithm produces edge map image that is single pixel continuous edge line so edge thinning process is eliminated. The continuity of the edge line in the proposed algorithm ensures that process of edge linking is unnecessary. In the proposed algorithm the abstraction of edge can also be determined by the use of the level of tree data structure. This feature, thus gives the freedom to the users in selection of range of bins to achieve the most appropriate results/outcome. It can be observed from the edge map image that each region within the body parts are clearly visible and isolated. The added advantage of this edge detection process is that it separated the ROI from the exterior background region. Experimentation results showed encouraging accuracy percentage with almost negligible values of over or under segmentation regions. Finally, the proposed algorithm is faster in execution time and less susceptible to noise to isolate regions. The average sensitivity and specificity of the proposed method is 0.97 and 0.96 respectively. The statistical analysis has proved that the derived edge map of the proposed method is very similar to other classical methods namely, LoG and Canny but it is significantly better than them due to its single pixel connected edge map which is very important for medical imaging.

ACKNOWLEDGMENT

The authors are obliged to Dr. Pradip Saha, MD, Radiology for his continuous participation in proposed work and Dr. Soma Chakraborty, MD, Radiology (Specialist in Mammography) for her expert opinions and comments. The authors are also appreciative to Mr. Sanjay Nag, Mr. Sumit Das and Ms. Sangita

Bhattacharjee for their contribution related to algorithm development, coding and documentation of the proposed work. The authors are especially grateful to Mr. Sisir Chatterejee for his expert opinions regarding mathematical and statistical modelling related to the proposed method.

REFERENCES

Bellotti, R., Carlo, F. D., Tangora, S., & Nunzio, G. D. (2006). A completely automated CAD system for mass detection in a large mammographic database. *Medical Physics*, *33*(8), 3066–3075. doi:10.1118/1.2214177 PMID:16964885

Bick, U., & Doi, K. (2000). Computer aided diagnosis tutorial on computer aided-diagnosis. CARS 2000, Hyatt Regency, San Francisco, CA.

Bottigli, U., Chiarucci, R., Golosio, B., Masala, G. L., Oliva, P., Stumbo, S., & Raso, G. et al. (2006). Superior performances of the neural network on the masses lesions classification through morphological lesion differences. *International Journal of Biomedical Science*, *1*(1), 56–63.

Canny, J. (1986). A computational approach to edge detection. *IEEE Transactions on Pattern Analysis and Machine Intelligence*, *8*(6), 679–698. doi:10.1109/TPAMI.1986.4767851 PMID:21869365

Cascio, D., Fauci, F., Magro, R., Raso, G., Bellotti, R., Carlo, F. D., & Torres, E. L. et al. (2006). Mammogram segmentation by contour searching and masses lesion classification with neural network. *IEEE Transactions on Nuclear Science*, *53*(5), 2827–2833. doi:10.1109/TNS.2006.878003

Cerello, P., Bagnasco, S., Bottigli, U., Cheran, S. C., Delogu, P., Fantacci, M. E., & Zanon, E. et al. (2005). GPCALMA: A grid based tool for mammographic screening. *Methods of Information in Medicine*, *44*(2), 244–248. PMID:15924184

Chang, C. Y. (2004). A contextual-based hopfield neural network for medical image edge detection. *IEEE International Conference on Multimedia and Expo (ICME)*. doi:10.1109/ICME.2004.1394374

Chidiac, H., & Ziou, D. (1999). *Classification of image edges. In Vision Interface 99* (pp. 17–24). Troise-Rivieres.

Davis, L. S. (1975). A survey of edge detection techniques. *Computer Graphics and Image Processing*, *4*(3), 248–260. doi:10.1016/0146-664X(75)90012-X

Doi, K., MacMahon, H., Katsuragawa, S., Nishikawa, R. M., & Jiang, Y. (1999). Computer-Aided diagnosis in radiology: Potential and pitfalls. *European Journal of Radiology*, *31*(2), 97–109. doi:10.1016/S0720-048X(99)00016-9 PMID:10565509

Frei, W., & Chen, C. (1977). Fast boundary detection: A generalization and a new algorithm. *IEEE Transactions on Computers*, *C-26*(10), 988–998. doi:10.1109/TC.1977.1674733

Giger, M. L., Huo, Z., Kupinski, M., & Vyborny, C. J. (2000). Computer-Aided diagnosis in mammography. In Handbook of Medical Imaging Medical Image Processing and Analysis. SPIE.

Gonzalez, R. C., & Woods, R. E. (2007). *Digital image processing* (3rd ed.). Upper Saddle River, NJ: Prentice Hall.

Gudmundsson, M., El-Kwae, E. A., & Kabuka, M. R. (1998). Edge detection in medical images using a genetic algorithm. *IEEE Transactions on Medical Imaging, 17*(3), 469–474. doi:10.1109/42.712136 PMID:9735910

Hajj, H. M., Nguyen, T. Q., & Chin, R. T. (1996). Multiscale edge detection for medical image enhancement. *18th Annual International Conference of the IEEE Engineering in Medicine and Biology Society.*

Huertas, A., & Medioni, G. G. (1986). Detection of intensity changes with sub pixel accuracy using laplacian-gaussian masks. *IEEE Transaction on Pattern Analysis and Machine Intelligence PAMI, 8*(5), 651–664. doi:10.1109/TPAMI.1986.4767838 PMID:21869362

Jassim, F. A. (2013). Semi-Optimal edge detector based on simple standard deviation with adjusted thresholding. *International Journal of Computers and Applications, 68*(2), 43–48. doi:10.5120/11555-6834

Ji, Q., & Haralick, R. M. (1999). Quantitative evaluation of edge detectors using the minimum kernel variance criterion.*ICIP 99, IEEE International Conference on Image Processing.*

Kao, C.-M., Pan, X., Hiller, E., & Chen, C.-T. (1998). A Bayesian approach for edge detection in medical ultrasound images. *IEEE Transactions on Nuclear Science, NS-45*, 3089–3098.

Karssemeijer, N., & Hendriks, J. H. C. L. (1997). Computer-Assisted reading mammograms. *European Radiology, 7*(5), 743–748. doi:10.1007/BF02742937 PMID:9166576

Kass, M., Witkin, A., & Terzopoulos, D. (1988). Snakes: Active contour models. *International Journal of Computer Vision, Kluwer Academic Publishers, 1*(4), 321–331. doi:10.1007/BF00133570

Lauria, A., Massafra, R., Tangaro, S. S., Bellotti, R., Delogu, F. P., Torres, E. L.,... Bottigli, U. (2006). GPCALMA: An Italian mammographic database of digitized images for research. *International Workshop on Breast Imaging Lecture Notes in Computer Science.* Springer. doi:10.1007/11783237_52

Lindeberg, T. (1998). Edge detection and ridge detection with automatic scale selection. *International Journal of Computer Vision, 30*(2), 117–156. doi:10.1023/A:1008097225773

Liu, L., Bland, P. H., Williams, D. M., Schunck, B. G., & Meyer, C. R. (1989). Application of robust sequential edge detection and linking to boundaries of low contrast lesions in medical images. *Computer Vision and Pattern Recognition, CVPR, 1989*, 582–587.

Maitra, I. K., Bhattacharjee, S., Bhattacharyya, D., Kim, T. H., & Bandyopadhyay, S. K. (2016). Adaptive edge detection technique towards features extraction from mammogram images. *Journal of Cancer Research Updates. LifeScience Global Publication, 5*(2), 47–58.

Marr, D., & Hildreth, E. (1980). Theory of edge detection. *Proceedings of the Royal Society of London. Series B, Biological Sciences, 207*(1167), 187–217. doi:10.1098/rspb.1980.0020 PMID:6102765

Masala, G., Tangaro, S., & Quarta, M. (2006). Classifiers trained on dissimilarity representation of medical pattern: A comparative study. *Il Nuovo Cimento C, 28*(6), 905–912.

Meyers, P. H., Nice, C. M. Jr, Becker, H. C., Nettleton, W. J. Jr, Sweeney, J. W., & Meckstroth, G. R. (1964). Automated computer analysis of radiographic images. *Radiology, 83*(6), 1029–1034. doi:10.1148/83.6.1029 PMID:14226800

Pellegrino, F. A., Vanzella, W., & Torre, V. (2004). Edge detection revisited. *IEEE Transactions on Systems, Man, and Cybernetics. Part B, Cybernetics, 34*(3), 1500–1518. doi:10.1109/TSMCB.2004.824147 PMID:15484920

Peng, J., & Rusch, P. H. (1991). Morphological filters and edge detection application to medical imaging.*The Annual Conference on Engineering in Medicine and Biology, 13*(1), 251-252. doi:10.1109/IEMBS.1991.683921

Prewitt, J. M. S. (1970). *Object enhancement and extraction. Picture processing and Psychopictorics.* Academic Press.

Roberts, L. G. (1965). Machine perception of 3-d solids. In Optical and Electro-Optical Information Processing. MIT Press.

Rosin, P. L., & Ioannidis, E. (2003). Evaluation of global image thresholding for change detection. *Pattern Recognition Letters, 24*(14), 2345–2356. doi:10.1016/S0167-8655(03)00060-6

Tasto, M. (1975). Automatische mammographie - Auswertung: Erkennung von Mikroverkalkungen. *Biomedizinische Technik, 20*, 273–274.

Technology Evaluation Center. (2002). *Computer-Aided Detection (CAD) in mammography.* Technology Assessment Program.

Thangam, S. V., SaiDeepak, K., Rai, H.G.N., & Mirajkar, P.P. (2009). An effective edge detection methodology for medical images based on texture discrimination. *Seventh International Conference on Advances in Pattern Recognition*, (pp. 227-231). doi:10.1109/ICAPR.2009.44

Vyborny, C. J., & Giger, M. L. (1994). Computer vision and artificial intelligence in mammography. *American Journal of Roentgenology, 162*(3), 699–708. doi:10.2214/ajr.162.3.8109525 PMID:8109525

Winsberg, F., Elkin, M., Macy, J. Jr, Bordaz, V., & Weymouth, W. (1967). Detection of radiographic abnormalities in mammograms by means of optical scanning and computer analysis. *Radiology, 89*(2), 211–215. doi:10.1148/89.2.211

Woods, N. C., Longe, O. B., & Roberts, A. B. C. (2012). A sobel edge detection algorithm based system for analysing and classifying image based spam. *Journal of Emerging Trends in Computing and Information Sciences, 3*(4), 506–511.

Yezzi, A., Kichenassamy, S., Kumar, A., Olver, P., & Tannenbaum, A. (1997). A geometric snake model for segmentation of medical imagery. *IEEE Transactions on Medical Imaging, 16*(2), 199–210. doi:10.1109/42.563665 PMID:9101329

Zeng, Y., Tu, C., & Zhang, X. (2008). Fuzzy-Set based fast edge detection of medical image. *Fuzzy Systems and Knowledge Discovery, 3*, 42–46.

Zhai, L., Dong, S., & Ma, H. (2008). Recent methods and applications on image edge detection. *Proceedings of the International Workshop on Education Technology and Training and International Workshop on Geoscience and Remote Sensing*. IEEE Computer Society. doi:10.1109/ETTandGRS.2008.39

Zhang, R., Ouyang, W., & Cham, W. K. (2009). Image edge detection using hidden Markov chain model based on the non-decimated wavelet. *International Journal of Signal Processing and Image Processing and Pattern, 2*(1), 109–118.

Chapter 8
Graph Theoretic Approaches for Image Analysis

Biplab Banerjee
Istituto Italiano Di Tecnologia, Italy

Sudipan Saha
SPANN Laboratory, India

Krishna Mohan Buddhiraju
IIT Bombay, India

ABSTRACT

Different graph theoretic approaches are prevalent in the field of image analysis. Graphs provide a natural representation of image pixels exploring their pairwise interactions among themselves. Graph theoretic approaches have been used for problem like image segmentation, object representation, matching for different kinds of data. In this chapter, we mainly aim at highlighting the applicability of graph clustering techniques for the purpose of image segmentation. We describe different spectral clustering techniques, minimum spanning tree based data clustering, Markov Random Field (MRF) model for image segmentation in this respect.

INTRODUCTION

Image analysis broadly refers to the techniques for extracting meaningful high level visual information from images. For example, given an image with several blob-like structures (Figure 1), the following questions are likely to arise:

- How many blobs are present in the image?
- What are the boundary pixels of each blob?
- Are the blobs of same kind?
- Do the blobs represent any natural clustering?

DOI: 10.4018/978-1-5225-1776-4.ch008

Figure 1. A typical image with multiple blobs

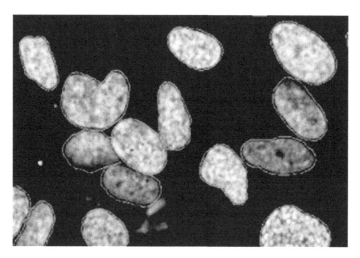

And the questions go on. However, in order to answer most of such questions, the first and foremost operation that needs to be performed on the image is undoubtedly *image segmentation*. Loosely speaking, segmentation is performed on an image to group the spatially consistent and spectrally or texturally homogeneous pixels together. The literature for image segmentation is very rich (Pal & Pal, 1993). There are hundreds of techniques for image segmentation involving thresholding, region merging, clustering jointly in the spatial-spectral domain etc. The main topic of the chapter, which is *graph based image analysis* provides an easy way of segmenting the image by exploiting the strengths of all the aforementioned techniques conveniently. This is one of the examples of the application of graphs in image analysis, which is arguably the most important one.

Apart from the domain of image analysis, graph based algorithms are very popular in all brunches of machine learning including:

- Classification (Goldberg, Zhu, & Wright, 2007),
- Manifold ranking (Yang, Zhang, Lu, Ruan, & Yang, 2013; Singer, 2006),
- Domain adaptation (Banerjee, Bovolo, Bhattacharya, Bruzzone, Chaudhuri, & Buddhiraju, 2015),
- Text summarization (Patil, Pharande, Nale, & Agrawal, 2015; Erkan & Radev, 2004) to name a few.

In image analysis, graphs are used for image filtering (Bougleux, Elmoataz, & Melkemi, 2007; Awate & Whitaker, 2006), morphology (Ta, Elmoataz, & Lézoray, 2011) in addition to the problem of image segmentation.

Going by the rich application domains and mathematical foundation, the highlight of the chapter will primarily be on the graph based algorithms for image segmentation. We have selected image segmentation as the task of segmentation is very important in computer vision as it bridges the semantic gap between low level pixels and high level semantic image objects. It is also one of the key stages towards visual scene understanding. Even after so many years from the inception of the topic, segmentation is still considered to be an open problem. Graph based image segmentation techniques allow joint spectral-spatial modeling of the images and pose the segmentation problem as an optimization problem. The main advantage of such methods over other image segmentation techniques is that the graph based segmentation methods are capable of preserving the image discontinuities while producing a smooth segmentation result. There are sophisticated graph algorithms which allow to model the segmentation problem from different perspectives. For example:

- The segmentation problem can be posed as a graph-cut problem at the pixel level so that similar pixels are grouped together at the cost of the pixels from different groups.
- Alternatively, the segmentation problem can be posed as graph node matching problem at the object level to segment out the similar objects while segmenting multiple images simultaneously. This is the standard co-segmentation problem.

Needless to mention, here we are interested in the unsupervised approaches for segmentation where the task is to group the similar image pixels together without being explicit about the semantic meanings of the clusters. In order to initiate this discussion, we will move in the following manner:

- We will first discuss how an image can efficiently be represented by a graph topology and why this is indeed a good representation. Further, we will mention a number of such graph topologies which are of interests.
- As graph based image segmentation essentially represents the underlying problem of graph clustering, next we will detail a number of powerful graph based data clustering paradigms in the light of *spectral clustering*, *minimum spanning tree based clustering* and the *max-flow min-cut* algorithm for Markov Random Field (MRF) models. We will try to mention the recent and relevant literatures in this respect.
- Finally, we will highlight some of the other interesting applications of graph for the purpose of image analysis.

Before actually diving deep into the main agenda of the chapter, a short discussion of some of the important concepts from graph theory (Bondy & Murty, 1976) is necessary to properly express the operations involved in the actual algorithms. This is further to note that, we will use natural images to show the effects of the algorithms. Table 1 mentions some of the frequently used mathematical symbols throughout the chapter. We will refer to these symbols unless explicitly specified.

A REFRESHER ON GRAPH THEORY

Formally, a graph G is represented by an ordered pair (V, E) where $V = \{V_1, V_2, ..., V_n\}$ represents the set of vertices (nodes) and $E = \{e_1, e_2, ..., e_m\}$ represents the set of edges (links). Ideally, an edge connects a pair of adjoining vertices. The edges can be weighted / unweighted, directed / undirected based on the given application.

Some of the basic paradigms related to graph theory are summarized in the following.

Table 1. Some frequent mathematical symbols used throughout the chapter

Mathematical Notation	Significance
$G(V,E)$	A graph with the vertex and edge set
m and n	Number of vertices and edges in the graph
$\mathcal{X} = \{X_1, X_2, ..., X_n\}$	A set of n data points
$T(V,E_T)$	The minimum spanning tree of G
$\{v_1, v_2, ..., v_n\}$	The set of vertices of $G(v_i = X_i)$
$\{e_1, e_2, ..., e_m\}$	The set of edges of G
κ	Number of clusters

- The number of edges connected to a given vertex denotes the *degree* of that vertex $(\deg(v_i))$. For a graph with n vertices, the maximum degree of a node is $n-1$. A vertex with degree 0 or 1 is known as the *isolated* or *pendant* vertex respectively.

It can be easily proved that the sum of the degrees of all the vertices is equal to twice the number of edges present in the graph.

$$\sum_{i=1}^{n} deg(v_i) = 2 * m$$

Further, it can be derived from the above result that the number of odd degree vertices in a graph is always even.

- For a directed graph, a vertex may have *in-degree* which counts the number of edges directed to that vertex and *out-degree* which counts the number of edges directed opposite to that vertex.
- If the degrees of all the vertices in V are equal, we call the corresponding G to be *regular*.
- If the degrees of all vertices in a graph are arranged in descending or ascending order, then the sequence obtained is known as the *degree sequence* of the graph.
- In a graph, if pair of vertices is connected by more than one edge, then those edges are called *parallel edges*. A graph having parallel edges is known as a *multi-graph*.
- In a graph, if an edge is drawn from vertex to itself, it is called a *loop*. A graph with no loops and no parallel edges is called a *simple graph*.
- A graph having no edges is called a *null graph*.
- A *path* in a graph is defined as an alternating sequence of vertices and edges. We say two vertices are *connected* if there exist a path between them. Otherwise, they are *disconnected*. Furthermore, if the starting and ending vertices of a path are similar, the path is called a *cycle*.

- A *walk* is a sequence of alternating vertices and edges, beginning and ending with vertices, where each edge's endpoints are the preceding and following vertices in the sequence. A walk is *closed* if its first and last vertices are the same and *open* if they are different.

- A subgraph(*H*) of *G* is a graph whose vertices are a subset of *V*. For a disconnected graph, each connected sub-graph represents a *connected component*.

- A complete subgraph is called a *clique*. If the deletion/addition of an additional node/edge fails to preserve the clique property, we call the clique to be a *maximum clique*.

- A simple graph $G=(V,E)$ with vertex partition $V=\{V_1,V_2\}$ is called a *bipartite graph* if every edge of E joins a vertex in V_1 to a vertex in V_2.

- A connected acyclic graph is called a *tree*. In addition, a disjoint collection of trees is called a forest.

- A *covering graph* is a subgraph which contains either all the vertices or all the edges corresponding to some other graph. A subgraph which contains all the vertices is called an *edge covering* whereas a subgraph which contains all the edges is called a *vertex covering*.

- A subset V_{cov} of V is called a *vertex covering* of G, if every edge of G is incident to or covered by a vertex in V_{cov}. A vertex covering V_{cov} of graph G is said to be *minimal vertex covering* if no vertex can be deleted from V_{cov}.

- A subgraph M of G is called a *matching M(G)* if each vertex of G is incident to at most one edge in M. It alternatively means that the degree of each node in M is either 0 or 1. The matching is said to be maximal if no other edge of G can be added to M.

- A graph can exist in different forms having the same number of vertices, edges along with the same edge connectivity. Such graphs are called *isomorphic graphs*.

Broadly, the relevant notions from the graph theoretical point of view are mentioned above. A detailed study of the same can be found in (West, 2001). Many real world problems can be posed as graph analysis problems. There are certain polynomial algorithms to solve many of such problems whereas some of them are NP-hard in nature. However, those problems have direct connection to the traditional machine learning or image analysis problems. Some of them are:

- **The Identification of the Shortest Path between a Pair of Nodes in a Graph:** We can further generalize the problem as: single source shortest and and all pair shortest path. We will see that the min-cut problem, which is a way to perform graph based clustering can alternatively be solved as a max-flow problem from a source to a sink node throughout the graph.

- **To Check whether Two Graphs Are Isomorphic:** The problem can be tackled in different ways for directed and undirected graphs. For unweighted graph, the graph topology is explored for this purpose. Whereas for the case of weighted graphs, the edge weights are also considered in conjunction to the graph topology. In many cases, it is required to match some portions of a pair of graphs. This is known as *subgraph isomorphism*. (Sub)graph isomorphism can be used to match similar image objects from multiple images. Applications like stereo matching (Bleyer & Gelautz, 2007), domain adaptation for the classification of remote sensing image pairs (Banerjee et al., 2015) make use of the graph isomorphism explicitly.

- **To Find the Distance between Two Graphs:** The distance between two graphs can be calculated in term of a graph kernel. The graph kernels usually explore the similarities in the number of random walks, the number of isomorphic subgraphs or the number of maximum common subgraphs to perform the matching task (Airola et al., 2008) (Bunke & Shearer, 1998). In addition, there are some approaches where one of the graphs is transformed by a set of primitive operations to construct the other graph. The minimum number of such operations required form a measure of similarity in this respect (e.g. graph edit distance (Neuhaus & Bunke, 2007)).

There are many such interesting problems other than the aforementioned ones. There are many problems like the Traveling Salesman Problem (TSP), which, if transformed to a graph theoretic representation, allows trivial solutions. In this chapter, we are primarily interested about the graph-cut problem which aims at removing a set of edges from a connected graph to generate a number of connected components. The problem is combinatorial in nature, hence, quickly becomes exponential as the number of edges increases in the graph. However, there are some approximation algorithms which provide polynomial time solution to the graph-cut problem. Our motive is to discuss a few such approximation algorithms.

Prior to that, let us first observe how we can obtain the corresponding graph based representation of an image. Further, we will see that the image segmentation problem is indeed equivalent to the graph-cut problem. Then the actual algorithms will be discussed.

IMAGE REPRESENTATION USING GRAPHS

Coming back to the application of graphs in image analysis, let us first consider the case of representing a set of data items using graph. We will straightway consider that the image pixels are the data items in this chapter. However, any vector can be the data item while being represented by a graph topology. Specifically in the domain of image analysis, it is assumed that each pixel shares its properties with the neighborhood pixels. Graph topologies can capture this neighborhood information in the underlying graph structure inherently. As a result, such adjacent pixels are connected by edges whereas the edges are weighted by the difference of the spectral properties of the corresponding pixels. In this way, graph structures are capable of jointly modeling the spatial-spectral properties of the image jointly.

In Figure 2, eight immediate neighbors of the pixel p can be observed and it is expected all these pixels share almost similar characteristics unless some of the pixels are edge pixels. We can connect the 8-neighbors of p with p to form a local graph. A connection of such local graphs produces a global grid-graph based representation of the image.

Formally, let us consider a set of n data items, defined by the notation $\mathcal{X} = \{X_1, X_2, ..., X_n\}$ where $X_i \in \mathbb{R}^d$ for d-dimensional Euclidean space. Graph based representation allows to model these n data items in an organized fashion preserving the locality structure efficiently. Extending the previous notation, let us consider that data points are represented by the nodes of $G(V=\chi)$. The edges define the links between the data items. If it is required that the closest pair of data points need to be connected, then E is modeled accordingly. The edge weight (E_w) can be defined based on some of the valid distance measures (L_p-norm, Gaussian Radial Basis Function distance etc.) between a pair of data items (X_i, X_j).

Specifically for a color image (I), we can consider that χ represents the pixels of I and each pixel consists of the spectral values in a 3-dimensional space. Let us further consider that each pixel is connected to the pixels in its 4 or 8-neighborhood. This gives a grid graph representation of I (Figure 3).

It is clear from the above discussion that based on the application at hand, different graph topologies are possible. Some of them which are widely used in machine learning and image analysis are:

Figure 2. The concept of 8-neighborhood in an image

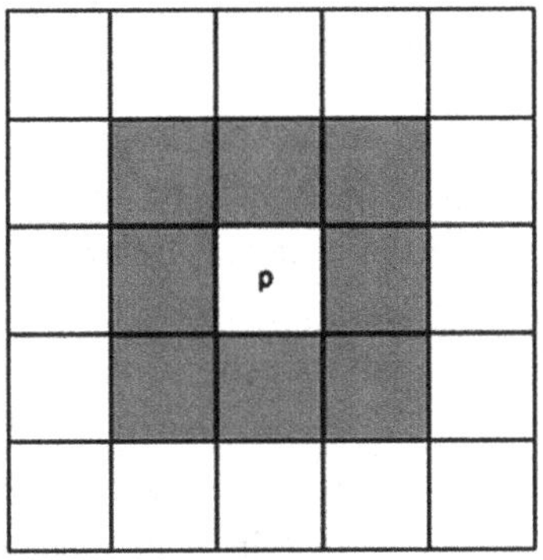

Figure 3. Grid graph representation of an image

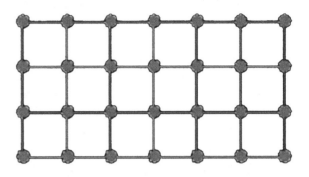

- **Complete Graph:** If there exists an edge $e \in E$ for every pair of the vertices $(v_i, v_j), v_i, v_j \in V$, we call G to be a complete graph.
- **Nearest Neighbor Graph:** In this case, every vertex is connected to its nearest vertex in the space. For instance, we already mentioned the situation where every pixel is connected to its 4 or 8-neighbors. Similar idea can be used to find the closest points in a feature space.
- **ϵ-Neighborhood Graph:** According to the ϵ-neighborhood topology, a node is connected to all the nodes within a distance of ϵ. Alternatively, we can say the the maximum edge weight possible in this case is ϵ.
- **Spanning Tree:** The sub-graph H of simple graph G is called a spanning tree of G if:
  - H is a tree.
  - H   contains all vertices of G.

Kirchoff's theorem is useful in finding the number of spanning trees that can be formed from a connected graph.

A minimum spanning tree of a weighted graph is the spanning tree having least cumulative edge weight. It is clear from the discussion that several spanning trees are possible for a given graph. There exist two well-known greedy algorithms for constructing the minimum spanning tree for a graph - *Prim's* and *kruskal's* algorithm (Kruskal, 1956) in $O(|V|+|E|)$. We will discuss in detail regarding the construction of spanning tree for a graph in subsequent sections.

Given a graph G which is constructed based on a topology, the next step is to represent and store G efficiently in a computer. Two of the traditional graph representation strategies are:

- **Adjacency Matrix:** For a graph with n vertices, the corresponding adjacency matrix (A) is an $n \times n$ matrix where each row or column represents a node. For a weighted graph, each entry of A represents the weight of the edge connecting the corresponding vertices. For a unweighted graph, the entries are either 0 or 1 representing the absence or presence of an edge between a pair of vertices. The matrix is symmetric, positive-semi-definite for a undirected graph.

This representation is easier to implement and follow. Removing an edge takes $O(1)$ time. Queries like whether there is an edge from vertex v_i to vertex v_j can efficiently be done in $O(1)$. At the same time, it consumes space in the order of $O(n^2)$.

- **Adjacency List:** An array of linked lists with size n is used in this case. The ith entry in the array represents the linked list of vertices adjacent to the ith vertex. This representation can also be used to represent a weighted graph. The weights of edges can be stored in nodes of linked lists.

Graph based representations for images are possible at multiple levels. At the primitive level, we construct a grid-graph over image pixels. However, the size of the graph adjacency matrix increases with the resolution of the image. Further, for a grid-graph representation, the adjacency matrix is inherently sparse. Hence, the grid-graph representation is not encouraged in practice due to its poor space handling. Hence, graph representations are preferred at higher level on image objects as numbers of objects are always far less than the number of pixels present in the image.

Let us consider a simple example of multi-level image segmentation. Given a color image I where each pixel x_{ij} is represented by three color channels, the final goal is to assign a class label to each such pixel, as already explained. For images with high spatial resolutions, it is not recommended to use a single level segmentation strategy to segment I as the segmentation may get affected by the presence of spurious edges in the image. Multi-level segmentation is useful in such scenarios which partitions the image in successive stages. Let us consider such a typical case where the image is initially over-segmented by some spatial segmentation strategy line *watershed transform*, *mean-shift* etc. Currently, the smallest entity is an image region obtained from the spatial segmentation. If we perform a merging of such small segments based on graph clustering, first we need build a graph with the regions as nodes and by defining appropriate edge weights on some feature space. There are two alternatives possible in this respect:

- The graph can be defined in the feature space, i.e. a pair of regions, which are close in the underlying feature space are connected by an edge.
- The graph can be defined in the image space, i.e., pair of regions are connected by an edge if they are closely located in the spatial domain. However, their feature difference can be used in this case to define the corresponding edge weight.

Figure 4 depicts a Region Adjacency graph (RAG) of the superpixels obtained from an image. Superpixel segmentation is a type of over-segmentation to the image which divided the whole image into a number of small quasi-homogeneous regions. Graph clustering can be adopted to perform merging of the super-pixels efficiently. RAG is another popular graph topology used specifically in this respect where adjacent regions are connected by edges. Through graph clustering, we can decide further where we can merge a number of adjoining regions to make bigger regions.

The number of edge connection will vary based on the specific topology chosen to construct the graph. Some sophisticated graph clustering technique can be used now to cluster the regions efficiently.

As highlighted above, the graph clustering problem is analogous to the graph-cut problem. We will now discuss the graph-cut problem and mention a number of cut measures in this regard. A good cut measure avoids irregular shaped clusters and handles outliers properly.

Figure 4. The region adjacency graph from image pixels

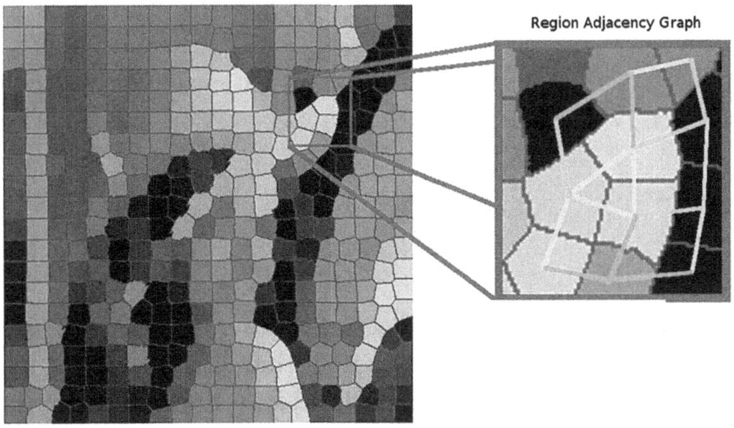

THE IDEA OF *CUT* IN A GRAPH AND ITS RELATION TO DATA CLUSTERING

Given the above definitions, let us define the notion of a *cut* in a graph. This is important because the idea of graph-cut is closely related to the problem of data clustering using a graph. Let us look at the problem more closely.

Let us again consider that we are given a set of data items $\chi = \{X_i\}_{i=1}^n$ where $X_i \in \mathbb{R}^d$. Let us also assume that the data come from κ clusters. According to the definition of data clustering, the idea is to obtain the κ subgroups by exploiting the data.

Given such a scenario, we first build a weighted graph $G(V,E)$ using χ as the node set and any of the aforementioned topologies. It is understood that the edges connecting data items from the same cluster have less weight measures than the edges connecting data items from different clusters. The idea of graph based clustering is to identify such *inconsistent* edges which span multiple clusters and remove them. Alternatively, this is equivalent to the problem of *graph cut*.

A cut in G can be of two types:

- A vertex $v_i \in V$ is called a *cut vertex* of a simple graph $G(V,E$, if $V-v$ (set-difference of V and v_i) results in a disconnected graph. Removing a cut vertex from a graph breaks it in to two or more subgraphs.
- An edge $e_i \in E$ is called a *cut edge* if of G if $E-e_i$ results in a disconnected graph. Data clustering is analogous to finding the inconsistent cut edges from the graph.

One of the well-known graph based clustering techniques which is spectral clustering is mostly based on the solution of the graph-cut problem. In order to achieve such a goal, the spectral clustering algorithms use a subset of eigenvectors from the Laplacian matrix of the corresponding graph to be partitioned that are solutions for the relaxation of some graph-cut problem.

In this context, the κ-way partitioning problem deals with the elimination of the edges from the graph in order to produce κ subgraphs (clusters). Different criteria can be considered while highlighting the set of edges to be eliminated. We will discuss a number of such measures next.

Let us consider first that $W(C_r, C_t) = \sum_{v_i \in C_r, v_j \in C_t} A_{ij}$ defines the total edge weights connecting the subgraphs C_r and C_t.

In view of the above, the *min-cut* problem with respect to the -way graph partitioning aims at choosing a partition $\{C_1, C_2, \ldots, C_K\}$ and is defined as:

$$cut(C_1, C_2, \ldots, C_k) = \frac{1}{2} \sum_{i=1}^{k} W(C_i, C_{i'})$$

Here the factor 1/2 is introduced for notational consistency to ensure that each edge is counted exactly once. Min-cut problem is generally easy to solve for $\kappa = 2$. However, for larger κ, the solution becomes difficult. It may even happen that a cluster with a single vertex is formed. As a remedy to this problem, a size constraint is introduced to the min-cut formulation. There are two variants to the simple min-cut in this regard, called *ratio-cut* and *normalized-cut*:

$$ratio\text{-}cut(C_1, C_2, \ldots, C_K) = \frac{1}{2} \sum_{i=1}^{K} \frac{W(C_i, C_{i'})}{|C_i|}$$

$$normalized\text{-}cut(C_1, C_2, \ldots, C_K) = \frac{1}{2} \sum_{i=1}^{K} \frac{W(C_i, C_{i'})}{vol(C_i)}$$

where $|C_i|$ and $vol(C_i)$ denotes the number of nodes in c_i and the sum of degrees of all the nodes in C_i. Both the aforementioned objective functions try to perform a *balanced* cut of G. However, introduction of this balancing condition makes then min-cut problem NP-hard. In addition, the graph-cut problem is explicitly combinatorial in nature. Spectral clustering is one of the ways to solve the relaxed versions of these problems. Relaxing normalized-cut leads to normalized spectral clustering. Relaxing ratio-cut leads to unnormalized spectral clustering.

GRAPH BASED DATA CLUSTERING TECHNIQUES

In this section, we will deal with different graph based data clustering techniques with the application to image segmentation. Specifically, we will consider three spectral graph clustering techniques, namely, *min-cut*, *ratio-cut* and *normalized-cut* and the minimum spanning tree based graph clustering technique.

To give the users a little more insight on the graph based clustering techniques, consider the data points of Figure 5. The data are spread in two half-moon structure. It can be observed that data from two different classes are present in the space. We can come to this conclusion by observing the pairwise similarities of the points. Now consider that k-means or fuzzy c-means clustering is used to cluster the points. It is highly unlikely that such clustering methods will be able to cluster the data in the desired shape because for distance based clustering techniques, the data within the rectangles are close to each other. However, in real scenario, this is something we are not looking for. Hence, the only option to take into account the pairwise similarities is through the graph structure.

Figure 5. A sample dataset and the corresponding graph based clustering

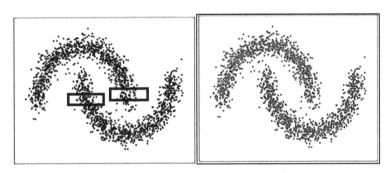

Spectral Graph Clustering

The set of eigenvalues of an adjacency matrix represents the spectrum of the corresponding graph. The spectrum is a very important factor in the study of similarity between two graphs. If two graphs are similar, then the adjacency matrix of one can be viewed as a permutation operator implemented on the other, thus their eigenvalues are the same. The goal of spectral clustering is to cluster data that is connected but not necessarily compact or clustered within convex boundaries. Alternatively, given a set of n points (pixels) in some d -dimensional feature-space with pairwise similarities encoded into the weighted adjacency matrix A, the goal of spectral clustering is to partition the data into groups through the process of Eigen-space projection so that points within a group are similar and points in different groups are dissimilar.

Let us look at the term *similar* more closely. Affinity or similarity is a metric that determines how close two points are in the feature space. In general, any distance measure in the Euclidean space can be used for this purpose. Alternatively, it is possible to learn a distance metric in a supervised fashion. This learning process models the distance measures emphasizing the relevant features of the data samples effectively. The domain of metric learning is very vast and is equipped with a number of good algorithms. A detailed survey of distance metric learning can be obtained in the work by Yang and Jin (2006). We will consider throughout this chapter that we already have a metric for the distance measure.

Gaussian RBF kernel is one of the most popular distance measures used. From the graph theoretic terminology, given a pair of points X_i and X_j, the entry in the corresponding weighted adjacency matrix A_{ij} is obtained through the RBF distance measure. It is also possible to learn the matrix A from the available data (Jordan & Bach, 2004).

For Gaussian RBF kernel $(A_{ij} \to 1)$ if the points are close enough in the feature space and 0 otherwise. This is similar to the statement that the distance values are high for the samples in the same cluster whereas low for the samples in different clusters. Further, this kernel accounts for the irregularities in the data well. However, it is possible that samples in the same cluster reside far apart in the feature space. We aim at transforming the space in such a situation in order to preserve our notion for cluster formation.

Apart from using the Gaussian RBF kernel directly, it is possible to accomplish the task using the notion of graph Laplacian.

Spectral clustering requires the definition of a graph Laplacian and the idea of Eigenvalue decomposition of a symmetric matrix. we will cover these topics first and then will proceed to the spectral graph clustering algorithms.

Eigenvalue Decomposition Problem

A vector τ of dimension $(d \times 1)$ is an eigenvector of a square matrix $A_{n \times n}$ iff it satisfies the linear equation

$$A\tau = \lambda\tau$$

where the scalar term λ is known as the eigenvalue corresponding to τ. Broadly speaking, the vector τ is special in the sense that it only gets extended or shortened when transformed by the matrix A.

Given a matrix A, the corresponding eigenvalue-eigenvector pairs can be obtained by solving the *characteristic polynomial* equation, solutions of which are eigenvalues of A and the set of all the eigenvalues is called the *spectrum* of A. For each λ, we can calculate the corresponding eigenvectors analytically.

The number of times that each λ occurs in the solution to the characteristic equation defines the *algebraic multiplicity* of that eigenvalue. Secondly, since, for an eigenvalue λ, we have $\det(A-\lambda I)=0$, i.e. $(A-\lambda I)$ is a singular matrix, and the linear transformation it defines has a non-trivial kernel. The dimension of this kernel is then said to be the *geometric multiplicity* of the eigenvalue.

The eigenvalue decomposition of A is given by

$$A = Q\Lambda Q^{-1}$$

where the ith column of Q is the eigenvalue τ_i of A and Λ is the diagonal matrix whose diagonal elements are the corresponding eigenvalues.

The product of the eigenvalues of A is equal to $\det(A)$ and the sum of the eigenvalues signifies the *trace* of A. The eigenvectors of A and A^{-1} are the same.

The Concept of Graph Laplacian

In addition to simply representing a graph G, the adjacency matrix A associated with G also serves two other purposes. It acts as an operator mapping a vector X to the vector AX and it is used to define a quadratic form mapping X to $X^T A X$. Laplacian matrix is the most natural choice when defining a quadratic form.

Let $D_{n \times n}$ be the degree matrix of the graph $G(V,E)$ with n nodes where each node denotes a data point X_i in some d-dimension. It is to be noted that we will use the notation X_i or v_i to refer to the ith data point or the ith node of G alternatively as they represent the same quantity. D is a diagonal matrix where each diagonal element represents the degree of the corresponding node in G. If $A_{n \times n}$ is the weighted adjacency matrix of G calculated, the unnormalized graph Laplacian L is then defined as $L=D-A$.

It can be proved that the graph Laplacian is the lower order approximation of the RBF kernel.

There are some very important and interesting properties of L apart from being a symmetric and positive semi-definite matrix which have direct consequences to the spectral clustering paradigm. Let us look at them more closely.

- According to the *Matrix-Tree* theorem (Mohar, Alavi, Chartrand, & Oellermann, 1991), for a pair of vertices (v_i, v_j) of G the absolute value of the determinant of the reduced L (unnormalized

Laplacian) produced with elimination of the ith row and the jth column of L is equal to the number spanning trees of G.

- Given a function f on the vertices of the graph, the Laplacian quadratic form is:

$$f^T L f = \sum_{(u,v) \in E} (f(u) - f(v))^2$$

From the above equation, it is obvious that Laplacian can be used to measure the smoothness of function f and the above quadratic form is non-negative. If we let f to be a constant vector, then the quadratic form evaluates to 0. So, smallest eigenvalue of the Laplacian (λ_1) is 0.

- It can be proved that a graph G has κ connected components iff algebraic multiplicity of the smallest eigenvalue (0) in the Laplacian is κ. Here connected component (for an undirected graph) is defined as a connected subgraph such that no edge links any vertex of the subgraph with rest of the graph. The proof is beyond the scope of this chapter, but sacrificing some mathematical rigor it can be said that when G has κ connected components, its Laplcian matrix can be decomposed into a block diagonal matrix with κ blocks, each with eigenvalue 0 having multiplicity 1. Algebraic multiplicity of 0 for the entire Laplacian matrix is equal to sum of algebraic multiplicity for each blocks, thus equal to the number of blocks. Further, if the vertices i and j are connected, then in one of the eigenvectors corresponding to the eigenvalue 0, i^{th} and j^{th} component will be set to 1.
- Using the above properties, Laplacian matrix can be used for data clustering. The idea is to construct a graph from the dataset such that different clusters belong to different connected component. Then we can look at the multiplicity of the eigenvalue 0 to discover number of different connected components and the eigenvectors corresponding to those to find the connected vertices. The main challenge lies in constructing the graph so that connected components reflects different clusters, as performance of clustering will entirely depend on it. One simple but effective approach is building a k-NN graph where each point in dataset corresponds to a vertex of the graph and an edge exists between it and its k nearest neighbors.
- The most remarkable advantage of the cluster discovery using above approach is that the discovered clusters capture shape of clusters much better than mere Euclidean distance based approaches.
- As obvious from the above discussion, if the graph is not connected, second smallest eigenvalue (λ_2) is also equal to 0. But here we are more interested to explore the significance of λ_2 when the graph is completely connected and hence $\lambda_2 > 0$. λ_2 is related to the task of dividing a graph into two pieces without cutting too many edges, i.e. graph partitioning..
- Let H be a subset of vertices of graph G. Let $\partial(H)$ denote set of all the edges connecting H to rest of the graph. We can define a ratio called isoperimetric ratio, as:

$$\theta(H) = |\partial(H)| / |H|$$

- Then the isoperimetric number or Cheeger constant is defined as:

$$\theta_G = \min_{|S| \leq n/2} \theta(S)$$

where n is number of vertices of G. Intuitively, Cheeger constant is an index to measure how well connected a graph is. If the Cheeger constant is small in magnitude, then there exist two large sets of vertices with only few edges between them. Larger Cheeger constant indicates any possible partition of graph into two parts will have a lot of edges between them.

- Interestingly it can be shown that $\theta_G \geq \lambda_2 / 2$. The proof is beyond the scope of this chapter, but readers can refer to the work by Bondy and Murty (1976). Thus larger λ_2 implies larger θ_G, which implies well connected graph. Fiedler (1973) called λ_2 as *algebraic connectivity* of a graph. Further it can be shown that the eigenvector τ_2 corresponding to the eigenvalue λ_2 can be used to provide an assignment to each vertex of the graph for optimal partitioning of the graph.
- λ is an eigenvalue of L_G with eigenvector of τ if and only if λ is an eigenvalue of L_N with eigenvector $D^{1/2}\tau$.
- λ is an eigenvalue of L_G with eigenvector τ if and only if λ and τ solve the generalized eigenproblem $L\tau = \lambda D\tau$.
- 0 is an eigenvalue of L_G with the constant vector 1 as eigenvector and is the same for L_N with eigenvector $D^{1/2}1$.

The Generalized Spectral Clustering Problem

We will now discuss three spectral clustering algorithms, namely, the unnormalized case and the normalized algorithms of (Ng, Jordan, & Weiss, 2002; Shi & Malik, 1998).

In each of the algorithms, it is considered that a set of data points χ is represented by a weighted graph $G(V,E)$ where the graph structure follows some predefined topology. The task is to cluster χ into κ clusters using the spectral clustering method.

Given this, the first algorithm of spectral clustering for unnormalized Laplacian is mentioned as follows:

1. Project the data χ into $G(V,E)$, i.e. each X_i is denoted by v_i.
2. Define a graph adjacency (affinity) matrix A using any distance measure.
3. Construct the graph Laplacian from A.
4. Solve an Eigenvalue decomposition problem $L\tau = \lambda D\tau$ where (λ,τ) represents the eigenvalue-eigenvector pair).
5. Select κ eigenvectors corresponding to the κ smallest eigenvalues to define a κ dimensional subspace.
6. Perform clustering in this subspace using k-means.
7. This gives an approximation of the clustering of the data in the original space.

The method by (Ng et al., 2002) is based on the generalized normalized Laplacian L_G. L_G is also known as the random walk Laplacian. The algorithm is summarized as the following:

1. Project the data χ into $G(V,E)$, i.e. each X_i is denoted by v_i.
2. Define a graph adjacency (affinity) matrix A using any distance measure.
3. Construct the graph Laplacian from A.
4. Solve an Eigenvalue decomposition problem $L\tau = \lambda D\tau$ where (λ,τ) represents the eigenvalue-eigenvector pair).

5. Select κ eigenvectors corresponding to the κ smallest eigenvalues to define a κ dimensional subspace.
6. Perform clustering in this subspace using k-means.
7. This gives an approximation of the clustering of the data in the original space.

Finally, the algorithm by Shi and Malik (1998) is given for L_N in the following manner:

1. Project the data χ into $G(V,E)$, i.e. each X_i is denoted by v_i.
2. Define a graph adjacency (affinity) matrix A using any distance measure.
3. Construct the graph Laplacian from A.
4. Compute the first κ eigenvector of L_N. Let $U \in \mathbb{R}^{n \times \kappa}$ be the matrix containing the eigenvectors as columns.
5. A new matrix $T \in \mathbb{R}^{n \times \kappa}$ is formed by normalizing the rows of U to 1.
6. Perform clustering of T in this subspace using k-means.
7. This gives an approximation of the clustering of the data in the original space.

All of the aforementioned algorithms look rather similar, apart from the fact that they use three different graph Laplacians. The main trick in all the cases is to change the representation of the data points $X_i \in \mathbb{R}^d$ to the points $Y_i \in \mathbb{R}^\kappa$. This change of representation is indeed useful as it enhances the cluster properties in the data so that the clusters can be represented well in the new induced feature space and further be detected by any traditional clustering algorithm.

The graph topology selected for a specific application sometimes makes the graph-cut problem easier to handle. We prefer a representation which is minimum as well as connected as it allows the handling less amount of data and direct inference is possible in polynomial time. We will consider such a topology, the minimum spanning tree in this respect and will mention how simple clustering algorithms can be designed specifically for MST.

Figure 6 depicts a number of segmentation results based on the multi-level normalized-cut approach (Shi & Malik, 2000).

A Graph-Cut View of Spectral Clustering

Given that the data clustering problem in the feature space is equivalent to the graph-cut problem, spectral clustering can be derived as an approximation to such graph partitioning problem effectively.

If we consider ratio-cut minimization problem, given a partition V into sets C_1, C_2, C_k of n data items in χ, we define κ indicator vectors

$$h_j = (h_{1,j}, ..., h_{n,j})', 1 \leq j \leq \kappa,$$

by

$$h_{i,j} = \begin{cases} \dfrac{1}{\sqrt{|C_j|}}, & \text{if } v_i \in C_j \\ 0, & \text{otherwise} \end{cases}$$

Figure 6. Some segmentation outputs based on normalized-cut
Source: Shi & Malik, 2000.

Then we can define a combined matrix $H \in \mathbb{R}^{n \times \kappa}$ as the matrix containing those κ indicator vectors in its columns. Columns in H are orthonormal to each other, hence, $H'H = I$. It can be shown that

$$\frac{cut(C_i, C_{i'})}{|A_i|} = h_{i'} L h_i = (H'LH)_{ii}$$

So,

$$ratio\text{-}cut(C_1, C_2, ..., C_\kappa) = \sum_{i=1}^{\kappa} (H'LH)_{ii} = Tr(H'LH)$$

Now, if we relax the problem by allowing entries of matrix H to take any arbitrary real value, the problem of minimizing

$$RatioCut(C_1, C_2, ..., C_\kappa)$$

becomes:

$$\min_{H \in \mathbb{R}^{n \times \kappa}} Tr(H'LH) \text{ subject to } H'H = I$$

The above equation is a standard trace minimization problem, which can be solved by Rayleigh-Ritz theorem and solution is given by matrix H containing first κ eigenvectors of L as columns. Thus matrix H is subspace-projected used in the unnormalized spectral clustering algorithm. Thus relaxation of ratio-cut leads to unnormalized spectral clustering algorithm. Similarly it can be shown that approximating normalized-cut leads to normalized spectral clustering algorithm.

MINIMUM SPANNING TREE BASED CLUSTERING

The minimalistic graph representation for a set of data items in a structured fashion is undoubtedly the minimum spanning tree (MST). A spanning tree of a graph is just a subgraph that contains all the vertices and is a tree. A graph may have many spanning trees. Further, for a weighted graph, many spanning trees are possible with different cumulative edge weights. However, we are interested in the one with minimum cumulative edge weight. This specific tree is known as the MST. There may be several minimum spanning trees of the same weight having a minimum number of edges. In particular, if all the edge weights of a given graph are the same, then every spanning tree of that graph is minimum.

This representation is very popular due to certain reasons:

- As compared to other graph topologies, MST contains the least number of edges. So, inference can be performed on an MST in polynomial time in all the cases.
- However, MST based graph-cut is extremely easy. Deletion of an edge from the MST makes the tree disconnected. From the point of view of data clustering, this is quite exciting as the deletion of each edge is equivalent to the construction of a new cluster. Further, the MST based clustering resembles the hierarchical clustering where a root dataset is iteratively divided into a number of base clusters.

Apart from its usage in in efficient data representation and data clustering, MST is hugely popular in domains like Taxonomy, Bio-informatics, Circuit design etc.

Given a weighted graph $G(V,E)$, there are multiple ways to obtain the minimum spanning tree:

- A randomized algorithm is expected to obtain the same in linear time (Karger, Klein, & Tarjan, 1995). Such algorithms generally employ a random sampling technique along with some linear-time verification algorithms to obtain the MST of the underlying graph. A *provably optimal deterministic comparison based minimum spanning tree algorithm* is developed by Pettie and Ramachandran (2002). This algorithm poses the MST construction problem as a search problem for multiple decision trees. However, though it is said that the time requirement of this algorithm is linear, but the time required for the step involving the construction of the decision tree in unknown. Hence, the name of the algorithm is kept in a stochastic manner.
- There are several parallel algorithms for obtaining the MST of a graph. Such algorithm is capable of solving the problem at $O(\log(N))$ with N number of processors which is quite remarkable.

- It is usually little difficult to obtain the MST for a complete graph as it requires the exploration of a huge number of edges depending upon the number of nodes. However, there are some algorithms (Frieze, 1985) that perform the task efficiently and can scale up well.
- However, in general, greedy algorithms are employed to obtain the MST for a given graph. Two well-known algorithms in this regard are the Prim's and the Kruskal's algorithms.

The Prim's algorithm grows the MST $T(V,E_T)$ of G considering one edge at a time. Initially, T contains an arbitrary vertex. In each step, T is augmented with the least-weight edge (u,v) such that u is in T and v is still in $G-T$. The run-time of this algorithm is either

$$O\left(|E_T|\log|V|\right) \text{ or } O\left(|E_T|+|V|\log|V|\right)$$

depending on the data-structures used.

On the contrary, the Kruskal's algorithm finds a subset of the edges of G that forms a tree with all the vertices from V, where the total weight of all the edges in the tree is minimized. If the graph is not connected, then it finds a minimum spanning forest in this regard. The average case running time of the Kruskal's algorithm is $O(\log|E_T|)$. There is an extension of the traditional Kruskal's algorithm which is known as the *reverse-delete algorithm*.

Given a set of data points $\chi = \{X_1, X_2, \ldots, X_n\}$, $X_i \in \mathbb{R}^d$ represented as graph $G(V,E)$, we now know that it is possible to construct the MST $T(V,E_T)$ using any of the aforementioned algorithms. The task of data clustering can easily be accomplished in T by exploiting the properties of T. Generally speaking, if the edges of T is weighted in such a way that a large weight means better similarity between the adjoining pair of nodes (points), then the process to find κ clusters from T means the deletion of $\kappa-1$ edges from T. This cut operation creates κ connected components where each component represents a cluster.

Figure 7 depicts such a scenario. Given a set of points, an MST is built of the data in the feature space. It can be observed that the edges connecting the points within a cluster have lesser weights as compared to the edges residing within a cluster. As mentioned above, the clustering is straight-forward and aims at finding the edges spanning multiple clusters.

However, this approach is largely affected by the presence of outliers in data. Zahn (1971) introduced an application of MST in clustering a point set. The clustering algorithm proposed by them is based on

Figure 7. An MST representation of a set of data points

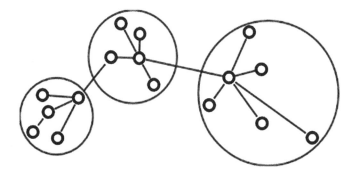

the assumption that the edges which span multiple clusters are substantially different from their neighboring edges which reside within the clusters. Päivinen (2005) proposed a scale-free MST (SFMST) clustering algorithm which builds a scale invariant network and outputs clusters with highly connected vertices. A cost-effective fast MST based partitional data clustering strategy has been introduced by Edla and Jana (2013), which performs clustering in quadratic time and also detects the outliers properly. Non-parametric mutual information based optimization technique is used to cluster an MST by Müller et al. (2012). An approximation algorithm is proposed to solve the optimization problem which is inherently hard. The well-known cluster validity measure based on the ratio between the inter-cluster variance and intra-cluster variance is used to construct the energy function for MST based clustering by Jana and Naik (2009). Two Euclidean distance based measures for MST clustering namely Euclidean MST (EMST) and Zahn's Euclidean MST (ZEMST) are introduced by Grygorash, Zhou, and Jorgensen (2006). Both the methods explore the consistency rules mentioned in (Zahn, 1971).

Most of the aforementioned methods consider that the number of clusters present in the data is already known. In contrast to that, we are interested in exploiting the properties of MST for data clustering in cases where the numbers of clusters are unknown to the algorithm. We will mention two recent MST based clustering algorithm in this respect:

- In the first of them by Banerjee, Varma, Buddhiraju, and Eeti (2014), the algorithm checks the edges of the MST iteratively and decides whether that edge can be deleted to construct two clusters.
- The second algorithm in this line by Banerjee, Mishra, Varma, and Mohan (2013) defines an optimization function for efficient graph-cut and iteratively explores it to cluster the data represented by the MST.

In both the cases, it is inherently considered that the weights of the edges inside a connected component (cluster) are lesser compared to the ones connecting multiple diverse connected components.

Non-Parametric Data Clustering Using MST: Algorithm 1

Banerjee et al. (2014) proposed a multi-level segmentation algorithm for multi-spectral remote sensing images. It is worth mentioning at this point that a multi-spectral image pixel is represented usually by more than 3 spectral bands capturing different properties of the Earth surface. In this algorithm, the input image is first over-segmented by mean-shift clustering (Comaniciu & Meer, 2002). Mean-shift is a spatial clustering strategy and is based on the properties of the gradient to the kernel density estimate. Mean-shift clustering based image segmentation preserves the edges of the image and perform an initial noise removal. Hence, most of the fine details are preserved even after the segmentation. Now, considering the regions produced after this stage as nodes, an MST is constructed in a newly defined feature space. The proposed clustering algorithm now clusters the regions to produce the final compact segmentation of the image.

Let us consider that the task is to segment an image I having d spectral bands. The image is initially segmented by an adaptive mean-shift. The interested readers are encouraged to read the paper to find details regarding the adaptive mean-shift algorithm proposed in this respect. Let us also consider that

$$\chi = \{R_1, R_2 \ldots, R_n\}$$

represent the regions found after this stage. A set of discriminative features needs to be extracted from each of the regions and to further cluster the regions in the feature space.

Hence, objects found after the over-segmentation step undergo a feature extraction stage. Mean spectral value of the regions along with some statistical texture features are considered for this purpose. Shape features are not taken into account as the objects belonging to a given class may have different sizes and shapes at different geographical locations.

Gray level co-occurrence matrix (GLCM) (Haralick, 1979) based texture features are considered as these kind of features can classify images with micro-textural elements. This concept is key in classifying different classes of remotely sensed satellite images. GLCM is defined as the distribution of the co-occurring values within a given offset in the image plane. It represents the distance and angular spatial relationship over an image sub-region of specific size. The GLCM used here is direction invariant. Hence the average of all four spatial arrangements depicting 0, 45, 90 and 135 degree angular deviations are used. A pixel offset of 1 and a quantization level of 256 are also considered. From the co-occurrence matrix, many texture parameters (Haralick, 1979) can be calculated. Entropy, energy, homogeneity and contrast are selected for this case to capture the relative gray level randomness and brightness of a given region. Hence for a d-band image, the regions found after the previous step are represented in a $(d+4)$-dimensional feature space and the data items in the new space are further clustered using the proposed MST based clustering algorithm.

Given a set of regions

$$R_1, R_2 \dots, R_n, (R_i \in \mathbb{R}^{(d+4)})$$

with unknown underlying probability distribution functions, a graph $G(V,E)$ is constructed with vertex set V and edge set E where each of the R_i's is represented as a $(d+4)$ dimensional feature vector by a node in the graph. The edge between a given pair of vertices R_i and R_j is weighted (A_{ij}) by a modified Gaussian Radial Basis distance of the corresponding feature vectors. The kernel hyper-parameter (γ) which reflects the neighborhood effects on the distance measure, is fixed heuristically. With this new distance measure, the value of A_{ij} is small if R_i and R_j are similar to each other in some sense whereas A_{ij} increases in case the regions differ substantially. An MST $T(V,E_T)$ of G is constructed henceforth using the Kruskal's approach.

The proposed clustering method checks iteratively whether a given edge of the tree can be deleted to form two compact sub-clusters. The edges are considered in the descending order of the corresponding edge weights because it is assumed that edges with larger weights are the ones which span different clusters. Algorithm 1 describes the proposed clustering process. Let W store the edges of T in descending order of their corresponding edge weights. As mentioned, deletion of an edge creates two sub-trees in T and an edge with sufficiently large weight may connect nodes or data items from two different clusters.

Algorithm 1.

Input: $T(V,E_T)$, A list W which stores the edge weights in descending order

Output: Array L of cluster labels of the vertices of T

1: **for** i=1 to size(W) **do**

2: Consider the (sub)tree where the $E_{T_{W(i)}}$ belongs to. { $E_{T_{W(i)}}$ is the edge in E_T having weight $W(i)$.}

3: Let T_1 and T_2 be the two Connected Components (CC) adjacent to $E_{T_{W(i)}}$.

4: Calculate ν_1 and ν_2 corresponding to T_1 and T_2 where $\nu_j (j \in \{1,2\})$ is defined as:

$$\nu_j = M_j + (\alpha_j \times \sigma_j)$$

{M_j and σ_j define the mean and standard deviation of the weights of the edges contained in T_j. α_j is calculated using Algorithm 2}

5: **if** $W(i) > \min(\nu_1, \nu_2)$ **then**

6: Delete $E_{T_{W(i)}}$ to generate two separate CC's T_1 and T_2.

7: Label the points of the two CC's and store the labels in L.

8: **else**

9: Break loop.

10: **end if**

11: **end for**

It can be noted that ν is a measure of the cluster compactness, i.e., it signifies how close the data points of a given cluster reside. If a given edge $E_{T_{W(i)}}$ has drastically larger weight value than the average edge weights of its two adjoining CCs, then it can be presumed that $E_{T_{W(i)}}$ spans two different clusters and hence can be deleted. The parameter α defines a tolerance per CC. Given a CC, the corresponding α controls the gap allowed in the feature space between this CC and any other CC.

In order to find for the ith CC, the boundary samples of the data points represented by the nodes of that component are found out using the BORDER algorithm (Xia et al., 2006). BORDER employs the Border kNN join and reverse kNN to find out the boundary points of a dataset. It is selected here as BORDER has been found to work well even in case of high dimensional data (Xia, Hsu, Lee, & Ooi, 2006). The average width of each CC is obtained by calculating the average Euclidean distance of all the pairs of such boundary points. Hence, for the ith CC, α_i is calculated as $\alpha_i = \dfrac{D_i}{M_i}$ where D_i and M_i define the average width of the CC and the average weight of all the edges present in the CC respectively. If the weight of a given edge is larger than the minimum of the ν values of its adjacent connected components, the edge is deleted. It indicates that the edge to be deleted has higher weight than the representative edge weights of both the adjacent CCs.

Algorithm 2. Calculate α_i for a given T_i

1: Use BORDER algorithm to find out the set of data points ($\{R_k\}$) of T_i which resides along the boundary in the feature space.

2: D_i= average width of the points of T_i in the feature space. {D_i is calculated by averaging the pairwise distances of all the points of $\{R_k\}$.}

3: $\alpha_i = \dfrac{D_i}{M_i}$

A typical output of the segmentation result of this method for a medium resolution multi-spectral remote sensing image can be observed in Figure 8.

Figure 8. A typical multi-level segmentation technique with MST based region merging
Source: Banerjee et al., 2014.

 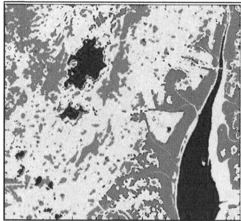

Non-Parametric Data Clustering Using MST: Algorithm 2

The other algorithm in the same line follows identical structure of merging a set of over-segmented regions using a non-parametric MST based clustering algorithm. However, in contrast to the previous technique, here an optimization function is proposed for edge-cut from the MST and the edges are iteratively removed from the MST until the function is optimized.

Here a kNN-MST based graph topology has been adopted which is capable of capturing the distribution of the data items in the feature space and it can be inferred easily by considering the weight of a given edge whether the edge spans two different clusters or resides within a given cluster. The graph topology is organized in such a way that conforms to the structure of a line graph. Such representation has not been used yet for the purpose of data clustering. However, as will see next, it possesses enough potential in this respect.

Graph Construction

The steps followed for constructing the MST-kNN graph given χ are:

1. For each $X_i \in \chi$, add an edge E_{X_i,X_j} between X_i and X_j where X_j is the first nearest neighbor of X_i. The edge is weighted by the Euclidean distance between X_i and X_j. Although any other distance measure can be used.
2. Once step 1 is completed for all the points, the results will be a set of connected components.
3. For each component, find its nearest component using single linkage Euclidean distance. This information can alternatively be found from the MST of G.

$$w(C_{i1}, C_{i2}) = \min\{A(\xi_{i1}, \xi_{i2})\}, i1 \neq i2$$

Here C_{i1} and C_{i2} represent two separate connected components. ξ_{i1} and ξ_{i2} represent the closest data points belonging to C_{i1} and C_{i2} respectively. Hence, for a given C_{i1}, the above steps identifies the particular C_{i2} for which $w(C_{i1}, C_{i2})$ is the smallest. The closest pair of data points of C_{i1} and C_{i2} are now connected by an edge and the edge is included in E.

4. Step 3 is repeated until G is minimally connected. Let us call the new graph $G_M(V, E_M)$.

The advantages of this graph topology are:

- The graph is minimally connected.
- The spatial distribution of the data items are completely captured with this kind of graph construction.
- Noisy data points can now be identified by checking the size of a connected component obtained after the kNN based graph construction.
- The graph inherently exploits the properties of MST to capture the nearest neighbor information effectively.

Clustering G_M

Algorithm 3 details the clustering procedure. Let us mention the stages of the clustering algorithm first. Then we will define the optimization function proposed in this respect to define the notion of cluster purity.

Algorithm 3.
Input: $G_M(V, E_M)$, A list W is created which stores the edge weights in descending order
Output: Array L of labels of the vertices of G_M
1: **for** $i = 1$ to size(W) **do**
2: Find the sub-tree where $E_{M_{W(i)}}$ is present and delete $E_{M_{W(i)}}$. {Deletion of edges from a minimally connected graph results in $\kappa+1$ connected components}
3: Now for the forest obtained, calculate cluster validity measure (τ). A forest is a set of disconnected graphs.
4: **end for**
5: Find the κ for which τ attains the maximum value.
6: Remove the largest $\kappa-1$ number of edges from and the result will be number of clusters.

The Proposed Cluster Validity Index

According to Algorithm 3, the entire clustering process is carried out based on the proposed cluster validity measure (τ). The measure is maximized then the clustering is near optimal. A set of edge properties are encoded in defining the validity measure. τ(index) for a random index is defined as:

$$\tau(index) = \frac{1}{\sum\limits_{i=1}^{index} M_{C_{w_i}}} + \sum\limits_{1 \leq i,j \leq index, i \neq j} D(S_{C_i}, S_{C_j}) + \frac{1}{\sum\limits_{i=1}^{index} \max_{C_{w_i}}}$$

The particular index which maximizes τ(index)is considered as the optimal number of clusters. The first term of the equation defining τ(index)ensures that the summation of the edge weights of a connected component attains minimum possible value if the underlying cluster is compact and optimal (No under or over clustering involved). According to the second term, the single linkage distance between a cluster and its *most similar* cluster (1 nearest neighbor) attains the maximum possible value in the optimal scenario. The third term indicates the maximum edge weight per connected component will be minimized at the point of optimal clustering.

All the terms impose some valid constraints to the overall data clustering problem. A combination of such constraints are expected to enhance the clustering output largely.

MARKOV RANDOM FIELD (MRF) OPTIMIZATION USING THE MAX-FLOW MIN-CUT ALGORITHM

Many problems in the domain of computer vision can be formulated in form of a random field of discrete random variables. Examples in this aspect range from low-level vision such as image segmentation, optical flow and stereo reconstruction, to high-level vision such as object recognition. The goal is typically to infer the most probable values of the random variables, known as Maximum a Posteriori (MAP) estimation. This has been widely studied in several areas of Computer Science and the resulting algorithms have greatly helped in obtaining accurate and reliable solutions to many problems. These algorithms are extremely efficient and can find the globally optimal solutions for an important class of models in polynomial time. Hence, they have led to a significant increase in the use of random field models in computer vision and machine learning in general.

Probabilistic Graphical Models (PGM) (Koller & Friedman, 2009) are primarily used for structured prediction and integrates the power of probability theory and graph topology properly. The inherent idea with the PGM is to represent a family of distribution functions in terms of a set of conditional independence statements. PGM can be either directed (better known as the Bayesian networks) or undirected (better known as the Markov networks). Both the representations have certain pros and cons. In image analysis, undirected graphical models are preferred given the bi-direction interactions among the pixels in a neighborhood. To motivate the readers further on the applicability of the PGM for different image analysis tasks, let us consider the problem of pixel classification. In simple terms, given a set of training pixels, a classification model like Naive Bayes aims at building a prediction model for new pixels. However, there are some inherent image properties which such a model fails to capture entirely. For instance, the local smoothness property of images, which ensures that adjoining pixels tend to have similar class labels is not considered explicitly by Naive Bayes. A structured predictor model can use such high level domain specific information for inference. This is why graphical models have gained enormous popularity in computer vision domain over the years (Li, 2009).

Here, we will mainly focus on the MRF models and will define the optimization problem for MAP inference to solve different computer vision tasks. We will then mention how such problem can be solved using the graph-cut formulation properly.

An MRF is formally specified for an given image I by:

- A set of sites $\mathcal{S} = \{1, 2, \ldots, n\}$ which corresponds to the n pixel locations in I. These are the observed measurements like image pixel values $\{X_i\}_{i=1}^{n}$.

- A set of random variables $\{w_i\}_{i=1}^{n}$ associated with each of the sites. These variables represent the unknown quantities. For example, for the edge detection task, such variables represent the presence or absence of edge at a given pixel value. Similarly, for the task of pixel classification, they represent the predicted label for each pixel.

- A set of neighbors $\{\mathcal{N}_i\}_{i=1}^{n}$ at each of the n sites.

To be an MRF, the model must satisfy the Markov property which states that:

$$\Pr\left(w_i \mid w_{\mathcal{S}-i}\right) = \Pr\left(w_i \mid w_{\mathcal{N}_i}\right)$$

In other words, the model should be conditionally independent of all of the other variables given its neighbors. Such neighboring pixels form the *Markov blanket* for the pixel under consideration. Consequently, we can consider an MRF to describe the joint probability of the variables as a product of a set of non-negative potential functions ($\phi_j[.]$) so that:

$$\Pr(w) = \frac{1}{Z} \prod_{j=1}^{J} \phi_j\left[w_{\mathcal{C}_j}\right]$$

The value of $\phi_j[.]$ depends on the state of a subset of variables $\mathcal{C}_j \subset \{1, 2, \ldots, n\}$ which is similar to a clique. Z is called the *partition function* and is a normalizing constant that ensures that the result is a valid probability distribution. Based on the Hammersely-Clifford theorem (Geman & Graffigne, 1986), we can say that $\Pr(W)$ is alternatively a Gibbs distribution represented by,

$$\Pr(w) = \frac{1}{Z} \exp\left[-\sum_{j=1}^{J} \nu_j\left[w_{\mathcal{C}_j}\right]\right]$$

where $\nu = -\log[\phi[.]]$ is the cost function. Since MRF is a generative model, we need to apply the Bayes theorem to infer the posterior probability of the unknown world states (random variables) as:

$$\Pr\left(w_{1,2,\ldots,n} \mid x_{1,2,\ldots,n}\right) = \frac{\displaystyle\prod_{i=1}^{n} \Pr\left(X_i \mid w_i\right) \Pr\left(w_{1,2,\ldots,n}\right)}{\Pr\left(X_{1,2,\ldots,n}\right)}$$

where we assume that the conditional probability $\displaystyle\prod_{i=1}^{n} \Pr\left(X_i \mid w_i\right)$ factorizes into a product of individual terms associated with each pixels.

Under the notion of MAP inference, we seek to obtain:

$$\hat{w}_{1,2,\dots,n} = \underset{w_{1,2,\dots,n}}{\arg\max} \Pr\left(w_{1,2,\dots,n} \mid X_{1,2,\dots,n}\right)$$

$$= \underset{w_{1,2,\dots,n}}{\arg\max} \left[\prod_{i=1}^{n} \Pr\left(X_i \mid w_i\right) \Pr\left(w_{1,2,\dots,n}\right)\right]$$

$$= \underset{w_{1,2,\dots,n}}{\arg\max} \left[\sum_{i=1}^{n} \log\left[\Pr\left(X_i \mid w_i\right)\right] + \log\left[\Pr\left(w_{1,2,\dots,n}\right)\right]\right]$$

where we transformed the results of the Bayes rule into log domain. The task is to choose the prior term in this respect which models the interactions between the random variables. One of the most popular measures used in this respect is the pairwise MRF model which is expressed as:

$$= \underset{w_{1,2,\dots,n}}{\arg\max} \left[\sum_{i=1}^{n} \log\left[\Pr(X_i \mid w_i)\right] - \sum_{(k,l)\in\mathcal{C}} \left[\nu(w_k, w_l, \theta)\right]\right]$$

$$= \underset{w_{1,2,\dots,n}}{\arg\min} \left[\sum_{i=1}^{n} - \log\left[\Pr(X_i \mid w_i)\right] + \sum_{(k,l)\in\mathcal{C}} \left[\nu(w_k, w_l, \theta)\right]\right]$$

$$= \underset{w_{1,2,\dots,n}}{\arg\min} \sum_{i=1}^{n} U_i(w_i) + \underset{(k,l)\in\mathcal{C}}{P_{kl}}(w_k, w_l)$$

where U denotes the *unary* term at pixel i. This is a cost for observing the data at pixel i given the state w_i and is usually expressed as a negative log-likelihood. Similarly, the pairwise term P_{kl} is the cost of placing labels w_k and w_l at the neighboring locations k and l. Further, this term occurs due to the clique cost $\nu[w_k, w_l, \theta]$ from the MRF prior for parameter θ. Note that, we have omitted the term including the partition function as it is constant with respect to the state variables.

We usually assume a parametric model like Gaussian to represent the data and define the unary potential accordingly. Let us consider the pairwise potential for binary image labeling task where each pixel can have labels from $\{0,1\}$. In this case, we usually set $P(0,1)$ $P(1,0)$ to a high value to highlight the label discrepancy. At the same time $P(0,0)$ and $P(0,1)$ are set to 0 to assure a smooth solution. We can further incorporate any discontinuity prior like the edge information in the pairwise term.

Three situation occur based on the set of the world-states as follows:

- In case of binary MRFs ($w_i \in \{0,1\}$), the costs for different combinations of adjacent labels are sub-modular. Exact inference can be performed in this case.
- In case of multi-label MRFs ($w_i \in \{1, 2, \dots, \mathcal{K}\}$), the costs are again sub-modular and exact inference is tractable.
- However, the inference is intractable in case of multi-label MRFs. However, good approximation techniques exist in some cases.

There are many ways to solve pairwise MRF model including simulated annealing, Iterated Conditional Model (ICM) (Dubes, Jain, Nadabar, & Chen, 1990) and graph-cut (Veksler, 2007). Due to this sub-modularity, the MAP estimation problem can alternatively be reduced to an instance of the max-flow problem in a graph. We will not go into detail of the actual max-flow min-cut algorithm (Ford & Fulkerson, 1962) used in this respect. However, there are two alternative solutions possible here based on the properties of the pairwise term P. The alpha-expansion algorithm can only be used when P is metric. If it is otherwise semi-metric, the alpha-beta swap algorithm is adopted.

Further, in contrast to the traditional MRF models which define the prior term as a generative model of the image data, it is possible to explore the observed image and make the pairwise term dependent on the actual pixel values. Such a model directly calculates the conditional probability of the world states given the image. One such discriminative log-linear model is the Conditional Random Field (CRF) (Lafferty, McCallum, & Pereira, 2001).

The application of MRFs and CRFs are vast in the domain of computer vision. Some of the applications in this respect are:

- Image de-noising (Malfait & Roose, 1997),
- Medical image segmentation (Pham, Xu, & Prince, 2000),
- Monocular depth estimation (Saxena, Chung, & Ng, 2008),
- Semantic image segmentation (Nowozin, Gehler, & Lampert, 2010) etc.

SOME EXTENDED APPLICATION OF GRAPH THEORY IN IMAGE ANALYSIS

Apart of the graph-cut based techniques for the purpose of image segmentation, there exists a number of application of graph in image analysis.

The natural grid graph representation is helpful for morphological image processing (Soille, 2013). Certain specific graph topologies have been proposed like the Delaunay triangle, Khalimksy grid, Perfect fusion grid etc. to satisfy some inherent properties of the Jordan curve theorem which states that a closed curve divides a space into two mutually exclusive regions for image structures. With graph structure, sophisticated definition for basic morphological operations like dilation, erosion etc. can be defined for not only binary images but gray scale images also. A detailed review of different graph theoretic morphological image analysis techniques can be found in the work by Najman and Cousty (2014).

Given the part based representation of objects, graph structures are a natural choice. For example a human face can be considered as a deformable graph of different face parts like eyes, nose, mouth etc. (Figure 9) (Felzenszwalb, McAllester, & Ramanan, 2008). The edge weight of such graph is not fixed as face is not a rigid object. However the number of nodes in such a deformable graph is fixed. This structure allows an MRF like formulation of the underlying objects and graph matching techniques can be allowed to match a pair of object instances for their category.

Graphs are used extensively in image retrieval. One direction in this respect is oriented towards the active learning paradigm where a set of images are fed to an external agent for the labeling task. Those labels are used further to refine the inference model. One important issue here is to select the images which are to be used for this external labeling. Such images should have high discriminative properties and contain information not yet captured. Graph structures in the image space can be used to select such images easily (Zhou & Huang, 2003).

The problem of domain adaptation deals with the data classification problem where the training and test samples are obtained from related but not identical distributions. Examples include training a recognition system on the images obtained by a webcam and then to test the model on images captured

Figure 9. A part model for human face
Source: Felzenszwalb et al., 2008.

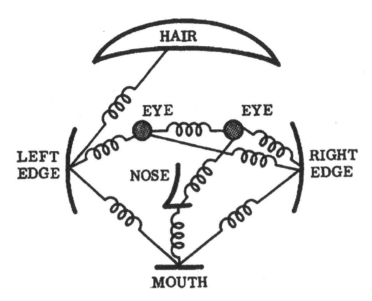

by an SLR camera. Similarly, in the case of multi-temporal image analysis, it is not always possible to annotate training samples from all the images from the sequence. One solution to alleviate the need of training pixel generation for all the images is to propagate the training information from some of the images (source domain) to others (target domain). This is again the problem of domain adaptation. One solution in this respect is to match the training pixel classes of the source domains to the pixel clusters of the target domain. The concept of graph node matching can be used for such purpose effectively. A cross-domain graph node matching based domain adaptation techniques is proposed in (Banerjee et al., 2015).

There are many more applications of graphs in image analysis. it is further possible to relax a given problem as one of the problems involving graphs which is expected to provide a relaxation to the problem in near polynomial time.

CONCLUSION

We discussed the applications of graphs for high level image analysis tasks. The problem of image segmentation has always attracted the research community as it is inherently a difficult problem. The segmentation problem can be solved efficiently using the notion of graph clustering. We discussed a number of graph clustering techniques in detail in this regard. We mentioned the spectral clustering; clustering based on spanning trees and theoretically analyzed the solutions. Then we mentioned some more applications of graphs on vision.

REFERENCES

Airola, A., Pyysalo, S., Björne, J., Pahikkala, T., Ginter, F., & Salakoski, T. (2008, June). A graph kernel for protein-protein interaction extraction. In *Proceedings of the workshop on current trends in biomedical natural language processing* (pp. 1-9). Association for Computational Linguistics. doi:10.3115/1572306.1572308

Awate, S. P., & Whitaker, R. T. (2006). Unsupervised, information-theoretic, adaptive image filtering for image restoration. *IEEE Transactions on Pattern Analysis and Machine Intelligence, 28*(3), 364–376. doi:10.1109/TPAMI.2006.64 PMID:16526423

Banerjee, B., Bovolo, F., Bhattacharya, A., Bruzzone, L., Chaudhuri, S., & Buddhiraju, K. M. (2015). A novel graph-matching-based approach for domain adaptation in classification of remote sensing image pair. *IEEE Transactions on Geoscience and Remote Sensing, 53*(7), 4045–4062. doi:10.1109/TGRS.2015.2389520

Banerjee, B., Mishra, P. K., Varma, S., & Mohan, B. K. (2013, October). A novel graph based clustering technique for hybrid segmentation of multi-spectral remotely sensed images. In *International Conference on Advanced Concepts for Intelligent Vision Systems* (pp. 274-285). Springer International Publishing. doi:10.1007/978-3-319-02895-8_25

Banerjee, B., Varma, S., Buddhiraju, K. M., & Eeti, L. N. (2014). Unsupervised multi-spectral satellite image segmentation combining modified mean-shift and a new minimum spanning tree based clustering technique. *IEEE Journal of Selected Topics in Applied Earth Observations and Remote Sensing, 7*(3), 888–894. doi:10.1109/JSTARS.2013.2266572

Bleyer, M., & Gelautz, M. (2007). Graph-cut-based stereo matching using image segmentation with symmetrical treatment of occlusions. *Signal Processing Image Communication, 22*(2), 127–143. doi:10.1016/j.image.2006.11.012

Bondy, J. A., & Murty, U. S. R. (1976). *Graph theory with applications* (Vol. 290). London: Macmillan. doi:10.1007/978-1-349-03521-2

Bougleux, S., Elmoataz, A., & Melkemi, M. (2007, May). Discrete regularization on weighted graphs for image and mesh filtering. In *International Conference on Scale Space and Variational Methods in Computer Vision* (pp. 128-139). Springer Berlin Heidelberg. doi:10.1007/978-3-540-72823-8_12

Bunke, H., & Shearer, K. (1998). A graph distance metric based on the maximal common subgraph. *Pattern Recognition Letters, 19*(3), 255–259. doi:10.1016/S0167-8655(97)00179-7

Comaniciu, D., & Meer, P. (2002). Mean shift: A robust approach toward feature space analysis. *IEEE Transactions on Pattern Analysis and Machine Intelligence, 24*(5), 603–619. doi:10.1109/34.1000236

Dubes, R. C., Jain, A. K., Nadabar, S. G., & Chen, C. C. (1990, June). MRF model-based algorithms for image segmentation. In *Pattern Recognition, 1990. Proceedings., 10th International Conference on* (Vol. 1, pp. 808-814). IEEE. doi:10.1109/ICPR.1990.118221

Edla, D. R., & Jana, P. K. (2013). Minimum spanning tree based clustering using partitional approach. In *Proceedings of the International Conference on Frontiers of Intelligent Computing: Theory and Applications (FICTA)* (pp. 237-244). Springer Berlin Heidelberg. doi:10.1007/978-3-642-35314-7_28

Erkan, G., & Radev, D. R. (2004). LexRank: Graph-based lexical centrality as salience in text summarization. *Journal of Artificial Intelligence Research*, *22*, 457–479.

Fattah, M. A., & Ren, F. (2008). Automatic text summarization. *World Academy of Science. Engineering and Technology*, *37*, 2008.

Felzenszwalb, P., McAllester, D., & Ramanan, D. (2008, June). A discriminatively trained, multiscale, deformable part model. In *Computer Vision and Pattern Recognition, 2008. CVPR 2008. IEEE Conference on* (pp. 1-8). IEEE. doi:10.1109/CVPR.2008.4587597

Fiedler, M. (1973). Algebraic connectivity of graphs. *Czechoslovak Mathematical Journal*, *23*(2), 298–305.

Ford, L. R. Jr, & Fulkerson, D. R. (2015). *Flows in networks*. Princeton university press.

Frieze, A. M. (1985). On the value of a random minimum spanning tree problem. *Discrete Applied Mathematics*, *10*(1), 47–56. doi:10.1016/0166-218X(85)90058-7

Geman, S., & Graffigne, C. (1986, August). Markov random field image models and their applications to computer vision. In *Proceedings of the International Congress of Mathematicians* (Vol. 1, p. 2).

Goldberg, A. B., Zhu, X., & Wright, S. J. (2007, October). Dissimilarity in graph-based semi-supervised classification. In Artificial Intelligence and Statistics (Vol. 34, p. 52).

Grygorash, O., Zhou, Y., & Jorgensen, Z. (2006, November). Minimum spanning tree based clustering algorithms. In *2006 18th IEEE International Conference on Tools with Artificial Intelligence (ICTAI'06)* (pp. 73-81). IEEE. doi:10.1109/ICTAI.2006.83

Haralick, R. M. (1979). Statistical and structural approaches to texture. *Proceedings of the IEEE*, *67*(5), 786–804. doi:10.1109/PROC.1979.11328

Jana, P. K., & Naik, A. (2009, December). An efficient minimum spanning tree based clustering algorithm. In *Methods and Models in Computer Science, 2009. ICM2CS 2009. Proceeding of International Conference on* (pp. 1-5). IEEE. doi:10.1109/ICM2CS.2009.5397966

Jordan, F. R. B. M. I., & Bach, F. (2004). Learning spectral clustering. *Advances in Neural Information Processing Systems*, *16*, 305–312.

Karger, D. R., Klein, P. N., & Tarjan, R. E. (1995). A randomized linear-time algorithm to find minimum spanning trees.[JACM]. *Journal of the Association for Computer Machinery*, *42*(2), 321–328. doi:10.1145/201019.201022

Koller, D., & Friedman, N. (2009). *Probabilistic graphical models: Principles and techniques*. MIT Press.

Kruskal, J. B. (1956). On the shortest spanning subtree of a graph and the traveling salesman problem. *Proceedings of the American Mathematical Society*, *7*(1), 48–50. doi:10.1090/S0002-9939-1956-0078686-7

Lafferty, J., McCallum, A., & Pereira, F. (2001, June). Conditional random fields: Probabilistic models for segmenting and labeling sequence data. In *Proceedings of the eighteenth international conference on machine learning, ICML* (Vol. 1, pp. 282-289). IEEE.

Li, S. Z. (2009). *Markov random field modeling in image analysis*. Springer Science & Business Media.

Malfait, M., & Roose, D. (1997). Wavelet-based image denoising using a Markov random field a priori model. *IEEE Transactions on Image Processing, 6*(4), 549–565. doi:10.1109/83.563320 PMID:18282948

Mohar, B., Alavi, Y., Chartrand, G., & Oellermann, O. R. (1991). The Laplacian spectrum of graphs. *Graph theory, combinatorics, and applications, 2*(871-898), 12.

Müller, A. C., Nowozin, S., & Lampert, C. H. (2012, August). Information theoretic clustering using minimum spanning trees. In *Joint DAGM (German Association for Pattern Recognition) and OAGM Symposium* (pp. 205-215). Springer Berlin Heidelberg. doi:10.1007/978-3-642-32717-9_21

Najman, L., & Cousty, J. (2014). A graph-based mathematical morphology reader. *Pattern Recognition Letters, 47*, 3–17. doi:10.1016/j.patrec.2014.05.007

Neuhaus, M., & Bunke, H. (2007). Bridging the gap between graph edit distance and kernel machines. World Scientific Publishing Co., Inc.

Ng, A. Y., Jordan, M. I., & Weiss, Y. (2002). On spectral clustering: Analysis and an algorithm. *Advances in Neural Information Processing Systems, 2*, 849–856.

Nowozin, S., Gehler, P. V., & Lampert, C. H. (2010, September). On parameter learning in CRF-based approaches to object class image segmentation. In *European conference on computer vision* (pp. 98-111). Springer Berlin Heidelberg. doi:10.1007/978-3-642-15567-3_8

Päivinen, N. (2005). Clustering with a minimum spanning tree of scale-free-like structure. *Pattern Recognition Letters, 26*(7), 921–930. doi:10.1016/j.patrec.2004.09.039

Pal, N. R., & Pal, S. K. (1993). A review on image segmentation techniques. *Pattern Recognition, 26*(9), 1277–1294. doi:10.1016/0031-3203(93)90135-J

Pettie, S., & Ramachandran, V. (2002). An optimal minimum spanning tree algorithm. *Journal of the ACM, 49*(1), 16–34. doi:10.1145/505241.505243

Pham, D. L., Xu, C., & Prince, J. L. (2000). Current methods in medical image segmentation 1. *Annual Review of Biomedical Engineering, 2*(1), 315–337. doi:10.1146/annurev.bioeng.2.1.315 PMID:11701515

Saxena, A., Chung, S. H., & Ng, A. Y. (2008). 3-d depth reconstruction from a single still image. *International Journal of Computer Vision, 76*(1), 53–69. doi:10.1007/s11263-007-0071-y

Shi, J., & Malik, J. (1998, January). Motion segmentation and tracking using normalized cuts. In *Computer Vision, 1998. Sixth International Conference on* (pp. 1154-1160). IEEE.

Shi, J., & Malik, J. (2000). Normalized cuts and image segmentation. *IEEE Transactions on Pattern Analysis and Machine Intelligence, 22*(8), 888–905. doi:10.1109/34.868688

Singer, A. (2006). From graph to manifold Laplacian: The convergence rate. *Applied and Computational Harmonic Analysis*, *21*(1), 128–134. doi:10.1016/j.acha.2006.03.004

Soille, P. (2013). *Morphological image analysis: principles and applications.* Springer Science & Business Media.

Ta, V. T., Elmoataz, A., & Lézoray, O. (2011). Nonlocal pdes-based morphology on weighted graphs for image and data processing. *IEEE Transactions on Image Processing*, *20*(6), 1504–1516. doi:10.1109/TIP.2010.2101610 PMID:21193378

Veksler, O. (2007, June). Graph cut based optimization for MRFs with truncated convex priors. In *2007 IEEE Conference on Computer Vision and Pattern Recognition* (pp. 1-8). IEEE. doi:10.1109/CVPR.2007.383249

West, D. B. (2001). *Introduction to graph theory* (Vol. 2). Upper Saddle River, NJ: Prentice hall.

Yang, C., Zhang, L., Lu, H., Ruan, X., & Yang, M. H. (2013). Saliency detection via graph-based manifold ranking. In *Computer Vision and Pattern Recognition, 2008. CVPR 2008. IEEE Conference on* (pp. 3166-3173). IEEE. doi:10.1109/CVPR.2013.407

Chapter 9
Utilizing Architecture Aspects for in Data Mining for Computer System Design

Chantana Chantrapornchai
Kasetsart University, Thailand

Sathaporn Srakaew
Silpakorn University, Thailand

Aree Kaegjing
Silpakorn University, Thailand

Warot Piyanuntcharatsr
Silpakorn University, Thailand

Songchok Krakhaeng
Silpakorn University, Thailand

ABSTRACT

Data mining has been a popular technique. It has been for many applications in many areas nowadays. In this chapter, we are interested in utilizing architecture features and apply data mining techniques for a computer design. Since data mining requires lot of collected data for building models, the relevant data needs to be properly generated. We demonstrate the applications and their methodology starting from data set generation, feature extraction, modeling and evaluations. Important characteristics of the architecture are considered for data set generation and feature extractions: particularly, the instruction set, and memory access pattern features. The chapter utilizes these features given with observations for building the models for cache prediction, branch prediction, and malware detection.

INTRODUCTION

Data mining has been popularly used in many areas. This chapter reveals another usage of data mining for computer architecture design. Typical computer designs need a lot of simulations to find out the proper architecture. Benchmark applications need to be simulated to get the traces of memory usages and instruction usages. For instance, to find the proper cache system, possible cache design parameters are such as cache size, block size, associativity etc. All the possible parameters have to be explored by

DOI: 10.4018/978-1-5225-1776-4.ch009

running benchmark simulations to obtain these traces. There is a huge search space when combining these parameters and the simulation for each case is time consuming.

Constructing the proper data mining model for each application requires the repeated process. In this chapter, we suggest to use data mining approach to build the prediction model for facilitating computer architecture design. Benchmark traces are collected and possible design parameters are explored for these traces to produce the training data. After that, the model is built and is reused to predict for other traces.

We demonstrate the methodology starting from extracting trace data related to instruction set, and memory trace behaviors. Depending on a goal, relevant traces or behaviors are recorded. Different tools are used for each case and different accuracy measurements are used.

For a cache model prediction, memory reference addresses are collected. The prediction model is used to select a proper cache model for given application data traces. Thus, in the beginning after selecting benchmark application, a profiling tool to collect the memory address references must be explored. Such tools may give both instruction and data addresses. The profiling tool will execute the application and record addresses accessed. However, the address collection depends on an assumed CPU architecture such as the number of cores. A cache model contains many parameters such as direct-mapped, 2-way, 4-way, fully-set associative, etc., the block size, cache capacity, bus width, word size, etc. Then, a cache simulation tool is used for a given set of traces, how these parameters affect the cache system miss rate. The cache parameters with the minimal number of misses are selected. In some case, the profiling tool includes a cache simulation tool. The precision and recall are metrics for correctness of the derived model.

For a branch prediction model, branch instruction addresses must be recorded as well as each branch condition results and target branch addresses. The goal is to create a model for branch prediction. The input of the model is a current branch address. The output is the prediction (taken/not taken). It considers branch history for each branch. For example, in the previous iteration, the same branch is taken or not. If so, the branch target address is fetched and the instruction at the branch target address is fetched into the program counter. If not, the instruction address following the branch instruction is fetched. A selected instruction-profiling tool needs to collect branch addresses, branch target addresses and branch condition results. The accuracy is the metric for correctness of the derived model.

For malware detection model, instruction execution sequences, in particular, the sequence of instruction addresses executed are recorded. The detection model takes a file as an input and decides whether the file contains certain malwares or not. The model is scoped with a selected set of malwares. The instruction execution of infected files for each malware is inspected. Features are extracted from these. For example, frequency of the instructions executed, the number and types of co-occurrences of instructions, statistics of instruction hex code etc. are recorded. These are used to train the model. The derived model is evaluated by precision and recall metrics.

In the following section, we describe the background related to architecture characteristics, e.g. memory and instruction sets. Then, the related work is discussed. Methodology is explained next. At last, we present the conclusion and discussion.

BACKGROUND

The features related to computer architecture that are useful in this research work are presented in this section: the background knowledge about instruction, memory and conditional branch.

Instructions, Addresses, and Branches

Every CPU has its own instruction set where each instruction set has particular characteristics such as the type of instructions, addressing modes, registers, etc. When a typical program is executed, the code must be loaded into the memory and the program counter is set to start execution at the beginning address of the code before starting execution. The code program is loaded in a code memory, called *instruction cache* and the data used in the program, usually in data segment region such as variables, are allocated in the data memory, or *data cache*.

When an application runs, a program counter (PC) increases to the next address in sequence by default. However, there are cases where PC is changed to another instruction address further away. This is due to conditional branch, jump, procedure call and return instructions. Thus, the instruction addresses executed in a program may not be consecutive.

Most programs contain branch instructions averagely 20% (Malishevsky, et. al., n.d.). Executing a branch instruction causes CPU to stalls since CPU needs to know the outcome of the branch instruction before the next instruction address is loaded. The number of stall cycles depends on a microarchitecture, or particularly types and the number of pipeline stages. Since the branch instructions are not avoidable, effect of the branch stalls must be reduced by some mechanism, i.e., branch prediction which is the method to predict the next instruction to execute. This allows the next instruction resulting from a branch condition to be fetched early.

The program may access data in memory in the contiguous region (known as spatial locality) or may access data memory addresses that are apart but they are accessed often in a certain time period (temporal locality). Knowing the pattern of memory address and program address references will be useful for designing the memory system. The memory hierarchy that is suitable for such reference patterns will reduce the number of stalls due to cache misses, speeding up total execution time of an application.

Branch prediction methods are classified as static branch prediction and dynamic branch prediction (Xiao et. al. 2006). The static branch prediction is where the prediction is never changed. For example, we always predict that the branch instruction addressed at 0x1000 is always not taken. This means the branch will not make the PC change to the target branch address. Meanwhile, the PC will just be increased by the instruction bytes. With this kind of prediction, the CPU will always fetch the following instruction after the branch instruction into the pipeline. Or if the prediction is always taken, the CPU will always fetch the instruction at the branch target address into the pipeline after the branch instruction. However, in this case, there is a need to know the branch target in advance. For static branch prediction, the prediction is never changed in static. The same prediction is used for every branch. The implementation can be done by the compiler where it will insert the proper predicted instruction in the branch delay slot or next address after the branch instruction. To help speedup the calculation of branch target address buffer, there may be a cache of branch targets called Branch Target Buffer (BTB) (Xiao et.al. 2006). During the fetch cycle, the PC is used to lookup in the BTB to obtain the branch target along if it is the branch instruction address.

For the dynamic branch prediction, we keep a history of the previous branches' results. The history is used to decide whether a current branch will be taken or not. The simple dynamic branch prediction one is the 2-bit counter scheme or sometimes is called, *saturating* counter. For this case, the prediction is changed when the 2 previous predictions are wrong. The other example is the global predictor or one-level predictor or bimodal predictor structure where the branch address is used to hash the counter to be used. The prediction value is extracted from the counter.

Memory System

Figure 1 presents the traditional memory hierarchy consisting of several levels. The memory level closest to the CPU is usually the smallest, fastest and the most expensive and the farther ones are less expensive, slower and bigger. The memory system has an inclusive property: the data resided in the upper level must as well be in the lower levels.

When a CPU requests a particular memory address, it needs to search in the memory level closest to it. If the requested memory address is there, it can access the data and may move it to the registers inside. If not, the required data needed to be transferred from where it is found to the closet level. The transfer may cause a lot of time if the data is found in the lowest memory level such as hard disk. The whole cache system performance is measured by the miss rate, calculated by the number of misses (when the request data is not found in the closest memory level) divided by the total number of memory requested in the program. Designing the effective cache needs to consider a cache configuration that affects the miss rate.

Total cache capacity is one of important parameters. Ideally, a cache should be large enough to hold all needed data during the whole execution. Thus, there would be no cache misses and the total performance will not be affected by memory at all. However, the size of cache is limited. It is enough to hold only the *working set* which contains the data required over a certain period. For a memory hierarchy system, the nearer the cache to CPU, the smaller size it is. Typical cache L1 size is 64KB or 128KB. With nowadays applications, it is not possible to hold all required data used by the application. Some data will be spilled into L2, L3, and main memory correspondingly. Selecting data to be replaced is determined by a *replacement policy*.

The cache must be divided into equal blocks. The data are stored in block, implying consecutive addresses inside one block. Data transferred to put in cache are in a unit of block of given size. Selecting block size is difficult. It is usually determined from the total number of blocks that can reside in a cache. It, therefore, determines the variety of addresses among blocks. The block size also affects the

Figure 1. Memory hierarchy

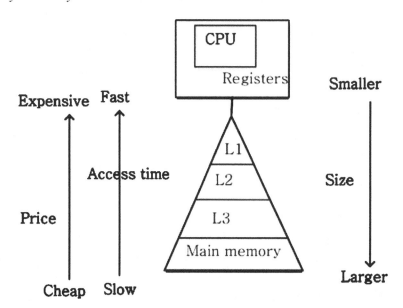

transfer time between the lower level and the upper level memories since the data must be transferred and is used to fill the whole block. Larger block size causes a long latency time to transfer and leads to fewer total number of blocks in a cache, but inducing long consecutive addresses. This is a favor to spatial locality where it is likely that data in consecutive addresses should be referenced in a sequence. However, too large block size may cause too many consecutive addresses that are not relevant in the same block. Also, when the total number of blocks in cache is small, there is not a variety of address regions that can be in the cache, which may not enough to hold a current working set. Picking the right block size needs a special consideration.

Replacement policy is another parameter needed when all blocks in a cache are filled up. When a new required data block arrives, and there is no empty block to store, some block must be replaced. The typical replacement policy is Least Recently Used (LRU), Pseudo LRU, First-in First-out (FIFO), Optimal methods etc. The replacement policy can complicate hardware design as well as prolong the latency of the transfer time.

Locality is a relevant concept in cache design. The main principle is to hold a required data in the nearest cache level as much as possible. The required data is usually determined by temporal and spatial factors. For spatial locality, it is observed that the address next to a current one is likely to be referred soon. For example, we usually write a loop to access, e.g. A[1],A[2],..,A[i+1], etc. iteratively. On the other hand, the temporal locality required the working set to hold data with in a time interval. For example a code such as

for (i=0;i< N; i++)

A[i] = B[i]+C[i];

Arrays A, B, and C are required in each iteration but these arrays are not located in the consecutive addresses. Each array may be allocated to different blocks. Having many blocks in the cache can accommodate this.

Perceptron and LVQ

There are many kinds of models used for prediction. In the following, we concentrate on a neural network model in our examples. Among these, the simplest one is the perceptron where we use in our prototype. The perceptron is the network where the inputs are in the vector form, totally R inputs. Each input is multiplied with the weights in a weight vector $W=[w_{11},w_{12}..w_{1R}]$. They are sent to the transfer function $f = \sum_{i=1}^{R} w_{1i} p_i$, described by Figure 2. There are many kinds of transfer function. An example one is $f(n)$ $= -1,$ if $n < 0,$ and $f(n) = 1,$ otherwise.

For multiplayer perceptron (MLP), it is extended from the above perceptron using a set of (many) simple units with weighted connections between them. MLPs are classified as a type of Artificial Neural Network (ANN). Many learning algorithms can be used to set the weights. Figure 3 shows an example of MLP with 2 hidden layers, where there are *inputs (x)* and *outputs (y)* layers. Hidden layers map inputs from previous layer's output, weight them and pass through an activation function.

Figure 2. Perceptron network

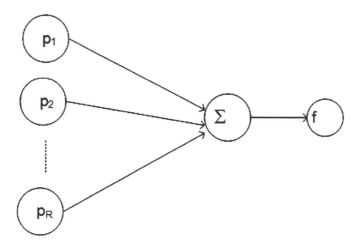

Figure 3. Multilayer perceptron

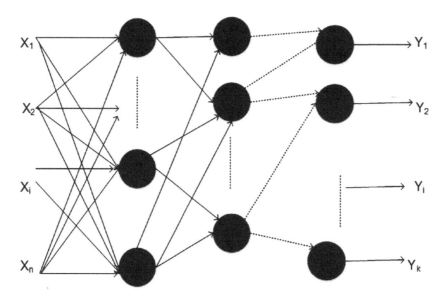

Further, LVQ also has the network structure similar to the self-learning network. The difference is that the neuron output is specified as the classification results, as shown in Figure 4.

For each class, there is a group of neuron outputs, where x is an input to the network. The neuron output that is closed to x is the winner. The network will adjust the weight vectors of the winner neuron and others as in the following equation.

$$w_{ij}^{new} = \begin{cases} w_{ij}^{old} + r\left(x_i - w_{ij}^{old}\right) & if\ correctly\ classified \\ w_{ij}^{old} - r\left(x_i - w_{ij}^{old}\right) & otherwise \end{cases}$$

Figure 4. LVQ network

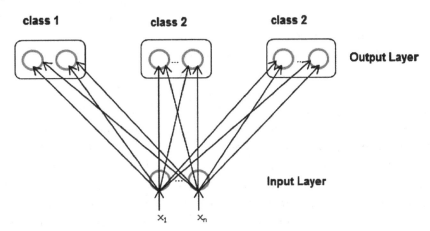

In the above equation, *r* is the learning rate. The weight vector is changed so that it is closed to the inputs. On the other hands, if the winner neuron gives the wrong classification results, the neuron has the penalty. Its weight is changed to be far apart from the inputs as in Figure 5.

RELATED WORK

There were many works that applied data mining to architecture design. Ozisikyilmaz et. al. (2006) presented architectural characteristics that were useful for data mining for workload characterization. The characteristics were a number of data references, bus accesses, instruction decodes, resource related stalls, CPI, cache misses (L1/L2), the number of branch mispredictions. These features were captured using VTune Performance Analyzer.

For example, in dynamic branch prediction, the branch misprediction traces must be collected during the run. Jiménez (2003) studied a branch prediction with perceptron. They compared the predictor with *gshare* and tested against 12 of SPEC2000 benchmark. The experiments varied the hardware budget

Figure 5. The learning of LVQ

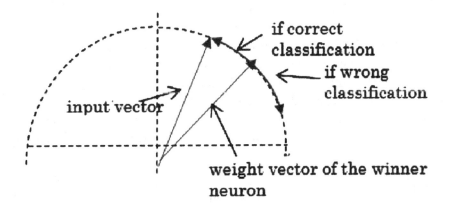

(capacity), and found a proper history length for each kind of perceptron. The trace was obtained from simulation and experiments for the path length predictor were performed. The path-based approach can run faster than the perceptron approach.

Ribas et. al. (2003) presented a branch prediction scheme using the neural network. They considered the perceptron and generated the branch stream where the number of taken branches was varied. The performance of the perceptron was always more than 50% accurate. The accuracy increases according to the largest percentage occurrence between taken and not-taken branches.

Egan et. al. (2003) applied the neural network to perform the dynamic branch prediction. They proposed to use the neural network in the second-level pattern history table (PHT). The approach exploits the large history with the training before the prediction and the LVQ predictor was used. The approach was applied to Stanford integer benchmark suite. Osofisan and Afunlehin (2007) focused on the super-scalar architecture with the dynamic branch prediction using the neural network. The neural network can be implemented as a hardware branch predictor. The experiments were tested on SpecInt95 where 8 benchmarks were considered. The trace of branches was collected for the training set. They used LVQ predictor in particular and modified the simple superscalar simulator to integrate to the neural network predictor. The architecture of the neural network was selected by training results.

Steven et. al. (2001) presented the LVQ neural network for the dynamic branch prediction. Three variations of the history registers were considered: the multiple local history register, global history register, and the combinations of them. Four back propagation networks were used. The authors simulated on Stanford integer benchmarks (eight C programs). Wang and Chen (2005) studied three kinds of machine learning algorithms. They studied perceptron, path-based and LVQ for dynamic branch prediction. The history length was varied and the bubble sort was tested with one input set. Yeh and Patt (1991) used the two-level adaptive branch predictor. They tested against SPEC benchmark and compared the performance with a static branch predictor. The cases with varying branch history length were tested.

Deibel and Sikorski (2003) presented an interesting comprehensive report that used perceptron for the branch prediction. They adapted the use of perceptron and performed the experiments in varying factors. They studied the impact of enlarging the perceptron table size, performance when using the local history, using set associative and the victim cache.

Bellare et. al. (2006) presented the report using perceptron's in the dynamic branch prediction. They tried on the kernel-based perceptron and hybrid predictor where several predictors may be used depending on the outcome, tested on the 1st JILP CBP-1 data set. They assumed the hardware budget of 64K. Several perceptron tables were used and one perceptron was selected at a time adaptively, called adaptive information processing. The adaptive information processing method gave the better performance than that of the traditional *gshare* (McFarling, 1993).

Some work studied data mining for cache prediction. Elakkumanan et. al. (2005) used data mining for cache hierarchy determination. They focused on commercial applications. Cache capacity and the number of levels were important parameters. The decision tree C4.5 and Apriori method were used to build prediction models. The SIMICS was used to simulate instructions for Enterprise Linux. Silva et. al. (2007) presented the efficient cache analysis that can run in a single pass. They evaluated various cache models for Mediabench. The evaluation time was faster by 70% compared to ADPCM approach. Data mining was used for cache prefetching by Fang et.al. (2006). They focused on enhancing the network storage system with prefetching.

Najari and Lotfi (2014) surveyed techniques in data mining for malware prediction. They divided the techniques for detection methods into the techniques based on signature and based on behavior.

The use of instruction traces for malware prediction was considered in the second kind. Some previous work was based on pattern matching of the string of hexadecimal values obtained by binary instructions. Some kept data as a tuple of positions and values while some considered the assembly-level instructions (Keung, et.al. 2005). For example, Choudhary and Saharan (2012) used data mining technique, SVM and neural net classifiers, in malware detection. They considered abstract assembly and selected top *L* features. IDApro was applied to generate the assembly code.

The work by Kumar and Mishra (2013) used the sequence alignment algorithm to detect malware. They considered HEX-code and ASCII code transformation. The artificial neural network model is used for prediction. The tests for viral and worm were considered. Tabish, Shafiq, and Muddassar (2009) applied the statistical approach to classify malware. They considered three types of files:DOC, EXE, JPG, MP3, PDF, and ZIP. The 52 features were considered which included 1,2,3,4 grams of 13 statistical features. 6 types of malware were considered. Rieck et.al. applied machine learning, e.g., clustering and classification, for malware detection. They proposed an incremental approach for behavior-based analysis. The behavior of malware binaries on a daily basis was collected.

Pratheema, Prabha, and Kavitha (2012) applied the naive bayes, KNN, and J48 to classify malware. Their approach considered a HEX code with N-grams as features. 15 subfamilies were considered with the total of 1056 samples. Baldangombo, Nyamjav, and Horng (2013) calculated information gain to detect malware. They extracted features from features of Windows PE file and applied PCA with three classifiers:

- SVM,
- J48, and
- Naïve Bayes.

Since our interest is in the use of profiling tools for study architectures, previous works motivate us in the analysis of these large data for architecture design, using data mining. These works differ in the benchmarks considered, profiling tools, features to study, and type of model used. In general, the whole process starts with application benchmarks selection. The applications should be standard, open-sourced, and represent a target application group which the designed system runs. The inputs need to be selected properly along with the benchmarks. There are many profiling tools for architecture characteristics. Each of them has different focuses. Some gives dynamic characteristics during the run time while some gives static features obtained at compile time. For dynamic profiling, the tools should be simple, easy to install, easy to customize, do not require the binary to recompile etc. Static profiling depends on compiler options and instruction sets. After profiling, these data needs to be analyzed where customized programs need to be developed. All these are considered as preprocessing which is important to data mining. Then, a proper data mining method is selected.

METHODOLOGY

To create the prediction model, relevant trace data according to the benchmark program must be collected. Figure 6 summarizes the methodology and examples in our case study. The three steps depend on the application. The first step involves data collection which requires direct profiling tools and mechanism to summarize the data from the profiling tools. Column "Tools" exhibits the tool name used in our example. Column "Models" present the model we tried in the experiments and Column "Metrics" is how to verify the quality of the derived model.

Data Gathering

Data gathering is very important in model constructions. First, we address the profiling approaches used in this work for collecting architectural features, starting from traces which includes instruction and memory addresses, branches addresses and branch target addresses, as well as instruction mixes, co-occurrences of the instructions and memory addresses.

Depending on applications, proper architectural features are collected. For instance, for cache prediction model, we need the memory traces of benchmark applications, i.e., how each interesting application accesses the memory addresses. Specifically, there are two kinds of memory addresses: instruction memory addresses, data memory addresses. Instruction memory, normally, refers to the memory that stores the code when running where it is usually an instruction cache. Data memory refers to the memory that stores data during the program executions, or data cache. To collect these memory traces, dynamic profiling tools are needed to run while running the benchmark application. Dynamic profiling tools

Figure 6. Methodology and example case studies

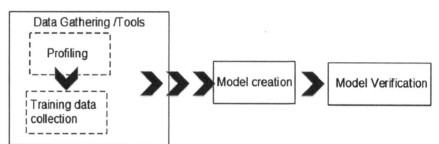

Applications	Architectural features	Tools	Models	Metrics
Cache model prediction	Memory reference addresses -Cache parameters: Capacity, associativity, block size etc.	Intel Pintools	Perceptron	Confusion matrix
Malware detection	Instruction mixes Instruction execution sequences -Instruction frequencies -Instruction co-occurrence N-Grams -Statistical values of instruction opcode	IDAPro	Decision tree	Precision / Recall
Branch prediction	Branch address Branch condition results Branch target address -Branch history length	Deassembler	Perceptron LVQ	Accuracy

need to collect data accurately, have low execution overhead, and need not require the applications to be compiled specifically.

To profile the application behavior, the addresses of executing instructions are collected. As in Figure 6, for cache memory design, the memory reference trace must be collected. The address trace is used to simulate with cache parameters for finding cache miss rates. For branch prediction, we need to collect branch address, target address, and branch condition outcome traces. For malware detection, profile the instruction mixes, and instruction execution sequences. Programs to count instruction frequency, co-occurences, and statistical opcode values are easily developed.

Intel Pintool, (Chi-Keung et. al., 2005; Luk et. al., 2005) such as *insmix, inscount, calltrace, strace* etc. can be advantageous for measuring the instruction type percentage, the total instruction count, calling sequence and stack trace etc. These tools can be modified to gather only interesting events at a sample interval to reduce the profiling execution time. However, this must be tuned properly so as to balance between profiling time and the accuracy of profile data.

For branch instructions which cause significant stall cycles, one needs to know specifically where the addresses of branch instructions are and whether the branches are taken or not. Using Pintools, we can select to monitor only branch instruction addresses, by customizing from *opcodemix, brtaken, br_target_addr* and *itrace* to obtain only the address of branch instruction, results (taken/not taken), and the target address. The information is used for training the branch predictor. IDA from Hex-Rays (Hex-Ray, n.d.) is also an example tool for deassemblers which can map the binary code back to assembly instructions. Figure 7 displays the equivalent of binary codes and assembly instructions using IDAPro. The left side shows the binary code while the right side shows the assembly derived.

Or if the benchmark code is not too complicated, using deassembler tool to map the code to assembly instruction. Then, we can manually step and record the branch target addresses and branch outcomes for every branch instruction in the code

For the memory references, the tools *pinatrace, dcache* are used to collected memory addresses access, and access type (Read (2) /Write (3)) as in Figure 8. The addresses are in hex values (64-bit long). The tools generate an address per access while running the benchmark. The total number of traces is considerably large. The huge trace file needs to be split in a proper size for further feature extraction and supervised learning.

Figure 7. Transformation from the binary to abstract assembly

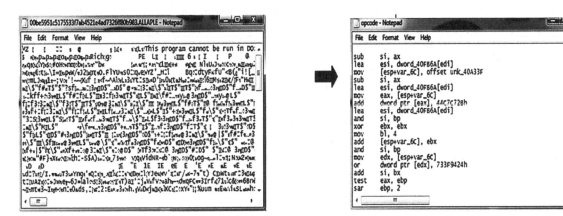

Figure 8. Example of memory traces collected by Pin Tool

```
2 7fffc790be98
2 7fffc790bea8
2 7fffc790beb0
3 f56054
2 7fffc790bec0
2 f53f8c
2 7fffc790bec8
3 7fffc790beb0
2 f56050
3 7fffc790bea8
2 605640
3 7fffc790be90
```

The Use of N-Grams

Once the benchmark program is viewed as binary instructions, the sequence of codes is analyzed to inspect individual instruction occurrences such as the frequency of the particular type of instructions and/or addressing modes. Also, the co-occurrences of the instructions are observed. The co-occurrences imply dependencies between instructions, which reflect some code pattern or memory access pattern. For instance, consecutive memory address reference shows spatial locality required for certain application. In another example, sequence of instruction addresses representing a loop body reflects the code attached due to a malware program.

Consider the example of the analysis of memory trace for finding cache model. Observing the memory access pattern, consider the parameter such as block size. What we are particularly interested in is the trace patterns that lead to the proper block size. Based on the locality observation, we observe the co-occurrences of addresses as well as the distances between them, and their frequencies. The distance implies the locality and temporal locality. The frequencies of each address as well as the length of contiguous addresses are counted. There are many possibilities to consider co-occurrences and contiguous addresses. There is a need to limit a window size for counting the co-occurrences such as between 64 addresses above and below. Programs to count the co-occurrences and distances as well as frequencies of contiguous addresses are developed based on the window size. After counting all these, top five frequently found distances of the found co-occurrences are extracted as features.

As another example of using N Grams, based on the instructions, similarly, there are a large number of instruction traces. They are divided into blocks of sizes 50KB, 100KB, etc. The block size is similar to the window size as in the previous case. One may also study the effect of window size for consecutive instructions. The frequency of individual instructions, two consecutive instructions and three consecutive instructions are counted. Then, the ranking of these N Grams are considered as features.

For example, consider as hexadecimal code "4db6ffda0dce0ebb". We can calculate 1,2,3 grams as:

- **1 gram:** We obtain 4d | b6 | ff | da | 0d.
- **2 gram:** We obtain 4db6 | b6ff | ffda | da0d | 0dce
- **3 gram:** We obtain 4db6ff | b6ffda | ffda0d | da0dce | 0dce0e

Table 1 presents 14 popular instructions commonly found in malwares (Daniel, 2007). One may rely on these for limiting the considered opcodes. Figure 9 is an example assembly derived using IDAPro. In Figure 10, it is seen that 1,2, and 3 consecutive opcodes are counted. Here, only opcodes are considered while in the extension, the addressing modes or operands can be considered together with opcodes.

Model Creation

Once traces extracted from the profiler tools as well as the extracted features are collected, the next step is to build the model. Given inputs for each application, the model is created by training data.

Cache Model Prediction

For memory address traces, collected from Pintools, using an existing cache simulator tool, such as SMPCache (SMPCache, 2015) with possible cache parameters, e.g., block size, associativity, replacement

Table 1. Frequent malware opcodes

No.	Opcode
1	mov
2	push
3	call
4	pop
5	cmp
6	jz
7	jmp
8	lea
9	add
10	test
11	retn
12	jnz
13	xor
14	and

Source: Daniel, 2007.

Figure 9. Logical assembly example

Figure 10. Opcode selection for three cases

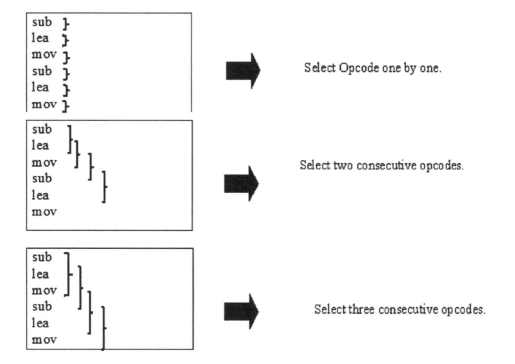

policy etc. to record cache misses as a training data. Further since there are many possible parameters, the limitation of variables will help reduce the exploring space. For instance, we may restrict the set of parameters, e.g., possible block size needs to be 64K, 128K and 256K. The replacement policy is fixed to be LRU and assuming direct-mapped approach. The misses, with the extracted features from training data are used to build the prediction model.

In our example case, the parameters are fixed as following:

- Processor in SMP = 1,
- Cache coherence protocol = MESI,
- Scheme for bus arbitration = Random,
- Word wide (bits) = 64,
- Mapping = Fully-Associative,

- Replacement policy = LRU,
- Main memory size = 512 Kbyte,
- Cache size = 32 KB.

The block size is varied among 256,512, or 1,024 bytes. The block size, which gives the lowest miss rate, is the output answer for training. N Grams calculation of address, co-occurrences, and frequency for each length of contiguous memory address give us totally 31 attributes totally including top 10 maximum distances of co-occurrence pairs, top 10 frequencies of addresses, 5 maximum lengths of contiguous addresses and their frequencies. The output of the predication model specifies the block size, either 256,512 or 1024 bytes.

Using a multilayer perceptron, parameters are learning rate, the number of hidden layers and momentum. For training a multilayer perceptron, these values are varied to find the best perceptron for a given training data set.

From our cache prediction model, using benchmark set from NUMineBench (Narayanan et. al.,2006), for applications: KMeans, SVM and Baysian, first, we try to find the proper number of hidden layers, between 1-20 using learning rate=0.3 and momentum=0.2. When the best case gives the best precision and recall is when the number of hidden layers is 2 and 8. Secondly, for the number of hidden layers=2 and 8, varying the learning rate between 0.1 to 1.0, to find the model with the best accuracy/precision/ recall. Finally, the derived model contains 30-nodes input 3-node output, 2 hidden layers, learning rate=1, momentum=0.9.

Branch Prediction Model

For branch prediction model, as a simple test, we select sorting algorithms as benchmarks on random input sets: quicksort and selection sort. From both sorting algorithms, the number of branches is bounded to the number of items, we inspect that the number of branches are varied due to the following:

- The number of items to be sorted.
- The relation of sorting items: such as whether the items are sorted in the reversed order or not, whether the items are sorted in part or not.
- The item values which should not be varied too much.

The random inputs are generated to the algorithm. The input value to be sorted is ranged -100 to 100. The number of elements in a set tested is 20,30,40, and 50. We select various methods for sampling. First, a program computer is written to random the number for three sets. Secondly, we draw elements with putting the items back after drawing and without putting it back. We random the range and sort the items.

To collect the branch address, the source code of sorting algorithms in C is transformed in the assembly using *gcc* and *objdump*. The *objdump* gives the assembly listing and branch addresses. The selection sort has 4 branch addresses at 119,15*b*,18*d*,1*c*6 and the quicksort has 5 branch addresses *b*,50,91,*dd*,107

For example, the following program is the assembly part of quicksort.

8: 8b 45 0c mov eax,DWORD PTR [ebp+12]

b: 3b 45 10 cmp eax,DWORD PTR [ebp+16]

e: 0f 8d dc 01 00 00 jge 1f0 <_quick_sort+0x1f0>

From the sorting code, we insert the code to count the number of taken, and untaken branches. We run the perceptron and LVQ predictors with various factors: the history length, the data size, the types of inputs.

The dynamic perceptron predictor contains two-dimensional weighted array where branch address is used as an input to select the proper row in perceptron table. It is interesting to see how long the branch history is needed in order to gain a high accuracy. The history length implies the hardware cost. The column of this array is the branch history. Considering the history of each branch, each prediction value is computed based on the weight properly. The prediction is compared to the real outcome and the weight values are updated and shifted for the next round. The following steps show how we use the perceptron for the branch prediction (Wang & Chen, 2005).

1. Let h be as the history length. $G[i]=0$, for every element, $j=1..h$ as a global predictor.
2. Let W be the weight matrix, where rows are the program counter (PC) and columns are the history indices. Every element of $W[i][j]$ is initialized to 0.
3. Let $i=PC \bmod n$
4. If G[j]=0 (not taken) then $y_{out}=W[i][0]-W[i][j+1]$ and $y_{out}=W[i][0]+W[i][j+1]$ otherwise.
5. If then prediction is taken, otherwise it is not taken.

In the above code, h is the limit of the boundary of the history length. The prediction is the variable *prediction* bit. The current output is determined by. Also, for the weight updated, the prediction and the real outcome are compared. If they are not same or, the weight is updated depending on the real outcome. If the real outcome is taken, $W[i][j]$ is increased by 1 or if the outcome is not taken, the weight $W[i][j]$ is decreased by 1 as in the symmetric transfer function. After that, the global register is left-shift by 1 bit position and we put the outcome in the corresponding $G[j]$. The overall picture of the perceptron predictor is in Figure 11. The array of weight W is the perceptron table. is the prediction value computed. The branch outcome is used for online training and updating the perceptron.

Another prediction model is using LVQ. The weight update approach is different. The training and the update are in the same loop. LVQ requires learning rate r and a stopping condition should be given. Input vector X is given as the two least significant bits of the branch PC to the bits in $G[h]$. Two weight vectors are used where which stores all 0's and stores all 1's. For example, when $h=4$, and $W_1=[1,1,1,1,1,1]$. The two bits of program counter (PC) combines with 4 bits in G when $h=4$ becomes 6 elements of. The two weight vectors implied two classes: taken-branch and not-taken branch.

The loop of updating the weight is as in Wang and Chen (2005). The prediction is done by calculating Euclidian distance from the input vector X to the initial weight vector for $j=0$ and 1. If it is closer to then is updated by the comparing the outcome to the class. If they are the same, $W_i(new)=W_i(old)+r(X-W_i(old))$. Otherwise,. Then, the learning rate is reduced and when the stopping condition is met, the loop stops.

It is seen that the weight is updated while the branch is executed. Figure 12 shows how to integrate the predictor to the program traces (Bellare, Kanni, and Sen, 2006). From the program source, the profiling is done during the execution. These information are fed to the perceptron predictor.

Figure 11. The perceptron predictors
Source: Jiménez and Lin, 2001.

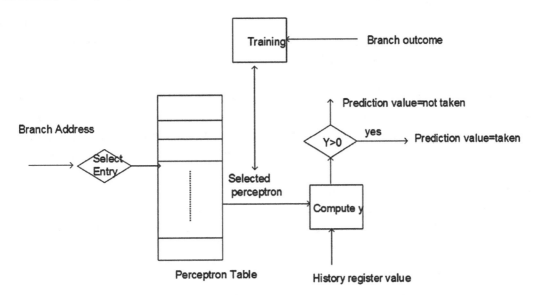

Figure 12. Architecture of using the predictor

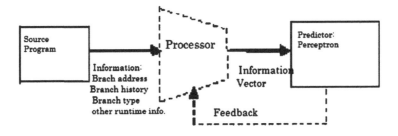

Malware Decision Tree

Another use of instruction traces is to create a malware prediction model from based on a decision tree J48 based on selected N Gram patterns. The data set was originally obtained from CWSanbox dividing into reference data set and application data set. The reference data set has 1,200 files used for training. They belong to malware classes: Allapple, Podhuha, Virut, each for 300 files. The normal files of types are DOC, JPG, EXE, 100 files each. The application data set has 3,251 files. Each contains malware class Allapple, Podhuha, Virut, where each class has 890, 8, and 2,053 files respectively. Each normal file for DOC, JPG and, EXE type has 100 files each.

The prototype model considers two kinds of feature sets: statistical values of opcode and instruction sequence behavior. For the statistical features, the instruction opcodes are transformed into the hexadecimal code (Tabish, Shafiq, & Muddassar, 2009). The statistical values, such as Simpson's index, Canberra distance, Minskowski distance, Manhantance distance, Chevbychev distance, Bray Curtts distance, angular separation, correlation coefficient,entropy, Kullback - Leibler Divergence, Itakura-

Saito Divergence, total variation (Cover & Thomas, 1991), are calculated as 1,2,3 grams and the top 10 features for each gram are selected features.

The input file is divided into blocks where we consider 50KB, 100KB, and the file size. The effect of block size to the model accuracy is studied for the statistical feature test. Thirteen statistical values are computed and each will be considered as 1,2,3 grams. Totally there are 39 features. The feature frequency is counted and used to model the decision tree.

Consider using assembly instruction features. The operand types are omitted in this example. The sequence of consecutive instructions are considered as 1,2,3 consecutive instructions and 1,2,3 grams. The consecutive instructions with top frequencies are selected. Totally, 58 attributes are obtained which are from 1 instruction for 14 attributes, from 2 consecutive instructions, for 17 attributes and from 3 consecutive instructions, for 26 attributes.

The threshold is used to justify whether the file is attached to malware. For example, threshold 0.5 means that the file must contain more than 50% malware blocks; then, the file is considered malware. Otherwise, it is classified as a normal file. The output results will report that the file is malware or not and it may be classified as which types. Figure 13 shows the tree derived from the reference data set

Figure 13. Decision tree of using N-Gram assembly instructions

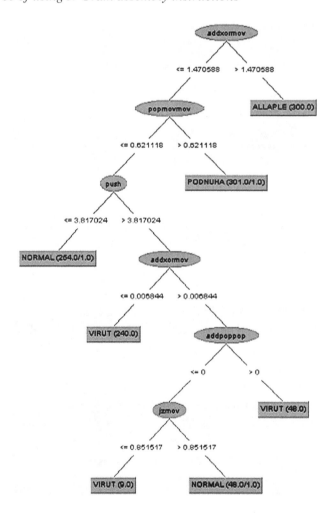

after 10-fold cross validation. Only six instructions are considered in the tree to justify the malware class. Frequency threshold of the instructions are on the tree edge.

Model Verification Metrics

Different models use different metrics. The following lists the metrics for our sample applications.

Confusion Matrix

For cache model prediction, we predict a proper block size for a given memory trace. We perform 10-fold cross validation where the miss rate of the training data are known. The predicted block size is compared to the trained data miss rate for each block size. If the predicted block size yields the lowest miss rate, it is a correct prediction. Then, we test against with 45 unknown data sets. Table 2 displays the sample confusion matrix. The table shows 100% accuracy. This is due to the variety of input memory traces since the experiments consider the only three benchmarks: KMeans, SVM and Baysian, with inputs. The memory traces for each benchmarks obtained are a lot but have the similar pattern though the inputs to each benchmark is different.

Precision/Recall/Accuracy

Consider the reference data set and application data set for malware detection model in Tables 3-4. Tables 5-6 are precision/recall/F-measure values for the approaches using statistical features and assembly instructions. In Table 5, Podnuha has the highest TP. Normal has the high FP rate. Allapple has high precision in the application set. From all the tests, Virut is wrongly classified as Normal for the most number of instances (118 instances from the confusion matrix). Allapple has the highest precision values for the application set. In Table 6, all the data sets (reference set, application set, 10-fold cross validation) has a TP rate about 1. Podnuha and Normal have the TP rate 1 for the application set. The FP is also very small for all the data sets. Virut has the highest precision for the application set while in the statistical approach, Allapple has the highest precision value. From the confusion matrix, Virut has the wrong instances as Normal only 5 instances and Virut is wrongly classified to Podnuha for 47 instances in the application set. However, compared to the statistical approach, Virut is wrongly classified into Normal for 1,148 instances.

Table 2. Confusion matrix

Class		Predicted		
		256	512	1024
Actual	256	15	0	0
	512	0	15	0
	1024	0	0	15

Table 3. Reference data set

Types	Total Files	Min Size (KB)	Max Size (KB)	Average Size (KB)
ALLAPLE	300	57	837	71
PODNUHA	300	109	109	109
VIRUT	300	13	1,139	139
DOC	100	22	1,734	653
JPG	100	10	2,101	387
EXE	100	29	944	114

Table 4. Application data set

Types	Total Files	Min Size (KB)	Max Size (KB)	Average Size (KB)
ALLAPLE	890	56	176	70
PODNUHA	8	122	122	122
VIRUT	2,053	12	1,036	281
DOC	100	22	1,715	229
JPG	100	10	2,186	396
EXE	100	80	150	86

Table 5. TP, FP, precision, recall, f-measure of the statistical methods

	TP	FP	Precision	Recall	F-Measure
Reference Set					
Allapple	0.99	0.001	0.997	0.99	0.993
Podnuha	1	0.001	0.997	1	0.998
Virut	0.973	0.003	0.99	0.973	0.996
Normal	0.993	0.009	0.974	0.993	0.997
Application Set					
Allapple	0.978	0.001	0.997	0.987	0.987
Podnuha	1	0.001	0.667	1	0.8
Virut	0.94	0.025	0.985	0.94	0.962
Normal	0.943	0.042	0.695	0.943	0.801
10-Fold Cross Validation					
Allapple	0.973	0.009	0.973	0.973	0.973
Podnuha	1	0.002	0.993	1	0.997
Virut	0.903	0.02	0.938	0.903	0.92
Normal	0.937	0.031	0.909	0.937	0.923

Figure 14 shows the graphical results of the correctness by classes for the N-Gram using statistical features. "size" is the block size of the divided instruction binary file. The statistical method performs better when the block size is large. When the block size equals to the file size, it is best. Figure 15 shows the graphical results of the correctness by classes for the N-Grams of assembly instructions. Rather than dividing into blocks, the whole file is considered. The method performs well for all the cases. Consider assembly instruction is more meaningful than using statistical values. Table 7 compares the performance of each method on the application set. It is seen that both performs well on Podnuha in general.

Accuracy

Accuracy is the direct comparison between actual answers and predicted one. For example in branch prediction, the predicted outcome is taken but the real answer is not taken. This is misprediction. Thus,

Table 6. TP rate, FP rate, precision, recall, f-measure (abstract assembly)

	TP	FP	Precision	Recall	F-Measure
Reference Set					
Allapple	1	0	1	1	1
Podnuha	1	0.001	0.997	1	0.998
Virut	0.99	0	1	0.99	0.995
Normal	1	0.002	0.993	1	0.997
Application Set					
Allapple	0.998	0	0.998	0.999	0.999
Podnuha	1	0.015	0.14	1	0.246
Virut	0.975	0	1	0.975	0.987
Normal	1	0.002	0.984	1	0.992
10-Fold Cross Validation					
Allapple	1	0.001	0.997	1	0.989
Podnuha	0.997	0.002	0.993	0.992	0.995
Virut	0.983	0	1	0.983	0.992
Normal	1	0.003	0.99	1	0.995

Figure 14. Comparison of percent correctness for each malware type for different block size of statistical features

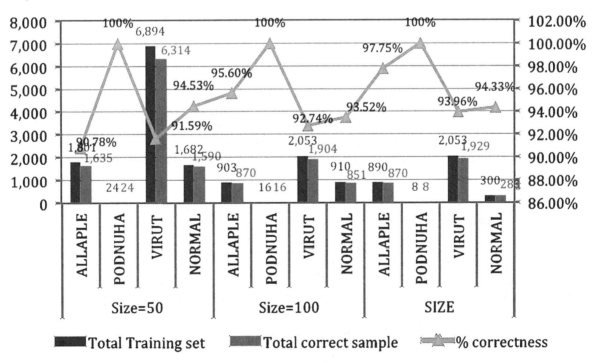

Figure 15. Comparison of percent correctness for each malware type for different block size of assembly instructions

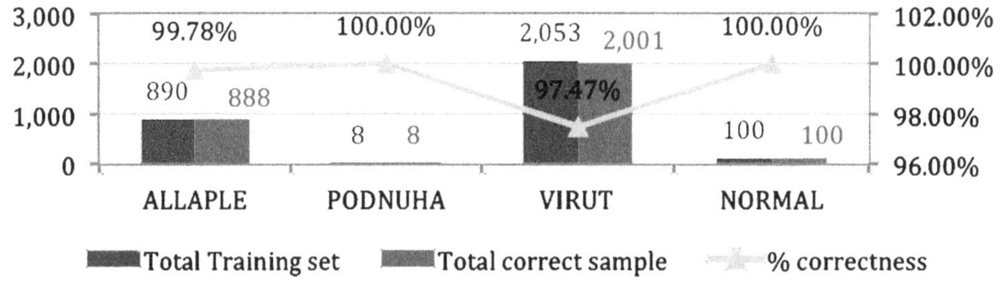

Table 7. Summary of the performance of each approach

Items	Statistical Method	Abstract Assembly Method
Number of correctly classified instances	95.04%	98.39%
Number of incorrectly classified instances	4.95%	1.661%
Highest TP rate	1 (Podnuha)	1 (Podnuha,Normal)
Highest FP rate	0.042 (Normal)	0.015 (Podnuha)
Highest Precision	0.997 (Allapple)	1 (Virut)
Highest Recall	1 (Podnuha)	1 (Podnuha,Normal)
Confusion matrix maximum error	118 instances (Virut classified as Normal)	47 (Virut classified as Pohnuha)

we compute the percentage of the total number of correct prediction is divided by the total number of branch addresses executed.

For branch prediction, the model includes branch history length since it is interesting to see how long is the branch history that we need in order to gain a high accuracy. In Table 8, the comparison of prediction accuracy is displayed between to perceptron and LVQ predictors. The longer the history is, the better correctness. The optimal one for this case is length 4. The LVQ predictor is another variation of perceptron where the weight updated scheme is different. The experiments vary the history length (the number of columns of weight matrix) against two kinds of sorting algorithm benchmarks. The more study can be done in a multidimensional way to inspect the effect of data size against the accuracy of the predictors as well as the history length. Also, the specific predictor for each branch accuracy can also be reported.

Table 8. History length vs. percent correctness

Type	Sort	History Length									
		h=1	h=2	h=3	h=4	h=5	h=6	h=7	h=8	h=9	h=10
Perceptron	Selection	67.96	88.78	88.83	83.53	84.28	84.20	85.00	84.70	84.72	78.58
Perceptron	Quicksort	59.08	65.23	65.56	61.39	63.84	64.70	63.74	66.31	66.80	67.86
LVQ	Selection	69.56	85.48	72.95	91.63	92.10	93.08	93.16	92.58	93.19	93.20
LVQ	Quicksort	55.43	64.28	56.99	72.60	72.58	72.27	72.21	72.40	72.38	72.62

Figure 16 compares the performance of both predictors varying the length of the history. We average the prediction correctness for all the cases. For each method, the more the history length is, the better the percentage of correctness. The history length of 4 gives about the optimal performance for the graph in Figure 16. LVQ is obviously better than the perceptron predictor.

From Figure 17, it is seen that LVQ and perceptron for the selection sort all performs better than those of the quicksort. Also, the LVQ performs better than the perceptron in both sorting about 10%. For all the LVQ cases, the history length about 2 is best. For perceptron, the history length about 2 is best.

Figure 16. Percent correctness of varying history length for both predictors

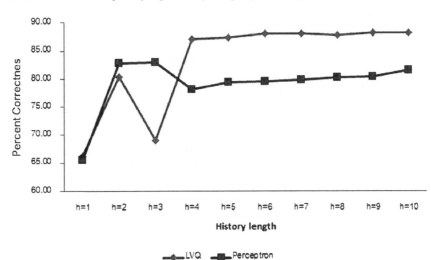

Figure 17. Percent correctness of the prediction for various sorting and neural network

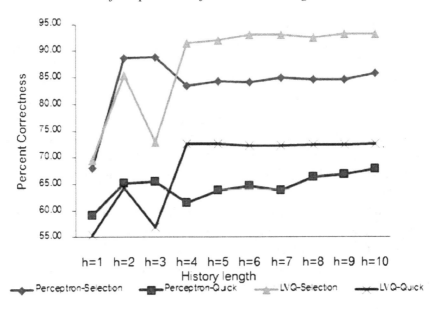

Figure 18. Percent correctness of the prediction for various data size for each branch for quicksort (LVQ)

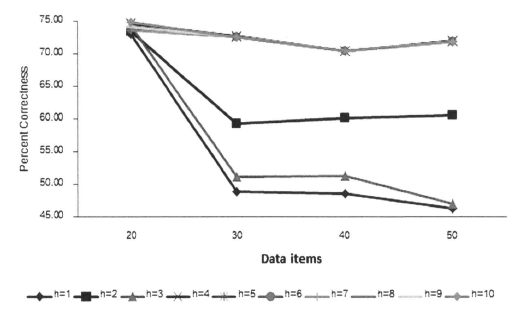

Figure 18 implies that the size of data items to be sorted affect the correctness of the predictors. With more data items for sorting, the percentage of correctness is reduced. This is true for all the history length test cases.

FUTURE RESEARCH DIRECTIONS

There are rooms for research improvements in architecture design. There are many profiling tools and each has focus on different aspects. Profiling tools generate a lot of characteristics which can be inspected and for architecture design.

As in our example, we use Pintool that collects profiles about instructions and memory traces. This tool can profile many more events such as stack trace, procedure call, etc. With the profile data, features or patterns can be extracted to find out certain problems. The typical patterns that are interesting are such as memory footprint, instruction traces, calling traces, stack traces. There are not a lot of works that utilize these traces by data mining and used them to improve the architecture or catching suspicious.

For example, previous work has used instruction sequences to detect malware code. One extension is to detect a block of repeated code or memory access violation, as well as consider sequence of calling traces. Besides, considering the nature of malwares or type of malwares can help detect specific patterns for each kind. The model besides perceptron may be challenging to use, for example, consider associative rules or deep learning.

We have seen a number of works utilizing perceptron for branch prediction. Using other kinds of predictor would also be interesting. Creating predictors for specific embedded architecture is also possible together with specific benchmark class.

Utilize memory traces for cache prediction model with data mining is a rare work. One of the reason is a lot of work is needed to collect memory traces. Also, to simulate these traces with all possible factors takes very long time. Thus, it is challenging to use branch and bound approach to cut down testing space so that training data can be effectively prepared.

Besides all these three applications, there are possibility of using application traces to find out proper number of CPUs, virtual memory size, bus bandwidth, networking etc., with proper feature extraction.

CONCLUSION

In this chapter, we describe the case study of using architectural features in data mining for designing the prediction model for system and software design. The examples include the use of instruction sets' feature for designing malware detection, the use of memory trace to design cache model, and the use of branch address to design branch prediction model. Importantly, static code analysis can be done with IDA while the instrumental profiler tool, Pintool, is used to collect memory address reference of the running application, instruction types, instruction addresses and kinds of instructions executed in the application. The profiling tool can collect more information such as stack trace, calling sequence etc. These information then is analyzed to for feature extractions. The observation of each design case is considered to establish extracted features. For instance, for cache prediction model, the memory reference pattern is observed to look for spatial locality and temporal locality which are necessary for the cache perform well. For malware prediction, the instruction sequence or pattern is observed. The pattern may exhibit repeated code and can imply the code portion that makes the normal program infect. For all these, N grams are commonly used for observing the combination or contiguous sequences of memory addresses and code addresses. These are used to construct training data. From then, the training data is used to create the prediction model. The model parameters are investigated to derived the suitable model. Then the model is verified using *n*-fold cross validation against the training set.

REFERENCES

Baldangombo, U., Nyamjav, J., & Horng, S. J. (2013). *A Static Malware Detection System Using Data Mining Methods*. Retrieved from https://arxiv.org/abs/1308.2831

Bellare, K., Kanni, P., & Sen, S. (2006). *Dynamic branch prediction using machine learning. Technical report*. University of Massachusetts at Amherst.

Chi-Keung, L. (2005). Pin: Building customized program analysis tools with dynamic instrumentation. *SIGPLAN*, *40*(6), 190–200. doi:10.1145/1064978.1065034

Choudhary, R., & Saharan, R. (2012). Malware detection using data mining techniques. *International Journal of Information Technology and Knowledge Management*, *5*, 85–88.

Cover, T. M., & Thomas, J. A. (1991). *Elements of Information Theory*. Wiley Interscience. doi:10.1002/0471200611

Daniel, B. (2007). Opcodes as predictor for malware. *Int. J. Electron. Secur. Digit. Forensic*, *1*(2), 156–168. doi:10.1504/IJESDF.2007.016865

Deibel, N., & Sikorski, K. (2003). *Exploring perceptrons in branch prediction.* Retrieved from https://courses.cs.washington.edu/courses/cse548/02wi/files/pdf/final/Kevin-and-Nick.pdf

Egan, C., Steven, G., Quick, P., Anguera, R., Steven, F., & Vintan, L. (2003). Two-level branch prediction using neural networks. *Journal of Systems Architecture, 49*(12-15), 557–570. doi:10.1016/S1383-7621(03)00095-X

Elakkumanan, P., Liu, L., Vankadara, V. K., & Sridhar, R. (2005). CHIDDAM: a data mining based technique for cache hierarchy determination in commercial applications. In *Proceedings of 48th Midwest Symposium on Circuits and Systems.* doi:10.1109/MWSCAS.2005.1594493

Fang, X., & Sheng, O. R. L. (2006). A Data-Mining-Based Prefetching Approach to Caching for Network Storage Systems. *INFORMS Journal on Computing, 18*(2), 267–282. doi:10.1287/ijoc.1050.0142

Hex-Rays. (n.d.). *IDA* [Software]. Retrieved from https://www.hex-rays.com/index.shtml

Jiménez, D. A. (2003). Fast path-based neural branch predictions. In *Proceedings of the 36th International Symposium on Microarchitecture* (MICRO-36). doi:10.1109/MICRO.2003.1253199

Jiménez, D. A., & Lin, C. (2001). Dynamic branch prediction with perceptrons. In *Proceedings of High-Performance Computer Architecture* (pp. 197–206). HPCA.

Kumar, V., & Mishra, S. K. (2013). Detection of malware by using sequence alignment strategy and data mining techniques. *International Journal of Computers and Applications, 61*, 16–19.

Luk, C. K., Cohn, R., Muth, R., Patil, H., Klauser, A., Lowney, G., & Hazelwood, K. et al. (2005). Pin: Building customized program analysis tools with dynamic instrumentation. *Proceedings of SIGPLAN, 40*(6), 190–200. doi:10.1145/1064978.1065034

Malishevsky, A., Beck., D., Schmid, A., & Landry, E. (n.d.). *Dynamic Branch Prediction.* Retrieved from http://web.engr.oregonstate.edu/~benl/Projects/branch_pred/

McFarling, S. (1993). *Combining branch predictor. Technical report.* Digital Western.

Najari, S. & Lotfi, I. (2014). Malware Detection Using Data Mining Techniques. *International Journal of Intelligent Information Systems, 3*(6–1), 33–37.

Narayanan, R., & Ozisikyilmaz, B. (2006). MineBench: a benchmark suite for data mining workloads. In *Proceedings of IEEE International Symposium on Workload Characterization.* doi:10.1109/IISWC.2006.302743

Osofisan, P. B., & Afunlehin, O. A. (2007). Application of neural network to improve dynamic branch prediction of superscalar microprocessors. *The Pacific Journal of Science and Technology, 8*(1), 80–97.

Ozisikyilmaz, B., Narayanan, R., Zambreno, J., Memik, G., & Choudhary, A. (2006). An Architectural Characterization Study of Data Mining and Bioinformatics Workloads. In *Proceedings of IEEE International Symposium on Workload Characterization.* doi:10.1109/IISWC.2006.302730

Pratheema, A., Prabha, M., & Kavitha, P. (2012). Malware Classification through HEX conversion and mining. In Proceedings of International Conferenece on EGovernance & Cloud Computing Sevices (EGov '12).

Ribas, V. M., Figueiredo, M. F., & Goņoalves, R. A. (2003). Simulating a simple neural network on branch prediction. *Acta Scientiarum Technology*, *25*(2), 153–160.

Silva, A., Esmeraldo, G., Barros, E., & Viana, P. (2007). Cache-Analyzer: design space evaluation of configurable-caches in a single-pass. In *Proceedings of International Workshop on Rapid SystemProto-typing*, (pp. 3–9). doi:10.1109/RSP.2007.15

SMPCache. (2015). *Simulator for cache memory systems on symmetric multiprocessors* [software]. Retrieved from http://arco.unex.es/smpcache/SMPCacheEnglish.htm

Steven, G., Anguera, R., Egan, C., Steven, F., & Vintan, L. (2001). Dynamic branch prediction using neural networks. In *Proceedings of Euromicro Symposium on Digital Systems Design*, (pp. 178–185). doi:10.1109/DSD.2001.952279

Tabish, S. M., Shafiq, M. Z., & Muddassar, F. (2009). Malware detection using statistical analysis of byte-level file content. In *Proceedings of the ACM SIGKDD Workshop on CyberSecurity and Intelligence Informatics*. Paris, France: ACM. doi:10.1145/1599272.1599278

Wang, Y., & Chen, L. (2005). *Abstract dynamic branch prediction using machine learning*. Retrieved from https://www.cs.utexas.edu/~lin/papers/hpca01.pdf

Xiao, F., Olivia, R., Liu, S., Wei, G., & Balakrishna, R. I. (2006). A data-mining-based prefetching approach to caching for network storage systems. *INFORMS Journal on Computing*, *18*(2), 267–282. doi:10.1287/ijoc.1050.0142

Yeh, T. Y., & Patt, Y. N. (1991). Two-level adaptive training branch prediction. In *Proceedings of the 24th Annual International Symposium on Microarchitecture* (MICRO 24). doi:10.1145/123465.123475

ADDITIONAL READING

Ahmadi, M., Ulyanov, D., Semenov, S., Trofimov, M., & Giacinto, G. (2015). Novel feature extraction, selection and fusion for effective malware family classification. Retrieved from http://arxiv.org/abs/1511.04317

Cachegrind: a cache and branch-prediction profiler. (n.d) Retrieved from http://valgrind.org/docs/manual/cg-manual.html

Feizollah, A., Anuar, N. B., Salleh, R., Wahid, A., & Wahab, A. (2015). A review on feature selection in mobile malware detection. *Digital Investigation*, *13*(June), 22–37. doi:10.1016/j.diin.2015.02.001

Jiang, Q., Zhao, X., & Huang, K. (2011). A feature selection method for malware detection, *Information and Automation (ICIA), InProceeding of 2011 IEEE International Conference on*, Shenzhen, 2011, 890–895.

Jiménez, D. A., & Lin, C. (2002). Neural methods for dynamic branch prediction Retrieved from: https://www.cs.utexas.edu/~lin/papers/tocs02.pdf

Kath, A., Paranjape, N., & Kulkarni, S. PandiPrediction, V. (n.d.) *System for L1 Data Cache*, Retrieved from http://www-users.cs.umn.edu/~kath/report_aca.pdf

Steven, G., Anguera, R., Egan, C., Steven, F., & Vintan, L. (2015) Dynamic branch prediction using neural networks. Retrieved from http://webspace.ulbsibiu.ro/lucian.vintan/html/neuralbr.pdf

KEY TERMS AND DEFINITIONS

Branch History: We typically record the past results of each branch. How much we record is called *history length* which affects the buffer size used to store them.

BTB: BTB stands for branch target buffer, which is a special buffer or cache that stores the branch target address for a particular branch instruction. It is very useful when CPU executes a branch instruction, it will lookup the branch target address in this cache to speedup the branch address computation.

Instruction Set Architecture: A structure of the assembly instructions used for a particular type of CPUs. It implies the types of instructions, and the form the addressing mode, i.e., how the operand of the instructions can be accessed.

Malware: The malicious program with the bad intention to harm the system.

SMP: Symmetric Multiprocessing is a kind of processing that assumes centralized shared memory and homogenous computers.

Spatial Locality: The program feature that uses consecutive data memory area over time.

Stall Cycle: The cycle of that the CPU is idle.

Temporal Locality: The program feature that reuses certain set of data during a period of time.

Chapter 10

On the Implementation of a Digital Image Watermarking Framework Using Saliency and Phase Congruency

Abhishek Basu
RCC Institute of Information Technology, India

Susmita Talukdar
Infosys Ltd., India

ABSTRACT

In this paper, a saliency and phase congruency based digital image watermarking scheme has been projected. The planned technique implants data at least significant bits (LSBs) by means of adaptive replacement. Here more information is embedded into less perceptive areas within the original image determined by a combination of spectral residual saliency map and phase congruency map. The position of pixels with less perceptibility denotes the most unimportant region for data hiding from the point of visibility within an image. Therefore any modification within these regions will be less perceptible to one observer. The model gives a concept of the areas which has excellent data hiding capacity within an image. Superiority of the algorithm is tested through imperceptibility, robustness, along with data hiding capacity.

INTRODUCTION

Digital domain provides various advantages like noise immunity, flexibility of implementation, easy data storage, low power consumption, scalability etc. over analog domain, as published by Pelgrom (2010). However all the natural signals are analog, digitizations is required for processing by means of sampling and quantization. Though due to quantization some information loss is occur in the form of quantization error but this error can be minimized by altering the number of quantization levels as per Freeman (2005). In addition to that signal processing are simpler and more reliable in digital domain with lower

DOI: 10.4018/978-1-5225-1776-4.ch010

cost. As a result technology switches over to digital domain, according to Proakis (2007) and Salivahanan and Gnanapriya (2011). This technology swap creates a revolution in information technology and data transmission over digital channels or in World Wide Web as published by Wolinsky Art (1999). Over and above the immense advantages offered by the Digital domain creates a boom in digital systems by means of digital consumer devices, according to the publication of Dhir (2004).

The enormous popularity of internet along with digital consumer devices like digital cameras, scanners etc, has become an indispensable part of people's live. At the same time as the popularity increases, access and storage of digital information become very easier. Accordingly a budding quantity of personal information about the users in addition to other digital data is stored in electronic form and that is generally transferred using unrestricted electronic means, as published by Feghhi Jalal et al. (1999). This effortless accessibility of digital information and the simplicity of the digital systems have left the contents over the digital media extremely insecure, in reference with Bidgoli Hossein (2006) and Furht Borko and Kirovski Darko (2006). This shows the way to the emerging problems like Copyright Protection as proposed by Farhadzadeh and Voloshynovskiy (2014), Nasir et al. (2007), Gertz Michael & Jajodia Sushil (2007) Wu Zhijun, (2014) and Zhang D et al (2009), Authenticity in print by Dal Park Geum et al. (2007), Eswaraiah R. & Reddy E.S., (2014), Otum Hazem Munawer Al (2014) & Wu Yongdong (2006), integrity verification and security of the digital information as proposed by Hosmer Chet, (2002), Li Chang-Tsun et al. (2010), Lynch C., (2000) & White paper, Digimarc Corporation (2004). As a result, the need for mechanisms to protect such information is undeniable.

Digital edition of information possesses intrinsic advantages of portability; efficiency and accuracy of information content, but alternatively, this production also place a severe intimidation of perfect and illegal replica in unlimited number as mentioned by Bandyopadhyay M. N., (2005), Horowitz Paul & Hill Winfield, (1989) & Pohlmann Ken C., (1992). To solve this challenging problem on the subject of data transmission in network surrounding, information hiding came as an efficient solution. Protecting copyright has initiated research to discover ways to hide copyright information or serial into digital data; the second one can help to identify copyright infringement, and the first one to take legal action as published by Anderson R., (1996), Wayner Peter, (2009) & Wei Chang Bao, (2014). Information hiding is a prospective means for copyright protection, authentication and integrity verification as well as intellectual property right protection as proposed by Kang X, Wei S., (2008) & Lo ChunChin et al. (2014).

Information hiding ensures the safety of data from corruption and helps to ensure privacy as well as secure communication. Now the idea of secret communication is very old, from ancient age people are trying to maintain the secrecy of massage as mentioned in Janeczko Paul B., (2006), Jung Ki-Hyun, Yoo Kee-Young, (2014) & Kahn David, (1996). Starting since Homer's Ilaid, stories by Herodotus, Kautilya's Arthasastra, Vatsayana's Kamasutra etc. the concealment of massage is one of the important task worldwide in different era as mentioned in Herodotus, (1972), Homer, (1972) & Kautilya, (1992).

Information hiding can be classified as:

Steganography

Steganography is the process of writing massage in such an ambiguous way that only sender and receptor can figure out the existence of the massage as printed in Aura, T. (1996), Craver, S. (1997) & Simmons, G. J. (1984). The word steganography is of Greek origin and means "concealed writing" appeared from the Greek words "steganos" which stands for "covered or protected", and "graphein" meaning "to write" as per Johannes Trithemius, (1606). The advantage of steganography, over cryptography is that it protects equally messages and communicating parties but cryptography protects the contents of a message as mentioned in Anderson, R. J., and F. A. P. Petitcolas (1998), Anderson, R. J. (1996), Cachin, C. (1998) & Möller, S. et al. (1998).

Digital Watermarking

Digital watermarking is the technique of embedding information/watermark into a digital signal in such a manner that it must be intricate to exterminate as published by Eskicioglu Ahmet M, Delp Edward J (2001) & Lenarczyk Piotr, Piotrowski Zbigniew, (2013). If the digital signal is copied, then the information embedded within the signal is also carried in the copy. The watermark might enclose further information together with the identity of the customer of a particular copy of the objects, Singh Amrik, Kaur Balpreet, (2014). Every proprietor has a sole watermark or can also place dissimilar watermarks in different objects, the marking algorithm embed the watermark into the object. The detection algorithm confirms the object determining together the owner and the integrity of the object, Shih Frank Y., (2008) & Lua Wei et al. (2006).

Cryptography

Cryptography is the process of modifying ordinary information into meaningless cipher text and decryption in the reverse. The word came from Greek sound "kryptos" which means "hidden, secret", and "graphein" meaning "to write", Smith Laurence Dwight, (1955). Cryptology is almost synonymous with encryption, the translation of information from a legible state to gibberish. The sender retained the capability to decrypt the information and thus avoid unwanted persons being able to interpret it as mentioned in Douglas R. Stinson, (2005) & Goldreich Oded, (2001).

Digital watermarking is very much correlated to steganography and cryptography, however it has several inherent advantages which make it admired and superior as published in Desai H. V., (2012), Grover Derrick, (2001) & Helor Hagit Zabrodsky (2001). The advantages are

- Robustness of watermarking is superior to steganogtaphy.
- Watermarks are inseparable from the digital signal in which they are embedded.
- Watermarks can shield the content even after they are decoded.
- Original signal itself is not modulated after embedding.

As a result digital watermarking is chosen in this article as security mechanism to ensure authentication, privacy and secure communication.

Digital watermarking is a promising area for research in computer science, signal processing and communication. Watermarking is basically a digital communication scheme in which a data, called watermark, tag or label embedded into a multimedia article in such a way that the watermark can be recognized or extracted later to make a claim about the object. The article may be an image or audio or video or text only Hartung Frank et al. (1998), Kabir Muhammed N et al.(2013) & Yeung M.M., (1998). One of the popular applications of watermarking is to provide evidence of ownership of digital image by embedding copyright declaration [60-61].

The similarity among paper watermarking and digital watermarking is very noticeable. In case of paper watermark an identifiable image or pattern appears in different shade of darkness and brightness when paper facing light. In late 13th century paper watermark was first introduced in Italy to represent format, quality identification and ownership proof. Later this use of watermark quickly spread across Europe, Emery, O. (1958), Weiner, J., and K. Mirkes. (1972). Till date nations are using watermark to protect legal papers, currencies and postage stamps from forgery, Jaseena K.U., Anita John (2011). A watermark is created on paper during extraction of excess water from paper-fiber pulp by pressing a water-coated light roller which is imprinted with a pattern, Biermann Christopher J., (1996). The idea of digital watermark came from this inspiration of paper watermark. The idea of watermarking first introduced by Tanaka et al. (1990) and the term digital/electronic watermarking is originally used by Tirkel et al. (1993). Since 1995, digital watermarking starts gaining appreciation and attention of researchers and become a promising field for research, Roche, S., and J.-L. Dugelay, (1998). However the three main requirements of watermarking technique are Imperceptibility, Robustness and Data hiding capacity and there is tradeoffs among them, Chandramouli, R. (2002), Dautzenberg C. and Boland F., (1994), Liu N et al. (2006) & Seitz Juergen, (2005). As a consequence digital watermarking still remains an open area for investigation. Digital watermarking techniques can be categorized into different classes in a variety of ways. The watermarking can be applied in spatial domain as well as in frequency domain. In spatial domain techniques the watermark is straightforwardly embedded into the host data, Gyum Kim Won et al. (1999), Lin PhenLan, (2001), Megalingam, R.K. (2010), Mukherjee D.P. (2004) & Mohanty Saraju P. et al. (2006). In frequency domain techniques, host data is primarily converted into frequency domain using different transforms like discrete Fourier transform (DFT), Ming Li Dong (2012), discrete cosine transform (DCT) Patra (2010), Fourier-Mellin transform, Dong Zheng, Jiying Zhao, (2003), or wavelet transform, Lalitha (2013) etc. and then embedded to the frequency domain coefficients. Frequency domain schemes are more robust in comparison with the spatial domain techniques although spatial domain offers facility of real time implementation throughout Hardware realization as of lesser computational complexity, Grgic Mislav (2009) & Maity Santi P (2009). Based on the type of digital object techniques can be divided into four categories and they are:

- Image Watermarking,
- Video Watermarking,
- Audio Watermarking, and
- Text Watermarking (Su, 1998; Singh, 2011).

However image is the most preferred multimedia object for researchers to test different watermarking technique. According to essentiality of data for watermark extraction, the watermarking techniques are Non-blind/Private Watermarking and Blind/Public Watermarking, Ping Dong et al. (2005). In Non-blind technique the original digital content is required to perform the extraction process form watermarked content, Minamoto T., Ohura R., (2012). In Blind technique the original digital content is not required to perform the extraction process, Zheng PanPan et al. (2014). Along with the human sensitivity of vision, the digital watermarks are further classified into three different types as follows: visible watermark, invisible watermark and dual watermark, Mohanty, S.P., Bhargava, B.K. (2008), Dhanalaks R., haiyalnayaki (2010). Visible watermarks become perceptible to an observer on inspection, Yip Shu-Kei et al. [2006]. Invisible watermarks are not visible to a viewer and it can be recovered only with suitable decoding system, Bhagyashri S.Kapre, Joshi M.Y., (2011), Craver, S. et al. (1998), & Cox I.J. et al. (1996). Dual watermarks are a combination of visible and invisible watermark, Yu Lin Pei (2009). From application viewpoint watermarks are source based or destination based, Servetto, S.D. (1996). A source-based watermark is a unique watermark embedded in all the copies of a particular digital object which need to be distributed and the watermark is used for authentication of object as well as impairment detection. In case of destination based watermark each digital copy required for distribution gets a unique watermark which used to mark out the buyer in the case of unlawful reselling, Podilchuk Christine I., Zeng Wenjun, (1998), Podilchuk Christine I., Zeng Wenjun, (1997). The requirements of watermarking schemes mainly focus on imperceptibility, robustness and embedding capacity but they continuously conflict with each other, Dehkordi, A.B. et al. (2011), Kuppusamy K., Thamodaran K., (2012) & Li Qing-Cheng, Hua Dong Zhen, (2008). Imperceptibility: Every processing related to an object will cause a significant loss of information or quality. Imperceptibility refers to the quality measures required to check the invisibility of the embedded watermarks inside an object without degrading the perceptual quality of watermarking. Ideally, there will be no perceptible difference between the watermarked and original signal, Jianquan Xie (2009), Smith Joshua R. & Comiskey Barrett O., (1996), Tu Shu-Fen, Hsu Ching-Sheng, (2008), Yang Hong-Mei et al. (2007) & Xun Jin, JongWeon Kim, (2012). However, this creates trouble in terms of robustness, as because achieving excellent imperceptibility means watermark always in perceptually insignificant portion of the host signal, Su J.K., Girod B., (1999) & Usman Imran et al. (2008).

Robustness: Robustness is the proof that the watermark can survive against signal impairment. Apart from intentional impairment, common signal processing operations can cause a threat to the extraction and detection of watermark; therefore it is desirable to create a watermarking scheme that can endure those operations, Chimanna, M.A., Khot, S.R., (2013), Cox I. and Linnartz J.-P. (1997) & Lina Shinfeng D. et al. (2010). Though, this starts problem with respect to imperceptibility, Matheson Lesley R. (1998), Bae Ki-Hyeok, Jung Sung-Hwan, (2001) & Verma Harsh K, (2009).

Embedding Capacity

Watermark embedding capacity usually refers to the quantity of information that can be embedded into a host object, as proposed by Anderson Ross, (1996), Awan, I. et al. (2006), Choo Hyon-Gon, Kim Whoi-Yul, (2004), Smithal B. & Navas K.A., (2007) & Tseng Hsien-Wen, Chang Chin-Chen, (2004). A high embedding capacity is normally attained at the price of either robustness or imperceptibility, or both, Akhaee Mohammad Ali et al. (2009), Bender W. et al. (1995), Jianquan Xie et al (2009).

A watermarked object is likely to face several intentional or non intentional signal impairments during transmission through channel, Song Chunlin (2010), Kutter M et al. (2000). Such impairments are termed as attacks Voloshynovskiy S. et al. (2000), Craver, S. et al. (1998) & Huang Chun-Hsiang, Wu Ja-Ling (2004). The attacks may be summarized as: compression like JPEG, MPEG Phi-Bang Nguyen et al. (2012) & Biswas Satyen et al. (2005); geometric distortions like cropping, rotation, scaling Licks Vinicius, Jordan Ramiro, (2005) & Tsang K.F., Au O.C., (2001); common signal processing operations like filtering, adding noise etc, as printed by Can, Y.S., Alagoz, F., (2013) & Hadi Ahmed Hassan, (2013). In addition to that some other intentional attacks are also available like printing, scanning, rewatermarking etc., Keskinarkaus A. et al. (2012), Chiu Yen-Chung, & Tsai Wen-Hsiang, (2006), Solanki Kaushal (2005) & Uhl Jutta Hämmerle et al. (2008). Such attacks degrade the quality of watermark and create a trouble in extraction and detection of watermark information, Voloshynovskiy S. et al. (2000) & Garzia F. (2013).

Considering the requirements of watermarking process and different intentional or non intentional signal impairments during transmission, fair benchmarking and performance evaluation are necessary for watermarking methods as mentioned by Macq B. et al. (2004), Hanjalic A. et al (2000) & Perez Meana

Hector, (2007). Measurement of quality is of critical importance in watermarking because quality is a key determinant for data reception and transmission control, Eckert Michael P. & Bradley Andrew P., (1998), Kullback S. & Leibler R. A., (1951). There are basically two classes of distortion assessment approaches. The first are mathematically defined which measures mean squared error (MSE), peak signal to noise ratio (PSNR), root mean squared error (RMSE) etc. The second class of measurement methods considers human visual system (HVS) characteristics in an attempt to incorporate perceptual quality measures, as mentioned in Saha S. et al. (2013), Avcıbaş İsmail (2001), Qian Jiansheng (2014) & Chopra Deepshikha et al.(2014). The most commonly used mathematical measurements are comprised of two main types - first one is the subjective measurement while the other is the objective measurement as printed in Żurawski Cezary, Skodowski Piotr, (2014), Arnold Michael (2008), Brandão Tomás, (2005), Sha Wang et al. (2014) & Zheng Dong (2003). These metrics use the original object as a reference to compare it with the impaired object. Objective measurement can be further divided into two classes: full-reference and no-reference, Lin Ma et al. (2012) & Farias M.C.Q., Akamine W.Y.L. (2012). Quality metrics are classified into six clusters in a broader way, based on the type of information they are using. The categories are: Pixel difference-based measures; Correlation-based measures; Edge-based measures; Spectral distance-based measures; Context-based measures and Human Visual System-based measures, Avcibas Ismail (2002), Eskicioglu M., Fisher P. S. (1995) & Kale K. V., Manza Ramesh Raybhan, (2008).

Watermarking algorithms can be implemented for spatial domain as well as for frequency domain. Frequency domain techniques are more robust in comparison with the spatial domain techniques but spatial domain provides facility in terms of lower computational complexity, higher perceptual quality and higher embedding capacity as printed in Shih FrankY., Wu Scott Y.T. (2003), Caldelli Roberto (2010), Megalingam, R.K. (2010), Baisa L. Gunjal, R.R. Manthalkar, (2011) & Nyeem Hussain (2013)]. Moreover real time implementation through hardware realization is also possible for spatial domain techniques because of lesser computational complexity, Chen Feifei et al. (2012), Vadde, S. et al. (2004), Ghosh, S.et al. (2009) & Joshi, A.M. et al. (2011). Software implementations have been developed due to the ease of use, upgrading and flexibility but at the cost of limited speed problem and vulnerability to the offline attack. On the contrary hardware realization offers advantage over the software in terms of less area, low execution time and low power, Scaria, A. et al. (2011) & Selvan M Thamarai, Kumar K Ashok, (2014). Hardware realization mark the digital object inside the system to authenticate the original data content right at the origin and guarantee the tamper proof in real time, Garcia M.Lopez et al. (2014) & Hala Farouk, Magdy Saeb. (2004). Hardware implementation varied from model to model. From programmable hardware implementation point of view the models can be realized either by Digital Signal Processor (DSP) or Field Programmable Gate Array (FPGA) or their mixed applications as referred in Qi Xiaojun, Qi Ji (2007), Cassuto Yuval et al. (2011), Carline Dylan, Coulton Paul, (2002), Maity Hirak Kumar, Maity Santi P., (2014), Qian Zhihong et al. (2012), Karthigaikumar P, Baskaranc Anumol, K, (2011), Kirovski Darko & Malvar Henrique S. (2003), Zoican, S (2005) & Hernandez Jose Juan Garcia et al (2011). Moreover Application Specific Integrated Circuits (ASIC) can also be used for real time implementation of digital watermarking algorithms, Karthigai P., Baskaran K. (2011), Garimella, A. et al. (2004) & Karthigaikumar P., Baskaran K. (2011).

The proposal of the work is regarding digital image watermarking technique based on Spectral Residual saliency map and phase congruency of an image in which the watermark will be implanted in the less prominent areas of the image. Saliency map represents visual saliency of a corresponding visual sense topographically as mentioned in A Basu et al. (2015). Spectral Residual Saliency is a fast and robust saliency detection model which does not depend on features, categories, or any other forms of past information of the objects. Here the spectral residual of an image is extracted in spectral domain by studying the log-spectrum of the input image. The corresponding saliency map is constructed in spatial domain thereafter, Hou Xiaodi & Zhang Liqing, (2007).On the other hand Phase Congruency detects corners and edges of the objects in an image. Here Peter Kovesi's model for Phase congruency has been used which utilizes a highly localized operator that can be used to identify both edges and corners in a contrast invariant way which helps to track the features of the images under varying illumination conditions with fixed thresholds, Kovesi Peter (2003). In this proposed technique data hiding is utmost at those positions where perceptibility and phase congruency values are low, Itti L. & Koch C. (2000), Itti L. & Koch C. (2001) & Basu A., Sarkar. S.K. (2013). By adaptive least significant bit (LSB) substitution method, the watermark is embedded in the original image, Shih FrankY., Wu Scott Y.T. (2003) & Asatryan David & Asatryan Naira (2009). Since the bits of the watermark are hidden at least significant positions of image, imperceptibility is better. The data is concealed at several places and multiple times to enhance the robustness and data hiding capacity, A Basu et al. (2011). This initial introduction about the proposed work is followed by some other sections like related works, description of the steps of watermark embedding and the extraction, experimental results and discussions, finally conclusion and references.

RELATED WORKS

According to the requirement and functioning domain, different types of watermarking methods have been developed. In initial paragraph a brief review on some state of the digital watermarking techniques are offered.

A local polar harmonic transform based robust digital watermarking algorithm was developed by Xiang-yang et al. (2015). The algorithm can produce watermarked image with high transparency and better robustness against general signal processing impairment and geometric distortions. Liu et al. (2016), proposed watermarking scheme of encrypted image which is based on comprehensive sensing. In this method the original image is encrypted with comprehensive sensing method. Then watermark information is implanted within the encrypted image by Scalar-Costa scheme. The analysis of the technique shows superiority in terms of robustness and embedding capacity. A digital image authentication scheme is projected by Wójtowicz and Ogiela (2015). The technique is based on bimodal biometric watermarking and abolishes the concept of authentication via password. The algorithm use fingerprint along with iris biometrics as watermark and embed them in an independent domain of the original image used as cover. The experimental outcomes ensure that the proposed scheme enables authentication of images with a significant accuracy level. AL-Nabhani et al. (2015) projected a digital image watermarking algorithm with high robustness using discrete wavelet and probabilistic neural network. The approach use discrete wavelet transform with a Haar filter to implant binary watermark information in selected coefficient blocks of original image and a probabilistic neural network is used to extract the watermark information. The experimental results show that the technique maintains the balance between imperceptibility and robustness. A fragile digital image watermarking scheme for image authentication and tamper detection in stereoscopic image is proposed by Zhou Wujie et al. (2016). The scheme use binocular just noticeable difference technique to embed the watermark. The results reveal the fact that projected technique got better security with balanced hiding capacity and imperceptibility. Hu Hwai-Tsu & Ling-Yuan Hsu (2016) proposed a blind digital image watermarking scheme with mixed modulation.

Quantization index modulation and Relative modulation is used for watermark embedding. For the period of the watermark implanting, the relative modulation acts on the Discrete Cosine Transform coefficients with small estimation differences. When the estimation difference exceeds preset boundary condition the Quantization index modulation takes over. A digital image watermarking based on Bidiagonal singular value decomposition is proposed by Mardanpour Malihe et al. (2016). Shearlet transform which is based on the study of multi-resolution with multi-directional and advances presentation of multidimensional data used here for transform. Better edge representation of this transform helps the scheme to achieve high imperceptibility and improved robustness. Khandare Shrinivas & Shrawankar Urmila (2015) presents a digital image watermarking algorithm based on bit depth plane for secured and classified data transmission. The procedure is a two part process. In first part the image converted into classified information by means of maximum likelihood classification and fuzzy model. In second part the classified image is secured with copyright information by image bit depth plane watermarking and get ready for transmission. A reversible fragile watermarking scheme for hologram authentication is proposed by Chan Hao-Tang et al. (2015). The algorithm embeds watermark to hologram image in transform domain, then store the image in spatial domain with restricted resolution which provide transparency to the watermarked image. The investigational outcome confirms the imperceptibility, robustness and hiding capacity. Boubiche Djallel Eddine et al. (2015) proposed an efficient fragile watermarking based scheme to protect the data aggregation integrity within heterogeneous wireless sensor networks. The projected security algorithm based on a dynamic embedding mechanism along with a cross-layer approach. The performance evaluation suggests the superiority of the technique with low communication and computation overhead along with energy efficiency. A watermarking framework using image depth map to improve the robustness of the watermark is proposed by Mohagheghe Hoda et al. (2015). The planned approach is an adaptive image watermarking based on perceptual image quality which define the regions of embedding with different depths. The embedding procedure used is Singular Value decomposition with Discrete Cosine Transform. The result analysis showed a good balance between visual quality and robustness. Chotikawanid Piyanart et al. (2015) presented a digital image watermarking method in homomorphic field. The scheme use to take out the low variational illumination component from the color host image. Based on this component a binary watermark is implanted within host image. A spatial domain based digital image watermarking process is described by Thongkor Kharittha et al. (2015). The blind method use regularized filter to implant watermark within the blue color component of host color image. A color image based watermarking method in the sparse domain is proposed by Sadreazami H. et al. (2015). A statistical model is designed based on the multivariate Cauchy distribution which used in designing the watermark detector. A wavelet domain based digital image watermarking algorithm is projected by Muhammad Nazeer and Bibi Nargis (2015). The scheme use partial pivoting lower and upper triangular based decomposition to factorize the watermark into a permutation matrix which embedded into particular sub-bands of a cover image. Andalibi Mehran & Chandler Damon M. (2015) proposed a scheme for invisible watermarking with a logo which is adaptively texturize. The main concept of this technique is to transform the logo into a set of textures that perceptually go with the textures of the original host image during embedding. Shah Prasanna et al. (2015) present a robust digital watermarking technique with Singular Value Decomposition and Discrete Wavelet Transform. The projected approach decomposes both original image and watermark image by means of Discrete Wavelet Transform followed by Singular Value Decomposition in LL band. After that finds out the singular values of every subband and changes these values with the watermark by scaling. A new watermark decoder in the contourlet domain is designed by Sadreazami Hamidreza et al. (2016). The proposed multiplicative decoder uses the standard inverse Gaussian Probability Density Functions as a prior for the contourlet coefficients of images. Makbol Nasrin M., et al. (2016) proposed a digital image watermarking design which utilizes the characteristics of human visual system. The projected scheme is a block-based approach which exploits the entropy and edge entropy as human visual system distinctiveness for the preference of major blocks to embed watermark which is binary in nature. Hernández Manuel Cedillo et al. (2015) presented a hybrid watermarking technique to facilitate the detection of illegal copies of digital color image, using a customer robust authentication. The experimental outcomes establish the fact that the scheme maintains image imperceptibility with excellent robustness. A double purpose spatial domain algorithm for image cryptography and digital image watermarking is represented by Ghosh Sudip et al. (2015). In this proposed technique a key is generated using Extended Hamming Code corresponding to each watermarked pixel. During extraction the watermark can be taken out blindfold with the watermarked image along with the key. A digital watermarking algorithm for copyright protection using identity based technique is proposed by Kumar Ashwani et al. (2015). The scheme serves a significant role in E-commerce where buyer and sellers identity is an important issue. The projected approach allows the proprietor to produce the watermarked content by private watermark key. In case of multiple ownership claims an arbiter will resolve it by means of time stamping.

This subsection present some methods of watermarking in spatial domain which has been proposed because watermarking methods in spatial domain are easy to implement, have lower computational complexity, higher perceptual quality and higher embedding capacity and also requires minimal computational power as mentioned in Shih FrankY., Wu Scott Y.T. (2003) & Asatryan David & Asatryan Naira (2009).

In this paragraph a brief review related to phase congruency and saliency based watermarking techniques has been represented.

There is a tradeoff between the imperceptibility and robustness to maintain the quality of the image while increasing the probability of the extraction of the watermark by the intended people after different attacks. To deal with the problem the results of the human visual system (HVS) was introduced in watermarking research. The HVS makes final evaluations on the quality of images which are then processed and displayed for improved outcome Basu A. et al. (2011). Cox I.J et. al. (1996) & Cox I.J et. al. (1996) projected a robust invisible watermarking technique in spectral domain where the watermark was proposed to be implanted in the perceptually significant components of a signal in order to make it robust against noise and malicious impairments. On the other hand, the alteration of these components degraded the perceptual quality of the signal. Koch C., Ullman S. (1985) introduced the idea of a saliency map to achieve pre attentive selection. This is an explicit two-dimensional map that encodes the saliency of objects in the visual environment. Sur A. et. al. (2009) proposed a spatial domain adaptive image watermarking scheme which embeds watermark to the least salient pixels of the image and thus the corresponding watermarked images have less perceptual error with respect to HVS based watermarking techniques. Guo C. L. et al. (2008) demonstrated the fact that the phase spectrum is the key to calculate the saliency map and proposed a model called phase spectrum of Fourier transform (PFT) to detect saliency. Graph-based visual saliency (GBVS) recognition was presented in 2006 by Harel J. (2006) and that can predict human fixations, although very expensive in terms of computational complexities. Another saliency based digital watermarking model is given in Basu Abhishek et al. (2015) where the authors have used Itti-Koch saliency model and adaptive LSB replacement to embed the watermark into the less perceptible area of an image to improve the imperceptibility. Gradient based edge detection methods were developed by Marr D. & Hildreth E. C. (1980), Canny J. F. (1983) & (1986) and others but those were sensitive to image illumination variations. A model of feature perception called the Local Energy Model was developed by Morrone M. C. (1986) and Morrone, M.C., Owens, R.A. (1987). This model was not based on the use of local intensity gradients for feature detection. Kovesi Peter, (2000) described a new corner and edge detector developed from the phase congruency model of feature detection which is highly localized and has responses that are invariable to image contrast. Hou Xiaodi & Zhang Liqing, (2007) projected an approach based on spectral residual, to detect saliency map which is faster and more robust against alteration. X. Cui et al. (2009) proposed a Temporal Spectral Residual scheme which is a motion saliency detection model for video content analysis. A survey of watermarking techniques applied to multimedia is presented by Tong Liu., Qiu Zheng-ding, (2002). The survey of digital watermarking-based image authentication techniques is given in Vidyasagar (2005). Asymmetric watermarking techniques, also named public key digital watermarking system is also an interesting area of research and a Survey of Public Key Digital Watermarking schemes is given by Xie Rongsheng et al. (2007). Phase congruency (PC) presents a dimensionless quantity which is a good measure of the significant feature points with high information (or entropy) and low in redundancy within an image Morrone, M.C., Owens, R.A. (1987). Phase congruency method proposed by Morrone, M.C., Burr, D.C., (1988) presented an algorithm to distinguish features according to the phase information, and has been used into face recognition Bezalel, E., Efron, U. (2005), palm-print verification. Punsawad, Y., Wongsawat, Y. (2009) & Struc, V., Pavesic, N. (2009), iris recognition Osman, Z. (2011) and remotely sensed image feature detection Xiao, P.F. et al. (2006) & Ahmed, Z. et al. (2009). Additionally, phase congruency method has been introduced into Image quality assessment (IQA) Liu, Z., Laganiere, R. (2007) & Zhang, L. et al. (2011). For image application, lots of techniques have been detailed using several filters bank. In recent times, PC model has been further customized and extended to two proportions for edges and corners extraction by means of log Gabor filters bank as mentioned in Kovesi P. D. (1996), (1999) & (2003). Moreover, PC model has been used in medical area like face alignment, Huang Y et al. (2004), noise removal from iris image, Huang Y et al. (2004), feature extraction of chromosomes, Kyan M. et al. (2001) using Morlet wavelets and ultrasonic liver characterization, Cao Guitao et al. (2005). In other words, the stretched Gabor filters have been used to extract of 2D images features, Robbins B. & Owens R. (1997). Also, this model has been successfully used to analyze text images based on Gabor wavelets, Chan W. & Coghill G. (2001). Additionally, PC is probably best implemented using monogenic filters, Felsberg M. and Sommer G. (2001). The choice of quadrature filters for 1-D signal is studied in, C. Ronse (1995). A great theoretical and mathematical study of this model has been developed in, Boukerroui, D. et al.(1999). Few watermarking techniques using phase part of a signal are available in literature. Ruanaidh, J.J.K.O. et al. (1996) presents a watermarking technique of digital images based on phase. Design of a robust watermarking technique using polynomial phase exponentials is given in, Mobasseri Bijan G. et al. (2005). Sang Jun & Alam Mohammad S. (2008) proposed a binary-phase-only-filter (BPOF)-based watermarking scheme which is a fragile watermarking, utilizing the phase information of an image. An adaptive secure watermarking scheme which uses double random-phase encoding technique is projected by Li Jianzhong & Chen Xiaojing (2009). Yao Susu et el. (2010) present a robust and efficient image registration method for HDR image reconstruction. This method uses phase congruency to remove illumination changes in the different-exposed images, Wang Wei et al. (2010). A scheme for digital image copyright protection based on robust watermarking has been presented. The protection scheme uses advantage of the feature points of phase congruency detector to locate the watermark hiding positions and to improve the watermark detection ratio, X. Cui et al. (2009). Several watermarking algorithms have been developed depending on these visual models. Huang, J., Shi, Y.Q. (1998) developed a human visual perception based spread spectrum dependent watermarking scheme where brightness and texture sensitivity were considered in DCT domain and the watermark sequences are inserted into low frequency coefficients. Kim, Y.S. et al. (1999) used wavelet transform instead of DCT. Here the changing rate of a sinusoidal pattern per subtended visual angle is the estimation of visual weight of watermark in each wavelet transfer band. Lee, H.K.et al. (2005) introduced a ROI-based medical image watermarking. This was a non-blind approach as there the interested portions of the watermark were embedded into the non ROI areas. This scheme is robust only against JPEG compression impairments. In Chu, Y. et al. (2006) watermarking method watermark was inserted in the interior of ROI. Que, D. et al. (2006) present an improved robustness against image patching and cropping with help of HVS based watermarking scheme. More other ROI dependent watermarking was proposed by Ni, R., Ruan, Q. (2006) and Fan, Y.C. et al. (2008) present a scheme where watermark was embedded into ROI (selected by the user) of the image. Instead of selecting ROI areas by user, Mohanty, S.P., Bhargava, B.K. (2008) used various influencing features of HVS like intensity, contrast, edginess, texture and location in their watermarking scheme. Another saliency based watermarking technique described by Niu, Y. et al. (2011). It can be used as a guide to optimize image watermarking to assist image watermarking by producing a visual saliency modulated JND profile.

In this paper, the objective of the proposed scheme is to improve robustness as well as the imperceptibility and hiding capacity while maintaining the overall security.

WATERMARK EMBEDDING AND EXTRACTION

The process of digital image watermarking proposed here aims to attain the trade-off between robustness and imperceptibility of the watermarked image through increasing the data hiding capacity i.e. the intention is to increase the strength of the watermark by embedding multiple copies of the logo in an effective way such that more bits are embedded in less noticeable segments while introducing less bits within more salient regions as proposed by Itti L. & Koch C. (2001).

The Figure 1 shows the process of encrypting a watermark in an image. The Phase Congruency (Peter Kovesi's Model) and Spectral Residual Saliency Map of the original grayscale image of dimension 256X256 are obtained separately at first. Image Averaging is done on the Phase Congruency of the original image and the saliency map. Hiding capacity estimation is done based on the average image and main regions where the watermarks can be hidden are approximated. On the basis of data hiding capacity of the image, the 16X16 binary watermark is implanted into it by adaptive LSB replacement process. More bits of the original image are replaced by the bits of the watermark where the original image is not noticeable. Accordingly the Watermarked image is obtained. The Figure 2 shows the process of extracting a watermark from a watermarked image. The Phase Congruency (Peter Kovesi's Model) and Spectral Residual Saliency Map of the original grayscale image are obtained as in the previous step. Image Averaging is done on the Phase Congruency of the original image and the saliency map and based on it hiding capacity estimation is done as before. On the basis of original image & hiding capacity in the original image, LSB is extracted from the pixels of the watermarked image. Adaptive symmetry of the bits of the identical order, extracted from different regions of the watermarked image based on the saliency, is calculated to extract the embedded binary watermark.

Figure 1. Block diagram of watermark encoder

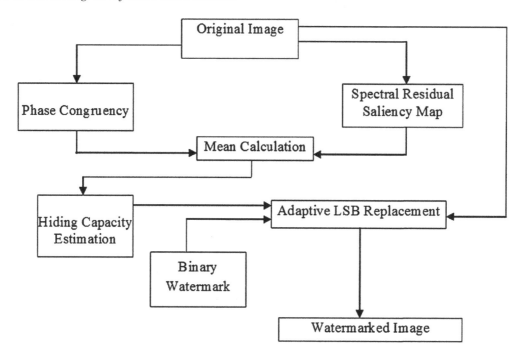

Figure 2. Block diagram of watermark decoder

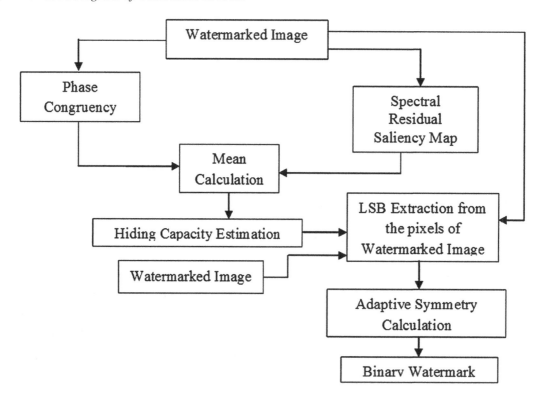

Phase Congruency Detection

Phase congruency can be taken as a measure of feature consequences in digital images and a method of edge detection that is mostly robust against changes in illumination and contrast. The measurement of phase congruency at a point in a signal can be geometrically represented as Figure 3.

Suppose, each of the Fourier components of a signal, at a location x in the signal, has amplitude $A_m(x)$ and phase angle $\theta_m(x)$. The Fourier components are local and complex valued. Here Figure 3 represents these local Fourier components as complex vectors adding head to tail. The magnitude of the vector from the starting point to the end point is $|E(x)|$, where $E(x)$ is the Local Energy. So the phase congruency according to Morrone M. C. et al. (1986) is given as:

$$P_c(x) = \frac{|E(x)|}{\sum_m A_m(x)} \tag{1}$$

where, $\sum_m A_m(x)$ is the overall path length taken by the local Fourier components to reach the end point and m is the number of local Fourier components.

If all the Fourier components are in phase, all the complex vectors would be aligned and the phase congruency will be 1 or otherwise it will have a minimum value of 0.This phase congruency can be expressed as a function of the cosine of the deviation of each phase component from the mean as below:

$$P_c(x) = \frac{\sum_m A_m(\cos(\theta(x) - \bar{\theta}(x)))}{\sum_m A_m(x)} \tag{2}$$

Figure 3. Polar diagram of a signal for measuring phase congruency

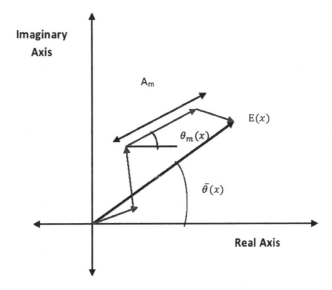

This measure of phase congruency is noise sensitive and does not provide good localization. So Kovesi Peter (1996) & (1999) developed a modified measure of phase Congruency as given below

$$P_c(x) = \frac{\sum_m \left\lfloor \mathcal{W}(x) A_m(x) \left(\left(\cos(\theta(x) - \bar{\theta}(x)) \right) \right) - \left| \sin(\theta(x) - \bar{\theta}(x)) \right| \right) - \mathcal{T}_n \right\rfloor}{\sum_m A_m(x) + \epsilon}$$

(3)

where $\mathcal{W}(x)$ denotes the weight for frequency spread, $\mathcal{T}_n$ is the noise threshold, constant ϵ is included to avoid division by zero. This equation provides a more localized response, Kovesi Peter, (2000).

Spectral Residual Saliency Map Detection

According to Hou Xiaodi & Zhang Liqing, (2007), to get the saliency map of an image by this approach, the image is taken into frequency domain by means of Fourier transform. According to scale invariance property proposed by Kim, Y.S. (1999) et al. & Lee, H.K. et al. (2005).

$$\mathrm{E}\{Amp(f)\} \propto \frac{1}{f}$$

(4)

where, $Amp(f)$ is the amplitude of the average Fourier spectrum of the collection of natural images.

Log spectrum of $Amp(f)$,

$$L(f) = log\{Amp(f)\}$$

(5)

and $Amp(f)$ can be estimated through the convolution of the input image as below

$$Amp(f) = d_m(f) * L(f)$$

(6)

where $d_m(f)$ is a local average filter that can be represented as an $m \times m$ matrix:

$$d_m(f) = \frac{1}{m^2} \begin{pmatrix} 1 & \cdots & 1 \\ \vdots & \ddots & \vdots \\ 1 & \cdots & 1 \end{pmatrix}$$

(7)

Thus the spectral residual $S_r(f)$ can be obtained as:

$$S_r(f) = \left(L(f) - Amp(f) \right)$$

(8)

To obtain the saliency map $S(x)$ and get back to the spatial domain inverse Fourier transform has to be performed:

$$S(x) = G(x) * \mathcal{F}^{-1}\left[\exp\left(S_r(f) + P(f)\right)\right]^2 \tag{9}$$

where $G(x)$ denotes a Gaussian filter and $P(f)$ is the phase spectrum of the image.

To obtain the object map $O(x)$ a threshold is considered and the object map is determined a

$$O(x) = \begin{cases} 1, & if \ S(x) > threshold \\ 0, & otherwise \end{cases} \tag{10}$$

Mean Calculation

Let the original gray-scale image be I_{o_m} of size C✕D and W_b be the binary watermark with size of P✕Q and illustrated as:

$$I_{o_m} = \left\{X(a,b)\right\}, 0 \le a < C, 0 \le b < D, X(a,b) \in \left\{0,1,\ldots,255\right\} \tag{11}$$

$$W_b = \{Y(i,j)\}, 0 \le i < P, 0 \le j < Q, Y(i,j) \in \left\{0,1\right\} \tag{12}$$

Let, S_m is the Spectral Residual Saliency map and P_c is the Phase Congruency of the original gray-scale image I_{o_m}.

Let A_m is the averaged image of size C✕D, where,

$$A_m = \frac{P_c + S_m}{2} \tag{13}$$

Hiding Capacity Estimation

From the generated saliency map, a hiding capacity map is created by using high embedding strength in less perceptible saliency areas and a low embedding strength in more perceptible saliency areas, to gain superior watermark invisibility and to improve the hiding capacity of the embedded watermark.

$$\mathcal{F}_{temp_m} = 0 \ \& \ m, where, 0 \le \mathcal{F}_m < 0.1000 \tag{14}$$

$$\mathcal{F}_{temp_m} = 0.25 \ \& \ m = 2, where, 0.1000 \le \mathcal{F}_m < 0.2500 \tag{15}$$

$$\mathcal{F}_{temp_m} = 0.50 \; \& \; m = 3, where, 0.2500 \le \mathcal{F}_m < 0.3500 \tag{16}$$

$$\mathcal{F}_{temp_m} = 0.75 \; \& \; m = 4, where, 0.3500 \le \mathcal{F}_m < 0.6000 \tag{17}$$

$$\mathcal{F}_{temp_m} = 1.00 \; \& \; m = 5, where, 0.6000 \le \mathcal{F}_m \tag{18}$$

Here $\mathcal{F}_{temp_m}$ are the color regions into which $\mathcal{F}_m$ is divided and m numbers are the index of the regions. No data is hidden in the region $m = 5$ i.e. the region of $\mathcal{F}_{temp_m} = 1.00$.

Encoder and Decoder

Let, $\mathcal{D}_b$ is the function of converting Decimal to Binary and B_d is the function of converting Binary to Decimal. The adaptive LSB watermarking is defined as functions $\left(\mathcal{F}_{enc}, \mathcal{F}_{dec} \right)$.

$$\mathcal{D}_b \left\{ I_{o_m} \right\} = \mathcal{B} I_{o_m} \tag{19}$$

$$\mathcal{B} I_{o_m} (0, \mathcal{M}) \leftarrow \mathcal{W}_b \tag{20}$$

where $\mathcal{M} = \{0,1,2,3,...,7\}$ and $m = \{0,1,2,3,4,5\}$ and $\mathcal{M} \le 2$ for $m = 1,2$, $\mathcal{M} \le 1$ for $m = 3,4$. The watermark can be inserted in each region i.e. $\mathcal{F}_{temp_m}$.

So here,

$$\mathcal{F}_{enc} : B_d \left\{ \mathcal{B} I_{o_m} \left(0, \mathcal{M} \right) \right\} \rightarrow I_w \tag{21}$$

and, I_w is the watermarked image of size C$\times$D.

Likewise, for decrypting the watermark,

$\mathcal{F}_{temp_m}$, I_{o_m} and I_w are compared to get the watermark that has been hidden in I_{o_m} for each value of m. Let the regions in I_w be

$$E_m = \left\{ E_m \left(p, q \right) \right\}, where \; 0 \le p < C, 0 \le q < D, E_m \left(p, q \right) \in \{0,1,...,255\} \tag{22}$$

$$\mathcal{D}_b \left\{ \mathcal{E}_m \right\} = \mathcal{B} \mathcal{E}_m \tag{23}$$

Now if $Count_m$ be the function to count binary '0' and '1' in LSBs of each pixel of $\mathcal{E}_m$ in the following manner and the function returns the value of majority to $\mathcal{C}_{bit_m}$ where

$$C_{bit_m} = \left\{ C_{bit_m}\left(g,h\right) \right\}, where \leq g < P, 0 \leq h < Q, C_{bit_m}\left(g,h\right) \in \{0,1\} \tag{24}$$

Then,
For $m = 4$ and $\mathcal{F}_{temp_m} = 0$

$$C_{bit_m} = Count_m \left\{ \mathcal{B}E_m(0,2), \mathcal{B}E_m(0,1), \mathcal{B}E_m(0,0) \right\} \tag{25}$$

For $m = 3$ and $\mathcal{F}_{temp_m} = 0.25$

$$C_{bit_m} = Count_m \left\{ \mathcal{B}E_m(0,2), \mathcal{B}E_m(0,1), \mathcal{B}E_m(0,0) \right\} \tag{26}$$

For $m = 2$ and $\mathcal{F}_{temp_m} = 0.50$

$$C_{bit_m} = \left\{ \mathcal{B}E_m(0,1) \right\} \tag{27}$$

For $m = 1$ and $\mathcal{F}_{temp_m} = 0.75$

$$C_{bit_m} = \left\{ \mathcal{B}E_m(0,1) \right\} \tag{28}$$

Let, $Count$ be the function to count binary '0' and '1' for value at the same positions for $C_{bit_4}, C_{bit_3}, C_{bit2}$ and the function returns the value of majority to

$$C = C(g,h), where\ 0 \leq g < P, 0 \leq h < Q, C_{bit_m}\left(g,h\right) \in \{0,1\} \tag{29}$$

Then,

$$C = Count \left\{ C_{bit_4}, C_{bit_3}, C_{bit2} \right\} \tag{30}$$

where C is the decrypted binary watermark.
Hence, following the above processes we get:

$$\mathcal{F}_{dec} : I_w \rightarrow c, where\ C \equiv W_b \tag{31}$$

RESULTS AND DISCUSSION

The following segment reports the experimental outcomes of the proposed scheme. Five grayscale test images of size 256×256 and one binary watermark image of size 16×16 have been used to study the performance of the proposed algorithm by means of imperceptibility and robustness. The binary watermark image is given in Figure 4 and the test gray scale images are given in Figure 5. Figure 6 presents the Phase Congruency maps for original grayscale images; Figure 7 represents Spectral Residual Saliency Maps of the original grayscale images. Figure 8 presents Mean images of the Phase Congruency Map and the Saliency map of the original grayscale images. Hiding capacity estimation maps based on the mean images has been offered in Figure 9, where different shades represent different hiding capacity. The darker region represents the less perceptible saliency region whereas the brighter region represents the more perceptible saliency region. Figure 10 display the watermarked Images.

In this context, imperceptibility infers the invisibility of the embedded watermark in the original images without corrupting the perceptual quality of watermarked image. As an outcome of embedding,

Figure 4. Binary watermark (logo)

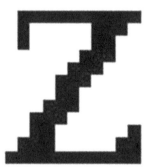

Figure 5. Original grayscale images (i) cloth (ii) forest (iii) natural (iv) nature (iv) space

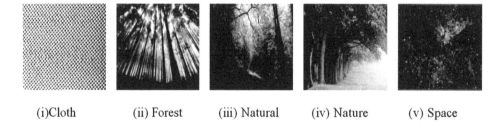

(i)Cloth   (ii) Forest   (iii) Natural   (iv) Nature   (v) Space

Figure 6. Phase congruency of the original grayscale images

Figure 7. Spectral residual saliency map of the original grayscale images

Figure 8. Mean of the saliency map and phase congruency of the original grayscale images

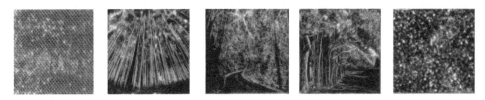

Figure 9. Hiding capacity estimation based on the mean of phase congruency and saliency map

Figure 10. Watermarked images

original image go through quality loss which is calculated using some well-known quality measures to test the invisibility of the implanted watermark in terms of imperceptibility. Table 1 and Table 2 tabulates the number of quality measures required to check the imperceptibility of the watermarks in the watermarked images.

If any means of planned or accidental processing is made on the image, a significant amount of quality degradation or information loss will occur. So, robustness of the proposed technique is tested against different attacks such as Contrast, Crop, Negative, Addition of Noise, Rotation and Resizing. Figure 11 provides recovered watermarks after different image impairments. The results against different attacks are presented in Figure 12 using bar charts.

NCC (Normalized Cross Correlation) in the domain of signal processing is cross-correlation which is a measurement of similarity between two series as a function of the lag of one relative to the other. In addition to that NCC is the normalized form of cross-correlation. NCC=1 refers that the original and the

Table 1. The performance results of imperceptibility

Original Images	SNR	PSNR	MSE	IF	LMSE	UIQI
CLOTH	39.5955	43.1328	3.1608	0.9999	0.0037	0.9997
FOREST	36.0240	43.2727	3.0606	0.9998	0.0127	0.9996
NATURAL	34.1891	43.2708	3.0620	0.9996	0.0479	0.9995
NATURE	35.9442	43.2847	3.0522	0.9997	0.0463	0.9995
SPACE	31.7889	43.2800	3.0555	0.9993	0.0042	0.9983

Table 2. The performance results of imperceptibility

Original Images	MSSIM	NQM	NAE	AD	MD
CLOTH	0.9996	39.6147	0.0046	0.4224	7
FOREST	0.9958	36.0518	0.0075	0.4066	7
NATURAL	0.9938	34.2365	0.0100	0.3968	7
NATURE	0.9927	35.9635	0.0073	0.4019	7
SPACE	0.9938	31.8359	0.0112	0.4083	7

Figure 11. Recovered watermarks after different image impairments (i) contrast, (ii) crop, (iii) gaussian noise, (iv) salt & pepper noise, (v) negative, (vi) resize, (vii) rotation (30), (viii) rotation (180)

| (i) | (ii) | (iii) | (iv) | (v) | (vi) | (vii) | (viii) |

extracted watermarks from attacked images are totally similar. Values of NCC above 0.9 also referred as good results related to cross-correlation.

SM (Similarity Measurement) is also a parameter to measure similarity between the embedded and the extracted watermarks. The value of SM for all the attacks is 1, which infers that the embedded and extracted watermarks from attacked watermarks are identical.

PCC (Pearson Correlation Coefficient) is a measure of the linear correlation (dependence) between two variables X and Y, giving a value between +1 and −1 inclusive, where 1 is total positive correlation, 0 is no correlation, and −1 is total negative correlation, Zhao Zhiying et al. (2015). Here it is used to measure the correlation between the original and the decrypted watermarks.

WDR stands for Watermark to Document ratio. More negative WDR implies that the encrypted and the decrypted watermarks are more similar.

In case of WPSNR (Weighted Peak Signal to Noise Ratio) infinite value means the embedded and the extracted watermarks are totally same i.e. more the value, better is the result.

MI and Joint Entropy are also used here to measure the similarity between the original watermark and the pulled out watermark from attacked images. For both the case 0.034 is the value which implies that the extracted watermarks are exactly same the original one i.e. they are not affected the attacks, Srivastava A. (2003).

Figure 12. Performance against attacks

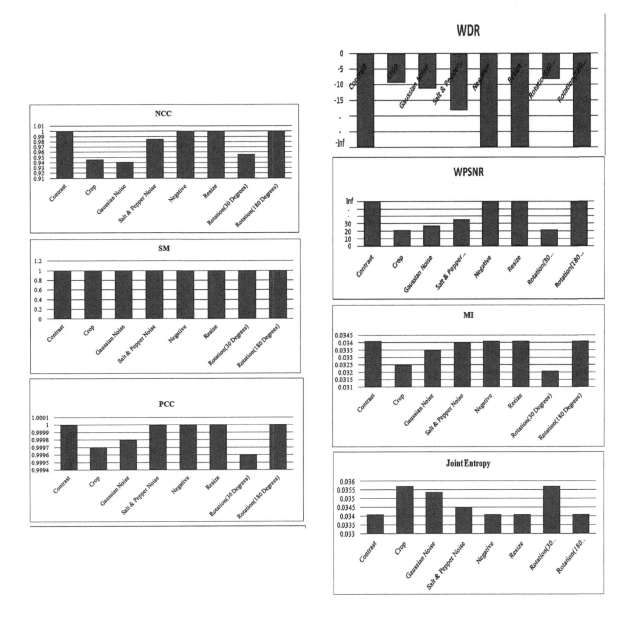

To confirm the performance of the projected approach, an assessment among some modern algorithms is offered in Table 2. The result validates better imperceptibility and enhanced hiding capacity of the technique.

CONCLUSION

In this projected article the authors endeavored to present some theoretical learning as well as simulations on copyright protection with the help of digital watermarking. The multimedia data used for

Table 3. Performance results comparison

Sl. No.	Method	PSNR (dB)	Capacity (BPP)
Saliency Based Watermarking			
1.	Proposed Method	43.25	2.8
2.	Saliency based (VAM) method, Sur A. et al. (2009)	--	0.0017
Several Other Spatial Domain Watermarking			
3.	Exhaustive LSB Substitution, Chang, C. et al. (2003)	38.3425	3
5.	Block based Algorithm, C.C.Chang et al, (1999)	38.3220	3
6.	Pair wise LSB matching, Xu, H. et al. (2010)	35.05	2.25
7.	Mielikainen's method, Mielikainen, J (2006)	33.05	2.2504
11.	PWLC Data Hiding, Chang-Lung Tsai et al. (2005)	48.35	0.68

experimental set up are grayscale and binary images. The technique proposed in this chapter is a spatial domain based digital image watermarking scheme which is a combination of saliency map and phase congruency map that used as a classifier to distinguish the main features of the original images. Based on the calculated features the secret copyright information is embedded within the original image which required to be protected. As a result robustness of the watermarked image become fighting fit. Moreover the imperceptibility of the scheme is also enhanced as the copyright set in within the non salient regions of the original image. The experimental outcomes also ensure that the proposed algorithm stands against different type of intentional and unintentional image impairment techniques with better hiding capacity. In addition to that the projected method is evaluated against some other state of the art algorithm. The result of assessment recommends that estimated scheme can be an efficient tool for copyright protection and authentication. In future other technique may be used other than LSB replacement to improve the effectiveness of the watermarking efficiently.

REFERENCES

Abhishek, B., Susmita, T., Nabanita, S., Avradeeta, K., Lal, C. S., & Kumar, S. S. (2015). On the Implementation of a Saliency based Digital Watermarking.*2nd International Conference on Information systems Design and Intelligent Applications.*

Ahmed, Z., Sayadi, M., & Faniech, F. (2009). Satellite images features extraction using phase congruency model. *Internat. J. Comput. Sci. Network Security, 9*(2), 192–197.

Al-Nabhani, Jalab, Wahid, & Noor. (2015). Robust watermarking algorithm for digital images using discrete wavelet and probabilistic neural network. *Journal of King Saud University – Computer and Information Sciences, 27*, 393-401.

Ali, Mohammad, Ebrahim, Bulent, & Farokh. (2009). Robust Scaling-Based Image Watermarking Using Maximum-Likelihood Decoder With Optimum Strength Facto, IEEE Transactions on Multimedia, 11(5), 822-833.

Amit, D. (2004). *The Digital Consumer Technology Handbook: A Comprehensive Guide to Devices, Standards, Future Directions, and Programmable Logic Solutions*. Elsevier.

Amrik & Balpreet. (2014). An Integrated SVD and Visibility Restoration Digital Watermarking. *International Journal of Advanced Research in Computer Science and Software Engineering, 4*(1).

Anderson, R. (1996). Information Hiding. *Proceedings of the first Workshop on Information Hiding, (LNCS) (vol. 1174). Springer Verlag.*

Anderson, R. J. (1996). Stretching the Limits of Steganography. In *Information Hiding: First International Workshop, Proceedings*, (LNCS), (vol. 1174, pp. 39–48). Springer.

Anderson, R. J., & Petitcolas, F. A. P. (1998). On The Limits of Steganography. *IEEE Journal on Selected Areas in Communications, 16*(4), 474–481.

Art, W. (1999). *The history of the Internet and the World Wide Web*. Enslow Publishers.

Asatryan & Asatryan. (2009). *Combined Spatial and Frequency Domain Watermarking*. Computer Science and Information Technologies.

Ashwani, K., Ghrera, S.P., & Vipin. (2015). A New and Efficient Buyer-Seller Digital Watermarking Protocol Using Identity Based Technique for Copyright Protection. *Third International Conference on Image Information Processing.*

Aura, T. (1996). Practical Invisibility in Digital Communication. In *Information Hiding: First International Workshop, Proceedings*, (LNCS), (vol. 1174, pp. 265–278). Springer.

Awan, I., Gilani, S. A. M., & Shah, S. A. (2006). Utilization of Maximum Data Hiding Capacity in Object-Based Text Document Authentication. In *International Conference on Intelligent Information Hiding and Multimedia Signal Processing.*

Bandyopadhyay, M. N. (2005). *Introduction to Signals and Systems and Digital Signal Processing*. PHI Learning Pvt. Ltd.

Bao. (2014). Image Copyright Protection Watermark Algorithm Based on Spread Spectrum Technology. Applied Mechanics and Materials, 602-605, 3272-3277.

Basu, A., Das, T. S., & Sarkar, S. K. (2011). Robust Visual Information Hiding Framework Based on HVS Pixel Adaptive LSB Replacement (HPALR) Technique. *Int. Jnl of Imaging & Robotics, 6*(A11), 71–98.

Basu, A., & Sarkar, S.K. (2013). On the Implementation of Robust Copyright Protection Scheme using Visual Attention Model. *Information Security Journal: A Global Perspective, 22*(1), 10-20.

Basu, A., Talukdar, S., Sengupta, N., Kar, A., Chakraborty, S. L., & Sarkar, S. K. (2015). On the Implementation of a Saliency based Digital Watermarking. *2nd International Conference on Information systems Design and Intelligent Applications*. doi:10.1007/978-81-322-2250-7_44

Bender, W., Gruhl, D., & Morimoto, N. (1995). Techniques for data hiding. *Proceedings of the Society for Photo-Instrumentation Engineers, 2420*, 40. doi:10.1117/12.205315

Bezalel, E., & Efron, U. (2005). Efficient face recognition method using a combined phase congruency/ Gabor filter bank technique. *Proceedings of the Society for Photo-Instrumentation Engineers, 5908*, 437–444. doi:10.1117/12.618226

Bhagyashri, S., & Kapre, J. M. Y. (2011). All frequency band DWT-SVD robust watermarking technique for color images in YUV color space. *IEEE International Conference on Computer Science and Automation Engineering (CSAE)*. doi:10.1109/CSAE.2011.5952684

Biermann. (1996). Handbook of Pulping and Papermaking (2nd ed.). Academic Press.

Borko, F., & Darko, K. (2006). *Multimedia Encryption and Authentication Techniques and Applications*. CRC Press.

Boukerroui, D., Noble, J., & Brady, V. (1999). *On the Choice of Band-Pass Quadrature Filters. Technical report, MVL*. Oxford University.

Braudaway, G. W., Magerlein, K. A., & Mintzer, F. (1996). *Color Correct Digital Watermarking of Images*. US patent No. 5,530,759.

Cachin, C. (1998). An Information-Theoretic Model for Steganography. In *Proceedings of the Second International Workshop on Information Hiding*. doi:10.1007/3-540-49380-8_21

Caldelli, Filippini, & Becarelli. (2010). Reversible Watermarking Techniques: An Overview and a Classification. *EURASIP Journal on Information Security*.

Can, Y. S., & Alagoz, F. (2013). Robust frequency hopping and direct sequence spread spectrum audio watermarking technique on wavelet domain. *International Conference on Electronics, Computer and Computation (ICECCO)*. doi:10.1109/ICECCO.2013.6718308

Canny, J. F. (1983). *Finding edges and lines in images* (Master's thesis). MIT.

Canny, J. F. (1986). A computational approach to edge detection. *IEEE Transactions on Pattern Analysis and Machine Intelligence, 8*(6), 679–698. doi:10.1109/TPAMI.1986.4767851 PMID:21869365

Cedillo, H. M., Cedillo, H. A., Balbuena, C. A. R., García, U. F., Nakano, M. M., & Meana, H. M. P. (2015). Customer Authentication of Digital Imaging Using Hybrid Watermarking. *International Conference on Mechatronics, Electronics and Automotive Engineering*.

Chan, W., & Coghill, G. (2001). Text analysis using local energy. *Pattern Recognition, 34*(12), 2523–2532. doi:10.1016/S0031-3203(00)00155-2

Chandramouli, R., Memon, N., & Rabbani, M. (2002). Digital Watermarking. Encyclopedia of Imaging Science and Technology.

Chang, C. C., Hsiao, J. Y., & Chan, C. S. (2003). Finding optimal least significant- bit substitution in image hiding by dynamic programming strategy. *Pattern Recognition, 36*(7), 1583–159. doi:10.1016/S0031-3203(02)00289-3

Chang, C. C., Hwang, K. F., & Hwang, M. S. (1999). A block based digital watermarks for copy protection of images. In *Proceedings of fifth Asia-Pacific Conference on Communications/ Fourth Optoelectronics and Communications Conference*. doi:10.1109/APCC.1999.820427

Chang-Tsun, L., Chih-Yuan, C., & Yue, L. (2010). On the Reputability of Device Identification and Image Integrity Verification Using Sensor Pattern Noise. *Social Informatics and Telecommunications Engineering, 41*, 19–25.

Chet, H. (2002). Proving the Integrity of Digital Evidence with Time. *International Journal of Digital Evidence, 1*(1), 1–7.

Chimanna, M. A., & Khot, S. R. (2013). Robustness of video watermarking against various attacks using Wavelet Transform techniques and Principle Component Analysis. *International Conference on Information Communication and Embedded Systems.* doi:10.1109/ICICES.2013.6508357

Choo, H-G. (2004). Data-Hiding Capacity Improvement for Text Watermarking Using Space Coding Method, Digital Watermarking. Lecture Notes in Computer Science, 2939, 593–599.

Chopra, Purohit, & Gaur. (2014). Quality Evaluation for LSB Replacement Watermarking of Grayscale Images. *International Journal of Advanced Research in Computer and Communication Engineering, 3*(5).

Chu, Y., Zhang, Y., Zhang, S., & Ye, X. (2006). Region of Interest Fragile Watermarking for Image Authentication. *First International Multi-Symposiums on Computer and Computational Sciences, 1,* 726–731.

Chunlin, S., Sudirman, S., Merabti, M., Jones, D. L. (2010). Analysis of Digital Image Watermark Attacks. *7th IEEE International Conference on Consumer Communications and Networking Conference.*

Cox, I., & Linnartz, J.-P. (1997). Public watermarks and resistance to tampering. *Proc. IEEE Conf. on Image Processing.* doi:10.1109/ICIP.1997.632226

Cox, I. J. (1996). Secure Spread Spectrum Watermarking of Images, Audio and Video. *Proc IEEE International Conf. on Image Processing, ICIP-96.* doi:10.1109/ICIP.1996.560429

Cox, I. J. (1996). A Secure Robust Watermark for Multimedia. In *Proc. of First International Workshop on Information Hiding.* Springer-Verlag.

Cox, I. J., Kilian, J., Leighton, T., & Shamoon, T. (1996). A Secure Robust Watermarking for Multimedia. In *Proc. of First International Workshop on Information Hiding,* (LNCS), (vol. 1174, pp. 185-206). Springer-Verlag.

Craver, S. (1997). *On Public-Key Steganography in the Presence of an Active Warden. Technical Report RC 20931.* IBM.

Craver, S., Memon, N., Yeo, B-L., & Yeung, M.M. (1998). Resolving rightful ownerships with invisible watermarking techniques: limitations, attacks, and implications. *IEEE Journal on Selected Areas in Communications, 16*(4), 573 - 586.

Craver S., Memon N., Lock, Y. B., & Yeung, M.M. (1998). Resolving rightful ownerships with invisible watermarking techniques: limitations, attacks, and implications. *IEEE Journal on Selected Areas in Communications, 16*(4), 573-586.

Cui, X., Liu, Q., & Metaxas, D. (2009). Temporal Spectral Residual: Fast Motion Saliency Detection. In *Proceeding: MM 2009 Proceedings of the 17th ACM International Conference on Multimedia.*

Darko, K., & Malvar, H. S. (2003). Spread-Spectrum Watermarking of Audio Signals. *IEEE Transactions on Signal Processing, 51*(4), 1020–1033. doi:10.1109/TSP.2003.809384

Dautzenberg, C., & Boland, F. (1994). *Watermarking images.* Dept. of Electrical Engineering, Trinity College.

David, K. (1996). The History of Steganography. *Lecture notes in Computer Science, 1174,* 1-7.

Dehkordi, A. B., Esfahani, S. N., & Avanaki, A. N. (2011). Robust LSB watermarking optimized for local structural similarity. *19th Iranian Conference on Electrical Engineering (ICEE).*

Derrick, G. (2001). Data Watermarking: Steganography And Watermarking Of Digital Data. *Journal of Computer Law & Security Review, 17*(2), 101–104. doi:10.1016/S0267-3649(01)00204-7

Desai, H. V. (2012). Steganography, Cryptography, Watermarking: A Comparative Study. *Journal of Global Research in Computer Science, 3*(12), 33–35.

Dhanalaks,, R., & Haiyalnayaki. (2010). Dual Watermarking Scheme with Encryption. *International Journal of Computer Science and Information Security, 7*(1), 248–253.

Digimarc Corporation. (2004). *Enhancing Personal Identity Verification with Digital Watermarks.* White Paper. Author.

Dong, Brankov, Galatsanos, Yang, & Davoine. (2005). Digital watermarking robust to geometric distortions. *IEEE Transactions on Image Processing, 14*(12), 2140-2150.

Dong, M. L., Dian, H. W., & Jie, L. (2012). A novel robust blind watermarking algorithm based on wavelet and Fractional Fourier Transform. *IEEE 14th International Conference on Communication Technology.*

Dong, Z., Jiying, Z., James, W. T., & Filippo, S. (2003). Image quality measurement by using digital watermarking. *IEEE International Workshop on Haptic, Audio and Visual Environments and their Applications.* doi:10.1109/HAVE.2003.1244727

Dylan, C., & Paul, C. (2002). A Novel Watermarking Technique for LUT Based FPGA Designs. *Lecture Notes in Computer Science, 2438,* 1152–1155. doi:10.1007/3-540-46117-5_129

Eckert Michael, P., & Bradley Andrew, P. (1998). Perceptual quality metrics applied to still image compression. *Signal Processing, 70*(3), 177–200. doi:10.1016/S0165-1684(98)00124-8

Eddine, B. D., Sabrina, B., & Azeddine, B. (2015). A Cross-Layer Watermarking-Based Mechanism for Data Aggregation Integrity in Heterogeneous WSNs. *IEEE Communications Letters, 19*(5), 823–826. doi:10.1109/LCOMM.2015.2409057

Emery, O. (1958). Des filigranes du papier. *Bulletin de l'Association technique de l'industrie papetière, 6,* 185–188.

Eskicioglu, M., & Fisher, P. S. (1995). Image Quality Measures and Their Performance. *IEEE Transactions on Communications, 43*(12), 2959–2965. doi:10.1109/26.477498

Eskicioglu Ahmet, M., & Delp Edward, J. (2001). An overview of multimedia content protection in consumer electronics devices. *Signal Processing Image Communication, 16*(7), 681–699. doi:10.1016/S0923-5965(00)00050-3

Eswaraiah, R., & Reddy, E. S. (2014). A Fragile ROI-Based Medical Image Watermarking Technique with Tamper Detection and Recovery. *Fourth International Conference on Communication Systems and Network Technologies (CSNT).* doi:10.1109/CSNT.2014.184

Fan, Y. C., Chiang, A., & Shen, J. H. (2008). ROI-based watermarking scheme for JPEG 2000', *Circuits, Systems &. Signal Processing, 27*(5), 763–774.

Farhadzadeh, F., & Voloshynovskiy, S. (2014). Active Content Fingerpriting. *IEEE Transactions on Information Forensics and Security, Vol, 9*(6), 905–920. doi:10.1109/TIFS.2014.2315531

Farias, M.C.Q., & Akamine, W.Y.L. (2012). On performance of image quality metrics enhanced with visual attention computational models. *IEEE Electronics Letters, 48*(11), 631-633.

Farouk & Saeb. (2004). Design and Implementation of a Secret Key Steganographic Micro-Architecture Employing FPGA. *Date Conference.*

Feifei, C., Yuhui, L., Bo, L., & Lian, Y. (2012). FPGA-based adaptive image watermark embedding method and implementation. *IET International Conference on Information Science and Control Engineering.*

Felsberg, M., & Sommer, G. (2001). The monogenic signal. *IEEE Transactions on Signal Processing, 12*(12), 3136–3144. doi:10.1109/78.969520

Frank, H., Peter, E., & Bernd, G. (1998). Digital Watermarking of MPEG-4 Facial Animation Parameters. *Computers & Graphics, 22*(4), 425–435. doi:10.1016/S0097-8493(98)00032-6

Freeman Roger, L. (2005). *Fundamentals of Telecommunications.* John Wiley & Sons. doi:10.1002/0471720941

Garimella, A., Satyanarayana, M. V. V., Murugesh, P. S., & Niranjan, U. C. (2004). ASIC for digital color image watermarking. *IEEE 11th Digital Signal Processing Workshop.*

Garzia, F. (2013). *Handbook of Communications Security.* WIT Press.

Geum, D. P., Dae-Soo, K., & Kee-Young, Y. (2014). Lossless Codebook-Based Digital Watermarking Scheme with Authentication. *11th International Conference on Information Technology: New Generations (ITNG).*

Ghosh, S., Ray, P., Maity, S. P., & Rahaman, H. (2009). Spread Spectrum Image Watermarking with Digital Design. *IEEE International Advance Computing Conference.* doi:10.1109/IADCC.2009.4809129

Guitao, C., Pengfei, S., & Bing, H. (2005). Ultrasonic Liver Characterization Using Phase Congruency. *Proceedings of the 2005 IEEE Engineering in Medicine and Biology 27th Annual Conference.*

Gunjal & Manthalkar. (2011). An overview of transform domain robust digital image watermarking algorithms. *Journal of Emerging Trends in Computing and Information Sciences, 2*(1).

Guo, C. L., Ma, Q., & Zhang, L. M. (2008). Spatio-temporal saliency detection using phase spectrum of quaternion Fourier transforms. *IEEE Conference on Computer Vision and Pattern Recognition.*

Hamidreza, Omair, & Swamy. (2016). Multiplicative Watermark Decoder in Contourlet Domain Using the Normal Inverse Gaussian Distribution. *IEEE Transactions on Multimedia, 18*(2), 19 -207.

Hämmerle, U. J., Andreas, U., & Hartmut, W. (2008). Multiple re-watermarking using varying non-stationary mra with parameterized wavelet filters. *Proceedings of the 10th ACM workshop on Multimedia and security.* doi:10.1145/1411328.1411340

Hanjalic, A., & Langelaar, G. C. (2000). Benchmarking the DEW watermarking algorithm. Advances in Image Communication, 8, 273–297.

Hao-Tang, C., Wen-Jyi, H., & Chau-Jern, C. (2015). Digital Hologram Authentication Using a Hadamard-Based Reversible Fragile Watermarking Algorithm. *Journal of Display Technology, 11*(2), 193–203. doi:10.1109/JDT.2014.2367528

Harel, J., Koch, C., & Perona, P. (2006). *Graph-based visual saliency.* Neural Information Processing Systems.

Hassan. (2013). Robust Image Watermarking Against Different Attacks: Noising, (Jpeg) Compression, And Filtering. *Journal of Babylon University/Pure and Applied Sciences, 21*(6).

Hernandez, J. J. G., Feregrino, U. C., Rene, C., & Carolina, R. (2011). On the Implementation of a Hardware Architecture for an Audio Data Hiding System. *Journal of Signal Processing Systems for Signal, Image, and Video Technology, 64*(3), 457–468. doi:10.1007/s11265-010-0503-8

Herodotus,. (1972). *The Histories* (R. Selincourt, Trans.). Middlesex, UK: Penguin.

Hoda, M., Nader, K., & Shadrokh, S. (2015). Framework for Watermark Robustness Adjustment Using Image Depth Map. *23rd Iranian Conference on Electrical Engineering.*

Homer,. (1972). *The Iliad* (R. Fragels, Trans.). Middlesex, UK: Penguin.

Hong, L., Di, X., Rui, Z., Yushu, Z., & Sen, B. (2016). Robust and hierarchical watermarking of encrypted images based on Compressive Sensing. *Journal of Signal Processing: Image Communication, 45*, 41–51.

Hong-Mei, Y., Yong-quan, L., Xiao-Dong, W., & Shu-juan, J. (2007). A DWT- based evaluation method of imperceptibility of watermark in watermarked color image. *International Conference on Wavelet Analysis and Pattern Recognition.* doi:10.1109/ICWAPR.2007.4420663

Horowitz & Hill. (1989). *The Art of Electronics* (2nd ed.). Cambridge University Press.

Hossein, B. (2006). Handbook of Information Security, Key Concepts, Infrastructure, Standards, and Protocols. John Wiley and Sons.

Hsien-Wen, T., & Chin-Chen, C. (2004). High Capacity Data Hiding in JPEG-Compressed Images. *Informatica, 15*(1), 127–142.

Huang & Wu. (2004). Attacking visible watermarking schemes. *IEEE Transactions on Multimedia, 6*(1), 16-30.

Huang, J., & Shi, Y. Q. (1998). Adaptive Image Watermarking Scheme Based on Visual masking. *Electronics Letters*, *34*(8), 748–750. doi:10.1049/el:19980545

Huang, Y., Lin, S., Stan, Z., Lu, H., & Shum, V. (2004). Face Alignment under Variable Illumination. *IEEE International Conference on Automatic Face and Gesture Recognition.*

Huang, Y., Lin, S., Stan, Z., Lu, H., & Shum, V. (2004). Noise removal and impainting model for iris image. *International Conference on Image Processing.*

Hussain, N., Wageeh, B., & Colin, B. (2013). A Review of Medical Image Watermarking Requirements for Teleradiology. *Journal of Digital Imaging*, *26*(2), 326–343. doi:10.1007/s10278-012-9527-x PMID:22975883

Hwai-Tsu, H., & Ling-Yuan, H. (2016). A mixed modulation scheme for blind image watermarking. *International Journal of Electronics and Communications*, *70*(2), 172–178. doi:10.1016/j.aeue.2015.11.003

Imran, U., Asifullah, K., Rafiullah, C., & Abdul, M. (2008). *Towards a Better Robustness-Imperceptibility Tradeoff in Digital Watermarking*. Innovations and Advanced Techniques in Systems, Computing Sciences and Software Engineering.

İsmail, A. (2001). *Image Quality Statistics And Their Use In Steganalysis and Compression* (PhD Thesis). Institute for Graduate Studies in Science and Engineering, Uludağ University.

Ismail, A., Bulent, S., & Khalid, S. (2002). Statistical Evaluation of Image Quality Measures. *Journal of Electronic Imaging*, *11*(2), 206–223. doi:10.1117/1.1455011

Itti, L., & Koch, C. (2000). A saliency-based search mechanism for overt and covert shifts of visual attention. *Vision Research*, *40*(10-12), 1489–1506. doi:10.1016/S0042-6989(99)00163-7 PMID:10788654

Itti, L., & Koch, C. (2001). Computational Modeling of Visual Attention. *Nature Reviews. Neuroscience*, *2*(3), 194–203. doi:10.1038/35058500 PMID:11256080

Jalal, F., Jalil, F., & Peter, W. (1999). *Digital Certificates: Applied Internet Security* (Vol. 1). Addison-Wesley.

Janeczko Paul, B. (2006). *Top Secret: A Handbook of Codes, Ciphers and Secret Writing*. Candlewick Press.

Jaseena, & John. (2011). Text Watermarking using Combined Image and Text for Authentication and Protection. *International Journal of Computer Applications, Volume*, *20*(4).

Jianquan, X., Qing, X., Dazu, H., & Duosi, X. (2010). Research on imperceptibility index of image Information Hiding. *Second International Conference on Networks Security Wireless Communications and Trusted Computing (NSWCTC)*. doi:10.1109/NSWCTC.2010.148

Jiansheng, Q., Dong, W., Li, L. C. D., & Xuesong, W. (2014). Image quality assessment based on multiscale representation of structure. *Digital Signal Processing*, *33*, 125–133. doi:10.1016/j.dsp.2014.06.009

Jianzhong, L., & Xiaojing, C. (2009). An adaptive secure watermarking scheme using double random-phase encoding technique. *2nd International Congress on Image and Signal Processing, CISP '09.*

Jin &, Kim. (2012). Imperceptibility Improvement of Image Watermarking Using Variance Selection, Computer Applications for Web, Human Computer Interaction. *Signal and Image Processing, and Pattern Recognition Communications in Computer and Information Science, 342*, 31–38.

Joshi, A. M., Darji, A., & Mishra, V. (2011). Design and implementation of real-time image watermarking. *IEEE International Conference on Signal Processing, Communications and Computing*. doi:10.1109/ICSPCC.2011.6061762

Juergen, S. (2005). *Digital Watermarking for Digital Media, Idea Group Inc*. IGI.

Jun, S., & Alam, M. S. (2008). Fragility and Robustness of Binary-Phase-Only-Filter-Based Fragile/Semifragile Digital Image Watermarking. *IEEE Transactions on Instrumentation and Measurement, 57*(3).

Kabir, M. N., Omar, T., & Alginahi, Y. M. (2013). Evaluation of Watermarking Approaches for Arabic Text Documents. *International Journal of Computer Science and Information Security, 11*(3), 49–54.

Kale, K. V. (2008). Advances in Computer Vision and Information Technology. I. K. International Pvt Ltd.

Kang, X., & Wei, S. (2008). Identifying tampered regions using singular value decomposition in digital image forensics. In *Proc. international conference on computer science and software engineering*. doi:10.1109/CSSE.2008.876

Karthigai, P., & Baskaran, K. (2011). An ASIC implementation of a low power robust invisible watermarking processor. *Journal of Systems Architecture: The EUROMICRO Journal, 57*(4), 404–411. doi:10.1016/j.sysarc.2010.03.008

Karthigaikumar, P., & Baskaran, K. (2011). FPGA and ASIC implementation of robust invisible binary image watermarking algorithm using connectivity preserving criteria. *Microelectronics Journal, 42*(1), 82–88. doi:10.1016/j.mejo.2010.08.023

Karthigaikumar, P., & Baskaranc Anumol, K. (2011). FPGA Implementation of High Speed Low Area DWT Based Invisible Image Watermarking Algorithm. *International Conference on Communication Technology and System Design*.

Kaushal, S., Upamanyu, M., Manjunath, B. S., & Shiv, C. (2005). Modeling the Print-Scan Process for Resilient Data Hiding, Security, Steganography, and Watermarking of Multimedia Contents. *SPIE, 5681*, 418-429.

Kautilya. (1992). *The Arthashastra* (L. N. Rangarajan, Trans.). Penguin Books India.

Keskinarkaus, A., Pramila, A., & Seppänen, T. (2012). Image watermarking with feature point based synchronization robust to print–scan attack. *Journal of Visual Communication and Image Representation, 23*(3), 507–515. doi:10.1016/j.jvcir.2012.01.010

Kharittha, T., Pipat, S., & Thumrongrat, A. (2015). Digital Image Watermarking based on Regularized Filter. *14th IAPR International Conference on Machine Vision Applications*.

Ki-Hyeok, B., & Sung-Hwan, J. (2001). A study on the robustness of watermark according to frequency band. *IEEE International Symposium on Industrial Electronics*. doi:10.1109/ISIE.2001.932024

Kim, Y. S., Kwon, O. H., & Park, R. H. (1999). Wavelet Based Watermarking Method for Digital Images Using The Human Visual System. *Electronics Letters*, *35*(6), 466–468. doi:10.1049/el:19990327

Koch, C., & Ullman, S. (1985). Shifts in selective visual attention: Towards the underlying neural circuitry. *Human Neurobiology*, *4*, 219–227. PMID:3836989

Kovesi, P. (2003). Phase Congruency Detects Corners and Edges.*Australian Pattern Recognition Society Conference.*

Kovesi, P. D. (1996). *Invariant Measures of Image Features from Phase Information* (PhD thesis). University of Western Australia.

Kovesi, P. D. (1999). Image features from phase congruency. *Videre: Journal of Computer Vision Research*, *1*, 1–26.

Kovesi, P. D. (2003). Phase congruency detects corners and edges. *The Australian Pattern Recognition Society Conference*. DICTA.

Kullback, S., & Leibler, R. A. (1951). On Information and Sufficiency.*Annals of Mathematical Statistics*, *22*(1), 79–86. doi:10.1214/aoms/1177729694

Kumar, M. H., & Maity, S. P. (2014). FPGA implementation of reversible watermarking in digital images using reversible contrast mapping. *Journal of Systems and Software*, *96*, 93–104. doi:10.1016/j.jss.2014.05.079

Kuppusamy, K., & Thamodaran, K. (2012). Optimized Image Watermarking Scheme Based On PSO. *Procedia Engineering*, *38*, 493–503. doi:10.1016/j.proeng.2012.06.061

Kutter, M., Voloshynovskiy, S., & Herrigel, A. (2000). The watermark copy attack. Security and Watermarking of Multimedia Content II, 3971.

Kyan, M., Guan, L., Arnison, R., & Cogswell, C. (2001). Feature Extraction of Chromosomes from 3-D Confocal Microscope Images. *IEEE Transactions on Bio-Medical Engineering*, *48*(11), 1306–1318. doi:10.1109/10.959326 PMID:11686629

Lalitha, N. V., & Rao, S. (2013). DWT - Arnold Transform based audio watermarking. *IEEE Asia Pacific Conference on Postgraduate Research in Microelectronics and Electronics*. doi:10.1109/PrimeAsia.2013.6731204

Lee, H. K., Kim, H. J., Kwon, S. G., & Lee, J. K. (2005). ROI Medical Image Watermarking Using DWT and Bit-Plane. *Asia-Pacific Conference on Communications.*

Lin, P.-L. (2001). Oblivious Digital Watermarking Scheme with Blob-Oriented and Modular-Arithmetic-Based Spatial-Domain Mechanism. *Journal of Visual Communication and Image Representation*, *12*(2), 136–151. doi:10.1006/jvci.2000.0454

Lina Shinfeng, D., Shieb, S-C., & Guoa, J.Y. (2010). Improving the robustness of DCT-based image watermarking against JPEG compression. *Computer Standards & Interfaces*, *32*(1–2), 54–60.

Liu & Qiu. (2002). The survey of digital watermarking-based image authentication techniques. *ICSP'02 Proceedings.*

Liu, N., Amin, P., Ambalavanan, A., & Subbalakshmi, K. P. (2006). An Overview of Digital Watermarking. In Multimedia Security Technologies for Digital Rights Management. Academic Press.

Liu, Z., & Laganiere, R. (2007). Phase congruence measurement for image similarity assessment. *Pattern Recognition Letters*, *28*(1), 166–172. doi:10.1016/j.patrec.2006.06.019

Lo, Hu, Chen, & Chang. (2014). Probability-Based Image Authentication Scheme for Indexed Color Images. *Journal of Electronic Imaging*, *23*(3).

Lopez, G. M., Ramos, L. R., Miguel, H. O., & Canto, N. E. (2014). *Embedded System for Biometric Online Signature Verification. IEEE Transactions on Industrial Informatics, 10*(1), 491–501.

Thamarai & Ashok. (2014). Low Power Implementation of an Invisible-Robust Image Watermarking Encoder using Xilinx FPGA. *Journal of Nanoscience and Nanotechnology*, *2*(1).

Lynch C., (2000). Authenticity and Integrity in the Digital Environment: An Exploratory Analysis of the Central Role of Trust. In *Authenticity in a Digital Age*. CLIR.

Ma, L., Weisi, L., Deng, C., & King, N. N. (2012). Image Retargeting Quality Assessment: A Study of Subjective Scores and Objective Metrics. *IEEE Journal of Selected Topics in Signal Processing, Volume*, *6*(6), 626–639. doi:10.1109/JSTSP.2012.2211996

Macq, B., Dittmann, J., & Delp, E. J. (2004). Benchmarking of image watermarking algorithms for digital rights management. *Proceedings of the IEEE, 92*(6), 971-984. doi:10.1109/JPROC.2004.827361

Maity, S. P., Kundu, M. K., & Seba, M. (2009). Dual Purpose FWT Domain Spread Spectrum Image Watermarking in Real-Time. *Computers & Electrical Engineering*, *35*(2), 415–433. doi:10.1016/j.compeleceng.2008.06.003

Makbol, N. M., Ee, K. B., & Rassem, T. H. (2016). Block-based discrete wavelet transform singular value decomposition image watermarking scheme using human visual system characteristics. *IET Image Process.*, *10*(1), 34–52. doi:10.1049/iet-ipr.2014.0965

Malihe, M., Mohammad, Z., & Chahooki, A. (2016). Robust transparent image watermarking with Shearlet transform andbidiagonal singular value decomposition. *International Journal of Electronics and Communications*, *70*(6), 790–798. doi:10.1016/j.aeue.2016.03.004

Marr, D., & Hildreth, E. C. (1980). Theory of edge detection. *Proceedings of the Royal Society of London. Series B, Biological Sciences*, *207*(1167), 187–217. doi:10.1098/rspb.1980.0020 PMID:6102765

Matheson, L. R., Mitchell, S. G., Shamoon, T. G., Tarjan, R. E., & Francis, Z. (1998). Robustness and security of digital watermarks, Financial Cryptography. *Lecture Notes in Computer Science*, *1465*, 227–240. doi:10.1007/BFb0055486

Megalingam, R. K., Nair, M. M., Srikumar, R., Balasubramanian, V. K., & Sarma, V. S. V. (2010). Performance Comparison of Novel, Robust Spatial Domain Digital Image Watermarking with the Conventional Frequency Domain Watermarking Techniques. *International Conference on Signal Acquisition and Processing*. doi:10.1109/ICSAP.2010.79

Megalingam, R. K., Nair, M. M., Srikumar, R., Balasubramanian, V. K., & Sarma, V. S. V. (2010). Performance Comparison of Novel, Robust Spatial Domain Digital Image Watermarking with the Conventional Frequency Domain Watermarking Techniques. *International Conference on Signal Acquisition and Processing*. doi:10.1109/ICSAP.2010.79

Mehran, A., & Chandler, D. M. (2015). Digital Image Watermarking via Adaptive Logo Texturization. *IEEE Transactions on Image Processing, 24*(12), 5060–5073. doi:10.1109/TIP.2015.2476961 PMID:26353371

Michael, A., Peter, B., & Walter, V. (2008). *Subjective and Objective Quality Evaluation of Watermarked Audio. In Digital Audio Watermarking Techniques and Technologies: Applications and Benchmarks*. IGI Global.

Michael, G., & Sushil, J. (2007). *Handbook of Database Security: Applications and Trends*. Springer Science & Business Media.

Mielikainen, J. (2006). LSB matching revisited. *IEEE Signal Processing Letters, 13*(5), 285–287. doi:10.1109/LSP.2006.870357

Minamoto, T., & Ohura, R. (2012). A Non-blind Digital Image Watermarking Method Based on the Dual-tree Complex Discrete Wavelet Transform and Interval Arithmetic. *Ninth International Conference on Information Technology: New Generations*. doi:10.1109/ITNG.2012.129

Mislav, G., Kresimir, D., & Mohammed, G. (2009). Recent Advances in Multimedia Signal Processing and Communications. Springer Science & Business Media.

Mobasseri Bijan, Zhang, Amin, & Dogahe. (2005). Designing robust watermarks using polynomial phase exponentials. *ICASSP*.

Mohanty, S.P., & Bhargava, B.K. (2008). Invisible Watermarking Based on Creation and Robust Insertion–Extraction of Image Adaptive Watermarks. *ACM Transactions on Multimedia Computing, Communications, and Applications, 5*(2), 12:1–12:22.

Mohanty, S. P., Parthasarathy, G., Elias, K., & Nishikanta, P. (2006). A Novel Invisible Color Image Watermarking Scheme using Image Adaptive Watermark Creation and Robust Insertion-Extraction. In *Proceeding of the 8th IEEE International Symposium on Multimedia (ISM '06)*. doi:10.1109/ISM.2006.7

Mohanty Saraju, P., & Bhargava Bharat, K. (2008). Invisible Watermarking Based on Creation and Robust Insertion-Extraction of Image Adaptive Watermarks. *ACM Transactions on Multimedia Computing, Communications, and Applications, 5*(2), 1–24. doi:10.1145/1413862.1413865

Möller, S., Pfitzmann, A., & Stirand, I. (1996). Computer Based Steganography: How It Works and Why Therefore Any Restrictions on Cryptography Are Nonsense, At Best, *in Information Hiding:First International Workshop, Proceedings*.

Morrone, M. C., & Burr, D. C. (1988). Feature detection in human vision: A phase dependent energy model. *Proceedings of the Royal Society of London. Series B, Biological Sciences, 235*(1280), 221–245. doi:10.1098/rspb.1988.0073 PMID:2907382

Morrone, M. C., & Owens, R. A. (1987). Feature detection from local energy. *Pattern Recognition Letters, 6*(5), 303–313. doi:10.1016/0167-8655(87)90013-4

Morrone, M. C., Ross, J., Burr, D. C., & Owens, R. (1986). Mach bands are phase dependent. *Nature, 324*(6049), 250–253. doi:10.1038/324250a0

Mukherjee, D. P., Maitra, S., & Acton, S. T. (2004). Spatial domain digital watermarking of multimedia objects for buyer authentication. *IEEE Transactions on Multimedia, Volume, 6*(1), 1–15. doi:10.1109/TMM.2003.819759

Nasir, I., Weng, Y., & Jiang, J. (2007). A new robust watermarking scheme for color image in spatial domain.*Proc. third international IEEE conference on signal image technologies and internet-based system.* doi:10.1109/SITIS.2007.67

Nazeer, M., & Nargis, B. (2015). Digital image watermarking using partial pivoting lower and upper triangular decomposition into the wavelet domain. *IET Image Process., 9*(9), 795–803. doi:10.1049/iet-ipr.2014.0395

Nguyen, Beghdadi, & Luong. (2012). Perceptual watermarking robust to JPEG compression attack. *5th International Symposium on Communications Control and Signal Processing (ISCCSP).*

Ni, R., & Ruan, Q. (2006). Region of Interest Watermarking Based on Fractal Dimension.*Proc. Int. Conf. Pattern Recognition, 3,* 934–937.

Niu, Y., Kyan, M., Ma, L., & Beghdadi, A. (2011) A Visual Saliency Modulated Just Noticeable Distortion Profile for Image Watermarking. *European Signal Processing Conference.*

Oded, G. (2001). Foundations of Cryptography Volume 1: Basic Tools. Cambridge University Press.

Osman, Z. (2011). *Iris Recognition Using Phase Congruency.* IICMS.

Otum, H. M. A. (2014). Semi-fragile watermarking for grayscale image authentication and tamper detection based on an adjusted expanded-bit multi-scale quantization-based technique. *Journal of Visual Communication and Image Representation, 25*(5), 1064–1081. doi:10.1016/j.jvcir.2013.12.017

Patra, J. C., Phua, J. E., & Rajan, D. (2010). DCT domain watermarking scheme using Chinese Remainder Theorem for image authentication. *IEEE International Conference on Multimedia and Expo.* doi:10.1109/ICME.2010.5583326

Pei, Jung, & Chang. (2009). Dual Digital Watermarking for Internet Media Based on Hybrid Strategies. *IEEE Transactions on Circuits and Systems for Video Technology, 19*(8), 1169-1177.

Pelgrom Marcel, J. M. (2010). *Analog-to-Digital Conversion.* Springer Science & Business Media. doi:10.1007/978-90-481-8888-8

Perez. (2007). *Advances in Audio and Speech Signal Processing: Technologies and Applications.* IGI.

Peter, K. (1996). *Invariant Measures of Image Features from Phase Information* (PhD thesis). The University of Western Australia.

Peter, K. (1999). Image features from phase congruency. *Videre: Journal of Computer Vision Research, 1*(3), 1–26.

Peter, K. (2000). Phase Congruency: A Low-Level Image Invariant. *Psychological Research Psychologische Forschung, 64*(2), 136–148. doi:10.1007/s004260000024 PMID:11195306

Peter, W. (2009). *Disappearing Cryptography: Information Hiding: Steganography & Watermarking* (3rd ed.). Morgan Kaufmann.

Petitcolas, F. A. P., & Anderson, R. J. (1998). Weaknesses of Copyright Marking Systems. In *Multimedia and Security Workshop at ACM Multimedia '98.*

Piotr, L., & Zbigniew, P. (2013). Parallel blind digital image watermarking in spatial and frequency domains. *Telecommunication Systems, 54.* doi:10.1007/s11235-013-9734-x

Piyanart, C., Kharittha, T., Pipat, S., & Amornraksa, T. (2015). Digital Image Watermarking on Illumination Component. *14th IAPR International Conference on Machine Vision Applications.*

Podilchuk & Wenjun. (1998). Image-Adaptive Watermarking Using Visual Models. *IEEE Journal on Selected Areas in Communication, 16*(4).

Podilchuk, C., & Delp, E. (2001). Digital Watermarking Algorithms and Applications. *IEEE Signal Processing Magazine, 18*(4), 33–46. doi:10.1109/79.939835

Podilchuk, C. I., & Wenjun, Z. (1997). Perceptual Watermarking of Still Images, *Workshop on Multimedia Signal Processing, USA, Electronic Proceedings.* doi:10.1109/MMSP.1997.602662

Pohlmann,. (1992). *The Compact Disc Handbook.* Oxford University Press.

Prasanna, S., Toshanlal, M., Ankit, S., Vivek, G., & Amit, K. (2015). A DWT-SVD Based Digital Watermarking Technique for Copyright Protection. *International Conference on Electrical, Electronics, Signals, Communication and Optimization.*

Proakis,. (2007). *Digital Signal Processing: Principles, Algorithms, And Applications.* Pearson Education India.

Punsawad, Y., & Wongsawat, Y. (2009). *Palmprint image enhancement using phase congruency.* IEEE ROBIO.

Qing-Cheng, L., & Zhen, H. D. (2008). Novel Text Watermarking Algorithm Based on Chinese Characters Structure. *Computer International Symposium on Science and Computational Technology.*

Que, D., Zhang, L., Lu, L., & Shi, L. (2006). A ROI Image Watermarking Algorithm Based on Lifting Wavelet Transform.*Proc. Int. Conf. Signal Processing.* doi:10.1109/ICOSP.2006.345979

Robbins, B., & Owens, R. (1997). 2-D feature detection via local energy. *Image and Vision Computing, 15*(5), 353–368. doi:10.1016/S0262-8856(96)01137-7

Roche, S., & Dugelay, J.-L. (1998). Image Watermarking Based on the Fractal Transform. In *Workshop on Multimedia Signal Processing.* IEEE.

Rongsheng, X., Wu, K., Du, J., & Li, C. (2007). Survey of Public Key Digital Watermarking Systems. *Eighth ACIS International Conference on Software Engineering, Artificial Intelligence, Networking, and Parallel/Distributed Computing.*

Ronse, C. (1995). *The phase congruence model for edge detection in two dimensional pictures: A mathematical study* (PhD thesis). University Louis Pastern.

Ross, A. (1996). Lecture notes in computer science: Vol. 1174. *Information Hiding*. Springer.

Ruanaidh, J. J. K. O., Dowling, W. J., & Boland, F. M. (1996). Phase watermarking of digital images. *International Conference on Image Processing, Proceedings*. doi:10.1109/ICIP.1996.560428

Ruderman, D. (1994). The Statistics of Natural Images. *Network (Bristol, England)*, *5*(4), 517–548. doi:10.1088/0954-898X_5_4_006 PMID:10057546

Sadreazami, H., Ahmad Omair, M., & Swamy, M. N. S. (2015). A Robust Multiplicative Watermark Detector for Color Images in Sparse Domain. *IEEE Transactions on Circuits and Systems—II. Express Briefs*, *62*(12), 1159–1163.

Saha, S., Tahtali, M., Lambert, A., & Pickering, M. (2013). Perceptual dissimilarity metric: A full reference objective image quality measure to quantify the degradation of perceptual image quality. *IEEE International Symposium on Signal Processing and Information Technology*. doi:10.1109/ISSPIT.2013.6781902

Salivahanan, S., & Gnanapriya, C. (2011). *Digital signal processing*. Tata McGraw-Hill Education.

Satyen, B., Das Sunil, R., & Petriu Emil, M. (2005). An Adaptive Compressed MPEG-2 Video Watermarking Scheme. IEEE Transactions on Instrumentation and Measurement, 54(5), 1853-1861.

Scaria, A., Badari Nath, D., Devi, M. N., & Mohankumar, N. (2011). Hardware Implementation of SVD Based Colour Image Watermarking in Wavelet Domain. *International Conference on Process Automation, Control and Computing (PACC)*.

Servetto, S. D., Podilchuk, C. I., & Ramchandran, K. (1998). Capacity Issues In Digital Image Watermarking. *International Conference on Image Processing*.

Shih Frank, Y. (2008). *Digital Watermarking and Steganography: Fundamentals and Techniques*. CRC Press.

Shih Frank, Y., & Wu Scott, Y. T. (2003). Combinational image watermarking in the spatial and frequency domains. *Pattern Recognition, 36*(4), 969–975. doi:10.1016/S0031-3203(02)00122-X

Shih Frank, Y., & Wu Scott, Y. T. (2003). Combinational image watermarking in the spatial and frequency domains. *Pattern Recognition*, *36*(4), 969–975. doi:10.1016/S0031-3203(02)00122-X

Shrinivas, K., & Urmila, S. (2015). Image bit depth plane digital watermarking for secured classified image data transmission. *Procedia Compute Science*, *78*, 698–705.

Shu-Fen, T., & Ching-Sheng, H. (2008). An Imperceptible Watermarking Scheme Using Variation and Modular Operations. *International Conference on Multimedia and Ubiquitous Engineering*.

Simmons, G. J. (1984). The Prisoners' Problem and the Subliminal Channel, in Advances in Cryptology. *Proceedings of CRYPTO*. Plenum Press.

Sin-Joo, L., & Sung-Hwan, J. (2001). *A survey of watermarking techniques applied to multimedia*. Pusan: Korea.

Smith Joshua, R., & Comiskey Barrett, O. (1996). Modulation and Information Hiding in Images. *Proceedings of the First Information Hiding Workshop*. doi:10.1007/3-540-61996-8_42

Smith Laurence Dwight. (1955). *Cryptography: The Science of Secret Writing*. Courier Dover Publications.

Smithal, B., & Navas, K. A. (2007). *Spatial Domain- High Capacity Data Hiding in ROI Images*. IEEE-ICSCN.

Srivastava, A., Lee, A., Simoncelli, E., & Zhu, S. (2003). On Advances in Statistical Modeling of Natural Images. *Journal of Mathematical Imaging and Vision*, *18*(1), 17–33. doi:10.1023/A:1021889010444

Stinson, D. R. (2005). *Cryptography: Theory and Practice* (3rd ed.). CRC Press.

Struc, V., & Pavesic, N. (2009). Phase congruency features for palm-print verification. *IET Signal Process.*, *3*(4), 258–268. doi:10.1049/iet-spr.2008.0152

Su, J. K., Frank, H., & Bernd, G. (1998). Digital Watermarking of Text, Image, and Video Documents. *Computers & Graphics*, *22*(6), 687–695. doi:10.1016/S0097-8493(98)00089-2

Su, J. K., & Girod, B. (1999). On the Robustness and Imperceptibility of Digital Fingeerprints. *Int. Conf. on multimedia Computing & System*.

Sudip, G., De Sayandip, M. S. P., & Hafizur, R. (2015). A Novel Dual Purpose Spatial Domain Algorithm for Digital Image Watermarking and Cryptography Using Extended Hamming Code. *International Conference on Electrical Information and Communication Technology*.

Sur, A., Sagar, S. S., Pal, R., Mitra, P., & Mukhopadhyay, J. (2009). A New Image Watermarking Scheme using Saliency Based Visual Attention Model. *Proceedings of IEEE Annual India Conference*. doi:10.1109/INDCON.2009.5409402

Susu, Y., Jinghong, Z., Li, Z., & Yao, W. (2010). Robust Image Registration Using Phase Congruency. *2nd International Conference on Signal Processing Systems (ICSPS)*.

Tanaka, K., Nakamura, Y., & Matsui, K. (1990). Embedding secret information into a dithered multi-level image. In *Proc. IEEE Military Communications Conference*. doi:10.1109/MILCOM.1990.117416

Tew & Wong. (2014). An Overview of Information Hiding in H.264/AVC Compressed Video. *IEEE Transactions on Circuits and Systems for Video Technology, 24*(2), 305-319.

Tirkel, A. Z., Rankin, G. A., Van Schyndel, R. M., Ho, W. J., Mee, N. R. A., & Osborne, C. F. (1993). *Electronic Water Mark. Digital Image Computing: Techniques and Applications 1993*. Macquarie University.

Tomás. (2005). Image communication quality assessment based on watermarking, an overview. *Internal Report, v0.02 – Instituto de Telecomunicações*.

Trithemius, J. (1606). Data hiding method in binary images based on block masking for key authentication. *Information Sciences*, *277*, 188–196.

Tsai, C.-L., Chiang, H.-F., Fan, K.-C., & Chung, C.-D. (2005). Reversible data hiding and lossless reconstruction of binary images using pair-wise logical computation mechanism. *Pattern Recognition*, 38.

Tsang, K. F., & Au, O. C. (2001). A Review on Attacks, Problems and Weakness of Digital Watermarking and the Pixel Reallocation Attack. Security and Watermarking of Multimedia Content III, 4314, 385-393.

Vadde, S., Agarwal, A., & Ganesan, S. (2004). *Real -Time adaptive Digital Image Watermarking.* IEEE Electro/Information Technology Conference.

Verma, Singh, & Kumar. (2009). Robustness of the Digital Image Watermarking Techniques against Brightness and Rotation Attack. *International Journal of Computer Science and Information Security, 5*(1).

Vidyasagar, P. M., Song, H., & Elizabeth, C. (2005). A Survey of Digital Image Watermarking Techniques. *3rd IEEE International Conference on Industrial Informatics.*

Vinicius, L., & Ramiro, J. (2005). Geometric Attacks on Image Watermarking Systems. *IEEE MultiMedia, 12*(3), 68–78. doi:10.1109/MMUL.2005.46

Vipula, S. (2011). *Digital Watermarking: A Tutorial. Journal of Selected Areas in Telecommunications,* 10–21.

Voloshynovskiy, S., Pereira, S., & Pun, T. (1999), Watermark attacks. *Erlangen Watermarking Workshop.*

Voloshynovskiy, S., Pereiraa, S., Herrigelb, A., Baumgartnerb, N., & Pun, T. (2000). Generalized watermarking attack based on watermark estimation and perceptual remodulation. *Proc. SPIE: Security and Watermarking of Multimedia Content.* doi:10.1117/12.384990

Wang, S., Jiying, Z., James, T. W., & Filippo, S. (2004). Image quality measurement by using watermarking based on discrete wavelet transform. *22nd Biennial Symposium on Communications.*

Wei, L., Hongtao, L., & Fu-Lai, C. (2006). Feature based watermarking using watermark template match. *Applied Mathematics and Computation, 177*(1), 377–386. doi:10.1016/j.amc.2005.11.015

Wei, W., Jinyan, W., Chengxi, W., & Pu, D. (2010). A Novel Watermarking Algorithm Based on Phase Congruency Corner Detection and SVD. *Fifth International Conference on Frontier of Computer Science and Technology.*

Weiner, J., & Mirkes, K. (1972). *Watermarking.* Appleton, WI: The Institute of Paper Chemistry.

Wioletta, W., & Ogiela, M. R. (2016). Digital images authentication scheme based on bimodal biometric watermarking in an independent domain. *Journal of Visual Communication and Image Representation, 38*, 1–10. doi:10.1016/j.jvcir.2016.02.006

Won, Chan, & Won. (1999). A watermarking scheme for both spatial and frequency domain to extract the seal image without the original image. *Fifth International Symposium on Signal Processing and Its Applications.*

Wujie, Z., Lu, Y., Zhongpeng, W., Mingwei, W., Ting, L., & Lihui, S. (2016). Binocular visual characteristics based fragile watermarking schemefor tamper detection in stereoscopic images. *International Journal of Electronics and Communications, 70*(1), 77–84. doi:10.1016/j.aeue.2015.10.006

Xiang-yang, W., Yu-nan, L., Shuo, L., Hong-ying, Y., Pan-pan, N., & Yan, Z. (2015). A new robust digital watermarking using local polar harmonic transform. Journal of Computers and Electrical Engineering, 46, 403–418.

Xiao, P. F., Feng, X. Z., & Zhao, S. H. (2006). Feature detection from IKONOS pan imagery based on phase congruency. In *Proc. SPIE, Image and Signal Processing for Remote Sensing XII*. doi:10.1117/12.689595

Xiaodi, H., & Liqing, Z. (2007). Saliency Detection: A Spectral Residual Approach. *IEEE Conference on Computer Vision and Pattern Recognition*.

Xiaojun, Q., & Ji, Q. (2007). A robust content-based digital image watermarking scheme. *Signal Processing, 87*(6), 1264–1280. doi:10.1016/j.sigpro.2006.11.002

Xie, J., Xie, Q., & Huang, D. (2009). A Robust High Capacity Information Hiding Algorithm Based on DCT High Frequency Domain. *International Symposium on Computer Network and Multimedia Technology*.

Xu, H., Wanga, J., & Kim, H. J. (2010). Near-optimal solution to pair wise LSB matching via an immune programming strategy. *Information Sciences, 180*(8), 1201–1217. doi:10.1016/j.ins.2009.12.027

Xuejuan, Z., Xiaochun, C., & Li, J. (2013). Geometric attack resistant image watermarking based on MSER. *Frontiers of Computer Science, 7*(1), 145–156. doi:10.1007/s11704-013-2174-7

Yen-Chung, C., & Wen-Hsiang, T. (2006). *Copyright Protection against Print-and-Scan Operations by Watermarking for Color Images Using Coding and Synchronization of Peak Locations in Frequency Domain. Journal of Information Science and Engineering, 22*, 483–496.

Yeung, M. M. (1998). Digital Watermarking. *Communications of the ACM, 41*(7), 31–33. doi:10.1145/278476.278484

Yip, Au, Ho, & Wong. (2006). Lossless Visible Watermarking. *IEEE ICME*.

Yongdong, W. (2006). Nonlinear collusion attack on a watermarking scheme for buyer authentication. *IEEE Transactions on Multimedia, Volume, 8*(3), 626–629. doi:10.1109/TMM.2006.870720

Yuval, C., Michael, L., & Shay, M. (2011). Real-Time Digital Watermarking System for Audio Signals Using Perceptual Masking. Signal and Image Processing Lab, Faculty of EE, Technion IIT, Haifa, Israel.

Zabrodsky, H. H. (2001). Watermarking and Copyright Labeling of Printed Images. *Journal of Electronic Imaging, 10*(3), 794–803. doi:10.1117/1.1382612

Zhang, D., Wu, B., Sun, J., & Huang, H. (2009). A new robust watermarking algorithm based on DWT. In *Proc. second international congress on image and signal processing*. doi:10.1109/CISP.2009.5303924

Zhang, L., Zhang, L., Mou, X., & Zhang, D. (2011). FSIM: A feature similarity index for image quality assessment. *IEEE Transactions on Image Processing, 20*(8), 2378–2386. doi:10.1109/TIP.2011.2109730 PMID:21292594

Zhao, Z., Wang, X., Zhang, W., & Zhu, Z. (2015). A Community-Based Approach to Identifying Influential Spreaders. *Entropy, 17*, 2228-2252. Retrieved from www.mdpi.com/journal/entropy

Zheng, D., & Zhao, J. (2003). RST invariant digital image watermarking: importance of phase information. *Canadian Conference on Electrical and Computer Engineering*. doi:10.1109/CCECE.2003.1226012

Zheng, P.-P., Feng, J., Li, Z., & Zhou, M. (2014). A Novel SVD and LS-SVM Combination Algorithm for Blind Watermarking. *Neurocomputing, 142*, 520–528. doi:10.1016/j.neucom.2014.04.005

Zhihong, Q., Lei, C., Weilian, S., Tingkai, W., & Huamin, Y. (2012). *Recent Advances in Computer Science and Information Engineering* (Vol. 5). Springer Science & Business Media. doi:10.1007/978-3-642-25766-7_29

Zhijun, W. (2014). *Information Hiding in Speech Signals for Secure Communication, Syngress*. Elsevier.

Zoican, S. (2005). Digital signal processing system for digital watermarking implementation. *7th International Conference on Telecommunications in Modern Satellite, Cable and Broadcasting Services.*

Żurawski & Skodowski. (2014). Standard Deviation-Based Image Fidelity Measure For Digital Watermarking. *Przegląd Elektrotechniczny, 90*(5).

Chapter 11
A Hybrid System Based on FMM and MLP to Diagnose Heart Disease

Swati Aggarwal
NSIT, India

Venu Azad
Government Girls PG College, India

ABSTRACT

In the medical field diagnosis of a disease at an early stage is very important. Nowadays soft computing techniques such as fuzzy logic, artificial neural network and Neuro- fuzzy networks are widely used for the diagnosis of various diseases at different levels. In this chapter, a hybrid neural network is designed to classify the heart disease data set the hybrid neural network consist of two types of neural network multilayer perceptron (MLP) and fuzzy min max (FMM) neural network arranged in a hierarchical manner. The hybrid system is designed for the dataset which contain the combination of continuous and non continuous attribute values. In the system the attributes with continuous values are classified using the FMM neural networks and attributes with non-continuous value are classified by using the MLP neural network and to synthesize the result the output of both the network is fed into the second MLP neural network to generate the final result.

INTRODUCTION

The task of classification is an emerging trend in research. Soft computing techniques such as artificial neural networks, fuzzy logic and neuro-fuzzy networks are widely used for the classification purpose. Among these technologies, artificial neural networks have emerged as well – known solution for tackling pattern recognition and classification task (Devijver & Kittler, 1982; Duda & Hart, 1973; Fukunaga, 1972). Indeed, artificial neural networks are used for classification in many different fields, e.g. stock market prediction, medical prognosis and diagnosis, industrial fault detection and classification (Quteishat, 2007). In the medical field, artificial neural networks (ANNs) are deployed as diagnostic decision sup-

DOI: 10.4018/978-1-5225-1776-4.ch011

port systems that help physicians diagnose diseases in the presence of uncertainty and imprecision. The system developed using artificial neural networks can be useful in assisting the physician arrive at an informed decision quickly, e.g. by learning from past cases with similar features in a large database of electronic patient records and inferring the diagnosis for the current patient with proper justifications (Seera & Lim, 2014).

The diseases such as Heart Diseases, Hepatitis, different types of Cancer, and Diabetics are major epidemics in India. The most popular among the above mentioned disease is Cardiovascular disease which is also called as heart disease, which occur due improper functioning of some of heart components. There are various types of heart diseases like coronary artery diseases, hypertension, and hyperlipidemia. The cardiovascular diseases (CVDs) or heart disease is the number one cause of death globally, more people die annually due to CVDs (cardio vascular diseases) than any other disease (WHO, guidelines). According to WHO (World Health Organization) report, CVDs (cardio vascular diseases) has become a modern epidemic. So, there is a need to detect or diagnose CVDs (cardio vascular diseases) at an early stage. In general, whenever a person feels some sickness he/she directly go the physician. A physician initially asks the basic symptoms, the person feeling and draw a conclusion that by which diseases the person is suffering from. Sometimes the disease is very complex and a physician can't draw a conclusion just by looking at the patient's symptoms, in such cases the physician ask the patient for some medical test like blood test, LFT (liver function test), KFT (Kidney function test), CT-SCAN, ECG (Electrocardiogram), PET (Proton emission test for cancer detection) etc.. Similarliy, there are a number of medical tools used to predict CVDs, such as electrocardiography (ECG), magnetic resonance angiography (MRA) etc., but using these measurements in home health care is inconvenient due to expensive cost and invasive measurement (DONG et al., 2010). The physician looks at the results of these medical test reports and then draw a conclusion. But sometime the patient doesn't satisfy with the physician's consensus. The patient consults some other doctor/physician to confirm the disease. This procedure takes a longer time than usual and sometimes it will be too late to diagnose a disease. To reduce the diagnosis time and improve the diagnostic precision it has become more of a demanding issue to develop reliable and powerful medical decision support system to support the yet and still increasingly complicated diagnosis decision process (Yan et. al., 2006).

There are many other factors which motivated us to carry out the research work in the area of diagnosis of diseases using soft computing techniques such as artificial neural network (NN), genetic algorithms (GAs), fuzzy logic (FL), and evolutionary computation. Soft computing combines these mechanisms as FL and NN (FL-NN), NN and GA (NN-GA) and FL and GA (FL-GA). In our study, we have used NN along with the hybrid combination of FL (fuzzy logic) and NN (neural network) in parallel. From past few years, the phenomenal growth can be seen in bio-informatics and medical informatics by using computational/evolutionary techniques for interpretation and analysis of biological and medical data (Yardimci, 2009). These soft computing techniques can be used in a number of ways in the field of medical and biological data like they can be used for diagnosis of diseases, regime selection, prediction of failure and success of a particular treatment of a disease, robotic assisted surgeries and drug prediction on the basis of symptoms or the data available. We have chosen the diagnostic science in which the clinical parameter derived from laboratory test and obtained by examining the patient are used to predict that whether the person is suffering from any kind of abnormality or the person is healthy. In developing countries where medical information is not so much flourished, as the medical experts are very less in comparison to the patients and medical facilities are hardly available to the remote areas these automated system provides the improved health care services. These systems are reliable, cost effective and easy to operate, with the help of this system the early diagnosis of diseases not only save the lives but also save a huge operating cost incurred at a later stage of a disease. These classification systems are not only beneficial for the patient, but also help the medical practitioner to take decision regarding the diagnosis of a particular disease and it also help the domain users like medical interns to grab the idea about the causes of a disease.

In this chapter, we will discuss a few methods which use soft computing techniques to diagnose heart disease. As there are a number of soft computing techniques each having its own benefits such as fuzzy logic which deals with the imprecision or incomplete information which is very frequently found in medical records, neural networks are able to learn themselves, genetic algorithms are used for the optimization purpose. To take their advantage of two more techniques we can combine the two or more concepts. There are various schemes of integrating the fuzzy logic with neural network neuro-fuzzy networks and fuzzy neural network. Various methodologies (Bagher–Ebadian et al., 2004; Chu et al., 2005; Kovalerchuk et al., 1997; Zahlmann et al., 2000) have been proposed to implement medical decision making which include fuzzy logic, neural network or a combination of these techniques with others. A medical diagnosing system is one which generates a diagnostic decision on the basis of input presented to the system (Zahlmann et al., 2000)

To detect any disease a physician has to analyze the symptoms or risk factor (which may cause disease). Different researchers use a different set of risk factors or symptoms as input to diagnose type of heart diseases. In this work the input parameter or the symptoms (risk factors) include age, smoking habit, height, weight, obesity, chest pain, blood pressure level and few laboratory tests based results the data set chosen is the combination of continuous and non – continuous data set.

Literature Review

Over the years, researchers have developed various classification systems to diagnose various types of diseases, some of which are presented here. In several areas of medical services, including diseases diagnosing, prescribing medicine data mining techniques have been applied (Tang et al., 2005). In research by Tang et al. (2005) the decision tree induction algorithm is one of the most important methods for classification; it uses two kinds of data: training and testing, training data are used to construct the decision tree. Decision Tree algorithms include CART (Classification and Regression Tree), ID3 (Iterative Dichotomized 3) and C4.5. Expert systems are an application of artificial intelligence technique, that can be applied to detection of diseases and prescribing regimen to the patient, for example MYCIN (Shortliffe, 1976), INTERNIST (Miller et al.), and CADIAG-2 (Adlassing, 1982) are the expert system, which are designed to prescribe antibiotics, according to symptoms, but these expert systems are used for diagnosis and prognosis of multiple diseases.

Yan et al. (2006) presents a multi-layer perceptron neural network with 40 input parameters is used to diagnose five different types of heart diseases. The multilayer perceptron used in this paper consist of three layers, the input layer, the hidden layer and the output layer. The number of nodes in each layer is as follows, the input layer contains 40 nodes each corresponds to one input variable. These 40 input variables are coded using binary (0, 1), ternary (-1, 0, 1) and by using a three value ordinal scales, the number of nodes in the hidden layer is decided by using a cascade learning process, which is 15 and the output layer contain 5 nodes each node represent the one heart disease on interest. This network is trained by using back propagation algorithm. BP (back propagation) is one of the simplest and most general methods for supervised learning of MLP (Duda et al., 2001). The back propagation algorithm augmented with the momentum term, the adaptive learning rate, the forgetting mechanics, and an optimized algorithm based on the conjugate gradient method is adopted. The data set used by the system is the data of 352 patients who, having different kind of heart diseases. The results show that the system achieves the high accuracy of about 91% of all cases.

WNN are based on wavelet transformation theory and used for approximating arbitrary nonlinear function. Wavelet neural networks can also be applied for diseases classification useful to diagnose coronary artery disease at different level (Tkacz & kostka, 2000). Radial basis function (RBF) neural networks and a variation of RBF that is generalized regression neural network (GRNN) are also used to prescribe the medicine to a heart patient based on the symptoms and patient details (Hannan et al., 2010). The work of Hannan et al. (2010) uses two neural networks, i.e. RBF (radial bases function) and GRNN (Generalize regression neural network) and a Gaussian Radial Basis Function (GRBF) to train the networks. The total 300 record of patients is collected for the study and data is encoded first. If people have some specific symptom at a particular place, then it is encoded as one (1) otherwise they encode it using zero (0). This encoded data is used to train the RBF and GRNN, the GRNN architecture consists of four layers: input layer, pattern layer, summation layer and output layer. The number of input units in the input layer depends on the total number of the observation parameters. RBFN consists of three layers: an input layer, a hidden (kernel) layer, and an output layer. In the output layer 52 medicines are used, if the medicine is used to treat the patient, it is defined by one and if it is not used to cure the patient it is defined by the zero. The experimental result shows that the output given by RBFN is satisfactory and is verified by the doctor which shows the usefulness of artificial neural network to predict the medicine.

In Anooj (2012) a diagnosing system is designed to diagnose the heart diseases based on the weighted fuzzy rules. The proposed CDSS (Clinical decision support system) works in two phases, in the first phase; they have used the mining technique, attribute selection and attribute weight age method to obtain the weighted fuzzy rules. Then, the Mamdani fuzzy inference system is constructed in accordance with the weighted fuzzy rules and chosen attributes. The weighted fuzzy rules are given to the Mamdani fuzzy inference system so that the system can learn these rules and the risk prediction can be carried out on the designed fuzzy system.There are various schemas to integrate FL and NN such as fuzzy neural network (FNN), fuzzy learning vector quantization (FLVQ) and fuzzy probabilistic neural network (FPNN). The work of SHI et al. (2010) describes a hierarchal network of pure FNNs, FPNNs, and FLVQs is presented to diagnose three typical frequently encountered CVDs, where different sub-network consume different group of input parameters. In Sekar et al. (2012) the researcher constructed a hierarchal network by fusing diverse sub-networks like FLVQ, FPNN at different level according to their performance in the diagnosis of the CVD (cardiovascular disease). It uses hemodynamic parameter derived from the non-invasive sphygmogram (SPG). Variance analysis method is used for the feature extraction. This method categorizes the input into three groups, i.e. sensitive, auxiliary, and replenish, these classes contain the HDP (Hemodynamic Parameters) parameter according to their relevancy to diagnose the heart diseases. A hierarchical network with diverse sub-NN is constructed to classify the input with a classification accuracy of 59.72%.

In the work of Pal et al. (2012) fuzzy logic is combined with expert system to diagnose CAD (coronary artery disease) by using clinical parameters. Researcher proposed a methodology consist of knowledge acquisition, design of a CAD (coronary artery disease) screening system using fuzzy rule based inference system. The expert system proposed by Pal et al. (2012) is a fuzzy rule base system which is used to classify the diseases. This system is used to predict the risk based on the 11 clinical parameters. Their work focuses on rule organization using the concept of modules, meta-rule base, rule address storage in tree representation and rule consistency checking for efficient search of a large number of rules in the rule base. The fuzzy inference engine of this expert system selects fuzzy rules and uses Mamdani inference mechanism to produce fuzzy output. For better rule organization the concept of modules and Meta rules are used. The overall accuracy obtained by applying proposed fuzzy expert system is 84.20%. In Kahramanli and Allahverdi (2008) a hybrid system comprises of artificial neural network and fuzzy neural network is presented to diagnose the diabetes and heart diseases. The system is proposed for the data set that contains the fuzzy values as well as crisp values. The hybrid neural network is constructed with the help of artificial neural network (ANN) and the fuzzy neural networks (FNN). The ANN (artificial neural network) is used to consume the crisp data, whereas the FNN (fuzzy neural networks) is used to consume the fuzzy data. The ANN (artificial neural network) used in this study is the multilayer perceptron neural network trained using the back-propagation learning algorithm. The FNN (fuzzy neural network) uses the fuzzy values. In the hybrid system, crisp data are standardized first and given to the input of ANN1, fuzzifiable data is fuzzified and given to the input of the FNN the results of FNN are defuzzified and presented to the input of ANN2 along with the output of ANN1 if the output given by the ANN2 is incorrect the weights are updated otherwise we stop the network training. The usefulness of the hybrid system is checked on two data set the Pima Indians Diabetes and the Cleveland heart disease data set taken from the University of California at Irvin.

The further work carried by the Kahramanli is presented in the Kahrmanli and Allahverdi (2009) in which they have proposed a rule extraction algorithm based on the AIS approach i.e. artificial Immune system. Artificial Immune System, it is a particular type of an Artificial Immune System developed to solve optimization problems. It is a computational technique inspired by the ideas coming from the immunology and used to develop the adaptive system capable of solving different domain problem (Seredynski & Bouvry, 2007). Here Opt-aiNET algorithm is developed for the extraction of rules for the Hybrid neural network to classify the data. This algorithm takes all input attributes into consideration and extracts the rules efficiently. The introduction of the rule extraction algorithm shows a great improvement in the accuracy of the system. A hybrid model is presented in Seera and Lim (2014). The hybrid intelligent system comprises of fuzzy min - max neural network, classification and regression tree and the random forest. This model is designed in such a way that the advantage of all three components can be exploited. The fuzzy min - max neural network enable the system to learn incrementally from the data samples and due to the CART (classification and regression tree) the system is able to predict and justify the output generated by the system; the high classification accuracy is achieved with the help of random forest. Here three data sets are used to evaluate the systems performances which are Breast Cancer Wisconsin, Pima Indians diabetes and liver disorders. All the data set is first normalized and then FMM (fuzzy min - max) neural network is used to classify the data, after that the CART (classification and regression tree) is used to extract the rules to justify the output generated by the system, from the CART - RF (classification and regression tree – Random Forest) is generated by the help of bagging method in tandem with random attribute selection. The experimental result shows that the system achieves higher accuracy rate for all three data sets.

In KIYAN and YILDIRIM (2004) statistical neural network like RBF (radial basis function), GRNN (general regression neural network), PNN (Probabilistic neural network) and MLP (multilayer perceptron) neural networks are used to classify WCBD (Wisconsin breast cancer data) data set the overall accuracy of these systems > 96%. In the work of kochurani and Aji (2007) a neuro fuzzy based approach is implemented for the CAD (coronary artery diseases) diagnosis. In the work of Palaniappan and Awang (2008) an intelligent heart diseases predication system was developed by using data mining techniques which include Decision Trees, Neural Network, and Naive Bayes. In Turkoglu et al. (2002) an expert system is developed which is used to diagnose heart valve diseases by extracting features from the Doppler Ultrasound and the back propagation neural network is used to classify the extracted features. In Chen et al. (2000) a self – organizing map (SOM) neural network is used to examine breast sonography tumor data set with accuracy 85.6%. In Panchal and Verma (2006) Digital mammogram is used to extract the features and an auto associator neural network is used to classify these extracted features and achieve the accuracy of 94%. In Singh and Dr. Gupta (2011) Biopsy images are used to examine the breast cancer, these images are first preprocessed using image processing techniques such as adaptive thresholding based segmentation and watershed segmentation method, then a classification algorithm based on feed –forward neural network is used to classify each cancer object into four object types. In Cascio et al. (2006) a supervised learning neural network is utilized for the classification of breast cancer in this a set of representative features were extracted and used for detection of masses in mammography images. In Tingting and Nandi (2007) SVM (Support Vector Machine) along with its variant like L_1-SVM, L_2-SVM and μ-SVM as well as combinations of SOM-RBF (Self organizing map – radial basis function) is also used to improve the classification accuracy of malignant tumor in WBCD (Wisconsin breast cancer data) data set. A highly accurate classification model for cancer from microarray data which identify the smallest set of genes for classification is constructed by using a fuzzy neural network and support vector machine (SVM) (Wang et al., 2007). In reference Lin (2008) a supervised learning model, i.e. a multilayer perceptron neural network (MLPNN) is used to classify the patterns of Scoliosis spinal deformity by using features obtained from the central axis curve of spinal deformity. A multilayer perceptron with genetic based algorithm is developed for automated identification of exudates pathologies in retinopathy images (Osareh et al., 2009). In Ji et al. (2012) a fuzzy k-prototype clustering technique is developed and used the same for the diagnosis of heart diseases. The work presented in Held et al. (2006) introduced a neuro-fuzzy model for classification and knowledge acquisition from the training set of sleep – awake states of infants, and different stages were developed for healthy infant of 6 months and onwards.

In Emre Comak et al. (2005) designed a clinical decision support system on the basis of feature extracted from the Doppler signals and uses least square support vector machine and back propagation artificial neural network to classify the extracted features. The research work presented in Ma and Wang (2012) designed a model for forecasting meteorological factors that could significantly affect hypertension using the multilayer feed forward neural network. In Das et al. (2008) a SAS based software 9.1.3 is designed to diagnose valvular heart disease and in the center of this proposed system an ensemble of the neural network is used that can create a new model by combining the posterior probabilities from multiple predecessor models. In the research of Azar (2013) a multilayer perceptron neural network (MLPNN) with fast learning algorithm is developed to predict the post – dialysis blood urea concentration. In Maglogiannis et al. (2009) presented a support vector machine based classifier to diagnose the heart valve diseases. The system identifies the heart valve disease on the bases of heart sound. In Mousa et al. (2005) wavelet analysis and hybrid network, i.e. fuzzy-neural network (FNN) is used to classify mammography image taken from MIAS (Mammographic image analysis) data set. In Verma et al. (2009) a soft cluster neural network is proposed for classification of digital mammograms, the concept of soft cluster is introduced as a pattern may fall in more than one group. The digital mammograms are first preprocessed to extract the features than soft cluster neural networks are used to classify. In Franco et al. (2007) a constructive algorithm that creates compact neural network architecture was developed to classify the early breast cancer in patients.

The literature review presented in this section shows that soft computing techniques such as artificial neural networks, fuzzy logic, genetic algorithm and expert system have proved their effectiveness in the diagnosis of various kinds of diseases and the Clinical decision support system developed by using these techniques can assist a medical expert at arriving a particular decision regarding the diagnosis of a disease. The various properties of the artificial neural network and fuzzy logic like their self learning capabilities, robustness, self-organization (i.e. To create an own organization with the information received during training), fault tolerance and their ability to deal with the imprecise information or vague information make us to choose these concepts to design a classifier or a decision support system to diagnose the heart diseases which is the major epidemic in India. In this paper a hybrid model is designed on the basis of artificial neural network and fuzzy min – max neural network which works in two stages. The proposed system is a hybrid system which is used to diagnose the heart diseases. The heart diseases data set is the combination of continuous value and the non-continuous values, so our motivation is to design such a system in which continuous values are fed to the fuzzy min max neural network and the non continuous values are given to the artificial neural network and the output generated by these two networks is again given to an artificial neural network to generate the cumulative results. The artificial neural network used in this system is the multilayer perceptron neural network. The fuzzy min - max neural network algorithm is a classification method that separates the joint input space into classes of any size with non-linear boundaries.

The content of this chapter is organized as follows:

- Section 1 contains the introduction about the need of a classifier to diagnose a diseases and use of soft computing to design the model,
- In section 2 the literature review is summarized which gives an insight about the usefulness of neural network and fuzzy logic and their combination in medical field to diagnose various kinds of diseases,
- In section 3 the architecture of the proposed hybrid system is given along with the detailed description of the architecture and the learning algorithm of multilayer perceptron neural network and fuzzy min max neural network and later in this section the construction of multilayer perceptron neural network and fuzzy min max neural network is given.
- In section 4 the details of the data set used for this experiment are given, followed by the data preprocessing for the experiment and k-fold cross validation method for performance analysis is described. Section 4 is followed by the
- Section 5 in which conclusion about the system and its performance is mentioned.
- The further enhancement strategy to improve the performance of the hybrid system and the proposed future objective are given in section 6 which is followed by the
- Section 7 which includes the reference and bibliography.

ARCHITECTURE OF THE PROPOSED SYSTEM

The architecture of the proposed system is the combination of the multilayer perceptron neural network and the fuzzy min-max neural network. The motive behind using these two networks is that the data set comprises of two types of values, i.e. continuous and non-continuous data set. Non- continuous values are used by the MLPNN (multilayer perceptron neural network) to classify the data. A multilayer perceptron is a mathematical model for the classification of non-linear data into different classes. Similarly, we have used fuzzy min - max neural network to classify the continuous values as this network is introduced for classification and clustering by P.K. Simpson in 1992 in two parts Simpson (1992,1993). The fuzzy min-max (FMM) will use hyperboxes in n-dimensional input pattern to represent the different classes, FMM's simple yet powerful learning algorithm helps in the incremental learning of the data, which motivates us to use the fuzzy min-max (FMM) in combination with multilayer perceptron neural network to classify the data having continuous as well as non - continuous values.

In this chapter a hybrid neural network is designed to classify whether a person is a heart patient or not on the basis of the clinical parameter available. The hybrid neural network includes the fuzzy min-max (FMM) neural network and multilayer perceptron (MLP) neural network. The data set is partitioned into two parts, i.e. continuous data and non-continuous data. The continuous data is utilized by the fuzzy min - max neural network, whereas non-continuous data is used by the multilayer perceptron neural network. A second multilayer perceptron neural network is used to generate the cumulative result by combining the output generated by the fuzzy min - max neural network and the multilayer perceptron neural network. The description of these neural networks is given as follows.

Multilayer Perceptron Neural Network

In Simpson (1992) the various properties of artificial neural networks are mentioned which are desirable for the task of pattern classification problem, which are listed in Quteishat and Lim (2008) are as follow:

- **On-Line Learning:** An artificial neural network classifier must be able to learn the input pattern and to adapt itself to the new data without forgetting the previously learned data patterns. This is so called "stability – plasticity dilemma" (Simpson, 1992; Carpenter & Grossberg, 1987).
- **Nonlinear Separability:** An artificial neural network should be able to decide the decision regions which separate classes of different shapes and size.
- **Decision Boundaries:** An artificial neural network should be able to define class boundaries so that the misclassification rate can be minimized.
- **Learning Time:** An artificial neural network should be able to learn the input pattern in a short time span.
- **Soft And Hard Classification:** An artificial neural network should be able to provide both hard as well as soft decisions means it provide the classification as well as the mechanism to validate and verify the results.
- **Tuning Parameters:** An artificial neural network must have some tuning parameters so that the network can adjust according to the different classification problem as each classification problem have its own unique set of parameters.
- **Nonparametric Classification:** An artificial neural network should not depend on the previous or a priori information as this information is not available for the entire classification problem.

All these properties led us to use the artificial neural network as a classifier and the one we choose for our research work is a multilayer perceptron neural network.

Multilayer Perceptron Neural Network Architecture

A multilayer perceptron is a model that can be used as a mathematical model of classification for non-linear data into different classes. It is the most popular and frequently used neural network architecture (Bishop, 1995; Hand, 1997; Ripley, 1996). An MLP is a neural network that can be defined as an artificial neural network consists of a large number of interconnected processing nodes known as neurons that act as a microprocessor. Neural networks (NN) are in consideration due to its self-adaptation, robustness, and performing the nonlinear mapping between the input feature and the desired output (DONG et al., 2010).

The layer of neuron or the microprocessor arranged in an orderly fashion to form a network which is known as a multilayer perceptron neural network. The MLP is feed-forward network architecture consists of two layers with one or more than one hidden layers; these layers are called the input layer, hidden layer, the output layer. The hidden layer and output layers are the processing layers and map the input to output class unlike the input layer. The input layer takes the external data; this external data is fed into input layer. No processing is done at input layer only the weighted sum of the inputs and the present bias is calculated and it serves as the input to the hidden layer neurons. Unlike input layer the hidden layer and the output layer are the processing layers and these layers use transformation function to generate the output. At hidden layer a transformation function is used to map the weighted sum of the inputs to intermediate outputs. This intermediate output act as input to next hidden layer or to the output layer, again a transformation function is used in output layer to calculate the final output. The mechanisms of the network work in successive layer until the outputs are generated at each output node. The results can be explained as the different output nodes represent different class or category of the input pattern when output is obtained one can expect a high output value on correct class node and low output values on the rest of the other output class (Yan et al., 2006). The architecture of the MLP neural network (Multilayer perceptron neural network) is given in Figure 1.

Figure 1. Architecture of multilayer perceptron neural network

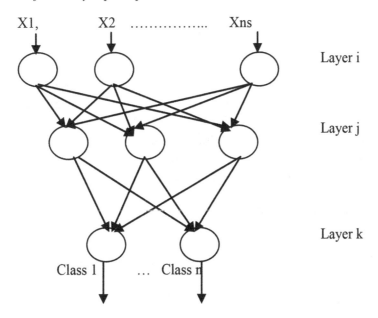

Each node in MLP is a processing element which performs following function:

1. Compute the weighted sum of the input along with the present bias

Process this weighted sum of input using an activation function to compute the output generated by that neuron.

$$y_{inj} = \sum_{i=0}^{n} x_i w_{ij} + \theta_j \tag{1}$$

$$y_j = f\left(y_{inj}\right) \tag{2}$$

where V_J is the weighted sum of inputs x_1, x_2, $x_{3...}$ x_p and bias θ_j for j^{th} neuron, W_{ji} is the connection weight between input x_i, and neuron j, and $f(.)$ is the activation function of the jth neuron, and Y_j is the output of the jth neuron.

The activation functions are applied to the net input to calculate the output. There are a number of activation functions such as Identity activation function, Binary step activation function, Bipolar step activation function, Binary sigmoidal function (logistic sigmoidal function, Bipolar sigmoidal function and the Ramp Function (Sivanandm & Deepa, 2011).

The sigmoidal function is commonly used and is defined in Equation 3.....

$$F\left(a\right) = \frac{1}{\left(1 + e^{-\alpha}\right)} \tag{3}$$

Multilayer Perceptron Neural Network Learning Algorithm

The most commonly used learning algorithm for the Multilayer perceptron neural network is BP (Back Propogation) algorithm; it is one of the simplest and the most general method for the supervised training of the multilayer perceptron neural network (MLPNN) (Duda et al., 2001). After determining the architecture of MLPNN (multilayer perceptron neural network) the weights of the network have to be computed by using a training procedure based on the input pattern and the desired output. The basic back propagation algorithm (Bishop, 1995; Duda et al., 2001) can be explained as follows:

Step 1: Initialize all the connection weights *W* with small randomly chosen values from a pseudorandom sequence generator.

Step 2: Repeat until convergence (either when the error *E* is below a preset value or until the gradient $\frac{\partial E\left(t\right)}{\partial W}$ is smaller than a preset value).

    Step 2.1: Compute the update using $\Delta W\left(t\right) = -\eta \left[\frac{\partial E\left(t\right)}{\partial W}\right]$.

    Step 2.2: Update the weights with $W\left(t+1\right) = W\left(t\right) + \Delta W(t)$.

Step 2.3: Compute the error $E\left(t+1\right)$.

where t is the number of iterations, W is the weights assigned to the connection and η is the learning rate. The E is the error and it can be chosen as mean square error (MSE) function of the actual output and the desired output which can be defined as:

$$E = \cfrac{1}{2\left(\sum_{j=1}^{n}\left(d_j - y_j\right)^2\right)} \qquad (4)$$

where d_j is the desired output and y_j is the actual output.

There are two common strategies to the train the neural network: the first one is the incremental training strategy (Shigetoshi et al., 1995) and the second is batch training strategy (Jang et al., 1997). Usually an incremental training strategy is faster and more efficient for the system with a large set of data as training set (Yan et al., 2006).

The Fuzzy Min-Max Neural Network

The original fuzzy min - max neural network algorithm was first introduced by Simpson in two articles (Simpson, 1992, 1993). In (Gabrys & Bargiela, 2000; Xi et al., 2001; Rizzi et al., 2002) the recursive algorithms based on fuzzy min max neural network were proposed. The FMM neural network is used for classification that separates the input variable space into classes of any size. The fuzzy min - max neural networks (FMMNN) classifier is a supervised learning method which is based on the hybrid neural network and the fuzzy logic concept. A characteristic of the fuzzy min - max neural network classifier is that all the input variables for learning and classification are required to be numerical, continuously valued variable (Rey-del-castillo & Cardenosa, 2011). Most of the time we have categorical data instead of numerical data, the best way to deal this problem is that replace the categorical data with numerical data and use it as a continuous data. But this procedure implicitly defines a metric for categories, which may not be suitable (Brouwer, 2002). A fuzzy min -max neural network can be used as a classifying model which takes the n input variable which must be continuous or numerical in nature and produces output as a label or a category of the discrete set of categorical values. The Fuzzy min - max neural network is formed by using the hyperboxes with fuzzy sets (Quteishat et al., 2008). A hyperbox can be defined by its minimum and maximum points defined in R_n which is the Cartesian product of a closed interval on the real line, and there corresponding membership functions are used to create a fuzzy subset in the n-dimensional pattern space. The FMM (fuzzy min max) neural network is a three layer feed forward network architecture, it consists of the input layer, i.e. F_A that contain input nodes equal to the number of dimensions of the input pattern, the hidden layer or hyperbox layer i.e. F_B each node in the hidden layer is denoted by hyberbox fuzzy set and the connection between the input layer and the hyperbox fuzzy set layer are the min- max points and the transfer function or the activation function is the hyperbox membership function, and the third layer is output layer i.e. F_C, it contains nodes equal to the number of classes or labels of the category. The fuzzy min - max neural network is an incremental learning system. In the incremental learning process the system learns when new information is received, i.e. FMM initially look for a hyperbox that can fit the new input pattern if no such hyperbox is found, it adds a new hyperbox to the system for the new input data pattern is given to the FMM (fuzzy min - max) neural network. The operation of classification is based on the hyperbox fuzzy sets defined in the n-dimensional pattern space. Thus, the input space is the n-dimensional unit cube

$$I^n = [0,1] \times [0,1] \times [0,1] \times .... [0,1].$$

A hyperbox is a n-dimensional pattern space which defines the membership degree of an input pattern with that hyperbox. Although it is possible to use hyperbox with an arbitrary range of values in any dimension, the fuzzy min-max neural network only uses values between 0 to 1and if the data is not in the range of [0, 1] we normalize the data. A hyperbox is defined by using its minimum and maximum points as shown in Figure 2, a hyperbox fuzzy set is defined as B_j, is

$$B_j = \left\{ X, V_j, W_j, b\left(X, V_j, W_j\right) \right\} \forall X \in I^n \tag{5}$$

where X is the input space,

$V_j = (V_{j1}......V_{jn})$ is the hyperbox minimum,

$W_j = (W_{j1}......W_{jn})$ is the maximum and

$b\left(X, V_j, W_j\right)$ is the membership function, where all pattern within the hyperbox have full- class membership.

The transfer function or the activation function of a hyperbox fuzzy set can be defined by equation 6 which is discussed later in this chapter.

Figure 3 shows an example of how the hyperboxes are aggregated to form nonlinear boundaries in two class classification.

Figure 2. Hyperbox in R³ defined from its minimum and maximum point

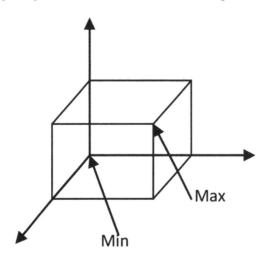

Figure 3. Fuzzy min-max hyperbox along the boundary of a two-class problem

Class 1

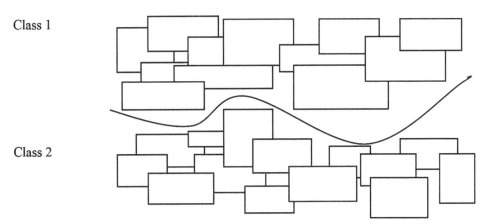

Class 2

Network Architecture

Figure 4 shows the three layer feed-forward neural network architecture. Layer 1 is the input layer consisting of 2n nodes 2 nodes for each input pattern corresponding to the input of hyperbox minimum X_{hi}^l and maximum X_{hi}^u. Layer 2 is the hyperbox layer or hidden layer node each node in this layer represent a hyperbox fuzzy set. The connection weights between the input layer and the hyperbox layer are the hyperbox fuzzy set minimum (v_{ji}) and the hyperbox fuzzy set maximum (w_{ji}) points. The connection weights between the input layer nodes (layer1) and the hyberbox fuzzy set layer nodes (layer 2) takes value between the interval of 0 and 1 both inclusive and are stored in matrix V and W The transformation function of the hyperbox layer is given as follows

$$b_j\left(x_h\right) = \min_{i=1,2,...n}\left(\min\left(\left[1-g\left(x_{hi}-w_{ji},\gamma\right)\right],\left[1-g\left(v_{ji}-x_{hi},\gamma\right)\right]\right)\right) \qquad (6)$$

Figure 4. Fuzzy min max neural network architecture

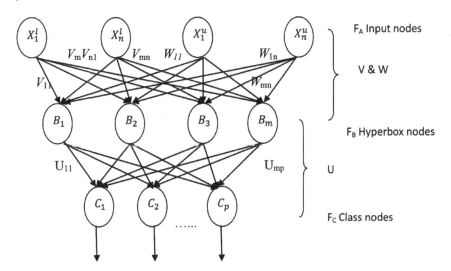

where g is the ramp threshold function of two parameters and γ is a parameter which regulates how fast the membership function decreases.

$$g(x, y) = \begin{cases} 1, & if \ x \cdot y > 1 \\ x \cdot y, & if \ 0 \le x \cdot y \le 1 \\ 0, & if \ x \cdot y < 0 \end{cases} \qquad (7)$$

The hyperbox fuzzy set membership function defines the degree to which the input pattern x_h falls inside of the B_j hyperbox fuzzy set. The value of membership function for a particular input pattern is 1 if it fully belongs to B_j hyperbox fuzzy set and becomes zero as the input pattern move away from the hyperbox B_j. The variable γ is the convergence parameter which regulates how fast the membership value of a fuzzy hyperbox decreases; when the distance between X_h input pattern and B_j hyperbox increases (Seera & Lim, 2014).

Layer 3 is the output layer (Fc) which contain nodes equal to the number of classes or labels in which input pattern has to be classified. The connection between the hyperbox layer (F_B) and the output layer (F_C) are the binary values stored in matrix U. The values are assigned to Matrix U by using the following equation.

$$U_{jk} = \begin{cases} 1, & if \ b_j \ is \ hyperbox \ for \ class \ C_k \\ 0, & otherwise \end{cases} \qquad (8)$$

where bj is the second layer node, i.e. hyperbox layer node and C_k is the kth third layer node. The output layer node presents the degree to which the input pattern X_h fits within the class k. The transfer function for each of the third layer node is defined as

$$C_k = \max_{j=1,2,.m} b_j U_{jk} \qquad (9)$$

The transfer function or the activation function in layer 3 can be defined as the union of the hyperbox membership functions according to the above expression. The result for the X_h pattern can be interpreted as the X_h input pattern belongs to the k_{th} class for which the C_k value is the greatest. There are two ways in which the output of layer 3 i.e. output layer class nodes can be used. If a soft decision is required, the outputs are used directly. If a hard decision is required, the layer 3 nodes with the highest value is determined and its value is set to one to indicate that it is the best matched pattern class, while the remaining values are set equal to zero (Quteishat et. al., 2010), based on the winner take all approach described in Kohonen (1984).

Figure 4 shows the network architecture of the fuzzy min max neural network

Learning Algorithm of Fuzzy Min Max Neural Network

The fuzzy min - max neural network follows the incremental learning methodology. It learns incrementally in a single pass through the data. It processes the existing pattern classes as new information is received. It also has the capacity of adding new pattern classes online (Quteishat & Lim, 2008). The learning algorithm in fuzzy min - max neural network is based on expansion/contraction process. The

FMM learning methodology can be described in a three step expansion –contraction process (Rey-del-castillo & Cardenosa, 2011) including the initialization step, and these three steps are repeated for each training input pattern. The training process starts with a training set D which contain a set of M ordered pair $\{X_h, d_h\}$, where

$$X_h = (X_{h1}, X2, X3, \ldots . X_{hn}) \varepsilon I^n$$

is the input pattern and $d_h \varepsilon \{1, 2, \ldots 3\}$ is the index of one of the p classes label. The learning process start with choosing an ordered pair from the set D and find a hyperbox B_j that can be expanded to fit the input pattern in that hyperbox. If a suitable hyperbox is found, the hyperbox is expended by resetting its minimum and maximum points this process sometime lead to overlapping of hyperboxes. The overlapping of hyperboxes can be categories as interclass (it means that one input data pattern belongs to more than one classes which is practically not true) overlapping and intraclass overlapping. If the hyperboxes from different classes overlapped each other, the contraction process start and the overlapped hyperboxes are eliminated from the fuzzy min max neural network. But the intraclass overlapping is free from elimination or contraction process as it does not affect the system's performance. In case, no hyperbox is found that can fit the new input data pattern a new hyperbox is added to the system. The learning process forms classes that are non- linearly separable and the boundaries of these non-linearly separable classes are defined between two classes with the points which have equal membership degree for both the classes. The existing classes can be refined over time and new classes are added without retraining, thereby reducing the total training time (Rey-del-castillo & Cardenosa, 2011). The learning process can be described in following four steps which include the initialization step also.

1. Initialization,
2. Hyperbox expansion,
3. Hyperbox overlapping test,
4. Hyperbox contraction.

Initialization

The input given to the FMM is an ordered pair of the form as given below

$$\{X_h, d_h\}$$

where

$$X_h = [X_h^l, X_h^u]$$

is the hth input pattern in a form of lower X_h^l, and upper X_h^u and

$$d_h \varepsilon \{1, 2, 3 \ldots P\}$$

is the index of one of the p class. When a new hyperbox is added to the system its minimum V_j and maximum W_j points are initialized. The value of V_j and W_j is set initially to

$$V_j = 1 \text{ and } W_j = 0 \tag{10}$$

The initialization is done in such a way that when j^{th} hyperbox is adjusted for the first time using the input pattern X_h its min and max points are identical to the hth input pattern.

$$V_j = X_h^l \text{ and } W_j = X_h^u \tag{11}$$

Hyperbox Expansion

When a new input pattern is presented to the system, the fuzzy min - max neural network filter the system and found a hyperbox that can fit the presented input pattern i.e. an expandable hyperbox with a highest membership degree is found. This expandable hyberbox is then extended according to the input pattern up to a certain limit (a predefined value). If an expandable hyperbox is not found, a new hyperbox for that class will be added. A hyperbox B_j is expanded only if it satisfies the following condition

$$\theta \geq \underset{i=1,...n}{\forall} \left(\max\left(W_{ji}, X_{hi}^u \right) - \min\left(V_{ji}, X_{hi}^l \right) \right) \tag{12}$$

where $0 \leq \theta \leq 1$ is a user –defined threshold that determine the maximum size of a hyperbox. If the expansion criterion is met, the minimum and the maximum points of a hyperbox are adjusted according to the input pattern, as follows:

$$V_{ji}^{new} = \min\left(V_{ji}^{old}, X_{hi} \right) \forall i, i = 1, 2, .. n \tag{13}$$

$$W_{ji}^{new} = \max\left(W_{ji}^{old}, X_{hi} \right) \forall i, i = 1, 2, .. n \tag{14}$$

Hyperbox Overlapping Test

The hyperbox overlapping can be defined as, when one or more dimension of a hyperbox fall/overlap/coincide with the dimension of some other hyperboxes. The hyperbox overlapping test determines the overlapped hyperboxes from different classes. The overlapping is of two types one is interclass hyperbox overlap i.e. when the hyperbox from different classes overlap and another is intraclass hyperbox overlapping in which hyperbox belonging to same class overlap. The intraclass hyperbox overlapping doesn't cause much problem but the interclass overlapping is fatal it shows that a single input pattern belongs to two different classes or category at the same time, which is impractical because a pattern at a time can belong to a single class. Our aim is to remove the interclass hyperbox overlapping. There are some formulas or mathematical equations which help us to determine the overlapped hyperboxes in a fuzzy min max neural network. Consider the following four cases when $\delta^{old} = 1$ initially

Case 1:

$$V_{ji} < V_{ki} < W_{ji} < W_{ji}, \delta^{new} = \min\left(W_{ji} - V_{ki}\delta^{old}\right), \delta^{new} = \min\left(W_{ji} - V_{ki}\delta^{old}\right) \tag{15}$$

Case 2:

$$V_{ki} < V_{ji} < W_{ki} < W_{ji}, \delta^{new} = \min\left(W_{ki} - V_{ji}\delta^{old}\right) \tag{16}$$

Case 3:

$$V_{ji} < V_{ki} < W_{ki} < W_{ji}, \delta^{new} = \min\left(\min\left(W_{ki} - V_{ji}, W_{ji} - V_{ki}\right), \delta^{old}\right) \tag{17}$$

Case 4:

$$V_{ki} < V_{ji} < W_{ji} < W_{ki}, \delta^{new} = \min\left(\min\left(W_{ji} - V_{ki}, W_{ki} - V_{ji}\right), \delta^{old}\right) \tag{18}$$

where j represents the hyperbox B_j expanded in the previous step, i.e. hyperbox expansion step and k denotes the hyperbox B_k of another class currently being tested for possible overlapping. If the condition $\delta^{old} - \delta^{new}$ is satisfied, then the $\Delta = I$ and $\delta^{old} = \delta^{new}$. If this condition is true, then there is overlap in the Δth dimension, and the test for overlapping continues for the next dimensions. Otherwise, the overlapping test stops and the minimum overlap index variable (Δ) is set to indicate that the further hyperbox contraction step is not necessary to perform (Quteishat et al., 2010), and if the above mentioned condition is not true, i.e. If any overlapping is detected between the hyperboxes of two different classes the hyperbox contraction process is followed and the hyperbox contraction process is described in the next section.

Hyperbox Contraction Process

If the overlapping occurs between the hyperbox of different class, we have to eliminate the overlapping by minimally adjusting each of the overlapped hyperbox. If $\Delta > 0$ then only Δ^{th} dimensions of the two overlapped hyperbox are contracted, we must save the index of the overlapping hyperbox dimension in the hyperbox overlapping step so that we can go to adjusting stage without examining the overlapping cases again and again (Gabrys & Bargiela, 2000). If all the dimensions of two hyperbox overlapped only one dimension among the n dimension which has minimum overlapping is adjusted to keep the hyperbox size as large as possible. The following four cases are considered for proper adjustment of the overlapped hyperboxes and Δ is the dimension to be contracted.

Case 1:

$$v_{j\Delta} < v_{k\Delta} < w_{j\Delta} < w_{k\Delta}, w_{j\Delta}^{new} = v_{k\Delta}^{new} = \frac{w_{j\Delta}^{old} + v_{k\Delta}^{old}}{2} z$$

Case 2:

$$v_{k\Delta} < v_{j\Delta} < w_{k\Delta} < w_{j\Delta}, w_{k\Delta}^{new} = v_{j\Delta}^{new} = \frac{w_{k\Delta}^{old} + v_{j\Delta}^{old}}{2}$$

Case 3a:

$$v_{j\Delta} < v_{k\Delta} < w_{k\Delta} < w_{j\Delta} \ and \ (w_{k\Delta} - v_{j\Delta}) < (w_{j\Delta} < v_{k\Delta}), v_{j\Delta}^{new} = w_{k\Delta}^{old}$$

Case3b:

$$v_{j\Delta} < v_{k\Delta} < w_{k\Delta} < w_{j\Delta} \ and \ (w_{k\Delta} - v_{j\Delta}) > (w_{j\Delta} < v_{k\Delta}), w_{j\Delta}^{new} = v_{k\Delta}^{old}$$

Case 4a:

$$v_{k\Delta} < v_{j\Delta} < w_{j\Delta} < w_{k\Delta} \ and \ (w_{k\Delta} - v_{j\Delta}) < (w_{j\Delta} < v_{k\Delta}), w_{k\Delta}^{new} = v_{j\Delta}^{old}$$

Case 4b:

$$v_{k\Delta} < v_{j\Delta} < w_{j\Delta} < w_{k\Delta} \ and \ (w_{k\Delta} - v_{j\Delta}) > (w_{j\Delta} < v_{k\Delta}), v_{k\Delta}^{new} = w_{j\Delta}^{old}$$

The Hybrid Neural Network

The architecture of the hybrid neural network is seen in Figure 5. It consists of two multilayer perceptron neural networks and a fuzzy min max neural network. The hybrid neural network works in two stages in first stage a multilayer perceptron (MLP) neural network and a fuzzy min mix neural network (FMMNN) is utilized to classify crisp, i.e. non continuous attributes and continuous data attributes respectively the output of previous stage acts as the input to the second stage and in second stage again a multilayer perceptron neural network with different configuration is used to obtain the final output. The working procedure of the hybrid neural network is given as follow:

Step 1: Provide the input data sample.
Step 2: Partition the data into two parts, i.e. continuous and non continuous data set
Step 3: Encode the continuous data and non- continuous data separately are as follow.
  ◦ For continuous data, we use the normalization to encode the data so the data falls in the range of 0 and 1 (both inclusive). The formula used for normalization is given as follows:

$$X_{i=0to1} = \frac{X_i - X_{min}}{X_{max} - X_{min}} \qquad (19)$$

where X_i is the data point and X_{min} is the minimum value among all the data points and X_{max} is the maximum value among all the data points.

Figure 5. Block diagram of the proposed hybrid system

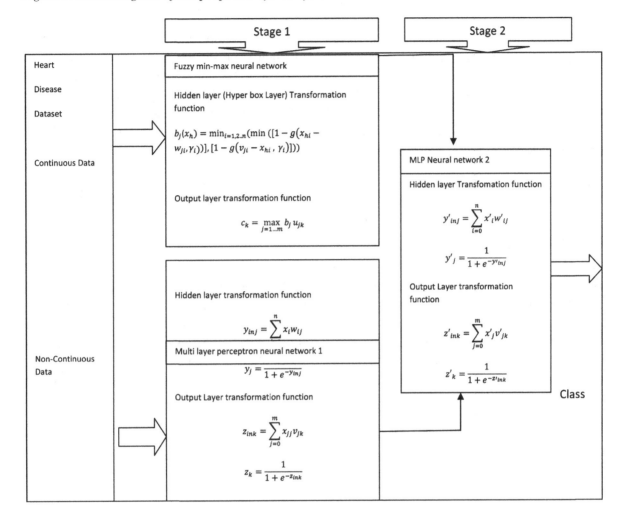

- For non continuous data where variable have two independent attributes such as sex and painloc are encoded with binary values (0,1) i.e. 1 represent male and 0 represent female. Variable with three independent attributes such as restecg are encoded using ternary values (-1, 0, 1), and for the variables having four independent attributes, we use four value logic (-1,-0.5, 0.5, 1).

Step 4: Construct the multilayer perceptron neural network with suitable number of hidden layer neuron for the non-continuous data in stage one

Step 5: Construct the FMM neural network and present the continuous data to FMM neural network and obtain the results in stage one

Step 6: Present the output of Step 4 and Step 5 to the multilayer perceptron neural network in stage two.

Step 7: If the obtained result matches with the expected result stop the training otherwise continue with the training of the network.

Implementation of the Hybrid Neural Network

In this section we discuss how the architecture of the proposed hybrid neural network is implemented and we also discuss the algorithm to implement the MLP (multilayer perceptron neural network) in stage 1 and stage 2 and the fuzzy min - max neural network in stage 1. The above mention architecture of the proposed hybrid neural network is implemented with the help of MATLAB software, the algorithms to implement the above neural network are discussed below, but before discussing the algorithm we have to preprocess the data and partition the data into continuous and non- continuous data set. The algorithms are given as follows:

Construction of MLP (Multilayer Perceptron) Neural Network

MLP1 [(Input Feature: Sex, Cp, Fbs, Restecg, Exang, Slope, Ca, Thal, Num), (Output Feature: Class)]

Input layer: The input layer of MLP1 (i.e. multilayer perceptron neural network in stage 1) consists of 8 nodes, each corresponds to the 8 non - continuous attributes of the Cleveland heart diseases data set.

Hidden layer: In the proposed system, there is only one hidden layer with 15 nodes. The number of nodes in the hidden layer plays a significant role in network's ability to classify the input. So, we have to carefully choose the number of hidden layer neuron for the system here we used a cascade learning algorithm described in Yan et al. (2006) to find the number of nodes (neuron) in the hidden layer. In the cascade learning algorithm Yan et al. (2006) consider two parameter accuracy and convergence speed which they want to optimize but we concentrated only on the accuracy parameter of the network which is more important for the classification of data. The algorithm is as follows:

Step 1: Initialize the number of neurons in hidden layer with small value hidden layer neuron i = 4 for current network

Step 2: for i=1:20

Create a multilayer perceptron network with i number of neurons

Train the network with current configuration (given in Table 1)

Test the network with a test data set and compute the average accuracy of the network.

Increment the hidden layer neuron by unit value i.e. 1.

Step 3: End

Output Layer: The output layer consists of one node whose output is used as intermediate results which is further processed in stage 2.

Algorithm to Implement Fuzzy Min - Max Neural Network

FMM [(Age, Trestbps, Chol,Thalach, Oldpeak), (class)]

Step 1: Initialization - The input $\{X_h, d_h\}$ to FMM is initialized with the given input, i.e. the value of continuous attributes such as age, Trestbps etc. in the form of upper bound and lower bound as input to FMM is given in upper bound and lower bound form. The input layer consists of 10 nodes

Table 1. The training parameters

The Training Parameter for MLP1	Values
No. of epochs	2000
Preset learning rate	0.07
Error precision target	0.5
Transfer function in both layer	Logsig
Training Parameters for MLP2	**Values**
No. of epochs	2000
Preset learning rate	0.06
Error precision target	0.5
Transfer function in both layer	Logsig
Statistical Parameters of FMM	**Values**
γ (used in transformation function of hyperbox fuzzy set as a convergence parameter)	0.1
θ (used to determine the maximum size of a hyperbox)	0.9

as for 5 continuous attributes as FMM takes two nodes for each input attribute. Initialize the value of V_j and W_j with $V_j = 1$ and $W_j = 0$;

Step 2: Hyperbox Expansion - For each new input pattern $\{X_h, d_h\}$ an expandable hyperbox is searched and if found it is checked whether we can expand it or not. If the condition specified in Equation 12 is satisfied the minimum and maximum point of hyperbox are adjusted according to the Equation 13 and 14. The value of θ in equation 10 is set to $\theta = 0.9$ which is randomly selected. If no hyperbox is found to fit the input pattern a new hyperbox B_j is created

Hyperbox overlapping and contraction process: The hyperbox B_j created in previous step is checked with rest of the hyperboxes to check whether it overlap with the hyperbox of other class. This overlapping test is conducted by using Equation 15 to 18.

If any overlapping is found we adjust the B_j hyperbox by using contraction process discussed in section Learning Algorithm of Fuzzy Min Max Neural Network

In this step a hyperbox B_j is constructed whose parameters are defined as follow:

$$B_j = \left\{ X, V_j, W_j, b\left(X, V_j, W_j\right)\right\} \forall X \in I^n \tag{20}$$

$$b_j\left(x_h\right) = \min_{i=1,2,..n}\left(\min\left(\left[1 - g\left(x_{hi} - w_{ji}, \gamma\right)\right], \left[1 - g\left(v_{ji} - x_{hi}, \gamma\right)\right]\right)\right) \tag{21}$$

where g is the ramp threshold function defined by the equation given below and the value of γ is set to be 0.1.

$$g(x,y) = \begin{cases} 1, & if \ x \cdot y > 1 \\ x \cdot y, & if \ 0 \le x \cdot y \le 1 \\ 0, & if \ x \cdot y < 0 \end{cases} \qquad (22)$$

Step 3: Now the Connection weights between the hyperbox fuzzy set layer and output layer are initialized and stored in matrix U. Matrix U contains binary values which are assigned on the basis of the following equation

$$U_{jk} = \begin{cases} 1, & if \ b_j \ is \ hyperbox \ for \ class \ C_k \\ 0, & otherwise \end{cases} \qquad (23)$$

where B_j is the hyperbox and C_k is the kth third layer node. The output layer consists of two nodes, one for each class and the output is obtained by applying the activation function given as:

$$C_k = \max_{j=1,2,.m} b_j U_{jk} \qquad (24)$$

The result of the X_h pattern can be interpreted as the X_h input pattern belongs to the kth class for which the C_k value is the greatest.

Construction of MLP2 In Stage 2

MLP2 [(X₁, X₂, X₃, Num), (class)]

The construction of Multilayer perceptron neural network is done similar to the multilayer perceptron neural network in stage 1 except the difference of nodes in different layer.

- **Input Layer:** Input layer consists of 3 nodes as the result generated by mlp1 is a $1 \times N$ matrix and the output generated by the FMM is $2 \times N$ matrix which combined form the input matrices for MLP1 (multilayer perceptron neural network) of size $3 \times N$ where N is the number of input pattern presented in stage 1.
- **Hidden Layer:** The hidden layer consists of 8 number of nodes determined using the cascade learning algorithm discussed in construction of MLP1.
- **Output Layer:** The output layer of MLP2 consists of 1 node. If the output generated is 1 means the person is a heart diseases patient and if the output is 0 means the person is healthy.

Summary about the System

The classifier designed contains 2 multilayer perceptron neural network and one fuzzy min max neural network. MLP1(multilayer perceptron neural network in stage 1) contain 8 input layer nodes, 15 hidden layer nodes and 1 output layer nodes, whereas the MLP2 (multilayer perceptron neural network in stage 2) contain 3 input layer nodes, 8 hidden layer nodes and 1 output layer node. The fuzzy min – max neural network contain 10 input layer nodes for five input attributes, total 22 hyperboxes are created in hidden layer or hyperbox fuzzy set layer out of which 13 hyperboxes are generated for class 1 and 9 are generated for class 2 the value of training parameters and the statistical variable used in the training of these neural networks are summarized in Table 1.

EXPERIMENTAL RESULTS AND DISCUSSION

In this section we have used the Cleveland heart disease data set available at the UCI machine learning repository (http://archive.ics.uci.edu/ml/datasets/Heart+Disease) it contains 76 attributes, but among all the attributes only 14 attributes are used for the experiment. These attributes are the combination of continuous and non continuous data. The data set contains 303 attributes and our aim is to diagnose the presence and absence of the heart disease, among the 303 instances, 139 instances are heart patient and 164 instances are non heart patient. The details of the continuous and non continuous data with detailed description are given in Table 2.

Table 2. Details of the continuous and non–continuous data set attributes

#	Name of Attribute	Category (Continuous/Non Continuous)	Value Range
1	age	Continuous	Age in years (0- 100 years)
2	Sex	Non-continuous	Sex (1 = male; 0 = female)
3	Cp	Non-continuous	Chest pain type -- Value 1: typical angina -- Value 2: atypical angina -- Value 3: non-anginal pain -- Value 4: asymptomatic
4	Trestbps	Continuous	resting blood pressure (in mm Hg on admission to the hospital)
5	Chol	Continuous	serum cholestoral in mg/dl
6	Fbs	Non- Continuous	(fasting blood sugar > 120 mg/dl) (1 = true; 0 = false)
7	Restecg	Non- Continuous	resting electrocardiographic results -- Value 0: normal -- Value 1: having ST-T wave abnormality (T wave inversions and/or ST elevation or depression of > 0.05 mV) -- Value 2: showing probable or definite left ventricular hypertrophy by Estes' criteria
8	Thalach	Continuous	maximum heart rate achieved
9	Exang	Non- Continuous	exercise induced angina (1 = yes; 0 = no)
10	Oldpeak	Continuous	ST depression induced by exercise relative to rest
11	Slope	Non- Continuous	the slope of the peak exercise ST segment -- Value 1: upsloping -- Value 2: flat -- Value 3: downsloping
12	Ca	Non- Continuous	number of major vessels (0-3) colored by flourosopy
13	Thal	Non- Continuous	3 = normal; 6 = fixed defect; 7 = reversable defect
14	Num	Non- Continuous	diagnosis of heart disease (angiographic disease status) -- Value 0: < 50% diameter narrowing -- Value 1: > 50% diameter narrowing

Data Set Preprocessing and Performance Assessment Methodology

Before performing the experiment with data set we have to preprocess the data as the data available at UCI repository contain the missing values, i.e. the value of some attributes in a record is null. In the Cleveland heart disease data set the number of missing values of different attribute is different and before feeding the input into the neural networks we have to process these missing values. There are a number of ways to deal with the missing values the missing values can be dealt either by removing the records with missing values or filling the missing values. If we deal with missing values by removing the records it will reduce the size of data set available which results in less generalized performance of the networks. There are different methods used for filling the missing values, in our research work we use a substitution mean method of Bishop (1995) in which the missing value is replaced by the mean or average of the other values of the same attribute. As far as the accuracy is concerned, it is found that the mean substitution method has a comparable performance as the ANN- Based approach of Erkki et al. (1998) but demand less computing effort.

After filling the missing values we have to prepare the data according to the hybrid neural network.

First, we have to partition the data into continuous and non – continuous data set for Multilayer layer perceptron neural network and for fuzzy min max neural network, respectively. The continuous data set consists of the five attributes which are Age, Trestbps (resting blood pressure (in mm Hg on admission to the hospital)), Chol (serum cholestoral in mg/dl), Thalach (maximum heart rate achieved), Oldpeak (ST depression induced by exercise relative to rest), and the data set contain eight non continuous attributes such as Sex, Cp(chest pain type), Fbs (fasting blood sugar), Restecg (resting electro-cardiographic results), Exang (exercise induced angina), Slope (the slope of the peak exercise ST segment), Ca (number of the major vessels) and Thal. The continuous data is first normalized by using the normalization equation described in the section The Hybrid Neural Network and then presented to the FMM neural network. It is necessary to normalize the data before feeding it into the fuzzy min - max neural network as a fuzzy min - max neural network work only with values between 0 and 1 this is because the size of a hyperbox is bounded with the limits between 0 and 1 if we use a hyperbox of smaller size it only contain few input pattern which increases the total number of hyperboxes in a network and if we use hyperboxes of larger size the which can contain larger number of hyperboxes reduces the size of the network but the classification performance is very low (Quteishat & Lim, 2008). Non - continuous data is encoded according to the rules defined in the section The Hybrid Neural Network i.e. The hybrid neural network section and presented to the multilayer perceptron neural network.The output obtained from fuzzy min max neural network with continuous data and the output obtained from multilayer perceptron neural network with non – continuous attributes form the intermediate results and also act as the input to the next stage i.e. The combined output of FMM (Fuzzy min-max neural network) and MLP (Multilayer perceptron neural network) is given again to another multilayer perceptron neural network in second stage. The output generated by the multilayer perceptron neural network in stage two is the final output of the hybrid neural network presented in this research work now this output is analyzed to assess the system's performance and to determine the effectiveness of the hybrid neural network in diagnosis of the cardiovascular diseases (CVD).

In artificial neural network based classifier performance assessment is critically important as the system depends on the selecting training set and testing set (Embrechts et al., 2001), specially for the data set that contain a smaller sized data set. In ANN (Artificial neural network) based classifier entire data set is divided into two disjoint subsets one is the training set which is used to determine the system parameters and second is the testing set which is used to evaluate the diagnostic accuracy and the network generalization (Yan et al., 2006). The researcher had discussed various methods to assess the generalization of the neural networks: the cross –validation method, the holdout method, the bootstrapping method are used to estimate the accuracy of the system.

K-Fold Cross Validation Method Based Performance Analysis

The results of the proposed system are analyzed by using the k-fold cross validation method to generalize the system performance. K-fold cross validation method is used to estimate the accuracy of the system, it is also known as rotation estimation in this the accuracy is calculated by dividing the overall number of correct classification by the total number of instances in the data set (Kohavi, 1995). To generalize the performance of the system a four– fold cross validation method is used. In this method the 303 instances of Cleveland heart disease data set are divided into four equal segments S1, S2, S3, and S4 and four different experiments are performed on following sets:

1. S2 + S3 + S4 set is used for training and S1 for testing
2. S1 + S3+ S4 set is used for training and S2 for testing
3. S1 +S2 + S4 set is used for training and S3 for testing
4. S1 + S2 + S3 set is used for training and S4 for testing

We have used specificity, sensitivity and accuracy as the performance measurement matrices given in Karalolis et al. (2010) these matrices are common is medical applications are discussed as follows:

1. **True Positive (TP):** It denotes the number of heart disease patient classified correctly by the hybrid neural network.
2. **True Negative (TN):** It denotes the number of patients not having heart diseases correctly classified by the system.
3. **False Positive (FP):** It denotes the number of healthy patients wrongly classified as a heart disease patient by the system.
4. **False Negative (FN):** It denotes the number of heart disease patient classified as a healthy patient by the system.

The above mentioned performance metrics are calculated as follows

1. **Specificity:** It is the percentage of healthy people classified correctly.

$$Specificity = \frac{TN}{TN + TP} \tag{25}$$

2. **Sensitivity:** It is the percentage of the abnormal patient (patient who is suffering from the heart diseases) classified correctly.

$$Sensitivity = \frac{TP}{TP + FN} \tag{26}$$

3. **Accuracy:** It is the percentage of the correct classification

Acc=Total no of correct classification/Total no of instances

After performing the experiment the system's performance is determined with the help of above mentioned performance parameters and metrics. The accuracy on both the data set is measured and summarized in Table 3 whereas the above performance metrics are also calculated and presented in Table 4.

The results of the proposed study are also compared with some other results which are given in Table 5, from the below table, we can see that the proposed approach for the classification of heart disease performs much better.

From Table 5, we can see that the proposed system performs much better than the above mentioned methods but the accuracy of the system still needs improvement as there are some other methods which perform much better than the proposed system such as one is the hybrid system proposed by Kahramanli & Allahverdi, 2008 having the accuracy of 86.8%. We would like to further carry out this work as an FMM feature of incremental learning helps to avoid the retraining of the system when a new record is presented to the system, the hyperboxes are adjusted according to the new data record.

PROPOSED FUTURE RESEARCH OBJECTIVE

The work carried out through this research shows that soft computing techniques are able to handle the vagueness, imprecision and linguistic terms associated with the medical field. Here we have used Cleveland heart disease data set to employ the usefulness of neural network and fuzzy logic. In our previous

Table 3. the accuracy measure for Cleveland heart diseases data set

Data Set	Accuracy (%)
Training Data	93.06
Testing Data	83.16

Table 4. Sensitiviy, accuracy and specificity measure for Cleveland heart diseases training data set

Performance Measure	%
Accuracy	93.06
Sensitivity	91.08
Specificity	92.27

Table 5. Comparison of classification accuracy with the proposed study

Method	Accuracy	References
Proposed Method	83.16	Suggested approach in this study
LVQ	82.9	Ster and Dobnikar
C-MLP2LN	82.5	RA, Estimated
FSM (Feature Space Mapping)	82.2	Rafal Admaczak
MLP+BP	81.3	Ster, Dobnikar, and RafalAdmaczak
CART	80.8	Ster, and Dobnikar
CDSS based on weighted fuzzy rules	72.65	P.K. Anooj

works we have worked on two data sets, i.e. Cleveland heart disease data set and the mammography mass data set. In our previous work Rathi and Aggarwal (2013) mammography mass data set is classified with MLP with different number of hidden layers. MLP with one hidden layer with 16 neurons is trained using back propagation algorithm and a second configuration in which we use two hidden layer neuron with a number of neurons 6, 5 respectively. The result obtained from experiment shows that the network achieves high accuracy of 87.91% in first configuration and 88.75% in the second configuration.

Later in two statistical neural networks and their FNN are used as classifier for the classification of mammographic masses in breast cancer. RBF is trained with 720 hidden layer nodes with the spread constant of 1.0. The FNN uses the same network configuration with fuzzified input. The result obtained from experiment shows that the fuzzy neural networks perform better than the neural networks with improved accuracy, of 2-3%, among the four networks fuzzy radial basis neural network achieve high accuracy of 90%

In our present work we have presented a hybrid neural network, which is designed to classify the heart disease data set. The hybrid system consists of the fuzzy min - max neural network and multilayer perceptron neural network working in parallel and the results of these two networks are again given to the second multilayer perceptron neural network, so the cumulative results can be obtained. The system is designed for the data set that contains the continuous as well as non-continuous variable. Fuzzy min-max neural network is used to classify the continuous data and MLP is used to classify the non-continuous data. A k-fold cross validation method is used to generalize the system's performance. The results obtained from the study shows that the proposed system can classify the data set with 93.66% accuracy. The further work can be extended to improve the efficiency of the hybrid system and we would like to work on the following areas to improve the system's performance and make them more reliable so that the model or the clinical decision support system can be implemented to classify or to diagnoses the diseases in real time environment. The future work will focus on the robustness of hybrid model for real world data. Besides providing the explanatory rules, the capabilities of handling the missing data are an another important feature in medical applications (Lim et al., 2005)

- We would like to integrate this work with the real world problem so that it helps the medical expert to arrive at a particular decision without much delay and save the life of the patient as well as money.
- The problem with real world data is that it contain missing values in some records which affect the diagnostic capability of the model so we want to devise a more efficient method of data imputation (fill - in the missing values with appropriate values) and integrate this method with the hybrid system to handle missing values so that the system can perform better.
- Our next area to improve is the values of some constant used in the construction of multilayer perceptron neural network and fuzzy min max neural network, as discussed in section 3 where the implementation is given for the above mention neural network we can see that we have taken some random values of learning rate, γ (convergence parameter), and θ (which is used to determine the maximum size of a hyperbox) and we know they play significant role in network's prediction capability, training time and the size of the network varies according to these parameters so we have to choose they wisely or we have to derive some method to determine the value of these parameters so that the optimal value of above mentioned parameters is used to design the classifier models.

- Till now we have designed binary classifiers which can predict that either person is suffering from a particular diseases or the person is normal, but this is not the case with every kind of diseases some time a diseases can have more than one category for example, if we consider the case of coronary artery diseases they can be of various kind like Hypertension, Coronary heart diseases, Rheumatic Valvular heart diseases, chronic cor pulmonale, and congential heart diseases (Yan et al., 2006) so we want to extend our binary classifier into a m- class classifier which gives the exact classification or diagnosis of diseases based on the symptoms of a person.

- Our next area of focus is the knowledge acquisition, which means extracting the information captured in the neural network for the reasoning purpose. The hybrid model designed in this chapter doesn't state that how it arrive at a particular decision, i.e. it can't explain that why it has classified a particular input pattern into class 1 or class 2. The artificial neural networks are treated as black boxes because the information learned from them can't be interpreted by the human beings (Naveen et al., 2012) so we have to overcome this drawback by integrating the ANN (artificial neural networks) with some knowledge extraction mechanism. Our focus is to integrate our hybrid model with some other technique which can extract rules from the model in the form of If <condition> then < consequence>. For example, if a person's age is>50 and sex is male and the resting blood pressure is > 130 mm/Hg etc. Then the person is a heart disease patient. There are various methods to extract the rule from a neural network like CART (Classification and regression tree), DT (Decision Tree), Neuro - fuzzy inference systems etc.

CONCLUSION

In this chapter a hybrid neural network is designed to classify the heart disease data set in two classes, class 1 represents person having heart diseases and class 2 represent people who are normal. The proposed hybrid system works in two stages. The hybrid system consists of the fuzzy min - max neural network and multilayer perceptron neural network working in parallel in stage one and the results of these two networks obtained are again given to the second stage multilayer perceptron neural network, and the multilayer perceptron neural network produces the cumulative results. The system is designed for the data set that contains the continuous as well as non-continuous variable. Fuzzy min - max neural network is used to classify the continuous data and this data has to be normalized in the range of 0 to 1 (both inclusive) as a fuzzy min - max neural network works only between the range of 0 and 1, and MLP is used to classify the non-continuous data. A k-fold cross validation method is used to generalize the system's performance. In the evaluation of the system's performance the value of k in k-fold cross validation method is kept equal to 4 which means the experiment is performed four times with different set of input pattern for training and testing. The Accuracy of the training data set and the testing data set along with the different performance matrics are summarized in Tables 3 and 4. The results obtained from the study shows that the proposed system can classify the data set with 93.56% accuracy which prove its effectiveness in the field of medical prognosis and diagnosis. A comparative evaluation of the proposed system is done with some other diagnosis model which is presented in Table 5 and it shows that we still need to improve the system's accuracy of classification. Our objective to design this system is to provide a portable device with CDSS (Clinical decision support system) enabled software that can be used in stand-alone mode at various locations and which can perceive medical data from different medical software and also works in manual mode also so that better medical facilities can be provided in remote areas. This is a revolutionary technique which is very helpful in the developing countries like India, where medical facilities are rarely available in remote areas and people are not aware about such technologies.

REFERENCES

Adlassing, K. P. (1982). *CADIAG-2 computer assisted medical diagnosis using fuzzy subsets in approximate reasoning in decision analysis*. Amsterdam: North Holland Publishing Company.

Anooj, P. K. (2012). Clinical decision support system: Risk level prediction of heart disease using weighted fuzzy rules. *Journal of King Saud University – Computer and Information Sciences, 24*, 27 – 40.

Azar, A. T. (2013). Fast neural network learning algorithm for Medical Applications. *Neural Computing & Applications, 23*(3-4), 1019–1034. doi:10.1007/s00521-012-1026-y

Bagher–Ebadian, H., Soltanian-Zadeh, H., Setayeshi, S., & Smith, S. T. (2004). Neural network and fuzzy clustering approach for automatic diagnosis of coronary heart disease in nuclear medicine. *IEEE Transactions on Nuclear Science, 51*(1), 184–192. doi:10.1109/TNS.2003.823047

Bishop, C. M. (1995). *Neural networks for pattern recognition*. Oxford, UK: Oxford University Press.

Brouwer, R. K. (2002). A feed-forward network for input which is both categorical and quantitative. *Neural Networks, 15*(7), 881–890. doi:10.1016/S0893-6080(02)00090-4 PMID:14672165

Carpenter, G. A., & Grossberg, S. (1987). A massively parallel architecture for a self organizing neural pattern recognition machine. *Computer Vision Graphics and Image Processing, 37*(1), 54–115. doi:10.1016/S0734-189X(87)80014-2

Cascio, D., Fauci, F., Magro, R., Raso, G., Ballotti, R., & De Carlo, F. et al.. (2006). Mammogram segmentation by contour searching and mass lesion classification with neural network. *IEEE Transactions on Nuclear Science, 53*(5), 2827–2833. doi:10.1109/TNS.2006.878003

Chen, D. R., Chang, R. F., & Huang, Y. L. (2000). Breast cancer diagnosis using self organizing map for sonography. *Ultrasound in Medicine & Biology, 26*(3), 405–411. doi:10.1016/S0301-5629(99)00156-8 PMID:10773370

Chu, F., Jin, G., & Wang, L. (2005). Cancer diagnosis and protein secondary structure prediction using Support Vector Machines. *StudFuzz, 177*, 343–363.

Comak, E., Arslan, A., & Turkoglu, I. (2007). A decision support system based on support vector machines for diagnosis of the heart valve diseases. *Computers in Biology and Medicine, 37*(1), 21–27. doi:10.1016/j.compbiomed.2005.11.002 PMID:16426598

Das, R., Turkoglu, I., & Sengur, A. (2009). Diagnosis of valvular diseases through neural network ensembles. *Computer Methods and Programs in Biomedicine, 93*(2), 185–191. doi:10.1016/j.cmpb.2008.09.005 PMID:18951649

Devijver, P., & Kittler, P. (1982). *Pattern recognition: A Statistical Approach*. Prentice-Hall.

Dong, M. C., Shi, J., Sekar, B. D., & Lei, W. K. (2010). Cardiovascular diseases risk detection using modified t-s fuzzy neural networks. *Computer and Automation Engineering (ICCAE), 2010 The 2nd International Conference on.*

Duda, R. O., & Hart, P. E. (1973). *Pattern Classification and Scene analysis.* New York: Wiley Publication New York.

Duda, R. O., Hart, P. E., & Strok, D. G. (2001). *Pattern classification.* New York: Willy Publication New York.

Embrechts, M. J., Arciniegas, F. A., Breneman, C. M., Bennett, K. P., & Lockwood, L. (2001). Bagging neural network sensitivity analysis for feature reduction for In-silico drug design. *Proceedings of INNS-IEEE International joint Conference on Neural Networks,* (pp. 2478–2482). doi:10.1109/IJCNN.2001.938756

Franco, L., Subirats, J. L., Molina, L., Alba, E., & Jerez, J. M. (2007). Early breast cancer prognosis prediction and rule extraction using a new constructive neural network algorithm. *Computational and Ambient intelligence. Lecture Notes in Computer Science, 4507,* 1004–1011. doi:10.1007/978-3-540-73007-1_121

Fukunaga, K. (1972). *Introduction to Statistical Pattern Recognition.* New York: Academic Press New York.

Gabrys, B., & Bargiela, A. (2000). General fuzzy min – max neural network for clustering and classification. *IEEE Transactions on Neural Networks, 11*(32), 769–783. doi:10.1109/72.846747 PMID:18249803

Hand, D. J. (1997). *Construction and Assessment of Classification Rules.* New York: Wiley Publication New York.

Hannan, S. A., Manza, R. R., & Ramteke, R. J. (2010). Generalized regression neural network and Radial basis function for heart disease diagnosis. *International Journal of Computer Applications, 7*(13).

Held, C. M., Heiss, J. E., Esteveg, P. A., Perez, C. A., Garrido, M., & Algarinn, C. (2006). Extracting fuzzy rules from polysomnographic recordings for infant sleep classification. *IEEE Transactions on Bio-Medical Engineering, 53*(10), 1954–1962. doi:10.1109/TBME.2006.881798 PMID:17019859

Jang, J. S. R., Sun, C. T., & Mizutani, E. (1997). *Neuro-Fuzzy And Soft Computing.* Prentice Hall.

Ji, J., Pang, W., Zhou, C., Yan, X., & Wang, Z. (2012). A fuzzy k-prototype clustering algorithm for mixed numerical and categorical data. *Knowledge-Based Systems, 30,* 129–135. doi:10.1016/j.knosys.2012.01.006

Kahrmanli, H., & Allahverdi, N. (2008). Design of a hybrid system for the diabetes and heart diseases. *Expert Systems with Applications, 35*(1-2), 82–89. doi:10.1016/j.eswa.2007.06.004

Kahrmanli, H., & Allahverdi, N. (2009). Extracting rules for classification problems: AIS based approach. *Expert Systems with Applications, 36*(7), 10494–10502. doi:10.1016/j.eswa.2009.01.029

Karalolis, M. A., Moutiris, J. A., Hadjipanayi, D., & Pattichis, C. S. (2010). Assessment of the risk factors of coronary heart events based on data mining with decision trees. *IEEE Transactions on Information Technology in Biomedicine, 14*(3), 559–564. doi:10.1109/TITB.2009.2038906 PMID:20071264

Kiyan, T., & Yildirim, T. (2004). Breast cancer diagnosis using statistical neural networks. *Journal of Electronic and Electrical Engineering, 4*(2), 1149–1153.

Kochurani, O. G., & Aji, S. (2007). A neuro fuzzy decision tree model for predicting the risk in coronary artery disease. *IEEE 22nd International Symposium on Intelligent Control*, (pp. 166 – 171).

Kohavi, R. (1995). A study of cross validation and bootstrap for accuracy estimation and model selection. *Proceeding of International Joint Conference on Artificial Intelligence*.

Kohonen, T. (1984). *Self-Organization and Associative Memory*. Berlin, Germany: Springer-Verlag.

Kovalerchuk, B., Triantaphyllou, E., Ruiz, J. F., & Clayton, J. (1997). Fuzzy logic in computer aided breast cancer diagnosis: Analysis of lobulation. *Artificial Intelligence in Medicine, 11*(1), 75–85. doi:10.1016/S0933-3657(97)00021-3 PMID:9267592

Lim, C. P., Leong, J. H., & Kuan, M. M. (2005). A hybrid neural network system for pattern classification task with missing features. *IEEE Transactions on Pattern Analysis and Machine Intelligence, 27*(4), 648–653. doi:10.1109/TPAMI.2005.64 PMID:15794170

Lin, H. (2008). Identification of spinal deformity classification with total curvature analysis and artificial neural network. *IEEE Transactions on Bio-Medical Engineering, 55*(1), 376–382. doi:10.1109/TBME.2007.894831 PMID:18232388

Ma, Y. X., & Wang, S. G. (2012). The applications of artificial neural network in medical meteorology. *Future Control and Automation. Lecture Notes in Electrical Engineering, 172*, 237–242. doi:10.1007/978-3-642-31006-5_29

Maglogiannis, I., Loukis, E., Zafiropoulos, E., & Stasis, A. (2009). Support vector machine-based identification of heart valve diseases using heart sounds. *Computer Methods and Programs in Biomedicine, 95*(1), 47–61. doi:10.1016/j.cmpb.2009.01.003 PMID:19269056

Miller, R. A., People, H. E., & Myres, J. D. (n. d.). INTERNIST-1: An experimental computer based diagnostic consultant for general internal medicine. *New Engl. J. Med., 307*, 468 – 476.

Mousa, R., Munib, Q., & Moussa, A. (2005). Breast cancer diagnosis system based on wavelet analysis and fuzzy-neural. *Expert Systems with Applications, 28*(4), 713–723. doi:10.1016/j.eswa.2004.12.028

Mu, T., & Nandi, A. K. (2007). Breast cancer detection from FNA using SVM with different parameter tuning systems and SOM-RBF classifier. *Journal of the Franklin Institute, 344*(3-4), 285–311. doi:10.1016/j.jfranklin.2006.09.005

Naveen, N., Ravi, V., & Rao, C. R. (2012). Rule extraction from DEWNN to solve classification and regression problems. *Proceedings of Third International Conference, SEMCCO 2012*. doi:10.1007/978-3-642-35380-2_25

Osareh, A., Shadgar, B., & Markham, R. (2009). A computational intelligence based approach for of exudates in diabetic retinopathy images. *IEEE Transactions on Information Technology in Biomedicine, 13*(4), 535–545. doi:10.1109/TITB.2008.2007493 PMID:19586814

Pal, D., Mandana, K. M., Pal, S., Sarkar, D., & Chakrabobrty, C. (2012). Fuzzy expert system approach for coronary artery disease screening using clinical parameters. *Knowledge-Based Systems*, *36*, 162–174. doi:10.1016/j.knosys.2012.06.013

Palaniappan, S., & Awang, R. (2008). Intelligent heart disease prediction system using data mining techniques.*IEEE/ACS International Conference on Computer System and Applications (AICCSA 2008) 2008*, (pp. 108 – 115). doi:10.1109/AICCSA.2008.4493524

Panchal, R., & Verma, B. (2006). Characterization of breast abnormality patterns in digital mammograms using auto –associator neural network. *ICONIP*, *3*(4234), 127–136.

Quteishat, A., & Lim, C. P. (2008). A modified fuzzy min-max neural network with rule extraction and its application to fault detection and classification.*Applied Soft Computing*, *8*(2), 985–995. doi:10.1016/j.asoc.2007.07.013

Quteishat, A., Lim, C. P., & Tan, K. S. (2010). A modified fuzzy min - max neural network with a ge-netic – algorithm based rule extractor for pattern classification. *IEEE Transactions on Systems, Man, and Cybernetics. Part A, Systems and Humans*, *40*(3), 641–650. doi:10.1109/TSMCA.2010.2043948

Rathi, V., & Aggarwal, S. (2013). Mammography mass classification of breast cancer using multilayer perceptron network.*7th International Conference on Advanced Computing and Communication Tech-nologies*.

Rey-del-castillo, P., & Cardenosa, J. (2011). Fuzzy min - max neural networks for categorical data:application to missing data imputation. *Neural Computing & Applications*, *21*(6), 1349–1362. doi:10.1007/s00521-011-0574-x

Ripley, B. D. (1996). *Pattern Recognition and Neural Networks*. Cambridge, UK: Cambridge University Press. doi:10.1017/CBO9780511812651

Rizzi, A., Panella, M., & Frattale Mascioli, F. M. (2002). Adaptive resolution min - max classifiers. *IEEE Transactions on Neural Networks*, *13*(2), 402–414. doi:10.1109/72.991426 PMID:18244441

Seera, M., & Lim, C. P. (2014). A hybrid intelligent system for medical data classification. *Expert Sys-tems with Applications*, *41*(5), 2239–2249. doi:10.1016/j.eswa.2013.09.022

Sekar, B. D., Dong, M. C., Shi, J., & Hu, X. Y. (2012). Fused hierarchical neural network for cardio-vascular disease diagnosis. *IEEE Sensors Journal*, *12*(3), 644–650. doi:10.1109/JSEN.2011.2129506

Seredynski, F., & Bouvry, P. (2007). Anomaly detection in TCP/IP networks using immune systems paradigms. *Computer Communications*, *30*(4), 740–749. doi:10.1016/j.comcom.2006.08.016

Shi, J., Dong, M. C., Sekar, B. D., & Lei, W. K. (2010). Fuzzy neural networks to detect cardiovascular diseases hierarchically. *IEEE 10th International Conference on Computer and Information Technology*.

Shigetoshi, S., Toshio, F., & Takanori, S. (1995). A neural network architecture for incremental learning. *Neurocomputing*, *9*(2), 111–130. doi:10.1016/0925-2312(94)00061-V

Shortliffe, E. H. (1976). *Computer Based Medical Consultations: MYCIN*. New York: Am Elsevier.

Simpson, P. K. (1992). Fuzzy min-max neural network part-1: Classification. *IEEE Transactions on Neural Networks, 3*(5), 776–778. doi:10.1109/72.159066 PMID:18276476

Simpson, P. K. (1993). Fuzzy min-max neural network part-1: Clustering. *IEEE Transactions on Fuzzy Systems, 1*(1), 32–45. doi:10.1109/TFUZZ.1993.390282

Singh, S., & Gupta, P. R. (2011). Breast cancer detection and classification using neural network. *International Journal of Advanced Engineering Science and Technologies, 6*(1), 4 - 9.

Sivanandm, S. N., & Deepa, S. N. (2011). Principles of Soft Computing (2nd ed.). Wiley Publication India.

Tang, T. I., Zheng, G., Huang, Y., Shu, G., & Wang, P. (2005). A comparative study of medical data classification methods based on decision tree and system reconstruction analysis. *IEMS, 4*(1), 102–108.

Tkacz, E. J., & kostka, P. (2000). An application of wavelet neural network for classification of patient with coronary artery disease based on HRV analysis. *Proceeding of the Annual International Conference on IEEE Engineering in Medicine and Biology,* (pp. 1391 - 1393). doi:10.1109/IEMBS.2000.897999

Turkoglu, I., Arslan, A., & Illkay, E. (2002). An expert system for the diagnosis of the heart valve diseases. *Expert Systems with Applications, 23*(3), 229–236. doi:10.1016/S0957-4174(02)00042-8

UC Irwin Machine Learning Repositry. (n.d.). *Cleveland Heart Disease Data Set.* Retrieved from http://archive.ics.uci.edu/ml/datasets/Heart+Disease

Verma, B., McLeod, P., & Klevansky, A. (2009). A novel soft cluster neural network for the classification of suspicious area in digital mammograms. *Pattern Recognition, 42*(9), 1845–1852. doi:10.1016/j.patcog.2009.02.009

Wang, L., Chu, F., & Xie, W. (2007). Accurate cancer classification using expression of very few genes. *IEEE/ACM Transactions on Computational Biology and Bioinformatics, 4*(1), 40–53. doi:10.1109/TCBB.2007.1006 PMID:17277412

World Health Organization. (n.d.). *Prevention of cardiovascular disease: Pocket guideline for assessment and management of cardiovascular risk.* Retrieved from http://www.who.int/cardiovascular_diseases/guidelines/

Xi, C., Dongming, J., & Zhijian, L. (2001). Recursive training for multi resolution fuzzy min - max neural network classifier.*6th International Conference Solid–State and Integrated Circuit Technology Proceedings,* (pp. 131 - 134).

Yan, H., Jiang, Y., Zheng, J., Peng, C., & Li, Q. (2006). A Multi-Layer Perceptron based medical decision support system for heart disease diagnosis. *Expert Systems with Applications, 30*(2), 272–281. doi:10.1016/j.eswa.2005.07.022

Yardimci, A. (2009). Application of soft computing to medical problems.*Ninth International Conference on Intelligent Systems Design and Application,* (pp. 614 – 619). doi:10.1109/ISDA.2009.168

Zahlmann, G., Scherf, M., Wegner, A., Obermaier, M., & Mertz, M. (2000). Situation assessment of glaucoma using a hybrid fuzzy neural network. *IEEE Engineering In Medicine And Biology, 19*(1), 84–91. doi:10.1109/51.816247 PMID:10659433

Chapter 12
A Combinational Fuzzy Clustering Approach for Microarray Spot Segmentation

Ong Pauline
Universiti Tun Hussein Onn Malaysia (UTHM), Malaysia

Zarita Zainuddin
Universiti Sains Malaysia (USM), Malaysia

ABSTRACT

Due to microarray experiment imperfection, spots with various artifacts are often found in microarray image. A more rigorous spot recognition approach in ensuring successful image analysis is crucial. In this paper, a novel hybrid algorithm was proposed. A wavelet approach was applied, along with an intensity-based shape detection simultaneously to locate the contour of the microarray spots. The proposed algorithm segmented all the imperfect spots accurately. Performance assessment with the classical methods, i.e., the fixed circle, adaptive circle, adaptive shape and histogram segmentation showed that the proposed hybrid approach outperformed these methods.

INTRODUCTION

Microarray study, consisting of a glass slide that contains samples with thousands of genes arranged in a rectangular grid, makes it possible to monitor the expression levels of thousands of genes simultaneously (Zainuddin & Ong, 2011). This technique has emerged as cutting-edge technology in bioinformatics. It is particularly important in distinguishing between the subtypes of the heterogeneous tumors. Different genes are expressed in the cells of heterogeneous tumors. By studying and contrasting the gene expression profiles from a microarray experiment, information about the types and amounts of mRNA present in the tumors can be obtained. This variation makes it possible to discriminate among the subtypes of tumors. Hence, gaining insight into the cellular mechanism and determining the pathway of the biological reaction are no longer obstacles.

DOI: 10.4018/978-1-5225-1776-4.ch012

The typical microarray experiment runs as follows (Amaratunga & Cabrera, 2004):

1. **Microarray Experiment Preparation:** The extracted mRNA from control samples and experimental samples are labeled with fluorescent dyes, cy3 (green color) and cy5 (red color), respectively. Both labeled samples are mixed and poured onto the microarray slides, where the hybridization will take place based on the base-pair complementarities.
2. **Microarray Image Scanning:** After the hybridization, the slides are scanned by a laser, and the fluorescent dye in the labeled samples is excited by the laser. The emitted detectable light is captured by a scanner. Samples with more bound, labeled probes will fluoresce more intensely. A gene expression matrix with rows corresponding to the single gene and columns correspond to the single sample is obtained by using image processing software to quantify the fluorescence intensities.
3. **Microarray Data Normalization:** Transformation and normalization of the microarray data are completed to improve the comparability of different gene expression level values between different microarrays within an experiment.
4. **Gene Selection:** The gene expression matrix consists of an overwhelming number of genes relative to the number of samples. A majority of such genes is probably irrelevant in discriminating between the subclasses of the heterogeneous cancers. To overcome the problem of over-fitting, various statistical and clustering approaches have been proposed to select the most discriminative genes as the input features to the classifier (Algamal & Lee, 2015a, 2015b; Park, Jung, Lee, & Lim, 2015; Ray, Ganivada, & Pal, 2015; Zainuddin & Ong, 2011).
5. **Classification:** Different classifiers such as machine learning, decision trees, and statistical approaches have been developed to separate the subclasses of the heterogeneous cancers (Algamal & Lee, 2015a; Garro, Rodríguez, & Vázquez, 2016; Tsai, Wang, Lee, Lin, & Chiu, 2015; Zainuddin & Ong, 2011).

It thus can be seen that preparation of the microarray experiment as well as the data analysis involved many interdependent phases. All processing stages at current state highly rely on the precision from earlier steps. Occurrence of erroneous measurements and vagueness at any interdependent phases that may deteriorate the quality of a microarray experiment is undesirable. Specifically, preciseness in finding the representative gene expression values for the spots in a microarray image is the most crucial. Compensation for the miscalculation of the spot intensities during the image analysis at later stages is difficult. Therefore, the primary task in microarray image manipulation is to extract the information from the image, including the spot size and shape, image orientation, spot intensities and distance between the spots. In this study, segmentation of the gene spots is the main concern. An intuitive mean in extracting representative quantifiers for the regular spots as well as the faulty spots is proposed.

The objectives of this study can be summarized as follows:

- To formulate a novel edge detection technique, *i.e.*, the wavClust algorithm based on the combination of the wavelet and fuzzy clustering approaches
- To evaluate the effectiveness of the proposed wavClust algorithm in microarray image segmentation
- To compare the segmentation quality of the proposed wavClust algorithm with other state-of-art methods in microarray image segmentation

The problem statement is given in block diagram, as shown in Figure 1.

Figure 1. Problem statement in block diagram

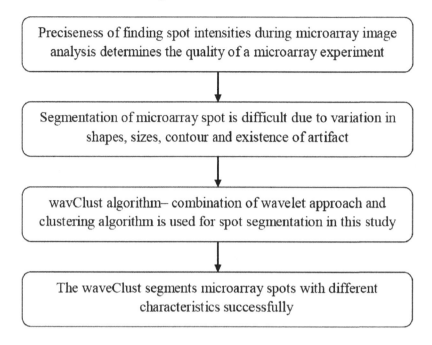

BACKGROUND

In the image processing stage, an RGB image is generated after the microarray image scanning. The scanned image must be converted into spot intensities before the pattern discovery or class prediction takes place. Thus, assigning an intensity value to every spot is the core of the image processing. The obtained spot intensity values must reflect the amount of labeled samples that are hybridized to the probe as reliable as possible.

Basically, the processing of the scanned image can be decomposed into three steps (Amaratunga & Cabrera, 2004):

1. **Addressing/Gridding:** Identifying the location of each spot.
2. **Segmentation:** Separating the pixels into foreground (spot of interest) and background (pixels that are not belong to a spot).
3. **Quantification:** Assigning the intensity value to each segmented spot.

An ideal microarray image with zero uncertainty for all spots, consistent pre-defined morphology, and invariant spot intensity from the background is the most wanted. However, this is probably a utopia, since variations and noise are always happening during the microarray experiment that spans from sample preparation to storage of image file format. For example, storage of the microarray images with lossy data compression will lead to blur spots. Dipping pins of the probe spotting machine might bend over time and cause irregularity in the printed spots, where it will impair the consistency of the pre-defined morphology. A rotated microarray image can be obtained, if any offset of the glass slide or dipping pins took place. Hybridization and spotting errors, such as the unattached fluorescent dye, salt deposits from evaporated solvents, slide material, ambient temperature, humidity as well as the presence of dust particles or dirt on the glass slide lead to variations also. Thus, deviations from the ideal microarray image are originated from these variations and noise, where these deviations can be categorized into four main problems (Bozinov & Rahnenführer, 2002):

- **Size Variation:** Spots have different diameters,
- **Contour Variation:** Spots have different shapes,
- **Normalization:** Spots with high background and low foreground,
- **Artifact:** Spots with smeared area.

The quality of spot segmentation is unassured, due to the image degradations which are affected by the aforementioned variations and noise. Therefore, any proposed spot segmentation approach must be able to resolve these potential obstacles. Several commercial software and research packages have been developed for the spot segmentation purpose, which can be classified into four different categories (Amaratunga & Cabrera, 2004):

- Fixed Circle Segmentation,
- Adaptive Circle Segmentation,
- Adaptive Shape Segmentation,
- Histogram Segmentation.

The simplest way to separate the spots from the background is by using the fixed circle segmentation approach, where a circle with constant diameter is fitted to all the spots on the microarray image. This approach is based on the assumptions that all the spots are in circular shape and with the same size. Software packages, such as ScanAlyze, GenePix, QuantArray and Spot-On are some of the customized softwares that implement this fixed circle algorithm. For example, in ScanAlyze software package, the user needs to define the number of columns of spots, number of rows of spots, spot width, spot height and the spacing between the centers of the spots. A grid with these predefined parameters will be formed on the microarray image. Next, the user needs to adjust, drag and resize the grid manually, until it was aligned perfectly with the microarray image, which proves to be very tedious and time-consuming.

The adjustable radius of the circle in the adaptive circle segmentation improves over the fixed circle segmentation approach. It allows the fitting of circular masks with different diameters to different spots on the image. This algorithm is implemented in the software packages, such as GenePix and ScanAlyze.

Even though the adaptive circle segmentation resolves the problem:

- By allowing the circular mask to have adjustable radius, it still assumes that all the spots are in circular shape, similar to the assumption made in fixed circle segmentation. Both of these implementations ignore the occurrence possibility of irregular shapes as stated in the problem, and
- In practice, these segmentation procedures provide a poor fit as the spots are rarely perfectly circular and they tend to vary in size.

Multiple attempts have suggested some ways in dealing with this setback. Adaptive shape segmentation that detects the contour variation has been proposed. One of such methods is the seeded growing region algorithm. The seeded region growing algorithm has been implemented in the Spot, which is a freeware written in the R programming language and AlphaArray. This proposed spot finding method is adaptable to the spots with various shapes and sizes, but it is non-robust and sensitive to the input initialization. If the starting seeds for the foreground and background region were not chosen properly, this algorithm might not be able to detect the contour of the spots accurately.

Histogram segmentation is another alternative in analyzing the contour of the gene spots, which has been implemented in the packages of ImaGene, QuantArray, TIGR Spotfinder and DeArray. In the histogram segmentation, a mask is placed over each spot and the histogram of the pixel intensities within the mask is formed. Next, the pixel intensities within the mask are examined. If the pixel intensity is higher than the threshold value, it will be assigned as foreground, or if the pixel intensity is lower than the threshold value, it will be assigned as background. The simplicity of this intensity-based segmentation approach is interesting, but it still faces some drawbacks. Since the pixel is classified as the foreground based on its intensity value, the resulting foreground does not necessarily connected. Determining of the threshold value may be ambiguous.

Apart from the previous segmentation techniques, several image analysis methods have been adopted in addressing the microarray spot segmentation. Paun *et al.* applied a contour-based approach for microarray image segmentation, in which they showed that the proposed method outperformed the Affymetrix GeneChip Operating Software (Păun, Li, Cheng, Tusa, & Păun, 2015). Instead of using a fixed circle or adaptive circle segmentation approach, Bergermann et al. (2004) used an adaptive ellipse in separating the spot from the background. Lukac and Plataniotis (2007) proposed a vector edge operator in the microarray spots localization. They proved that the proposed edge detection method outperformed the conventional edge detectors, such as Canny and Sobel operators, and it was more robust in handling the microarray images with noise. Sterpone (2009) proposed a dual-core architecture in analyzing the microarray image, where the Prewitt kernels were applied in finding the edges of the spots. He showed that the proposed architecture has speeded up the computation time needed by the edge detection execution and has improved over the data-driven and template-based approaches. Followed from this piece of work, Kornaros (2010)used a multi-core architecture with the Sobel edge detector in spot segmentation. Biju *et al.* (2015) examined the effectiveness of different clustering approaches in cDNA microarray images, in which the fuzzy local information c means was reported to give the best segmentation accuracy.

Athanasiadis et al. (2009) compared the segmentation abilities of fuzzy Gaussian mixture model and Gaussian mixture model in dealing with microarray spot segmentation. They showed that the former approach gave a better recognition rate, however, they did not consider the segmentation of problematic spots. Instead of using the Gaussian mixture model, Athanasiadis et al. (2009) proposed a new segmentation method, which combined the stationary wavelet transform with Markov random field model. Performance assessment showed that their model is superior to the FCM clustering algorithm, Spot and ScanAlyze software packages. Integration of snake model and the Fisher criterion was proposed by Ho and Hwang (Jinn & Wen-Liang, 2008). They compared their segmentation model with the commercial software GenePix and Spot. The performance assessment demonstrated that this proposed model outperformed the rest, even in handling the spots with artifacts and inner holes. Integration of histogram approach with the unsupervised classification based on Gaussian-kernelized FCM in separating the spot from background pixels was suggested by Daskalakis (Daskalakis, Glotsos, Kostopoulos, Cavouras, & Nikiforidis, 2009).

Abbaspour et al. (2006) proposed a spot segmentation method based on the hybridization of multidimensional clustering and shape constraints. They were aware of the problem of the inner holes in the spot and they discarded the objects which are higher/smaller than an upper/lower bound. Segmentation of spots with inner holes and scratches by using the adaptive pixel clustering was suggested by Bozinov and Rahnenfuher (2002). The superiority of the proposed method has been shown in their final segmentation results. Followed from that, apart from the segmentation of the spots with inner holes and scratches, Li et al. (2005) extended their work in studying the blank spot by using model-based clustering algorithm. It outperformed the segmentation results by Spot and Spot-On in localizing the spots with variations and noise.

MAIN FOCUS OF THE CHAPTER

A method that combines the spatial edge detection method based on wavelet approach and the shape independent advantages based on clustering algorithm was proposed in discriminating the foreground and background of the microarray spots.

The wavelet-based edge detection was proposed by Mallat et al. (1989). It looks for points where the gradient of the image intensity has a modulus which is locally maximum, since an edge is a contour where the pixel intensities have sharp transitions. A brief introduction for the wavelet transform (WT) edge detection is given as follows:

Let $\theta(x,y)$ be a smoothing function, whose double integral is nonzero. Next, let $\psi^1(x,y)$ and $\psi^2(x,y)$ be the two wavelet functions, where it is the first order derivative of smoothing function $\theta(x,y)$ with x and y, respectively, such that

$$\psi^1(x,y) = \frac{\partial \theta(x,y)}{\partial x} \text{ and } \psi^2(x,y) = \frac{\partial \theta(x,y)}{\partial y}$$

Let

$$\psi^1_s(x,y) = \frac{1}{s^2}\psi^1\left(\frac{x}{s},\frac{y}{s}\right) \text{ and } \psi^2_s(x,y) = \frac{1}{s^2}\psi^2\left(\frac{x}{s},\frac{y}{s}\right).$$

For any function

$$f(x,y) \in L^2(R^2),$$

the WT of $f(x,y)$ at the scale s with respect to $\psi^1(x,y)$ and $\psi^2(x,y)$ will have two components, *i.e.*,

$$W^1_s f(x,y) = f * \psi^1_s(x,y) \text{ and } W^2_s f(x,y) = f * \psi^2_s(x,y)$$

respectively. Hence,

$$\begin{pmatrix} W_s^1 f(x,y) \\ W_s^2 f(x,y) \end{pmatrix} = \begin{pmatrix} f * \psi_s^1(x,y) \\ f * \psi_s^2(x,y) \end{pmatrix}$$

$$= \begin{pmatrix} f * \left(s \dfrac{\partial \theta_s}{\partial x} \right)(x,y) \\ f * \left(s \dfrac{\partial \theta_s}{\partial y} \right)(x,y) \end{pmatrix}$$

$$= \begin{pmatrix} s \dfrac{\partial}{\partial x}(f * \theta_s)(x,y) \\ s \dfrac{\partial}{\partial y}(f * \theta_s)(x,y) \end{pmatrix}$$

$$= s \begin{pmatrix} \dfrac{\partial}{\partial x}(f * \theta_s)(x,y) \\ \dfrac{\partial}{\partial y}(f * \theta_s)(x,y) \end{pmatrix} = s \vec{\nabla}(f * \theta_s)(x,y)$$

The two components of WT are proportional to the coordinates of the gradient vector of $f(x,y)$ smoothed by smoothing function $\theta(x,y)$ at the scale s. If the modulus of the gradient vector of a point is maximum in the direction where the gradient vector points to, it will be assigned as an edge point. The orientation of the gradient vector indicates the direction where the partial derivative of $f(x,y)$ has an absolute value which is maximized. This is the direction where $f(x,y)$ has the sharpest variation.

For a dyadic sequence, the two components for the WT of $f(x,y)$ with respect to $\psi^1(x,y)$ and $\psi^2(x,y)$ become $W^1 f(2^j, x, y)$ and $W^2 f(2^j, x, y)$. The modulus for the WT at dyadic scale 2^j is now defined as:

$$Mf(2^j, x, y) = \sqrt{\left| W^1 f(2^j, x, y) \right|^2 + \left| W^2 f(2^j, x, y) \right|^2}$$

and the angle between the gradient vector and the horizontal is given as:

$$Af(2^j, x, y) = \arg \tan \left(\frac{W^2 f(2^j, x, y)}{W^1 f(2^j, x, y)} \right)$$

At each scale of 2^j, edges are defined as the points (x,y), where the modulus $Mf(2^j, x, y)$ is maximum along the gradient direct by $Af(2^j, x, y)$.

The transformation of a two-dimensional image is done separately using a pair of high-pass (HP) and low-pass (LP) filter, as shown in Figure 2. A one-dimensional transformation is applied to the rows first, and it followed by the one-dimensional transformation to the columns of the image. The low-pass filter produces coarse approximation coefficients, whereas the high-pass filter outputs the detail coefficients. The size of the approximation coefficients and detail coefficients decreases by a factor of 2 at each successive decomposition. Subsequently, the approximation and detail coefficients are subjected to further decomposition into approximation and detail coefficients at next level as well along the column vectors,

Figure 2. Wavelet transform for image

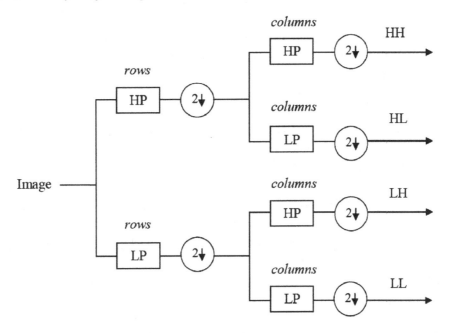

as illustrated in Figure 2. An image will be decomposed into four parts of sub-bands by the cascading filters. There are four possibilities for the filtering process, i.e.

1. Low-pass filter to rows, followed by low-pass filter to columns (LL coefficients)
2. Low-pass filter to rows, followed by high-pass filter to columns (HL coefficients)
3. High-pass filter to rows, followed by low-pass filter to columns (LH coefficients)
4. High-pass filter to rows, followed by high-pass filter to columns (HH coefficients)

The component of LL contains the low frequency information, HL contains the high frequency vertical information, LH contains the high frequency horizontal information whereas HH contains the high frequency diagonal information. The WT can be implemented recursively on the LL component until the desired level. Mallat *et al.* proved that the implementation of the one-dimensional WT is a scheme with perfect reconstruction. However, the two-dimensional WT does not possess this characteristic. As a result of this separable transformation along the horizontal and vertical directions only, the standard WT works efficiently in detecting the horizontal and vertical edges, but it can only capture very limited directional information. Thus, it might perform inadequately for locating more complex discontinuities in an image.

A modified wavelet approach in the edge detection is proposed, where clustering algorithm and OR operator will be incorporated in enhancing the edge detection process. The flow of the proposed algorithm is as follows:

- **Multi-Scale Wavelet-Based Edge Detection:** First, the conventional two-dimensional WT was applied to the image. As a result, the image is decomposed into four subbands, i.e. the LL, HL, LH and HH components. Since the edge information are always carried in the subbands with high frequencies, exploiting the HL, LH and HH subbands further will reflect more details about the edge information.

- **Clustering of Images with High Frequencies:** Clustering algorithm was applied on the HL, LH and HH images to reveal more details about the edge information. Edge detection intends to separate the edge from the background, the number of clusters was chosen as 2. Thus, clustering on the subband images is a discrete 2-center problem with the objective to identify every pixel in the image as edge or as background.
- **Forming the Edge Map with OR Operator:** From the previous procedure, all the pixels in the subband images have been assigned to either as edge or as background. Next, OR operator was applied in forming an edge map. The subband images HL, LH and HH carries the edge information along the horizontal, vertical and diagonal direction, respectively. This information is now combined in the edge map by using the OR operator. A simple rule was applied. A pixel will be assigned as edge line, if it was classified as an edge in at least two subband images. If this criterion is not satisfied, the pixel will be allocated to edge line or background region based on the edge detection results from the conventional wavelet decomposition.
- **Edge Detection Result Combination:** Finally, the edge detection results from the multiscale wavelet-based approach and the clustering-based approach were combined to produce a final segmented image. For simplicity, we denote this proposed approach as wavClust algorithm. The pseudocode of the wavClust algorithm is presented in Table 1, whereas the pseudocode of the utilized clustering algorithm - Modified Point Symmetry-based Fuzzy C-Means (MPSFCM), is presented in Table 2 (Zainuddin & Ong, 2013).

SOLUTIONS AND RECOMMENDATIONS

The superiority of the proposed wavClust algorithm was examined using a variety of real microarray spots. A Daubechies wavelet (Db3) was chosen as the smoothing function in the three-scale dyadic wavelet-based edge detection. If a coarser scale is selected, information about the fine edges are lost. A three-scale dyadic is not extremely fine or coarse. The clustering algorithm of MPSFCM will be applied in identifying the real edges from the subband images (Zainuddin & Ong, 2013). Seven spots which represent one or more typical problem that are often encountered in microarray images were chosen. The spot segmentation results using the wavClust algorithm on different spots are illustrated in Figure 3. The comparison of the proposed wavClust algorithm with other existing spot segmentation approaches, *i.e.* the fixed circle segmentation, adaptive shape segmentation (seeded region growing) and the histograms segmentation, as well as the innovative spot segmentation approach based on fuzzy Gaussian mixture model (FGMM) (Athanasiadis, Cavouras, Spyridonos, et al., 2009), were shown in Figure 3, too.

The first spot in Figure 3 is a simple well-formed circular spot. All the aforementioned existing methods should deliver a satisfactory result. As expected, the spot segmentation with wavClust performed adequately. The second spot is an irregular spot with no artifact. The contour is not round, which is probably due to the retrieval of the spotting pin. In detecting the outer line for an irregular spot, all the methods gave satisfactory segmentation results, except for the fixed circle method. Circle used in the fixed circle segmentation is not representative for the spots with irregular shapes, artifacts or scratch. A circular mask with fixed radius was applied for all the spots. Thus, the segmentation is based on the spatial properties of the spots, and does not consider the pixel intensities. It was noticeable from Figure

Table 1. Pseudocode of the wavClust algorithm

Procedure: Input: Image X, number of clusters K, number of wavelet decomposition level n	

Step 1:	**Apply multi-scale wavelet-based edge detection**
	for i = 1:n
	    for each row of image
	        do the one-dimensional decomposition
	    end for
	    for each column of image
	        do the one-dimensional decomposition
	    end for
	end for

Step 2:	**Perform clustering on the obtained HL, LH and HH sub-images** for each sub-image cluster each pixel as edge (class 1) or background (class 0) using MPSFCM algorithm as in Algorithm 2 end for

Step 3:	**Apply OR operator to form the edge map**
	for each pixel p_i
	    if (class pixel p_i in HL = 1 and class pixel p_i in LH = 1) OR (class pixel p_i in HL = 1 and class pixel p_i in HH = 1)
	        Assign pixel p_i as edge
	    else
	        Assign pixel p_i as background
	    end if
	end for

Step 4:	**Combine the edge detection result from edge map and WT**
	for each pixel p_i
	    if (class pixel p_i in edge map = 1 and class pixel p_i in LL sub-image = 0)
	        Assign pixel p_i as edge
	    end if
	end for

Output: Segmented image	

Table 2. Pseudocode of the modified point symmetry-based fuzzy c-means

Step 1:	**Initialization** Initialize the membership matrix u_{ij} randomly, where $u_{ij} \in [0,1]$, $\sum_{i=1}^{K} u_{ij} = 1, \forall j = 1, \ldots, N$ and K is the number of cluster centers.
Step 2:	**Coarse-Tuning** Use the conventional fuzzy C-means algorithm to update the cluster centers c_i, where $i = 1, \ldots, K$.

continued on following page

Table 2. Continued

Step 3:	**Fine-Tuning 1**
	For each pixel p_i, calculate
	$$DSL(p_i, c_k, p_j) = \begin{cases} 1 - \dfrac{|d_i - d_j|}{d} & if \quad 0 \leq d_j / d_i \leq 2 \\ 0 & otherwise \end{cases}$$
	where $d_i = \overline{p_i c_k}$ and $d_j = \overline{p_j c_k}$, and
	$$OSL(p_i, c_k, p_j) = \frac{v_i \cdot v_j}{2 \| v_i \| \| v_j \|} + 0.5$$
	where $v_i = \overrightarrow{p_i c_k}$ and $v_j = \overrightarrow{c_k p_j}$.
	Find out the set Sb_{ik} of all candidate symmetrical pixel p_j for each p_i, such that
	$$OSL(p_i, c_k, p_j) \geq \beta(= 0.97) \text{ and } DSL(p_i, c_k, p_j) \geq \alpha(= 0.6).$$
Step 4:	**Fine-Tuning 2**
	Compute the SSL for each pixel p_i, where
	$$SSL(p_i, c_k, p_j) = \max_{1 \leq j \leq N, p_j \in C_k} \sqrt{\frac{DSL^2(p_i, c_k, p_j) + OSL^2(p_i, c_k, p_j)}{2}}$$
	If the value for $SSL(p_i, c_k{}^*)$ is the largest and the most symmetrical pixel p_j, relative to $c_k{}^*$ belongs to Sb_{ik}, assign pixel p_i to the cluster center $c_k{}^*$.
	Otherwise, assign pixel p_i to the cluster center $c_k{}^{**}$ with the shortest distance.
	Next, update the membership matrix u_{ij} based on the criterion that if
	$$SSL(p_i, c_k{}^*) > \theta \in [0,1], \; u_{ij} = \begin{cases} u_{ij} = 1, & if \quad j = k \\ u_{ij} = 0, & if \quad j \neq k \end{cases}$$
	Otherwise, update the membership matrix u_{ij} based on the criterion that
	$$u_{ij} = \frac{1}{\displaystyle\sum_{k=1}^{c} \left(\frac{d_{ji}}{d_{ki}}\right)^{2/(m-1)}}$$
Step 5:	**Updating**
	Update the new cluster center for K clusters by
	$$c_k^{new} = \frac{\displaystyle\sum_{i=1}^{n} u_{ji}^m p_i}{\displaystyle\sum_{i=1}^{n} u_{ji}^m}, \text{ where } p_i \in c_k.$$
Step 6:	**Continuation**
	If there are no changes or the iterations reach a predefined maximum value, then stop. Otherwise, go to Step 3.

Figure 3. Comparative results of the wavClust algorithm with other existing spot segmentation approaches

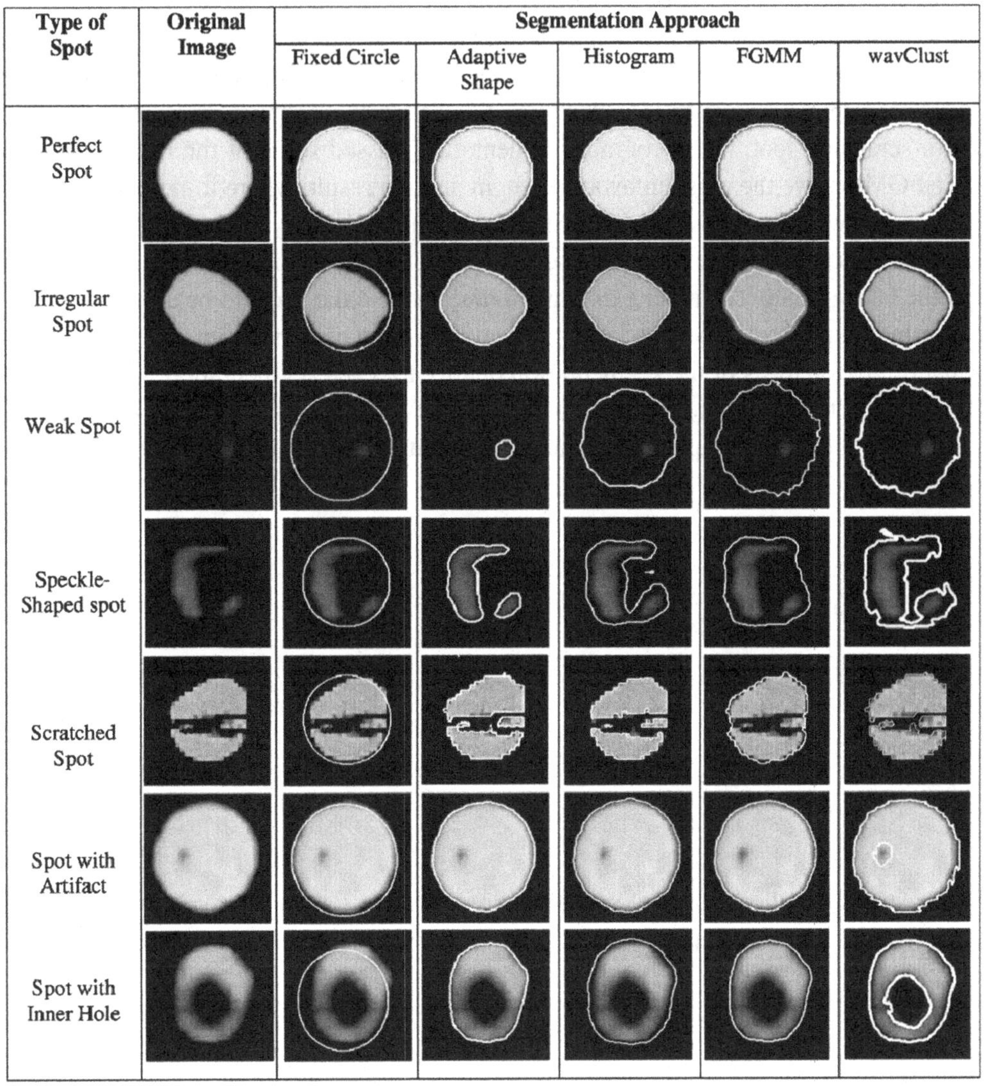

3, fixed circle segmentation performed well in detecting the edge of the perfect spot. In other cases, the segmentation results were very disappointing. Despite of its simplicity, the fixed circle used in the segmentation was not representative on many occasions. It included some of the background as the spot, or it missed some of the region in the spot. For example, in segmenting the spot with inner hole, the fixed circle segmentation method misrepresented the shape of the spot where the inner hole was included as part of the foreground. In segmenting the scratched spot also, there are considerable pixels mistakenly assigned to the foreground by fixed circle segmentation.

The third microarray spot in Figure 3 is a spot with very low overall expression. This will imply that the pixel intensities between the background and spot are certainly close to each other In dealing with the weak spot, only the histogram segmentation, FGMM and the wavClust method performed well in the spot segmentation. The seeded region growing algorithm used in the adaptive shape segmentation was not performed adequately. The misclassification of the pixels was probably due the difficulty in selecting a set of pixels as the seed for the foreground and background regions. Thus, if the initial seed was not chosen correctly, the seeded region growing algorithm did poorly in the edge detection.

The adaptive shape segmentation approach and the FGMM produced spurious edges in segmenting the speckle-shaped spot, whereas histogram method and the proposed wavClust gave a good solution. In detecting a scratched spot, the histogram segmentation missed some of the region in the center of the spot. The FGMM gave the most unfavorable segmentation result, where it includes in the scratched region as the spot as well. For the spot with artifacts and inner hole, only the proposed wavClust method segmented the artifacts and inner hole accurately. All the pixels in the artifacts and inner hole were excluded as the background. The other existing approaches take the spots to be all the pixels inside the outer contour. Including the artifacts and inner hole may lead to bias in the intensity estimation.

Next, quantitative analysis of the segmentation quality for each segmentation approach is shown in Table 3. For quantitative evaluation, an empirical goodness method, $F(I)$, that does not require prior knowledge of the real edge was applied to evaluate the quality of segmentation (Jianqing & Yang, 1994), which is given as:

$$F(I) = \sqrt{R} \times \sum_{i=1}^{R} \frac{e_i^2}{\sqrt{A_i}}$$

where

$$e_i^2 = \sum_{p \in C_i} (x_p - c_i)^2$$

I is the image and R is the number of segmented regions. Let C_i denotes the set of pixels in region i, then we have A_i as the number of pixels in C_i. Let x_p denotes the feature vector of pixel p and

$$c_i = \left(\sum_{p \in C_i} c_p \right) / A_i$$

Table 3. Quantitative evaluation on microarray spot segmentation results

Type of Spot	F(I) (*1.0e+5)				
	Microarray Segmentation Approach				
	Fixed Circle	Seeded Region Growing	Histogram	FGMM	wavClust
Perfect Spot	2.2436	1.8774	2.6001	**1.2483**	0.9299
Irregular Spot	2.8536	**0.5591**	0.7663	1.3264	0.5083
Weak Spot	0.1589	0.3968	**0.0968**	0.2890	0.0711
Speckle Spot	0.7978	0.8675	**0.5116**	1.1426	0.4455
Scratched Spot	3.9278	**0.8220**	0.9323	2.2517	0.7883
Artifact Spot	4.1016	2.0446	**2.0114**	2.1936	1.6839
Donut Spot	3.1639	2.0785	1.7205	**1.6186**	1.4876

is defined as the feature centroid of C_i. The assumption for a good segmentation quality is when $F(I)$ achieves a lower value.

From Table 3, the best segmentation results obtained by the wavClust algorithm for all the spots concerned will be used for comparison purposes. The best segmentation results achieved by the other segmentation approaches for each type of spot are highlighted in the table.

The segmentation approaches postulate that pixels in the same region have the similar features and homogeneity. Therefore, a good segmentation will achieve more homogeneity within the regions, and it indicates a lower value for the validity function $F(I)$. As demonstrated by the images in Figure 3, the proposed wavClust algorithm produces better segmentation results. Its superiority as compared with other existing microarray spot segmentation platforms is verified quantitatively in Table 3. As shown in this table, the wavClust algorithm improves the segmentation accuracy over the rest, since the smallest value for $F(I)$ validity criterion was achieved for all the spots concerned. As expected, the fixed circle segmentation demonstrates the highest value for $F(I)$, except in segmenting the weakly expressed spot, which agrees with our visual inspection in Figure 3.

Due to the microarray manufacturing imperfection, spots with irregular shape, inner holes, scratches and artifacts are often found in microarray image. A more rigorous approach in ensuring successful image analysis is appreciated. Solely spatial and solely distributional edge detection methods are not performing well in addressing the aforementioned problems. Purely spatial shape segmentation methods are unable to find the spot when it has been divided into more than one region, for example, the scratched spot and the spot with artifacts and inner hole. Purely distribution shape segmentation methods are facing problem with the spots with low expression value, since there is no sharp transition between the foreground and background. A hybrid method based on the spatial and distributional approaches seems to be a more promising solution. Therefore, the wavClust algorithm that combines the merits from the spatially adaptive wavelet edge detection method and distributional intensity-based clustering algorithm was proposed. From the experimental simulations, the proposed wavClust produces better segmentation results in detecting the spot contour. The promising potential and the effectiveness of this proposed approach suggests another alternative in addressing the issues in image segmentation.

FUTURE RESEARCH DIRECTIONS

This work hopefully provides another insight for the microarray spot segmentation using the combinational fuzzy clustering approach, specifically, the wavClust algorithm. However, much effort needs to be done for further improvement. Utilizing a bivalence mask in the clustering results can provide a better representation of the presumed location of the edges. Implementation of the proposed wavClust algorithm is not only limited to microarray spot segmentation. Its potential benefit in edge detection can be extended to other applications, such as number plate segmentation, pedestrian movement detection, face recognition, text segmentation, biometric thumb print detection and medical image segmentation or any other applications that require image processing.

Developing an automated microarray image spot segmentation package in the future, which includes the process of gridding, segmentation and quantification using the proposed wavClust algorithm, will be an interesting research to pursue. The developed software will provide an alternative to the existing microarray spot segmentation packages and algorithms.

CONCLUSION

A novel edge detection approach based on the hybridization of wavelet transform and clustering algorithms, i.e. wavClust algorithm was proposed. Its implementation in segmenting the perfect spot, irregular spot, speckled-spot and blur spot as well as in detecting the artifacts and inner hole within a spot were computed. The segmentation results for the wavClust algorithm are reassuring, since successful spot segmentation was accomplished even when the spots are contaminated with various variations and noise. Comparison with the well-developed spot segmentation methods verifies the robustness of the proposed wavClust algorithm in handling the spots with different contours and conditions.

REFERENCES

Abbaspour, M., Abugharbieh, R., Podder, M., Tripp, B. W., & Tebbutt, S. J. (2006). *Hybrid spot segmentation in four-channel microarray genotyping image data.* Paper presented at the Signal Processing and Information Technology, 2006 IEEE International Symposium on.

Algamal, Z. Y., & Lee, M. H. (2015a). Penalized logistic regression with the adaptive LASSO for gene selection in high-dimensional cancer classification. *Expert Systems with Applications, 42*(23), 9326–9332. doi:10.1016/j.eswa.2015.08.016

Algamal, Z. Y., & Lee, M. H. (2015b). Regularized logistic regression with adjusted adaptive elastic net for gene selection in high dimensional cancer classification. *Computers in Biology and Medicine, 67*, 136–145. doi:10.1016/j.compbiomed.2015.10.008 PMID:26520484

Amaratunga, D., & Cabrera, J. (2004). *Exploration and analysis of DNA microarray and protein array data.* Wiley.

Athanasiadis, E. I., Cavouras, D. A., Glotsos, D. T., Georgiadis, P. V., Kalatzis, I. K., & Nikiforidis, G. C. (2009). Segmentation of complementary DNA microarray images by wavelet-based Markov random field model. *Information Technology in Biomedicine. IEEE Transactions on, 13*(6), 1068–1074. doi:10.1109/TITB.2009.2032332

Athanasiadis, E. I., Cavouras, D. A., Spyridonos, P. P., Glotsos, D. T., Kalatzis, I. K., & Nikiforidis, G. C. (2009). Complementary DNA microarray image processing based on the fuzzy Gaussian mixture model. *Information Technology in Biomedicine. IEEE Transactions on, 13*(4), 419–425. doi:10.1109/TITB.2008.907984

Bergemann, T. L., Laws, R. J., Quiaoit, F., & Zhao, L. P. (2004). A statistically driven approach for image segmentation and signal extraction in cDNA microarrays. *Journal of Computational Biology, 11*(4), 695–713. doi:10.1089/cmb.2004.11.695 PMID:15579239

Biju, V. G., & Mythili, P. (2015). Fuzzy clustering algorithms for cDNA microarray image spots segmentation. *Procedia Computer Science, 46*, 417–424. doi:10.1016/j.procs.2015.02.039

Bozinov, D., & Rahnenführer, J. (2002). Unsupervised technique for robust target separation and analysis of DNA microarray spots through adaptive pixel clustering. *Bioinformatics (Oxford, England), 18*(5), 747–756. doi:10.1093/bioinformatics/18.5.747 PMID:12050071

Daskalakis, A., Glotsos, D., Kostopoulos, S., Cavouras, D., & Nikiforidis, G. (2009). A comparative study of individual and ensemble majority vote cDNA microarray image segmentation schemes, originating from a spot-adjustable based restoration framework. *Computer Methods and Programs in Biomedicine*, *95*(1), 72–88. doi:10.1016/j.cmpb.2009.01.007 PMID:19278747

Garro, B. A., Rodríguez, K., & Vázquez, R. A. (2016). Classification of DNA microarrays using artificial neural networks and ABC algorithm. *Applied Soft Computing*, *38*, 548–560. doi:10.1016/j.asoc.2015.10.002

Jianqing, L., & Yang, Y. H. (1994). Multiresolution color image segmentation. *Pattern Analysis and Machine Intelligence. IEEE Transactions on*, *16*(7), 689–700. doi:10.1109/34.297949

Jinn, H., & Wen-Liang, H. (2008). Automatic microarray spot segmentation using a snake-fisher model. *Medical Imaging. IEEE Transactions on*, *27*(6), 847–857. doi:10.1109/TMI.2008.915697

Kornaros, G. (2010). A soft multi-core architecture for edge detection and data analysis of microarray images. *Journal of Systems Architecture*, *56*(1), 48–62. doi:10.1016/j.sysarc.2009.11.004

Li, Q., Fraley, C., Bumgarner, R. E., Yeung, K. Y., & Raftery, A. E. (2005). Donuts, scratches and blanks: Robust model-based segmentation of microarray images. *Bioinformatics (Oxford, England)*, *21*(12), 2875–2882. doi:10.1093/bioinformatics/bti447 PMID:15845656

Lukac, R., & Plataniotis, K. N. (2007). Vector edge operators for cDNA microarray spot localization. *Computerized Medical Imaging and Graphics*, *31*(7), 510–522. doi:10.1016/j.compmedimag.2007.06.002 PMID:17707611

Mallat, S. G. (1989). A theory for multiresolution signal decomposition: The wavelet representation. *Pattern Analysis and Machine Intelligence. IEEE Transactions on*, *11*(7), 674–693. doi:10.1109/34.192463

Park, D., Jung, E.-Y., Lee, S.-H., & Lim, J. (2015). A composite gene selection for DNA microarray data analysis. *Multimedia Tools and Applications*, *74*(20), 9031–9041. doi:10.1007/s11042-013-1583-9

Păun, M., Li, Y., Cheng, Y., Tusa, I., & Păun, A. (2015). Segmenting microarray images using a contour-based method. *Theoretical Computer Science*, *608*, 108–118. doi:10.1016/j.tcs.2015.07.036

Ray, S. S., Ganivada, A., & Pal, S. K. (2015). *A granular self-organizing map for clustering and gene selection in microarray data. IEEE Transactions on Neural Networks and Learning Systems*. doi:10.1109/TNNLS.2015.2460994

Sterpone, L. (2009). A novel dual-core architecture for the analysis of DNA microarray images. *Instrumentation and Measurement. IEEE Transactions on*, *58*(8), 2653–2662. doi:10.1109/TIM.2009.2015695

Tsai, M.-H., Wang, H.-C., Lee, G.-W., Lin, Y.-C., & Chiu, S.-H. (2015). A decision tree based classifier to analyze human ovarian cancer cDNA microarray datasets. *Journal of Medical Systems*, *40*(1), 1–8. doi:10.1007/s10916-015-0361-9 PMID:26531754

Zainuddin, Z., & Ong, P. (2011). Reliable multiclass cancer classification of microarray gene expression profiles using an improved wavelet neural network. *Expert Systems with Applications*, *38*(11), 13711–13722. doi:10.1016/j.eswa.2011.04.164

Zainuddin, Z., & Ong, P. (2013). Design of wavelet neural networks based on symmetry fuzzy C-means for function approximation. *Neural Computing & Applications*, *23*(1), 247–259. doi:10.1007/s00521-013-1350-x

ADDITIONAL READING

Angulo, J., & Serra, J. (2003). Automatic analysis of DNA microarray images using mathematical morphology. *Bioinformatics (Oxford, England)*, *19*(5), 553–562. doi:10.1093/bioinformatics/btg057 PMID:12651712

Baldi, P., & Long, A. D. (2001). A Bayesian framework for the analysis of microarray expression data: Regularized t-test and statistical inferences of gene changes. *Bioinformatics (Oxford, England)*, *17*(6), 509–519. doi:10.1093/bioinformatics/17.6.509 PMID:11395427

Ball, C. A., Sherlock, G., Parkinson, H., Rocca-Sera, P., Brooksbank, C., Causton, H. C., & Holstege, F. et al. (2002). Standards for microarray data. *Science*, *298*(5593), 539. doi:10.1126/science.298.5593.539b PMID:12387284

Brown, M. P., Grundy, W. N., Lin, D., Cristianini, N., Sugnet, C. W., Furey, T. S., & Haussler, D. et al. (2000). Knowledge-based analysis of microarray gene expression data by using support vector machines. *Proceedings of the National Academy of Sciences of the United States of America*, *97*(1), 262–267. doi:10.1073/pnas.97.1.262 PMID:10618406

Chen, Y., Dougherty, E. R., & Bittner, M. L. (1997). Ratio-based decisions and the quantitative analysis of cDNA microarray images. *Journal of Biomedical Optics*, *2*(4), 364–374. doi:10.1117/12.281504 PMID:23014960

DeRisi, J., Penland, L., Brown, P. O., Bittner, M. L., Meltzer, P. S., Ray, M., & Trent, J. M. et al. (1996). Use of a cDNA microarray to analyse gene expression patterns in human cancer. *Nature Genetics*, *14*(4), 457–460. doi:10.1038/ng1296-457 PMID:8944026

Dudoit, S., Yang, Y. H., Callow, M. J., & Speed, T. P. (2002). Statistical methods for identifying differentially expressed genes in replicated cDNA microarray experiments. *Statistica Sinica*, *12*(1), 111–140.

Efron, B., Tibshirani, R., Storey, J. D., & Tusher, V. (2001). Empirical Bayes analysis of a microarray experiment. *Journal of the American Statistical Association*, *96*(456), 1151–1160. doi:10.1198/016214501753382129

Golub, T. R., Slonim, D. K., Tamayo, P., Huard, C., Gaasenbeek, M., Mesirov, J. P., & Caligiuri, M. A. et al. (1999). Molecular classification of cancer: Class discovery and class prediction by gene expression monitoring. *Science*, *286*(5439), 531–537. doi:10.1126/science.286.5439.531 PMID:10521349

Lee, J. W., Lee, J. B., Park, M., & Song, S. H. (2005). An extensive comparison of recent classification tools applied to microarray data. *Computational Statistics & Data Analysis*, *48*(4), 869–885. doi:10.1016/j.csda.2004.03.017

Leung, Y., & Hung, Y. (2010). A multiple-filter-multiple-wrapper approach to gene selection and microarray data classification.[TCBB]. *IEEE/ACM Transactions on Computational Biology and Bioinformatics*, *7*(1), 108–117. doi:10.1109/TCBB.2008.46 PMID:20150673

Leung, Y. F., & Cavalieri, D. (2003). Fundamentals of cDNA microarray data analysis. *Trends in Genetics*, *19*(11), 649–659. doi:10.1016/j.tig.2003.09.015 PMID:14585617

Lim, L. P., Lau, N. C., Garrett-Engele, P., Grimson, A., Schelter, J. M., Castle, J., & Johnson, J. M. et al. (2005). Microarray analysis shows that some microRNAs downregulate large numbers of target mRNAs. *Nature*, *433*(7027), 769–773. doi:10.1038/nature03315 PMID:15685193

Mallat, S. (1999). *A wavelet tour of signal processing*. Academic press.

Mallat, S., & Hwang, W. L. (1992). Singularity detection and processing with wavelets. *Information Theory. IEEE Transactions on*, *38*(2), 617–643.

Mallat, S., & Zhong, S. (1992). Characterization of signals from multiscale edges. *IEEE Transactions on Pattern Analysis and Machine Intelligence*, *14*(7), 710–732. doi:10.1109/34.142909

Mallat, S. G. (1989). Multifrequency channel decompositions of images and wavelet models. *Acoustics, Speech and Signal Processing. IEEE Transactions on*, *37*(12), 2091–2110.

Quackenbush, J. (2001). Computational analysis of microarray data. *Nature Reviews. Genetics*, *2*(6), 418–427. doi:10.1038/35076576 PMID:11389458

Quackenbush, J. (2002). Microarray data normalization and transformation. *Nature Genetics*, *32*(Supp), 496–501. doi:10.1038/ng1032 PMID:12454644

Schena, M., Shalon, D., Davis, R. W., & Brown, P. O. (1995). Quantitative monitoring of gene expression patterns with a complementary DNA microarray. *Science*, *270*(5235), 467–470. doi:10.1126/science.270.5235.467 PMID:7569999

Tibshirani, R., Hastie, T., Narasimhan, B., & Chu, G. (2002). Diagnosis of multiple cancer types by shrunken centroids of gene expression. *Proceedings of the National Academy of Sciences of the United States of America*, *99*(10), 6567–6572. doi:10.1073/pnas.082099299 PMID:12011421

Yang, Y. H., Buckley, M. J., Dudoit, S., & Speed, T. P. (2002). Comparison of methods for image analysis on cDNA microarray data. *Journal of Computational and Graphical Statistics*, *11*(1), 108–136. doi:10.1198/106186002317375640

Yang, Y. H., Buckley, M. J., & Speed, T. P. (2001). Analysis of cDNA microarray images. *Briefings in Bioinformatics*, *2*(4), 341–349. doi:10.1093/bib/2.4.341 PMID:11808746

Yang, Y. H., Dudoit, S., Luu, P., Lin, D. M., Peng, V., Ngai, J., & Speed, T. P. (2002). Normalization for cDNA microarray data: A robust composite method addressing single and multiple slide systematic variation. *Nucleic Acids Research*, *30*(4), e15–e15. doi:10.1093/nar/30.4.e15 PMID:11842121

Zainuddin, Z., & Pauline, O. (2015). An effective fuzzy C-means algorithm based on symmetry similarity approach. *Applied Soft Computing*, *35*, 433–448. doi:10.1016/j.asoc.2015.06.021

KEY TERMS AND DEFINITIONS

Addressing: The first stage in microarray image processing where the location of each spot is identified.

Clustering: The action of grouping together of patterns into dissimilar clusters with respect to a similarity measure.

Fuzzy C-Means: The classical clustering algorithm which categorizes the patterns into more than one cluster, where the degree of belongingness of each pattern to a respective cluster is specified by a membership function.

Image Segmentation: The action of grouping together of pixels in an image into dissimilar regions with respect to a similarity measure.

Microarray: A cutting-edge technology in bioinformatics which is used to monitor the expression levels of thousands of genes simultaneously.

Microarray Image Processing: Microarray image analysis which consists of processes of gridding, segmentation and quantification.

Quantification: The last stage in microarray image processing where each segmented spot is assigned with an intensity value, corresponding to the expression level of each gene.

Wavelet Transform: A flexible time-frequency analysis, which narrows when observing high frequency phenomena and widens when analyzing low frequency behavior.

Chapter 13
Proficient Clustering algorithm for Wireless Sensor Networks

Nivetha Gopal
University College of Engineering Ariyalur, India

Venkatalakshmi Krishnan
University College of Engineering Tindivanam, India

ABSTRACT

Enhancing the energy efficiency and maximizing the networking lifetime are the major challenges in Wireless Sensor Networks (WSN).Swarm Intelligence based algorithms are very efficient in solving nonlinear design problems with real-world applications.In this paper a Swarm based Fruit Fly Optimization Algorithm (FFOA) with the concept of K-Medoid clustering and swapping is implemented to increase the energy efficiency and lifetime of WSN. A comparative analysis is performed in terms of cluster compactness,cluster error and convergence. MATLAB Simulation results show that K-Medoid Swapping and Bunching Fruit Fly optimization (KMSB-FFOA) outperforms FFOA and K-Medoid Fruit Fly Optimization Algorithm (KM-FFOA).

INTRODUCTION

Wireless Sensor Networks (WSN) comprises of numerous tiny sensor nodes that are capable of sensing various environmental effects and transmitting them wirelessly to an information collecting agent. These sensor nodes are deployed in vast numbers in the regions where it is difficult to oversee by the people (Amgoth & Jana, 2015; Aslam, Phillips, Robertson, & Sivakumar, 2011; Anastasi, Conti, Di, & Passarella, 2009; Li, Xu, Xiong, Yang, Zhang, Chen, & Xu, 2011). The sensor nodes in wireless sensor networks are normally fueled by battery, which is undesirable, even difficult to revived or supplanted. Sensor nodes have to rely on batteries for sensing, communication and information gathering. Sensor nodes are significantly constrained in available resources including storage, computational capacity, however energy accounts for the most restrictive of all factors because it affects the operational lifetime of WSN. As a result, sensor nodes must automatically collaborate with each other to create a self-organized network, and must be outfitted with energy efficient modules and protocols to minimize energy consumption and

DOI: 10.4018/978-1-5225-1776-4.ch013

ensure long network lifetime (Rault, Bouabdallah, & Challal, 2014; Min, Wei-ren, Chang-jiang, & Ying, 2010; Jung, Lim, Ko, & Park, 2011). In this manner, enhancing the energy efficiency and maximizing the networking lifetime are the significant challenges in sensor networks. Therefore the optimal use of these valuable energy resources becomes imperative. Generally, energy conservation should be possible in taking after ways energy-efficient routing, clustering, effective scheduling of sensor states to interchange between sleep and active nodes and data compression to decrease the extent of transmitted information. This paper addresses the issues such as energy-efficient routing and clustering. Wireless communication is the significant source of energy drainage in WSN. It is crucial that the transmission energy (E) which mainly dominates the overall energy consumption is proportional to the distance (d) between transmitter and receiver, i.e., $E \propto d^{\lambda}$, where λ is the path loss exponent. Subsequently, minimization of transmission distance can reduce the energy consumption. In recent years, researchers have done a lot of studies and proved that clustering is a compelling process in enhancing energy efficiency and lifetime of wireless sensor networks (Chamam, & Pierre,2010; Halgamuge, Guru, & Jennings,2003). In order to acquire a faster and efficient solution of the clustering and routing with the above issues, a swarm Intelligence based optimization approaches is exceedingly alluring. Numerous metaheuristic algorithms are intended for optimization, though they are not generally proficient and furthermore there may be different issues such as memory limit, computational efficiency, and computing resources (Yang, & Karamanoglu, 2013; Yang, 2013). SI-based algorithms are very efficient in tackling nonlinear design issues with real-world applications such as function optimization, traveling salesman problem, route planning, image segmentation, spam detection, data clustering and functional modules detection in protein-protein interaction network. Recently the U.S. military is exploring swarm systems for controlling unmanned vehicles. The European Space Agency is pondering about an orbital swarm for self-assembly and interferometry. NASA is researching the utilization of swarm innovation for planetary mapping.Anthony Lewis and Bekey discusses the likelihood of using swarm intelligence to control nanobots inside the body for the purpose of killing cancer tumors. Swarm intelligence (SI) is a relatively novel field that was initially defined as "Any attempt to design algorithms or distributed problem-solving devices inspired by the aggregate manner of social creepy crawlies and other animal creatures" (Abraham, 2008; Crina Grosan, 2006). The main rationale behind this fact lies in the observation that these insect societies, as a collective unit, do actually solve routing problems. They need to discover and establish paths that can be used by the single insects to effectively move back and forth from the nest of the colony to sources of food. More over swarm intelligence algorithms show a number of properties, such as self-organization, adaptivity, scalability and robustness that are highly desirable in modern large-scale artificial systems (Saleem, Caro & Farooq, 2011; Ducatelle, Di & Gambardella, 2010).All these advantages make SI design interesting for modern networks such as the wireless sensor networks. The main objective of this paper is to develop an energy efficient cluster based swarm intelligence routing algorithms for WSNs with the consideration of low energy consumption of the sensor nodes for drawing out network lifetime. This paper is illustrated as follows:

1. Section 1 depicts related works,
2. Section 2 describes Swarm based routing protocol.
3. Network model is described in section 3,
4. Section 4 explains simulation and results and
5. Finally, section 5 concludes this paper.

RELATED WORKS

Jiang, Zang, Zhao, & Shi (2010), have proposed a clustering algorithm called BACCA for radar sensor networks using ant colony optimization algorithm. Kumar and Thomas enhanced energy efficiency and network lifetime in wireless sensor networks using improved Ant Colony Optimization (ACO). Aryaand Sharma (2012) describes Analysis and Optimization of Energy of Sensor Node Using ACO in Wireless Sensor Network. In ant colony based algorithms the movement of an ant is controlled by pheromone, which will dissipate after some time. Without such time-dependent dissipation, ant algorithms will lead to premature convergence to the local solutions. This premature convergence is because of its lacks of crossover, and thus the subspace exploitation ability is very limited. Kuila and Jana proposed a Particle Swarm Optimization (PSO) based energy efficient clustering and routing algorithm for wireless sensor networks.PSO can have high mobility in particles with a high degree of exploration. Its advantage is that it helps speed up the convergence by drawing toward the present best, while at the same time it may lead to premature convergence, even though this may not be the true optimal solution of the problem of interest. The authors Hatamlou, Abdullah and Pour (2012) explain energy efficient cluster formation using cuckoo search. Cuckoo Search has strong mutation at both local and global scales, while good mixing is carried out by using solution similarity, which also plays the role of equivalent hybrid. Without the explicit use of current best solution premature convergence is observed as in Cuckoo Search.

Hatamlou, Abdullah and Pour in 2012 proposed a combined methodology for clustering based on k-means and gravitational search algorithm. Tang, Fong and Deb integrates K-means algorithm with nature inspired algorithms ant colony, cuckoo search, bat, wolf and made a comparative analysis in terms of objective function value and convergence. Y. Lin et al proposed PM-Kmeans algorithm which integrates K-means clustering optimization and Particle Swarm Optimization.But the k-means clustering methods mentioned above is not guaranteed to converge to the global optimum and often terminates at a local optimum. The outcomes may rely upon the initial random selection of cluster centers. To obtain good results in practice, it is common to run the k-means algorithm multiple times with different initial cluster centers. The k-means method is also not suitable for discovering clusters with nonconvex shapes or clusters of very different size. The k-means algorithm is sensitive to outliers because such objects are far from most of the information, and thus, when assigned to a cluster, they can significantly distort the mean estimation of the cluster. This inadvertently influences the task of different assignment of objects to clusters. Based on this literature review the focus of this work is to develop a energy efficient clustering routing protocol using swarm intelligence algorithm.

SWARM INTELLIGENCE BASED CLUSTERING ROUTING PROTOCOL

The downside of the k-means clustering algorithm gave rise to the so called k-medoid algorithm, where each cluster is represented by one of its points called medoid. A medoid can be defined as the object of a cluster whose average dissimilarity to all the objects in the cluster is minimal and it is a most centrally located point in the cluster. This way of representing clusters is more robust to noise and outliers as compared to k-means because it minimizes a sum of pairwise dissimilarities instead of a sum of squared Euclidean distances (Koutroumbas, 2006; Xing & Gao, 2014).This section describes the proposed swarm intelligence algorithm to overcome the drawbacks in ACO, PSO, Cuckoo Search with the integration of k-medoid clustering to enhance the energy efficiency in WSN. Wen-Tsao Pan in 2012 proposed a sort of Drosophila inspired algorithm, called Fruit Fly Optimization Algorithm (FFOA) which is a novel evolutionary computation and optimization strategy. The FFOA is a new methodology for discovering global optimization taking into account the swarm conduct of organic fruit flies. With the exceptional olfactory, fruit flies can perceive the odor using an osphoresis organ in the air even the food source is beyond 40 meters and fly towards the food location, then fruit fly swarm will use vision to fly towards so far best smell position, this implies that fruit flies will be around the so far best smell position at a fast speed. While searching, a fly also sends and receives information from its neighbors and makes comparison about the so far best location and fitness (Wang, 2013). FFOA has applied to many of optimization problems as multidimensional knapsack problem (Choubey, 2014), travelling and salesman problem (Liu, 2012), PID controller (Zheng & Wang, 2014), semiconductor final testing and scheduling problem (Li, 2013), neural network parameter optimization (Lei, 2014) and so on. FFOA has the downside that it is only used for one dimensional problem (Karaboga, Okdem & Ozturk, 2012).It becomes obviously that Euclidean distance used is not suitable for high dimensional issues and also the complexity to calculate the distance between flies is an extremely lengthy procedure. Smell concentration judgment value (S) is also a one dimensional in FFOA. To defeat these issues in FFOA, a cluster based fruit fly optimization algorithm with the concept of k-medoid grouping and swapping is executed to expand the efficiency and to enhance the convergence speed. Clustering is the procedure of grouping a set of data objects into multiple groups or clusters so that objects inside a cluster have high similarity, but are very dissimilar to objects in other clusters (Karaboga & Ozturk, 2011; Kogan, 2007). Cluster analysis has broad applications, including business intelligence, image pattern recognition, Web search, biology, and security. Cluster analysis can also be used as a data mining tool to gain insight into the data distribution, or as a preprocessing step for other data mining algorithms (Attea & Khalil, 2012).FFOA is actualized in clustered structure using i) K-Medoid clustering algorithm (KM-FFOA) and ii) K- Medoid Swapping and Bunching algorithm (KMSB-FFOA).

PROPOSED ALGORITHMS

FFOA is actualized in clustered structure using

1. K-Medoid clustering algorithm (KM-FFOA), and
2. K- Medoid Swapping and Bunching algorithm (KMSB-FFOA).

K-Medoid Clustering Fruit Fly Optimization Algorithm (KM-FFOA)

In K-medoid Clustering Fruit Fly Optimization Algorithm (KM-FFOA)clustering is formed using k-medoid clustering method and route optimization is done using fruit fly optimization algorithm.The main steps in the algorithms are as follows

Step 1: **Initialization** The random initial position of 'n'fruit flies
Step 2: Preprocessing (Cluster Formation)

```
for all fruit flies n
        a. select 'm' random fruit flies as cluster medoids
           where m = √ (n/2)  (by rule of thumb)
        b. calculate Manhattan distance of all fruit flies with all cluster
medoids and assign fruit flies to the cluster that have nearest medoids
      end
```

Step 3: Random direction of clusters searching food source using

$C_i(X) = C_i(X\_axis) + Random\ Value$

$C_i(Y) = C_i(Y\_axis) + Random\ Value$

Step 4: As the location of food cannot be known, the distance between cluster medoids to the origin is estimated before the decision value of smell concentration (S)

$$Dist_i = \sqrt{\sum\left(C_m\_X\right)^2 + \sum\left(C_m\_Y\right)^2}$$
$$S_i = 1 / Dist_i$$

Step 5: Calculate the smell concentration of every bunch as

$Cluster\_Smell(i) = \sum S_{ik}$, where k is number of flies in the clusters, i=1,2,3...m

Substitute smell concentration value in the Fitness function

$Smell_i = Function(Cluster\_Smell)$

Step 6: Determine the cluster medoid fruit fly with the maximum smell concentration

$[bestSmell, bestIndex] = max(Smell_m)$

Find the best smell concentration value then the clusters moves toward the position by their vision.

$Smellbest = bestSmell$
$C_m(X\_axis) = C_m\_X(bestIndex)$
$C_m(Y\_axis) = C_m\_Y(bestIndex)$

Step 7: Repeat steps 3-6, and judge the best smell concentration.

K-Medoid Swapping and bunching Fruit Fly Optimization Algorithm (KMSB - FFOA)

In K- Medoid Swapping and Bunching algorithm (KMSB-FFOA)clustering is formed using k-medoid clustering method and swapping and route optimization is done using fruit fly optimization algorithm. The main steps in the algorithms are as follows

Step 1: **Initialization** The random initial position of 'n'fruit flies
Step 2: Preprocessing (Cluster Formation)

```
    for all fruit flies n
        a. Select, 'm'  random fruit flies as cluster medoids
                where  m = √ (n/2)  (by rule of thumb)
        b. Calculate Manhattan distance of all fruit flies with all cluster
medoids and assign fruit flies to the cluster that have nearest medoids
        c. For each medoid  fruit fly  'm'
                for each non-medoid  fruit flies 'oⱼ',where j=n-m
            i. Swap m and o and compute the total distance cost of the
clusters using
                Distance cost Cᵢ(x, m) = ∑ ᵈᵢ₌₁ | Cᵢ (xᵢ) – Cᵢ  (mᵢ) |
        d. Select the cluster with the low total distance cost
                e. Repeat steps 2 (b) to 2 (d) until there is no change in the
medoids.
                    end
            end
end
```

Step 3: Random direction of food searching using

$C_i(X)=C_i(X\_axis)+$Random Value
$C_i(Y)=C_i(Y\_axis)+$Random Value

Step 4: As the location of food cannot be known, the distance between medoids to the origin is estimated before the decision value of smell concentration (S)

$$\text{Dist}_i=\sqrt{\sum\left(C_m\_X\right)^2 +\sum\left(C_m\_Y\right)^2}$$
$$S_i = 1 / \text{Dist}_i$$

Step 5: Calculate the smell concentration of each cluster as

$$\text{Cluster\_Smell}(i)=\sum S_{ik} \text{ where k is number of flies in the clusters}$$

Substitute the smell concentration value in the Fitness function

Smell$_i$=Function(Cluster_Smell)

Step 6: Determine the cluster medoid fruit fly with the maximum smell concentration among the cluster medoids fruit flies

[bestSmell,bestIndex]=max(Smell$_m$)

Find the best smell concentration value then the clusters moves toward the position by vision.

Smellbest=bestSmell
C_m(X_axis)=C_m_X(bestIndex)
C_m(Y_axis)=C_m_Y(bestIndex)

Step 7: Repeat steps 3-6, and judge the best smell concentration.

SIMULATION AND RESULTS

A Random deployment of fifty nodes in a sensor field of 50 m× 50 m is shown in Figure 1a) According to rule of thumb five fruit flies are randomly chosen as cluster medoids as depicted in Figure 1b). K-Medoid FFOA clustering is done by assigning each fruit flies to the nearest cluster medoids as in Figure 1c). K-Medoid Swapped and Bunching FFOA is formed using step 2 in KMSB-FFOA as shown in Figure 1d). We performed extensive experiments on the proposed algorithms using MATLAB.We made an analysis on cluster quality or compactness, cluster error and convergence speed.

Cluster Compactness

Silhouette refers to a method of interpretation and validation of consistency within clusters of data. The technique provides a succinct graphical representation of how well each object lies within its cluster. It was first described by Peter J. Rousseeuw in 1986.The silhouette coefficient is used to measure the cluster compactness.For each flies f_0 calculate $a(f_0)$ as the average distance between f_0 and all other flies in the cluster to which f_0 belongs. Similarly, $b(f_0)$ is the minimum average distance from f_0 to all clusters to which f_0 doesnot belong. The silhouette coefficient of f_0 is then defined as

$$S(f_0) = b(f_0) - a(f_0) / \max\{a(f_0), b(f_0)\} \qquad (4)$$

The value of the silhouette coefficient is between −1 and 1. The smaller the coefficient value, more the Cluster compactness (Han, 2012 ; Koutroumbas, 2006). As is a measure of how dissimilar is to its own cluster, a small value means it is well matched. Furthermore, a large implies that is badly matched to its neighboring cluster. Simulation plot in Figure 2 shows the silhouette plot of the KM-FFOA and the KMSB-FFOA of each cluster. It is also depicted that due the concept of medoid selection and swapping KMSB-FFOA has high cluster compactness than KM-FFOA. The average $S(f_0)$ over all nodes of

Figure 1. a) Random deployment of fruit flies b) random selection of cluster medoids c) cluster formation using KM-FFOA d) cluster formation using KMSB-FFOA

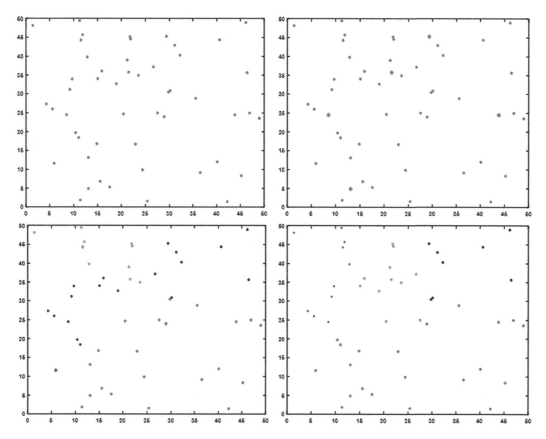

Figure 2. Silhouette value a) KMFFOA b) KMSB-FFOA

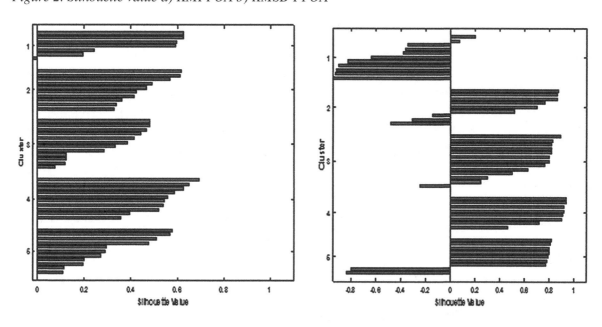

Table 1.

S.No	Algorithm	Average Silhouette Value
1	KM-FFOA	0.4229
2	KMSB-FFOA	0.1796

a cluster is a measure of how tightly grouped all the nodes in the cluster are.As mentioned in Table 1. KMSB-FFOA has low average silhouette coefficient value than KM-FFOA which shows high cluster compactness and quality.

Cluster Error

The Sum Squared Error is used to measure the error inside a cluster as Cluster Error (Ec).It is defined as the sum of the distances of each flies f_i to its mediod fly m_c in each cluster.It is expressed as

$$\text{Error}_c(c) = \sum \text{dist}(f_i, \text{medoid}(m_c)) \tag{5}$$

where i=number of flies in cluster and m_c =cluster medoid

Figure 3 shows the plot of Cluster Number to Cluster Error, which shows Cluster Error for KMSB-FFOA is very low than KM-FFOA.

Figure 3. Cluster Error a) KMFFOA b) KMSB-FFOA

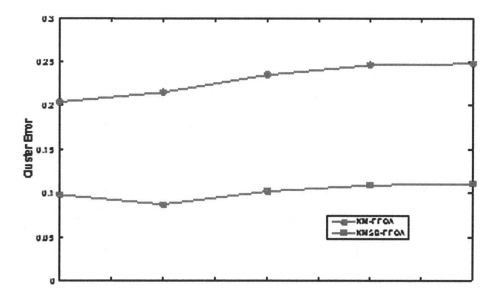

Table 2.

S.No	Algorithm	Number of Iterations
1	KM-FFOA	43
2	KMSB-FFOA	35

Convergence

Convergence is defined as the iteration number where the value of objective function becomes changeless (Karaboga, Okdem & Ozturk, 2012).The number of iterations needed to find an optimal or a stable solution determines the overall computational efforts and the performance of an algorithm. A better algorithm should use less computations and minimum number of iterations. As shown in Table 2. KMSB-FFOA reaches the convergence value in less number of iterations than FFOA and KM-FFOA.

CONCLUSION

In this paper a swarm based fruit fly optimization algorithm is implemented in clustered form with random K-Medoid clustering and Swapped K-Medoid clustering. Simulation results reveals that KMSB-FFOA has high convergence speed, low cluster error, high cluster quality, high energy available, and maximum network lifetime than KM-FFOA and FFOA.

REFERENCES

Ajith Abraham, S. D. (2008). Swarm intelligence algorithms for data clustering. Soft computing for Knowledge Discovery and Data mining, (pp. 279-313).

Amgoth, T., & Jana, P. K. (2015). Energy-aware routing algorithm for wireless sensor networks. *Computers & Electrical Engineering*, *41*, 357–367. doi:10.1016/j.compeleceng.2014.07.010

Anastasi, G., Conti, M., Di, M., & Passarella, A. (2009). Energy conservation in wireless sensor networks : A survey. *Ad Hoc Networks*, *7*(3), 537–568. doi:10.1016/j.adhoc.2008.06.003

Arya, R., & Sharma, S. C. (2015). Analysis and optimization of energy of sensor node Using ACO in wireless sensor network. *Procedia Computer Science*, *45*, 681–686. doi:10.1016/j.procs.2015.03.132

Aslam, N., Phillips, W., Robertson, W., & Sivakumar, S. (2011). A multi-criterion optimization technique for energy efficient cluster formation in wireless sensor networks. *Information Fusion*, *12*(3), 202–212. doi:10.1016/j.inffus.2009.12.005

Attea, B., & Khalil, E. (2012). A new evolutionary based routing protocol for clustered heterogeneous wireless sensor networks. *Applied Soft Computing*, *12*(7), 1950–1957. doi:10.1016/j.asoc.2011.04.007

Camilo, T., Carreto, C., Jorge, S., & Boavida, F. (2006). An energy-efficient ant-based routing algorithm for wireless sensor networks,*ANTS 2006, LNCS 4150. Springer-Verlag Berlin Heidelberg, 2006*, 49–59.

Chamam, A., & Pierre, S. (2010). A distributed energy-efficient clustering protocol for wireless sensor networks. *Computers & Electrical Engineering, 36*(2), 303–312. doi:10.1016/j.compeleceng.2009.03.008

Choubey, N. S., & Ph, D. (2014). Fruit fly optimization algorithm for travelling salesperson problem. *Journal of Computer Applications, 107*(18), 22–27. doi:10.5120/18851-0385

Crina Grosan, A. A. (2006). *Swarm Intelligence in data mining. Studies in Computational Intelligence*. Springer Verlag.

Das, K. N., & Singh, T. K. (2014). Drosophila food-search optimization. *Applied Mathematics and Computation, 231*, 566–580. doi:10.1016/j.amc.2014.01.040

Ducatelle, F., Di, G. A., & Gambardella, L. M. (2010). Principles and applications of swarm intelligence for adaptive routing in telecommunications networks. *Swarm Intelligence, 4*(3), 173–198. doi:10.1007/s11721-010-0040-x

Halgamuge, M. N.,Guru, S. M., & Jennings, A. (2003). Energy efficient cluster formation in wireless sensor networks. *10th International Conference on Telecommunications, 2003. ICT 2003*. doi:10.1109/ICTEL.2003.1191668

Hatamlou, A., Abdullah, S., & Nezamabadi-Pour, H. (2012). A combined approach for clustering based on K-means and gravitational search algorithms. *Swarm and Evolutionary Computation, 6*, 47–52. doi:10.1016/j.swevo.2012.02.003

Hinchey, M.G., Sterritt, R., & Rouff, C. (2007). Swarms and swarm intelligence. IEEE Journal *on* Computers, 111-113.

Jiang, T., Zang, W., Zhao, C., & Shi, J. (2010). An energy consumption optimized clustering algorithm for radar sensor networks based on an ant colony algorithm. *EURASIP Journal on Wireless Communications and Networking*.

Jiawei Han, M. K. (2012). *Data mining concepts and techniques*. Morgan Kaufmann Publishers, Elsevier.

Jung, W.-S., Lim, K.-W., Ko, Y.-B., & Park, S.-J. (2011). Efficient clustering-based data aggregation techniques for wireless sensor networks. *Wireless Networks, 17*(5), 1387–1400. doi:10.1007/s11276-011-0355-6

Karaboga, D., Okdem, S., & Ozturk, C. (2012). Cluster based wireless sensor network routing using artificial bee colony algorithm. *Wireless Networks, 18*(7), 847–860. doi:10.1007/s11276-012-0438-z

Karaboga, D., & Ozturk, C. (2011). A novel clustering approach: Artificial Bee Colony (ABC) algorithm. *Applied Soft Computing, 11*(1), 652–657. doi:10.1016/j.asoc.2009.12.025

Kogan. (2007). *Introduction to clustering large and high-dimensional data* (1st ed.). Cambridge University Press.

Koutroumbas, S. T. (2006). *Pattern Recognition*. Elseiver.

Kuila, P., & Jana, P. K. (2014). Energy efficient clustering and routing algorithms for wireless sensor networks: Particle swarm optimization approach. *Engineering Applications of Artificial Intelligence, 33*, 127–140. doi:10.1016/j.engappai.2014.04.009

Kumar, A., & Thomas, A. (2012). Energy efficiency and network lifetime maximization in wireless sensor networks using improved ant colony optimization. *Procedia Engineering*, *38*, 3797–3805. doi:10.1016/j.proeng.2012.06.435

Lewis, M. A., & Bekey, G. A. (1992). The behavioral self-organization of nanorobots using local rules. *International Conference on Intelligent Robots and Systems*. IEEE.

Li, G. Y., Xu, Z., Xiong, C., Yang, C., Zhang, S., Chen, Y., & Xu, S. (2011). Energy-efficient wireless communications: Tutorial, survey, and open issues. *IEEE Wireless Communications*, *18*(6), 28–35. doi:10.1109/MWC.2011.6108331

Li, H. G.-Q., Guo, S., Li, C., & Sun, J. (2013). A hybrid annual power load forecasting model based on generalized regression neural network with fruit fly optimization algorithm. *Knowledge-Based Systems*, *37*, 378–387. doi:10.1016/j.knosys.2012.08.015

Lin, Y., Tong, N., Shi, M., & Fan, K. (2012). *K-means optimization clustering algorithm Based on Particle Swarm Optimization and Multiclass Merging*. Academic Press.

Ling Wang, X.-Z.-y. (2013). A novel binary fruit fly optimization algorithm for solving the multidimensional knapsack problem. *Knowledge-Based Systems*, *48*, 17–23. doi:10.1016/j.knosys.2013.04.003

Liu, Y. W. (2012). A modified fruit-fly optimization algorithm aided PID controller designing. *IEEE 10th World Congress on Intelligent Control and Automation* (pp. 233-238). Beijing, China: IEEE.

Min, X., Wei-ren, S., Chang-jiang, J., & Ying, Z. (2010). Energy efficient clustering algorithm for maximizing lifetime of wireless sensor networks. *AEÜ. International Journal of Electronics and Communications*, *64*(4), 289–298. doi:10.1016/j.aeue.2009.01.004

Rault, T., Bouabdallah, A., & Challal, Y. (2014). Energy efficiency in wireless sensor networks: A top-down survey. *Computer Networks*, *67*(March), 104–122. doi:10.1016/j.comnet.2014.03.027

Saleem, M., Di Caro, G. A., & Farooq, M. (2011). Swarm intelligence based routing protocol for wireless sensor networks: Survey and future directions. *Information Sciences*, *181*(20), 4597–4624. doi:10.1016/j.ins.2010.07.005

Tang, R., Fong, S., & Deb, S. (2012). *Integrating nature-inspired optimization algorithms to K-means clustering*. Academic Press.

Xing, B., & Gao, W.-J. (2014). *Innovative computational intelligence: A rough guide to 134 Clever algorithms*. Academic Press.

Xiujuan Lei, M. D. (2014). Chaotic fruit fly optimization algorithm. *Advances in Swarm Intelligence 5th International Conference, ICSI 2014* (pp. 74-85). Springer.

Yang, X. (2013). *Swarm intelligence based algorithms: A critical analysis. Evolutionary Intelligence*. Springer.

Yang, X.-S. (2013). *Nature-inspired optimization algorithms* (1st ed.). Elsevier.

Yang, X. S., & Karamanoglu, M. (2013). Swarm intelligence and bio-inspired computation: An overview. Swarm Intelligence and Bio-Inspired Computation. Elsevier.

Yuan, X., Dai, X., Zhao, J., & He, Q. (2014). On a novel multi-swarm fruit fly optimization algorithm and its application. *Applied Mathematics and Computation, 233*, 260–271. doi:10.1016/j.amc.2014.02.005

Zang, H., Zhang, S., & Hapeshi, K. (2010). A Review of nature-inspired algorithms. *Journal of Bionics Engineering, 7*, S232–S237. doi:10.1016/S1672-6529(09)60240-7

Zheng, X., Wang, L., & Wang, S. (2014). A novel fruit fly optimization algorithm for the semiconductor final testing scheduling problem. *Knowledge-Based Systems, 57*, 95–103. doi:10.1016/j.knosys.2013.12.011

Chapter 14
A Study on Hybridization of Intelligent Techniques in Bioinformatics

Peyakunta Bhargavi
Sri Padmavati Mahila University, India

S. Jyothi
Sri Padmavati Mahila University, India

D. M. Mamatha
Sri Padmavati Mahila Univeristy, India

ABSTRACT

This chapter aims to study the use of Hybridization of intelligent techniques in the areas of bioinformatics and computational molecular biology. These areas have risen from the needs of biologists to utilize and help interpret the vast amounts of data that are constantly being gathered in genomic research. Also describes the kind of methods which were developed by the research community in order to search, classify and mine different available biological databases and simulate biological experiments. This chapter also presents the hybridization of intelligent systems involving neural networks, fuzzy systems, neuro-fuzzy system, rough set theory, swam intelligence and genetic algorithm. The key idea was to demonstrate the evolution of intelligence in bioinformatics. The developed hybridization of intelligent techniques was applied to the real world applications. The hybridization of intelligent systems performs better than the individual approaches. Hence these approaches might be extremely useful for hardware implementations.

INTRODUCTION

Intelligent systems which may offer humanlike experience like domain information, uncertain reasoning, and adaptation to a noisy and time-varying environment, are vital in endeavor sensible computing issues. Hybrid intelligent system could be a promising area of modern machine intelligence. An elementary stimulant to the investigations of hybrid intelligent systems is that the awareness within the educational

DOI: 10.4018/978-1-5225-1776-4.ch014

communities that combined approaches may be necessary if the remaining robust issues in hybrid intelligent system are to be resolved. The combination of various learning and adaptation techniques are used to overcome individual limitations and to attain cooperative effects through the hybridization or fusion. Hybridization of intelligent systems are becoming a very important problem solving methodology poignant researchers and practitioners in areas starting from science, technology, business and commerce. In recent years, these techniques have contributed to an oversized range of recent intelligent system designs. Most of those hybridization approaches follow an ad hoc design methodology justified by success in certain application domains. Hybridization of various intelligent systems is an innovative approach to construct computationally intelligent systems consisting of artificial neural network, fuzzy inference systems, rough set, approximate reasoning and bio inspire algorithms like evolutionary computation, swarm intelligence and Ant colony technologies so on.

Bioinformatics and machine biology are involved with the utilization of computation to know biological phenomena and to acquire and exploit biological information, increasingly large scale information.

Strategies from bioinformatics and computational biology are increasingly used to augment or leverage ancient laboratory and observation-based biology. These strategies became crucial in biology as a result of recent changes in our ability and determination to acquire massive large biological information sets, and as a result of the ever present, in biological insights that have come back from the exploitation of these information. This transformation from a data-poor to a data-rich field began with DNA sequence data, however is currently occurring in several different areas of biology. DNA sequence analysis (Sathish et al, 2012) is attractive to computer scientists because of the availability of digital information. However, there are many challenges related to this area such as:

1. Parsing a genome in order to find the segments of DNA sequence with various biological roles.
2. DNA sequence analysis (Sathish et al, 2012) is engaging to computer scientists owing to the provision of digital data.

However, there are several challenges associated with this area such as:

1. Parsing a genome so as to search out the segments of DNA sequence with numerous biological roles. As an example, encryption proteins and RNA, and dominant once and wherever those molecules are expressed.
2. Aligning the sequences in DNA sequences so as to check for similarity or variations.

The alignment procedure may be performed locally (DNA fragment level) or globally (genome level). DNA arrays or DNA Chips were projected in the late Eighties by many researchers severally for the aim of DNA sequencing and therefore the technology was named DNA sequencing by Hybridization.

Hybridization of intelligent system is a well-established paradigm with current systems having many of the characteristics of biological computers and capable of performing a variety of tasks that are difficult to do using conventional techniques. It is a methodology involving adaptive mechanisms and/or an ability to learn that facilitate intelligent behavior in complex and changing environments, such that the system is perceived to possess one or more attributes of reason, such as generalization, discovery, association and abstraction. The objective of this article is to present to the hybridization of intelligent system and bioinformatics research communities some of the state-of-the-art in hybridization of intelligent system applications to bioinformatics and motivate research in new trend-setting directions. In this chapter, we present an overview of the hybridization of intelligent system techniques in bioinformatics. We will show how hybridization of intelligent system techniques including neural networks, restricted Boltzmann machine, deep belief network, fuzzy logic, rough sets, evolutionary algorithms (EA), genetic algorithms (GA), swarm intelligence, artificial immune systems and support vector machines, could be successfully employed to tackle various problems such as gene expression clustering and classification, protein sequence classification, gene selection, DNA fragment assembly, multiple sequence alignment, and protein function prediction and its structure. We discuss some representative methods to provide inspiring examples to illustrate how hybridization of intelligent system can be utilized to address these problems and how bioinformatics data can be characterized by hybridization of intelligent system. Challenges to be addressed and future directions of research are also presented and an extensive bibliography is included.

Hybrid Intelligent Systems

In Recent years several adaptive hybrid soft computing frameworks have been developed for model expertise, decision support, image and video segmentation techniques, process control, mechatronics, robotics and complicated automation tasks(Abraham, 2005; Hiwarkar et al, 2013). Many of these approaches use a combination of different knowledge representation schemes, decision making models and learning strategies to solve a computational task. This integration aims at overcoming the limitations of individual techniques through hybridization or the fusion of various techniques. These ideas have led to the emergence of several different kinds of intelligent system architectures (Kandel et al, 1992). The well-known fact is that intelligent systems can provide human-like expertise such as domain knowledge, uncertain reasoning, and adaptation to a noisy and time-varying environment. These are important in tackling practical computing problems. Experience has shown that it is crucial, in the design of hybrid systems, to focus primarily on the integration and interaction of different techniques rather than to merge different methods to create ever-new techniques. Techniques already well understood should be applied to solve specific domain problems within the system. Their weaknesses must be addressed by combining them with complementary methods. Nevertheless, developing hybrid intelligent systems is an open-ended concept rather than restricting to a few technologies. That is, it is evolving those relevant techniques together with the important advances in other new computing methods.

Hybrid intelligence system is a well-established paradigm (Abraham, 2005), where new theories with a sound biological understanding have been evolving. The current experimental systems have many of the characteristics of biological computers (Hu et al, 2011) and are beginning to be built to perform a variety of tasks that are difficult or impossible to do with conventional computers. Computational intelligence is not an easy task. In the current research pursuits, this area is heterogeneous with a combination of technologies like neural networks, fuzzy systems, evolutionary computation, swarm intelligence, and probabilistic reasoning. The recent trends are to integrate different components to take advantage of complementary features and to develop a synergistic system. Hybrid architectures like neuro-fuzzy systems, evolutionary-fuzzy systems, evolutionary neural networks, evolutionary neuro-fuzzy systems, rough-neural, rough-fuzzy, etc. are widely applied for real world problem solving. The integration of different learning and adaptation techniques, to overcome individual limitations and achieve synergetic effects through hybridization or fusion of these techniques, has in recent years contributed to an emergence of large number of new superior class of intelligence known as Hybrid Intelligence.

The various hybrid intelligent architectures are broadly classified into four different categories based on the system's overall architecture namely stand-alone, transformational, hierarchical hybrid and integrated hybrid systems (Abraham, 2005; Medsker, 1995). Fused architectures are the first true form of integrated intelligent systems. They include systems which combine different techniques into one single computational model. They share data structures and knowledge representations. Another approach is to put the various techniques side-by-side and focus on their interaction in a problem-solving task. This method can allow integration of alternative techniques and exploiting their mutuality. The benefits of integrated models include robustness, improved performance and increased problem-solving capabilities. Finally, fully integrated models can provide a full range of capabilities such as adaptation, generalization, noise tolerance and justification.

The Hybrid Intelligent System shown in Figure 1 is implemented using traditional hardware components and software techniques. Neural networks, Fuzzy systems, bio inspired algorithms and machine learning algorithms are well established and useful technologies in hybrid intelligent systems. Many development tools and environments are available for each and few environments are now specifically coming for the development of hybrid neural networks and bio inspired algorithms.

Bioinformatics

For the past few decades there is a massive growth in biological information. Such information coming in the form of genomes, protein sequences, gene expression data and so on. This information has led to the absolute need for effective and efficient computational tools to store, analyze and interpret the multifaceted data. Bioinformatics and computational biology both involve the use of techniques including applied mathematics, informatics, statistics, computer science, artificial intelligence, chemistry, and biochemistry to solve biological problems on the molecular level. Often research in computational biology overlaps with systems biology. The major research efforts in this field include sequence alignment, gene finding, genome assembly, protein structure alignment, protein structure prediction, prediction of

Figure 1. Intelligent technologies used in hybrid intelligent technologies

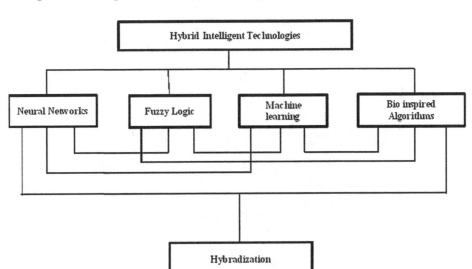

gene expression and protein-protein interactions, and the modelling of evolution. In other words, the bioinformatics can be described as an application of computational methods to make biological discoveries. Here the ultimate attempt of this field is to develop new insights into the science of life as well as creating a global perspective, from which the unifying principles of biology can be derived.

The term bioinformatics was introduced by Paulien Hogeweg in 1979. Bioinformatics is for the study of informatics processes in biotic systems. In the late 1980s it was most importantly used in genomics and genetics, particularly in those areas of genomics involving large-scale DNA sequencing. Bioinformatics can also be defined as the application of computer technology to the management of biological information. Bioinformatics involves the manipulation, searching and data mining of DNA sequence data. The development of techniques to store and search DNA sequences have widely used in the advances like computer science, especially string searching algorithms, machine learning and database theory. In other applications such as text editors, even simple algorithms for this problem usually suffice, because these algorithms exhibit worst case behaviour due to their small number of distinct characters in DNA sequencing. The Data sets representing entire genomes' are worth of DNA sequences, such as those that are produced by the Human Genome Project. These are difficult to use without observations that are labelled the locations of genes and regulatory elements on each chromosome. Regions of DNA sequence that have the characteristic patterns associated with protein or RNA coding genes can be identified by gene finding algorithms. These algorithms allow researchers to predict the presence of particular gene products in an organism even before they have been inaccessible experimentally. The primary goal of bioinformatics is to increase the understanding of biological processes. Figure 2 and Figure 3 represent general human cell structure and DNA structure respectively (Google).

Figure 2. An overview of a typical human cell
(Courtesy of Google)

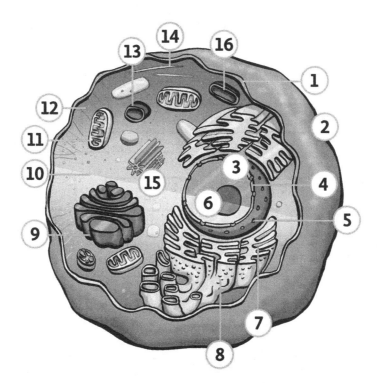

Figure 3. An overview of a DNA
Source: Google

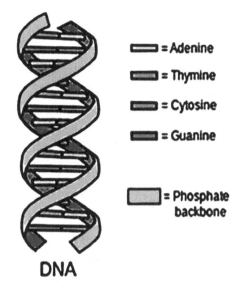

1. **Plasma Membrane (or Cell Surface Membrane):** A phospholipid bilayer that contains choles-terol and proteins. It is a fluid layer that surrounds the cell and enables it to communicate with its neighbours and detect and respond to changes in the environment. It also acts as a physical barrier, controlling what can enter and exit the cell.
2. **Extracellular Matrix:** The material in between cells that holds tissues together, usually made of scaffolding proteins such as collagen. Important for cell-to-cell signalling.
3. **Nucleus:** The information centre of the eukaryotic cell, where the DNA is stored, replicated and copied into messenger RNA (mRNA) through transcription.
4. **Nuclear Envelope:** Double membrane that separates the contents of the nucleus from the cytoplasm.
5. **Nuclear Pores:** Gaps in the nuclear envelope that allow substances to move in and out of the nucleus.
6. **Nucleolus:** Part of the nucleus that produces ribosomes.
7. **Endoplasmic Reticulum (ER):** An extensive network of membranes. Rough ER is studded with ribosomes and is a site where proteins are made, folded and moved to the Golgi apparatus. The roles of smooth ER include lipid and steroid synthesis and drug detoxification.
8. **Ribosomes:** Molecular machines, built from ribosomal RNA (rRNA) and protein, that make new proteins from mRNA through a process called translation. They are found as 'free ribosomes' in the cytoplasm and bound to the rough endoplasmic reticulum.
9. **Golgi Apparatus:** One of the wondrously complex membrane systems in the cytoplasm, which modifies, packages and directs newly made proteins to where they are needed.
10. **Cytoplasm:** Everything in the cell outside the nucleus; a viscous aqueous fluid (cytosol) contain-ing water, proteins, other organic and inorganic molecules, and organelles. This is the site of many biochemical reactions.
11. **Mitochondria (Singular: Mitochondrion):** Rod-shaped bodies in the cytoplasm that supply chemical energy to the rest of the cell. They are surrounded by a double membrane (envelope).

12. **Microfilaments:** These are made from repeating actin subunits. Responsible for cell movement and changes in shape, and make muscle contraction possible. The thinnest component of the cytoskeleton.

13. **Vacuole:** Internal bags, surrounded by a membrane, which cells use for storing food or waste.

14. **Microtubules:** Small, tubular assemblies of protein, made from repeating tubulin subunits, which help maintain the cell's internal structure and move organelles and cytoplasm using molecular motors. Part of the cytoskeleton.

15. **Centrioles:** A pair of organelles that organises microtubules into spindles on which chromosomes are separated when cells divide.

16. **Lysosomes:** Membrane-bound organelles that are the cell's rubbish disposal and recycling units; contain hydrolytic (digestive) enzymes.

Hybrid Intelligence in Bioinformatics

Hybrid intelligence system methods are now being applied to problems in molecular biology and bioinformatics. Few of them are application of neural networks, evolutionary algorithms, and clustering algorithms to DNA microarray experimental data analysis (Tuan et al, 2005) identifying and classifying gene functional patterns from the heterogeneous nonlinear time series micro array experiments. There are no hard and fast rules dictating which algorithms can be combined to give a hybrid, but as will be seen later, evolutionary methods are often favoured because they can be hybridized in a number of ways. Hybrid intelligence system can be used many ways in molecular biology research. The use of Hybrid intelligence system is for storing DNA sequence information and constructing the correct DNA sequences. Once genome sequences are stored and accessed, there is a need for comparative genome analysis across databases so that the organization and evolution of genomes can be studied. Such analyses may uncover relationships between model organisms, crops, domestic animals and humans. Visualization tools and Hybrid techniques are required to conduct these analyses. Many areas of biology rely on images for communicating their results. Hybrid tools and techniques are required for searching, describing, manipulating and analysing for features within these images. There is a need for Hybrid intelligence system that can predict the structure of a protein from its sequence of amino acids (Keedwell et al, *2005*).

Probabilistic Approaches

Probability is the branch of mathematics which is concerned with the likelihood that events will occur. This is also of particular importance to bioinformaticians as the interactions and reactions that occur in biological processes can often only be characterized by probability theory (Keedwell et al, *2005*). Probability theory can also be useful in determining the underlying structure of datasets or sequences. Bayes' Theorem, with a slight reinterpretation, allows reasoning of the form:

$$p(cause \mid effect) = [p(effect \mid cause) \times p(cause)] / p(effect)$$

Some of the earliest applications of Bayes' Theorem in artificial intelligence were in fact in the medical domain where knowledge of conditional probabilities concerning causal relationships in medicine were used to derive probabilities of diagnosis. Bayes' Theorem has found several other applications in artificial intelligence and a good source of material on Bayes' Theorem and such applications. Several links to work on Bayesian networks in computational molecular biology and bioinformatics can be found, including references to recent papers on Bayesian approaches to gene expression analysis and biological data integration. Such models, in addition to being used for determining the probability of a sequence being accepted or produced, can also be used for *learning*.

A typical problem in bioinformatics may consist of trying to identify the Markov Model that best fits the four short DNA sequences: AGTC, CAGC, TGC and AGC (note that the sequences need not be the same length). A more powerful Markov model than the simple one described above is required to handle this problem. Markov Models can be considered a true bioinformatics technique, with several applications in profile family characterization in homology search, gene finding.

Nearest Neighbor

SIMPA is an extended nearest neighbour method for predicting the secondary structures of proteins. Consider three short amino acid sequences and their known secondary structure conformations:

```
h h s s s s c          h s c c c c          h h s s c c
A T S L V F W          S T S G V V W          S C N G A F W
```

A hypothetical similarity matrix that identifies the relationships between individual amino acids based on various properties, such as charge, aromaticity and hydrophobicity SIMPA is an extended nearest neighbour technique since it essentially attributes a conformation to a residue in the new sample on the basis of nearest neighbour residues with known conformations in homologues. Nearest neighbour approaches generally work well when there are a few attributes and many samples (Keedwell et al, *2005*).

Decision Trees

Identification trees are probably the most widely applied intelligent technique. They have been used for a huge variety of applications in commerce and academia ranging from the sciences, through engineering to financial, commercial and risk-based applications. In fact, identification trees are most used in everyday life as they are often applied in the retail sector where they are used to determine and predict our shopping and spending habits. Practically every store has a loyalty scheme of some description, and the terabytes of data that are collected about customers contain salient information about how and why we behave in the way that we do. To discover this information from the data, it must be mined to reveal the interesting features and remove those that are irrelevant or noisy. It is in this process of data mining that identification trees have become most well known. Their success in these commercial areas can also benefit the field of bioinformatics as many problems in this field consist of large amounts of noisy data. As with many techniques, the success of the identification tree approach is due partly to its simplicity and efficiency. In terms of its execution, the identification tree is an algorithm that has few complex steps. The following section describes the notion of classification and the method that the identification tree uses to classify data taken from many domains, including those with very large databases such as bioinformatics (Keedwell et al, *2005*).

The prediction of secondary and tertiary protein structure from the underlying amino acid combinations is one of the most pressing problems in bioinformatics. The secondary structure determines how groups of amino acids form sub-structures such as the coil, helix or extended strand. The correct derivation of the secondary structure provides vital information as to the tertiary structure and therefore the function of the protein. There are various methods which can be used to predict secondary structure, including the DSSP approach which uses hydrogen bond patterns as predictors, the DEFINE algorithm which uses the distance between C-alpha atoms, and the P-CURVE method which finds regularities along a helicoidal axis. As might be expected, these disparate approaches do not necessarily agree with each other when given the same problem and this can create problems for researchers. The work by Selbig, Mevissen, and Lengauer (1999) develops the decision tree as a method for achieving consensus between these approaches by creating a dataset of predicted structures from a number of prediction methods for the same dataset. The correct structures for each of the protein elements in the training set is known, and this forms the classification for each of the records in the training set. The identification tree therefore creates rules of the form

```
IF Method1 = Helix AND Method2
         = Helix THEN Consensus = Helix
```

In this way, the identification tree can choose when it is prudent to use certain structure prediction methods and when to use others. This methodology ensures that prediction performance is at worst the same as the best prediction method, and in the best case should perform better than that.

Neural Networks

Neural networks have been developed as generalizations of mathematical models of biological nervous systems. In a simplified mathematical model of the neuron, synapses are represented by connection weights that modulate the effect of the associated input signals, and the nonlinear characteristic exhibited by neurons is represented by a transfer function (Strapasson et al, 2014). The neuron impulse is computed as the weighted sum of the input signals, transformed by the transfer function. The learning capability of an artificial neuron is achieved by adjusting the weights in accordance to the chosen learning algorithm. Most applications of neural networks fall into the following categories:

- Prediction,
- Classification,
- Data Association, and
- Data Conceptualization.

The behaviour of the neural network depends largely on the interaction between the different neurons. The basic architecture consists of three types of neuron layers: input, hidden, and output layers. In feed-forward networks the signal flow is from input to output units strictly in a feed-forward direction. The data processing can extend over multiple units, but no feedback connections are present, that is, connections extending from outputs of units to inputs of units in the same layer or previous layers. Recurrent networks contain feedback connections. Contrary to feed-forward networks, the dynamical properties of such networks are important. In some cases, the activation values of the units undergo a relaxation process such that the network will evolve to a stable state in which these activations do not change any more.

The famous algorithm to train a feed forward network is the back-propagation algorithm. The development phase of this algorithm is generally categorized into two specific branches, heuristic approach towards the back-propagation training optimization. Here the considerable research on ad-hoc modification of parameter is observed. This kind of algorithm is designed with variable learning rate where variations in learning rate depend on the performance index. With modification of several other parameters that are responsible to converge the algorithm also leads hinge on performance index of the algorithm. Another algorithm is the hybrid method of optimizing back propagation training. This hybridization is caused by incorporating two nature inspired methods. Genetic algorithm based back-propagation is one kind of hybridized method to optimize the neural network training. This method is slow in convergence because of its large search space. Population based approach is used in this algorithm, so this use fitness value of solution as a performance index. The other methods effectively applied to back-propagation for training optimization are artificial bee colony algorithm and particle swarm optimizations. In some cases it is observed that the hybridization method implemented in the back-propagation, training optimization updates the weight of each node in a neural network by implementing the standard optimization algorithm in training phase, and hence artificial bee colony method is indirectly responsible to modify the weight and bias of each neuron in optimization phase of back-propagation training. This may cause lot computation power, memory storage. As the non-linear least square method is involved in the optimization process for which this hybridization is not derivative-free, and so, there is a risk of tackling local minimum.

Classification and Dimensionality Reduction

Gene expression data is currently one of the hottest topics in bioinformatics and it looks set to be one of the most revealing analysis techniques used in biology. Microarray data is notoriously difficult to process, even after a successful experiment it is noisy and requires many statistical transformations to yield correct and normalized gene expression values. However, even once this is achieved, there are further difficulties in analysing this type of data, namely that the number of genes is so large that typical analysis methods can be completely ineffective in the face of the 'curse of dimensionality'. Gene expression experiments are often used to attempt to distinguish between diseased and normal individuals, or to distinguish between two types of a disease by solely using the expression values of genes taken from those individuals. This is of primary importance to medical science as a number of different cancers are very difficult to diagnose (Keedwell et al, *2005*). Single layer neural networks (or perceptrons) can be used as an effective method for reducing the number of genes to be considered in an analysis.

Identifying Protein Subcellular Location

Protein function is often closely related to its location within the cell and work undertaken by Cai, Liu, and Chou (2009) used a Kohonen neural network to predict where a protein was located, based on its amino acid make-up. As the number of discovered proteins increases, determining the subcellular location of such a protein can provide important clues as to its structure and function in the cell. The study was short, but it neatly showed the effectiveness of the Kohonen network in tasks such as this.

Designing Neural Networks for Bioinformatics

When designing NN for bioinformatics applications, there are common designing issues that needs to be addressed. Preprocessing of data involves feature presentation and input encoding. This is an important element which determines the performance and the information entered to the NN. In order to get the full benefit of the NN, the designer has to represent prior knowledge about sequence structure and functions. This allows the extraction of salient features in the given sequence. When considering proteins, they are made up of a combination of 20 amino acids and have various lengths. A sequence can be written using a defined alphabet set. But in biology these letters carry more information such as residue structure and function. It is well known that the Training/Test data set (Molecular sequence) Neural network model (Architecture, Learning algorithm, parameters) Feature representation and input encoding Classification/ Structure prediction Output encoding Pre-processing Post-processing amino acid side chain exhibits a large number of chemical and physical properties. The interaction of these side chains with one another and with the backbone of the protein determines its structure and function. Several important properties of amino acids like hydrophobisity, surface area, chemical properties, polarity, volume, secondary structure propensity, etc. have been encoded as prior knowledge when using as the input for NN (Tuan et al, 2005).

Some amino acids play more than one structural or functional role; therefore their properties need to be assessed considering the entire protein. These are known as protein context features which can be local or global. In order to represent these features; hydrophobic moment, hydrophobicity profile or amino acid frequency can be calculated and encoded to use in NN(Tuan et al, 2005). Another type of feature is the protein evolutionary feature which is normally represented in substitution matrices like PAM or BLOSUM. This information can be encoded and used in the NN. Neural network model has also a promising technique in DNA sequence analysis because this approach might well emerge the important aspects of intelligence that was not captured by symbolic and statistical methods. Neural networks have also been actively used in many bioinformatics applications such as DNA sequence prediction, protein secondary structure prediction, gene expression profile classification, and analysis of gene expression patterns.

The neural network system is designed to classify unknown sequences into predefined known classes. In other words, it maps molecular sequences (input) into sequence classes (output) as shown in the figure 1. The sequence strings are first converted by an n-gram sequence encoding method into input vectors of real numbers. Long n-gram input vectors can be compressed by a SVD method to reduce vector size dimension. The neural network then maps the sequence vectors into predefined classes according to sequence information embedded in the neural interconnections after network training. The neural networks used are three-layered, feed-forward networks that employ back-propagation or counter-propagation learning algorithms. The sequence encoding schema, used in the preprocessor, converts molecular sequences i.e., character strings into input vectors of the neural network classifier.

Back-Propagation (BP) Neural Networks

The BP neural networks used in the figure 1 were three layered, feed-forward networks. The size of the input layer (i.e., number of input units) was dictated by the sequence encoding schema chosen. As shown above, the size was m^n with n-gram encoding; and the size was the reduced dimension (k), if the n-gram vector is compressed by SVD. The output layer size was determined by the number of classes represented

Figure 4. A neural network system for molecular sequence classification

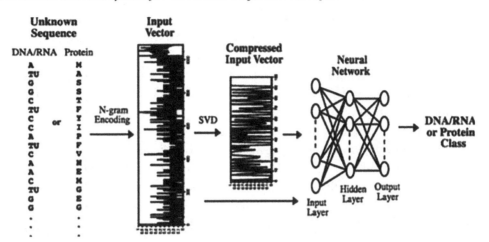

in the network, with each output unit representing one class. The hidden size was determined heuristically, usually a number between input and output sizes. Here the networks were trained using weight matrices initialized with random weights ranging from -0:3 to 0.3. Other network parameters included the learning factor of 0.3, momentum term of 0.2, a constant bias term of -1:0, and error threshold of 0.01. To speed up the BP training, a pedagogical pattern selection strategy was used to favor the selection of patterns producing high error values to the disadvantage of the patterns already mastered by the network. The pedagogical method achieved similar classification accuracy with only one third of training time, when compared to the commonly used uniform strategy (Wu et al, 1994).

Fuzzy Systems

Fuzzy Inference Systems (FISs) are generally composed of fuzzy rules, membership functions and a form of fuzzification / defuzzification. Any of these elements could be updated or modified to tune the FIS. The rules of the FIS follow the Mamdani method which is in the form of IF-THEN. A conventional fuzzy inference system makes use of a model of the expert who is in a position to specify the most important properties of the process. Expert knowledge is often the main source for designing fuzzy inference systems (Strapasson et al, 2014; Tuan et al, 2005). According to the performance measure of the problem environment, the membership functions, the knowledge base and the inference mechanism are to be adapted. Several research works continue to explore the adaptation of fuzzy inference systems. These include the adaptation of membership functions, rule bases and the aggregation operators. The input of Fuzzy membership is in the range of [0, 1]. The issue with the fuzzy systems is the uncertainty. Uncertainty is dealt with the probability and random variables.

Any biological sequence is a sequence of characters drawn from an alphabet. For DNA sequence, character set is {A, C, G, T}, character set is {A, R, N, D, C, Q, E, G, H, I, L, K, M, F, P, S, T, W, Y, V}. A sequence alignment is the process of identifying one-to-one correspondence among subunits of sequences. The biological sequences representing DNA, RNA, or proteins can also be seen as sentences derived from a formal grammar. DNA, RNA, or protein sequences are viewed as strings or formal languages on alphabets of four nucleotides A, C, G, T or A, C, G, U or 20 amino acids, respectively, a grammatical representation and an inference method can be applied to this problem for biological sequence analyses. The development of grammatical system is done by increasing number of yielded DNA and RNA and especially the stochastic grammars such as hidden Markov models (HMMs), are developed to predict the biological sequences.

Multiple sequences are also developed by fuzzy systems. Here the main objective is assembling data by approximate matching using fuzzy logic(Nasser et al). To achieve this several matches of two sub sequences are provided. Then based on the criterion specified by the user best match is picked. To demonstrate the use of fuzzy rules the dynamic programming is the most commonly used method. Fuzzy Logic is also used in approximate string matching using distance measures. In the application area of building genomes from sub sequences of nucleotides However, very little work has been done. This process becomes computationally expensive, because multiple comparisons have to be performed for each possible string pair. The accuracy of any fuzzy matching system is partially determined by the error model used. An accurate system reflects the mechanism responsible for the variations in the match. Therefore a flexible error metrics is desired that is generic for any fuzzy matching. Current sequencing methods tend to reject sequences that do not match with a high degree of similarity. This can lead to large amounts of data being rejected by algorithms that otherwise may be important in deriving a genomic sequence and the metabolic characteristics of such a sequence.

Neuro-Fuzzy

Over the last several years DNA analysis has seen tremendous development (Teodorescu, 2003). DNA includes huge amounts of data that must be interpreted. The operations in DNA analysis include the cognition of the type of organism to which the gene belongs, when the genetic material comes from different sources, the identification of specific segments in the DNA sequence, sections that represent the genes and the identification of the proteins the genes code, the prediction of the genes expression (Georgiou et al, 2013). Because of the huge amount of data in the genetic material, the operations must be automated. The first two tasks above are somewhat similar and may use similar tools. They are both essentially related to the identification of patterns in the genetic code. Several tools have been developed for these purposes, including Hidden Markov Models (HMM), statistical methods, and fuzzy and neural models that inherently reflect the statistics.

A novel approach is presented that deals with the genetic sequence prediction, based on its decomposition into four distance series and on the use of neuro-fuzzy predictors in a hierarchical pattern identification system. The syntagma gene prediction has several meanings, relating to the object of prediction and depending on the research context. One meaning is to predict the splice sites; another is to determine what the gene expression result would be.

Pattern Detection

The prediction task is approached from a fresh point of view and proposes a new type of gene prediction with a view to classify the genetic sequences, to determine the right splice sites and to classify the information they carry. For this purpose, pre-process the original, raw base sequence and first produce four base sequences, as A, C, G, and T respectively. The pre-processing steps are:

Step 1: Original base sequence

```
.....AGCATGCCA.......
```

Step 2: A-base sequence

```
. _A_ _ _A _ A _ _ _ A _.
C-base sequence
. _C_ _ C _ _ _ C _ _ C _.
G-base sequence
. _G _ _G _ _ G _ G _.
T-base sequence
._T_ _ _T_ _T_ _ _T_.
```

Details of Pre-Processing the Base Sequence

X-Base Sequence:._X_ _ _X_X_ →Low-pass filtering → Conditioning & normalization → Neuro-fuzzy predictor

X-Base Sequence:._X_ _ _X_X_ →High-pass filtering → Conditioning & normalization → Neuro-fuzzy predictor

Each of the four series is then pre-processed to derive the "trend" and the "fast varying" components. The low-pass filtering is performed by a 3-step MA filter, accordingto the formula:

$$y\big[n\big] = (x[n-1] + x[n] + x[n+1])3 \,. \tag{1}$$

To generate the final prediction, each of the two components is then predicted and the results are summed. The neuro-fuzzy system used in the prediction needs normalized values in the [-1, 1] interval, so, the distance series are also normalized according to

$$y[n] = 2.[x[n] - (x_{max} + x_{min}) / 2] / (x_{max} - x_{min}) \tag{2}$$

where $(x_{max} - x_{min})$ are the maximal and minimal elements in the series. To improve the prediction outcome, the exceptional events like the large distances and far out of the spreading range, if any, may first be eliminated. The predictor is a multi-fuzzy system network with inputs represented by the delayed samples, and the fuzzy cells are Sugeno type 0, with Gauss input membership functions. The formula $\mu(x) = \exp(-(x-a)^2 / \sigma)$ represents the membership degree μ of the input $x; a$ is the center and σ is the spreading of the input membership function. The input-output function of the neuro-fuzzy predictor is

$$y = \sum_{k=0}^{M} w_k \left[\sum_{l=1}^{N} \beta_{kl} . e^{\frac{(x_{n-k}-a_{kl})^2}{\sigma}} \bigg/ \sum_{l=1}^{N} e^{\frac{(x_{n-k}-a_{kl})^2}{\sigma}} \right] \tag{3}$$

Here M is the number of Sugeno fuzzy systems, N is the number of membership functions for each Sugeno fuzzy system, index $k = 0 \div M$, index $l = 1 \div N$, a_{kl} are the centers of the Gauss type membership functions, β_{kl} is the single tones and w_k *are* the weights.

The individual predictors may be of any type, but fuzzy neural network predictors have several advantages. The rational for using this type of predictor is based on the complexity of the input-output function of this predictor. The class predictor is given by the input-output function of the predicting system. This function is a ratio with sums of exponentials at the nominator and the denominator. Therefore, the capabilities of this type of predictor are higher than for simple fuzzy logic systems with triangular or other piecewise input and output membership functions. Also, the characteristic function of this predictor is more intricate than the sum of sigmoid functions, as in the case of a single layer perceptron. Compared to a MLP using sigmoid neurons, which has the characteristic function represented essentially by composed sigmoid functions, the characteristic function of this predictor is still more intricate, because it is a ratio of non-linear functions. Compared to a MLP using Gaussian RBF neurons, which has the characteristic function represented essentially by composed Gaussian RBF functions, the characteristic function of this predictor is still more intricate, for similar reasons as above. Regarding the number of parameters involved, showing the adaptation flexibility of the predictor, this predictor is similar to the one predictor that is discussed above. Moreover, by adding belief degrees to the rules of the TSK-fuzzy systems representing the neurons, the number of parameters is easily increased. Regarding the possibility to use various learning algorithms, including gradient type algorithms, gradient algorithms are easily adaptable to this predictor, in contrast to classic fuzzy systems with piecewise input and output membership functions, which do not accept classic gradient algorithms, because of the non-derivability of the function. The training set of the predictors refer to the adaptation of several sets of parameters, namely of the weights w_i output singletons, and parameters of the input membership functions, a_k, σ_k. The system described here uses implicit information, which means the information is included in the predictors, after appropriate training of data.

Particle Swarm Optimization

Particle swarm optimization (PSO) is a population-based stochastic optimization technique developed by (Kennedy et al, 1995). In the past years, PSO has been successfully applied in both the computer science and engineering. In the original PSO algorithm, each particle knows its best value (pbest), velocity, and position. Additionally, each particle knows the best value in its swarm (gbest). A particle modifies its position based on its current velocity and position. The velocity of each particle is calculated using

$$v_i^{k+1} = \omega v_i^k + c_1 r_1 (pbest_i - s_i^k) + c_2 r_2 (gbest^k - s_i^k) \tag{4}$$

where v_i^k, v_i^{k+1}, and s_i^k are the velocity vector, modified velocity vector, and positioning vector of particle i at generation k, respectively. $pbest_i$ is the best position found by particle i and $gbest^k$ is the best position found by the particle's in the entire swarm. c_1 and c_2 are the cognitive and social coefficients, respectively. These used to bias the search of a particle towards *pbest* and the best experience of the whole swarm *gbest*. ω is called inertia weight, which is employed to control the impact of the previous history of velocities on the current velocity of each particle. The ω parameter regulates the trade-off between the exploration and exploitation ability of the swarm. Large values of ω facilitate exploration and searching new areas, while small values of ω navigate the particles to more refined search. The velocity equation includes two different random parameters, represented by a variable, r_1 and r_2, sampled from uniform distribution between 0 and 1, i.e., $\_ U(0;1)^n$. The modified position vector, s_i^{k+1}, is obtained using

$$s_i^{k+1} = s_i^k + v_i^{k+1} \tag{5}$$

To allow the PSO algorithm to operate in binary problem spaces, the binary particle swarm optimization (BinPSO) algorithm has been introduced. It uses the concept of velocity converted to a probability that a bit takes on a value of 1 or 0. In Binary PSO, Equation 4 of updating a velocity remains unchanged, but Equation 5 of updating a position is re-defined by the following rule:

$$s_y^{k+1} = 0 \, if \, r3 \geq s(v_{ij}^{k+1})$$

$$1 \, if \, r3 \geq s(v_{ij}^{k+1}) \tag{6}$$

With $r3 \_ U(0;1)$ and s is the sigmoid function used to transform the velocity to a probability constrained to the interval [0:0; 1:0] as follows:

$$s(v_{ij}^{k+1}) = \frac{1}{1 + e^{-v_{ij}^{k+1}}} \tag{7}$$

In order to design a set of DNA sequences based on Bin PSO, a sequence is represented as binary vector, where A, C, G, and T, are encoded as 002, 012, 102, and 112, respectively. In order to find a set of n-sequences with $l - mer$ length, a search space of $(nXlX2)$ dimensions is required.

Rough Sets

The rough sets theory is a mathematical tool that can be used for processing and analyzing of inexact, uncertain, and vague datasets. Practically, rough set theory has been applied to the number of application domains such as medical diagnosis, engineering reliability, expert systems, empirical study of materials data, machine diagnosis, business failure prediction, activity-based travel modelling, travel demand analysis, solving linear programming and data mining.

In many applications classification of objects in the databases or information systems sources are based on rough set theory (Nordin et al, 2010). The technique in rough set theory has the ability to search objects in a multi-dimensional data space and determine the relationship between objects and its attributes. Therefore, rough sets theory method is useful for exploring DNA sequence patterns and ease to construct genomic sequence classification. Classification will help to improve DNA sequence similarity search performance.

An automatic classification and reduction of DNA sequence databases has become important for effective sequence similarity search problem. Both clustered and reduction dataset of DNA sequences can extract the sequence features that affect the similarity search performance. By constructing a relation between attributes, rough sets theory can eliminate the 'redundant' DNA sequences from a particular class of sequences.

The new mechanism to transform DNA sequence data into knowledge scheme is a fundamental task in homology searching process and other computational biology applications as well. The association of knowledge features into DNA sequence in the database makes the user to perceive the dataset in two-dimension and ease to formulate a classification based on some conditions. The rough sets theory provides a series of logic reasoning procedures to accomplish the formal transformation a set of sequence data into knowledge structure. It is based on the original data and does not need any external information such as static statistical parameters, therefore assumption requirements can be minimized and allowing the data to represent itself. Moreover, one of the advantages of rough sets theory is that programs implementing its methods may easily run on parallel computers.

Genetic Algorithms

A good deal of the success of the GA is based on its flexibility. The problem-independent nature of the GA is the reason it can be applied to so many domains without alteration of the algorithm itself. This problem independence is established through the use of a *chromosome* and *objective function*. The chromosome is a genetic representation of a single solution to the problem and its performance at solving that problem is evaluated by a function which relates the chromosome variables to the problem at hand. With bioinformatics being a relatively new science and genetic algorithms only finding popularity relatively recently, the number of applications of GAs to bioinformatics currently remains relatively small. A large portion of the work has concentrated on using GAs to process microarray data. Specifically, they have been used to 'reverse engineer' regulatory networks and also, in conjunction with neural networks, as a method of data mining gene expression data. The following sections describe the most current research into these topics (Keedwell et al, *2005*).

Reverse Engineering of Regulatory Networks

Gene expression or microarray data allows biologists unprecedented access to the workings of genes within a cell, and the expression values of many thousands of genes can be recorded simultaneously for a particular sample. This process can be applied repeatedly for a sample placed under stimuli, which then yields a trace of genetic activity for a number of genes over time. It is this trace and the interactions between genes over time which is of interest for a number of reasons. Another objective which is factored into the fitness function is that sparse matrices are required in this problem to remove the possibility of all genes having an effect on all other genes. A measure of the number of zero weights present in the chromosome is added so an individual solution fitness is based both on its solution and number of zeroes in the solution. The advantages of this process are that the GA uses gene regulatory network modelling and also makes use of the reverse engineering process to a certain extent. The results on artificial data are encouraging and suggest that the GA should be able to extract matrix-type gene regulatory networks from this type of data (Keedwell et al, *2005*).

Multiple Sequence Alignment

The task of comparing sequences is at the heart of bioinformatics. By comparing sequences of nucleic or amino acids, the similarity in structure between genes and proteins can be discovered. The ability to match two or more sequences according to the elements within those sequences is an extremely important one in bioinformatics as it allows new genes and proteins to be accurately compared with existing ones for which the structure and function are known. The comparison of these sequences can help in the discovery of similar genes across species and also help determine the phylogeny of those species. Genetic algorithms in particular have been successful in this domain, pioneered by the Sequence Alignment Genetic Algorithm (SAGA) (Keedwell et al, *2005*).

Genetic Programming Drug Discovery

This Drug discovery as a whole field is a 'hot topic' in bioinformatics as currently it takes a new drug compound between 10 and 12 years to get into mainstream usage. Much of this time is often spent testing the drug firstly in the laboratory and then later in organisms and animals. Whilst the laboratory testing stage of a drug is relatively cheap, it can also be frustrating as there will exist many compounds with similar properties that have to be tested. Pharmaceutical companies are constantly searching for automated methods to help them target their search in these initial stages. Langdon and Barrett showed that GP can be successfully used for determining the bioavailability of a set of compounds based on their structure. The bioavailability of a compound is one of a set of metrics and is designed to determine how well a drug will pass through the various bodily systems and, on reaching the active site, how much effect the drug will have. If taken orally, a drug is subject to many bodily mechanisms such as digestion, metabolism and excretion. Some compounds will be relatively unaffected by these processes whereas others will have practically no effect on their target because they have been broken down by these bodily functions before they can reach the target site (Keedwell et al, *2005*).

Genetic Programming for Functional Genomics

This research used some of the first reliable gene expression data taken from a set of experiments with a species of yeast, *Saccharomyces cerevisiae*. The data itself was collected in a time-course experiment where the yeast was exposed to a set of 79 different experimental conditions, including heat shock, reducing shock and sporulation (for more on this see Eisen *et al.*, 1998). Each of the genes had been assigned one of six classes – 'Histone', 'Proteasome', 'TCA Pathway', 'Respiratory Complex', 'Ribosome' and As mentioned previously, CA have found application in a number of science and engineering areas since their inception in the late 1940s. In recent times, though, they have been used in a variety of biological simulation applications where the notion is that the complex dynamical systems present in much of biology can be simplified and understood by applying discrete systems such as CA. What follows is a description of some of the most interesting work in this area using CA (Keedwell et al, *2005*).

Cellular Automata Model for Enzyme Kinetics

Cellular automata (CA) approach to model the reaction between an enzyme and substrate in water. The CA consists of a 110∗110 grid of cells (12 100 cells), each of which can take the values of one molecule of E (enzyme), S (substrate), P (product) and W(water); 69 per cent of the automaton was covered with water and 31 per cent was deemed to be space. When any ingredients are added, they are assumed to replace the water part of the automaton and therefore this cavity ratio was maintained. Each cell has a probability associated with its movement and its interaction with other molecules in the automaton. An enzyme molecule could react with the substrate, product and water molecules, but not with another enzyme. Molecules were determined to be adjacent according to a von Neumann neighbourhood, where the four adjoining cells (up, down, left and right) were determined to be interacting.

Sequencing the DNA molecule involves massive computation and reconstructing the original DNA sequence is an optimization search hence application of genetic algorithms (GAs) is quite justified in the DNA sequencing problem (Blazewicz et al, 2002; Douzono et al, 1998; Majje et a.l,2004). The performance of a GA in DNA sequencing through oligonucleotide hybridization method. They have constructed special kind of crossover and mutation operators. They also introduced special scoring scheme for detecting the repetitive units. The experiments showed construction of sub-sequences of length $N+1$ from hybridized probes of length N actually available from the biochemical experiment. For short sequences, the simulation produced near exact results. For example, when the length of the original DNA sequence is 12 and the number of probes (length $N=4$) is 8. Then the number of sub-sequences of length $N+1$ (i.e. 5) constructed is 7. Here the GA population size was equal to 20 and the number of generations needed was 8. The final sequence after the eighth generation was almost identical with the original sequence except that its length was 11. The GA solution suffered from early convergence of the population especially when the length of original DNA sequence reaches 22.

A hybrid genetic algorithm (HGA) solving the DNA sequencing problem with negative and positive errors was proposed (Blazewicz et al, 2002). Their method supplements a standard genetic approach by using greedy improvement. The size of oligos was set to 10. The lengths of original sequences were between 109 and 509, and lengths of oligos were 10. The experiments showed that HGA generated near optimal solutions, and similarities with original sequences were very high. For instances of cardinality 100, the HGA returned only original sequences. Similarity less than 100% was caused because of missing information about the last nucleotides in sequences. Even for large spectra of lengths reaching 500 with many errors of both types, the HGA composed sometimes-optimal sequences. The obtained solutions have the qualities from 98.3 to 100% of optimal values on the average. The applications of AI in DNA sequencing have been very fruitful in generating effective and competitive solutions. However, there is still a constant need for more advanced and sophisticated tools in computational molecular biology.

Neural-Genetic Algorithm for Analysing Gene Expression Data

The problems of gene expression analysis have been described in some detail previously in this book, so a short explanation will suffice here. Currently there are two types of microarray experimentation that are attracting interest in the literature: temporal analysis involves exploring the interactions of genes over time, and classification analysis attempts to discover those genes or groups of genes that are associated with a class value. The two analyses are driven by the goals of the experiment and the type of microarray experiments that have been performed by the biologist. This, in turn, dictates the type and scale of microarray data which is available for bioinformaticians to use. For determining gene – gene interactions in epidemiology, the probability of developing the disease is reflected by using a table of penetrance function values. All of the data in the experiment requires that at least two of the polymorphisms interacted with each other to create increased susceptibility to disease. None of the effects seen in the data could be determined solely by a main effect of one of the genes (Keedwell et al, *2005*).

GA-Knn Method

The genetic algorithm k nearest neighbour (GA-Knn) method makes use of a cosine-based Knn classification. This is slightly different from normal Knn classification in that each of the features in the data-set is weighted and the final classification predicted by the system for a new example is the sum of those weights. In this two-class example, a positive sum indicates one class and a negative sum, another. These weights are optimized by the GA by using the first N (where N is the number of features) elements of the chromosome to evolve the weights for classification. This constitutes the first section of optimization for the technique. The second N points of the chromosome are involved with changing the point of origin for the Knn classifier. When predicting the class of a new solution, the Knn classifier compute the 'nearest neighbour' based on the angle created when plotting a solution in two feature dimensions, between the origin and the test point. The similarity between the angle of the test point and points in the training set determines the nearest neighbour classification. However, if the origin is changed in one or both axes, a more optimal set of neighbours could be found. This constitutes the second part of the chromosome, where N points determine the offset of the origin for each feature. Finally, the k value for the Knn classifier is determined as a single integer at the end of the chromosome. Therefore the GA is involved with optimizing the weight, offset and k values for the cosine-based Knn classifier (Keedwell et al, *2005*) [25].

CONCLUSION

This chapter discusses the use of Hybridization of intelligent techniques in the areas of bioinformatics and computational molecular biology. These areas have risen from the needs of biologists to utilize and help interpret the vast amounts of data that are constantly being gathered in genomic research. This chapter also described the methods like hybridization of intelligent systems involving neural networks, fuzzy systems, neuro-fuzzy system, rough set theory, swam intelligence, genetic algorithms used in bioinformatics which were developed by the research community in order to search, classify and mine different available biological databases and simulate biological experiments with and without errors.

REFERENCES

Abraham, A. (2005). Hybrid intelligent systems: Evolving intelligence in hierarchical layers. Springer.

Blazewicz, J., Kasprzak, M., & Kuroczycki, W. (2002). Hybrid genetic algorithm for DNA sequencing with errors. *Journal of Heuristics*, *8*(5), 495–502. doi:10.1023/A:1016589707123

Courtesy, G. (n.d.). Retrieved from: https://bigpictureeducation.com/finding-your-way-around-cell

Douzono, H., Hara, S., & Noguchi, Y. (1998). An application of genetic algorithm to DNA sequencing by oligonucleotide hybridization. *Proceedings of the IEEE international joint symposia on intelligence and systems*. doi:10.1109/IJSIS.1998.685424

Georgiou, D. N., Karakasidis, T. E., & Megaritis, A. C. (2013). A short survey on genetic sequences, chous pseudo amino acid composition and its combination with fuzzy set theory. *The Open Bioinformatics Journal, 7*(1), 41–48. doi:10.2174/1875036201307010041

Hiwarkar, T. A., & Sridhar Iyer, R. (2013). New applications of soft computing, artificial intelligence, fuzzy logic & genetic algorithm in bioinformatics. *International Journal of Computer Science and Mobile Computing, 2*(5), 202–207.

Hu, Y.J., Hu, Y.H., & Ke, J.B. (2011). The modified DNA identification classification on fuzzy relation. *Applied Mechanics and Materials, 48-49*, 1275-1281.

Kandel, A., & Langholz, G. (Eds.). (1992). *Hybrid architectures for intelligent systems*. CRC Press.

Keedwell, E., & Narayanan, A. (2005). *Intelligent bioinformatics*. John Wiley & Sons, Ltd. doi:10.1002/0470015721

Kennedy, J., & Eberhart, R. C. (1995). Particle swarm optimization. *Proc. of IEEE International Conference on Neural Networks*. doi:10.1109/ICNN.1995.488968

Liu, H.-C., Yih, J.-M., Lin, W.-C., & Liu, T.-S. (2009). Fuzzy c-means algorithm based on pso and maha-lanobis distances. *International Journal of Innovative Computing, Information, & Control, 5*(12b), 5033–5040.

Majje, C., & Sahoo, G. (2004). *DNA sequencing by oligonucleotide hybridization: A genetic algorithm approach, proceedings of the international conference on genetics and evolutionary computation*. Seattle, WA: GECCO.

Medsker, L. R. (1995). *Hybrid intelligent systems*. Kluwer Academic Publishers.

Nasser, S., Vert, G. L., & Nicolescu, M. (n.d.). *Multiple sequence alignment using fuzzy logic*. Retrieved from: http://www.cse.unr.edu/~bioinfor/papers/cibcb-mfgs.pdf

Nordin, M., Rahman, A., Yazid, M., Saman, M., Ahmad, A., & Tap, O. A. M. (2010). Applying rough set theory for DNA sequence database classification and reduction. *International Journal of Biomedical Soft Computing and Human Sciences, 16*(2), 115–124.

Sathish, K. S., & Duraipandian, N. (2012). An effective identification of species from DNA sequence: A classification technique by integrating DM and ANN. *International Journal of Advanced Computer Science and Applications, 3*(8).

Strapasson, R. A., Woiciechowski, A. L., Letti, L. A. J., & Soccol, C. R. (2014). *Some applications of artificial intelligence on biotechnology*. Academic Press.

Teodorescu, H-N. (2003). Genetics, gene prediction, and neuro-fuzzy systems – The context and a program proposal. *FSAI, 9*(1–3), 15–22.

Tuan, D., Beck, P. D., & Crane, D. (2005). *Fuzzy clustering of stochastic models for molecular phylogenetics*. Academic Press.

Wakasa, Y., Tanaka, K., Akashi, T., & Nishimura, Y. (2010). Pso-based simultaneous tuning method for pid controllers and dead-zone compensators and its application to ultrasonic motors. *International Journal of Innovative Computing, Information, & Control, 6*(10), 4593–4604.

Wu, C. H., & Shivakumar, S. (1994). Back-propagation and counterpropagation neural networks for phylogenetic classification of ribosomal RNA sequences. *Nucleic Acids Research, 22*(20), 4291–4299. doi:10.1093/nar/22.20.4291 PMID:7937158

ADDITIONAL READING

Cao, J., & Xiong, L. (2014). Protein sequence classification with improved extreme learning machine algorithms, BioMed Research International. *Article ID, 103054*, 12.

Wu, C. H., Berry, M., Shivakumar, S., & McLarty, J. (1995). Neural networks for full-scale protein sequence classification: Sequence encoding with singular value decomposition. *Machine Learning, 21*(1-2), 177–193. doi:10.1007/BF00993384

Chapter 15
Adaptive Clustering Techniques and Their Applications

Deepthi P. Hudedagaddi
VIT University, India

B. K. Tripathy
VIT University, India

ABSTRACT

With the increasing volume of data, developing techniques to handle it has become the need of the hour. One such efficient technique is clustering. Data clustering is under vigorous development. The goal of clustering is to determine the intrinsic grouping in a set of unlabeled data. Several data clustering algorithms have been developed in this regard. Data is uncertain and vague. Hence uncertain and hybrid based clustering algorithms like fuzzy c means, intuitionistic fuzzy c means, rough c means, rough intuitionistic fuzzy c means are being used. However, with the application and nature of data, clustering algorithms which adapt to the need are being used. These are nothing but the variations in existing techniques to match a particular scenario. The area of adaptive clustering algorithms is unexplored to a very large extent and hence has a large scope of research. Adaptive clustering algorithms are useful in areas where the situations keep on changing. Some of the adaptive fuzzy c means clustering algorithms are detailed in this chapter.

Learning to read clusters is not something your eyes do naturally. It takes constant practice.
-Bill Cosby

INTRODUCTION

Human beings have been applying clustering techniques subconsciously as per the situation and hence adapting to the environment. This has helped him in understanding or solving real world problems. Clustering is the unsupervised classification of patterns (observations, data items or feature vectors) into groups (or clusters) (Bijuraj, 1993). A cluster is a collection of data objects that are similar to one

DOI: 10.4018/978-1-5225-1776-4.ch015

another within the same cluster and are dissimilar to the objects in other clusters(Han,2011). Clustering is a challenging field of research in which its potential applications pose their own special requirements and they are

- Scalability.
- Ability to deal with different types of attributes.
- Discovery of clusters with arbitrary shape.
- Minimal requirements for domain knowledge to determine input parameters.
- Ability to deal noisy data.
- Incremental clustering and insensitivity to the order of input records.
- High dimensionality.
- Constraint-based clustering.
- Interpretability and usability.

Different Clustering Methods

Clustering methods can be classified into the following categories

- Partitioning Method.
- Hierarchical Method.
- Density-based Method.
- Grid-Based Method.
- Model-Based Method.
- Constraint-based Method.

Partitioning Method

Suppose we are given a database of 'n' objects and the partitioning method constructs 'k' partition of data. Each partition will represent a cluster and k $\leq$ n. It means that it will classify the data into k groups, which satisfy the following requirements

- Each group contains at least one object.
- Each object must belong to exactly one group.

For a given number of partitions (say k), the partitioning method will create an initial partitioning. Then it uses the iterative relocation technique to improve the partitioning by moving objects from one group to other.

Hierarchical Methods

This method creates a hierarchical decomposition of the given set of data objects. We can classify hierarchical methods on the basis of how the hierarchical decomposition is formed. There are two approaches here

- Agglomerative Approach.
- Divisive Approach.

Agglomerative Approach

This approach is also known as the bottom-up approach. In this, we start with each object forming a separate group. It keeps on merging the objects or groups that are close to one another. It keep on doing so until all of the groups are merged into one or until the termination condition holds.

Divisive Approach

This approach is also known as the top-down approach. In this, we start with all of the objects in the same cluster. In the continuous iteration, a cluster is split up into smaller clusters. It is down until each object in one cluster or the termination condition holds. This method is rigid, i.e., once a merging or splitting is done, it can never be undone.

Approaches to Improve Quality of Hierarchical Clustering

Here are the two approaches that are used to improve the quality of hierarchical clustering –

Perform careful analysis of object linkages at each hierarchical partitioning.

Integrate hierarchical agglomeration by first using a hierarchical agglomerative algorithm to group objects into micro-clusters, and then performing macro-clustering on the micro-clusters.

Density-Based Method

This method is based on the notion of density. The basic idea is to continue growing the given cluster as long as the density in the neighborhood exceeds some threshold, i.e., for each data point within a given cluster, the radius of a given cluster has to contain at least a minimum number of points.

Grid-Based Method

In this, the objects together form a grid. The object space is quantized into finite number of cells that form a grid structure. The major advantage of this method is fast processing time. It is dependent only on the number of cells in each dimension in the quantized space.

Model-Based Methods

In this method, a model is hypothesized for each cluster to find the best fit of data for a given model. This method locates the clusters by clustering the density function. It reflects spatial distribution of the data points. This method also provides a way to automatically determine the number of clusters based on standard statistics, taking outlier or noise into account. It therefore yields robust clustering methods.

Constraint-Based Method

In this method, the clustering is performed by the incorporation of user or application-oriented constraints. A constraint refers to the user expectation or the properties of desired clustering results. Constraints provide us with an interactive way of communication with the clustering process. Constraints can be specified by the user or the application requirement(Jain,1999).

Applications of Data Clustering

Clustering is useful in several exploratory pattern analysis, grouping, decision making, and machine learning situations including data mining, document retrieval, image segmentation and pattern classification. Some of the real world applications of clustering methods are as follows:

- **Marketing:** Finding groups of customers with similar behavior given a large database of customer data containing their properties and past buying records;
- **Biology:** Classification of plants and animals given their features;
- **Libraries:** Book ordering;
- **Insurance:** Identifying groups of motor insurance policy holders with a high average claim cost; identifying frauds;
- **City-Planning:** Identifying groups of houses according to their house type, value and geographical location;
- **Earthquake Studies:** Clustering observed earthquake epicenters to identify dangerous zones; and
- **WWW:** Document classification; clustering weblog data to discover groups of similar access patterns.

ADAPTIVE CLUSTERING APPROACH AND METHODS

Adaptive clustering uses external feedback to improve cluster quality; past experience serves to speed up execution time. It supports the reuse of clustering by memorizing what worked well in the past. It has the capability of exploring multiple paths in parallel when searching for good clusters.

Differences between Adaptive Clustering and Other Clustering Techniques

Most clustering techniques assume a well defined distinction between the clusters so that each pattern can only belong to one cluster at a time. This supposition can neglect the natural ability of objects existing in multiple clusters. For this reason and with the aid of fuzzy logic, fuzzy clustering can be employed to overcome this weakness. The membership of a pattern in a given cluster can vary between 0 and 1. In adaptive clustering, one single pattern can have different degrees of membership in various clusters. A pattern belongs to the cluster where it has the highest membership value. Adaptive clustering algorithms model this kind of data.

Different Adaptive Clustering Algorithms Developed So Far

Several clustering algorithms like FCM, RCM, IFCM, RFCM and RIFCM have been developed till date, which have been further extended to both kernel based and possibilistic versions such that their efficiency is increased and these can be applied to more number of applications. FCM with respect to adaptive clustering has already been developed. Although Fuzzy C-means algorithm shows strengths in many areas, it lacks the abilityto determine the appropriate number of clusters for pattern classification and requires theuser to define the correct number of clusters. Many applications of clustering like patternrecognition or intrusive data classification require the clustering algorithm to decide on the proper number of clusters, as the correct number of classes is not a priori known.

APPLICATIONS OF ADAPTIVE CLUSTERING

Adaptive clustering algorithms as of now have been applied for image segmentation techniques whereas these can also be applied for pattern recognition, data mining and document retrieval.

Case Study 1: Cluster Number Adaptive FCM Algorithm for Image Segmentation

Image segmentation is one of the most difficult and challenging problems in a number of applications, and this low-level vision task is also one of the most crucial steps toward computer vision (Bagherjei-ran,2005; Geweniger, 2013; Kamal, 1996; Teppola, 1999). Classically, image segmentation is defined as an inverse problem which consists of achieving a compact region-based description of the image by decomposing it into meaningful or spatially multiple coherent regions, which are homogeneous with respect to one or more characteristics such as color or texture. From an implementation point of view, image segmentation can be treated as a clustering problem where the features describing a pixel correspond to a pattern, and each image region corresponds to a cluster. Therefore, many clustering algorithms, especially the fuzzy c-means algorithm (FCM), have widely been used to solve the segmentation problem. The success of this chiefly attributes to introduction of fuzziness for the belongingness of each image pixel, which makes the clustering methods able to retain more information from the original image than the crisp or hard segmentation methods (e.g., K-means). The advantages of the FCM are its simply straightforward implementation, fairly robust behavior, applicability to vector data and the ability of uncertainty data modeling.

Nevertheless, most of the FCM-based image segmentation algorithms assume a prior knowledge of the cluster number. While in many practical situations, the appropriate cluster number is unknown or impossible to determine, which has unneglectable impacts on the image segmentation quality. Therefore, how to automatically and accurately determine the cluster number to avoid over-segmentation or under-segmentation becomes a challenging task. To solve this problem, (Li,2010) developed an algorithm called automatic modified FCM cluster segmentation algorithm (AMFCM) that can automatically determine the optimal cluster number. However, the AMFCM algorithm requires iterative execution of the standard FCM with cluster number from 2 to maximum possible value until predefined optimal validation criteria is met, which will extremely increase the computational complexity. To improve the performance, an ant colony fuzzy c-means hybrid algorithm (AFHA) was proposed to overcome the FCM's sensitiveness to the initialization condition of cluster number in (Tan,2011). Essentially, the AFHA incorporated the ant system algorithm (AS) to the FCM to improve the compactness of the clustering results in the color feature space. However, its efficiency is still low due to computational complexity of the AS algorithm. To increase the AFHA's efficiency, an improved ant colony fuzzy c-means hybrid algorithm (IAFHA) was also introduced in (Tellaeche, 2011; Weinland, 2011). Specifically, the IAFHA added an ant sub-sampling-based method to modify the AFHA. Although the IAFHA's efficiency had been increased, it still suffers from high computational complexity. (Tan,2011) presented a histogram thresholding fuzzy c-means hybrid (HTFCM) approach which applied the histogram thresholding technique to estimate optimal cluster number in an image. Then, the standard FCM algorithm was utilized to improve the compactness of the clusters forming those uniform regions based on color feature. The above algorithms assume that the input images mostly contain uniformly colored objects, which is typically not true for natural images. In fact, the texture feature reflecting the spatial patterns of pixels at image block level has strong links with the human perception and in many practical scenarios the color-alone feature at pixel level is not sufficiently robust to accurately describe the image content (Blasco 2007; Yu 2010). The cluster number estimation of those FCM-based algorithms, such as AFHA, IAFHA and HTFCM, only considers color feature at pixel level which means that they could not determine accurate cluster number for complex images, especially natural images.

Here much emphasis is on cluster number adaptive segmentation for computer vision applications. To overcome the aforementioned disadvantages of those FCM-based segmentation algorithms, a novel cluster number estimation module is added prior to the standard FCM algorithm to obtain optimal cluster number. In this estimation module, instead of processing at pixel level, the image is first divided into many small rectangular image blocks. The Gray Level Co-occurrence Matrix (GLCM) feature extraction is completed and optimal cluster number at the block level is estimated. The novel estimation module is based on the coarse image, which makes its execution time very fast. Moreover, in contrast to the initialization module of the IAFHA and HTFCM algorithm only employing color feature, GLCM texture feature allows accurate cluster number estimation. Then, in the FCM clustering, in contrast to the algorithms like FCM_S (Ilea, 2005; Ahmed, 2002; Chen, 2004)that incorporate local spatial information in the objective function, Gabor filters (Chen, 2004; Clausi, 2005)are utilized for feature extraction for each pixel. The parameters of the Gabor filter are specified by the frequency, the orientation of the sinusoid, and the scale of the Gaussian function. Therefore, the feature vector extracted for each pixel implicitly incorporate local orientations and spatial frequencies information. The developed algorithm considers spatial information in the feature space instead of in the objective function, which makes the objective function quite simple. A large number of experiments were carried out to assess performance of the proposed segmentation algorithm, and experimental results have demonstrated that the CNAFCM algorithm could accurately determine cluster number and obtain better segmentation results (produce meaningful segmentation effectively) than those approaches such as AMFCM, AFHA, IAFHA and HTFCM.

The Standard FCM Algorithm

The FCM clustering algorithm was first introduced by Dunn (1973) and later extended by Bezdek (1984). This was based on Zadeh's fuzzy sets (Zadeh,1996). This algorithm has been used as one of the popular clustering techniques for image segmentation in pattern recognition. In the FCM, each image pixel has certain membership degree associated with each cluster centroid. These membership degrees have values in the range, indicating the strength of the association between that pixel and a particular cluster centroid. The FCM algorithm attempts to partition every image pixel into a collection of the fuzzy cluster centroids by minimizing the weighted sum of squared error objective function $Jm(U,C)$ (Bezdek, 2013; Reddi, 1984):subject to

$$\sum_{j=1}^{K} u_{ji}^{m} = 1, \ 1 < j < K \tag{2}$$

$$\sum_{i=1}^{N} u_{ji}^{m} < N, \ 1 \leq i \leq N \tag{3}$$

$$\sum_{i=1}^{N} \sum_{j=1}^{K} u_{ji}^{m} = N$$

where N is the total number of pixels in image, is the membership degree of ith pixel $c$to jth clustercentroid c_j, m is the exponential weight of membership degree which controls the fuzziness of the resulting partition, and $d_{ji} = \left\| x_i - c_j \right\|$ is the distance between x_i and c_j. It needs to be pointed out that the standard FCM algorithm would degenerate to hard c-means algorithm when $u_{ji} \in [0,1]$ and m=1.Let $U_i = (u_{1i}, u_{2i}, \ldots, u_{Ki})^T$be the set of membership degree ofx_i associated with each cluster centroids, then $U = (U_1, U_2, \ldots, U_N)$ is the membership matrix and $C = (c_1, c_2, \ldots, c_K)$is the set of cluster centroids.

The degree of compactness and uniformity of the cluster centroids greatly depend on the objective function of the FCM. In general, a smaller objective function of the FCM indicates a more compact and uniform cluster centroid set. Unfortunately, there is no close form solution to produce minimization of the objective function. To achieve the optimization of the objective function, an iteration process must be carried out by the FCM algorithm. The key steps of the FCM can be described in Table 1.

$$u_{ji} = \frac{1}{\sum_{k=1}^{K} \left(d_{ji} / d_{ki} \right)^{2/m-1}} \tag{3}$$

where $1 \leq j \leq K$ and $1 \leq i \leq N$. It should be noted that if $d_{ji}=0$ then $u_{ji}=1$ and set others membership degrees of this pixel to 0.

Table 1. The standard FCM algorithm

Steps	Algorithm
1	Randomly initialise fuzzy partition matrix C^0, set the iteration terminating threshold ϵ to a small number in range [0,1] and number of iteration q to 0.
2	Calculate U^q according to C^q with Equation 3
3	Compute C^{q+1} according to U^q with Equation 4.
4	Update U^{q+1} according to C^{q+1} with Equation 3.
5	Compare U^{q+1} with U^q if $\left\| U^{q+1} - U^q \right\| \leq \varepsilon$ stop iteration. Else q=q+1,repeat steps 3,4 until $\left\| U^{q+1} - U^q \right\| \leq \varepsilon$. Finally optimal membership matrix U is obtained. Based on U, final segmentation image is obtained.

$$c_j = \frac{\sum_{i=1}^{N} u_{ji}^m X_i}{\sum_{i=1}^{N} u_{ji}^m} \tag{4}$$

where $1 \leq j \leq K$ and X_i is the multidimensional feature vector of ith pixel.

Developed Algorithm

Basic Idea

As previously mentioned, the performance of the FCM-based segmentation algorithm is often affected by the cluster number which is manually initialized. Therefore, the core idea of this algorithm is to obtain a solution to overcome the FCM's sensitiveness to the cluster number by introducing a novel cluster number estimation module before the standard FCM clustering. The most important object in this estimation module is to accurately determine cluster number with minimal computation cost. Conventionally, feature vectors used in the FCM segmentation algorithm are usually extracted for each pixel. For an image with a typical size, hundreds of thousands of vector data will have to be processed if we directly do clustering at the pixel level. In fact, the notion of the region is well defined at the level of our visual perception, and the human eyes and brain are able to delineate regions that exhibit common spatial patterns, i.e., texture. In a certain sense, an image can be roughly considered as the composition of several different regions. Therefore, the texture is useful for identifying object or region of interest, and the task to estimate the region number can be performed at the coarse level, i.e., the image block level. In our work, the image block is a rectangular region widths = r x r pixels and the standard FCM algorithm is employed to determine the optimal cluster number within the range of 2 to predefined maximum search value, which best suits a given image according to cluster validity index. Specifically, the Gray Level Co-occurrence Matrix (GLCM) texture feature of each block is used to estimate all possible homogenous regions in the image. Compared with the large number of pixels in an image, block-level representation of an image usually has only several hundreds of blocks. Therefore, the feature extraction at the block level is utilized instead of the pixel level resulting in reducing the computational cost of the clustering. The method provides an attractive way to estimate cluster number with minimal time cost in comparison with those approaches such as AMFCM, AFHA, IAFHA and HTFCM.

GLCM Texture Feature Extraction

Gray Level Co-occurrence Matrix was proposed in Haralick (1973) and is widely used for texture analysis. It estimates the second-order statistics related to image properties by considering the spatial relationship of pixels (Tan & Isa, 2011; Ilea & Whelan, 2005). The GLCM is created by calculating how often a pixel with the intensity value i occurs in a specific spatial relationship to a pixel with the value j. The major two steps are as follow:

The first step is to determine co-occurring probabilities of all pairwise combinations of quantized grey levels (i,j) in the fixed-size spatial window given two parameters which are the distance between the pixel pair and their angular relation θ. θ. is quantized in four directions ($0°, 45°, 90°$ and $135°$) For rectangular r x r image segment I(x,y), gray levels i and j, the non-normalized GLCM 's P_{ij}'s are defined by:

Table 2. θ values for different directions

θ	0^0	45^0	90^0	135^0
θ_0	0	1	1	1
θ_1	1	1	0	-1

$$P_{ij}\left(\theta, d\right) = \sum_{x=1}^{r} \sum_{y=1}^{r} C\left\{\left(I\left(x,y\right) = i\right) \wedge I\left(x \pm d\theta_0, y \pm d\theta_1\right) = j\right\} \tag{5}$$

where C{ }=1 if the argument is true and C{ }=0 otherwise. The $\pm$ and $\mp$ signs in Equation (5) mean that each pixel pair is counted twice: once forward and once backward to make the GLCM diagonal symmetric. For each direction, θ_0 and θ_1 are shown in Table 2.

The second step is to apply statistics to the co-occurring probabilities. Statistics that identify some structural aspect of the arrangement of the co-occurring probabilities, which reflect some qualitative characteristic of the local image texture like smoothness or roughness, are applied to generate the texture feature vector. In this work five GLCM texture features, which are used to form a feature vector: 1) contrast (CON); 2) homogeneity (HOM); 3) angular second moment (ASM); 4) entropy (ENT); 5) correlation (COR) are calaculated. Finally, each image block generates a feature vector to describe its texture characteristics.

Cluster Validity

For an unsupervised clustering scheme, the segmentation quality depends on determining the cluster number according to cluster validity index. Several well-known cluster validity indexes for evaluation of the cluster quality could be adopted. One of the most fundamental indexes is the mean squared error (MSE) that could be described as follows:

$$MSE = \frac{1}{N} \sum_{j=1}^{K} \sum_{i \varepsilon S_j} \left\| x_j - c_j \right\| \tag{6}$$

It is quite clear from the concept of MSE that when cluster number is fixed, a good clustering algorithm should always generate results with small distortion. In other words, cluster centroids should be placed in such a way that they reduce the distances to data pieces as much as possible.

Another commonly used index is Bezdek's evaluation function V_{PC} (Bezdek,1974), which is defined as follows:

$$V_{PC} = \sum_{i=1}^{N} \sum_{j=1}^{K} u_{ji}^2 \Big/ N \tag{7}$$

This cluster validity evaluation function essentially measures the fuzziness of a clustering result. A smaller value V_{PC} indicates a fuzzier result. On the contrary, larger the value, the better the clustering result. For a crisp partition, achieves maximum value of 1.

A more recent validity evaluation index is the Xie-Beni function, which is defined as follows:

$$V_{XB} = \frac{\sum_{i=1}^{N} \sum_{j=1}^{K} u_{ji}^2 \left\| x_i - c_j \right\|}{N \min_{\forall \neq k} \left\| c_j - c_k \right\|}$$ (8)

According to research by Pal (1995) and Xie (1991), V_{XB} should decrease monotonically when K is close to N. When V_{XB} shows a smaller value, the result is presumably a better partition. In this work, the determination of the cluster number K_{opt} is carried out with combination of cluster validity index V_{PC} and V_{XB}.

FCM Clustering

Although the cluster number is appropriately estimated in cluster number estimation module, there still exists one problem to be resolved. For those FCM-based image segmentation algorithms such as AFHA, IAFHA and HTFCM, cluster assignment is based solely on the distribution of pixel attributes in the color feature space, and the spatial distribution of pixels in an image is not taken into consideration. The application of the FCM to complex scenes such as natural images will lead to over-segmented results since the spatial continuity is not enforced during the space partitioning process. The main approach is to introduce spatial constraints into the objective function of the FCM. Although the introduction of local spatial information to the corresponding objective functions solves the problem to some extent, it will also make the objective function more complicated at the same time, resulting in low efficiency.

The feature of a pixel depends on a number of factors, such as the spatial relation among pixels, their scale, and orientation. In contrast to many conventional approaches, the spatial connectivity information between pixels is extracted and embedded in the multi-dimensional feature vector of each pixel. Specifically, Gabor filters with a large number of oriented band pass filters with adaptive filter size, orientation, frequency and phase have been used to extract spatial features of the pixels. As such, spatial connectivity is guaranteed since a definite spatial connectivity constraint has been imposed during feature extraction. Gabor feature extraction details can be referred in Dunn (1973) and Bezdek (2013). Briefly, the standard FCM algorithm is used to cluster Gabor feature vectors of the pixels with the cluster number which has been estimated by the cluster number estimation module already, and then each pixel is labeled with its corresponding cluster to form final compact regions.

Pseudo Code

The outline of the developed segmentation algorithm, which automatically clusters the pixels of an image into different homogeneous regions when the cluster number is not known beforehand, is illustrated in Table 3.

Experiments Performed on Natural Images

In this subsection, the segmentation results are evaluated visually. Although synthetic test images are best for verifying the possibilities and limits of an algorithm, segmentation of natural images is a reliable

Table 3. Cluster Number Adaptive Fuzzy C Means Algorithm

Steps	Algorithm
1	Maximal search cluster number K_{max}. Divide input image into blocks with height r and width r'.
2	Extract GLSM feature vector f_B^j for each image block and obtain data set $F_B = \left\{ f_B^j \right\}_{j=1}^{Z}$, where Z is the number of data blocks.
3	For k=1 to K_{max} Do standard FCM on F_B and compute cluster validity measure on V_{PC}^k and V_{XB}^k . End for
4	With V_{PC}^k and V_{XB}^k determine optimal cluster number K_{opt}
5	Apply Gabor filter too extract texture feature f_p^i for each pixel and obtain set for
6	Perform standard FCM on F_p again with cluster number K_{opt}

evaluation indicator for image segmentation algorithms. In order to evaluate CNAFCM's performance with respect to the identification of perceptual homogenous regions, we have tested the proposed CNAFCM segmentation algorithm on a large number of complex natural images databases which includes images characterized by non-uniform textures, fuzzy borders, and low image contrast. For instance, we have compared our segmentation results with the ones by the color-based segmentation algorithm, i.e., HTFCM. From the result, it can be observed that the different regions produced by CNAFCM algorithm are well segmented and the shape of objects in the images is preserved. However, it can also be observed that the regions produced by HTFCM algorithm are mixed together (caused by over-estimation of regions), which cannot preserve the shape of objects in the images and makes it difficult to detect and recognize objects in the high-level vision applications.

Case Study 2: AFCM Algorithm for Image Segmentation in Presence of Intensity Inhomogenities (Pham,1999)

In this section, an algorithm with a new objective function for obtaining fuzzy segmentations of images with intensity inhomogeneities is explained. The objective function contains a multiplier field term

Figure 1. Natural image from the Berkeley database and segmentation results. a) original image; b) using proposed algorithm; b) using HTFCM algorithm

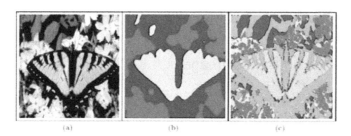

(a) (b) (c)

that models the brightness variation caused by the inhomogeneities. A method based on nonparametric density estimation for automatically obtaining initial values for the centroids needed in the algorithm is explained. Finally, a multigrid technique is described for the solution of the multiplier field during each iteration of the algorithm.

Objective Function

The standard FCM algorithm for scalar data seeks the membership functions u_k and the centroids v_k, such that the following objective function is minimized:

$$J_{FCM} = \sum_{ij} \sum_{k=1}^{C} u_k(i,j)^q \left\| y(i,j) - v_k \right\|^2 \tag{9}$$

where $u_k(i,j)$ is the membership value at pixel location (i, j) for class k such that $\sum_{k=1}^{C} u_k(i,j) = 1$ and $y(i, j)$ is the observed image intensity at location (i, j), and v_k is the centroid of class k. The total number of classes C is assumed to be known k. The parameter q is a weighting exponent on each fuzzy membership and determines the amount of 'fuzziness' of the resulting classification. For simplicity, it is assumed that $q = 2$ and the norm operator $\|. \|$ represents the standard Euclidean distance.

The FCM objective function is minimized when high membership values are assigned to pixels whose intensities are close to the centroid for its particular class, and low membership values are assigned where the pixel data is far from the centroid. An advantage of FCM is that if a pixel is corrupted by noise, then the segmentation will be changed by some fractional amount while in hard segmentations, the entire classification may change. Furthermore, in the segmentation of medical images, fuzzy membership functions can be used as an indicator of partial volume averaging, which occurs where multiple classes are present in a single pixel.

Performing a Picard iteration through the two necessary conditions leads to an iterative scheme for minimizing the objective function(Dunn, 1973; Bezdek, 1980). This is the standard FCM algorithm. The resulting fuzzy segmentation can be converted to a hard or crisp segmentation by assigning each pixel solely to the class that has the highest membership value for that pixel. This is known as a maximum membership segmentation.

A new objective function which preserves the advantages of FCM while being applicable to images with intensity inhomogeneities is introduced. In this approach, we model the brightness variation by multiplying the centroids by some unknown multiplier field $m(i, j)$, which is assumed to be smooth and slowly varying with respect to i and j. The two-dimensional AFCM algorithm seeks to minimize the following objective function with respect to u, v and m

$$J_{AFCM} = \sum_{ij} \sum_{k=1}^{C} u_k(i,j)^q \left\| y(i,j) - v_k \right\|^2 + \lambda_1 \sum_{ij} \left(\left(D_i * m(i,j)^2 \right) + D_j * m(i,j)^2 \right)$$

$$+ \lambda_2 \sum_{ij} \left(\left(D_{ii} * m(i,j)^2 \right) + 2(D_{ij} * * m(i,j))^2 \right) + (D_{jj} * * m(i,j))^2$$

where D_i and D_j are the standard forward finite difference operators (like derivatives in the continuous domain) along the rows and columns, and $D_{ii}=D_i*D_i$, $D_{ij}=D_i*D_j$ and $D_{jj}=D_j*D_j$ are second-order finite differences. The symbols * and ** denote the one- and two-dimensional discrete convolution operators, respectively. The last two terms, controlled by the parameters λ_1 and λ_2, are first and second order regularization terms operating on the multiplier field (not the membership functions).

The first order regularization term penalizes multiplier fields that have a large amount of variation. The second order term also penalizes, to a certain degree, the amount of variation but especially penalizes multiplier fields that possess discontinuities. If we assume that the membership functions $u_k(i, j)$ and the centroids v_k are known, then the multiplier field that minimizes J_{AFCM} is the field that makes the centroids close to the data, but is also slowly varying (as governed by the 1st and 2nd regularization terms) and smooth (as governed by the 2nd order term). Without the regularization terms, a multiplier field could always be found that would set the objective function to zero. The parameters λ_1 and λ_2 should be set according to the magnitude and the smoothness of the intensity inhomogeneity in the image. For an image with little or no inhomogeneities, larger values for λ_1 and λ_2 should be used, thereby reducing AFCM to standard FCM.

Algorithm Steps

The objective function J_{AFCM} can be minimized in a fashion similar to the standard FCM algorithm. Taking the first derivatives of J_{AFCM} with respect to $u_k(i, j)$, v_k and $m(i, j)$ and setting them equal to zero results in three necessary conditions for J_{AFCM} to be at a minimum. Using these conditions, the steps for our AFCM algorithm can then be described as follows:

1. Provide initial values for centroids, v_k, k = 1,..., C, and set the multiplier field m(i, j) equal to one for all (i, j).

2. Compute memberships as follows:

$$u_k(i, j) = \frac{\left\| y(i, j) - m(i, j)v_k \right\|^{-2}}{\sum_{i=1}^{C} \left\| y(i, j) - m(i, j)v_i \right\|^{-2}}$$

For all (i,j) and k=1,...,C

3. Compute new centroids as follows:

$$v_k = \frac{\sum_{ij} u_k(i, j)^2 m(i, j) y(i, j)}{\sum_{ij} u_k(i, j)^2 m(i, j)^2} \quad k=1,...,C$$

4. Compute new multiplier field by solving the following space-varying difference equation for m(i,j):

$$y(i, j)\sum_{k=1}^{C} u_k^2(i, j)v_k = m(i, j)\sum_{k=1}^{C} u_k^2(i, j)v_k^2 + \lambda_1(m(i, j) * *H_1(i, j)) + \lambda_2(m(i, j) * *H_2(i, j))$$

where $H_1(i,j) = D_i * \check{D}_i + D_j * \check{D}_j$ and $H_2(i,j) = D_{ii} * \check{D}_{ii} + 2(D_{ij} ** \check{D}_{ij}) + D_{jj} * \check{D}_{jj}$. Here the notation $\check{f}(i) = f(-i)$ is discussed.

5.   If the algorithm has converged, then quit. Otherwise, go to Step 2.

Convergence is said to be when the maximum change in the membership functions over all pixels between iterations is less than a threshold value. In practice, a threshold value of 0.01 is used. Steps 1 and 4 are discussed in more detail.

Initial Centroids

In order to minimize operator interaction and improve speed of convergence in AFCM, an automated method for determining the initial values of the centroids in Step 1 was used. The method finds the modes of a critically smoothed kernel estimator of the image histogram and is similar to the bump-hunting method described by Silverman (1993). The kernel estimator, $\hat{p}(x)$, is a non parametric estimator of the probability density function of a data set and is defined by

$$\hat{p}(x) = \frac{1}{nh} \sum_{ij} \phi\left(\frac{x - y(i,j)}{h}\right)$$

where ϕ is the kernel function, in this case a Gaussian function with zero mean and variance of one, and n is the total number of pixels. The h variable is called the window width or bandwidth parameter; larger values of h result in a smoother estimator of the density function.

It has been shown that the number of modes is a decreasing function of h (Silverman, 1993). Thus by starting with a large value of h and reducing it, one goes from a unimodal kernel estimate to an estimate with an increasing number of modes. The critical bandwidth parameter, h_{crit}, for C modes is defined as the minimum value of h such that $\hat{p}$ has C modes. For initializing the centroids, it is therefore desirable to use the mode locations of the critically smoothed kernel estimator. This can be accomplished in the following manner

1.   Set lower bound for h, h_{lo}, and upper bound, h_{hi}, to zero and 50 (or other large value such that $\hat{p}$ is unimodal), respectively.
2.   Compute kernel estimator with $h=(h+h_{lo})/2$.
3.   Count number of modes.
4.   If number of modes is less than or equal to C, let $h_{hi}=h$, and go to Step 2. If number of modes is greater than C, let $h_{lo}=h$, and go to Step 2.
5.   Repeat until the change in h between iterations is less than a threshold value and number of modes is equal to C.
6.   Use the location of the modes as initial centroids.

Threshold value in Step 5 is set to 0.01. Because a Gaussian kernel function is used, it is straight forward to analytically take first and second derivatives of the kernel estimator. Therefore, the number of modes can be determined by discretizing the range of pixel intensities and checking for zero crossings in the first derivative and for a negative value at the zero crossings in the second derivative.

Figure 2 shows an example of the kernel estimatorfor an MR image, which is shown in Figure 2(a). Figure 2(b) is a histogram of the pixel intensities(ignoring background intensities) and Figure 2(c) is aplot of the kernel estimator at the critical bandwidthparameter for three modes. The x-axis in theplots represents the pixel intensity. If h was slightlydecreased in the kernel estimator, additionalmodes would become evident at pixel intensities ofapproximately 50 and 90. Thus, as much detail aspossible from the original histogram is preservedin the kernel estimator such that three modes arepresent.

RESULTS

Figure 3 shows the results of applying the FCMand AFCM algorithms to segment an image of acryo-sectioned brain (from Toga et al., 1994).Fig. 3(a) is the original image. Strong intensityinhomogeneities due to non-uniform illuminationduring the photography are apparent in the image.

Both the FCM and AFCM algorithms were usedto segment the image into three classes corresponding to background, gray matter (GM) andFig. 2 white matter (WM). Figure. 3(b) and 3(c) show thecontours of where the GM membership function isequal to the WM membership function in theFCMandAFCM results, respectively. The FCMcontour provides an inaccurate representation ofthe GM-WM boundary. The AFCM algorithm,on the other hand, yields a much improved result.The values of λ_1 and λ_2 were set to 4×10^5 and 9×10^5, respectively.

CONCLUSION

The field of adaptive clustering calls for a tremendous amount of research. The Fuzzy C-means algorithm is altered so that it isinitialized based on the Membership Degree Matrix from the previous iteration. In a similar way, according to the scenario, FCM is being altered and made adaptable. Thenumber of pattern classes used in the clustering process is adaptively calculated.Comparisons done between the typical K-means algorithm and the proposed heuristicdemonstrate a better performance concerning the correct clustering percentage and theQuadratic Error factor. Work can also be done on extending the existing algorithms to algorithms with intuitionsitic features. Like the mentioned modifications for FCM, several work can be done in the direction of making IFCM,RCM,RFCM and RIFCM adaptable to the scenarios.

REFERENCES

Ahmed, M. N., Yamany, S. M., Mohamed, N., Farag, A. A., & Moriarty, T. (2002). A modified fuzzy c-means algorithm for bias field estimation and segmentation of MRI data. *IEEE Transactions on Medical Imaging, 21*(3), 193–199. doi:10.1109/42.996338 PMID:11989844

Figure 2. A kernel estimator example: (a) an MR image; (b) histogram of pixel intensities; (c) critically smoothed kernel estimator for 3 modes

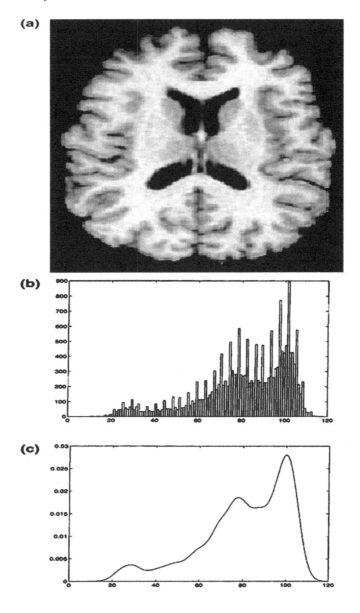

Figure 3. Cryosectioned brain image: (a) original image; (b)FCM GM-WM contour; (c)AFCM GM-WM contour

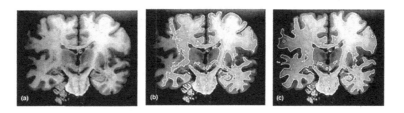

Bezdek, J. C. (2013). *Pattern recognition with fuzzy objective function algorithms*. Springer Science & Business Media.

Bezdek, J. C., Ehrlich, R., & Full, W. (1984). FCM: The fuzzy c-means clustering algorithm. *Computers & Geosciences*, *10*(2-3), 191–203. doi:10.1016/0098-3004(84)90020-7

Bijuraj, L. V. (2013). Clustering and its applications. In *Proceedings of National Conference on New Horizons in IT-NCNHIT* (p. 169)

Blasco, J., Aleixos, N., & Molto, E. (2007). Computer vision detection of peel defects in citrus by means of a region oriented segmentation algorithm. *Journal of Food Engineering*, *81*(3), 535–543. doi:10.1016/j.jfoodeng.2006.12.007

Chen, S., & Zhang, D. (2004). Robust image segmentation using FCM with spatial constraints based on new kernel-induced distance measure. *IEEE Transactions on Systems, Man, and Cybernetics. Part B, Cybernetics*, *34*(4), 1907–1916. doi:10.1109/TSMCB.2004.831165 PMID:15462455

Clausi, D. A., & Deng, H. (2005). Design-based texture feature fusion using Gabor filters and co-occurrence probabilities. *IEEE Transactions on Image Processing*, *14*(7), 925–936. doi:10.1109/TIP.2005.849319 PMID:16028556

Dunn, J. C. (1973). *A fuzzy relative of the ISODATA process and its use in detecting compact well-separated clusters*. Academic Press.

Geweniger, T., Kästner, M., & Villmann, T. (2013). Border sensitive fuzzy vector quantization in semi-supervised learning. In ESANN.

Han, J., Pei, J., & Kamber, M. (2011). *Data mining: Concepts and techniques*. Elsevier.

Haralick, R. M., Shanmugam, K., & Dinstein, I. H. (1973). Textural features for image classification. *IEEE Transactions on Systems, Man, and Cybernetics*, *3*(6), 610–621. doi:10.1109/TSMC.1973.4309314

Ilea, D. E., & Whelan, P. F. (2005). An adaptive unsupervised segmentation algorithm based on color-texture coherence. IEEE Transactions on Image Processing.

Jain, A. K., Murty, M. N., & Flynn, P. J. (1999). Data clustering: A review. *ACM Computing Surveys*, *31*(3), 264–323. doi:10.1145/331499.331504

Kamal, S., & Burk, L. I. (1996). FACT: A new neural network-based clustering algorithm for group technology. *International Journal of Production Research*, *34*(4), 919–946. doi:10.1080/00207549608904943

Läuter, H. (1988). Silverman, BW: Density Estimation for Statistics and Data Analysis. Chapman & Hall.

Li, Y. L., & Shen, Y. (2010). An automatic fuzzy c-means algorithm for image segmentation. *Soft Computing*, *14*(2), 123–128. doi:10.1007/s00500-009-0442-0

Pal, N. R., & Bezdek, J. C. (1995). On cluster validity for the fuzzy c-means model. *IEEE Transactions on Fuzzy Systems*, *3*(3), 370–379. doi:10.1109/91.413225

Pham, D. L., & Prince, J. L. (1999). An adaptive fuzzy C-means algorithm for image segmentation in the presence of intensity inhomogeneities. *Pattern Recognition Letters*, *20*(1), 57–68. doi:10.1016/S0167-8655(98)00121-4

Reddi, S. S., Rudin, S. F., & Keshavan, H. R. (1984). An optimal multiple threshold scheme for image segmentation. *IEEE Transactions on Systems, Man, and Cybernetics*, *SMC-14*(4), 661–665. doi:10.1109/TSMC.1984.6313341

Tan, K. S., & Isa, N. A. M. (2011). Color image segmentation using histogram thresholding–Fuzzy C-means hybrid approach. *Pattern Recognition*, *44*(1), 1–15. doi:10.1016/j.patcog.2010.07.013

Tellaeche, A., Pajares, G., Burgos-Artizzu, X. P., & Ribeiro, A. (2011). A computer vision approach for weeds identification through Support Vector Machines. *Applied Soft Computing*, *11*(1), 908–915. doi:10.1016/j.asoc.2010.01.011

Teppola, P., Mujunen, S. P., & Minkkinen, P. (1999). Adaptive Fuzzy C-Means clustering in process monitoring. *Chemometrics and Intelligent Laboratory Systems*, *45*(1), 23–38. doi:10.1016/S0169-7439(98)00087-2

Weinland, D., Ronfard, R., & Boyer, E. (2011). A survey of vision-based methods for action representation, segmentation and recognition. *Computer Vision and Image Understanding*, *115*(2), 224–241. doi:10.1016/j.cviu.2010.10.002

Xie, X. L., & Beni, G. (1991). A validity measure for fuzzy clustering. *IEEE Transactions on Pattern Analysis and Machine Intelligence*, *13*(8), 841–847. doi:10.1109/34.85677

Yu, Z., Au, O. C., Zou, R., Yu, W., & Tian, J. (2010). An adaptive unsupervised approach toward pixel clustering and color image segmentation. *Pattern Recognition*, *43*(5), 1889–1906. doi:10.1016/j.patcog.2009.11.015

Zadeh, L. A. (1996). *Fuzzy sets, fuzzy logic, and fuzzy systems: Selected papers by Lotfi A Zadeh* (Vol. 6). World Scientific. doi:10.1142/2895

Compilation of References

Abadi, D. J. (2008). *Query execution in column-oriented database systems* (PhD Thesis). Massachusetts Institute of Technology. Retrieved from http://cs-www.cs.yale.edu/homes/dna/papers/abadiphd.pdf

Abadi, D., Boncz, P., Harizopoulos, S., Idreos, S., & Madden, S. (2013). The design and implementation of modern column-oriented database systems. *Foundations and Trends in Databases*, *5*(3), 197–280. doi:10.1561/1900000024

Abbaspour, M., Abugharbieh, R., Podder, M., Tripp, B. W., & Tebbutt, S. J. (2006). *Hybrid spot segmentation in four-channel microarray genotyping image data.* Paper presented at the Signal Processing and Information Technology, 2006 IEEE International Symposium on.

Abhishek, B., Susmita, T., Nabanita, S., Avradeeta, K., Lal, C. S., & Kumar, S. S. (2015). On the Implementation of a Saliency based Digital Watermarking.*2nd International Conference on Information systems Design and Intelligent Applications.*

Abraham, A. (2005). Hybrid intelligent systems: Evolving intelligence in hierarchical layers. Springer.

Adlassing, K. P. (1982). *CADIAG-2 computer assisted medical diagnosis using fuzzy subsets in approximate reasoning in decision analysis.* Amsterdam: North Holland Publishing Company.

Aggarwal, C. C., & Reddy, C. K. (2014). Data Clustering Algorithms and Applications. CRC Press.

Aggarwal, C., & ChengXiang, Z. (Eds.). (2012). Comprehensive survey driven book on text mining with chapters contributed by prominent researchers in the field. In Mining Text Data. Springer.

Aggarwal, C., & Yu, P. (2001). Outlier Detection for High Dimensional Data. In *Proceedings of the ACM SIGMOD International Conference on Management of Data.* doi:10.1145/376284.375668

Ahmed, M. N., Yamany, S. M., Mohamed, N., Farag, A. A., & Moriarty, T. (2002). A modified fuzzy c-means algorithm for bias field estimation and segmentation of MRI data. *IEEE Transactions on Medical Imaging*, *21*(3), 193–199. doi:10.1109/42.996338 PMID:11989844

Ahmed, Z., Sayadi, M., & Faniech, F. (2009). Satellite images features extraction using phase congruency model. *Internat. J. Comput. Sci. Network Security*, *9*(2), 192–197.

Airola, A., Pyysalo, S., Björne, J., Pahikkala, T., Ginter, F., & Salakoski, T. (2008, June). A graph kernel for protein-protein interaction extraction. In *Proceedings of the workshop on current trends in biomedical natural language processing* (pp. 1-9). Association for Computational Linguistics. doi:10.3115/1572306.1572308

Ajith Abraham, S. D. (2008). Swarm intelligence algorithms for data clustering. Soft computing for Knowledge Discovery and Data mining, (pp. 279-313).

Algamal, Z. Y., & Lee, M. H. (2015a). Penalized logistic regression with the adaptive LASSO for gene selection in high-dimensional cancer classification. *Expert Systems with Applications, 42*(23), 9326–9332. doi:10.1016/j.eswa.2015.08.016

Algamal, Z. Y., & Lee, M. H. (2015b). Regularized logistic regression with adjusted adaptive elastic net for gene selection in high dimensional cancer classification. *Computers in Biology and Medicine, 67*, 136–145. doi:10.1016/j.compbiomed.2015.10.008 PMID:26520484

Ali, Mohammad, Ebrahim, Bulent, & Farokh. (2009). Robust Scaling-Based Image Watermarking Using Maximum-Likelihood Decoder With Optimum Strength Facto, IEEE Transactions on Multimedia, 11(5), 822-833.

Allen, J. F. (1984). Towards a general theory of action and time. *Artificial Intelligence, 23*(2), 123–154. doi:10.1016/0004-3702(84)90008-0

Al-Nabhani, Jalab, Wahid, & Noor. (2015). Robust watermarking algorithm for digital images using discrete wavelet and probabilistic neural network. *Journal of King Saud University – Computer and Information Sciences, 27*, 393-401.

Amaratunga, D., & Cabrera, J. (2004). *Exploration and analysis of DNA microarray and protein array data.* Wiley.

American Medical Association. (2010). *Getting the most for our health care dollars: Medical liability reform.* Chicago, IL: American Medical Association. Retrieved on 30 December 2015 from http://www.allhealth.org/briefingmaterials/AMASharedDecisionMaking-1936.pdf

Amgoth, T., & Jana, P. K. (2015). Energy-aware routing algorithm for wireless sensor networks. *Computers & Electrical Engineering, 41*, 357–367. doi:10.1016/j.compeleceng.2014.07.010

Amin, S. U., Agarwal, K., & Beg, R. (2013). Data mining in clinical decision support systems for diagnosis, prediction and treatment of heart disease. *International Journal of Advanced Research in Computer Engineering & Technology, 2*(1), 218–223.

Amit, D. (2004). *The Digital Consumer Technology Handbook: A Comprehensive Guide to Devices, Standards, Future Directions, and Programmable Logic Solutions.* Elsevier.

Amrik & Balpreet. (2014). An Integrated SVD and Visibility Restoration Digital Watermarking. *International Journal of Advanced Research in Computer Science and Software Engineering, 4*(1).

Ananthanarayana, V. S., Narasimha Murthy, M., & Subramanian, D. K. (2001). Multi-dimensional semantic Clustering of large databases for Association rule mining. Pattern Recognition, 939-941

Anastasi, G., Conti, M., Di, M., & Passarella, A. (2009). Energy conservation in wireless sensor networks : A survey. *Ad Hoc Networks, 7*(3), 537–568. doi:10.1016/j.adhoc.2008.06.003

Anastasiu, D. C., Gao, B. J., & Buttler, D. (2011, October). A framework for personalized and collaborative clustering of search results. In *Proceedings of the 20th ACM international conference on Information and knowledge management* (pp. 573-582). ACM. doi:10.1145/2063576.2063662

Anderson, R. J. (1996). Stretching the Limits of Steganography. In *Information Hiding:First International Workshop, Proceedings*, (LNCS), (vol. 1174, pp. 39–48). Springer.

Anderson, R. (1996). Information Hiding. *Proceedings of the first Workshop on Information Hiding, (LNCS) (vol. 1174). Springer Verlag.*

Anderson, R. J., & Petitcolas, F. A. P. (1998). On The Limits of Steganography. *IEEE Journal on Selected Areas in Communications, 16*(4), 474–481.

Anne. (2011). *Challenges for process mining in medicine.* Retrieved on 30 August 2013 from http://www.techcrunch.com

Anooj, P. K. (2012). Clinical decision support system: Risk level prediction of heart disease using weighted fuzzy rules. *Journal of King Saud University – Computer and Information Sciences, 24,* 27 – 40.

Art, W. (1999). *The history of the Internet and the World Wide Web.* Enslow Publishers.

Arya, R., & Sharma, S. C. (2015). Analysis and optimization of energy of sensor node Using ACO in wireless sensor network. *Procedia Computer Science, 45,* 681–686. doi:10.1016/j.procs.2015.03.132

Asatryan & Asatryan. (2009). *Combined Spatial and Frequency Domain Watermarking.* Computer Science and Information Technologies.

Ashwani, K., Ghrera, S.P., & Vipin. (2015). A New and Efficient Buyer-Seller Digital Watermarking Protocol Using Identity Based Technique for Copyright Protection. *Third International Conference on Image Information Processing.*

Aslam, N., Phillips, W., Robertson, W., & Sivakumar, S. (2011). A multi-criterion optimization technique for energy efficient cluster formation in wireless sensor networks. *Information Fusion, 12*(3), 202–212. doi:10.1016/j.inffus.2009.12.005

Athanasiadis, E. I., Cavouras, D. A., Glotsos, D. T., Georgiadis, P. V., Kalatzis, I. K., & Nikiforidis, G. C. (2009). Segmentation of complementary DNA microarray images by wavelet-based Markov random field model. *Information Technology in Biomedicine. IEEE Transactions on, 13*(6), 1068–1074. doi:10.1109/TITB.2009.2032332

Athanasiadis, E. I., Cavouras, D. A., Spyridonos, P. P., Glotsos, D. T., Kalatzis, I. K., & Nikiforidis, G. C. (2009). Complementary DNA microarray image processing based on the fuzzy Gaussian mixture model. *Information Technology in Biomedicine. IEEE Transactions on, 13*(4), 419–425. doi:10.1109/TITB.2008.907984

Attea, B., & Khalil, E. (2012). A new evolutionary based routing protocol for clustered heterogeneous wireless sensor networks. *Applied Soft Computing, 12*(7), 1950–1957. doi:10.1016/j.asoc.2011.04.007

Aura, T. (1996). Practical Invisibility in Digital Communication. In *Information Hiding:First International Workshop, Proceedings,* (LNCS), (vol. 1174, pp. 265–278). Springer.

Awan, I., Gilani, S. A. M., & Shah, S. A. (2006). Utilization of Maximum Data Hiding Capacity in Object-Based Text Document Authentication. In *International Conference on Intelligent Information Hiding and Multimedia Signal Processing.*

Awate, S. P., & Whitaker, R. T. (2006). Unsupervised, information-theoretic, adaptive image filtering for image restoration. *IEEE Transactions on Pattern Analysis and Machine Intelligence, 28*(3), 364–376. doi:10.1109/TPAMI.2006.64 PMID:16526423

Azar, A. T. (2013). Fast neural network learning algorithm for Medical Applications. *Neural Computing & Applications, 23*(3-4), 1019–1034. doi:10.1007/s00521-012-1026-y

Bagher–Ebadian, H., Soltanian-Zadeh, H., Setayeshi, S., & Smith, S. T. (2004). Neural network and fuzzy clustering approach for automatic diagnosis of coronary heart disease in nuclear medicine. *IEEE Transactions on Nuclear Science, 51*(1), 184–192. doi:10.1109/TNS.2003.823047

Baldangombo, U., Nyamjav, J., & Horng, S. J. (2013). *A Static Malware Detection System Using Data Mining Methods.* Retrieved from https://arxiv.org/abs/1308.2831

Bandyopadhyay, M. N. (2005). *Introduction to Signals and Systems and Digital Signal Processing.* PHI Learning Pvt. Ltd.

Banerjee, M., & Islam, S. M. (2015). Tackling Curse of Dimensionality for Efficient Content Based Image Retrieval, In *Pattern Recognition and Machine Intelligence: 6th International Conference, PReMI 2015.* Springer. doi:10.1007/978-3-319-19941-2_15

Banerjee, B., Bovolo, F., Bhattacharya, A., Bruzzone, L., Chaudhuri, S., & Buddhiraju, K. M. (2015). A novel graph-matching-based approach for domain adaptation in classification of remote sensing image pair. *IEEE Transactions on Geoscience and Remote Sensing*, *53*(7), 4045–4062. doi:10.1109/TGRS.2015.2389520

Banerjee, B., Mishra, P. K., Varma, S., & Mohan, B. K. (2013, October). A novel graph based clustering technique for hybrid segmentation of multi-spectral remotely sensed images. In *International Conference on Advanced Concepts for Intelligent Vision Systems* (pp. 274-285). Springer International Publishing. doi:10.1007/978-3-319-02895-8_25

Banerjee, B., Varma, S., Buddhiraju, K. M., & Eeti, L. N. (2014). Unsupervised multi-spectral satellite image segmentation combining modified mean-shift and a new minimum spanning tree based clustering technique. *IEEE Journal of Selected Topics in Applied Earth Observations and Remote Sensing*, *7*(3), 888–894. doi:10.1109/JSTARS.2013.2266572

Bao. (2014). Image Copyright Protection Watermark Algorithm Based on Spread Spectrum Technology. Applied Mechanics and Materials, 602-605, 3272-3277.

Barnett, V., & Lewis, T. (1994). *Outliers in Statistical Data*. Chichester, UK: John Wiley and Sons; doi:10.1016/0169-2070(95)00625-7

Basu, A., & Sarkar, S.K. (2013). On the Implementation of Robust Copyright Protection Scheme using Visual Attention Model. *Information Security Journal: A Global Perspective, 22*(1), 10-20.

Basu, A., Das, T. S., & Sarkar, S. K. (2011). Robust Visual Information Hiding Framework Based on HVS Pixel Adaptive LSB Replacement (HPALR) Technique. *Int. Jnl of Imaging & Robotics*, *6*(A11), 71–98.

Basu, A., Talukdar, S., Sengupta, N., Kar, A., Chakraborty, S. L., & Sarkar, S. K. (2015). On the Implementation of a Saliency based Digital Watermarking. *2nd International Conference on Information systems Design and Intelligent Applications*. doi:10.1007/978-81-322-2250-7_44

Batal, I., Valizadegan, H., Cooper, G. F., & Hauskrecht, M. (2012). A Temporal pattern mining approach for classifying electronic health record data. *ACM Transactions on Intelligent Systems and Technology*, *4*(4), 63. PMID:25309815

Bellare, K., Kanni, P., & Sen, S. (2006). *Dynamic branch prediction using machine learning. Technical report*. University of Massachusetts at Amherst.

Bellotti, R., Carlo, F. D., Tangora, S., & Nunzio, G. D. (2006). A completely automated CAD system for mass detection in a large mammographic database. *Medical Physics*, *33*(8), 3066–3075. doi:10.1118/1.2214177 PMID:16964885

Bender, W., Gruhl, D., & Morimoto, N. (1995). Techniques for data hiding. *Proceedings of the Society for Photo-Instrumentation Engineers*, *2420*, 40. doi:10.1117/12.205315

Berenson, M. L., & Levine, D. M. (2012). *Basic business statistics: Concepts and Applications* (12th ed.). Boston, MA: Prentice Hall.

Bergemann, T. L., Laws, R. J., Quiaoit, F., & Zhao, L. P. (2004). A statistically driven approach for image segmentation and signal extraction in cDNA microarrays. *Journal of Computational Biology*, *11*(4), 695–713. doi:10.1089/cmb.2004.11.695 PMID:15579239

Berman, J. J. (2002). Confidentiality issues for medical data miners. *Artificial Intelligence in Medicine*, *26*(1-2), 25–36. doi:10.1016/S0933-3657(02)00050-7 PMID:12234715

Bezalel, E., & Efron, U. (2005). Efficient face recognition method using a combined phase congruency/Gabor filter bank technique. *Proceedings of the Society for Photo-Instrumentation Engineers*, *5908*, 437–444. doi:10.1117/12.618226

Bezdek, J. C. (1981). *Pattern Recognition with Fuzzy Objective Function Algorithms*. Plenum Press.

Bezdek, J. C. (2013). *Pattern recognition with fuzzy objective function algorithms*. Springer Science & Business Media.

Bezdek, J. C., Ehrlich, R., & Full, W. (1984). FCM: The fuzzy c-means clustering algorithm. *Computers & Geosciences*, *10*(2-3), 191–203. doi:10.1016/0098-3004(84)90020-7

Bhagyashri, S., & Kapre, J. M. Y. (2011). All frequency band DWT-SVD robust watermarking technique for color images in YUV color space. *IEEE International Conference on Computer Science and Automation Engineering (CSAE)*. doi:10.1109/CSAE.2011.5952684

Bick, U., & Doi, K. (2000). Computer aided diagnosis tutorial on computer aided-diagnosis. CARS 2000, Hyatt Regency, San Francisco, CA.

Biermann. (1996). Handbook of Pulping and Papermaking (2nd ed.). Academic Press.

Bijuraj, L. V. (2013). Clustering and its applications. In *Proceedings of National Conference on New Horizons in IT-NCNHIT* (p. 169)

Biju, V. G., & Mythili, P. (2015). Fuzzy clustering algorithms for cDNA microarray image spots segmentation. *Procedia Computer Science*, *46*, 417–424. doi:10.1016/j.procs.2015.02.039

Bishop, C. M. (1995). *Neural networks for pattern recognition*. Oxford, UK: Oxford University Press.

Blasco, J., Aleixos, N., & Molto, E. (2007). Computer vision detection of peel defects in citrus by means of a region oriented segmentation algorithm. *Journal of Food Engineering*, *81*(3), 535–543. doi:10.1016/j.jfoodeng.2006.12.007

Blazewicz, J., Kasprzak, M., & Kuroczycki, W. (2002). Hybrid genetic algorithm for DNA sequencing with errors. *Journal of Heuristics*, *8*(5), 495–502. doi:10.1023/A:1016589707123

Bleyer, M., & Gelautz, M. (2007). Graph-cut-based stereo matching using image segmentation with symmetrical treatment of occlusions. *Signal Processing Image Communication*, *22*(2), 127–143. doi:10.1016/j.image.2006.11.012

Bondy, J. A., & Murty, U. S. R. (1976). *Graph theory with applications* (Vol. 290). London: Macmillan. doi:10.1007/978-1-349-03521-2

Borko, F., & Darko, K. (2006). *Multimedia Encryption and Authentication Techniques and Applications*. CRC Press.

Bottigli, U., Chiarucci, R., Golosio, B., Masala, G. L., Oliva, P., Stumbo, S., & Raso, G. et al. (2006). Superior performances of the neural network on the masses lesions classification through morphological lesion differences. *International Journal of Biomedical Science*, *1*(1), 56–63.

Bougleux, S., Elmoataz, A., & Melkemi, M. (2007, May). Discrete regularization on weighted graphs for image and mesh filtering. In *International Conference on Scale Space and Variational Methods in Computer Vision* (pp. 128-139). Springer Berlin Heidelberg. doi:10.1007/978-3-540-72823-8_12

Boukerroui, D., Noble, J., & Brady, V. (1999). *On the Choice of Band-Pass Quadrature Filters. Technical report, MVL*. Oxford University.

Bozinov, D., & Rahnenführer, J. (2002). Unsupervised technique for robust target separation and analysis of DNA microarray spots through adaptive pixel clustering. *Bioinformatics (Oxford, England)*, *18*(5), 747–756. doi:10.1093/bioinformatics/18.5.747 PMID:12050071

Bramer, M. (2013). *Principles of data mining*. London: Springer-Verlag. doi:10.1007/978-1-4471-4884-5

Braudaway, G. W., Magerlein, K. A., & Mintzer, F. (1996). *Color Correct Digital Watermarking of Images*. US patent No. 5,530,759.

Brouwer, R. K. (2002). A feed-forward network for input which is both categorical and quantitative. *Neural Networks, 15*(7), 881–890. doi:10.1016/S0893-6080(02)00090-4 PMID:14672165

Bruno, G., & Garza, P. (2012). Temporal pattern mining for medical applications. In *Data Mining: Foundations and Intelligent Paradigms* (pp. 9–18). Berlin: Springer. doi:10.1007/978-3-642-23151-3_2

Bunke, H., & Shearer, K. (1998). A graph distance metric based on the maximal common subgraph. *Pattern Recognition Letters, 19*(3), 255–259. doi:10.1016/S0167-8655(97)00179-7

Busch, V., & Van Stel, H. F. (2013). *Clustering of health-related behaviors, health outcomes and demographics in Dutch adolescents: A cross-sectional study.* BMC Public Health. doi:10.1186/1471-2458-13-1118

Cachin, C. (1998). An Information-Theoretic Model for Steganography. In *Proceedings of the Second International Workshop on Information Hiding.* doi:10.1007/3-540-49380-8_21

Caldelli, Filippini, & Becarelli. (2010). Reversible Watermarking Techniques: An Overview and a Classification. *EURASIP Journal on Information Security.*

Camilo, T., Carreto, C., Jorge, S., & Boavida, F. (2006). An energy-efficient ant-based routing algorithm for wireless sensor networks,*ANTS 2006, LNCS 4150. Springer-Verlag Berlin Heidelberg, 2006,* 49–59.

Canlas, R. D., Jr. (2009). *Data Mining in Healthcare: Current Applications and Issues* (Unpublished master dissertation). Carnegie Mellon University, Australia.

Canny, J. F. (1983). *Finding edges and lines in images* (Master's thesis). MIT.

Canny, J. (1986). A computational approach to edge detection. *IEEE Transactions on Pattern Analysis and Machine Intelligence, 8*(6), 679–698. doi:10.1109/TPAMI.1986.4767851 PMID:21869365

Can, Y. S., & Alagoz, F. (2013). Robust frequency hopping and direct sequence spread spectrum audio watermarking technique on wavelet domain. *International Conference on Electronics, Computer and Computation (ICECCO).* doi:10.1109/ICECCO.2013.6718308

Cao, H., Si, G., Zhang, Y., & Jia, L. (2008). A Density-based Quantitative Attribute Partition Algorithm for Association Rule Mining on Industrial Database.*American Control Conference Westin Seattle Hotel.*

Carpenter, G. A., & Grossberg, S. (1987). A massively parallel architecture for a self organizing neural pattern recognition machine. *Computer Vision Graphics and Image Processing, 37*(1), 54–115. doi:10.1016/S0734-189X(87)80014-2

Cascio, D., Fauci, F., Magro, R., Raso, G., Bellotti, R., Carlo, F. D., & Torres, E. L. et al. (2006). Mammogram segmentation by contour searching and masses lesion classification with neural network. *IEEE Transactions on Nuclear Science, 53*(5), 2827–2833. doi:10.1109/TNS.2006.878003

Cedillo, H. M., Cedillo, H. A., Balbuena, C. A. R., García, U. F., Nakano, M. M., & Meana, H. M. P. (2015). Customer Authentication of Digital Imaging Using Hybrid Watermarking. *International Conference on Mechatronics, Electronics and Automotive Engineering.*

Ceglar, A., & Roddick, J. F. (2006). Association mining.*ACM Computing Surveys,38*(2), 1–42. doi:10.1145/1132956.1132958

Celik, S., Logsdon, B., & Aase, S. I. (2014). Efficient dimensionality reduction for high-dimensional network estimation. In *Proc. 31st Int. Conf. Mach. Learn.,* (pp. 1953–1961).

Center of Medicare & Medicaid Services. (2007). *Security 101 for covered entities.* Retrieved on June 10, 2015 from: http://www.hhs.gov/ocr/privacy/hipaa/administrative/securityrule/security101.pdf

Cerello, P., Bagnasco, S., Bottigli, U., Cheran, S. C., Delogu, P., Fantacci, M. E., & Zanon, E. et al. (2005). GPCALMA: A grid based tool for mammographic screening. *Methods of Information in Medicine*, *44*(2), 244–248. PMID:15924184

Chamam, A., & Pierre, S. (2010). A distributed energy-efficient clustering protocol for wireless sensor networks. *Computers & Electrical Engineering*, *36*(2), 303–312. doi:10.1016/j.compeleceng.2009.03.008

Chandramouli, R., Memon, N., & Rabbani, M. (2002). Digital Watermarking. Encyclopedia of Imaging Science and Technology.

Chang, C. C., Hwang, K. F., & Hwang, M. S. (1999). A block based digital watermarks for copy protection of images. In *Proceedings of fifth Asia-Pacific Conference on Communications/ Fourth Optoelectronics and Communications Conference*. doi:10.1109/APCC.1999.820427

Chang, C. C., Hsiao, J. Y., & Chan, C. S. (2003). Finding optimal least significant- bit substitution in image hiding by dynamic programming strategy. *Pattern Recognition*, *36*(7), 1583–159. doi:10.1016/S0031-3203(02)00289-3

Chang, C. Y. (2004). A contextual-based hopfield neural network for medical image edge detection.*IEEE International Conference on Multimedia and Expo (ICME)*. doi:10.1109/ICME.2004.1394374

Chang-Tsun, L., Chih-Yuan, C., & Yue, L. (2010). On the Reputability of Device Identification and Image Integrity Verification Using Sensor Pattern Noise. *Social Informatics and Telecommunications Engineering*, *41*, 19–25.

Chan, W., & Coghill, G. (2001). Text analysis using local energy. *Pattern Recognition*, *34*(12), 2523–2532. doi:10.1016/S0031-3203(00)00155-2

Chechik, G., Sharma, V., Shalit, U., & Bengio, S. (2010). Large scale online learning of image similarity through ranking. *Journal of Machine Learning Research*, *11*, 1109–1135.

Chen, H., Fuller, S. S., Friedman, C., & Hersh, W. (2005). Knowledge management, data mining, and text mining in medical informatics. In Medical Informatics (pp. 3-33). Springer US. doi:10.1007/0-387-25739-X_1

Chen, D. R., Chang, R. F., & Huang, Y. L. (2000). Breast cancer diagnosis using self organizing map for sonography. *Ultrasound in Medicine & Biology*, *26*(3), 405–411. doi:10.1016/S0301-5629(99)00156-8 PMID:10773370

Chen, H., & Hu, J. (2013). *Proceedings of The Eighth International Conference on Bio-Inspired Computing: Theories and applications*. Springer.

Chen, S., & Zhang, D. (2004). Robust image segmentation using FCM with spatial constraints based on new kernel-induced distance measure. *IEEE Transactions on Systems, Man, and Cybernetics. Part B, Cybernetics*, *34*(4), 1907–1916. doi:10.1109/TSMCB.2004.831165 PMID:15462455

Chen, Y., Zhou, X. S., & Huang, T. (2001). One-class svm for learning in image retrieval. In *International Conference on Image Processing* (pp. 34-37).

Chet, H. (2002). Proving the Integrity of Digital Evidence with Time. *International Journal of Digital Evidence*, *1*(1), 1–7.

Chidiac, H., & Ziou, D. (1999). *Classification of image edges. In Vision Interface 99* (pp. 17–24). Troise-Rivieres.

Chi-Keung, L. (2005). Pin: Building customized program analysis tools with dynamic instrumentation. *SIGPLAN*, *40*(6), 190–200. doi:10.1145/1064978.1065034

Chimanna, M. A., & Khot, S. R. (2013). Robustness of video watermarking against various attacks using Wavelet Transform techniques and Principle Component Analysis. *International Conference on Information Communication and Embedded Systems*. doi:10.1109/ICICES.2013.6508357

Choo, H-G. (2004). Data-Hiding Capacity Improvement for Text Watermarking Using Space Coding Method, Digital Watermarking. Lecture Notes in Computer Science, 2939, 593–599.

Chopra, Purohit, & Gaur. (2014). Quality Evaluation for LSB Replacement Watermarking of Grayscale Images. *International Journal of Advanced Research in Computer and Communication Engineering, 3*(5).

Choubey, N. S., & Ph, D. (2014). Fruit fly optimization algorithm for travelling salesperson problem. *Journal of Computer Applications, 107*(18), 22–27. doi:10.5120/18851-0385

Choudhary, R., & Saharan, R. (2012). Malware detection using data mining techniques. *International Journal of Information Technology and Knowledge Management, 5*, 85–88.

Chu, F., Jin, G., & Wang, L. (2005). Cancer diagnosis and protein secondary structure prediction using Support Vector Machines. *StudFuzz, 177*, 343–363.

Chummun, M. R., Kirubarajan, T., Pattipati, K. R., & Bar-Shalom, Y. (2001). Fast data association Using Multidimensional Assignment with Clustering. *IEEE Transactions on Aerospace and Electronic Systems, 37*(3), 898–913. doi:10.1109/7.953245

Chunlin, S., Sudirman, S., Merabti, M., Jones, D. L. (2010). Analysis of Digital Image Watermark Attacks. *7th IEEE International Conference on Consumer Communications and Networking Conference.*

Churchill, G. A. Jr. (1995). *Marketing Research Methodological Foundations*. The Dryden Press.

Chu, Y., Zhang, Y., Zhang, S., & Ye, X. (2006). Region of Interest Fragile Watermarking for Image Authentication. *First International Multi-Symposiums on Computer and Computational Sciences, 1*, 726–731.

Cios, K. J., & Moore, G. W. (2002). Uniqueness of medical data mining. *Artificial Intelligence in Medicine, 26*(1), 1–24. doi:10.1016/S0933-3657(02)00049-0 PMID:12234714

Clausi, D. A., & Deng, H. (2005). Design-based texture feature fusion using Gabor filters and co-occurrence probabilities. *IEEE Transactions on Image Processing, 14*(7), 925–936. doi:10.1109/TIP.2005.849319 PMID:16028556

Cobos, C., Mendoza, M., & Leon, E. (2011, June). A hyper-heuristic approach to design and tuning heuristic methods for web document clustering. In Evolutionary Computation (CEC), 2011 IEEE Congress on (pp. 1350-1358). IEEE. doi:10.1109/CEC.2011.5949773

Comak, E., Arslan, A., & Turkoglu, I. (2007). A decision support system based on support vector machines for diagnosis of the heart valve diseases. *Computers in Biology and Medicine, 37*(1), 21–27. doi:10.1016/j.compbiomed.2005.11.002 PMID:16426598

Comaniciu, D., & Meer, P. (2002). Mean shift: A robust approach toward feature space analysis. *IEEE Transactions on Pattern Analysis and Machine Intelligence, 24*(5), 603–619. doi:10.1109/34.1000236

Concaro, S., Sacchi, L., Cerra, C., Fratino, P., & Bellazzi, R. (2011). Mining health care administrative data with temporal association rules on hybrid events. *Methods of Information in Medicine, 50*(2), 166–179. doi:10.3414/ME10-01-0036 PMID:21170468

Cooper, T., & Collman, J. (2005). Managing information security and privacy in healthcare data mining. In Medical Informatics (pp. 95-137). Springer US. doi:10.1007/0-387-25739-X_4

Costa, J. P., Cecílio, J., Martins, P., & Furtado, P. (2011). ONE: A Predictable and Scalable DW Model. Data Warehousing and Knowledge Discovery Lecture Notes in Computer Science.

Courtesy, G. (n.d.). Retrieved from: https://bigpictureeducation.com/finding-your-way-around-cell

Cover, T. M., & Hart, P. E. (1967). Nearest neighbor pattern classification. *IEEE Transactions on Information Theory, IT-13*(1), 21–27. doi:10.1109/TIT.1967.1053964

Cover, T. M., & Thomas, J. A. (1991). *Elements of Information Theory.* Wiley Interscience. doi:10.1002/0471200611

Cox, I. J. (1996). A Secure Robust Watermark for Multimedia. In *Proc. of First International Workshop on Information Hiding.* Springer-Verlag.

Cox, I. J., Kilian, J., Leighton, T., & Shamoon, T. (1996). A Secure Robust Watermarking for Multimedia. In *Proc. of First International Workshop on Information Hiding,* (LNCS), (vol. 1174, pp. 185-206). Springer-Verlag.

Cox, I. J. (1996). Secure Spread Spectrum Watermarking of Images, Audio and Video.*Proc IEEE International Conf. on Image Processing, ICIP-96.* doi:10.1109/ICIP.1996.560429

Cox, I., & Linnartz, J.-P. (1997). Public watermarks and resistance to tampering. *Proc. IEEE Conf. on Image Processing.* doi:10.1109/ICIP.1997.632226

Craver S., Memon N., Lock, Y. B., & Yeung, M.M. (1998). Resolving rightful ownerships with invisible watermarking techniques: limitations, attacks, and implications. *IEEE Journal on Selected Areas in Communications, 16*(4), 573-586.

Craver, S., Memon, N., Yeo, B-L., & Yeung, M.M. (1998). Resolving rightful ownerships with invisible watermarking techniques: limitations, attacks, and implications. *IEEE Journal on Selected Areas in Communications, 16*(4), 573 - 586.

Craver, S. (1997). *On Public-Key Steganography in the Presence of an Active Warden. Technical Report RC 20931.* IBM.

Crina Grosan, A. A. (2006). *Swarm Intelligence in data mining. Studies in Computational Intelligence.* Springer Verlag.

Cui, X., Liu, Q., & Metaxas, D. (2009). Temporal Spectral Residual: Fast Motion Saliency Detection. In *Proceeding: MM 2009 Proceedings of the 17th ACM International Conference on Multimedia.*

Daniel, B. (2007). Opcodes as predictor for malware. *Int. J. Electron. Secur. Digit. Forensic, 1*(2), 156–168. doi:10.1504/IJESDF.2007.016865

Darko, K., & Malvar, H. S. (2003). Spread-Spectrum Watermarking of Audio Signals. *IEEE Transactions on Signal Processing, 51*(4), 1020–1033. doi:10.1109/TSP.2003.809384

Das, K. N., & Singh, T. K. (2014). Drosophila food-search optimization. *Applied Mathematics and Computation, 231,* 566–580. doi:10.1016/j.amc.2014.01.040

Daskalakis, A., Glotsos, D., Kostopoulos, S., Cavouras, D., & Nikiforidis, G. (2009). A comparative study of individual and ensemble majority vote cDNA microarray image segmentation schemes, originating from a spot-adjustable based restoration framework. *Computer Methods and Programs in Biomedicine, 95*(1), 72–88. doi:10.1016/j.cmpb.2009.01.007 PMID:19278747

Das, R., Turkoglu, I., & Sengur, A. (2009). Diagnosis of valvular diseases through neural network ensembles. *Computer Methods and Programs in Biomedicine, 93*(2), 185–191. doi:10.1016/j.cmpb.2008.09.005 PMID:18951649

Das, S., Abraham, A., & Konar, A. (2008). Automatic clustering using an improved differential evolution algorithm. *Systems, Man and Cybernetics, Part A: Systems and Humans. IEEE Transactions on, 38*(1), 218–237.

Dautzenberg, C., & Boland, F. (1994). *Watermarking images.* Dept. of Electrical Engineering, Trinity College.

David, K. (1996). The History of Steganography. *Lecture notes in Computer Science, 1174,* 1-7.

Davis, L. S. (1975). A survey of edge detection techniques. *Computer Graphics and Image Processing, 4*(3), 248–260. doi:10.1016/0146-664X(75)90012-X

Dehkordi, A. B., Esfahani, S. N., & Avanaki, A. N. (2011). Robust LSB watermarking optimized for local structural similarity. *19th Iranian Conference on Electrical Engineering (ICEE).*

Deibel, N., & Sikorski, K. (2003). *Exploring perceptrons in branch prediction.* Retrieved from https://courses.cs.washington.edu/courses/cse548/02wi/files/pdf/final/Kevin-and-Nick.pdf

Deng, C., Xiaofei, H., & Jiawei, H. (2007). Spectral regression: a unified subspace learning framework for content-based image retrieval. *Proceedings of the 15th international conference on Multimedia.*

Derrick, G. (2001). Data Watermarking: Steganography And Watermarking Of Digital Data. *Journal of Computer Law & Security Review, 17*(2), 101–104. doi:10.1016/S0267-3649(01)00204-7

Desai, H. V. (2012). Steganography, Cryptography, Watermarking: A Comparative Study. *Journal of Global Research in Computer Science, 3*(12), 33–35.

DeSarbo, W. S., & Mahajan, V. (1984). Constrained classification: The use of a priori information in cluster analysis. *Psychometrika, 49*(2), 187–215. doi:10.1007/BF02294172

Desikan, P., Hsu, S., & Srivastava, J. (2011, April). *Data mining for health care management.* Paper presented at 2011 SIAM International Conference on Data mining, Mesa, AZ.

Devijver, P., & Kittler, P. (1982). *Pattern recognition: A Statistical Approach.* Prentice-Hall.

Dhanalaks,, R., & Haiyalnayaki. (2010). Dual Watermarking Scheme with Encryption. *International Journal of Computer Science and Information Security, 7*(1), 248–253.

Digimarc Corporation. (2004). *Enhancing Personal Identity Verification with Digital Watermarks.* White Paper. Author.

Doi, K., MacMahon, H., Katsuragawa, S., Nishikawa, R. M., & Jiang, Y. (1999). Computer-Aided diagnosis in radiology: Potential and pitfalls. *European Journal of Radiology, 31*(2), 97–109. doi:10.1016/S0720-048X(99)00016-9 PMID:10565509

Dong, Brankov, Galatsanos, Yang, & Davoine. (2005). Digital watermarking robust to geometric distortions. *IEEE Transactions on Image Processing, 14*(12), 2140-2150.

Dong, M. C., Shi, J., Sekar, B. D., & Lei, W. K. (2010). Cardiovascular diseases risk detection using modified t-s fuzzy neural networks. *Computer and Automation Engineering (ICCAE), 2010 The 2nd International Conference on.*

Dong, M. L., Dian, H. W., & Jie, L. (2012). A novel robust blind watermarking algorithm based on wavelet and Fractional Fourier Transform. *IEEE 14th International Conference on Communication Technology.*

Dong, X., & Pi, D. (2014). An Effective Method for Mining Quantitative Association Rules with Clustering Partition in Satellite Telemetry Data. *Second International Conference on Advanced Cloud and Big Data.* doi:10.1109/CBD.2014.12

Dong, Z., Jiying, Z., James, W. T., & Filippo, S. (2003). Image quality measurement by using digital watermarking. *IEEE International Workshop on Haptic, Audio and Visual Environments and their Applications.* doi:10.1109/HAVE.2003.1244727

Douzono, H., Hara, S., & Noguchi, Y. (1998). An application of genetic algorithm to DNA sequencing by oligonucleotide hybridization. *Proceedings of the IEEE international joint symposia on intelligence and systems.* doi:10.1109/IJSIS.1998.685424

Duan, L., Street, W. N., & Xu, E. (2011). Healthcare information systems: Data mining methods in the creation of a clinical recommender system. *Enterprise Information Systems, 5*(2), 169–181. doi:10.1080/17517575.2010.541287

Dube, S., El-Saden, S., Cloughesy, T. F., & Sinha, U. (2006). Content based image retrieval for MR image studies of brain tumors. *IEEE International conference on Engineering in Medicine and Biology*, (pp. 3337–3340).

Dubes, R. C., Jain, A. K., Nadabar, S. G., & Chen, C. C. (1990, June). MRF model-based algorithms for image segmentation. In *Pattern Recognition, 1990. Proceedings., 10th International Conference on* (Vol. 1, pp. 808-814). IEEE. doi:10.1109/ICPR.1990.118221

Ducatelle, F., Di, G. A., & Gambardella, L. M. (2010). Principles and applications of swarm intelligence for adaptive routing in telecommunications networks. *Swarm Intelligence, 4*(3), 173–198. doi:10.1007/s11721-010-0040-x

Duda, R. O., & Hart, P. E. (1973). *Pattern Classification and Scene analysis*. New York: Wiley Publication New York.

Duda, R. O., Hart, P. E., & Strok, D. G. (2001). *Pattern classification*. New York: Willy Publication New York.

Dunham Margaret, H. (2003). *Data Mining Introductory and Advanced Topics*. Prentice Hall, Pearson Education Inc.

Dunn, J. C. (1973). *A fuzzy relative of the ISODATA process and its use in detecting compact well-separated clusters*. Academic Press.

Dylan, C., & Paul, C. (2002). A Novel Watermarking Technique for LUT Based FPGA Designs. *Lecture Notes in Computer Science, 2438*, 1152–1155. doi:10.1007/3-540-46117-5_129

Eckert Michael, P., & Bradley Andrew, P. (1998). Perceptual quality metrics applied to still image compression. *Signal Processing, 70*(3), 177–200. doi:10.1016/S0165-1684(98)00124-8

Eddine, B. D., Sabrina, B., & Azeddine, B. (2015). A Cross-Layer Watermarking-Based Mechanism for Data Aggregation Integrity in Heterogeneous WSNs. *IEEE Communications Letters, 19*(5), 823–826. doi:10.1109/LCOMM.2015.2409057

Edla, D. R., & Jana, P. K. (2013). Minimum spanning tree based clustering using partitional approach. In *Proceedings of the International Conference on Frontiers of Intelligent Computing: Theory and Applications (FICTA)* (pp. 237-244). Springer Berlin Heidelberg. doi:10.1007/978-3-642-35314-7_28

Egan, C., Steven, G., Quick, P., Anguera, R., Steven, F., & Vintan, L. (2003). Two-level branch prediction using neural networks. *Journal of Systems Architecture, 49*(12-15), 557–570. doi:10.1016/S1383-7621(03)00095-X

Elakkumanan, P., Liu, L., Vankadara, V. K., & Sridhar, R. (2005). CHIDDAM: a data mining based technique for cache hierarchy determination in commercial applications. In *Proceedings of 48th Midwest Symposium on Circuits and Systems*. doi:10.1109/MWSCAS.2005.1594493

Elmasri, R., & Navathe, S. B. (2015). *Fundamentals of Database Systems* (7th ed.). Boston, MA: Pearson.

Embrechts, M. J., Arciniegas, F. A., Breneman, C. M., Bennett, K. P., & Lockwood, L. (2001). Bagging neural network sensitivity analysis for feature reduction for In-silico drug design.*Proceedings of INNS-IEEE International joint Conference on Neural Networks*, (pp. 2478 – 2482). doi:10.1109/IJCNN.2001.938756

Emery, O. (1958). Des filigranes du papier. *Bulletin de l'Association technique de l'industrie papetière, 6,* 185–188.

Erkan, G., & Radev, D. R. (2004). LexRank: Graph-based lexical centrality as salience in text summarization. *Journal of Artificial Intelligence Research, 22,* 457–479.

Eskicioglu Ahmet, M., & Delp Edward, J. (2001). An overview of multimedia content protection in consumer electronics devices. *Signal Processing Image Communication, 16*(7), 681–699. doi:10.1016/S0923-5965(00)00050-3

Eskicioglu, M., & Fisher, P. S. (1995). Image Quality Measures and Their Performance. *IEEE Transactions on Communications, 43*(12), 2959–2965. doi:10.1109/26.477498

Eswaraiah, R., & Reddy, E. S. (2014). A Fragile ROI-Based Medical Image Watermarking Technique with Tamper Detection and Recovery. *Fourth International Conference on Communication Systems and Network Technologies (CSNT)*. doi:10.1109/CSNT.2014.184

ETH. (2015). *Seminar for Statistics. Shapiro-wilk normality test*. Retrieved May 15, 2015, from http://stat.ethz.ch/R-manual/R-devel/library/stats/html/shapiro.test.html

European Union. (n.d.). *EU Member Countries*. Retrieved from http://europa.eu/about-eu/countries/index_en.htm

Eurostat. (n.d.). *The Statistical Office of the European Union*. Retrieved June 3, 2016, from http://ec.europa.eu/eurostat/search?p_auth=TbvilBdy&p_p_id=estatsearchportlet_WAR_estatsearchportlet&p_p_lifecycle=1&p_p_state=maximized&p_p_mode=view&_estatsearchportlet_WAR_estatsearchportlet_action=search&text=computer

Fahad, A., Alshatri, N., Tari, Z., Alamri, A., Khalil, I., Zomaya, A. Y., & Bouras, A. et al. (2014). A survey of clustering algorithms for big data: Taxonomy and empirical analysis. *IEEE Transactions on Emerging Topics in Computing*, 2(3), 267–279. doi:10.1109/TETC.2014.2330519

Fang, X., & Sheng, O. R. L. (2006). A Data-Mining-Based Prefetching Approach to Caching for Network Storage Systems. *INFORMS Journal on Computing*, 18(2), 267–282. doi:10.1287/ijoc.1050.0142

Fan, Y. C., Chiang, A., & Shen, J. H. (2008). ROI-based watermarking scheme for JPEG 2000', *Circuits, Systems &. Signal Processing*, 27(5), 763–774.

Färber, F., May, N., Lehner, W., Große, P., Müller, I., Rauhe, H., & Dees, J. (2012). The SAP HANA Database -- An Architecture Overview. *A Quarterly Bulletin of the Computer Society of the IEEE Technical Committee on Data Engineering*, 35(1),28–33.

Farhadzadeh, F., & Voloshynovskiy, S. (2014). Active Content Fingerpriting. *IEEE Transactions on Information Forensics and Security, Vol*, 9(6), 905–920. doi:10.1109/TIFS.2014.2315531

Farias, M.C.Q., & Akamine, W.Y.L. (2012). On performance of image quality metrics enhanced with visual attention computational models. *IEEE Electronics Letters*, 48(11), 631-633.

Farouk & Saeb. (2004). Design and Implementation of a Secret Key Steganographic Micro-Architecture Employing FPGA. *Date Conference*.

Fattah, M. A., & Ren, F. (2008). Automatic text summarization. *World Academy of Science. Engineering and Technology*, 37, 2008.

Feifei, C., Yuhui, L., Bo, L., & Lian, Y. (2012). FPGA-based adaptive image watermark embedding method and implementation. *IET International Conference on Information Science and Control Engineering*.

Felsberg, M., & Sommer, G. (2001). The monogenic signal. *IEEE Transactions on Signal Processing*, 12(12), 3136–3144. doi:10.1109/78.969520

Felzenszwalb, P., McAllester, D., & Ramanan, D. (2008, June). A discriminatively trained, multiscale, deformable part model. In *Computer Vision and Pattern Recognition, 2008. CVPR 2008. IEEE Conference on* (pp. 1-8). IEEE. doi:10.1109/CVPR.2008.4587597

Fiedler, M. (1973). Algebraic connectivity of graphs. *Czechoslovak Mathematical Journal*, 23(2), 298–305.

Flickner, M., Sawhney, H., Niblack, W., Ashley, J., Huang, Q., Dom, B., & Yanker, P. et al. (1995). Query by image and video content: The QBIC system. *Computer*, 28(9), 23–32. doi:10.1109/2.410146

Fogel, D. B. (1997). An introduction to genetic algorithms: Melanie Mitchell. MIT Press.

Ford, L. R. Jr, & Fulkerson, D. R. (2015). *Flows in networks*. Princeton university press.

Franco, L., Subirats, J. L., Molina, L., Alba, E., & Jerez, J. M. (2007). Early breast cancer prognosis prediction and rule extraction using a new constructive neural network algorithm. *Computational and Ambient intelligence. Lecture Notes in Computer Science*, *4507*, 1004–1011. doi:10.1007/978-3-540-73007-1_121

Frank, H., Peter, E., & Bernd, G. (1998). Digital Watermarking of MPEG-4 Facial Animation Parameters. *Computers & Graphics*, *22*(4), 425–435. doi:10.1016/S0097-8493(98)00032-6

Freeman Roger, L. (2005). *Fundamentals of Telecommunications*. John Wiley & Sons. doi:10.1002/0471720941

Frei, W., & Chen, C. (1977). Fast boundary detection: A generalization and a new algorithm. *IEEE Transactions on Computers*, *C-26*(10), 988–998. doi:10.1109/TC.1977.1674733

Frieze, A. M. (1985). On the value of a random minimum spanning tree problem. *Discrete Applied Mathematics*, *10*(1), 47–56. doi:10.1016/0166-218X(85)90058-7

Fukunaga, K. (1972). *Introduction to Statistical Pattern Recognition*. New York: Academic Press New York.

Gabrys, B., & Bargiela, A. (2000). General fuzzy min – max neural network for clustering and classification. *IEEE Transactions on Neural Networks*, *11*(32), 769–783. doi:10.1109/72.846747 PMID:18249803

Garimella, A., Satyanarayana, M. V. V., Murugesh, P. S., & Niranjan, U. C. (2004). ASIC for digital color image watermarking. *IEEE 11th Digital Signal Processing Workshop*.

Garro, B. A., Rodríguez, K., & Vázquez, R. A. (2016). Classification of DNA microarrays using artificial neural networks and ABC algorithm. *Applied Soft Computing*, *38*, 548–560. doi:10.1016/j.asoc.2015.10.002

Garzia, F. (2013). *Handbook of Communications Security*. WIT Press.

Gaynes, R., Richards, C., Edwards, J., Emori, T. G., Horan, T., Alonso-Echanove, J., & Tolson, J. et al. (2001). Feeding back surveillance data to prevent hospital-acquired infections. *Emerging Infectious Diseases*, *7*(2), 295–298. doi:10.3201/eid0702.010230 PMID:11294727

Geman, S., & Graffigne, C. (1986, August). Markov random field image models and their applications to computer vision. In *Proceedings of the International Congress of Mathematicians* (Vol. 1, p. 2).

Georgiou, D. N., Karakasidis, T. E., & Megaritis, A. C. (2013). A short survey on genetic sequences, chous pseudo amino acid composition and its combination with fuzzy set theory. *The Open Bioinformatics Journal*, *7*(1), 41–48. doi:10.2174/1875036201307010041

Geum, D. P., Dae-Soo, K., & Kee-Young, Y. (2014). Lossless Codebook-Based Digital Watermarking Scheme with Authentication. *11th International Conference on Information Technology: New Generations (ITNG)*.

Geweniger, T., Kästner, M., & Villmann, T. (2013). Border sensitive fuzzy vector quantization in semi-supervised learning. In ESANN.

Ghosh, S., & Dubey, S. K. (2013). Comparative Analysis of K-Means and fuzzy C-Means Algorithms. *International Journal of Advanced Computer Science and Applications*, *4*(4), 35–39. doi:10.14569/IJACSA.2013.040406

Ghosh, S., Ray, P., Maity, S. P., & Rahaman, H. (2009). Spread Spectrum Image Watermarking with Digital Design. *IEEE International Advance Computing Conference*. doi:10.1109/IADCC.2009.4809129

Giger, M. L., Huo, Z., Kupinski, M., & Vyborny, C. J. (2000). Computer-Aided diagnosis in mammography. In Handbook of Medical Imaging Medical Image Processing and Analysis. SPIE.

Goldberg, A. B., Zhu, X., & Wright, S. J. (2007, October). Dissimilarity in graph-based semi-supervised classification. In Artificial Intelligence and Statistics (Vol. 34, p. 52).

Goldberg, D. E. (2006). *Genetic algorithms*. Pearson Education India.

Gong, X., & Richman, M. B. (1995). On the application of cluster analysis to growing season precipitation data in North America east of the Rockies. *Journal of Climate, 8*(4), 897–931. doi:10.1175/1520-0442(1995)008<0897:OTAOCA>2.0.CO;2

Gonzalez, R. C., & Woods, R. E. (2007). *Digital image processing* (3rd ed.). Upper Saddle River, NJ: Prentice Hall.

Gonzalez, R. R., Gomez-Gil, J., Gomez-Gil, F. J., & Martínez-Martínez, V. (2014). *An SVM-Based Classifier for Estimating the State of Various Rotating Components in Agro-Industrial Machinery with a Vibration Signal Acquired from a Single Point on the Machine Chassis*. Academic Press.

Gray, J. (1992). *The Benchmark Handbook: For Database and Transaction Processing Systems*. San Francisco, CA: Morgan Kaufmann Publishers.

Grygorash, O., Zhou, Y., & Jorgensen, Z. (2006, November). Minimum spanning tree based clustering algorithms. In *2006 18th IEEE International Conference on Tools with Artificial Intelligence (ICTAI'06)* (pp. 73-81). IEEE. doi:10.1109/ICTAI.2006.83

Gudmundsson, M., El-Kwae, E. A., & Kabuka, M. R. (1998). Edge detection in medical images using a genetic algorithm. *IEEE Transactions on Medical Imaging, 17*(3), 469–474. doi:10.1109/42.712136 PMID:9735910

Guitao, C., Pengfei, S., & Bing, H. (2005). Ultrasonic Liver Characterization Using Phase Congruency. *Proceedings of the 2005 IEEE Engineering in Medicine and Biology 27th Annual Conference.*

Gun, S. R. (1998). SVM for classification and regression. University of Southampton.

Gunjal & Manthalkar. (2011). An overview of transform domain robust digital image watermarking algorithms. *Journal of Emerging Trends in Computing and Information Sciences, 2*(1).

Guo, C. L., Ma, Q., & Zhang, L. M. (2008). Spatio-temporal saliency detection using phase spectrum of quaternion Fourier transforms. *IEEE Conference on Computer Vision and Pattern Recognition.*

Hair, J. F., Black, W. C., Babin, B. J., & Anderson, R. E. (2010). *Multivariate Data Analysis, A Global Perspective*. Upper Saddle River, NJ: Pearson Prentice Hall.

Hajj, H. M., Nguyen, T. Q., & Chin, R. T. (1996). Multiscale edge detection for medical image enhancement. *18th Annual International Conference of the IEEE Engineering in Medicine and Biology Society.*

Halgamuge, M. N.,Guru, S. M., & Jennings, A. (2003). Energy efficient cluster formation in wireless sensor networks. *10th International Conference on Telecommunications, 2003. ICT 2003.* doi:10.1109/ICTEL.2003.1191668

Hamidreza, Omair, & Swamy. (2016). Multiplicative Watermark Decoder in Contourlet Domain Using the Normal Inverse Gaussian Distribution. *IEEE Transactions on Multimedia, 18*(2), 19 -207.

Hämmerle, U. J., Andreas, U., & Hartmut, W. (2008). Multiple re-watermarking using varying non-stationary mra with parameterized wavelet filters. *Proceedings of the 10th ACM workshop on Multimedia and security.* doi:10.1145/1411328.1411340

Hand, D. J. (1997). *Construction and Assessment of Classification Rules*. New York: Wiley Publication New York.

Han, J., Kamber, M., & Pei, J. (2011). *Data mining: Concepts and techniques*. Elsevier.

Hanjalic, A., & Langelaar, G. C. (2000). Benchmarking the DEW watermarking algorithm. Advances in Image Communication, 8, 273–297.

Hannan, S. A., Manza, R. R., & Ramteke, R. J. (2010). Generalized regression neural network and Radial basis function for heart disease diagnosis. *International Journal of Computer Applications, 7*(13).

Hao-Tang, C., Wen-Jyi, H., & Chau-Jern, C. (2015). Digital Hologram Authentication Using a Hadamard-Based Reversible Fragile Watermarking Algorithm. *Journal of Display Technology, 11*(2), 193–203. doi:10.1109/JDT.2014.2367528

Haralick, R. M. (1979). Statistical and structural approaches to texture. *Proceedings of the IEEE, 67*(5), 786–804. doi:10.1109/PROC.1979.11328

Haralick, R. M., Shanmugam, K., & Dinstein, I. H. (1973). Textural features for image classification. *IEEE Transactions on Systems, Man, and Cybernetics, 3*(6), 610–621. doi:10.1109/TSMC.1973.4309314

Harel, J., Koch, C., & Perona, P. (2006). *Graph-based visual saliency*. Neural Information Processing Systems.

Hassan. (2013). Robust Image Watermarking Against Different Attacks: Noising, (Jpeg) Compression, And Filtering. *Journal of Babylon University/Pure and Applied Sciences, 21*(6).

Hastie, T., Tibshirani, R., & Friedman, J. (2008). The Elements of Statistical Learning: Data Mining, Inference, and Prediction (2nd ed.). Retrieved from https://web.stanford.edu/~hastie/local.ftp/Springer/OLD/ESLII_print4.pdf

Hatamlou, A., Abdullah, S., & Nezamabadi-Pour, H. (2012). A combined approach for clustering based on K-means and gravitational search algorithms. *Swarm and Evolutionary Computation, 6*, 47–52. doi:10.1016/j.swevo.2012.02.003

Hawkins, D. (1980). *Identification of Outliers*. Chapman and Hall. doi:10.1007/978-94-015-3994-4

Hawkins, S., He, H. X., Williams, G. J., & Baxter, R. A. (2002). Outlier detection using replicator neural networks. In *Proceedings of the Fifth International Conference and Data Warehousing and Knowledge Discovery (DaWaK02)*.

Hays, T. (2012, December). *Medical data mining*. Speech made at The National Institute of Standards and Technology (NIST) Symposium. Retrieved on 30 December 2015 from http://www.nist.gov/healthcare/upload/Hays-Medical-Data-Mining-slides-for-web.pdf

Held, C. M., Heiss, J. E., Esteveg, P. A., Perez, C. A., Garrido, M., & Algarinn, C. (2006). Extracting fuzzy rules from polysomnographic recordings for infant sleep classification. *IEEE Transactions on Bio-Medical Engineering, 53*(10), 1954–1962. doi:10.1109/TBME.2006.881798 PMID:17019859

Henriques, R., Pina, S., & Antunes, C. (2013). Temporal mining of integrated healthcare data: Methods, revealings and implications. *SDM IW on Data Mining for Medicine and Healthcare*, 52-60.

Hernandez, J. J. G., Feregrino, U. C., Rene, C., & Carolina, R. (2011). On the Implementation of a Hardware Architecture for an Audio Data Hiding System. *Journal of Signal Processing Systems for Signal, Image, and Video Technology, 64*(3), 457–468. doi:10.1007/s11265-010-0503-8

Herodotus, . (1972). *The Histories* (R. Selincourt, Trans.). Middlesex, UK: Penguin.

Hex-Rays. (n.d.). *IDA* [Software]. Retrieved from https://www.hex-rays.com/index.shtml

Hinchey, M.G., Sterritt, R., & Rouff, C. (2007). Swarms and swarm intelligence. IEEE Journal *on* Computers, 111-113.

Hiwarkar, T. A., & Sridhar Iyer, R. (2013). New applications of soft computing, artificial intelligence, fuzzy logic & genetic algorithm in bioinformatics. *International Journal of Computer Science and Mobile Computing, 2*(5), 202–207.

Hoda, M., Nader, K., & Shadrokh, S. (2015). Framework for Watermark Robustness Adjustment Using Image Depth Map. *23rd Iranian Conference on Electrical Engineering.*

Hodge, V. J., & Austin, J. (2004). A survey of outlier detection methodologies. *Artificial Intelligence Review, 22*(2), 85–126. doi:10.1023/B:AIRE.0000045502.10941.a9

Homer, . (1972). *The Iliad* (R. Fragels, Trans.). Middlesex, UK: Penguin.

Hong, L., Di, X., Rui, Z., Yushu, Z., & Sen, B. (2016). Robust and hierarchical watermarking of encrypted images based on Compressive Sensing. *Journal of Signal Processing: Image Communication, 45*, 41–51.

Hong-Mei, Y., Yong-quan, L., Xiao-Dong, W., & Shu-juan, J. (2007). A DWT- based evaluation method of imperceptibility of watermark in watermarked color image. *International Conference on Wavelet Analysis and Pattern Recognition.* doi:10.1109/ICWAPR.2007.4420663

Horowitz & Hill. (1989). *The Art of Electronics* (2nd ed.). Cambridge University Press.

Hossein, B. (2006). Handbook of Information Security, Key Concepts, Infrastructure, Standards, and Protocols. John Wiley and Sons.

Hsien-Wen, T., & Chin-Chen, C. (2004). High Capacity Data Hiding in JPEG-Compressed Images. *Informatica, 15*(1), 127–142.

Hu, Y.J., Hu, Y.H., & Ke, J.B. (2011). The modified DNA identification classification on fuzzy relation. *Applied Mechanics and Materials, 48-49,* 1275-1281.

Huang & Wu. (2004). Attacking visible watermarking schemes. *IEEE Transactions on Multimedia, 6*(1), 16-30.

Huang, Y., Lin, S., Stan, Z., Lu, H., & Shum, V. (2004). Face Alignment under Variable Illumination. *IEEE International Conference on Automatic Face and Gesture Recognition.*

Huang, Y., Lin, S., Stan, Z., Lu, H., & Shum, V. (2004). Noise removal and impainting model for iris image. *International Conference on Image Processing.*

Huang, J., & Shi, Y. Q. (1998). Adaptive Image Watermarking Scheme Based on Visual masking. *Electronics Letters, 34*(8), 748–750. doi:10.1049/el:19980545

Huertas, A., & Medioni, G. G. (1986). Detection of intensity changes with sub pixel accuracy using laplacian-gaussian masks. *IEEE Transaction on Pattern Analysis and Machine Intelligence PAMI, 8*(5), 651–664. doi:10.1109/TPAMI.1986.4767838 PMID:21869362

Hussain, N., Wageeh, B., & Colin, B. (2013). A Review of Medical Image Watermarking Requirements for Teleradiology. *Journal of Digital Imaging, 26*(2), 326–343. doi:10.1007/s10278-012-9527-x PMID:22975883

Hwai-Tsu, H., & Ling-Yuan, H. (2016). A mixed modulation scheme for blind image watermarking. *International Journal of Electronics and Communications, 70*(2), 172–178. doi:10.1016/j.aeue.2015.11.003

Idreos, S., Groffen, F., Nes, N., Manegold, S., Mullender, K. S., & Kersten, M. L. (2012). Monetdb: Two decades of research in column-oriented database architectures. *A Quarterly Bulletin of the Computer Society of the IEEE Technical Committee on Data Engineering, 35*(1), 40–45.

Ilea, D. E., & Whelan, P. F. (2005). An adaptive unsupervised segmentation algorithm based on color-texture coherence. IEEE Transactions on Image Processing.

Imran, U., Asifullah, K., Rafiullah, C., & Abdul, M. (2008). *Towards a Better Robustness-Imperceptibility Tradeoff in Digital Watermarking.* Innovations and Advanced Techniques in Systems, Computing Sciences and Software Engineering.

İsmail, A. (2001). *Image Quality Statistics And Their Use In Steganalysis and Compression* (PhD Thesis). Institute for Graduate Studies in Science and Engineering, Uludağ University.

Ismail, A., Bulent, S., & Khalid, S. (2002). Statistical Evaluation of Image Quality Measures. *Journal of Electronic Imaging, 11*(2), 206–223. doi:10.1117/1.1455011

Ismail, M. A., & Kamel, M. S. (1989). Multidimensional data clustering utilizing hybrid search strategies. *Pattern Recognition, 22*(1), 75–89. doi:10.1016/0031-3203(89)90040-X

Itti, L., & Koch, C. (2000). A saliency-based search mechanism for overt and covert shifts of visual attention. *Vision Research, 40*(10-12), 1489–1506. doi:10.1016/S0042-6989(99)00163-7 PMID:10788654

Itti, L., & Koch, C. (2001). Computational Modeling of Visual Attention. *Nature Reviews. Neuroscience, 2*(3), 194–203. doi:10.1038/35058500 PMID:11256080

Jacob, S. G., & Ramani, R. G. (2012). Data mining in clinical data sets: A review. *International Journal of Applied Information Systems, 4*(6), 15–26. doi:10.5120/ijais12-450774

Jain, A. K. (2010). Data clustering: 50 years beyond K-means. *Pattern Recognition Letters, 31*(8), 651–666. doi:10.1016/j.patrec.2009.09.011

Jain, A. K., Murty, M. N., & Flynn, P. J. (1999). Data clustering: A review. *ACM Computing Surveys, 31*(3), 264–323. doi:10.1145/331499.331504

Jain, N., & Srivastava, V. (2013). Data mining techniques: A survey paper. IJRET. *International Journal of Research in Engineering and Technology, 2*(11), 1163–2319.

Jalal, F., Jalil, F., & Peter, W. (1999). *Digital Certificates: Applied Internet Security* (Vol. 1). Addison-Wesley.

Jana, P. K., & Naik, A. (2009, December). An efficient minimum spanning tree based clustering algorithm. In *Methods and Models in Computer Science, 2009. ICM2CS 2009.Proceeding of International Conference on* (pp. 1-5). IEEE. doi:10.1109/ICM2CS.2009.5397966

Janeczko Paul, B. (2006). *Top Secret: A Handbook of Codes, Ciphers and Secret Writing.* Candlewick Press.

Jang, J. S. R., Sun, C. T., & Mizutani, E. (1997). *Neuro-Fuzzy And Soft Computing.* Prentice Hall.

Jaseena, & John. (2011). Text Watermarking using Combined Image and Text for Authentication and Protection. *International Journal of Computer Applications, Volume, 20*(4).

Jassim, F. A. (2013). Semi-Optimal edge detector based on simple standard deviation with adjusted thresholding. *International Journal of Computers and Applications, 68*(2), 43–48. doi:10.5120/11555-6834

Jenatton, R., Obozinski, G., & Bach, F. (2010). Structured sparse principal component analysis. In *Proc. Int. Conf.Artif. Intell. Statist.,* (pp. 366–373).

Jensen, F. V., & Nielsen, T. D. (2007). *Bayesian networks and decision graphs.* London: Springer. doi:10.1007/978-0-387-68282-2

Jensen, R., & Shen, Q. (2008). *Computational Intelligence and Feature Selection: Rough and Fuzzy Approaches.* Wiley-IEEE Press. doi:10.1002/9780470377888

Jensi, R., & Jiji, D. G. W. (2014). *A survey on optimization approaches to text document clustering.* arXiv preprint arXiv:1401.2229

Jiang, T., Zang, W., Zhao, C., & Shi, J. (2010). An energy consumption optimized clustering algorithm for radar sensor networks based on an ant colony algorithm. *EURASIP Journal on Wireless Communications and Networking.*

Jianqing, L., & Yang, Y. H. (1994). Multiresolution color image segmentation. *Pattern Analysis and Machine Intelligence. IEEE Transactions on, 16*(7), 689–700. doi:10.1109/34.297949

Jianquan, X., Qing, X., Dazu, H., & Duosi, X. (2010). Research on imperceptibility index of image Information Hiding. *Second International Conference on Networks Security Wireless Communications and Trusted Computing (NSWCTC).* doi:10.1109/NSWCTC.2010.148

Jiansheng, Q., Dong, W., Li, L. C. D., & Xuesong, W. (2014). Image quality assessment based on multi-scale representation of structure. *Digital Signal Processing, 33*, 125–133. doi:10.1016/j.dsp.2014.06.009

Jianzhong, L., & Xiaojing, C. (2009). An adaptive secure watermarking scheme using double random-phase encoding technique. *2nd International Congress on Image and Signal Processing, CISP '09.*

Jiawei Han, M. K. (2012). *Data mining concepts and techniques.* Morgan Kaufmann Publishers, Elsevier.

Jiawei, H., & Kamber, M. (2001). Data mining: Concepts and techniques. San Francisco, CA: Morgan Kaufmann.

Ji, J., Pang, W., Zhou, C., Yan, X., & Wang, Z. (2012). A fuzzy k-prototype clustering algorithm for mixed numerical and categorical data. *Knowledge-Based Systems, 30*, 129–135. doi:10.1016/j.knosys.2012.01.006

Jiménez, D. A. (2003). Fast path-based neural branch predictions. In *Proceedings of the 36th International Symposium on Microarchitecture* (MICRO-36). doi:10.1109/MICRO.2003.1253199

Jiménez, D. A., & Lin, C. (2001). Dynamic branch prediction with perceptrons. In *Proceedings of High-Performance Computer Architecture* (pp. 197–206). HPCA.

Jin &, Kim. (2012). Imperceptibility Improvement of Image Watermarking Using Variance Selection, Computer Applications for Web, Human Computer Interaction. *Signal and Image Processing, and Pattern Recognition Communications in Computer and Information Science, 342*, 31–38.

Jinn, H., & Wen-Liang, H. (2008). Automatic microarray spot segmentation using a snake-fisher model. *Medical Imaging. IEEE Transactions on, 27*(6), 847–857. doi:10.1109/TMI.2008.915697

Ji, Q., & Haralick, R. M. (1999). Quantitative evaluation of edge detectors using the minimum kernel variance criterion. *ICIP 99,IEEE International Conference on Image Processing.*

John, S. (1996). SPRINT: A scalable Parallel Classifier for Data Mining. *22th International Conference on very large databases.*

Johnson, D. E. (2001). Web-based data analysis tools help providers, MCOs contain costs. *Health Care Strategic Management, 19*(4), 16. PMID:11329971

Jordan, F. R. B. M. I., & Bach, F. (2004). Learning spectral clustering. *Advances in Neural Information Processing Systems, 16*, 305–312.

Joshi, A. M., Darji, A., & Mishra, V. (2011). Design and implementation of real-time image watermarking. *IEEE International Conference on Signal Processing, Communications and Computing.* doi:10.1109/ICSPCC.2011.6061762

Juergen, S. (2005). *Digital Watermarking for Digital Media, Idea Group Inc.* IGI.

Ju, F., Sun, S., Gao, J., Hu, Y., & Yin, B. (2015). Image outlier detection and feature extraction via L1-normbased 2Dprobabilistic PCA. *IEEE Transactions on Image Processing*, *24*(12), 4834–4846. doi:10.1109/TIP.2015.2469136 PMID:26292341

Jung, W.-S., Lim, K.-W., Ko, Y.-B., & Park, S.-J. (2011). Efficient clustering-based data aggregation techniques for wireless sensor networks. *Wireless Networks*, *17*(5), 1387–1400. doi:10.1007/s11276-011-0355-6

Junrui, Y., & Feng, Z. (2010). An Effective Algorithm for Mining Quantitative Associations Based on Subspace Clustering.*International Conference on Networking and Digital Society*.

Jun, S., & Alam, M. S. (2008). Fragility and Robustness of Binary-Phase-Only-Filter-Based Fragile/Semifragile Digital Image Watermarking. *IEEE Transactions on Instrumentation and Measurement*, *57*(3).

Kabir, M. N., Omar, T., & Alginahi, Y. M. (2013). Evaluation of Watermarking Approaches for Arabic Text Documents. *International Journal of Computer Science and Information Security*, *11*(3), 49–54.

Kahrmanli, H., & Allahverdi, N. (2008). Design of a hybrid system for the diabetes and heart diseases. *Expert Systems with Applications*, *35*(1-2), 82–89. doi:10.1016/j.eswa.2007.06.004

Kahrmanli, H., & Allahverdi, N. (2009). Extracting rules for classification problems: AIS based approach. *Expert Systems with Applications*, *36*(7), 10494–10502. doi:10.1016/j.eswa.2009.01.029

Kale, K. V. (2008). Advances in Computer Vision and Information Technology. I. K. International Pvt Ltd.

Kamal, S., & Burk, L. I. (1996). FACT: A new neural network-based clustering algorithm for group technology. *International Journal of Production Research*, *34*(4), 919–946. doi:10.1080/00207549608904943

Kandel, A., & Langholz, G. (Eds.). (1992). *Hybrid architectures for intelligent systems*. CRC Press.

Kang, X., & Wei, S. (2008). Identifying tampered regions using singular value decomposition in digital image forensics. In *Proc. international conference on computer science and software engineering*. doi:10.1109/CSSE.2008.876

Kantardzic, M. (2011). *Data mining: concepts, models, methods, and algorithms*. John Wiley & Sons. doi:10.1002/9781118029145

Kao, C.-M., Pan, X., Hiller, E., & Chen, C.-T. (1998). A Bayesian approach for edge detection in medical ultrasound images. *IEEE Transactions on Nuclear Science*, *NS-45*, 3089–3098.

Karaboga, D., Okdem, S., & Ozturk, C. (2012). Cluster based wireless sensor network routing using artificial bee colony algorithm. *Wireless Networks*, *18*(7), 847–860. doi:10.1007/s11276-012-0438-z

Karaboga, D., & Ozturk, C. (2011). A novel clustering approach: Artificial Bee Colony (ABC) algorithm. *Applied Soft Computing*, *11*(1), 652–657. doi:10.1016/j.asoc.2009.12.025

Karalolis, M. A., Moutiris, J. A., Hadjipanayi, D., & Pattichis, C. S. (2010). Assessment of the risk factors of coronary heart events based on data mining with decision trees. *IEEE Transactions on Information Technology in Biomedicine*, *14*(3), 559–564. doi:10.1109/TITB.2009.2038906 PMID:20071264

Karger, D. R., Klein, P. N., & Tarjan, R. E. (1995). A randomized linear-time algorithm to find minimum spanning trees. [JACM]. *Journal of the Association for Computer Machinery*, *42*(2), 321–328. doi:10.1145/201019.201022

Karssemeijer, N., & Hendriks, J. H. C. L. (1997). Computer-Assisted reading mammograms. *European Radiology*, *7*(5), 743–748. doi:10.1007/BF02742937 PMID:9166576

Karthigaikumar, P., & Baskaranc Anumol, K. (2011). FPGA Implementation of High Speed Low Area DWT Based Invisible Image Watermarking Algorithm. *International Conference on Communication Technology and System Design.*

Karthigaikumar, P., & Baskaran, K. (2011). FPGA and ASIC implementation of robust invisible binary image watermarking algorithm using connectivity preserving criteria. *Microelectronics Journal, 42*(1), 82–88. doi:10.1016/j.mejo.2010.08.023

Karthigai, P., & Baskaran, K. (2011). An ASIC implementation of a low power robust invisible watermarking processor. *Journal of Systems Architecture: The EUROMICRO Journal, 57*(4), 404–411. doi:10.1016/j.sysarc.2010.03.008

Kass, M., Witkin, A., & Terzopoulos, D. (1988). Snakes: Active contour models. *International Journal of Computer Vision, Kluwer Academic Publishers, 1*(4), 321–331. doi:10.1007/BF00133570

Kaufman, L., & Rousseeuw, P. J. (2008). *Partitioning Around Medoids (Program PAM).* John Wiley & Sons, Inc.

Kaushal, S., Upamanyu, M., Manjunath, B. S., & Shiv, C. (2005). Modeling the Print-Scan Process for Resilient Data Hiding, Security, Steganography, and Watermarking of Multimedia Contents. *SPIE, 5681,* 418-429.

Kautilya. (1992). *The Arthashastra* (L. N. Rangarajan, Trans.). Penguin Books India.

Keedwell, E., & Narayanan, A. (2005). *Intelligent bioinformatics.* John Wiley & Sons, Ltd. doi:10.1002/0470015721

Keller, J. M., Gray, M. R., & Givens, J. A. Jr. (1985). A fuzzy K-nearest neighbor algorithm. *IEEE Transactions on Systems, Man, and Cybernetics, SMC-15*(4), 580–585. doi:10.1109/TSMC.1985.6313426

Kemper, A., & Neumann, T. (2011). HyPer: A hybrid OLTP&OLAP main memory database system based on virtual memory snapshots. In *Proceeding of the 27th International Conference on Data Engineering,* (pp, 195-206). Hannover, Germany: IEEE. doi:10.1109/ICDE.2011.5767867

Kennedy, J., & Eberhart, R. C. (1995). Particle swarm optimization. *Proc. of IEEE International Conference on Neural Networks.* doi:10.1109/ICNN.1995.488968

Keskinarkaus, A., Pramila, A., & Seppänen, T. (2012). Image watermarking with feature point based synchronization robust to print–scan attack. *Journal of Visual Communication and Image Representation, 23*(3), 507–515. doi:10.1016/j.jvcir.2012.01.010

Kharittha, T., Pipat, S., & Thumrongrat, A. (2015). Digital Image Watermarking based on Regularized Filter. *14th IAPR International Conference on Machine Vision Applications.*

Ki-Hyeok, B., & Sung-Hwan, J. (2001). A study on the robustness of watermark according to frequency band. *IEEE International Symposium on Industrial Electronics.* doi:10.1109/ISIE.2001.932024

Kim, Y. S., Kwon, O. H., & Park, R. H. (1999). Wavelet Based Watermarking Method for Digital Images Using The Human Visual System. *Electronics Letters, 35*(6), 466–468. doi:10.1049/el:19990327

Kiyan, T., & Yildirim, T. (2004). Breast cancer diagnosis using statistical neural networks. *Journal of Electronic and Electrical Engineering, 4*(2), 1149–1153.

Koch, C., & Ullman, S. (1985). Shifts in selective visual attention: Towards the underlying neural circuitry. *Human Neurobiology, 4,* 219–227. PMID:3836989

Kochurani, O. G., & Aji, S. (2007). A neuro fuzzy decision tree model for predicting the risk in coronary artery disease. *IEEE 22nd International Symposium on Intelligent Control,* (pp. 166 – 171).

Kogan. (2007). *Introduction to clustering large and high-dimensional data* (1st ed.). Cambridge University Press.

Kohavi, R. (1995). A study of cross validation and bootstrap for accuracy estimation and model selection. *Proceeding of International Joint Conference on Artificial Intelligence.*

Koh, H. C., & Tan, G. (2011). Data mining applications in healthcare. *Journal of Healthcare Information Management, 19*(2), 65. PMID:15869215

Kohli, S., & Mehrotra, S. (2016), A clustering approach for optimization of search result. Journal of Images and Graphics, 4(1), 63-66.

Kohonen, T. (1984). *Self-Organization and Associative Memory.* Berlin, Germany: Springer-Verlag.

Kolçe, E., & Frasheri, N. (2012, September). *A literature review of data mining techniques used in healthcare databases.* Paper presented at the ICT innovations 2012, Ohrid, Macadonia.

Koller, D., & Friedman, N. (2009). *Probabilistic graphical models: Principles and techniques.* MIT Press.

Kong, W. L., Teoh, E. K., Wang, J.-G., & Venkateswarlu, R. (2005). A framework of 2D Fisher discriminant analysis: Application to face recognition with small number of training samples. In *Proc. IEEE Int. Conf. Comput. Vis. Pattern Recognit.,* (pp. 1083–1088).

Kornaros, G. (2010). A soft multi-core architecture for edge detection and data analysis of microarray images. *Journal of Systems Architecture, 56*(1), 48–62. doi:10.1016/j.sysarc.2009.11.004

Kotsiantis, S. B. (2007). Supervised Machine Learning: A Review of Classification Techniques. *Informatica, 31,* 249–268.

Koutroumbas, S. T. (2006). *Pattern Recognition.* Elseiver.

Kovalerchuk, B., Triantaphyllou, E., Ruiz, J. F., & Clayton, J. (1997). Fuzzy logic in computer aided breast cancer diagnosis: Analysis of lobulation. *Artificial Intelligence in Medicine, 11*(1), 75–85. doi:10.1016/S0933-3657(97)00021-3 PMID:9267592

Kovesi, P. D. (1996). *Invariant Measures of Image Features from Phase Information* (PhD thesis). University of Western Australia.

Kovesi, P. D. (2003). Phase congruency detects corners and edges. *The Australian Pattern Recognition Society Conference.* DICTA.

Kovesi, P. (2003). Phase Congruency Detects Corners and Edges.*Australian Pattern Recognition Society Conference.*

Kovesi, P. D. (1999). Image features from phase congruency. *Videre: Journal of Computer Vision Research, 1,* 1–26.

Krizhevsky, A., Sutskever, I., & Hinton, G. E. (2012). Imagenet classification with deep convolutional neural networks. *Advances in Neural Information Processing Systems.*

Kruskal, J. B. (1956). On the shortest spanning subtree of a graph and the traveling salesman problem. *Proceedings of the American Mathematical Society, 7*(1), 48–50. doi:10.1090/S0002-9939-1956-0078686-7

Kuila, P., & Jana, P. K. (2014). Energy efficient clustering and routing algorithms for wireless sensor networks: Particle swarm optimization approach. *Engineering Applications of Artificial Intelligence, 33,* 127–140. doi:10.1016/j.engappai.2014.04.009

Kullback, S., & Leibler, R. A. (1951). On Information and Sufficiency. *Annals of Mathematical Statistics, 22*(1), 79–86. doi:10.1214/aoms/1177729694

Kumar, A., & Thomas, A. (2012). Energy efficiency and network lifetime maximization in wireless sensor networks using improved ant colony optimization. *Procedia Engineering, 38,* 3797–3805. doi:10.1016/j.proeng.2012.06.435

Kumar, M. H., & Maity, S. P. (2014). FPGA implementation of reversible watermarking in digital images using reversible contrast mapping. *Journal of Systems and Software*, *96*, 93–104. doi:10.1016/j.jss.2014.05.079

Kumar, V., & Mishra, S. K. (2013). Detection of malware by using sequence alignment strategy and data mining techniques. *International Journal of Computers and Applications*, *61*, 16–19.

Kuo, R. J., Lin, S. Y., & Shih, C. W. (2007). Mining association rules through integration of clustering analysis and ant colony system for health insurance database in Taiwan. Expert Systems with Applications, 794–808.

Kuppusamy, K., & Thamodaran, K. (2012). Optimized Image Watermarking Scheme Based On PSO. *Procedia Engineering*, *38*, 493–503. doi:10.1016/j.proeng.2012.06.061

Kutter, M., Voloshynovskiy, S., & Herrigel, A. (2000). The watermark copy attack. Security and Watermarking of Multimedia Content II, 3971.

Kwiatkowska, M., Atkins, M. S., Ayas, N. T., & Ryan, C. F. (2007). Knowledge-based data analysis: First step toward the creation of clinical prediction rules using a new typicality measure. Information Technology in Biomedicine. *IEEE Transactions on*, *11*(6), 651–660.

Kyan, M., Guan, L., Arnison, R., & Cogswell, C. (2001). Feature Extraction of Chromosomes from 3-D Confocal Microscope Images. *IEEE Transactions on Bio-Medical Engineering*, *48*(11), 1306–1318. doi:10.1109/10.959326 PMID:11686629

Laboratory for Biomedical Informatics. (2015). Retrieved on September 11, 2015, from http://www.labmedinfo.org/translational/temporal

Lafferty, J., McCallum, A., & Pereira, F. (2001, June). Conditional random fields: Probabilistic models for segmenting and labeling sequence data. In *Proceedings of the eighteenth international conference on machine learning, ICML* (Vol. 1, pp. 282-289). IEEE.

Lalitha, N. V., & Rao, S. (2013). DWT - Arnold Transform based audio watermarking. *IEEE Asia Pacific Conference on Postgraduate Research in Microelectronics and Electronics*. doi:10.1109/PrimeAsia.2013.6731204

Lauria, A., Massafra, R., Tangaro, S. S., Bellotti, R., Delogu, F. P., Torres, E. L., . . . Bottigli, U. (2006). GPCALMA: An Italian mammographic database of digitized images for research. *International Workshop on Breast Imaging Lecture Notes in Computer Science*. Springer. doi:10.1007/11783237_52

Läuter, H. (1988). Silverman, BW: Density Estimation for Statistics and Data Analysis. Chapman & Hall.

Lee, H. K., Kim, H. J., Kwon, S. G., & Lee, J. K. (2005). ROI Medical Image Watermarking Using DWT and Bit-Plane. *Asia-Pacific Conference on Communications*.

Lewis, M. A., & Bekey, G. A. (1992). The behavioral self-organization of nanorobots using local rules.*International Conference on Intelligent Robots and Systems*. IEEE.

Li, G. Y., Xu, Z., Xiong, C., Yang, C., Zhang, S., Chen, Y., & Xu, S. (2011). Energy-efficient wireless communications: Tutorial, survey, and open issues. *IEEE Wireless Communications*, *18*(6), 28–35. doi:10.1109/MWC.2011.6108331

Li, H. G.-Q., Guo, S., Li, C., & Sun, J. (2013). A hybrid annual power load forecasting model based on generalized regression neural network with fruit fly optimization algorithm. *Knowledge-Based Systems*, *37*, 378–387. doi:10.1016/j.knosys.2012.08.015

Lim, C. P., Leong, J. H., & Kuan, M. M. (2005). A hybrid neural network system for pattern classification task with missing features. *IEEE Transactions on Pattern Analysis and Machine Intelligence*, *27*(4), 648–653. doi:10.1109/TPAMI.2005.64 PMID:15794170

Lin, Y., Tong, N., Shi, M., & Fan, K. (2012). *K-means optimization clustering algorithm Based on Particle Swarm Optimization and Multiclass Merging.* Academic Press.

Lina Shinfeng, D., Shieb, S-C., & Guoa, J.Y. (2010). Improving the robustness of DCT-based image watermarking against JPEG compression. *Computer Standards & Interfaces, 32*(1–2), 54–60.

Lindeberg, T. (1998). Edge detection and ridge detection with automatic scale selection. *International Journal of Computer Vision, 30*(2), 117–156. doi:10.1023/A:1008097225773

Ling Wang, X.-Z.-y. (2013). A novel binary fruit fly optimization algorithm for solving the multidimensional knapsack problem. *Knowledge-Based Systems, 48*, 17–23. doi:10.1016/j.knosys.2013.04.003

Lin, H. (2008). Identification of spinal deformity classification with total curvature analysis and artificial neural network. *IEEE Transactions on Bio-Medical Engineering, 55*(1), 376–382. doi:10.1109/TBME.2007.894831 PMID:18232388

Lin, P.-L. (2001). Oblivious Digital Watermarking Scheme with Blob-Oriented and Modular-Arithmetic-Based Spatial-Domain Mechanism. *Journal of Visual Communication and Image Representation, 12*(2), 136–151. doi:10.1006/jvci.2000.0454

Lin, W., Orgun, M. A., & Williams, G. J. (2002). Mining temporal patterns from health care data. In *Data Warehousing and Knowledge Discovery* (pp. 222–231). Springer Berlin Heidelberg. doi:10.1007/3-540-46145-0_22

Li, Q., Fraley, C., Bumgarner, R. E., Yeung, K. Y., & Raftery, A. E. (2005). Donuts, scratches and blanks: Robust model-based segmentation of microarray images. *Bioinformatics (Oxford, England), 21*(12), 2875–2882. doi:10.1093/bioinformatics/bti447 PMID:15845656

Li, S. Z. (2009). *Markov random field modeling in image analysis.* Springer Science & Business Media.

Li, T., & Chen, Y. (2009). Hierarchical Clustering Ensemble Algorithm based Association Rules.*5th International Conference on Wireless Communications, Networking and Mobile Computing.* doi:10.1109/WICOM.2009.5305676

Liu & Qiu. (2002). The survey of digital watermarking-based image authentication techniques. *ICSP'02 Proceedings.*

Liu, N., Amin, P., Ambalavanan, A., & Subbalakshmi, K. P. (2006). An Overview of Digital Watermarking. In Multimedia Security Technologies for Digital Rights Management. Academic Press.

Liu, Y. W. (2012). A modified fruit-fly optimization algorithm aided PID controller designing. *IEEE 10th World Congress on Intelligent Control and Automation* (pp. 233-238). Beijing, China: IEEE.

Liu, H.-C., Yih, J.-M., Lin, W.-C., & Liu, T.-S. (2009). Fuzzy c-means algorithm based on pso and maha-lanobis distances. *International Journal of Innovative Computing, Information, & Control, 5*(12b), 5033–5040.

Liu, L., Bland, P. H., Williams, D. M., Schunck, B. G., & Meyer, C. R. (1989). Application of robust sequential edge detection and linking to boundaries of low contrast lesions in medical images. *Computer Vision and Pattern Recognition, CVPR, 1989*, 582–587.

Liu, Z., & Laganiere, R. (2007). Phase congruence measurement for image similarity assessment. *Pattern Recognition Letters, 28*(1), 166–172. doi:10.1016/j.patrec.2006.06.019

Li, Y. L., & Shen, Y. (2010). An automatic fuzzy c-means algorithm for image segmentation. *Soft Computing, 14*(2), 123–128. doi:10.1007/s00500-009-0442-0

Lo, Hu, Chen, & Chang. (2014). Probability-Based Image Authentication Scheme for Indexed Color Images. *Journal of Electronic Imaging, 23*(3).

Lopez, G. M., Ramos, L. R., Miguel, H. O., & Canto, N. E. (2014). *Embedded System for Biometric Online Signature Verification. IEEE Transactions on Industrial Informatics, 10*(1), 491–501.

Lowrance, W. W. (2002). Learning from experience: Privacy and the secondary use of data in health research. *The Journal of Biolaw & Business, 6*(4), 30–60. PMID:15072055

Lu, K., He, X., & Zeng, J. (2005). Image retrieval using dimensionality reduction. In J. Zhang, J. H. He, & Y. Fu (Eds.), Computational and Information Science (LNCS), (vol. 3314, pp. 775–781). doi:10.1007/978-3-540-30497-5_120

Lu, H., Plataniotis, K. N., & Venetsanopoulos, A. N. (2008). MPCA: Multilinear principal component analysis of tensor objects. *IEEE Transactions on Neural Networks, 19*(1), 18–39. doi:10.1109/TNN.2007.901277 PMID:18269936

Lukac, R., & Plataniotis, K. N. (2007). Vector edge operators for cDNA microarray spot localization. *Computerized Medical Imaging and Graphics, 31*(7), 510–522. doi:10.1016/j.compmedimag.2007.06.002 PMID:17707611

Lynch C., (2000). Authenticity and Integrity in the Digital Environment: An Exploratory Analysis of the Central Role of Trust. In *Authenticity in a Digital Age.* CLIR.

Lynch, C. A. (1988). Selectivity estimation and query optimization in large databases with highly skewed distribution of column values. In *Proceedings of the 14th International Conference on Very Large Data Bases (VLDB),* (pp. 240-251). San Francisco, CA: Morgan Kaufmann Publishers Inc.

Macq, B., Dittmann, J., & Delp, E. J. (2004). Benchmarking of image watermarking algorithms for digital rights management. *Proceedings of the IEEE, 92*(6), 971-984. doi:10.1109/JPROC.2004.827361

MacQueen, J. B. (1967). Some methods for classification and analysis of multivariate observations. In *Proceedings of the Fifth Symposium on Mathematical Statistics and Probability.* University of California.

Maglogiannis, I., Loukis, E., Zafiropoulos, E., & Stasis, A. (2009). Support vector machine-based identification of heart valve diseases using heart sounds. *Computer Methods and Programs in Biomedicine, 95*(1), 47–61. doi:10.1016/j.cmpb.2009.01.003 PMID:19269056

Maitra, I. K., Bhattacharjee, S., Bhattacharyya, D., Kim, T. H., & Bandyopadhyay, S. K. (2016). Adaptive edge detection technique towards features extraction from mammogram images. *Journal of Cancer Research Updates. LifeScience Global Publication, 5*(2), 47–58.

Maity, S. P., Kundu, M. K., & Seba, M. (2009). Dual Purpose FWT Domain Spread Spectrum Image Watermarking in Real-Time. *Computers & Electrical Engineering, 35*(2), 415–433. doi:10.1016/j.compeleceng.2008.06.003

Majje, C., & Sahoo, G. (2004). *DNA sequencing by oligonucleotide hybridization: A genetic algorithm approach, proceedings of the international conference on genetics and evolutionary computation.* Seattle, WA: GECCO.

Makbol, N. M., Ee, K. B., & Rassem, T. H. (2016). Block-based discrete wavelet transform singular value decomposition image watermarking scheme using human visual system characteristics. *IET Image Process., 10*(1), 34–52. doi:10.1049/iet-ipr.2014.0965

Ma, L., Weisi, L., Deng, C., & King, N. N. (2012). Image Retargeting Quality Assessment: A Study of Subjective Scores and Objective Metrics. *IEEE Journal of Selected Topics in Signal Processing, Volume, 6*(6), 626–639. doi:10.1109/JSTSP.2012.2211996

Malfait, M., & Roose, D. (1997). Wavelet-based image denoising using a Markov random field a priori model. *IEEE Transactions on Image Processing, 6*(4), 549–565. doi:10.1109/83.563320 PMID:18282948

Malihe, M., Mohammad, Z., & Chahooki, A. (2016). Robust transparent image watermarking with Shearlet transform andbidiagonal singular value decomposition. *International Journal of Electronics and Communications*, *70*(6), 790–798. doi:10.1016/j.aeue.2016.03.004

Malik, H., & Kender, J. R. (2006). High quality, efficient hierarchical document clustering using closed interesting item sets.*Proceedings of the Sixth International Conference on Data Mining (ICDM'06)*. IEEE. doi:10.1109/ICDM.2006.81

Malishevsky, A., Beck., D., Schmid, A., & Landry, E. (n.d.). *Dynamic Branch Prediction*. Retrieved from http://web. engr.oregonstate.edu/~benl/Projects/branch_pred/

Mallat, S. G. (1989). A theory for multiresolution signal decomposition: The wavelet representation. *Pattern Analysis and Machine Intelligence. IEEE Transactions on*, *11*(7), 674–693. doi:10.1109/34.192463

Marques, O., & Borko, F. (2002). MUSE: A content-based image search and retrieval system using relevance feedback. *Multimedia Tools and Applications*, *17*(1), 21–50. doi:10.1023/A:1014679605305

Marr, D., & Hildreth, E. (1980). Theory of edge detection. *Proceedings of the Royal Society of London. Series B, Biological Sciences*, *207*(1167), 187–217. doi:10.1098/rspb.1980.0020 PMID:6102765

Martinez, W. L., & Martinez, A. R. (2005). *Exploratory Data Analysis with MATLAB*. Boca Raton, FL: Chapman & Hall/CRC Press.

Masala, G., Tangaro, S., & Quarta, M. (2006). Classifiers trained on dissimilarity representation of medical pattern: A comparative study. *Il Nuovo Cimento C*, *28*(6), 905–912.

Matheson, L. R., Mitchell, S. G., Shamoon, T. G., Tarjan, R. E., & Francis, Z. (1998). Robustness and security of digital watermarks, Financial Cryptography. *Lecture Notes in Computer Science*, *1465*, 227–240. doi:10.1007/BFb0055486

Ma, Y. X., & Wang, S. G. (2012). The applications of artificial neural network in medical meteorology. *Future Control and Automation. Lecture Notes in Electrical Engineering*, *172*, 237–242. doi:10.1007/978-3-642-31006-5_29

McFarling, S. (1993). *Combining branch predictor. Technical report*. Digital Western.

Medsker, L. R. (1995). *Hybrid intelligent systems*. Kluwer Academic Publishers.

Megalingam, R. K., Nair, M. M., Srikumar, R., Balasubramanian, V. K., & Sarma, V. S. V. (2010). Performance Comparison of Novel, Robust Spatial Domain Digital Image Watermarking with the Conventional Frequency Domain Watermarking Techniques. *International Conference on Signal Acquisition and Processing*. doi:10.1109/ICSAP.2010.79

Mehran, A., & Chandler, D. M. (2015). Digital Image Watermarking via Adaptive Logo Texturization. *IEEE Transactions on Image Processing*, *24*(12), 5060–5073. doi:10.1109/TIP.2015.2476961 PMID:26353371

Mehrotra, S., & Kohli, S. (2015, October). Comparative analysis of K-Means with other clustering algorithms to improve search result. In *Green Computing and Internet of Things (ICGCIoT), 2015 International Conference on* (pp. 309-313). IEEE. doi:10.1109/ICGCIoT.2015.7380479

Mehrotra, S., & Kohli, S. (2016). Application of clustering for improving search result of a website. In *Information Systems Design and Intelligent Applications* (pp. 349–356). Springer India. doi:10.1007/978-81-322-2752-6_34

Mehrotra, S., & Kohli, S. (2016, March). The Study of the Usage of Data Analytic and Clustering Techniques for Web Elements. In *Proceedings of the ACM Symposium on Women in Research 2016* (pp. 118-120). ACM. doi:10.1145/2909067.2909089

Mehta, M., Agrawal, R., & Rissanen, J. (1996). A fast scalable classifier for data mining. In *proceedings of 5th International Conference on Extending Database Technology: Advances in Database Technology*. Springer Verlag. doi:10.1007/BFb0014141

Meyers, P. H., Nice, C. M. Jr, Becker, H. C., Nettleton, W. J. Jr, Sweeney, J. W., & Meckstroth, G. R. (1964). Automated computer analysis of radiographic images. *Radiology*, *83*(6), 1029–1034. doi:10.1148/83.6.1029 PMID:14226800

Michael, A., Peter, B., & Walter, V. (2008). *Subjective and Objective Quality Evaluation of Watermarked Audio. In Digital Audio Watermarking Techniques and Technologies: Applications and Benchmarks*. IGI Global.

Michael, G., & Sushil, J. (2007). *Handbook of Database Security: Applications and Trends*. Springer Science & Business Media.

Mielikainen, J. (2006). LSB matching revisited. *IEEE Signal Processing Letters*, *13*(5), 285–287. doi:10.1109/LSP.2006.870357

Miller, R. A., People, H. E., & Myres, J. D. (n. d.). INTERNIST-1: An experimental computer based diagnostic consultant for general internal medicine. *New Engl. J. Med., 307*, 468 – 476.

Milligan, G. W., & Cooper, M. C. (1987). Methodology review: Clustering methods. *Applied Psychological Measurement*, *11*(4), 329–354. doi:10.1177/014662168701100401

Milovic, B., & Milovic, M. (2012). Prediction and decision making in Health Care using Data Mining. *International Journal of Public Health Science*, *1*(2), 69–78.

Minamoto, T., & Ohura, R. (2012). A Non-blind Digital Image Watermarking Method Based on the Dual-tree Complex Discrete Wavelet Transform and Interval Arithmetic. *Ninth International Conference on Information Technology: New Generations*. doi:10.1109/ITNG.2012.129

Miner, G., Delen, D., Elder, J., Fast, A., Hill, T., & Nisbet, R. A. (2012). *Practical Text Mining and Statistical Analysis for Non-structured Text Data Applications*. Waltham, MA: Elsevier Inc.

Min, X., Wei-ren, S., Chang-jiang, J., & Ying, Z. (2010). Energy efficient clustering algorithm for maximizing lifetime of wireless sensor networks. *AEÜ. International Journal of Electronics and Communications*, *64*(4), 289–298. doi:10.1016/j.aeue.2009.01.004

Mishra, P., Padhy, N., & Panigrahi, R. (2013). The survey of data mining applications and feature scope. *Asian Journal of Computer Science & Information Technology*, *2*(4), 43–58.

Mislav, G., Kresimir, D., & Mohammed, G. (2009). Recent Advances in Multimedia Signal Processing and Communications. Springer Science & Business Media.

Mobasseri Bijan, Zhang, Amin, & Dogahe. (2005). Designing robust watermarks using polynomial phase exponentials. *ICASSP*.

Mohanty Saraju, P., & Bhargava Bharat, K. (2008). Invisible Watermarking Based on Creation and Robust Insertion-Extraction of Image Adaptive Watermarks. *ACM Transactions on Multimedia Computing, Communications, and Applications*, *5*(2), 1–24. doi:10.1145/1413862.1413865

Mohanty, S.P., & Bhargava, B.K. (2008). Invisible Watermarking Based on Creation and Robust Insertion–Extraction of Image Adaptive Watermarks. *ACM Transactions on Multimedia Computing, Communications, and Applications*, *5*(2), 12:1–12:22.

Mohanty, S. P., Parthasarathy, G., Elias, K., & Nishikanta, P. (2006). A Novel Invisible Color Image Watermarking Scheme using Image Adaptive Watermark Creation and Robust Insertion-Extraction. In *Proceeding of the 8th IEEE International Symposium on Multimedia (ISM '06).* doi:10.1109/ISM.2006.7

Mohar, B., Alavi, Y., Chartrand, G., & Oellermann, O. R. (1991). The Laplacian spectrum of graphs. *Graph theory, combinatorics, and applications, 2*(871-898), 12.

Möller, S., Pfitzmann, A., & Stirand, I. (1996). Computer Based Steganography: How It Works and Why Therefore Any Restrictions on Cryptography Are Nonsense, At Best, *in Information Hiding:First International Workshop, Proceedings.*

Monet D. B. B. V. (2015). *The column-store pioneer.* Retrieved May 15, 2015, from http://www.monetdb.org/Home

Moore, D. S., & McCabe, G. P. (2009). *Introduction to the Practice of Statistics* (6th ed.). New York, NY: W. H. Freeman and Company.

Morrison, D. G. (1967). Measurement problems in cluster analysis. *Management Science, 13*(12), B-775–B-780. doi:10.1287/mnsc.13.12.B775

Morrone, M. C., & Burr, D. C. (1988). Feature detection in human vision: A phase dependent energy model. *Proceedings of the Royal Society of London. Series B, Biological Sciences, 235*(1280), 221–245. doi:10.1098/rspb.1988.0073 PMID:2907382

Morrone, M. C., & Owens, R. A. (1987). Feature detection from local energy. *Pattern Recognition Letters, 6*(5), 303–313. doi:10.1016/0167-8655(87)90013-4

Morrone, M. C., Ross, J., Burr, D. C., & Owens, R. (1986). Mach bands are phase dependent. *Nature, 324*(6049), 250–253. doi:10.1038/324250a0

Mountrakis, G., Im, J., & Ogole, C. (2011). Support vector machines in remote sensing: A review. *ISPRS Journal of Photogrammetry and Remote Sensing, 66*(3), 247–259. doi:10.1016/j.isprsjprs.2010.11.001

Mousa, R., Munib, Q., & Moussa, A. (2005). Breast cancer diagnosis system based on wavelet analysis and fuzzy-neural. *Expert Systems with Applications, 28*(4), 713–723. doi:10.1016/j.eswa.2004.12.028

Mukherjee, D. P., Maitra, S., & Acton, S. T. (2004). Spatial domain digital watermarking of multimedia objects for buyer authentication. *IEEE Transactions on Multimedia, Volume, 6*(1), 1–15. doi:10.1109/TMM.2003.819759

Müller, A. C., Nowozin, S., & Lampert, C. H. (2012, August). Information theoretic clustering using minimum spanning trees. In *Joint DAGM (German Association for Pattern Recognition) and OAGM Symposium* (pp. 205-215). Springer Berlin Heidelberg. doi:10.1007/978-3-642-32717-9_21

Muralidhar, A., & Pattabiraman, V. (2015). An Efficient Association Rule Based Clustering of XML Documents. *2nd International Symposium on Big Data and Cloud Computing (ISBCC'15), Procedia Computer Science.* doi:10.1016/j.procs.2015.04.024

Mu, T., & Nandi, A. K. (2007). Breast cancer detection from FNA using SVMwith different parameter tuning systems and SOM-RBF classifier. *Journal of the Franklin Institute, 344*(3-4), 285–311. doi:10.1016/j.jfranklin.2006.09.005

Najari, S. & Lotfi, I. (2014). Malware Detection Using Data Mining Techniques. *International Journal of Intelligent Information Systems, 3*(6–1), 33–37.

Najman, L., & Cousty, J. (2014). A graph-based mathematical morphology reader. *Pattern Recognition Letters, 47,* 3–17. doi:10.1016/j.patrec.2014.05.007

Narayanan, R., & Ozisikyilmaz, B. (2006). MineBench: a benchmark suite for data mining workloads. In *Proceedings of IEEE International Symposium on Workload Characterization.* doi:10.1109/IISWC.2006.302743

Nasir, I., Weng, Y., & Jiang, J. (2007). A new robust watermarking scheme for color image in spatial domain.*Proc. third international IEEE conference on signal image technologies and internet-based system.* doi:10.1109/SITIS.2007.67

Nasser, S., Vert, G. L., & Nicolescu, M. (n.d.). *Multiple sequence alignment using fuzzy logic.* Retrieved from: http://www.cse.unr.edu/~bioinfor/papers/cibcb-mfgs.pdf

Naveen, N., Ravi, V., & Rao, C. R. (2012). Rule extraction from DEWNN to solve classification and regression problems. *Proceedings of Third International Conference, SEMCCO 2012.* doi:10.1007/978-3-642-35380-2_25

Nazeer, M., & Nargis, B. (2015). Digital image watermarking using partial pivoting lower and upper triangular decomposition into the wavelet domain. *IET Image Process., 9*(9), 795–803. doi:10.1049/iet-ipr.2014.0395

Neuhaus, M., & Bunke, H. (2007). Bridging the gap between graph edit distance and kernel machines. World Scientific Publishing Co., Inc.

Ng, A. Y., Jordan, M. I., & Weiss, Y. (2002). On spectral clustering: Analysis and an algorithm. *Advances in Neural Information Processing Systems, 2*, 849–856.

Nguyen, Beghdadi, & Luong. (2012). Perceptual watermarking robust to JPEG compression attack. *5th International Symposium on Communications Control and Signal Processing (ISCCSP).*

Ni, R., & Ruan, Q. (2006). Region of Interest Watermarking Based on Fractal Dimension.*Proc. Int. Conf. Pattern Recognition, 3*, 934–937.

Nisbet, R., Elder, J., & Miner, G. (2009). *Handbook of Statistical Analysis and Data Mining Applications.* Burlington, MA: Elsevier Inc.

Nitze, I., Schulthess, U., & Asche, H. (2012). Comparison of machine learning algorithms random forest, artficial neural network and support vector machine to maximum likelihood for supervised crop type classification.*Proceedings of the 4th GEOBIA.*

Niu, Y., Kyan, M., Ma, L., & Beghdadi, A. (2011) A Visual Saliency Modulated Just Noticeable Distortion Profile for Image Watermarking. *European Signal Processing Conference.*

Nordin, M., Rahman, A., Yazid, M., Saman, M., Ahmad, A., & Tap, O. A. M. (2010). Applying rough set theory for DNA sequence database classification and reduction. *International Journal of Biomedical Soft Computing and Human Sciences, 16*(2), 115–124.

Nowozin, S., Gehler, P. V., & Lampert, C. H. (2010, September). On parameter learning in CRF-based approaches to object class image segmentation. In *European conference on computer vision* (pp. 98-111). Springer Berlin Heidelberg. doi:10.1007/978-3-642-15567-3_8

Obenshain, M. K. (2004). Application of data mining techniques to healthcare data. *Infection Control and Hospital Epidemiology, 25*(8), 690–695. doi:10.1086/502460 PMID:15357163

Oded, G. (2001). Foundations of Cryptography Volume 1: Basic Tools. Cambridge University Press.

Osareh, A., Shadgar, B., & Markham, R. (2009). A computational intelligence based approach for of exudates in diabetic retinopathy images. *IEEE Transactions on Information Technology in Biomedicine, 13*(4), 535–545. doi:10.1109/TITB.2008.2007493 PMID:19586814

Osman, Z. (2011). *Iris Recognition Using Phase Congruency.* IICMS.

Osofisan, P. B., & Afunlehin, O. A. (2007). Application of neural network to improve dynamic branch prediction of superscalar microprocessors. *The Pacific Journal of Science and Technology*, *8*(1), 80–97.

Osowski, S., Siwekand, K., & Markiewicz, T. (2004). MLP and SVM Networks – a Comparative Study.*Proceedings of the 6th Nordic Signal Processing Symposium.*

Otum, H. M. A. (2014). Semi-fragile watermarking for grayscale image authentication and tamper detection based on an adjusted expanded-bit multi-scale quantization-based technique. *Journal of Visual Communication and Image Representation*, *25*(5), 1064–1081. doi:10.1016/j.jvcir.2013.12.017

Ozisikyilmaz, B., Narayanan, R., Zambreno, J., Memik, G., & Choudhary, A. (2006). An Architectural Characterization Study of Data Mining and Bioinformatics Workloads. In *Proceedings of IEEE International Symposium on Workload Characterization.* doi:10.1109/IISWC.2006.302730

Päivinen, N. (2005). Clustering with a minimum spanning tree of scale-free-like structure. *Pattern Recognition Letters*, *26*(7), 921–930. doi:10.1016/j.patrec.2004.09.039

Palaniappan, S., & Awang, R. (2008). Intelligent heart disease prediction system using data mining techniques.*IEEE/ACS International Conference on Computer System and Applications (AICCSA 2008) 2008*, (pp. 108 – 115). doi:10.1109/AICCSA.2008.4493524

Pal, D., Mandana, K. M., Pal, S., Sarkar, D., & Chakrabobrty, C. (2012). Fuzzy expert system approach for coronary artery disease screening using clinical parameters. *Knowledge-Based Systems*, *36*, 162–174. doi:10.1016/j.knosys.2012.06.013

Pal, N. R., & Bezdek, J. C. (1995). On cluster validity for the fuzzy c-means model. *IEEE Transactions on Fuzzy Systems*, *3*(3), 370–379. doi:10.1109/91.413225

Pal, N. R., & Pal, S. K. (1993). A review on image segmentation techniques. *Pattern Recognition*, *26*(9), 1277–1294. doi:10.1016/0031-3203(93)90135-J

Panchal, R., & Verma, B. (2006). Characterization of breast abnormality patterns in digital mammograms using auto –associator neural network. *ICONIP*, *3*(4234), 127–136.

Park, D., Jung, E.-Y., Lee, S.-H., & Lim, J. (2015). A composite gene selection for DNA microarray data analysis. *Multimedia Tools and Applications*, *74*(20), 9031–9041. doi:10.1007/s11042-013-1583-9

Patel, D., Hsu, W., & Lee, M. L. (2008, June). Mining relationships among interval-based events for classification. In *Proceedings of the 2008 ACM SIGMOD international conference on Management of data* (pp. 393-404). ACM. doi:10.1145/1376616.1376658

Patra, J. C., Phua, J. E., & Rajan, D. (2010). DCT domain watermarking scheme using Chinese Remainder Theorem for image authentication. *IEEE International Conference on Multimedia and Expo.* doi:10.1109/ICME.2010.5583326

Păun, M., Li, Y., Cheng, Y., Tusa, I., & Păun, A. (2015). Segmenting microarray images using a contour-based method. *Theoretical Computer Science*, *608*, 108–118. doi:10.1016/j.tcs.2015.07.036

Pei, Jung, & Chang. (2009). Dual Digital Watermarking for Internet Media Based on Hybrid Strategies. *IEEE Transactions on Circuits and Systems for Video Technology, 19*(8), 1169-1177.

Pelgrom Marcel, J. M. (2010). *Analog-to-Digital Conversion.* Springer Science & Business Media. doi:10.1007/978-90-481-8888-8

Pellegrino, F. A., Vanzella, W., & Torre, V. (2004). Edge detection revisited. *IEEE Transactions on Systems, Man, and Cybernetics. Part B, Cybernetics*, *34*(3), 1500–1518. doi:10.1109/TSMCB.2004.824147 PMID:15484920

Peng, J., & Rusch, P. H. (1991). Morphological filters and edge detection application to medical imaging. *The Annual Conference on Engineering in Medicine and Biology, 13*(1), 251-252. doi:10.1109/IEMBS.1991.683921

Pentland, A., Picard, R. W., & Sclaroff, S. (1996). Photobook: Content-based manipulation of image databases. *International Journal of Computer Vision, 18*(3), 233–254. doi:10.1007/BF00123143

Perez. (2007). *Advances in Audio and Speech Signal Processing: Technologies and Applications.* IGI.

Peter, K. (1996). *Invariant Measures of Image Features from Phase Information* (PhD thesis). The University of Western Australia.

Peter, K. (1999). Image features from phase congruency. *Videre: Journal of Computer Vision Research, 1*(3), 1–26.

Peter, K. (2000). Phase Congruency: A Low-Level Image Invariant. *Psychological Research Psychologische Forschung, 64*(2), 136–148. doi:10.1007/s004260000024 PMID:11195306

Peter, W. (2009). *Disappearing Cryptography: Information Hiding: Steganography & Watermarking* (3rd ed.). Morgan Kaufmann.

Petitcolas, F. A. P., & Anderson, R. J. (1998). Weaknesses of Copyright Marking Systems. In *Multimedia and Security Workshop at ACM Multimedia '98.*

Pettie, S., & Ramachandran, V. (2002). An optimal minimum spanning tree algorithm. *Journal of the ACM, 49*(1), 16–34. doi:10.1145/505241.505243

Pham, D. L., & Prince, J. L. (1999). An adaptive fuzzy C-means algorithm for image segmentation in the presence of intensity inhomogeneities. *Pattern Recognition Letters, 20*(1), 57–68. doi:10.1016/S0167-8655(98)00121-4

Pham, D. L., Xu, C., & Prince, J. L. (2000). Current methods in medical image segmentation 1. *Annual Review of Biomedical Engineering, 2*(1), 315–337. doi:10.1146/annurev.bioeng.2.1.315 PMID:11701515

Philbin, J., Chum, O., Isard, M., Sivic, J., & Zisserman, A. (2007). Object retrieval with large vocabularies and fast spatial matching. *Computer Vision and Pattern Recognition, CVPR'07, IEEE Conference.*

Piotr, L., & Zbigniew, P. (2013). Parallel blind digital image watermarking in spatial and frequency domains. *Telecommunication Systems, 54.* doi:10.1007/s11235-013-9734-x

Piyanart, C., Kharittha, T., Pipat, S., & Amornraksa, T. (2015). Digital Image Watermarking on Illumination Component. *14th IAPR International Conference on Machine Vision Applications.*

Podilchuk & Wenjun. (1998). Image-Adaptive Watermarking Using Visual Models. *IEEE Journal on Selected Areas in Communication, 16*(4).

Podilchuk, C. I., & Wenjun, Z. (1997). Perceptual Watermarking of Still Images, *Workshop on Multimedia Signal Processing, USA, Electronic Proceedings.* doi:10.1109/MMSP.1997.602662

Podilchuk, C., & Delp, E. (2001). Digital Watermarking Algorithms and Applications. *IEEE Signal Processing Magazine, 18*(4), 33–46. doi:10.1109/79.939835

Pohlmann, . (1992). *The Compact Disc Handbook.* Oxford University Press.

Prasanna, S., Toshanlal, M., Ankit, S., Vivek, G., & Amit, K. (2015). A DWT-SVD Based Digital Watermarking Technique for Copyright Protection. *International Conference on Electrical, Electronics, Signals, Communication and Optimization.*

Pratheema, A., Prabha, M., & Kavitha, P. (2012). Malware Classification through HEX conversion and mining. In Proceedings of International Conferenece on EGovernance & Cloud Computing Sevices (EGov '12).

Prewitt, J. M. S. (1970). *Object enhancement and extraction. Picture processing and Psychopictorics*. Academic Press.

Proakis, . (2007). *Digital Signal Processing: Principles, Algorithms, And Applications*. Pearson Education India.

Punj, G., & Stewart, D. W. (1983). Cluster analysis in marketing research: Review and suggestions for application. *JMR, Journal of Marketing Research, 20*(2), 134–148. doi:10.2307/3151680

Punsawad, Y., & Wongsawat, Y. (2009). *Palmprint image enhancement using phase congruency*. IEEE ROBIO.

Qing-Cheng, L., & Zhen, H. D. (2008). Novel Text Watermarking Algorithm Based on Chinese Characters Structure. *Computer International Symposium on Science and Computational Technology*.

QingLan, H., & Zhen. (2013). Multi-level Association rule mining based on clustering partition. *Third International Conference on Intelligent System Design and Engineering Applications*. IEEE.

Quan, W. (2012). *Kernel principal component analysis and its applications in face recognition and active shape models*. arXiv preprint arXiv:1207.3538

Que, D., Zhang, L., Lu, L., & Shi, L. (2006). A ROI Image Watermarking Algorithm Based on Lifting Wavelet Transform.*Proc. Int. Conf. Signal Processing*. doi:10.1109/ICOSP.2006.345979

Quinlan, J. R. (1987). Simplifying Decision Trees. *International Journal of Man-Machine Studies, 27*(3), 221–234. doi:10.1016/S0020-7373(87)80053-6

Quteishat, A., & Lim, C. P. (2008). A modified fuzzy min-max neural network with rule extraction and its application to fault detection and classification. *Applied Soft Computing, 8*(2), 985–995. doi:10.1016/j.asoc.2007.07.013

Quteishat, A., Lim, C. P., & Tan, K. S. (2010). A modified fuzzy min - max neural network with a genetic – algorithm based rule extractor for pattern classification. *IEEE Transactions on Systems, Man, and Cybernetics. Part A, Systems and Humans, 40*(3), 641–650. doi:10.1109/TSMCA.2010.2043948

Ramakrishnan, R., & Gehrke, J. (2003). *Database Management Systems* (3rd ed.). New York, NY: McGraw-Hill.

Raman, V., Lohman, G. M., Malkemus, T., Mueller, R., Pandis, I., Schiefer, B., . . . Liu, S. (2013). DB2 with BLU acceleration: so much more than just a column store. *Proceedings of the VLDB Endowment, 6*(11), 1080-1091. doi:10.14778/2536222.2536233

Rathi, V., & Aggarwal, S. (2013). Mammography mass classification of breast cancer using multilayer perceptron network.*7th International Conference on Advanced Computing and Communication Technologies*.

Rault, T., Bouabdallah, A., & Challal, Y. (2014). Energy efficiency in wireless sensor networks: A top-down survey. *Computer Networks, 67*(March), 104–122. doi:10.1016/j.comnet.2014.03.027

Ray, S. S., Ganivada, A., & Pal, S. K. (2015). *A granular self-organizing map for clustering and gene selection in microarray data. IEEE Transactions on Neural Networks and Learning Systems*. doi:10.1109/TNNLS.2015.2460994

Reddi, S. S., Rudin, S. F., & Keshavan, H. R. (1984). An optimal multiple threshold scheme for image segmentation. *IEEE Transactions on Systems, Man, and Cybernetics, SMC-14*(4), 661–665. doi:10.1109/TSMC.1984.6313341

Rey-del-castillo, P., & Cardenosa, J. (2011). Fuzzy min - max neural networks for categorical data:application to missing data imputation. *Neural Computing & Applications, 21*(6), 1349–1362. doi:10.1007/s00521-011-0574-x

Ribas, V. M., Figueiredo, M. F., & Goņoalves, R. A. (2003). Simulating a simple neural network on branch prediction. *Acta Scientiarum Technology, 25*(2), 153–160.

Ripley, B. D. (1996). *Pattern Recognition and Neural Networks*. Cambridge, UK: Cambridge University Press. doi:10.1017/CBO9780511812651

Rissanen, J. (1978, September). Modeling by shortest data description. *Automatica*, *14*(5), 465–471. doi:10.1016/0005-1098(78)90005-5

Rizzi, A., Panella, M., & Frattale Mascioli, F. M. (2002). Adaptive resolution min - max classifiers. *IEEE Transactions on Neural Networks*, *13*(2), 402–414. doi:10.1109/72.991426 PMID:18244441

Robbins, B., & Owens, R. (1997). 2-D feature detection via local energy. *Image and Vision Computing*, *15*(5), 353–368. doi:10.1016/S0262-8856(96)01137-7

Roberts, L. G. (1965). Machine perception of 3-d solids. In Optical and Electro-Optical Information Processing. MIT Press.

Roche, S., & Dugelay, J.-L. (1998). Image Watermarking Based on the Fractal Transform. In *Workshop on Multimedia Signal Processing*. IEEE.

Rongsheng, X., Wu, K., Du, J., & Li, C. (2007). Survey of Public Key Digital Watermarking Systems. *Eighth ACIS International Conference on Software Engineering, Artificial Intelligence, Networking, and Parallel/Distributed Computing.*

Ronse, C. (1995). *The phase congruence model for edge detection in two dimensional pictures: A mathematical study* (PhD thesis). University Louis Pastern.

Rosin, P. L., & Ioannidis, E. (2003). Evaluation of global image thresholding for change detection. *Pattern Recognition Letters*, *24*(14), 2345–2356. doi:10.1016/S0167-8655(03)00060-6

Ross, A. (1996). Lecture notes in computer science: Vol. 1174. *Information Hiding*. Springer.

Ruanaidh, J. J. K. O., Dowling, W. J., & Boland, F. M. (1996). Phase watermarking of digital images. *International Conference on Image Processing, Proceedings.* doi:10.1109/ICIP.1996.560428

Ruderman, D. (1994). The Statistics of Natural Images. *Network (Bristol, England)*, *5*(4), 517–548. doi:10.1088/0954-898X_5_4_006 PMID:10057546

Ruspini, E. (1970). Numerical methods for fuzzy clustering. *Information Sciences*, *2*(1), 319–350. doi:10.1016/S0020-0255(70)80056-1

Sadreazami, H., Ahmad Omair, M., & Swamy, M. N. S. (2015). A Robust Multiplicative Watermark Detector for Color Images in Sparse Domain. *IEEE Transactions on Circuits and Systems—II. Express Briefs, 62*(12), 1159–1163.

Saha, S., Tahtali, M., Lambert, A., & Pickering, M. (2013). Perceptual dissimilarity metric: A full reference objective image quality measure to quantify the degradation of perceptual image quality. *IEEE International Symposium on Signal Processing and Information Technology.* doi:10.1109/ISSPIT.2013.6781902

Saleem, M., Di Caro, G. A., & Farooq, M. (2011). Swarm intelligence based routing protocol for wireless sensor networks: Survey and future directions. *Information Sciences*, *181*(20), 4597–4624. doi:10.1016/j.ins.2010.07.005

Salembier, P., & Sikora, T. (2002). *Introduction to MPEG-7: Multimedia Content Description Interface*. New York, NY: John Wiley & Sons, Inc.

Salivahanan, S., & Gnanapriya, C. (2011). *Digital signal processing*. Tata McGraw-Hill Education.

Sanders, G., & Shin, S. (2001). Denormalization effects on performance of RDBMS. In *Proceedings of the 34th Annual Hawaii International Conference on System Sciences*. Maui, HI: IEEE Computer Society.

Sarvestani, A. S., Safavi, A. A., Parandeh, N. M., & Salehi, M. (2010, October). Predicting breast cancer survivability using data mining techniques. In *Software Technology and Engineering (ICSTE), 2010 2nd International Conference on* (Vol. 2, pp. V2-227). IEEE. doi:10.1109/ICSTE.2010.5608818

Sathish, K. S., & Duraipandian, N. (2012). An effective identification of species from DNA sequence: A classification technique by integrating DM and ANN. *International Journal of Advanced Computer Science and Applications*, *3*(8).

Satyen, B., Das Sunil, R., & Petriu Emil, M. (2005). An Adaptive Compressed MPEG-2 Video Watermarking Scheme. IEEE Transactions on Instrumentation and Measurement, 54(5), 1853-1861.

Saxena, A., Chung, S. H., & Ng, A. Y. (2008). 3-d depth reconstruction from a single still image. *International Journal of Computer Vision*, *76*(1), 53–69. doi:10.1007/s11263-007-0071-y

Scaria, A., Badari Nath, D., Devi, M. N., & Mohankumar, N. (2011). Hardware Implementation of SVD Based Colour Image Watermarking in Wavelet Domain. *International Conference on Process Automation, Control and Computing (PACC)*.

Scholkopf, B., Smola, A., & Muller, K. R. (1998). Nonlinear component analysis as a kernel eigenvalue problem. *Neural Computation*, *10*(5), 1299–1319. doi:10.1162/089976698300017467

Seera, M., & Lim, C. P. (2014). A hybrid intelligent system for medical data classification. *Expert Systems with Applications*, *41*(5), 2239–2249. doi:10.1016/j.eswa.2013.09.022

Sekar, B. D., Dong, M. C., Shi, J., & Hu, X. Y. (2012). Fused hierarchical neural network for cardiovascular disease diagnosis. *IEEE Sensors Journal*, *12*(3), 644–650. doi:10.1109/JSEN.2011.2129506

Seredynski, F., & Bouvry, P. (2007). Anomaly detection in TCP/IP networks using immune systems paradigms. *Computer Communications*, *30*(4), 740–749. doi:10.1016/j.comcom.2006.08.016

Servetto, S. D., Podilchuk, C. I., & Ramchandran, K. (1998). Capacity Issues In Digital Image Watermarking. *International Conference on Image Processing*.

Sharma, A., & Mansotra, V. (2014, March). Emerging applications of data mining for healthcare management-A critical review. In *Computing for Sustainable Global Development (INDIACom), 2014 International Conference on* (pp. 377-382). IEEE. doi:10.1109/IndiaCom.2014.6828163

Sharma, N., Bajpai, A., & Litoria, R. (2012). Comparison the various clustering algorithms of weka tools. *International Journal of Emerging Technology and Advanced Engineering*, *2*(5), 73–80.

Shi, J., & Malik, J. (1998, January). Motion segmentation and tracking using normalized cuts. In *Computer Vision, 1998. Sixth International Conference on* (pp. 1154-1160). IEEE.

Shi, J., Dong, M. C., Sekar, B. D., & Lei, W. K. (2010). Fuzzy neural networks to detect cardiovascular diseases hierarchically. *IEEE 10th International Conference on Computer and Information Technology*.

Shigetoshi, S., Toshio, F., & Takanori, S. (1995). A neural network architecture for incremental learning. *Neurocomputing*, *9*(2), 111–130. doi:10.1016/0925-2312(94)00061-V

Shih Frank, Y. (2008). *Digital Watermarking and Steganography: Fundamentals and Techniques*. CRC Press.

Shih Frank, Y., & Wu Scott, Y. T. (2003). Combinational image watermarking in the spatial and frequency domains. *Pattern Recognition, 36*(4), 969–975. doi:10.1016/S0031-3203(02)00122-X

Shi, J., & Malik, J. (2000). Normalized cuts and image segmentation. *IEEE Transactions on Pattern Analysis and Machine Intelligence*, *22*(8), 888–905. doi:10.1109/34.868688

Shin, S. K., & Sanders, G. L. (2006). Denormalization strategies for data retrieval from data warehouses. *Decision Support Systems*, *42*(1), 267–282. doi:10.1016/j.dss.2004.12.004

Shortliffe, E. H. (1976). *Computer Based Medical Consultations: MYCIN*. New York: Am Elsevier.

Shrinivas, K., & Urmila, S. (2015). Image bit depth plane digital watermarking for secured classified image data transmission. *Procedia Compute Science*, *78*, 698–705.

Shu-Fen, T., & Ching-Sheng, H. (2008). An Imperceptible Watermarking Scheme Using Variation and Modular Operations. *International Conference on Multimedia and Ubiquitous Engineering*.

Silahtaroglu, G. (2008). *Kavram ve Algoritmalarıyla Temel Veri Madenciliği*. Istanbul: Papatya Yayıncılık. (in Turkish)

Silva, A., Esmeraldo, G., Barros, E., & Viana, P. (2007). Cache-Analyzer: design space evaluation of configurable-caches in a single-pass. In *Proceedings of International Workshop on Rapid System Prototyping*, (pp. 3–9). doi:10.1109/RSP.2007.15

Simmons, G. J. (1984). The Prisoners' Problem and the Subliminal Channel, in Advances in Cryptology. *Proceedings of CRYPTO*. Plenum Press.

Simpson, P. K. (1992). Fuzzy min-max neural network part-1: Classification. *IEEE Transactions on Neural Networks*, *3*(5), 776–778. doi:10.1109/72.159066 PMID:18276476

Simpson, P. K. (1993). Fuzzy min-max neural network part-1: Clustering. *IEEE Transactions on Fuzzy Systems*, *1*(1), 32–45. doi:10.1109/TFUZZ.1993.390282

Singer, A. (2006). From graph to manifold Laplacian: The convergence rate. *Applied and Computational Harmonic Analysis*, *21*(1), 128–134. doi:10.1016/j.acha.2006.03.004

Singh, S., & Gupta, P. R. (2011). Breast cancer detection and classification using neural network. *International Journal of Advanced Engineering Science and Technologies*, *6*(1), 4 - 9.

Singhal, G., Panwar, S., Jain, K., & Banga, D. (2013). A comparative study of data clustering algorithms. *International Journal of Computers and Applications*, *83*(15), 41–46. doi:10.5120/14528-2927

Sin-Joo, L., & Sung-Hwan, J. (2001). *A survey of watermarking techniques applied to multimedia*. Pusan: Korea.

Sivanandm, S. N., & Deepa, S. N. (2011). Principles of Soft Computing (2nd ed.). Wiley Publication India.

Smith Joshua, R., & Comiskey Barrett, O. (1996). Modulation and Information Hiding in Images. *Proceedings of the First Information Hiding Workshop*. doi:10.1007/3-540-61996-8_42

Smith Laurence Dwight. (1955). *Cryptography: The Science of Secret Writing*. Courier Dover Publications.

Smithal, B., & Navas, K. A. (2007). *Spatial Domain- High Capacity Data Hiding in ROI Images*. IEEE-ICSCN.

SMPCache. (2015). *Simulator for cache memory systems on symmetric multiprocessors* [software]. Retrieved from http://arco.unex.es/smpcache/SMPCacheEnglish.htm

Soille, P. (2013). *Morphological image analysis: principles and applications*. Springer Science & Business Media.

Speights, K. (2013). 7 Countries with the highest health care costs. *Daily Finance*. Retrieved on September 14 2015 from http://www.dailyfinance.com/2013/06/15/7-countries-with-the-highest-health-care-costs/

Srivastava, A., Lee, A., Simoncelli, E., & Zhu, S. (2003). On Advances in Statistical Modeling of Natural Images. *Journal of Mathematical Imaging and Vision*, *18*(1), 17–33. doi:10.1023/A:1021889010444

Sterpone, L. (2009). A novel dual-core architecture for the analysis of DNA microarray images. *Instrumentation and Measurement. IEEE Transactions on, 58*(8), 2653–2662. doi:10.1109/TIM.2009.2015695

Steven, G., Anguera, R., Egan, C., Steven, F., & Vintan, L. (2001). Dynamic branch prediction using neural networks. In *Proceedings of Euromicro Symposium on Digital Systems Design*, (pp. 178–185). doi:10.1109/DSD.2001.952279

Stinson, D. R. (2005). *Cryptography: Theory and Practice* (3rd ed.). CRC Press.

Strapasson, R. A., Woiciechowski, A. L., Letti, L. A. J., & Soccol, C. R. (2014). *Some applications of artificial intelligence on biotechnology*. Academic Press.

Strehl, A., Gupta, G. K., & Ghosh, J. (1999). Distance Based Clustering of Association Rules.*Proceedings ANNIE Intelligent Engineering Systems through Artificial Neural Networks*.

Struc, V., & Pavesic, N. (2009). Phase congruency features for palm-print verification. *IET Signal Process., 3*(4), 258–268. doi:10.1049/iet-spr.2008.0152

Su, J. K., & Girod, B. (1999). On the Robustness and Imperceptibility of Digital Fingeerprints. *Int. Conf. on multimedia Computing & System*.

Sudip, G., De Sayandip, M. S. P., & Hafizur, R. (2015). A Novel Dual Purpose Spatial Domain Algorithm for Digital Image Watermarking and Cryptography Using Extended Hamming Code.*International Conference on Electrical Information and Communication Technology*.

Su, J. K., Frank, H., & Bernd, G. (1998). Digital Watermarking of Text, Image, and Video Documents. *Computers & Graphics, 22*(6), 687–695. doi:10.1016/S0097-8493(98)00089-2

Sundar, N. A., Latha, P. P., & Chandra, M. R. (2012). Performance analysis of classification data mining techniques over heart disease database. *International Journal of Engineering Science & Advanced Technology*.

Sun, J., Zhu, X., Zhang, C., & Fang, Y. (2012). Security and privacy for mobile health-care (m-Health) systems. In S. K. Das, K. Kant, & N. Zhang (Eds.), *Handbook on Securing Cyber-Physical Critical Infrastructure* (pp. 677–704). Elsevier. doi:10.1016/B978-0-12-415815-3.00027-3

Sur, A., Sagar, S. S., Pal, R., Mitra, P., & Mukhopadhyay, J. (2009). A New Image Watermarking Scheme using Saliency Based Visual Attention Model.*Proceedings of IEEE Annual India Conference*. doi:10.1109/INDCON.2009.5409402

Susu, Y., Jinghong, Z., Li, Z., & Yao, W. (2010). Robust Image Registration Using Phase Congruency.*2nd International Conference on Signal Processing Systems (ICSPS)*.

Tabish, S. M., Shafiq, M. Z., & Muddassar, F. (2009). Malware detection using statistical analysis of byte-level file content. In *Proceedings of the ACM SIGKDD Workshop on CyberSecurity and Intelligence Informatics*. Paris, France: ACM. doi:10.1145/1599272.1599278

Takabayashi, K., Ho, T. B., Yokoi, H., Nguyen, T. D., Kawasaki, S., Le, S. Q., & Yokosuka, O. et al. (2007). Temporal abstraction and data mining with visualization of laboratory data. *Studies in Health Technology and Informatics, 129*(2), 1304. PMID:17911925

Tanaka, K., Nakamura, Y., & Matsui, K. (1990). Embedding secret information into a dithered multilevel image. In *Proc. IEEE Military Communications Conference*. doi:10.1109/MILCOM.1990.117416

Tang, M., Zhou, Y., Cui, P., Wang, W., Li, J., Zhang, H., . . . Yan, B. (2009). Discovery of Migration habitats and routes of Wild Bird Species by Clustering and Association analysis. Springer.

Tang, R., Fong, S., & Deb, S. (2012). *Integrating nature-inspired optimization algorithms to K-means clustering.* Academic Press.

Tang, T. I., Zheng, G., Huang, Y., Shu, G., & Wang, P. (2005). A comparative study of medical data classification methods based on decision tree and system reconstruction analysis. *IEMS, 4*(1), 102–108.

Tan, K. S., & Isa, N. A. M. (2011). Color image segmentation using histogram thresholding–Fuzzy C-means hybrid approach. *Pattern Recognition, 44*(1), 1–15. doi:10.1016/j.patcog.2010.07.013

Tan, P. N., Steinbach, M., & Kumar, V. (2007). *Introduction to Data Mining.* Pearson Education.

Tasto, M. (1975). Automatische mammographie - Auswertung: Erkennung von Mikroverkalkungen. *Biomedizinische Technik, 20*, 273–274.

Ta, V. T., Elmoataz, A., & Lézoray, O. (2011). Nonlocal pdes-based morphology on weighted graphs for image and data processing. *IEEE Transactions on Image Processing, 20*(6), 1504–1516. doi:10.1109/TIP.2010.2101610 PMID:21193378

Technology Evaluation Center. (2002). *Computer-Aided Detection (CAD) in mammography.* Technology Assessment Program.

Tellaeche, A., Pajares, G., Burgos-Artizzu, X. P., & Ribeiro, A. (2011). A computer vision approach for weeds identification through Support Vector Machines. *Applied Soft Computing, 11*(1), 908–915. doi:10.1016/j.asoc.2010.01.011

Teodorescu, H-N. (2003). Genetics, gene prediction, and neuro-fuzzy systems – The context and a program proposal. *FSAI, 9*(1–3), 15–22.

Teppola, P., Mujunen, S. P., & Minkkinen, P. (1999). Adaptive Fuzzy C-Means clustering in process monitoring. *Chemometrics and Intelligent Laboratory Systems, 45*(1), 23–38. doi:10.1016/S0169-7439(98)00087-2

Tew & Wong. (2014). An Overview of Information Hiding in H.264/AVC Compressed Video. *IEEE Transactions on Circuits and Systems for Video Technology, 24*(2), 305-319.

Thamarai & Ashok. (2014). Low Power Implementation of an Invisible-Robust Image Watermarking Encoder using Xilinx FPGA. *Journal of Nanoscience and Nanotechnology, 2*(1).

Thangam, S. V., SaiDeepak, K., Rai, H.G.N., & Mirajkar, P.P. (2009). An effective edge detection methodology for medical images based on texture discrimination. *Seventh International Conference on Advances in Pattern Recognition,* (pp. 227-231). doi:10.1109/ICAPR.2009.44

The multidimensional data model. (n.d.). Retrieved August 5, 2016, from https://web.stanford.edu/dept/itss/docs/oracle/10g/olap.101/b10333/multimodel.htm

Tirkel, A. Z., Rankin, G. A., Van Schyndel, R. M., Ho, W. J., Mee, N. R. A., & Osborne, C. F. (1993). *Electronic Water Mark. Digital Image Computing: Techniques and Applications 1993.* Macquarie University.

Tkacz, E. J., & kostka, P. (2000). An application of wavelet neural network for classification of patient with coronary artery disease based on HRV analysis. *Proceeding of the Annual International Conference on IEEE Engineering in Medicine and Biology,* (pp. 1391 - 1393). doi:10.1109/IEMBS.2000.897999

Tomás. (2005). Image communication quality assessment based on watermarking, an overview. *Internal Report, v0.02 – Instituto de Telecomunicações.*

Torki, M., Elgammal, A., & Lee, C. S. (2010). Learning a joint manifold representation from multiple data sets. In *Proc. IEEE 20th Int.Conf. Pattern Recognit.,* (pp. 1068–1071). doi:10.1109/ICPR.2010.267

Transaction Processing Performance Council (TPC). (2013). *TPC Benchmark H Standard Specification Revision 2.17.0, 2014*. Retrieved May 15, 2015, from http://www.tpc.org/tpc_documents_current_versions/pdf/tpc-h_v2.17.1.pdf

Trithemius, J. (1606). Data hiding method in binary images based on block masking for key authentication. *Information Sciences*, *277*, 188–196.

Tsai, C.-L., Chiang, H.-F., Fan, K.-C., & Chung, C.-D. (2005). Reversible data hiding and lossless reconstruction of binary images using pair-wise logical computation mechanism. *Pattern Recognition*, 38.

Tsai, M.-H., Wang, H.-C., Lee, G.-W., Lin, Y.-C., & Chiu, S.-H. (2015). A decision tree based classifier to analyze human ovarian cancer cDNA microarray datasets. *Journal of Medical Systems*, *40*(1), 1–8. doi:10.1007/s10916-015-0361-9 PMID:26531754

Tsang, K. F., & Au, O. C. (2001). A Review on Attacks, Problems and Weakness of Digital Watermarking and the Pixel Reallocation Attack. Security and Watermarking of Multimedia Content III, 4314, 385-393.

Tuan, D., Beck, P. D., & Crane, D. (2005). *Fuzzy clustering of stochastic models for molecular phylogenetics*. Academic Press.

Turkoglu, I., Arslan, A., & Illkay, E. (2002). An expert system for the diagnosis of the heart valve diseases. *Expert Systems with Applications*, *23*(3), 229–236. doi:10.1016/S0957-4174(02)00042-8

UC Irwin Machine Learning Repositry. (n.d.). *Cleveland Heart Disease Data Set*. Retrieved from http://archive.ics.uci.edu/ml/datasets/Heart+Disease

Upstate Medical University. (2011). *Protecting patient confidentiality and security*. Retrieved on September 1 2015, from www.upstate.edu/forms/documents/F84037.pdf

Vadde, S., Agarwal, A., & Ganesan, S. (2004). *Real -Time adaptive Digital Image Watermarking*. IEEE Electro/Information Technology Conference.

Veksler, O. (2007, June). Graph cut based optimization for MRFs with truncated convex priors. In *2007 IEEE Conference on Computer Vision and Pattern Recognition* (pp. 1-8). IEEE. doi:10.1109/CVPR.2007.383249

Verma, Singh, & Kumar. (2009). Robustness of the Digital Image Watermarking Techniques against Brightness and Rotation Attack. *International Journal of Computer Science and Information Security, 5*(1).

Verma, B., McLeod, P., & Klevansky, A. (2009). A novel soft cluster neural network for the classification of suspicious area in digital mammograms. *Pattern Recognition*, *42*(9), 1845–1852. doi:10.1016/j.patcog.2009.02.009

Verma, M., Srivastava, M., Chack, N., Diswar, A. K., & Gupta, N. (2012). A comparative study of various clustering algorithms in data mining. *International Journal of Engineering Research and Applications*, *2*(3), 1379–1384.

Vidyasagar, P. M., Song, H., & Elizabeth, C. (2005). A Survey of Digital Image Watermarking Techniques. *3rd IEEE International Conference on Industrial Informatics.*

Vinicius, L., & Ramiro, J. (2005). Geometric Attacks on Image Watermarking Systems. *IEEE MultiMedia*, *12*(3), 68–78. doi:10.1109/MMUL.2005.46

Vipula, S. (2011). *Digital Watermarking: A Tutorial. Journal of Selected Areas in Telecommunications*, 10–21.

Voloshynovskiy, S., Pereiraa, S., Herrigelb, A., Baumgartnerb, N., & Pun, T. (2000). Generalized watermarking attack based on watermark estimation and perceptual remodulation. *Proc. SPIE: Security and Watermarking of Multimedia Content*. doi:10.1117/12.384990

Voloshynovskiy, S., Pereira, S., & Pun, T. (1999), Watermark attacks. *Erlangen Watermarking Workshop.*

Vyborny, C. J., & Giger, M. L. (1994). Computer vision and artificial intelligence in mammography. *American Journal of Roentgenology, 162*(3), 699–708. doi:10.2214/ajr.162.3.8109525 PMID:8109525

Wakasa, Y., Tanaka, K., Akashi, T., & Nishimura, Y. (2010). Pso-based simultaneous tuning method for pid controllers and dead-zone compensators and its application to ultrasonic motors. *International Journal of Innovative Computing, Information, & Control, 6*(10), 4593–4604.

Wang, Y., & Chen, L. (2005). *Abstract dynamic branch prediction using machine learning.* Retrieved from https://www.cs.utexas.edu/~lin/papers/hpca01.pdf

Wang, H., Cai, Y., Zhang, Y., Pan, H., Weifeng, L. v., & Han, H. (2014). Deep learning for content-based image retrieval: A comprehensive study. *Proceedings of the ACM International Conference on Multimedia.* ACM.

Wang, J., Li, J., & Wiederhold, G. (2001). Simplicity: Semantics-sensitive integrated matching for picture libraries. *IEEE Transactions on Pattern Analysis and Machine Intelligence, 23*(9), 947–963. doi:10.1109/34.955109

Wang, L., Chu, F., & Xie, W. (2007). Accurate cancer classification using expression of very few genes. *IEEE/ACM Transactions on Computational Biology and Bioinformatics, 4*(1), 40–53. doi:10.1109/TCBB.2007.1006 PMID:17277412

Wang, S., Jiying, Z., James, T. W., & Filippo, S. (2004). Image quality measurement by using watermarking based on discrete wavelet transform. *22nd Biennial Symposium on Communications.*

Wan, S. J., Wong, S. K. M., & Prusinkiewicz, P. (1988). An Algorithm for Multidimensional data clustering. *ACM Transactions on Mathematical Software, 14*(2), 153–162. doi:10.1145/45054.45056

Washio, T., Mitsunaga, Y., & Motoda, H. (2005). Mining Quantitative Frequent Item sets Using Adaptive Density-based Subspace Clustering. *Fifth IEEE International Conference on Data Mining (ICDM'05).* doi:10.1109/ICDM.2005.100

Wei, L., Hongtao, L., & Fu-Lai, C. (2006). Feature based watermarking using watermark template match. *Applied Mathematics and Computation, 177*(1), 377–386. doi:10.1016/j.amc.2005.11.015

Weiner, J., & Mirkes, K. (1972). *Watermarking.* Appleton, WI: The Institute of Paper Chemistry.

Weinland, D., Ronfard, R., & Boyer, E. (2011). A survey of vision-based methods for action representation, segmentation and recognition. *Computer Vision and Image Understanding, 115*(2), 224–241. doi:10.1016/j.cviu.2010.10.002

Wei, W., Jinyan, W., Chengxi, W., & Pu, D. (2010). A Novel Watermarking Algorithm Based on Phase Congruency Corner Detection and SVD. *Fifth International Conference on Frontier of Computer Science and Technology.*

West, D. B. (2001). *Introduction to graph theory* (Vol. 2). Upper Saddle River, NJ: Prentice hall.

Wilk, J., & Pelka, M. (2013). "Cluster analysis-symbolic vs. classical data", Acta Universitatis Lodziensis. *Folia Oeconomica, 286,* 205–213.

Williams, G., Baxter, R., He, H., Hawkins, S., & Gu, L. (2002). A Comparative Study for RNN for Outlier Detection in Data Mining. In *Proceedings of the 2nd IEEE International Conference on Data Mining.* doi:10.1109/ICDM.2002.1184035

Winsberg, F., Elkin, M., Macy, J. Jr, Bordaz, V., & Weymouth, W. (1967). Detection of radiographic abnormalities in mammograms by means of optical scanning and computer analysis. *Radiology, 89*(2), 211–215. doi:10.1148/89.2.211

Wioletta, W., & Ogiela, M. R. (2016). Digital images authentication scheme based on bimodal biometric watermarking in an independent domain. *Journal of Visual Communication and Image Representation, 38,* 1–10. doi:10.1016/j.jvcir.2016.02.006

Won, Chan, & Won. (1999). A watermarking scheme for both spatial and frequency domain to extract the seal image without the original image. *Fifth International Symposium on Signal Processing and Its Applications.*

Woods, N. C., Longe, O. B., & Roberts, A. B. C. (2012). A sobel edge detection algorithm based system for analysing and classifying image based spam. *Journal of Emerging Trends in Computing and Information Sciences, 3*(4), 506–511.

World Health Organization. (n.d.). *Prevention of cardiovascular disease: Pocket guideline for assessment and management of cardiovascular risk.* Retrieved from http://www.who.int/cardiovas cular_diseases/guidelines/

Wu, C. H., & Shivakumar, S. (1994). Back-propagation and counterpropagation neural networks for phylogenetic classification of ribosomal RNA sequences. *Nucleic Acids Research, 22*(20), 4291–4299. doi:10.1093/nar/22.20.4291 PMID:7937158

Wujie, Z., Lu, Y., Zhongpeng, W., Mingwei, W., Ting, L., & Lihui, S. (2016). Binocular visual characteristics based fragile watermarking schemefor tamper detection in stereoscopic images. *International Journal of Electronics and Communications, 70*(1), 77–84. doi:10.1016/j.aeue.2015.10.006

Wu, X., Zhu, X., Wu, G. Q., & Ding, W. (2014). Data mining with big data. *Knowledge and Data Engineering. IEEE Transactions on, 26*(1), 97–107.

Xiang-yang, W., Yu-nan, L., Shuo, L., Hong-ying, Y., Pan-pan, N., & Yan, Z. (2015). A new robust digital watermarking using local polar harmonic transform. Journal of Computers and Electrical Engineering, 46, 403–418.

Xiao, P. F., Feng, X. Z., & Zhao, S. H. (2006). Feature detection from IKONOS pan imagery based on phase congruency. In *Proc. SPIE, Image and Signal Processing for Remote Sensing XII.* doi:10.1117/12.689595

Xiaodi, H., & Liqing, Z. (2007). Saliency Detection: A Spectral Residual Approach. *IEEE Conference on Computer Vision and Pattern Recognition.*

Xiaojun, Q., & Ji, Q. (2007). A robust content-based digital image watermarking scheme. *Signal Processing, 87*(6), 1264–1280. doi:10.1016/j.sigpro.2006.11.002

Xi, C., Dongming, J., & Zhijian, L. (2001). Recursive training for multi resolution fuzzy min - max neural network classifier.*6th International Conference Solid–State and Integrated Circuit Technology Proceedings,* (pp. 131 - 134).

Xie, J., Xie, Q., & Huang, D. (2009). A Robust High Capacity Information Hiding Algorithm Based on DCT High Frequency Domain. *International Symposium on Computer Network and Multimedia Technology.*

Xie, X. L., & Beni, G. (1991). A validity measure for fuzzy clustering. *IEEE Transactions on Pattern Analysis and Machine Intelligence, 13*(8), 841–847. doi:10.1109/34.85677

Xing, B., & Gao, W.-J. (2014). *Innovative computational intelligence: A rough guide to 134 Clever algorithms.* Academic Press.

Xin, R. S., Rosen, J., Zaharia, M., Franklin, M. J., Shenker, S., & Stoica, I. (2013). Shark; k: SQL and Rich Analytics at Scale. In *Proceedings of the 2013 International Conference on Management of Data (SIGMOD),* (pp. 13-24). New York, NY: ACM. doi:10.1145/2463676.2465288

Xiujuan Lei, M. D. (2014). Chaotic fruit fly optimization algorithm. *Advances in Swarm Intelligence 5th International Conference, ICSI 2014* (pp. 74-85). Springer.

Xuejuan, Z., Xiaochun, C., & Li, J. (2013). Geometric attack resistant image watermarking based on MSER. *Frontiers of Computer Science, 7*(1), 145–156. doi:10.1007/s11704-013-2174-7

Xu, H., Wanga, J., & Kim, H. J. (2010). Near-optimal solution to pair wise LSB matching via an immune programming strategy. *Information Sciences, 180*(8), 1201–1217. doi:10.1016/j.ins.2009.12.027

Xu, R., & Wunsch, D. (2005). Survey of clustering algorithms. *Neural Networks. IEEE Transactions on, 16*(3), 645–678.

Yang, C. C., & Ng, T. D. (2009, June). Web opinions analysis with scalable distance-based clustering. In *Intelligence and Security Informatics, 2009.ISI'09. IEEE International Conference on* (pp. 65-70). IEEE.

Yang, C., Zhang, L., Lu, H., Ruan, X., & Yang, M. H. (2013). Saliency detection via graph-based manifold ranking. In *Computer Vision and Pattern Recognition, 2008. CVPR 2008. IEEE Conference on* (pp. 3166-3173). IEEE. doi:10.1109/CVPR.2013.407

Yang, X. S., & Karamanoglu, M. (2013). Swarm intelligence and bio-inspired computation: An overview. Swarm Intelligence and Bio-Inspired Computation. Elsevier.

Yang, F., Sun, T., & Zhang, C. (2009). An efficient hybrid data clustering method based on K-harmonic means and Particle Swarm Optimization. *Expert Systems with Applications, 36*(6), 9847–9852. doi:10.1016/j.eswa.2009.02.003

Yang, J., Estivill-Castro, V., & Chalup, S. (2002). Support vector clustering through proximity graph modeling. In *Proceedings of the 9th International Conference on Neural Information Processing, ICONIP '02* (pp. 898-903). doi:10.1109/ICONIP.2002.1198191

Yang, X. (2013). *Swarm intelligence based algorithms: A critical analysis. Evolutionary Intelligence.* Springer.

Yang, X.-S. (2013). *Nature-inspired optimization algorithms* (1st ed.). Elsevier.

Yang, Y., & Padmanabhan, B. (2005). Ghic: A Hierarchical Pattern-Based Clustering Algorithm for Grouping Web Transactions. *IEEE Transactions on Knowledge and Data Engineering, 17*(9), 1300–1304. doi:10.1109/TKDE.2005.145

Yan, H., Jiang, Y., Zheng, J., Peng, C., & Li, Q. (2006). A Multi-Layer Perceptron based medical decision support system for heart disease diagnosis. *Expert Systems with Applications, 30*(2), 272–281. doi:10.1016/j.eswa.2005.07.022

Yardimci, A. (2009). Application of soft computing to medical problems.*Ninth International Conference on Intelligent Systems Design and Application*, (pp. 614 – 619). doi:10.1109/ISDA.2009.168

Yeh, T. Y., & Patt, Y. N. (1991). Two-level adaptive training branch prediction. In *Proceedings of the 24th Annual International Symposium on Microarchitecture* (MICRO 24). doi:10.1145/123465.123475

Yen-Chung, C., & Wen-Hsiang, T. (2006). *Copyright Protection against Print-and-Scan Operations by Watermarking for Color Images Using Coding and Synchronization of Peak Locations in Frequency Domain. Journal of Information Science and Engineering, 22,* 483–496.

Yeung, M. M. (1998). Digital Watermarking. *Communications of the ACM, 41*(7), 31–33. doi:10.1145/278476.278484

Yezzi, A., Kichenassamy, S., Kumar, A., Olver, P., & Tannenbaum, A. (1997). A geometric snake model for segmentation of medical imagery. *IEEE Transactions on Medical Imaging, 16*(2), 199–210. doi:10.1109/42.563665 PMID:9101329

Yin, Y., & Yasuda, K. (2005). Similarity coefficient methods applied to the cell formation problem: A comparative investigation. *Computers & Industrial Engineering, 48*(3), 471–489. doi:10.1016/j.cie.2003.01.001

Yin, Y., & Yasuda, K. (2006). Similarity coefficient methods applied to the cell formation problem: A taxonomy and review. *International Journal of Production Economics, 101*(2), 329–352. doi:10.1016/j.ijpe.2005.01.014

Yip, Au, Ho, & Wong. (2006). Lossless Visible Watermarking. *IEEE ICME.*

Yiu, M. L., & Mamoulis, N. (2004). Clustering Objects on a Spatial Network. *Proceedings of the ACM Conference on Management of Data (SIGMOD)*.

Yongdong, W. (2006). Nonlinear collusion attack on a watermarking scheme for buyer authentication. *IEEE Transactions on Multimedia, Volume, 8*(3), 626–629. doi:10.1109/TMM.2006.870720

Yoo, I., Alafaireet, P., Marinov, M., Pena-Hernandez, K., Gopidi, R., Chang, J. F., & Hua, L. (2012). Data mining in healthcare and biomedicine: A survey of the literature. *Journal of Medical Systems, 36*(4), 2431–2448. doi:10.1007/s10916-011-9710-5 PMID:21537851

Yuan, X., Dai, X., Zhao, J., & He, Q. (2014). On a novel multi-swarm fruit fly optimization algorithm and its application. *Applied Mathematics and Computation, 233*, 260–271. doi:10.1016/j.amc.2014.02.005

Yunkai, G., Junrui, Y., & Yulei, H. (2008). An Effective Algorithm for Mining Quantitative Association Rules Based on High Dimension Cluster.*4th International Conference on Wireless Communications, Networking and Mobile Computing*. IEEE.

Yuval, C., Michael, L., & Shay, M. (2011). Real-Time Digital Watermarking System for Audio Signals Using Perceptual Masking. Signal and Image Processing Lab, Faculty of EE, Technion IIT, Haifa, Israel.

Yu, Z., Au, O. C., Zou, R., Yu, W., & Tian, J. (2010). An adaptive unsupervised approach toward pixel clustering and color image segmentation. *Pattern Recognition, 43*(5), 1889–1906. doi:10.1016/j.patcog.2009.11.015

Zabrodsky, H. H. (2001). Watermarking and Copyright Labeling of Printed Images. *Journal of Electronic Imaging, 10*(3), 794–803. doi:10.1117/1.1382612

Zadeh, L. A. (1996). *Fuzzy sets, fuzzy logic, and fuzzy systems: Selected papers by Lotfi A Zadeh* (Vol. 6). World Scientific. doi:10.1142/2895

Zahlmann, G., Scherf, M., Wegner, A., Obermaier, M., & Mertz, M. (2000). Situation assessment of glaucoma using a hybrid fuzzy neural network. *IEEE Engineering In Medicine And Biology, 19*(1), 84–91. doi:10.1109/51.816247 PMID:10659433

Zainuddin, Z., & Ong, P. (2011). Reliable multiclass cancer classification of microarray gene expression profiles using an improved wavelet neural network.*Expert Systems with Applications,38*(11), 13711–13722. doi:10.1016/j.eswa.2011.04.164

Zainuddin, Z., & Ong, P. (2013). Design of wavelet neural networks based on symmetry fuzzy C-means for function approximation. *Neural Computing & Applications, 23*(1), 247–259. doi:10.1007/s00521-013-1350-x

Zang, H., Zhang, S., & Hapeshi, K. (2010). A Review of nature-inspired algorithms. *Journal of Bionics Engineering, 7*, S232–S237. doi:10.1016/S1672-6529(09)60240-7

Zeng, Y., Tu, C., & Zhang, X. (2008). Fuzzy-Set based fast edge detection of medical image. *Fuzzy Systems and Knowledge Discovery, 3*, 42–46.

Zhai, L., Dong, S., & Ma, H. (2008). Recent methods and applications on image edge detection.*Proceedings of the International Workshop on Education Technology and Training and International Workshop on Geoscience and Remote Sensing*. IEEE Computer Society. doi:10.1109/ETTandGRS.2008.39

Zhang, C., & Zhang, S. (n.d.). *Association rule mining: models and algorithms*. Springer.

Zhang, D., Wu, B., Sun, J., & Huang, H. (2009). A new robust watermarking algorithm based on DWT. In *Proc. second international congress on image and signal processing*. doi:10.1109/CISP.2009.5303924

Zhang, J., Huang, H., & Wang, J. (2010). Manifold learning for visualizing and analyzing high-dimensional data. *IEEE Intelligent Systems, 25*(4), 54–61.

Zhang, L., Zhang, L., Mou, X., & Zhang, D. (2011). FSIM: A feature similarity index for image quality assessment. *IEEE Transactions on Image Processing, 20*(8), 2378–2386. doi:10.1109/TIP.2011.2109730 PMID:21292594

Zhang, R., Ouyang, W., & Cham, W. K. (2009). Image edge detection using hidden Markov chain model based on the non-decimated wavelet. *International Journal of Signal Processing and Image Processing and Pattern, 2*(1), 109–118.

Zhao, Z., Wang, X., Zhang, W., & Zhu, Z. (2015). A Community-Based Approach to Identifying Influential Spreaders. *Entropy, 17,* 2228-2252. Retrieved from www.mdpi.com/journal/entropy

Zheng, D., & Zhao, J. (2003). RST invariant digital image watermarking: importance of phase information. *Canadian Conference on Electrical and Computer Engineering.* doi:10.1109/CCECE.2003.1226012

Zheng, P.-P., Feng, J., Li, Z., & Zhou, M. (2014). A Novel SVD and LS-SVM Combination Algorithm for Blind Watermarking. *Neurocomputing, 142,* 520–528. doi:10.1016/j.neucom.2014.04.005

Zheng, X., Wang, L., & Wang, S. (2014). A novel fruit fly optimization algorithm for the semiconductor final testing scheduling problem. *Knowledge-Based Systems, 57,* 95–103. doi:10.1016/j.knosys.2013.12.011

Zhihong, Q., Lei, C., Weilian, S., Tingkai, W., & Huamin, Y. (2012). *Recent Advances in Computer Science and Information Engineering* (Vol. 5). Springer Science & Business Media. doi:10.1007/978-3-642-25766-7_29

Zhijun, W. (2014). *Information Hiding in Speech Signals for Secure Communication, Syngress.* Elsevier.

Zoican, S. (2005). Digital signal processing system for digital watermarking implementation. *7th International Conference on Telecommunications in Modern Satellite, Cable and Broadcasting Services.*

Żurawski & Skodowski. (2014). Standard Deviation-Based Image Fidelity Measure For Digital Watermarking. *Przegląd Elektrotechniczny, 90*(5).

About the Contributors

Siddhartha Bhattacharyya did his Bachelors in Physics, Bachelors in Optics and Optoelectronics and Masters in Optics and Optoelectronics from University of Calcutta, India in 1995, 1998 and 2000 respectively. He completed PhD in Computer Science and Engineering from Jadavpur University, India in 2008. He is the recipient of the University Gold Medal from the University of Calcutta for his Masters. He is currently the Professor and Head of Information Technology of RCC Institute of Information Technology, Kolkata, India. In addition, he is serving as the Dean of Research and Development of the institute from November 2013. Prior to this, he was an Associate Professor of Information Technology of RCC Institute of Information Technology, Kolkata, India from 2011-2014. Before that, he served as an Assistant Professor in Computer Science and Information Technology of University Institute of Technology, The University of Burdwan, India from 2005-2011. He was a Lecturer in Information Technology of Kalyani Government Engineering College, India during 2001-2005. He is a co-author of 3 books and the co-editor of 6 books and has more than 150 research publications in international journals and conference proceedings to his credit. He has got a patent on intelligent colorimeter technology. He was the convener of the AICTE-IEEE National Conference on Computing and Communication Systems (CoCoSys-09) in 2009. He was the member of the Young Researchers' Committee of the WSC 2008 Online World Conference on Soft Computing in Industrial Applications. He has been the member of the organizing and technical program committees of several national and international conferences. He served as the Editor-In-Chief of International Journal of Ambient Computing and Intelligence (IJACI) published by IGI Global, Hershey, PA, USA from 17th July 2014 to 06th November 2014. He was the General Chair of the IEEE International Conference on Computational Intelligence and Communication Networks (ICCICN 2014) organized by the Department of Information Technology, RCC Institute of Information Technology, Kolkata in association with Machine Intelligence Research Labs, Gwalior and IEEE Young Professionals, Kolkata Section and held at Kolkata, India in 2014. He is the Associate Editor of International Journal of Pattern Recognition Research. He is the member of the editorial board of International Journal of Engineering, Science and Technology and ACCENTS Transactions on Information Security (ATIS). He is also the member of the editorial advisory board of HETC Journal of Computer Engineering and Applications. He is the Associate Editor of the International Journal of Bio-Info Soft Computing since 2013. He is the Lead Guest Editor of the Special Issue on Hybrid Intelligent Techniques for Image Analysis and Understanding of Applied Soft Computing, Elsevier, B. V. He was the General Chair of the 2015 IEEE International Conference on Research in Computational Intelligence and Communication Networks (ICRCICN 2015) organized by the Department of Information Technology, RCC Institute of Information Technology, Kolkata in association with IEEE Young Professionals, Kolkata Section and held at Kolkata, India in 2015. He is the Lead Guest Editor of the Special Issue on

Computational Intelligence and Communications in International Journal of Computers and Applications (IJCA); Publisher: Taylor & Francis, UK in 2016. He is the Issue Editor of International Journal of Pattern Recognition Research since January 2016. He was the General Chair of the 2016 International Conference on Wireless Communications, Network Security and Signal Processing (WCNSSP2016) held during June 26-27, 2016 at Chiang Mai, Thailand. He is the member of the editorial board of Applied Soft Computing, Elsevier, B. V. His research interests include soft computing, pattern recognition, multimedia data processing, hybrid intelligence and quantum computing. Dr. Bhattacharyya is a senior member of Institute of Electrical and Electronics Engineers (IEEE), USA, Association for Computing Machinery (ACM), USA and International Engineering and Technology Institute, Hong Kong. He is a member of International Rough Set Society, International Association for Engineers (IAENG), Hong Kong, Computer Science Teachers Association (CSTA), USA, Asian Council of Science Editors (ACSE), UAE and International Association of Academicians, Scholars, Scientists and Engineers (IAASSE), USA. He is a life member of Computer Society of India, Optical Society of India, Indian Society for Technical Education and Center for Education Growth and Research, India.

Sourav De did his Bachelors in Information Technology from The University of Burdwan, Burdwan, India in 2002. He did his Masters in Information Technology from West Bengal University of Technology, Kolkata, India in 2005. He completed PhD in Computer Science and Technology from Indian Institute of Engineering & Technology, Shibpur, Howrah, India in 2015. He is currently an Associate Professor of Computer Science and Engineering in Cooch Behar Government Engineering College, West Bengal. Previous to this, he was an Assistant Professor in the Department of Computer Science and Information Technology of University Institute of Technology, The University of Burdwan, Burdwan, India since 2006. He served as a Junior Programmer in Apices Consultancy Private Limited, Kolkata, India in 2005. He has more than about 20 research publications in internationally reputed journals, international edited books and international IEEE conferences. He served as reviewer in several International IEEE conferences and also in several international editorial books. He has been the member of the organizing and technical program committees of several national and international conferences. He has been invited in different seminars as an expert speaker. He is a co-author of a proposed book on soft computing. His research interests include soft computing, pattern recognition, image processing and data mining. Dr. De is a member of IEEE, ACM, Computer Science Teachers Association (CSTA) and IAENG, Hong Kong. He is a life member of ISTE, India.

Indrajit Pan has done his B.E. in Computer Science and Engineering with Honors from The University of Burdwan in 2005, M. Tech. in Information Technology from Bengal Engineering and Science University, Shibpur in 2009 and Ph.D. (Engg.) from Indian Institute of Engineering Science and Technology, Shibpur in 2015. He is the recipient of BESU, University Medal for securing First rank in M. Tech. (IT). He has couple of National and International level research publications and Book Chapters to his credit. He has attended several International Conferences, National level Faculty development programs, workshops and symposiums. Indrajit is a Member of Institute of Electrical and Electronics Engineers (IEEE), USA and Association for Computing Machinery (ACM), USA.

Paramartha Dutta, born 1966, did his Bachelors and Masters in Statistics from the Indian Statistical Institute, Calcutta in the years 1988 and 1990 respectively.He afterwards completed his Master of Technology in Computer science from the same Institute in the year 1993 and Doctor of Philosophy in

Engineering from the Bengal Engineering and Science University, Shibpur in 2005 respectively. He has served in the capacity of research personnel in various projects funded by Govt. of India, which include DRDO, CSIR, Indian Statistical Institute, Calcutta etc. Dr. Dutta is now a Professor in the Department of Computer and System Sciences of the Visva Bharati University, West Bengal, India. Prior to this, he served Kalyani Government Engineering College and College of Engineering in West Bengal as full time faculty members. Dr. Dutta remained associated as Visiting/Guest Faculty of several Universities/ Institutes such as West Bengal University of Technology, Kalyani University, Tripura University to name some. He has coauthored eight books and has also five edited book to his credit. He has published about hundred eighty-five papers in various journals and conference proceedings, both international and national as well as several book chapters in edited volumes of reputed International publishing house like Elsevier, Springer-Verlag, CRC Press, John Wiley to name a few. Dr. Dutta has guided three scholars who already had been awarded their Ph. D. Presently, he is supervising six scholars for their Ph. D program. Dr. Dutta has served as editor of special volumes of several international journals published by publishers of International repute such as Springer, etc. Dr. Dutta, as investigator, could implement successfully projects funded by AICTE, DST of the Govt. of India. Prof. Dutta has served/serves in the capacity of external member of Boards of Studies of relevant departments of various Universities encompassing West Bengal University of Technology, Kalyani University, Tripura University, Assam University, Silchar to name a few. He had the opportunity to serve as the expert of several interview boards conducted by West Bengal Public Service Commission, Assam University, Silchar, National Institute of Technology, Arunachal Pradesh, Sambalpur University, etc. Dr. Dutta is a Life Fellow of the Optical Society of India (OSI), Computer Society of India (CSI), Indian Science Congress Association (ISCA), Indian Society for Technical Education (ISTE), Indian Unit of Pattern Recognition and Artificial Intelligence (IUPRAI) – the Indian affiliate of the International Association for Pattern Recognition (IAPR), Senior Member of Associated Computing Machinery (ACM), IEEE Computer Society, USA and IACSIT.

* * *

Swati Aggarwal is working as an Assistant Professor, NSIT, Dwarka. She has 10 years of research experience. Her research interests include Soft computing techniques, Big data and cloud computing.

Venu Azad is currently working as an Extension lecturer in Govt. Girls PG college Sec.14 Gurgaon, I have done B.Tech (Computer Science) from GCEW College Bilaspur, M.Tech(Computer Science) from ITM University Gurgaon. I have also Qualified UGC-NET June 2014 Exam and my research interest is classification and clustering using Soft computing techniques and designing the clinical decision support system.

Samir K. Bandyopadhyay is Professor of Computer Science and Engineering, University of Calcutta, India. He obtained his Ph.D. in Computer Science and Engineering in 1989 from University of Calcutta, M.Tech in Radio-Physics and Electronics in 1979 from University of Calcutta and B.E. in Electronics and Tele-Communication in 1975 from B.E. College, University of Calcutta. He is the Chairman of Science and Engineering Research Support Society (SERSC, Indian Part), Fellow of Computer Society of India, Sectional President of ICT of Indian Science Congress Association, 2008–2009, Senior Member of IEEE, Member of ACM, Fellow of Institution of Engineers (India), Fellow of Institution of Mammographic Density Estimation and Classification Electronics and Tele-Communication Engineering, India, Reviewer of International Journals IEEE Transactions on Neural Networks, ACM and Springer Publications. His fields of specialization are Bio-medical Engineering, Mobile Computing, Pattern Recognition, Graph Theory, Image Processing, Handwritten Signature Verification, Graphical Password Verification, etc. He has 25 years of Teaching and Research experience in the Post-graduate and under-graduate studies. He published books like Data structure Using C, Addison Wesley, 2003; C Language, Pearson Publication, 2010. He is author of more than 150 publications in National and International Journals and Conferences

Biplab Banerjee is currently working as a post-doctoral researcher at the Pattern Analysis & Computer Vision (PAVIS) group, Istituto Italiano di Tecnologia, Genova, Italy. He obtained his PhD from Indian Institute of Technology Bombay in 2015. His PhD thesis was selected for the 'Excellence in PhD thesis award' from IIT Bombay at the 53rd convocation. He spent the whole of 2015 as a post-doctoral researcher at the Image laboratory, GreyC-CNRS, Caen, France. He also completed visiting assignments at the Distributed and Remote Sensing lab, University of Trento and Department of Image and Signal Processing, Telecom-ParisTech, Paris, France. He works broadly in computer vision and machine learning and his specific research interests include action and activity recognition from videos, weakly-supervised object recognition, transfer learning for multi-temporal image analysis and graph based data clustering techniques. His works have been published in reputed journals and conferences from IEEE, Springers and ACM. He is also the referee for IEEE T. on Geoscience & Remote Sensing, IEEE JSTARS, IEEE Remote Sensing Letters, IEEE Signal Processing Letters etc.

Minakshi Banerjee received her B. Tech., M. Tech. in Radio Physics and Electronics in 1987 and 1990 respectively from the University of Calcutta. She obtained her PhD degree from Jadavpur University in 2008 for which the research work was carried out as a Senior Research Fellow (CSIR) in the Machine Intelligence Unit of Indian Statistical Institute, Kolkata. In 1992, she joined as a Technical Officer in Government of India and worked upto 1993. She had been working as a Systemspecialist in a software company (India Infopower International Pvt. Ltd.) and worked in different projects. Her research interests include Image Processing, Pattern Recognition, Soft Computing etc. Presently she is working as an Associate professor in the Department of Computer Science and Engineering of RCC Institute of information Technology Kolkata, India.

Bülent Başaran is an Associate Professor in the Faculty of Economics and Administrative Sciences at Bilecik Şeyh Edebali University in Turkey. He teaches Operations Management, Operations Research, and Statistics at the Faculty. He holds an M.B.A. from Illinois Institute of Technology and a Ph.D. from Uludağ University in Turkey. His research interests include reverse logistics, inventory management, quality management, cluster analysis, and cellular manufacturing.

Abhishek Basu received his B. Tech. in Electronics and Telecommunication Engineering from West Bengal University of Technology in year 2005, M. Tech. in VLSI Design from Institute of Radio Physics, Calcutta University, India in 2008 and Ph. D (Engg) from Jadavpur University in 2015. At present he is an Assistant Professor in the department of Electronics and Communication Engineering at RCC Institute of Information Technology, Kolkata, India. His field of interest spans digital image processing, visual information hiding, IP protection technique, FPGA based system design, low power VLSI Design and Embedded System Design.

P. Bhargavi is working as Assistant Professor in the Department of Computer Science, Sri Padmavathi Mahila Visvavidyalayam (SPMVV), Tirupati. Received her Ph.D. from Sri Padmavati Women's University, Tirupati. She has 18 years of professional experience. She is member in IEEE, CSI, ISTE, IASCIT, IAENG and, MEACSE. Her areas of interest is Data mining, Soft Computing and Big Data Analytics.

Krishna Mohan Buddhiraju received his PhD in Electrical Engineering from Indian Institute of Bombay in 1991. He is a Professor at the Centre of Studies in Resources Engineering and the current Head of the Centre. He is also an Institute Chair Professor of IIT Bombay. Prof. Krishna Mohan's interests include image processing and analysis, machine learning algorithms, spatial data security, and multimedia educational content development for satellite image analysis and geographic information systems. He has supervised over 50 PhD and M.Tech. students at IIT Bombay. Prof. Krishna Mohan Buddhiraju is a member of the Executive Council of Indian Society of Remote Sensing (ISRS), the highest level body of ISRS. representing academia. He is a life member of Indian Society of Remote Sensing, Indian Society of Geomatics and a member IEEE. He is a reviewer of manuscripts submitted to journals like IEEE Trans. on Geoscience and Remote Sensing, IEEE Geoscience and Remote Sensing Letters, SPIE Journal of Applied Remote Sensing, ASPRS Journal of Photogrammetry and Remote Sensing, Remote Sensing Letters, Journal of Indian Society of Remote Sensing. He has published over 100 papers in refereed international journals and conferences, and contributed to several books. He is reciepient of 2003 IETE M.N. Saha Memorial gold medal for Best Application Oriented Paper published in IETE Journal of Research, Indian Society of Remote Sensing National Geospatial Award for Excellence 2012. Prof. Krishna Mohan delivers every year invited lectures at a number of colleges and universities in India, and he also serves as a member of Board of Studies in programs related to Geoinformatics and Electronics and Communications areas. He conducted several 1-2 week courses on satellite image processing and analysis, basic to advanced.

Chantana Chantrapornchai obtained her Bachelor degree (Computer Science) from Thammasat University of Thailand in 1991. She graduated from Northeastern University at Boston, College of Computer Science, in 1993 and University of Notre Dame, Department of Computer Science and Engineering, in 1999, for her Master and Ph.D degrees respectively. Currently, she is an associated professor of Dept. of Computer Engineering, Faculty of Engineering, Kasetsart University, Thailand. Her research interests include: parallel computing, big data processing, semantic web, computer architecture and fuzzy logic.

Marlene Goncalves received her Ph.D. degree from Universidad Simón Bolívar, Venezuela. She is currently a Full Professor of Department of Computer Science & Information Technology at Universidad Simón Bolívar, Venezuela. Her research interests include database modeling, preference based queries and query processing. She has published over 53 papers in international journals, conferences and books in these areas since 2001.

Fatih Güneş is a research assistant in the department of Management Information Systems at Bilecik Şeyh Edebali University in Turkey. He studied computer science and mathematics at Technical University Stuttgart of Applied Sciences and after that he holds MS in Computer Engineering from Beykent University and is currently continues his PHD in Computer Engineering at Istanbul Commerce University. His research interests include Big Data, Internet of Things, Data Mining and Computer Networks.

Güney Gürsel is born in 1972 in İzmir / Turkey. He graduated from Military Academy in 1994 as systems engineer. He had his MSc. degree in information systems field in 2003 in Middle East Technical University (METU), and PhD in Medical Informatics field in 2012 again in METU. He is working in Command post of Gendarme Logistics, School ol of Technical and Auxiliary Forces, as head of computer systems department. He speaks advanced English. He is working in the fields of Healthcare Information Systems (HIS), Evaluation of HIS, End user expectations from HIS, Fuzzy logic application in HIS, Interoperability in HIS. He is married and has two kids.

Seikh Mazharul Islam received his B.Tech. degree in Computer Science and Engineering from Maulana Abul Kalam Azad University of Technology, West Bengal (formerly known as West Bengal University of Technology [WBUT]), India, in 2006 and M.E. degree in Information Technology from Indian Institutes of Engineering Science and Technology (IIEST) (formerly known as Bengal Engineering and Science University (BESU), Shibpur), India, in 2009. Currently, he is an assistant professor in the department of Computer Science and Engineering, RCC Institute of Information Technology, Kolkata, India. His research interests include Image processing, pattern recognition, machine learning, soft computing and graph mining.

S. Jyothi is working as Professor in the Department of Computer Science and Director of Computer Centre, Sri Padmavathi Mahila Visvavidyalayam (SPMVV), Tirupati. Dr. S. Jyothi is a Professor in Computer Science. She has 25 years teaching experience and 30 years research experience. She is handling core and electives subjects of Computer Science for post graduate and graduate level. 9 Ph.D., 7 M.Phil were awarded and 8 Ph.D. scholars are being guided under her supervision. She is senior member of IEEE & IACSIT, fellow of RSS, ISCA, IETE & SSARSC, member of IEEE GSRS & WS, ACM, IET, IAENG & Gyancity Research Labs and life member of CSI, ISTE, ISCA, IFERP, IUPRAI and ISRS. More than 150 papers published presented in International and National Journals and conferences. 8 books were authored and edited by her. Her areas of interest in Image Processing, Soft Computing, Data Mining, Big Data, Bioinformatics and Hyperspectra.

Aree Kaegjing graduate B.S. in Computer Science, from Silpakorn University, in 2014.

Neelu Khare has completed Ph.D from MANIT Bhopal and working as Associate Professor in IT, her areas of interest are data mining, Bio-informatics and soft computing.

Shruti Kohli is working as an Assistant Professor in the department of computer science in Birla Institute of Technology, Mesra, Noida centre. She did her Master Degree in Operational Research from the University of Delhi in 2001. She obtained Masters'; degree in Computer Application from IGNOU in 2002. She did her Mphil in Operational Research from University of Delhi in year 2004 and obtained the Ph.D in (Technology in the year 2012) from Birla Institute of Technology. The area of her doctoral research work was web intelligence. She has also cleared Digital Fundamental Course from Google Analytics Academy. Her area of interest includes Information retrieval, Operational Research, Data Mining, Web Analytics. At present she is guiding three PhD students in mainly in area of web intelligence and one in the area of Mobile Ad-Hoc Networks. She has already mentored two Mtech Scholars and currently mentoring 1 Mtech Scholar in the area of Semantic web. She has presented papers in many international and national conferences and had been a resource person in DST sponsored FDPs. She is an active blogger and has great interest Mobile Apps development. She had been conducting Mobile App workshop in college and is currently running Mobile Incubator Cell in her college. She is teaching subjects like web technology, Simulation & Modelling-Ecommerce and had written 2 course book on Web technology for Maharishi Dayanand University (MDU) and KKHSOU (Kirshna Kanta Handiqui State Open University). She has also co-authored a book on banking in which she highlighted role of IT in banking. She had been a member of program committee and review committee of many national international conferences and had been session chair and speaker in few conferences. She was presented best paper award in 2014 by South Asian University for presenting her research work in international workshop titled "Machine Learning and Text Analytics". She is in the advisory word of WARSE (Word Academic Research in Science and Engineering). She is active member of IEEE, IAENG International Society for Engineers and Soft Computing Research Society.

Songchok Krakhaeng graduated M.S. in Computer and Information Science, from Silpakorn University, in 2015. His research area is data mining.

Indra K. Maitra is Ph.D. in Computer Science from University of Calcutta and working as Sr. System Analyst at B. P. Poddar Institute of Management and Technology. He obtained Master in Computer Application (MCA) in the year 2002 from St. Xavier's College under IGNOU. He received award in 96th Indian Science Congress, 2009 at Shillong for the Best Poster in Computer Science. He is author of two books and more than 30 publications in National and International Journal and Conference. His working areas of specialization are Image Processing, Network Security, Data Structure, Programming Language, Computer Organization and Architecture, etc. He is now doing research in the Govt. of India funded project in the field of Biomedical Image Analysis and CAD.

D. M. Mamatha is working as Professor in the Department of Sericulure, Sri Padmavati Mahila Visvavidyalayam did her PhD in India and PostDoc in USA. Specialised in Insect Physiology, Recombinant bio pesticide development, Gene Expression, Bioinformatics and DNA Barcoding. she is a Fulbright scholar to University of California, Davis. She received Young Scientist and Achievement awards. She visited Singapore, USA, Thailand, Nepal, and Egypt. She is fellow of ISEC and ISCA. Her areas of Research are Biotechnology & Bioinformatics research in the field Insect Physiology and Recombinant biopesticide development.

Shashi Mehrotra is employed as an Assistant Professor in Information Technology department, Tecnia Institute of advance Studies, Delhi, India. Curently she is on study leave, and pursing Ph.D (CSE) from Birla Institute of Technology, Mesra, India. She did M.Tech in Computer Science Engineering in 2010. She obtained M.Phil degree in Computer Science in 2005 from Madurai Kamraj University, India. Her area of research is Data Mining, Text Mining and Data Analytics. She has presented papers in national & international conferences and seminars. She was presented best paper award in 2009 in National seminar on "Emerging Trends in Computing, Communication, control and Information Technology" organized by Institute of Technology and Management Gurgaon. She has also published papers in national and international journals and conference proceedings. She taught and mentored B.Tech, M.Tech and MCA, BCA students in her teaching career. She is life time member of Computer Society of India (CSI).

Ong Pauline received her Ph.D in applied mathematics from Universiti Sains Malaysia, Penang, Malaysia in year 2011, with specialiation in artificial neural networks. She is currently a senior lecturer with Universiti Tun Hussein Onn Malaysia, Johor, Malaysia. Her current research interests include artificial neural networks, mathematical modeling, and metaheuristic algorithm.

Warot Piyanuntcharatsr graduated B.S. (Computer Science) from Silpakorn University, in 2014.

Sudipan Saha obtained his M.Tech. (Electrical Engineering) from Indian Institute of Technology Bombay in 2014 where he worked at Signal Processing and Artificial Neural Networks Laboratory. Currently he is working as image processing engineer in semiconductor industry. His domain of expertise include computer vision, machine learning, digital signal processing.

Sathaporn Srakaew graduated B.S. in Computer Science from Silpakorn Universtiy, Thailand, in 2014.

Susmita Talukdar received her B.Tech in Electronics & Communication Engineering from RCC Institute of Information Technology, Kolkata, in the year 2015. She is currently a Systems Engineer in Infosys, working in Tandem technology. Her domain of interests include digital image processing, digital copyright protection, visual information hiding, Mainframe Technologies & Tandem systems.

B.K. Tripathy has received 03 gold medals for topping the list of candidates at graduation andpost-graduation level of Berhampur University. He was a Professor and Head of the department of Computer Science of Berhampur University till 2007. Dr. Tripathy is now working as a Senior Professor in School of Computing Science and Engineering, VIT University, Vellore, India. He has received research/academic fellowships from UGC,DST, SERC and DOE of Govt. of India for various academic pursuits. Dr.Tripathy has published more than 380 technical papersin different international journals, proceedings of reputed international conferences and edited research volumes. He has produced 25 PhDs, 13 MPhils and 4 M.S (By research) under his supervision. Dr. Tripathy has published two text books on Soft Computing and Computer Graphics. He was selected as honorary member of the American Mathematical Society from 1992-1994 for his distinguished contribution as a reviewer of American Mathematical Review. Dr. Tripathy has served as the member of Advisory board or Technical Programme Committee member of several International conferences inside India and abroad. Also, he has edited two research volumes for IGI publications and is editing three more research volumes. He is a life/senior member of IEEE, ACM, IRSS, CSI, ACEEE, OMSand IMS. Dr.Tripathy is an editorial board member/reviewer of more than 60 journals. He has guest edited some research journals. Dr. Tripathy has Technical grants for research projects from various funding agencies like UGC, DST and DRDO. His research interest includes Fuzzy Setsand Systems, Rough Sets and Knowledge Engineering, Data Clustering, Social Network Analysis, SoftComputing, Granular Computing, Content Based Learning, Neighbourhood Systems, Soft Set Theory, Social Internet of Things, Big Data Analytics, Theory of Multisets and List theory.

Index

A

Adaptive Circle Segmentation 329-330
Adaptive Shape Segmentation 329, 334, 337-338
AFCM algorithms 394
Apriori 78-82, 232
Architecture Design 225-226, 231, 233, 248
Artificial Neural Network (ANN) 135, 139, 171, 229, 233, 293-294, 296-301, 316, 359
Association Rules 74, 77-79, 81-82, 85-88, 142, 145, 150

B

Bayesian Network 140, 171
Binary Data 31, 33-34, 36, 39, 51, 71
Bioinformatics 326, 344, 358-362, 364-368, 374-375, 377
Boolean association 85, 87
Branch History 226, 232, 240, 246, 252
Branch Prediction 225-227, 231-232, 235, 239-240, 244, 246, 248-249
BTB 227, 252

C

Cache Design 225, 229
Cache Prediction 225, 232, 234, 239, 248-249
clinical parameter 294, 300
Cluster Compactness 213, 345, 351, 353
Cluster Error 345, 351, 353-354
clustering algorithms 28, 35, 79, 88, 96-98, 100, 103, 105-107, 201, 203, 206-207, 340, 364, 380, 383-384
C-means 35, 41, 202, 344, 384-386, 394
Column-stores 2-3
Computer-Aided Diagnosis (CAD) 161
content based image retrieval 109-110, 114, 132
Convex Polygon 82-83
cross validation 243, 249, 317, 319-320

D

Data Clustering 28-30, 41, 47, 65, 68, 75, 90, 112, 193, 201-202, 207, 209-211, 214, 216, 346, 380, 383
Data Mining 29-30, 35, 52, 59, 74, 82, 86, 135-154, 225-226, 231-233, 248-249, 295, 297, 348, 362, 365, 373-374, 383-384
Database Management Systems 2-3, 9, 15, 18
Decision tree 35, 52-54, 58-59, 139, 143, 232, 241-242, 295, 366
Dendrogram 48, 51, 71, 96
Denormalization 4-5, 9-10, 13, 15, 18, 25-27
Density based Clustering 85, 102-103
DICOM 160, 162, 173, 183
digital image watermarking 253, 258-261, 263, 274
Distance Measure 50, 66, 93-94, 203, 212
DNA Sequence 359, 362, 364, 368-370, 374, 376

E

Edge detection 159, 162-164, 166, 168-173, 181-183, 187-188, 261, 265, 330-331, 333-334, 338-340
Energy Efficiency 260, 345-347
Entropy 52-54, 56, 71, 162, 212, 241, 261-262, 272, 388
Execution Plans 2-3, 18

F

Fixed Circle Segmentation 329, 334, 337, 339
Fuzzy C-Means 35, 41, 202, 344, 384-385, 394
Fuzzy logic 135, 140, 172, 293-296, 299, 303, 318, 360, 370, 372, 383
Fuzzy min-max neural network 299, 303-304, 316, 319
Fuzzy sets 86, 303-304, 385
Fuzzy Systems 358, 360-361, 369-370, 372, 377

G

Genetic Algorithms 103-105, 135, 139-140, 294-295, 360, 374-377

Support Your Colleagues and Stay Current on the Latest Research Developments

Become a Reviewer

In this competitive age of scholarly publishing, constructive and timely feedback significantly decreases the turn-around time of manuscripts from submission to acceptance, allowing the publication and discovery of progressive research at a much more expeditious rate.

The overall success of a refereed journal is dependent on quality and timely reviews.

Several IGI Global journals are currently seeking highly qualified experts in the field to fill vacancies on their respective editorial review boards. Reviewing manuscripts allows you to stay current on the latest developments in your field of research, while at the same time providing constructive feedback to your peers.

Reviewers are expected to write reviews in a timely, collegial, and constructive manner. All reviewers will begin their role on an ad-hoc basis for a period of one year, and upon successful completion of this term can be considered for full editorial review board status, with the potential for a subsequent promotion to Associate Editor.

Join this elite group by visiting the IGI Global journal webpage, and clicking on "**Become a Reviewer**".

Applications may also be submitted online at:
www.igi-global.com/journals/become-a-reviewer/.

Applicants must have a doctorate (or an equivalent degree) as well as publishing and reviewing experience.

If you have a colleague that may be interested in this opportunity, we encourage you to share this information with them.

Any questions regarding this opportunity can be sent to:
journaleditor@igi-global.com.

Become an IRMA Member

Members of the **Information Resources Management Association (IRMA)** understand the importance of community within their field of study. The Information Resources Management Association is an ideal venue through which professionals, students, and academicians can convene and share the latest industry innovations and scholarly research that is changing the field of information science and technology. Become a member today and enjoy the benefits of membership as well as the opportunity to collaborate and network with fellow experts in the field.

IRMA Membership Benefits:

- **One FREE Journal Subscription**

- **30% Off Additional Journal Subscriptions**

- **20% Off Book Purchases**

- Updates on the latest events and research on Information Resources Management through the IRMA-L listserv.

- Updates on new open access and downloadable content added to Research IRM.

- A copy of the Information Technology Management Newsletter twice a year.

- A certificate of membership.

IRMA Membership $195

Scan code or visit **irma-international.org** and begin by selecting your free journal subscription.

Membership is good for one full year.

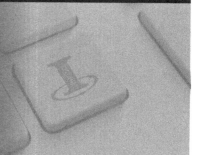

Printed in the United States
By Bookmasters